# The Rise *of the* Colored Races

*Keith Irvine*

# The Rise
## *of the* Colored
# Races

W · W · NORTON & COMPANY · INC ·
*New York*

D
21
.3
I75
1970

SBN 393 05392 X

FIRST EDITION

1 2 3 4 5 6 7 8 9 0

*To Aline*

# Contents

# Acknowledgments

MANY PEOPLE have helped me in various ways in the writing of this book, and many others have given me encouragement and support. I cannot hope to mention all of them, and merely ask that omissions will be forgiven. I have benefited from many suggestions and corrections. Such mistakes as may have occurred are, however, my responsibility, and mine alone.

Among those who have read parts of the manuscript, made suggestions or corrections, lent me books, or otherwise helped the work forward, are Mrs. Mary Anderberg; Miss Mary Benson; Dr. Robert S. Browne; Dr. Guy and Mrs. Bueno of Prensa y Radio Espanolas; Michael Caesar of Grenada; Denis and Winifred Courtney; Mrs. Gloria Davidson; Dr. Ato Dickson of the University of Ghana; Dr. Frank Erlach and Dr. Helen Erlach; Mr. Bob Fuhring; Dr. Arnold Kunst of the London School of Oriental and African Studies; Mr. Robin Miller of the United Nations Secretariat; Mr. Victor Perlo; Mrs. Derek Payton-Smith; Mrs. John A. Powelson; Mr. Enuga Reddy of the United Nations Secretariat; Dr. Emory Ross; the Reverend Michael Scott; Mrs. Anne Marie Stokes; and Mrs. Carol Thompson, Editor of *Current History*.

I also wish to thank various past and present officials of the Ghana Ministry of External Affairs (formerly the Ministry of Foreign Affairs), notably Mr. Daniel A. Chapman, Mr. H. R. Amonoo, Mr. Alex Quaison-Sackey, Mr. Nathan A. Quao, and Mr Victor Gbeho, as well as other Ghanaian friends, who read parts of the manuscript and gave me encouragement.

The friendly co-operation of the staff of the Croton Free Library at Croton-on-Hudson, New York, is also gratefully acknowledged. My thanks are due also to Mrs. Jane Herbert of Chicago for her research work.

I am particularly grateful to Mr. Peter Jacobsohn, who first pressed me to develop the idea of this book, and who continued to encourage me thereafter. Mr. Richard O. Boyer, as well as his wife Sophie, placed their profound and intimate knowledge of American history in general, and those parts of it relating to slavery and abolitionism in particular, at my disposal in long conversations that were of inestimable benefit. Mr. Eric Swenson, combining tact and understanding with pragmatism, has been the most patient of editors.

I am indebted to my mother, Mrs. Dorothy Stuart Irvine, for putting in long hours of research, particularly for the earlier chapters, in the New York Public Library. My daughters, Lilian, Dominique, and Madeline, helped with proofreading and showed cheerful forbearance throughout what has been a long ordeal. Finally, and most of all, I thank my wife, who participated in some of the research, and gave me constant encouragement and loyal support during these voyages of discovery.

ONE

The Rise of Color Consciousness

*"Civilization's going to pieces," exclaims Tom Buchanan in F. Scott Fitzgerald's* The Great Gatsby. *"I've gotten to be a terrible pessimist about things. Have you read* The Rise of the Colored Empires *by this man Goddard? . . . It's a fine book, and everybody ought to read it. The idea is if we don't look out the white race will be—utterly submerged. It's all scientific stuff; it's been proved."*

*Tom Buchanan, "nibbling at the edges of stale ideas," was, of course, referring to Lothrop Stoddard's* The Rising Tide of Color Against White World Supremacy, *a book that in 1920 reflected a concern with the question of color which is again occupying us today. Indeed, color is becoming the specter which haunts our time.*

*In the course of the last few hundred years the relationship between power and color has grown in significance. This has become manifest first by the emergence of white European dominion over other continents, and then, in a historic counterreaction, by the assertion of colored sovereignty in regions previously subject to white control. Invasion and withdrawal, suppression and concession, war and compromise—such extremes have represented the ebb and flow in a relationship whose story still remains only half told.*

*In this book I have outlined the historic background of the situation in which the world now finds itself. Paradoxically, it will be seen that it is the white Europeans themselves who initially propagated the two contradictory concepts that are now in conflict. The first of these is the idea of a social and political hierarchy based on skin color ("white supremacy" or its counterparts). The second is the idea of a world based on equal rights for all men.*

*With the gradual dissolution of white dominion in Asia and Africa we have entered into a transitional period in which we may assume that an international economy and a world community are slowly being formed. The question as to whether this world community will be based upon the principle of racial privilege or upon the principle of equal rights has yet to be decided. The rise of the colored world which has been gathering momentum from decade to decade now confronts the white world with a collective challenge that demands explicit replies. Upon the response much will depend.*

# Chapter 1

# The Ancient World

◧ MAN'S ORIGINS remain veiled from us. Investigation into our beginnings is being pursued more intensively, more scientifically, and upon a more widespread basis than ever before, but theories still remain theories, supported by evidence that is, however plausible, at best circumstantial.

In the field of prehistory, new techniques and explorations of geographical areas that were formerly virtually uninvestigated are leading to new hypotheses, and to the adaptation of old hypotheses to fit new evidence. One of the problems has been that in the past research was largely limited to Europe. Yet in much of the prehistorical era most of Europe was glaciated. The logical sequence for investigating the origins and early geographic distribution of man would have been to begin with Asia and Africa, and then to pursue the unfolding tale into its European and American settings. The fact that paleontological research tended to concentrate upon Europe and then North America was the result of an orientation that, however understandable for earlier decades, is now being corrected.

Phylogenetically, plants have been classified into five groups (including mosses), and animals into eight. As for man, however, even today there is still no more decisive agreement among authorities as to whether mankind consists of a single "race" or species or of several than there was when Charles Darwin stated in 1871 that

Man has been studied more carefully than any other animal, and yet there is the greatest possible diversity amongst capable judges whether he should be classified as a single species or race, or as two (Virey), as three (Jacquinot), as four (Kant), five (Blumenbach), six (Buffon), seven (Hunter), eight (Agassiz), eleven (Pickering), fifteen (Bory St. Vincent), sixteen (Desmoulins), twenty-two (Morton), sixty (Crawfurd), or as sixty-three, according to Burke.[1]

To which he went on to add that difficulties would continue to arise until some definition of the term "species" became generally acceptable. "We might as well attempt," he remarked, "without any definition to decide whether a certain number of houses should be called a village, town, or city."

Sixty-six years later, in words reminiscent of Darwin's, Rudolf Rocker restated the problem:

> For a long time we were content with the four races of Linnaeus, then Blumenbach produced a fifth and Buffon a sixth: Peschel followed at once with a seventh and Agassiz with an eighth. Till at length Haeckel was talking of twelve, Morton of twenty-two, and Crawford of sixty races—a number which was to be doubled a little later. So that as respectable a researcher as Luschan could with justice assert that it is just as impossible to determine the number of existing races of men as of the existing languages, since one can no more easily distinguish between a race and a variety than between a language and a so-called dialect. If a white North European is set beside a Negro and a typical Mongolian the difference is clear to any layman. But if one examines thoroughly the countless gradations of these three races one reaches a point at last where one cannot say with certainty where one race leaves off and the other begins.[2]

Conscious of the social importance of negating the doctrines of Nazi "race science" (which maintained, among other things, that different human "races" originated independently of one another), the overwhelming majority of scientific commentators from the 1930s to the present have taken pains to record their views that mankind is *probably* one species. This view has found its political reflection even in such documents as the Charter of the United Nations, the preamble of which speaks of "mankind," and of the "equal rights of men and women and of nations large and small."

Indeed, it may be said that while the belief that all men sprang from a common species, and that through mutation different varieties of men have come into being, is not universally accepted, it is common currency, and is accepted as probable by authorities as different as, for example, Charles Darwin, Teilhard de Chardin, and Ashley Montagu.[3] It would,

1. *The Descent of Man.*
2. *Nationalism and Culture* (1937).
3. "All the races agree in so many unimportant details of structure and in so many mental peculiarities that these can be accounted for only by inheritance from a common progenitor." (Charles Darwin, *The Descent of Man,* 1871)

"If the Science of Man can affirm nothing directly for or against monogeneticism (a single original couple), on the other hand it pronounces itself, it appears, decidedly in favor of monophyletism (a single phylum)." (Pierre Teilhard de Chardin, *The Human Phenomenon,* 1955)

"It is today generally agreed that all men belong to the same species, that all were probably derived from the same ancestral stock, and that all share in a common patrimony." (Ashley Montagu, *Man's Most Dangerous Myth,* 1952)

however, be surprising if universal agreement were to be achieved upon any subject, and a dissenting view is held by a few scientists, of whom Carleton S. Coon may be taken as typical.[4]

Some have used the image of the "Tree of Life" as a conceptual aid —a tree with various branches which, in turn, branch off again. Yet the image can mislead. As H. G. Wells puts it:

We have to remember that human races can all interbreed freely and that they separate, mingle, and reunite as clouds do. Human races do not branch out like trees with branches that never come together again. It is a thing we need to bear constantly in mind, this remingling of races at every opportunity.[5]

If we want to understand man's early origins, therefore, we have to imagine populations of unknown composition living in areas of the world that were probably quite different in character than they are today. The vast climatic changes that took place during periods of glaciation, as compared with the interglacial periods, resulted, for example, in the lowering of sea levels to many yards below present-day levels. Some areas that are now under cultivation were previously inundated. The contours of some coastlines were also entirely different. Areas that are now islands were sometimes joined by isthmuses to the mainland. Land bridges sometimes spanned places that were later eaten through by the waters to form straits. For instance, Herodotus, writing in the fifth century B.C., considered Sardinia to be the largest island in the world. Since both Sicily and Britain, which were within the geographic frontiers of knowledge in his day, both surpass Sardinia in size, it may be a justifiable inference that in the fifth century B.C. both Sicily and Britain were perhaps not islands. It is now thought likely that only shortly before the Roman invasion of Britain the waters of the North Sea—perhaps in some great storm—finally broke through the neck of land joining Britain to the mainland to mingle with the waters of the Atlantic. At the time when man first appeared on the earth, a land bridge may have connected Spain with North Africa, and another may have connected North America with Asia.

In the eighteenth century, for some obscure reason, shoals of herring began to desert the Baltic for the North Sea.[6] Human populations have also, in earlier times, suddenly begun to change their habitat, leaving areas that had formerly sustained them for long centuries. About 1,500 years ago, for example, the western Roman Empire collapsed as a result

---

4. "My thesis is, in essence, that at the beginning of our record, over half a million years ago, man was a single species, *Homo erectus*, perhaps already divided into five geographical races or sub-species. *Homo erectus* then evolved into *Homo sapiens* not once but five times, as each sub-species, living in its own territory, passed a critical threshold from a more brutal to a more sapient state." (Carleton S. Coon, *The Origin of Races*, 1962)

5. *A Short History of the World* (1946 edition).

6. The Swedes attributed the departure of the herring to the firing of British and other ships of war attending convoys.

of migrations of whole nations from Asia into Europe. Prince Peter Kropotkin, the Russian geographer, was of the opinion that the cause of these migrations was desiccation—a desiccation which dried up rivers and reduced lakes to mere ponds. The inhabitants of North West Mongolia and East Turkestan were thus obliged to move into lowlands to the west, driving the plains' dwellers before them, and setting in motion a "landslide" of peoples that was to continue for centuries.

Such "tidal" movements of humanity often left "puddles" of people behind. The crania of the Guanche people of the Canary Islands—who have now disappeared as a specific group, although the present populations of the islands are believed to be as much Guanche as Spanish in origin—were found to resemble the skulls of the Cro-Magnon people. It was therefore concluded that the Guanches were a people who, in the Canary Islands, had succeeded in surviving the glacial period. The Ainu of the Kurile Islands near Japan are a "Caucasian" group who originally occupied the whole of Japan. In North Africa, blonde hair and blue eyes, which still occasionally occur among the populations of the Maghreb, are believed to be genetically attributable to the Vandals—an ethnic group which was originally formed in Sweden, and which dissolved in North Africa in the sixth century A.D.

## Human Clouds

Human clouds have mingled and separated on occasions that can no longer be traced with any certainty. Unrelated glimpses, merely, are afforded us:

> The origin of the Berbers is obscure; although the fact that they had displaced an earlier indigenous population across the whole north-eastern fringe of the Sahara by the second millennium B.C. seems to be fairly conclusively proved by ancient Egyptian documents. On linguistic grounds it is usually conceded that they are non-African and most probably West Asiatic in origin.[7]

Herodotus told of some "wild young men"—Nasamonians of Libya—who drew lots for five of their number to go and explore the desert parts of Libya, and to see if they could penetrate further than anyone had done before. Having crossed, among other areas, "a tract which is wholly sand, very scant of water, and utterly and entirely desert," they came to a plain where trees were growing. They were proceeding to gather fruit from the trees when "there came upon them some dwarfish men, under the middle height, who seized them and carried them off . . ." They were finally led to a town "where all the men were of the height of their conductors, and black-complexioned. A great river flowed by the town, running from west to east, and containing crocodiles."

R. S. Rattray, in *Religion and Art in Ashanti* (1927), refers to the

7. C. B. McBurney, *The Stone Age of Northern Africa* (1960).

"pirafo," or dwarfs—"persons of both sexes, of a very diminutive stature, who are to be found in many Ashanti villages . . . I first came across these curious little people in some of the forest villages in the Brong country of Northern Ashanti, where I saw at least three in a single village. They were extremely shy, and at first always 'not at home' when I tried to visit them." Rattray suggested that these people were "possibly a reversion to a very diminutive forest race, possibly the original inhabitants of the Ashanti forests."[8]

Other writers have speculated that an old Negritic element existed in the population of parts of Southern and Western Europe. In support of this theory they referred to the Grimaldi fossils—the remains of sixteen prognathous individuals found in caves in the Italian Riviera in 1901. More recently, however, the theory has been challenged, and it does not now meet with general acceptance.

Thus from a few old bones, and from old manuscripts, or other evidence, we try to piece together what happened long ago. Only hints and glimpses are afforded us. Beyond that the distant past remains as dark as that night to which the mysterious Cimmerian people, whose identity still escapes us, gave their name.

It is not always clear, therefore, in considering the ancient world, precisely where the frontiers of skin coloration then lay. Let us nevertheless attempt to outline the approximate situation at the dawning of ancient civilizations—that is to say, when written records first began to be kept.

The following broad generalizations, based to some extent upon scholarly guesswork, and subject to much qualification and modification, and even dispute, may nevertheless be made:

*Black-skinned Peoples:* The ancestors of the black Africans of today had previously occupied a broad belt of territory that stretched through Africa and southern Asia. An influx of brown-skinned "Indo-Europeans" moving down into India split this great grouping into two parts. The western part of the black group then consolidated its position in Africa, into which its peoples moved deeper in a great southerly and westerly migration. In so doing they may have replaced or amalgamated with still earlier inhabitants. The eastern part of the black group was fragmented to some extent, although clear and widespread traces of it are to be found to this day in Southeastern Asia.

*Yellow-skinned Peoples:* Yellow-skinned nomadic peoples lived in northern Asia, from where they moved down into China. Other Asian peoples (ancestors of the "red skins") crossed from Asia to America, probably via a land bridge.

8. Ateliosis (dwarfism) has been given as a possible explanation for this phenomenon. It has been pointed out that while dwarfs are also encountered in Europe and America, nobody has postulated the existence in earlier times of a "race" of white dwarfs.

*White-skinned Peoples:* White nomadic peoples living in Asia and northern Europe moved west and south until they reached the Atlantic Ocean and the Mediterranean Sea.

*Brown-skinned Peoples:* The Middle East, the North African littoral, parts of Asia, and perhaps of Southern Europe, were occupied by brown-skinned peoples.

There are, to be sure, exceptions to these broad outlines, and certainly many more exceptions than we may ever know of. To take only one example, there were the Colchians, of whom Herodotus writes. The Colchians inhabited a district in what is now Soviet Georgia in the Caucasus, and their chief port, then named Phasis, corresponds to modern Poti. Herodotus wrote of them:

> There can be no doubt that the Colchians are an Egyptian race. Before I heard any mention of the fact from others, I had remarked it myself. After the thought had struck me, I made enquiries on the subject both in Colchis and in Egypt, and I found that the Colchians had a more distinct recollection of the Egyptians, than the Egyptians had of them. Still the Egyptians said that they believed the Colchians to be descended from the army of Sesostris. My own conjectures were founded, first, on the fact that they are black skinned and have woolly hair; which certainly amounts to very little, since several other nations are so too; but further, and more especially, on the circumstance that the Colchians, the Egyptians, and the Ethiopians, are the only nations who have practised circumcision from the earliest times.

It is believed that the Colchians have now been absorbed by intermarriage with the white populations of the region. Colchis was the fabled land of the Golden Fleece, from which Medea, daughter of King Aetees, came. Circe, the enchantress, who turned men into animals, is described by Homer in the *Odyssey* as "own sister to the magician Aetees, for they are both children of the sun." Circe, it may be noted, is sometimes portrayed as black.[9]

Certainly the black soldiers of "King Sesostris" (who was possibly a mythical character, or—more precisely—a composite one, to whom were ascribed jointly the exploits of Senusret I, Senusret III, and Rameses II) were neither the first nor the last black Africans to bear arms in Europe and the Middle East in classical times. The African troops who fought in the Trojan War, and those who later crossed the Alps with Hannibal and served him throughout his long Italian campaigns, may not have established any more Colchian kingdoms, but they certainly participated in that long process of intermingling which has almost invariably happened when different peoples have found themselves in propinquity.

If, however, "pockets" of blacks were to be found north of the "color frontier," so, too, there were signs of "pockets" of whites to the south. The legendary "white" origin of the Fulbe people (who are also known

9. See, for example, J. A. Rogers, *Nature Knows No Color Line* (1952), p. 33.

as the Fulani, the Fulah, or the Peuhls), has been the subject of much discussion. The first kings of Ghana, according to ancient chronicles compiled by Timbuktu scholars, were "white men" from the north. It is, of course, possible that the whiteness may have only been relative. We may doubt or believe as we wish—just as we may believe or doubt Henri Lhote's statement that in prehistoric times black Africa stretched much further north on the continent than it does now.

### "The Most Ancient of Mankind"

So far as early civilizations are concerned, we know that the Egyptians used to consider themselves "the most ancient of mankind,"[10] as both Herodotus and Plato have testified. Herodotus, however, recounted that since the reign of the Egyptian King Psammetichus, the Egyptians had yielded their claims to antiquity to the Phrygians. This was on account of an "experiment" conducted by Psammetichus to ascertain which was the most ancient nation.

> He took two children of the common sort, and gave them over to a herdsman to bring up at his folds, strictly charging him to let no one utter a word in their presence, but to keep them in a sequestered cottage. . . . His object therein was to know, after the indistinct babblings of infancy were over, what word they would first articulate. . . . The herdsman obeyed his orders for two years, and at the end of that time, on his one day opening the door of their room and going in, the children both ran up to him with outstretched arms, and distinctly said "Becos" . . .

—a word that proved to be the Phrygian word for "bread."

We may smile today at the naïveté of this early linguistic research, and at the conclusions drawn from it. Whether or not the Egyptians were, as they had believed, the oldest nation, there is reason to think that they may perhaps have been, if by "nation" we mean a social group which creates a higher civilization. Because the flood plain of the Nile made the planting of crops simple, the Nile valley was one of the first places, if not the first place, where mankind is believed to have abandoned the nomadic way of life in favor of agriculture. Certainly, Egyptian civilization, which dates back at least to 3400 B.C., is older than the Chinese or any other major civilization of the old world that is today known to us.[11]

If Egypt was, in fact, the first major world civilization, the question occurs, Did Egypt arise and spread its influence deeply into the African continent? Or, on the other hand, did Egypt draw heavily upon older African traditions, fashioning out of them a new synthesis? Diodorus Siculus, for example, writing during the first century B.C., spoke well of

10. The Ethiopians, however, considered themselves to be still older.
11. But recently it has been claimed that the city of Jericho has existed since 7800 B.C., that is, for almost 10,000 years. The evidence on which this claim is based has, however, been doubted by some authorities.

the civilized Ethiopians of Meroe (capital of the kingdom of Kush, to the south of Egypt, which stood in what is now the Sudan), and said that they were the first people to worship the gods, and that most Egyptian institutions were derived from their civilization. Egyptian knowledge of astronomy was also apparently derived from Kush. Ancient Africa has many a secret yet to yield—and many, no doubt, that it will always keep. What can we make, for example, of the assertion of Leo Frobenius that the Yoruba Holy City of Ife, where tradition maintains that man, both black and white, was first created, is identical with the capital of lost Atlantis?[12]

What of color consciousness in these early times? Always, in considering these questions, it is to Egypt that one returns in search of answers. For Egypt was the place above all others where the peoples of Africa, Asia, and Europe met and mingled. It would seem that early writers tended to refer to the Egyptians as if they were black-skinned people. Herodotus, in the passage already quoted about the Colchians, does so. Nor is this an isolated reference from his work. In recounting how the oracles of Dodoma in Greece and of Ammon in Libya came to be founded, he says that, according to the Thebans, two sacred women of Thebes were once carried off by the Phoenicians and sold, one in Greece, and one in Libya, and that they then founded the oracles in these two countries. The Dodonaeans, however, speaking figuratively, said that "two black doves flew away from Egyptian Thebes, and while one directed its flight to Libya, the other came to them." Herodotus adds that in his own opinion "by calling the dove black the Dodonaeans indicated that the woman was an Egyptian."

We have already referred to the tradition that Egypt derived certain religious institutions, as well as a knowledge of astronomy, from the Ethiopians. This fact alone is indicative of the closeness of contact that has always existed between Egypt and black Africa. The continuity of this contact has never been in doubt. Much, however, remains to be discovered about the varying forms it has taken. Military expeditions marched, at different epochs and with varying success, from Egypt to the south, and from the south against Egypt. Trade and religion provided further channels for exchange, and evidence has been found far afield. During the First World War, for example, a Belgian, in command of some troops in Katanga, ordered his men to dig deep holes in order to set up the posts of a hangar. As a result a small bronze statuette of Osiris was unearthed. A connection has been postulated between Shango, a West African thunder god who appears in storms riding upon a ram, and Ammon, the ram-headed sun god of the Egyptians, Greeks, and

12. See *The Voice of Africa* (1913).

Libyans.[13] Another connection has been seen between Ashanti custom and those of ancient Egypt.[14]

The interesting thing about all this is that there appears to be no justification for thinking that Egyptians linked skin color with social status. Slaves and rulers alike in Egypt's long history are known to have been both white and black. Egyptian paintings depict individuals of both colors, as well as others who are brown or reddish. Statues are likewise to be found with equally variegated physical features. It is noticeable, for example, that the characteristics of the sphinx are "negroid." African, Asian, and European dynasties alike have ruled over Egypt, of which only the Kushite, Persian, and Ptolemaic dynasties need be mentioned as examples. Indeed, there is abundant evidence, both pictorially and in written form, of the interrelationship among peoples of many races in Egypt. The passions which today are sometimes associated with the question of skin color, the ancient Egyptians would appear to have associated with loyalties to different gods, oracles, or religious cults.

In the minds of most Westerners of today, of course, a clear association exists between the institution of slavery and skin color. This is, no doubt, the heritage of the decision of white-skinned peoples in fairly recent centuries that black-skinned peoples might be enslaved. But the question of who properly should, and who should not, be enslaved did, periodically, perplex the ancient world. (In practice, the principle laid down by the Athenian representatives of the Melian Conference in the fifth century B.C. that "the strong do what they have the power to do and the weak accept what they have to accept" determined the answer.)

One theoretical attempt to provide a basis for a decision was put forward by the poet Hesiod in his story of the "four races" which succeeded one another—the golden, the silver, the bronze, and the copper. This idea is an adaptation of a scheme of Oriental origin, in which the Nubians were the people of gold (the word for "gold" was the Egyptian *nb* and the Coptic *noyb*), the Hittites the people of silver, the Cypriots the people of copper, and the Chalybes of Asia Minor a people of steel. The myth was circulated by the Phoenicians at a time when they were allied with Kushite Egypt, and appears to have had a political motivation in that it was claimed that the silver, bronze, and steel peoples had degenerated from the "aboriginal perfection of the Nubian 'golden race.' "[15]

The metallurgical scheme of Hesiod had a parallel in the theory of

13. Leo Frobenius, *The Voice of Africa* (1913).
14. Eva Meyerowitz, *Akan Traditions of Origin* (1952).
15. See Robert Eisler, *Metallurgical Anthropology in Hesiod and Plato and the Date of the Phoenician Lie* (Isis XI: 1949). Also c.f. E. Pittard's allusion to four races in Egypt—the Rot (reddish-brown), Nehusi (black), Namu (yellow), and Temehou (white).

"correspondences," which was given a brief revival by the French symbolist poets of the nineteenth century—notably Gérard de Nerval—and which, it was claimed, derived from the ancients. According to this theory there was a secret correspondence, or relationship, between superficially unrelated objects. Particular stars were related to particular flowers or mosses, and these in turn to metals, colors, and human dispositions. An understanding of astronomy played a large part in this.

Bases, of course, there were for classifying people, but the indications are that no particular significance was attached to skin color in ancient times. Certainly it is plausible that at a time when travel was slow, and when the world in consequence seemed vaster, the majority of mankind would consider all peoples who lived beyond their boundaries as strange and barbarian. Those of a different skin color would naturally appear as possessing yet one more superficial external difference in addition to other differences, such as those of language, of tribe, of environment, of religious belief, and of allegiance. Lord Bryce, the historian, stated that a survey of the facts "has shown us that down to the days of the French Revolution there had been very little in any country, or at any time, of self-conscious racial feeling." Strong as patriotism and national feeling might be, he added, men did not think of themselves in terms of ethnology.[16]

### Skin Color and the Greeks

The Greeks, of course, primarily through their special relationship with Egypt, were well acquainted with black- and brown-skinned peoples, and also knew much of other lands. Here again it is Herodotus who can provide us with further insights. In discussing the reasons for which, in his opinion, the Nile waters could not be formed of melted snow, he put forward three arguments, one of which was that in the land out of which the Nile flows "the natives of the country are black with the heat." The comment is interesting for two reasons. The first is that it confirms that in the fifth century B.C. the peoples who lived in those regions were indeed black. Today this may seem to us a truism. Yet in the tenth century B.C. the black Queen of Sheba (or Sabaea), from whom the Ethiopians claim descent, then ruled not in Africa, but over the southern part of the Arabian peninsula. The second is that the comment of Herodotus reveals something of his own belief—and presumably that of his Sophoclean contemporaries—concerning the reason for the difference in the color of men's skins. This belief was that skin color was due to environment, and not to any qualitative difference.

The Greeks, indeed, tended to divide humanity into two groups— Greeks and Barbarians. An expression of Greek sentiment on the subject

16. *Race Sentiment as a Factor in History* (1915).

of Barbarians—who were distinguished principally by being unacquainted with the Greek language—is to be found in the writings of Euripides, in which this passage occurs:

It accords with the fitness of things that Barbarians should be subject to Greeks, for Greeks are free men and Barbarians are slaves by nature.

Although four out of five of the population of ancient Greece were slaves, the blacks among them were not sufficiently numerous to attract any particular attention. The criteria for enslavement remained mainly political or cultural, rather than physical. In that eotechnic age,[17] when wind, water, and muscle were the sole generators of power, slavery was considered a practical necessity, and knew no color line.

As we have seen, the Greeks derived not only some proportion of their religion, but also their knowledge of astronomy from Kush and/or Ethiopia, via Egypt. It was the remoteness of Ethiopians and others that led to their being regarded as Barbarians. Who, whether black or white, being situated far from Greece could be regarded as other than unfortunate? The Greek poet Menander, writing of the unimportance of pedigree in comparison with moral qualities, says:

The man whose natural bent is good,
He, mother, he, though Aethiop, is nobly born.
A Scyth, you say? Pest! Anarcharsis was a Scyth!

The geographer Ptolemy placed the "uncivilized" blacks who lived beyond Napata and Kush at one pole, and Scythians at the other. The uncultured habits of these tribes, he said, were attributable to the fact that in their homes they were continually oppressed by the heat, just as the behavior of the savage Scyths was due to the fact that they had to endure constant cold.

The black Africans were also known to the Greeks as soldiers who had fought against them in both the Trojan and the Persian wars. (Memnon, who fought on the Trojan side, and who killed Antilochus, son of Nestor, and was himself killed by Achilles, was an Ethiopian). Quintus of Smyrna wrote that the Ethiopians at Troy excelled in battle. Certainly African troops were widely used as auxiliaries in the ancient world. The high esteem in which Odysseus held Eurybates of the "woolly hair" and the "sable skin" and the rank that he gave him as one of his heralds is also worth noting.

As in Egypt, so in Greece, depictions of both white and black individuals have come down to us from the artists of ancient days, although such Greek examples are considerably less numerous than those from Egypt. Some of the coinage of Phocis, Delphi, Lesbos, and Athens bears

17. Lewis Mumford's term for the age when wind was the main source of power.

the head of a black African who, according to some, was Delphos, the founder of Delphi, himself.

## Skin Color and the Romans

It was in the Roman civilization, rather than in the Egyptian or Greek, that the greater degree of international contact, both at home and abroad, appears to have taken place. The reputation of the Roman Empire has continued to exercise a compelling influence upon the pattern of history down to our own times. Have not certain Frenchmen, Britons, Italians, and Americans of our own century tended to view their respective nations as the destined "heirs of Rome"? The puissance of Rome's example is due, in effect, to its universalism.

How, then, could an Empire claiming universality not have knowledge of even the remotest places or peoples? Such knowledge, that is, as lay within its power to acquire. Northern Africa, from Mauritania to Egypt, had, by 30 B.C., become subject to Roman rule. Further south and east, however, the traces of the limits of Roman power and knowledge are less discernible. But the Romans are known to have been more knowledgeable about black Africa than was previously suspected. As Richard Jobson, the seventeenth-century English trader, eloquently commented, "The Romans, careful Relaters of their great victories, doe speak little of the interior parts of Affrica." The Carthaginians, in earlier times, did much to bar the trans-Sahara trade to them. Later, however, in the first century A.D., after the reduction of Carthage, and after the conclusion of an alliance between the Romans and their former enemies, the Libyan tribe of the Garamantes, more than one Roman expedition marched south across the desert. Suetonius Paulinus is believed to have reached the headwaters of streams that are tributary to the Niger. It is thought that Cornelius Balbus may have reached the Niger itself.[18] How far Septimus Flaccus penetrated into the "country of the black men" nobody can now tell. Julius Maternus and his men, accompanied by the King of the Garamantes, proceeded "towards the Aethiopians"; after four months of traveling they arrived at Agisymba, "a district or province of the Ethiopians where rhinoceroses congregate," which has been identified with the Lake Chad area.

It has been suggested that the custom, found in some parts of West Africa, of constructing an "atrium," or large entrance hall, in the houses of the more important personalities, as well as the widespread West African custom of offering libations to ancestors, have much in common with Roman practice. The fashion of wearing sandals and a cloth draped like a toga, followed by Ashanti and some other West African groups, provides an even more obvious parallel. Roman beads are also reported to have been discovered in the tombs of the Ashanti kings.

18. Henri Lhote, *The Search for the Tassili Frescoes* (1959).

On the Nile the Romans were for a relatively long period in communication with Kush, where, in 23 B.C., the Roman general Petronius conducted a punitive campaign after the Kushites had raided Philae and Aswan and pulled down the statues of the Emperor Augustus. A bronze head of Augustus was found hidden beneath the floor of the former royal palace of Meroe, once the capital of Kush, about fifty years ago. The Emperor Nero also sent two centurions to visit the Sudan and to report to him whether it was worth conquering. After reportedly traveling the entire length of the Nile, the centurions returned to Rome and told Nero that it was not.

The Roman legions had marched, of course, deep into Asia. Here again, however, their writ ran only some of the way. Contact with the other great empire on the planet—Cathay—was virtually nonexistent. The first Chinese empire of Ts'in sent emissaries west on a voyage of discovery, and through them "just brushed against the first Empire of Rome with the tips of its antennae," as Arnold Toynbee put it. But the buffer states between the two empires effectively held them apart, although it is reported that Romans and Chinese did engage together in "the silent trade," which was a method of silent or "dumb" bartering, not uncommon in the ancient world and in the Middle Ages, and which was often conducted by goods being left at some predetermined spot without the trading partners ever physically confronting one another.

In Rome, and in the Empire itself, we hear little of any repugnance for dark-skinned Africans. Rome, the greatest city of the ancient world, was also its melting pot. Herodian, writing in the third century A.D., called the population of Rome "variegated and commingled," and related how the Emperor Constantine stared at the sight of the Roman people, commenting on "how swiftly every type of man on earth congregates at Rome." "The hub of the globe," "the inn of the world,"—such were the expressions used to describe the Rome of those days. Cicero himself stated that immigration "overflowed Rome and blended her blood with that of every race" of the ancient world.

Ludwig Friedlander writes that

At Rome the gabble of a hundred speeches might be heard, the shapes and garb of every race rubbed shoulders. Moorish slaves led elephants from out of the Emperor's stables. There a troop of blond Germans of the Emperor's Life Guards were exercising in gleaming armour. The Egyptians, with shaven heads, in sweeping linen robes, were carrying the goddess Isis in procession. Behind a Greek professor a young Nubian was carrying his scrolls of books. Oriental princes . . . tattooed savages from Britain staring their eyes out at the marvels of the new world all about them.[19]

And again:

Roman courtesans received according to Martial visits from Parthians, Germans, Cilicians, Cappadocians, Egyptians, Nubians, Jews, Dacians, and Alani. At Augustus'

19. *Roman Life and Manners Under the Early Empire* (seventh edition: undated).

spectacle of a naval battle ( 2 B.C.), Ovid says the whole world was in Rome; at the consecration of the Flavian amphitheatre according to Martial, spectators foregathered from the farthest regions, Sarmatians, Sigambians, Arabians, Sabaeans, and Aethiopians.

Comparing the Roman Empire to empires of our own day, we must conclude that the barriers of color, language, and habits we know today were unknown in the Roman world. Similarly, just as barriers exist in modern times which were not there before, so in the ancient world forces for unity were at work which today have grown fainter under the insistent pressure of modern technological culture with its scarcely concealed impatience with the survivals of past eras. Lord Bryce, a Scotsman whom we have already quoted, sensed a connection between African tribal customs and those of the ancient world. "How thankful we should be, we men of the nineteenth century, if a Roman had taken the trouble fully to investigate the habits of our Celtic forefathers!" he remarked to H. A. Junod, the Swiss anthropologist. Leo Frobenius, in his *Voice of Africa,* also noted similarities between the religion of the Yorubas of West Africa and the pre-Christian religion of the ancient world. Like the Etruscans, the Yoruba built their temples on a plan divided into sixteen different quarters, and divided the horizon into sixteen sections for the purpose of divination. Sir James Frazer was also among those who first noted the close connection between ancient classical studies and modern anthropology. Contemporary educators in West Africa have more than once noted the ease with which their African students have understood passages in the Greek classics which have given considerable trouble to European or American schoolchildren. The metaphysical framework, no less than the technical one, was similar, and the imbalance of our own days had not yet occurred.

Yet if Rome did not know domination based on color, it knew and practiced domination based on conquest. Slavery in Rome, as in Greece, was an accepted norm—and yet was quite different in character to that which, over a thousand years later, sprang up in Europe and the Americas.

Under the Roman slave system a large proportion of physicians and sculptors were slaves, as also were some distinguished authors, not to speak of lesser literary lights, many imported from Greece. The well-known proposal that slaves should be distinguished by special dress, which was rejected lest they should become overly conscious of their overwhelming numerical strength and plot to seize the city, is also additional evidence that slaves were not marked out by color. Montesquieu, in the eighteenth century, commented on the unselective aspect of slavery in Rome. "There was a great circulation of men from all the universe," he wrote. "Rome received them as slaves and sent them back Romans."

As in Greece, slaves were to be found of every skin color. Nobody suggested that it should be otherwise; nor did anyone suggest that a system that was so self-evidently necessary to civilization at that time be abolished.

So far as the Roman Empire was concerned, men with dark skins as well as those with white could aspire to the most eminent of positions. Septimus Severus, Emperor of Rome from A.D. 193–211, who was born in Tripolitania, is said to have been at least partially of black African origin. He died at York, in England, where he had been reorganizing the Roman defenses against the Scottish tribes. His son Caracalla, whose mother was Syrian, succeeded him, and is credited with having done much to make possible the granting of Roman citizenship to men of all origins, instead of on the more restrictive basis previously practiced.

In the religious domain, Egyptian religion, in pre-Christian times, was immensely popular in Rome. Among the Christians a most notable African was Saint Augustine, himself a Berber, who was born in Carthage.

There can, in sum, remain little doubt that in antiquity skin color was by no means invested with the emotional significance that has in more recent times become attached to it. One would hardly wish to claim that antiquity constituted, from the social point of view, a "golden age." Despite its more renowned virtues and values it was anything but that. But the curse of acute color-consciousness, attended by all the raw passions and social problems that cluster around it—that, at least, antiquity was spared.

# Chapter 2

# "When the Earth Was Flat":
# The Scene Is Set

DURING THE Middle Ages—a period that may be defined as lasting from approximately 500 to 1500 A.D.—many of the shadows that hide earlier developments in mankind's history are dispelled, so that it is possible to gain a reasonably accurate concept of the moods, movements, and relationships of the earth's peoples in the period immediately before the emergence of modern racial mythology.

Commenting on the dissolution of the ancient world, Gobineau wrote that from the time of the Punic Wars among the Romans and of Pericles among the Greeks, the uniform civilization of the respective countries of the antique world, at bottom national in character, tended to break down more and more.

> The mixture of nations brought with it a mixture of civilizations. The result was a very complex and learned society, with a culture far more refined than before. But it had one striking disadvantage; both in Italy and in Hellas, it existed merely for the upper classes. . . . By the masses it was, at all times, merely tolerated. The peoples of Europe understood nothing of its Asiatic and African elements, those of Egypt had no better idea of what it brought them from Gaul and Spain, those of Numidia had no appreciation of what came to them from the rest of the world. . . . We have here the example of a civilization that is accepted and dominant, no longer through the convictions of the peoples who live under it, but by their exhaustion, their weakness, and their indifference.[1]

More immediately, the fall of the Roman Empire in the West may be

1. *The Inequality of Human Races* (1854).

said to have occurred as a result of the movement of peoples in Asia. The Huns, advancing across the Sarmatic Plain,[2] pushed the European Barbarian tribes against the "limes," or borders, of the Roman Empire. The Ostrogoths, defeated by the Huns, entered the Roman province of Pannonia (in the western part of what is now Hungary) in the fall of 376 A.D. Crossing the Danube with the permission of the Roman Emperor, they retained their rights of nationality and their organizational structure intact. The Ostrogoths were the first of several tribal groups to be so admitted by the Romans, and the decision to admit them proved a fatal one. The groups proved unassimilable, and their subsequent actions within the Empire led to its disintegration. The center of Empire moved to Byzantium, athwart the trade route between the Mediterranean and the countries of the East, while the Germanic element emerged to predominate in the disunited West.

The Middle Ages and the Age of Byzantium were, indeed, coeval. From the time of the fall of Rome to the Vandals in 455 A.D. until the capture of Constantinople by the Turks in 1453, the wealth and learning of Byzantium stood as a landmark to the age—a lighthouse, it might be said, throwing its rays out over the dark and stormy scenes of Christendom. For whereas Byzantium, and later Damascus and Baghdad, represented the centers of world civilization, medieval Christendom lived by faith rather than reason. It was as if the European psyche, after the insecurities and sudden reversals of fortune that marked the closing days of the Roman Empire in the West, had retreated into subjectivity. Religion was the dominant emotion—the historian Huizinga tells us that we can "never sufficiently realize the extreme excitability of the mediaeval soul." Passion is certainly not a state of mind conducive to the progress of learning or of objective enquiry concerning the nature of the world and of its peoples. Rumor, legend, and superstition were consequently frequently given the same valuation as objective fact.

In matters of fundamental importance, of course, it was the Church that proclaimed where truth lay. So far as ethnic differences were concerned, the Church, seeking as it did the spiritual unity of Christendom, proclaimed the doctrine that all Christians were the same kind of men. Mankind was divided into Christians on the one hand, and into Jews, Moslems, and other infidels on the other. All mankind was, nevertheless, as taught in the Bible, descended from Adam in the first place, and, later, from Noah. Observable racial differences were explained by the fact that some were descended from the children of Shem, some of Ham, and some of Japhet. Later commentators connected the children of Shem with Asia, of Ham with Africa, and of Japhet with Europe.

2. The Sarmatian tribes are believed to have been the ancestors of the Slavs.

*Myths and Fables*

Under ecclesiastical dominance, a European view of the physical world came to prevail in medieval times. It was far removed from that of Ptolemy. Although, during the Dark Ages, the Venerable Bede and some other writers believed that the earth was round, the majority held to the theory that the earth was flat, that Jerusalem lay at its center, and that the Garden of Eden, from which flowed the four Rivers of Paradise, was to be found somewhere in the hinterland of Asia. In Byzantium itself, more accurate conceptions prevailed, despite occasional revolts against Ptolemaic theory, such as that of the monk Cosmas Indicopleustes, who maintained that the earth was shaped like a rectangular room with the sky as its ceiling, and heaven on the first floor.

In Western Europe, where the majority of the population lived in villages and hamlets and were preoccupied with the problems of survival, questions of race and color remained immaterial, like most other things that existed beyond the horizon's rim. In a world in which lived giants such as Gog and Magog, headless men with eyes in their stomachs, and the troglodytes of Libya—single-footed cave-dwellers who shielded themselves from the heat of the sun by lying on their backs and using their huge feet as umbrellas—the fact that some variations of skin color were also reported among foreigners must have appeared as a minor detail. Even those individuals who had personal experience of relations with men of other colors through the Hunnish invasions, the struggles with the "Moors" or other followers of "Mahound,"[3] trade with the East, pilgrimages to Jerusalem, or the Crusades, do not appear to have viewed skin coloration per se as a badge indicating men's ultimate loyalties.

This is not to say that thought was not given to questions of the unknown. Fantasies and myths abounded, flourishing with all the more potency after the seventh century, when Christendom became invested with a Moslem "belt" that effectively insulated it from close contact with Africa, and also jeopardized contacts that existed with the East. We can get some idea of the concepts that prevailed in Western Europe before the time of Henry the Navigator and of Columbus from commentators of the time. Bartholomew Anglicus, writing about 1248 in *De Proprietatibus Rerum*, tells us:

Ethiopia,[4] blue men's land, had first that name of color of men. For the sun is nigh and roasteth and toasteth them. And so the color of men showeth the strength of the star, for there is considerable heat. . . . In this land be many nations with divers faces wonderly and horribly shapen. There be two Ethiopias, one in the East and the other

3. "Mahound" is an old European form of "Mohammed," and is sometimes synonymous with "Satan."
4. Africa was often referred to as "Ethiopia," "Abyssinia," "Libya," or "Nubia" in the Middle Ages.

is Mauretania in the West, and that is more near Spain. And then is Numidia and the Province of Carthage. Then is Getula, and at last against the course of the sun is the land that is hight Ethiopia Adusta, burnt, and fables tell that there beyond the Antipodes men that have their feet against our feet.[5]

Gervase of Tilbury, an English writer and traveler who eventually became marshal of the kingdom of Arles in the early thirteenth century, developed the theme that there was a connection between character and geography. "According to the diversities of the air," he wrote, "the Romans are grave, the Greeks fickle, the Africans sly, the Gauls fierce, the English of great ability, and the Teutons robust."

Later, in the fifteenth century, a Venetian physician, John Caderia, observed that the differences between south and north were due to the fact that the influence of the stars was weaker in the south and the signs of the zodiac less fortunate. "Therefore," he said, "the south is of necessity sterile and pestiferous. Because of the humidity of the south wind, it induces corruption of matter and mind. Men of the south, therefore, are savage, brutal, and often cannibals. To make matters worse, there is often a multitude of demons there."

Arab commentators tended to be more exact in their geographical conceptions than those of Christendom. Idrisi, the twelfth-century geographer, wrote in his *Geography* (often known as the *Book of Roger,* because his patron was Roger II of Sicily) not only a reasonably accurate description of the topography of the known world, but also the following description of the world itself, which may have appeared somewhat extravagant to some of his European contemporaries:

The land, as well as the waters, is immersed in space, as is the yolk in the middle of an egg, that is to say in a central position. . . . The earth is stable in the midst of space, and all created bodies are stable upon the surface of the earth, the air attracting towards it whatever is light, and the earth attracting towards it whatever is heavy, in the same way that a magnet attracts iron.

There were various Western myths and fables of the Middle Ages concerning nonwhite peoples or countries.[6] Among the legends which clustered around the name of Charlemagne, for example, is one in which one of his twelve paladins, Astolpho, flies to Abyssinia on the back of

5. That is, the "fables" told that the world was round. See also the quotation from Marlowe's "Tamburlaine the Great" at the beginning of Chapter 8, p. 184.
6. A curious legend that dates back to early times is that of the Seven Sleepers. In 250 A.D. seven young Christians of Ephesus, suffering from the persecution of the Emperor Decius, allowed themselves to be walled into a cavern to bear witness to their faith. Two centuries later they were allegedly discovered alive, but deep in a sleep, from which they were aroused. The legend, with its overtones of Resurrection, provided the basis for an agricultural fertility cult that was associated with the Pleiades (known as the "Seven Sleepers," as well as by their classic name of the "Seven Sisters"), which became widely disseminated through the dispersion of relics. The cult found adherence in regions as diverse as Yemen, Sumatra, Mali, Western Europe, North Africa, Afghanistan, Chinese Turkestan, and Ethiopia. The legend later entered into the Moslem religious tradition under the name of Ahl al-Kahf. In 1963 a religious fete consecrated to the Seven Sleepers was still being observed in Brittany, with speeches delivered in Breton, Latin, Greek, Arabic, and Kabyle.

a hippogriff[7] and, after various adventures there, including ridding Senapu, the King of Abyssinia, of a plague of harpies,[8] raises a black African army 100,000 strong with which he crosses the Nubian desert and lays siege to Bizerta, thereby taking the Saracens in the rear. Whether this story is pure fable or whether it has a basis in the unchronicled adventures of some Christian knight in the Dark Ages, a garbled version of whose exploits have come down to us via the lays of troubadours and the pages of epic fantasies, none can now say. The strategy is, however, precisely the same as that later attempted by the Portuguese prince, Henry the Navigator.

Another myth that appears to have associations with Africa is the myth of the River of Gold—the medieval "El Dorado"—which was apparently originally based on rumors of West African gold from the Senegal River. This was the "Golden Trade of the Moors" that later became one of the most closely guarded secrets of Islam. The river was said to flow through the land of Ghana—that is to say, the ancient kingdom of Ghana that existed from the fourth to the thirteenth century on the upper Niger— of which Idrisi had written that its two major towns were the most populous and the most involved in trade of any of those of black Africa. Idrisi also described how Africans came from all over the old Sudan to collect gold when the river Senegal rose in August, and added that the country's inhabitants "are rich; they possess gold in abundance."

Yet another myth is the legend of the Three Wise Men of the East, one of whom is frequently depicted as black. And perhaps the most comprehensive of all these myths was the legend of Prester John, the Christian priest-king who was said to be descended from the race of the Three Wise Men and who was the greatest monarch of the world. His land was said to be four months' journey across, and to contain seventy-two provinces. Among other marvels to be found in his domain were the lands of the Amazons, as well as those of the Brahmins, not to speak of such renowned examples of architecture as the Fountain of Youth and the Tower of Babel, of which the whole world had heard, and mineral resources that included rivers that ran gold, silver, and jewels.

The Prester John legend appears to have been based originally on information given to one Otto von Friesing by a Syrian bishop whom he met in Italy in 1145, and which apparently referred to a certain Buddhist tribal leader who had recently gained a victory in Central Asia against the Seljuk ruler of Persia. The legend gained extraordinarily in power and interest as a result of the subsequent forged "Letter of Prester John" of which surviving manuscript copies are addressed to the Emperor of

---

7. The hippogriff, according to medieval writers, resulted from crossing a gryphon and a mare. (The gryphon itself was allegedly a cross between an eagle and a lion.) Hippogriffs were admittedly rare, and inhabited only the far northern or else mountainous regions.
8. A harpy was a vulture with the head and breasts of a woman.

Byzantium, the Pope, and Frederick Barbarossa. In the subjective world of the Middle Ages, however, in which it was more important to know how the individual stood in relation to heaven and hell, rather than in relation to the points of the compass, the legend of Prester John flourished virtually uninvestigated, until at last his mythical realm was identified with that of Ethiopia—first by Jordan of Severac in about 1340, and then by the Portuguese adventurers who reached Ethiopia at the end of the fifteenth century. The identification of Prester John as the Negus of Ethiopia, however, did not at all disturb the believers in his legend. Most Europeans of the time had vague ideas as to the geographical manner in which the continents of Africa and Asia were separated, and often thought of them as completely contiguous.

## Byzantium

It was, however, the concept of the "glorious East" which above all fascinated the superstitious Western medieval mind, and around which the greatest number of legends clung. Byzantium itself, to those who did not live there, took on many of the attributes of a mythical city. It was the center of Christendom, and tales of its power and glory spread throughout the Empire over which it theoretically ruled. Even details of dress served to add to the exotic legend. As early as the fifth century the Roman toga was abandoned by the Byzantines in favor of long coats of stiff brocade. The scaramangium, the robe that every Byzantine noble wore on ceremonial occasions, was copied from a garment worn by the Huns, and that, in turn, had probably been inspired long before by the robes of Chinese mandarins.

Just as East and West met in Byzantine culture, so, too, did they in ethnic intermixture. Until the seventh century the intermixing that had characterized the Mediterranean cultures under Roman rule continued under that of the Byzantines. The loss of Egypt and of Syria to the Muslims, however, altered the pattern. Henceforth it was the peoples of Asia Minor—a conglomeration of Phrygian, Hittite, Gallic, Iranian, Semitic, and other stocks—that became predominant. Yet, even so, new elements continued to come in, notably Slavs and Armenians. The constant racial intermixing had been further encouraged both by an influx of immigrants seeking their fortunes, as well as by an outflow of Muslim emigrants to Europe. So Byzantines became converted to Islam, and Arabs to Christianity, as their interest prompted them. Thus we are told that the father of the epic hero Digenis Akritas was a Saracen[9] convert, and the Emperor Nicephorus I was of Arab blood. So mixed, indeed, was the blood of the Byzantines that racial prejudices were virtually

9. The word "Saracen" is derived from the Old French *sarrazin,* the late Greek *Sarakenos,* and the Arabic *sharkeyn,* meaning "eastern people" as opposed to *maghribe,* meaning "western people."

nonexistent. To adhere to Greek religion and to speak Greek were the two criteria of citizenship. Thus an alien who was converted and naturalized could marry any Byzantine, whatever his or her origin may have been. "It is true," writes Runciman, "that when Justinian II forced a senatorial lady to marry his own Negro cook, decent feeling was outraged,"[10] but the outrage, so far as we know, arose from the difference in social station rather than from ethnic difference.

How far Byzantine influence once spread into Africa remains unclear. There was trade with the Abyssinian kingdom of Axum, and the Abyssinians, in their turn, traded with Central Africa, often accompanied by Byzantine merchants. Frobenius traces an ancient Byzantine connection with the kingdom of Nupe in what is now Western Nigeria—before the "enemies of Jesus" (i.e. the Moslems) closed the road forever; a connection that he proves by the Byzantine patterns on carved beams and chased brass, by the crosses on the saddle pommels, and in the cruciform hilts of daggers.

## Slavery in the Middle Ages

While Byzantium, standing as it did at the crossroads of the world, athwart the great trade axis between the Mediterranean and the East, spread its fame far and wide, Western Europe remained culturally backward, a distant province of the civilized world. Superstition advanced at the expense of learning; knowledge of other regions grew less. Slavery was, moreover, widely practiced in medieval Christendom, although it gradually gave way under the influence of Christianity.

Slavery was distinctly and formally recognized by Christianity, and it is not without interest that, although the Fathers of the Church made much of the natural equality of mankind, the justification of slavery was sometimes based by the Fathers upon the Curse of Ham, of which so much was to be made in later centuries. Christianity, nevertheless, worked first to ameliorate the condition of slaves, and then for their eventual emancipation. Despite these efforts slavery in Europe lasted for 800 years after Constantine.

During the earlier Middle Ages, the city of Venice was a great slave mart, and there were repeated protests about the selling of Christian slaves there for delivery into pagan hands. From the end of the ninth century on, slaves from the Dalmatian coast were carried off (or bought there) by Venetians, who sold them to the harems of Egypt and Syria. Barcelona also engaged in the slave trade, using Moorish slaves captured in Spain. Until the tenth century Prague was the most important slave market of Middle Europe. (A Jewish merchant, Ibrahim Ibn Jaqub, who visited Prague during the reign of Otto the Great, expecting to

10. Steven Runciman, *Byzantine Civilization* (1933).

purchase men and women slaves, was evidently perplexed not to find the coveted blonde ware on sale, but only brown-skinned humans with dark hair). Slaves disappeared from Prague markets, however, during the reign of either the second or third Christian ruler of Bohemia. Most European slaves, however, did not appear to have been of any particular origin, although it will of course be recalled that the word "slave" itself is derived from "Slav." The connection that was later to link black skin with slavery had not yet, despite occasional references to the Curse of Ham, been established; indeed the first African slaves were not taken to Europe until 1442, when the Portuguese succeeded in outflanking the Muslim cordon that cut off Europe from black Africa.

By the twelfth century slavery in Europe had become very rare. In France it had been customary for slaves to be freed annually at certain ecclesiastical festivals, but by the thirteenth century there were no more slaves left to emancipate, so that the churches were obliged to release caged pigeons in their place "in memory of the ancient charity and that prisoners might still be freed in the name of Christ."[11]

## The Cross and the Crescent

In the earlier Middle Ages, the contacts of Western Europe with lands beyond Christendom were often with Arabs. Paradoxically, Charlemagne himself, who became the supposed prototype of the Christian crusader against the Saracen infidel, carefully cultivated friendly relations with Harun al-Rashid—a political friendship based on mutual opposition to Christian Byzantium. Lack of contact between Western Europe and Africa at that time is indicated by the fact that the most prized of the many gifts sent to Charlemagne by Harun al-Rashid was an elephant—named Abul Abbas,[12] after the first caliph of the Abbasid dynasty, Abu al-Abbas. Abul Abbas created a sensation when he first arrived at Aachen on July 20, 802, but he died suddenly eight years later during one of Charlemagne's campaigns into Saxony. The annalists recorded the loss, we are told, as if it were a member of the royal family. (Another sign of the superior Arab command of the human environment was the further present of a water clock—the first clock of any kind seen in Europe.)

The immediate cause of Europe's isolation during this period was the gradually more effective closing of the Mediterranean by the "Saracens"—a process which began in the middle of the seventh century with the capture of Syria by the Moslems, and which became virtually complete by the ninth century, when Charlemagne was crowned. The cultural effects of this change in the balance of power are represented

---

11. W. E. H. Lecky, *History of European Morals* (1930).
12. Three types of elephant originally existed—African, Indian, and North African. The North African elephants were exterminated by the wars of antiquity and by the Roman circuses. It is not known to what species Abul Abbas belonged.

by a material fact—that after 677 the royal chancellery of the Frankish Empire stopped using papyrus because, due to the Saracen blockade, papyrus could no longer be imported from Egypt. It was not until the eleventh century that Western trading ships were able to sail freely through the Mediterranean once more.

It may, indeed, be said that the birth of Western Europe as a cultural entity began at the time of Charlemagne, because it was at this time that the region was driven back upon its own resources and virtually isolated from the rest of the world. It is perhaps for this reason that in that age a certain provincialism was incorporated into the bloodstream of Western culture, the effects of which have been felt down to the present day, and which have had a bearing upon the rise of racial feelings.

By the eighth century the Arab caliphate had come not only to see itself but also to be seen by others as the center of world learning. The foundation of Islam in the year of the Hegira (the flight of Mohammed from Mecca), 622 A.D., is often viewed as the signal for a great outward expansion of the Arabs. In effect, although it was also this, it was rather the dynamic birth and rapid geographic growth of a new religion, which, by its early emphasis on conversion by the sword, gave special impetus to those racial groups which espoused it. These were the Arabs in the Middle East, the Arabs and later the Berbers in the Maghreb and in Spain, and the Fulbe in the savannah lands of West Africa.

Mecca, where the holy Kaaba lies, was the spiritual cradle of Islam, since Mohammed was a member of the Quraish tribe, the tribe of Mecca. The political capital of the new movement was removed, first to Medina, then to Damascus, and then again, in 750, to Baghdad, while the religion of Islam itself spread, in the most remarkable epic of conquest and conversion known to mankind, to the shores of the Atlantic in the West, and to the shores of the China Sea in the East. Although the outward expansion of Islam was originally aided by widespread religious and economic discontent with Byzantine and Persian rule in large areas of the Middle East, this circumstance was no more than a contributory factor to a development that stands as a permanent reminder of the unpredictability of the course of human events.

Immediately, the Umayyad caliphate became the symbol of oppression, and its policy of buttressing Arab privilege and asserting Arab racial superiority angered the Persians. In 750 A.D. Abu al-Abbas, supported by popular opinion, overthrew the Umayyad caliphate and established the Abbasid dynasty, under which learning and racial tolerance went hand in hand. Thus the period of Arab chauvinism in Islam's history closed, and a period in which it assumed a more international character became evident. The removal of the political capital from Damascus to Baghdad became symbolic of the change, and within fifty years Baghdad had become the center of world culture. Spain, North Africa, and other provinces that had acknowledged Umayyad rule, refused to recognize the Abbasids, although the Abbasids succeeded in conquering Sicily. The main result of the Abbasid succession was not, however, such adjustments of political boundaries, but the ending of Arab isolation on the one hand, and a productive fusion of Persian, Arab, and—later—Greek cultures with one another. The caliph Mamun was primarily responsible for encouraging Greek cultural influences in Baghdad, but in popular Western legend the character of the Abbasids is symbolized by the personality of Harun al-Rashid, of *Arabian Nights*[13] fame, who was Mamun's predecessor. It was as a consequence of this fusion of cultures that the internationalism and the cultural attainments of Islam, at this time, stood in striking contrast to a Europe which remained provincial in culture and uncouth in manners.

The cultural fertilization of Morocco and Spain by Islam is renowned, and, indeed, it was Islam that provided the conduit through which ancient Greek learning and the Greek tradition flowed once more, through the Iberian peninsula, into Western Europe to help stimulate the European Renaissance. Less widely known perhaps is the Islamic contribution to Sicily. Under Arab rule sugar cane and rice were introduced to the island from India; silkworms and mulberry trees from Persia; lemons, peaches, and apricots from Syria; and cotton and saffron, as well as pomegranates from Egypt and Arabia. It is also not without significance that the earliest extant European paper document was executed in Sicily, and the first European coin with a date in Arabic numerals was minted there in 1138.

Under the Normans, who had conquered the island by 1090, a fusion of Arabic and Latin culture had taken place that was dramatically expressed in the attitude of Frederick II (*Stupor Mundi*, or the "Wonder of the World," as he was called), who in the thirteenth century attracted Jewish and Muslim as well as Christian philosophers to his court, and thus, as H. G. Wells put it, "did much to irrigate the Italian mind with Saracenic influences."

Apart from Sicily and Italy it was the Iberian peninsula that constituted the main land bridge over which not only Greek learning but also African and Middle Eastern influences, as well as peoples, passed into Europe. During the eighth century the fortress of Ceuta was held for the Visigoths of Spain by a Count Julian. Julian engaged Arab support in an internal visigothic dispute with the result that, following a preliminary reconnaissance, a Berber army 7,000 strong landed at Gibraltar, under the generalship of the Arab leader Tarik,[14] on the last day of April, 711. The following year Tarik was joined by Muza, the Governor

---

13. Many of the tales of *The Arabian Nights* are of Persian origin.
14. The name "Gibraltar"—Gebel, or Djebel, Tarik—means "The Hill of Tarik."

of Mauretania, with a strong force of "Moors."[15] By 718 most of the peninsula had fallen to the invaders, who were only checked in their northward advance at Poitiers in France, in 732, by Charles Martel, after which the Muslim influence was pushed back to Spain. Eight more centuries were to pass before the descendants of the invaders from Africa were to be expelled from Iberia, and during the interval ethnic and cultural intermixture had proceeded so far that down to this day the saying "Africa begins at the Pyrenees" is a byword in Europe. In effect, it was essentially Islam that was expelled from Europe, and not the descendants of those who had been its followers. Even today both the architecture and the population not only of Spain, but also of parts of Southern France bear traces of the Arab-Berber invasion.

During the earlier centuries of Moorish rule in Spain, relations between the Arab rulers of al-Andalus (as their Spanish realm was called) and the "mozarabs" ("almost Arabs"), as their Christian subjects were named, remained generally those of tolerant coexistence. The tone was set by the marriage of the widow of Roderick (the Visigothic ruler overthrown by the Arabs) to the son and successor of Muza. The trend toward cultural and ethnic fusion of the disparate elements in al-Andalus was increased by the breaking of the political link with the caliphate at the time that the Abbasids overthrew the Umayyads. Subsequently, in the tenth century, large numbers of Berber troops were again brought over into Spain from North Africa, while yet another Berber invasion occurred with the irruption into the peninsula in 1090 of the Almoravides ("those vowed to God"). With the fanaticism of the newly converted, the Almoravides replaced the easy tolerance of the caliphate by a persecution of unbelievers. History was not slow to repeat itself, however, when after the Almoravide crusading fervor had become blunted through association with the society they had conquered, a fresh wave of conquering Berber zealots, this time the Almohades ("traditionists"), who came from the Atlas Mountains, arrived. Under the Almohades not only mozarabs but even Arabs themselves were persecuted. It was, indeed, from this time onward that the "Moors" of Spain became essentially Berber in ethnic composition. It was the intolerance, and the Moroccan power base, of the Almoravides and the Almohades that provoked the mozarabs and the Christian states of the north to unite in expelling the "Moors" from Spain, which they finally succeeded in doing in 1492.

One of the most important historic documents which emerges from the early Middle Ages is the *Chanson de Roland*. Of unknown authorship,[16] it draws heavily on oral traditions handed down from generation

15. The word "Moor" comes from the name of the Roman province of "Mauretania."
16. The quotations that follow are translated from the Oxford (Turoldus) version of the poem, which is generally admitted to be the oldest and finest of the eight versions extant.

to generation concerning the Christian-Moslem conflict in Spain, as formalized in the lays of the troubadors. It is of interest to note that in the poem there are several allusions not merely to Saracens from "Barbary," but also to black Africans, or to connections with black Africa. Ivory, for example, is mentioned more than once. It was of ivory that Roland's horn, or oliphant, was made, and the medieval word "oliphant" itself comes from "elephant." Baligant the Paynim also seats himself upon a throne of ivory upon his arrival in Saragossa. Presumably the ivory was procured from West Africa, as was that which was used by the ivory carvers of Dieppe in the fourteenth century. A number of the forces who attack the Christians are also from black Africa. Of the Saracen Abisme we are told, "black he is as melted pitch to see." After the Saracen leader Marsile takes flight the Chanson tells us:

> Yet there remains his uncle Marganice
> That governs Carthage, Alfrere and Garamile,
> And Ethiope, a land accursed and vile.
> In his command are all the Negro tribes;
> Thick are their noses, their ears are very wide;
> Full fifty thousand are gathered in their lines,
> Boldly and fast and furiously they ride,
> Yelling aloud the Paynim battle-cry . . .
> When Roland looks on these accursed tribesmen
> As black as ink from head to foot their hides are
> With nothing white about them but their grinders.

After the death of Roland, when Charlemagne himself engages the Saracens in yet another battle, the Chanson mentions no less than thirty columns of different nationalities as fighting on the Saracen side, and quotes the "Frankish geste" as authority for this information. Those cited include Nubians, "Sorbs and Servians," Negroes, Persians, Turks, Avars, Bulgarians, Huns, and Hungarians, as well as others, such Ugles and Ormalians, who are harder to identify. That this is not merely the imaginative embroidery of the medieval bards and anonymous chroniclers is indicated by the fact that Abd al-Rahman, who reigned over al-Andalus as a contemporary of Charlemagne, was convinced of the need for a standing army, and recruited for it not merely Berbers but no less than 40,000 Slavs from various parts of Southern Europe. It is small wonder that the Spanish language, in its various forms, reflects a history of extensive ethnic intermixture. The vocabulary is, of course, essentially formed of an admixture of Roman, Visigothic, and Arabic words.

## The Arabs and Africa

After their conquest of Egypt, the Arabs occupied the entire North African littoral, establishing their principal city at Kairwan in Tunisia. The Sahara checked their southward progress, although they occupied some oases. In the Maghreb itself, however, a long struggle between Arab and Berber began, of which the historic traces have remained discernible down to our own times. The persistence with which the Berbers have maintained themselves apart, without amalgamating with the Arabs, has been a constant source of astonishment to ethnologists. Indeed, in earlier times, the Berbers also preserved their separate and distinct identity despite the arrival in the Maghreb of Phoenicians, Romans, Vandals, and Jews.

In the eleventh century, after an apparently prolonged struggle, the Berbers drove out the Arabs, only to suffer a short time later a fresh invasion of 200,000 Bedouin Arabs—the Beni Soleim, who settled in Cyrenaica, and the Beni Hilal, who overran the lowlands of the Maghreb, effecting inestimable damage.

Trans-Sahara contact had, as we have seen, existed from the earliest times. Throughout the Middle Ages the Christians were frequently permitted to trade with and even to settle along the seaboard of the Maghreb. In 1034, for example, the Pisans, having recently conquered Sardinia, ventured to North Africa and for a time made themselves masters of Bona. Christians were forbidden, however, to use the trans-Sahara trade routes lest they penetrate the secret of the West African gold trade. This secret was that gold was obtainable only from certain African tribes, who would only exchange it for salt. The means of barter was the "silent trade." No Christian writer, therefore, has left us any firsthand account of the interior of West Africa during the Middle Ages. The only two Muslim travelers to have done so are the tenth-century Arab geographer, Ibn Haukal, and the fourteenth-century Berber writer, Ibn Battuta. Other Arab writers wrote at second hand, even though they often had excellent sources to draw upon. El-Bekri, for example, the eleventh-century writer, was a Spanish Arab who had access to the Cordoba archives, where many treasures of scholarship and knowledge concerning the known world, including Africa, were then stored.

Ibn Haukal visited the Tuareg capital of the Lemtuna nation, which was called Audoghast, as well as visiting Kumbi, the capital of Ghana. Both these towns lay between the Senegal and Niger rivers, and Ibn Haukal, observing the Niger flowing to the east, concluded, like many a traveler after him, that this was in fact the Nile. Ibn Battuta, arriving after Ghana had been overthrown, and when the successor kingdom of Mali was in the ascendant, visited the capital of Mali, as well as the town of Timbuktu. Of the African kingdoms south of the Sahara he reported:

> Perfect security reigns; one may live and travel there without fear of theft or rapine. They do not confiscate the goods of those white men who die in their country; even when the value is immense they do not tamper with them; on the contrary they place the heritage in the keeping of curators chosen from amongst the white men.

Ibn Battuta, who also confused the Niger with the Nile, traced its course as follows. After flowing to Timbuktu, he said, it flowed on to Koukou, and then to Mouli, the last of the Mali dependencies.

> The river flows afterwards from Mouli to Youfi [Nupe], one of the greatest countries of the Sudan, which is governed by a powerful sultan. White men are not allowed to penetrate here; they are killed before they can arrive. From here the Nile [*sic*] descends to the country of the Nubians, where they profess Christianity, and afterwards passes close by Dongola. . . . From Dongola the river descends to the cataracts.

Ibn Battuta describes the city of Mali as the capital of the Sudan, and said that it had a special quarter inhabited by the whites, where he lodged.

In East Africa, Arab settlements were made along the coast at ports such as Mogadiscio, Mombasa, and Kilwa "in the land of Zanj."[17] The Arab influence had arrived there by stages. After the Arab conquest of Egypt, which began in 639, there were periodic invasions of Nubia to the south, of which the first was led by the Arab governor of Egypt in 641–2. It was also during the seventh century that the Arabs moved to control the Red Sea, seizing the port of Massawa, and so striking a blow at Abyssinian control of the African coast of the Red Sea. As a result of this new racial trend, Arabs replaced Red Sea traders from the Mediterranean, and so cut off Abyssinia from the Mediterranean area. In the earlier period of Islam, however, Islamic Egypt and Christian Ethiopia coexisted without undue strain,[18] and it was not until Christian-Moslem feeling had become exacerbated that Ethiopia was driven to the extremity from which only the timely arrival of the Portuguese at the end of the fifteenth century rescued it. By joining with Christian Ethiopia, the Portuguese defeated the forces of Islam, thus helping to save the realm from extinction. Further to the south, on the East African coast, the Arab traders, beginning in the eighth century, established small settlements, but only succeeded in consolidating their hold in the thirteenth century. Here they found the hinterland already occupied by Black Africans, who had been slowly moving north between the fourth and the tenth centuries. It is of considerable interest that the Roman sailors' manual, called the Periplus of the Erythean Sea, published in the first century, described the East African coast down to Zanzibar, but made no mention of black men, whereas Ptolemy's geography, written in the second century, mentioned black men living in what is now the northern area of Mozambique. By the time that Masudi, the Arab geographer, wrote in the tenth century, black men had apparently moved north to the Kenya-Somali area.

Despite the commercial relations that existed between the Arabs of

17. Ibn Battuta visited these ports at an earlier stage of his protracted travels. At Kilwa he heard that gold dust was brought across the continent from "Youfi" (identified with Nupe in Nigeria) to Sofala, further down the coast.

18. Even throughout the Crusades, Abyssinian bishops continued to be consecrated in Cairo.

North Africa and the black men of the Western Sudan, Arab writers do not appear generally to have held black African society in high esteem. Ibn Haukal, for example, in his *Book of Ways and Provinces,* robbed posterity of many an interesting detail when he refused to describe the land of the African blacks "and the other peoples of the torrid zone," "because naturally loving wisdom, ingenuity, religion, justice and regular government, how could I notice such people as these." Al Masudi, also writing in the tenth century, commented upon physical differences between black Africans and Arabs, saying that the heat of the equatorial belt

predisposes in the humors a tendency to go to the upper parts of the body, hence the eyes are large, the lips thick, the nose flat and big and the head high. The crasis of the brain is therefore out of proportion and the mind cannot therefore perfectly manifest its action. The nicety of distinction and the action of understanding are confused.

Ibn Battuta, for his part, appeared primarily dissatisfied by the food and the value of the presents that he received, which he regarded as incommensurate with his status. He also complained of the nakedness of the women ("even in the month of Ramadan"), and the "singular morals" of the people, by which he meant the public acceptance of liaisons between men and women. On the other hand, he praised the Africans' high standard of justice, the assiduity with which they learned the Koran and insisted upon their children also learning it, even placing them in chains until they had performed this duty. He also appears to have yielded to the charm and orderly rhythm of life in the Sudan, and to have made several friends there. His description of stopping at a certain village on the Niger, near Timbuktu, to ask for provisions, is of interest, for he found the "Governor" of the village had a secretary who held in his hand a writing tablet, and later in his house he noticed a copy of the Kitab-el-Mohdich of El-Djeuzi[19]—two circumstances that contradicted a view still prevalent in the West that the interior of West Africa, before the coming of the Europeans, was a place characterized by complete illiteracy. The "Governor," he learned, had also "made the pilgrimage" to Mecca.

## "The Pilgrimage" and the Crusades

The medieval custom of making a pilgrimage was shared by Moslem and Christian alike. Whether the pilgrimage was to Mecca, Jerusalem, or to lesser shrines, the custom served more than anything else except warfare to disseminate knowledge of other peoples and other ways. For the Moslem the *haj* (pilgrimage) to Mecca brought together century after century travelers from countries as far removed as Morocco,

19. The Kitab-el-Mohdich is said to be a work concerned with the Maliki School of Islamic law, which is studied by Sunni Muslims. El-Djeuzi is not the original author, but a commentator.

Indonesia, Persia, Senegal, and China. Consequently an internationalist undercurrent was at work throughout the Moslem world that did much to promote both trade and an underlying cultural unity.

The Christians, for their part, traveled to the Holy Sepulcher in Jerusalem. Throughout the seventh, eighth, and ninth centuries pilgrims had free access to the Holy City, although in the tenth century a mad Fatimid caliph, ruling in Cairo, persecuted religious minorities, including Christians. The brief seizure of Jerusalem by the Seljuk Turks— descendants of the nomads of Asia who had crossed the Volga to sweep down to the shores of the Mediterranean—led the Emperor of Byzantium to ask Pope Urban II for mercenary troops to help to drive the Turks from Asia Minor. There followed a most remarkable series of incursions of Europeans into the Middle-Eastern area—incursions which began with the preaching of the First Crusade by Pope Urban II at Clermont Ferrand in France in 1095, and which virtually ended with the death of King Louis IX (Saint Louis) of France in 1270. Between these two dates cities were built and destroyed, kingdoms established and overthrown, alliances—some of them between Christian and Moslem—made and broken. The Crusades, in effect, before they were diverted from their original goal of the recapture of the Holy Sepulcher to serve ends of political expediency, were nothing less than a continuation of the pilgrimage to Jerusalem in military form. Apart from other considerations, the joint effort of an aroused Christendom did much to help Europeans transcend national antipathies. As Fulcher, the French priest-chronicler, wrote:

Who had ever heard of so many languages in one army before? Here were Franks, Flemings, Lotharingians, Bavarians, Normans, Angles, Scots, Italians, Britons, Greeks, and Armenians all together. . . . But even if we spoke such varied languages we were all brothers in God's love and seemed like close kinsmen.

But the grouping, however catholic, did not unite such a wide range of peoples as did the Meccan pilgrimages. Ethnically, so far as we know, the Crusaders were almost entirely white-skinned. At least one allusion, however, hints that there may have been other ethnic groupings involved, perhaps Mozarabs from Spain. In *The Crusade of Richard Coeur de Lion* the chronicler Ambroise, juxtaposing epochs as was so often done in order to invoke the name of Charlemagne, the hypothetical Great Crusader, wrote the following catchy lines, in which he refers not only to the inter-European solidarity among the Crusaders to which Fulcher had referred, but also mentioned the unimportance of skin color among them:

> When Charlemagne, that king so great
> Who conquered many a realm and state
> Set forth to wage his war in Spain

In the other war when Syria
Was lost and conquered and invaded
And Antioch likewise blockaded
And midst the strike and fierce onslaught
Of battles gainst the paynims fought
Where many of them lost their life
There was no quarrelling or strife
In those old days for men to quench
Of who was Norman and who French
Manceau Burgundian or who was Breton from Poitou
And who from England, who from Flanders
There were no bitter words or slanders
Cast, or tauntings harsh with scorn
But by each man was honor borne,
And all were called Franks, whether they
Were white of skin, or brown or bay
And when sin caused them to discord
The princes harmony restored.

In some ways, with the hindsight of history, it may be regretted not that the Holy Sepulcher was not preserved in a Christian kingdom of Jerusalem, but that the vast movement of peoples that the Crusades represented did not achieve a fusion of European and Arab cultures, as at times it seemed on the verge of doing. The philosophic aims of Frederick II (whatever his political aims may have been) were not dissimilar from those of some of the Templars and Hospitalers who, locked within their immeasurably strong castles in Syria, acquired first knowledge from and then reached understandings with their Arab neighbors. Some, indeed, pondered over certain changes in Christian dogma that would permit Christian and Moslem differences to be reconciled. When the Franks had at last been driven from the Holy Land, however, and the Templars returned to Europe, these unorthodox tendencies were used against them. Powerful enemies, jealous of their great wealth, succeeded in having the order suppressed on the grounds of heresy, after which the Templars' property was confiscated.

Essentially, however, whatever hopes might have flowered but did not, the Crusades represented a movement in which the peoples of Europe, led principally by the French, attempted to move to the eastern Mediterranean lands and to colonize them. The Crusades represented a war that lasted for almost 200 years, involving Europeans on the one side, and mixed forces of Arabs, Turks, and Kurds on the other. In all its various phases, therefore, from the first onset of the barons along the *Via Dei* to the final efforts of King Louis to fight his way to Cairo, it represented the earliest attempt by Europe at physical expansion, and it failed. Not only were the Crusaders driven from the eastern shores of the Mediterranean, not only was Byzantium weakened, so that it too was eventually overthrown, but also the Arabs themselves were weakened to such an extent that the Mongols were able to enter the Middle-Eastern arena in their turn.

As we saw earlier, until the time of the discovery of America, it was the "East" that fascinated Europe, and that stirred its imagination. "The East" was the East of Byzantium, the East of Cairo and of Baghdad, of India and of Persia—but also of Cathay. The Far East, however, remained even more legendary than the Near, for, whereas the pilgrimage to Jerusalem had long forged a link between Europe and the Middle East, it is probable that, until the thirteenth-century visits of the papal emissaries, and then of the Polos of Venice, no European had penetrated east of Baghdad. Even many of those who had engaged in the trade that had existed from Roman times, in silk and in the other products that came along the famous Silk Road which stretched from Antioch on the Mediterranean shore to distant China, had no clear concept of where those products originated. In the fourteenth century, however, many travelers were successful in reaching Cathay from Europe, and contacts were becoming increasingly numerous when two events—the Black Death of 1348 and the emergence of the Ottoman Turks across the trade route —cut off the links abruptly.

The Black Death affected the Arabs no less than it had affected the Europeans. Yet their links with the Far East—India, China, and the islands of the Pacific—were of too long standing to be seriously jeopardized. Centuries-old trading habits, no less than the Islamic religion itself, were in no way injured by the mortalities, and the Indian province of Sind did not cease to maintain its Moslem connection. A heavier blow, to the Arabs, was the attack of the Mongols. The sudden rise of Genghis Khan, the Mongol chieftain from the Gobi Desert who conquered Northern China and then spread his conquests to India and the Middle East, no less than to Eastern Europe, rivaled the earlier conquests of the Arabs themselves. Though the ethnic frontiers between Asia and the Middle East were to be stabilized once more, there was no question about the heavy price that had to be paid for this stability.

Commercially the Indian Ocean had long been the counterpart of the Mediterranean Sea in the trade of those nations which bordered its shores. Arab descriptions of China are, significantly, to be found from the ninth century onwards—adventurous Arab traders having penetrated not only north to Russia, but also east to China, and south to the southern tip of Africa. Having commented that the brotherhood of Islam knew "no difference of race or birth," H. A. R. Gibb goes on to add: "Throughout the Middle Ages the trade routes of Africa and Asia and the seaborne trade of the Indian Ocean were almost exclusively in the hands of the Muslim merchants."[20] China, however, does not appear to have been

20. Ibn Battuta, *Travels in Asia and Africa: 1325–54* (Introduction by H. A. R. Gibb).

an inactive partner in this trade. Even much earlier the presence of Chinese merchants on the coast of what is now Tanganyika was reported, and some enterprising fifteenth-century Chinese adventurers appear to have transported a Tanganyikan giraffe back to China under the impression that they had captured that elusive unicorn, or *ki-lin,* as they called it,[21] whose appearance, according to Chinese legend, represented divine confirmation of the virtue of the reigning emperor. Subsequently, however, the "inland," or isolationist, party in China overcame those in favor of foreign trade, and the direct connection with Africa was discouraged. The peripatetic Ibn Battuta had reported, however, that in the fourteenth century traveling on the China Sea was only done on Chinese ships. He went on to mention that "Abyssinians" (i.e., Africans) played a traditional role in the Indian Ocean trade. Abyssinians, he wrote, "are the guarantors of safety on the Indian Ocean; let there be but one of them on a ship and it will be avoided by the Indian pirates and idolaters." He himself embarked at Qandahar (Gandhar) upon a ship with fifty such Abyssinian men-at-arms, and he also reported that the owners of the big four-decker junks, built only in Zaytun and Canton, had a guard of archers and Abyssinians whenever they went ashore; while in Colombo the "wazir and ruler of the sea Jalasti" had with him about 500 Abyssinians.

Toward the end of the fifteenth century a series of changes took place in Europe that marked the passing away of the Middle Ages and the opening of a new chapter in world history. The collapse of the Crusades weakened papal authority, while the labor shortage that resulted from the Black Death undermined the social fabric of traditional relationships which constituted the feudal system. The fall of Constantinople led to an influx of learning and technical knowledge that reinforced the rising sea-power of the Western nations. Energies previously directed to the Middle East were now directed to new goals, and to seeking new horizons. Among the ships that set sail from Europe at this time was a small convoy comprising the *Nina,* the *Pinta,* and the *Santa Maria,* which, on October 12, 1492, sighted the island of San Salvador in the Caribbean, after sailing west from the Canaries for five weeks across the uncharted ocean. White-skinned Europeans had crossed the ocean and made contact with American Indians of Mongol origin. Mankind for the first time had made a contact around the globe that was never to be broken.

21. The *ki* is the male and the *lin* the female; the species is known as *ki-lin.*

# Chapter 3

# "A Wild Surmise": Europe's Expansion

*Or like stout Cortez when with eagle eyes*
*He star'd at the Pacific—and all his men*
*Look'd at each other with a wild surmise—*
*Silent, upon a peak in Darien.*
     *—John Keats*

THE BIRTH DATE of most great enterprises is usually known, yet often only the ending of those which come to disaster can be as clearly seen. As a small spring marks the point of departure of a stream, so it may be said that the activity of Prince Henry the Navigator[1] fed the stream of Portuguese discovery and expansion. Yet the Portuguese stream was soon joined by other European tributaries to form a river whose waters, in turn, have flowed on until they merged into the sea of world history.

The story of Europe's expansion has several facets: it is intertwined with such themes as that of the systematic exploration of the globe, of colonization, and of the struggle for trade and strategic supremacy among the European powers themselves. In this chapter we shall deal primarily with Europe's expansion beyond the limits of the Ptolemaic *oikumenikos*—the inhabited world as it had been known to the Greeks of antiquity, and then to medieval Europe. This expansion proved to be an expansion in consciousness no less than in physical and political influence. Although the initial aim of the movement was to turn the flank of

---

1. The name "Henry the Navigator" was popularized in the nineteenth century by British writers. Henry, in his own day, was known as the Enfante Dom Henrique.

Islam, which had hitherto cut off Europe from trade with the East (whose rich potential had been revealed by Marco Polo and others), the success of the techniques of discovery that were evolved soon invited the European nations of the Atlantic seaboard to proceed to explore the entire world. As a result, all the races of the world were eventually to be brought into relationship with one another.

It is generally considered that Henry the Navigator was primarily responsible for generating the original expansionist impulse. This is, no doubt, in a sense true. It was he who established the pattern of discovery down the West African coast that had as its goal the linking of Europe with India. It was he who fostered the improved techniques of ship design and of navigation and who financed the first voyages that were to lead to the new discoveries and the new trade patterns. Yet, on a philosophic level, we may recall Tolstoy's essay "The Forces That Move Nations" and conclude that the responsibility for European expansion may no more be attributed to Henry than the responsibility for the French invasion of Russia in 1812 may be laid to Napoleon. The great historical movement that we are examining came about as a result of innumerable small and daily decisions. Geographically it may also be argued that it was inevitable that such a movement should be initiated by the people of the Iberian peninsula. Here, where Europe and Africa face each other across the Straits of Gibraltar, if there had not been a Henry there would no doubt have been another Portuguese or Spaniard endowed with courage and imagination who would find himself confronted with the same elements in the same puzzle and so produce the same answer. European expansion may thus be said to have been as inevitable as the subsequent European colonization was inevitable, and as, in turn, the subsequent rejection of European hegemony by the people of other continents has proved to be inevitable.

Historically we may recall that whereas Henry was, in effect, the captain of a great enterprise that ended by being the enterprise of world discovery, the enterprise had had its precursors whose efforts, while they remain shadowy to us, were no doubt considerably better known to him.[2] It is suggested that some Norman seamen from Dieppe sailed down the West African coast a hundred years before the Portuguese, and that they established a series of trading stations there. One of these was said to have stood on the Senegal River; two more (named "Little Paris" and "Little Dieppe") on what is now the Liberian coast; and yet two more on what is now the coast of Ghana—one at Kormantin, and the other at "La Mine d'Or" (Elmina).[3] Only the wars in France, it is said, led to

2. "Till the age of print and reference libraries, discoveries were soon lost. Everything had to be refound, re-explored, restated a thousand times . . ." (Joyce Cary, *Britain and West Africa,* 1946).

3. The Elmina settlement was said to have been founded in 1382. All the settlements were said to have been abandoned forty years later.

the abandonment of Dieppe's West African settlements. Oral tradition supports the claims of the Dieppois, for Dieppe to this day is called "The Town of Ivory" from its famous craft of ivory carving—an industry that is said to date from the very earliest times, and that, in an Atlantic seaport, might logically be founded upon a West African connection. Norman sailors were, of course, familiar with Mediterranean waters, and it was a Norman who discovered the Canary Islands in the fourteenth century.

It also appears possible that the Genoese may have visited West Africa in the fourteenth century. In the Laurentian Portulano—a collection of maps made by the Genoese in 1351—Africa is for the first time delineated as a continent. This information may, however, have been obtained from the Arabs during the Crusades.

It was, nevertheless, Prince Henry who established, in the initial stages, the pattern of European discovery, no less than of colonization and of domination over non-European peoples. The fifth son of John I of Portugal and of his English queen (herself the daughter of John of Gaunt), he participated with honor in the capture of the Moorish city of Ceuta by the Portuguese in 1415. The moving spirit of the enterprise, Henry had wished to continue his direct assault upon the Western flank of Islam by going on to capture Tangier and Gibraltar,[4] thereby seizing for the benefit of Christendom in general and the Portuguese in particular the western Mediterranean terminals of the trans-Sahara trade. The concept was bold and imaginative, but his more cautious royal father, pleased with one isolated success, would not agree. Nevertheless, Henry's imagination had been stimulated by what he had heard in Ceuta (of which he was appointed Governor), about the gold trade of Africa,[5] just as later it was to be stirred by the information given him by his brother Peter, who returned in 1428 from travels in Europe and the Near East bringing with him a copy of Marco Polo's *Travels*, which had been given him by the Venetians, and which he translated for the benefit of Henry.

Upon the rocky promontory of Sagres—the most southwesterly point of Europe—Henry established his headquarters. Here he recruited mapmakers, pilots, captains, astrologers, shipbuilders, mathematicians, and adventurers to serve his cause. Here he fitted out his craft, trained sailors and navigators, and year by year sent ships south upon voyages of exploration. His behavior was the more remarkable as Portugal had no strong incentive to discovery or colonization. There was, on the contrary, a shortage of manpower in Portugal, and the nascent national tradition,

4. At this time the "Moors" still occupied Granada in southern Spain. (Portugal had driven out the Moors and received Castilian acknowledgment of its claim to its national territory by 1267). In 1437 Henry attempted to pursue his original plan and to capture Tangier, but because of insufficient preparation the attempt failed. In 1458, however, he participated in the taking of Alcacar, a port halfway between Ceuta and Tangier. This small success in frontal assault upon Islam was by far outweighed by the results of his maritime endeavors.
5. While in Ceuta he is said to have heard from "the Moors of Timbuktu."

such as it was, was of hostility to neighboring Castile rather than of foreign adventure.

Henry's motives for launching his campaign of discovery have been the subject of speculation. The Portuguese chronicler Azurara, who as a contemporary may be regarded as one of the more authoritative commentators, identified six separate reasons for his actions:[6]

1) [Henry] desired to know what lands there were beyond the Canary Islands and a cape called Bojador, for up to that time no one knew, whether by writing or the memory of man, what there might be beyond this cape.

He also added, as part of the first reason:

Some believed that St. Brandan[7] had passed it. Others said that two galleys[8] had gone thither and never returned. But it seems to us that this cannot be in any way true, for it is not credible that if the said galleys had gone thither, other ships would not have undertaken to discover what had become of them. And the Infante Dom Henrique desired to know the truth of this; for it seemed to him that if he or some other lord did not essay to discover this, no sailor or merchant would undertake this effort, for it is very sure that these do not think to navigate otherwise than to places where they already know that they will find their profit. And seeing that no other prince was concerning himself with the matter, he sent his ships to these countries in order to acquire certitude, and this for the service of God and of the King Dom Duarte, his brother and seigneur.

2) If in these territories there should be any population of Christians, or any harbours where men could enter without peril, they could bring back to the realm many merchandises at little cost, by reason that there would be no other person on these coasts who would negotiate with them; and that in like manner one could carry to these regions merchandise of the realm, of which the traffic would be of great profit to the natives.

3) It was said that the power of the Moors of this land of Africa was very much greater than was generally thought, and that there were among them neither Christians nor other races. And because every wise man is moved by desire to know the strength of his enemy, the Infante devised means to send his people in quest of information in order to know the full extent of the Infidels' power.

4) During one and thirty years of battles with the Moors, the Infante had never found Christian King or Seigneur outside this kingdom, who for the love of Our Lord Jesus Christ was willing to aid him in this war. He desired to know whether in those regions there might be any Christian princes in whom the charity and love of Christ were strong enough to cause them to aid him against these enemies of the faith.

5) [In order that] lost souls should be saved.

6) [The astrological reason, from which all the others proceed," that as Henry was born on March 4th, 1394, he was under the influence of] the Ram, which is in the

---

6. In the quotations from Azurara which follow, the first five reasons cited are taken from *Conquests and Discoveries of Henry the Navigator,* by Gomes Eannes de Azurara, translated by Bernard Miall (1936). The sixth reason, passed over in the Miall translation, is translated from a French edition of Azurara, *Chronique de Guinée,* published in the series *Mémoires de l'Institut Français d'Afrique Noir* (1960).

7. St. Brandan, Brendan, Brenainn, or Borandon, an Irish missionary (484–577), was widely credited in medieval times with having traveled on a seven-year voyage to the Land of Paradise which lay to the west and northwest of Ireland. Until 1755 St. Brandan's Isle was mapped as lying five degrees west of the Canaries.

8. In the 1375 map of West Africa by Abraham Cresques there is a picture of the Catalan galley of Jacme Ferrer, who sailed from Mallorca for the River of Gold in 1346 and never returned. The River of Gold was the Senegal River.

House of Mars, with the Sun in the ascendant, and is the Lord of the Eleventh House in which he is accompanied by the Sun. And because the said Mars was in Aquarius which is of the House of Saturn and the house of hope, this indicated that this prince was bound to engage in great and noble conquests, and above all he was bound to attempt the discovery of things which were hidden from other men, and secret.

The matter has been expressed in contemporary terms by Sir Percy Sykes as follows:

The original design of the Prince, who was the greatest man of his age, was to out-flank the Moors by sea, to join forces with Prester John, who was now identified with the Prince of Ethiopia, and thus crush the Moslems. As time passed, Prince Henry aimed rather at the development of commerce, whereby he could strengthen Portugal in her crusades against the Moslems, whose cruisers were often met with at sea. He was the first statesman to realize that oceans were not barriers, but rather great high-ways for commerce, and that sea-power would win dominion.[9]

In 1418–19 Henry's eccentric conduct, as it was at first generally con-sidered, produced its first result—the discovery of the little island of Porto Santo in the Madeiras. This was followed shortly after by the discovery of Madeira itself. With the Madeiras colonized, the discovery of the Azores followed in 1431–32. Despite these first fruits of explora-tion, however, Cape Bojador—a barrier more psychological than physical —constantly blocked the sea-road south. As Azurara wrote:

Although many set out, none dared to go beyond this cape. . . . And this, to tell the truth, was not by reason of any courage or lack goodwill, but . . . the idea of discovering if legends were true seemed full of menace. "How shall we pass beyond the limits established by our elders?" "What profit can the Infante win from the loss of our souls and our bodies? For plainly we should be as men taking their own lives."

Cape Bojador ("The Bulging Cape") was popularly supposed to be the point beyond which the world came to an end. Here, a hundred miles south of the Canaries, according to the tales of mariners, the sea began to boil with that same heat of the sun that turned all men black. Here, too, the waters ran over the edge of the world, carrying with them any ship that dared to sail so far. Those who had approached the nearest testified to having seen the waters curve steeply away over the horizon.[10] Cape Bojador, in every sense, marked one of the limits of medieval Europe. It was in 1434 that one of Henry's captains, Gil Eannes, more courageous than his predecessors (who, like Eannes himself, had returned from voyage after voyage to make excuses to Henry), finally sailed down to Bojador, stood offshore to avoid shoals, and so rounded the cape. He found nothing more spectacular than the same sandy coastline, trending south. Landing in a small boat he found no sign of life, except for a little cluster of St. Mary's roses—the same species that grow in Portugal. By

9. *A History of Exploration* (1950).
10. One of the last occasions on which the fear of reaching the world's end off the West African coast was recorded was in 1456, when the two captains who sailed to the Gambia with Diogo Gomes insisted that they return home because "they were at the limits of the ocean."

passing Bojador, however, one age had begun to pass, and another, the Age of Discovery, to arrive. A potent myth had been dismantled, opening the way to a rational examination first of West Africa's geography, and then of the geography of the entire world. Some of the immediate results of the crumbling of the medieval frontiers of the mind were to be seen in the fact that by the end of the century European ships would have rounded the Cape of Good Hope, reached India, and sailed west to the Americas. By 1522 the *Victoria,* surviving ship of Magellan's expedition, arrived in Seville, having circumnavigated the globe.

By the time of Henry's death in 1460, Portuguese caravels,[11] pushing ever further south down the West African coast, had reached Sierra Leone. As the implications of his enterprise dawned upon the courts of Europe, the Portuguese grew increasingly secretive.[12] What has been called the "conspiracy of silence" ensured that only the King of Portugal and his advisers would know in detail the results of exploration by Portuguese ships in Africa. Because of this, details of many of the early voyages remain unknown to us. Some records, however, are available, such as, for example, the journals of Cadamosto,[13] a Venetian captain who sailed to the Gambia in 1455 and 1456 with the red cross of Prince Henry's Order of Christ[14] on his sails. Cadamosto's relations with the Senegambians were generally good: he engaged in successful trade and less successful religious discussion with them, and on one occasion demonstrated the bagpipes to his hosts, thereby causing much astonishment since at first they believed the instrument to be some kind of animal that he had taught to sing. Cadamosto was, however, one of the exceptions. Most other captains held their tongues.

There was increasing reason why silence should be maintained. Other European nations—especially Spain—were growing interested in the West African trade in gold dust, ivory, slaves, and black pepper that the Portuguese had begun to establish. But Henry had foreseen the possibility of Spanish or other European competition, and had taken diplomatic action to guard against it by petitioning the international authority of the age—the Pope—to sanction his discoveries in the name of Portugal alone. His petition was granted, and in 1445 Pope Eugenius IV issued a bull confirming that all new territory beyond Cape Bojador

11. The caravel was developed by Henry at Sagres. Its lateen rig, borrowed from the Arabs, enabled it to sail close to the wind, as square-rigged ships could not. In the fifteenth and sixteenth centuries the caravel, in one form or another, was the standard type of ship used in European exploration.

12. In 1481, when Columbus was still in the service of Portugal, the Portuguese Cortes petitioned the King to exclude Genoese immigrants from the realm, as they were good for nothing except to steal important secrets about Portugal's trade with Africa and the Western Islands. Genoese were in fact later excluded from the African trade, but not before Columbus himself had sailed to West Africa.

13. Cadamosto was the first European to record seeing the Southern Cross.

14. Henry financed his activities from the revenues of the Order of Christ, of which he was the Grand Master. The Order of Christ, which was the supreme pontifical order, was founded in 1318 on the abolition of the Templars. Despite this source of revenue, when Henry died he was heavily in debt.

be conceded to the crown of Portugal, that Henry's Order of Christ be given spiritual jurisdiction over the new lands and all converts made in them, and that those who died on voyages of discovery be granted the same indulgences as those who had fallen in the Crusades. Pope Nicholas V confirmed this in a bull issued in 1450, and in 1454 issued yet another bull granting Henry the monopoly of exploration as far east as India. A five-year war between Portugal and Castile over the question of succession was concluded, after the defeat of the Portuguese, by the Treaty of Alcacovas in 1479—according to the terms of which, among other things, the Canary Islands were ceded to Spain, but Portuguese sovereignty south of the Canaries was recognized. The terms of the treaty were confirmed by another papal bull, *Aeterni Regis,* issued by Sixtus IV in 1481.

Protected by papal sanction, therefore, Portuguese discovery in Africa was steadily pursued throughout the fifteenth century. In 1471 Fernando Po discovered the island named after him, as well as the bend to the south of the West African coastline. In 1438 Diogo Cao arrived off the mouth of the Congo River (which he called the Zaire). In 1488 Bartolomeu Dias rounded the Cape of Good Hope,[15] while Pero da Covilhan, sent out via the Mediterranean route at the same time as Dias, visited India, East Africa, and Mecca before he arrived, in 1493, in Ethiopia,[16] and established contact with Prester John—the Negus, Alexander.

Spain could hardly remain pleased with the Portuguese successes, but could do little at first to change the situation in her own favor, being still occupied with efforts to expel the Moors from her own borders. Spanish ships, which attempted to participate in the West African trade did so at considerable risk, since, under a decree of John II, the crews of all foreign ships captured in this Portuguese sphere of influence were to be thrown to the sharks. The situation changed completely, however, with the return of Columbus from the Americas in 1493 with unknown types of birds, beasts, vegetables, and human beings from the "Indies." The event immediately precipitated a diplomatic crisis between Portugal and Spain.

## The Pope Divides the World

Driven to the mouth of the Tagus by a westerly cyclone, with only a single sail left, Columbus's caravel *Nina,* on his return, had dropped

15. Dias named the Cape *Cabo Tormentoso* ("Cape of Storms"), but his patron, King John II of Portugal, had this changed to the "Cape of Good Hope." King John, incidentally, already knew the lay of the land. Two Portuguese Jews, Joseph of Lamego and the Rabbi Abraham of Beja, who preceded da Covilhan overland to the Persian Gulf, told him of the existence of the Arab settlements on the East African coast, and also that during bad weather some Arab ships had been driven west round the Cape, reporting the northern trend of the west coast on their return.

16. Covilhan found it easier to arrive than to depart. The following year—1494—the Negus Alexander and his young son both died, to be succeeded by Naod, who received Covilhan "with much favour" but refused his petition that he might be allowed to leave the country. As a contemporary later wrote, "Neyther would his successors permit that Ulysses to returne, a man of many languages and much usefull for his experience in the world."

anchor at 9 A.M. on March 4, 1493, four miles from Lisbon. As a result he was first interviewed not by his sponsors, Ferdinand and Isabella of Spain, but by their rival, John II of Portugal. By the time he arrived at the court of Spain, the Spanish sovereigns—warned that John was reported to be hurriedly preparing a Portuguese fleet to sail to the "Indies" —had already approached the Pope to obtain title to the new discoveries. It was their good fortune that the Pope, Alexander VI, was a Spaniard who owed his election, and other favors, to them. The actions of the Pope in the months that followed reflect the different diplomatic pressures applied by Portugal and Spain, although in the final analysis there was no doubt that he was committed to the Spanish cause. His first act, upon being approached by Ferdinand and Isabella, was to issue a bull— *Inter Caetera* of May 3, 1493,[17] which stated that, whereas Columbus had sailed "toward the Indians," Spanish possession was confirmed of the islands and countries discovered or to be discovered, providing that they ha never been the possession of any Christian prince. At this point Portugal made representations to the Pope, claiming that according to the Treaty of Alcacovas, and especially according to the bull *Aeterna Regis* of 1481, Portugal had been given sovereignty "beyond [i.e., south of] the Canaries." This, King John claimed, gave Portugal title to all discoveries south of a demarcation line running from east to west through the Canaries—that is, along latitude 28° north—whether those discoveries were on the African side of the ocean or anywhere farther west.

On June 12, 1493, a Spanish envoy, visiting Rome on a diplomatic mission reflecting, so far as is publicly known, Spanish preoccupations of a purely European character, strongly complained to the Pope concerning his attitude on various questions, including the harboring of Moors expelled from Spain. A week later, on June 19, the Spanish Ambassador to Rome dropped a diplomatic hint to the Pope by preaching a sermon in which he alluded to the new discoveries of Columbus, saying that Christ had recently given Spain "other unknown islands towards the Indians." Shortly after this, Alexander issued two further bulls—*Eximiae Devotionis* (confirming the previous *Inter Caetera* of May 3, and a second *Inter Caetera*, predated May 4), which gave satisfaction to the Spanish monarchs. It established a demarcation line running not from east to west through the Canaries, as the Portuguese desired, but longitudinally from the North Pole to the South, 100 leagues west of the Azores and the Cape Verde Islands. This line, in effect, divided the world beyond the bounds of Christendom between Portugal and Spain, with Spain to possess all that lay to the west of the line, and Portugal all that lay to the east. It is believed, incidentally, that the man who

17. The existence of the first bull, *Inter Caetera* of May 3, was forgotten for 350 years, because it had been mistakenly identified with the second bull of the same name dated May 4, which was in fact not promulgated until at least a month later.

suggested this longitudinal line was Columbus, who was advisor to Ferdinand and Isabella during the 1493 negotiations.[18]

Portugal then made representations to Spain in which dissatisfaction with the demarcation line was expressed, because King John said he expected to make discoveries, including a continent, "very profitable and richer than all the others," between the demarcation line and Africa.[19] These representations had the effect of alarming Ferdinand and Isabella, who thereupon prevailed upon the Pope to issue yet a fourth bull, dated September 26, 1493, and entitled *Dudum Siquidem*, in which he stated that "we amplify and extend our aforesaid gift . . . to all islands and mainlands whatsoever, found and to be found . . . in sailing or travelling toward the west or south, whether they be in regions occidental, or meridional and oriental and of India." It also declared all previous grants concerning these lands to be null and void, even if there had been previous possession.

In the face of such overwhelming papal support for Spanish designs upon the trade of the Indies, Portugal had no recourse except to cease dealing with the Pope, and to negotiate directly with Ferdinand and Isabella. The result was the Treaty of Tordesillas, which was concluded between Spain and Portugal on June 7, 1494. According to this treaty, the demarcation line was maintained, but was moved to the meridian running 370 leagues west of the Cape Verde Islands. As a result of this, Portugal obtained title to Brazil, and peaceful relations between the two powers were maintained.

However, under the terms of the treaty it was provided that a joint cruise should take place from the Canaries west to the demarcation line, after which, having held a conference in mid-ocean to confirm that the right place had been reached, the participating vessels should sail south until they reached land, where a pillar should be set up. Each party was to consist of "pilots, astrologers, seamen and others." In view of the fact that this arrangement was later judged to be "unprofitable," the two powers decided, in 1495, to abandon the cruise, and instead to content themselves with keeping each other informed of new discoveries made. As Samuel Eliot Morison has added:

Considering the differences of opinion as to a ship's position among the pilots of Columbus's fleet, the impossibility of determining longitude, and the lack of knowledge of compass variation, the failure of this joint cruise to come off is a sad loss to the humors of maritime history.[20]

18. In a letter written to Ferdinand and Isabella on his third voyage in 1500, Columbus remarked that 100 leagues west of the Azores he found "a very great change in the sky, the stars, the air temperature, and in the ocean," as well as compass variation. He also added cryptically: "On reaching that line it is as if you had put a hill below the horizon." The sixteenth-century historian Las Casas made the further claim that whereas on the Portuguese side of the line "many are the lice that breed," they began to die forthwith as soon as the ship sailed over to the Spanish zone.

19. Whether John II of Portugal was in fact in possession of evidence pointing to the existence of Brazil, or whether he was merely making a blind bargain, still remains a subject of speculation.

20. *Admiral of the Ocean Sea: A Life of Christopher Columbus* (1942).

Only after Pope Alexander VI and John II of Portugal had both died did the papacy confirm the Treaty of Tordesillas. This was done by Pope Julius II in the bull *Ea Quae,* issued in 1506. Papal confirmation was of advantage to Portugal, since it prevented any return to the demarcation line proposed by Spain, 100 leagues west of the Azores. Meanwhile the Treaty of Tordesillas served the immediate purpose of avoiding conflict between Portugal and Spain, until a fresh collision of interests occurred in the Pacific, where the ships of the two powers next began to impinge upon each other's activities. Spain thereupon claimed that the Tordesillas line of demarcation should merely be prolonged down the other side of the globe, thus dividing the world into two equal halves. Portugal, however, claimed that Tordesillas had merely established the principle that the Portuguese had the right to sail east to the Indies, and the Spanish to sail west, so that whatever happened in the Indies and Pacific area would depend on which power held de facto control there— which Portugal did. In maintaining her argument Portugal succeeded in obtaining the support of Pope Leo X (who had been pleased by the gift of a performing elephant, sent him by Albuquerque, the Portuguese viceroy in India), and in 1514, he issued a bull, *Praecelsae Devotionis,* granting to Portugal all lands that might be taken from heathen peoples in Africa, India, and any other regions which might be reached by sailing eastward.

In 1519 Magellan, a Portuguese who had entered the service of Spain, set out from Seville and, having sailed round the tip of South America through the Straits later named after him, reached the Pacific. Although he died in the course of the voyage, the survivors of his expedition continued to the Moluccas—that is to say, the Spice Islands, which were perhaps the most coveted prize of European endeavor in the Indies. Here they established a Spanish garrison at Tidore, after which the sole surviving vessel returned to Spain, thus completing the first circumnavigation of the globe. A further Spanish venture into the Pacific having failed, and the Portuguese being demonstrably in control in that region, Charles V of Spain prepared to come to terms with Portugal. According to the Treaty of Saragossa, concluded in 1529 though opposed by the Spanish Cortes, Charles yielded his claim to the Moluccas in return for 350,000 ducats, and a line of demarcation was established in the Pacific, running from north to south 17° east of the islands. The Spanish-Portuguese contest was at an end.

Thus, at the height of the Age of Discovery, Africa, Asia, and the Americas were divided up between the two small powers of the Iberian peninsula. The Treaty of Tordesillas became the prototype of innumerable subsequent settlements of colonial disputes between European powers, establishing the principle of dividing disputed areas into "zones of influence." The schism in Christendom between Catholic and Protestant countries prevented, meanwhile, the further development of the papacy as an effective international authority with recognized moral influence and legal jurisdiction in colonial questions.

As for the conflict between Islam and Christianity that had permeated the later Middle Ages, this gave way to the age of European hegemony. Beleaguered Christendom, which in 1453 had witnessed the fall of Byzantium to the Turks, and which barely succeeded in halting the Muslims before the walls of Vienna, now found itself suddenly established within a totally new and favorable context. Not only had Prince Henry's scheme succeeded, not only had the Moors been outflanked and the Far East trade gained, but also a hundred new lands had been discovered in all of which, thanks to their ships and guns, the Europeans found themselves at an advantage. Within a few brief years the threat of Islamic domination subsided to relatively insignificant proportions.

The pace of discovery was such that this transformation occurred within a few years. In 1500, while news of the voyage of Columbus had spread rapidly, little was known of its nature, except perhaps that some new islands had been discovered in the west. Even Columbus himself appears to have been somewhat confused about his achievement, believing to the end that the isthmus of Panama was the Malay Peninsula, and that Cuba was the province of Mangi in Cathay—a part of the Asian mainland.[21] By 1515, however, the realization of the existence and the importance of the new-found lands and peoples of Africa, Asia, and the Americas had become widespread. Within a scant fifteen years the European concept of the world had changed beyond recognition. Even though some further adjustments in that concept—for example, the implications of Balboa's sighting of the Pacific in 1513 after crossing the isthmus of Panama—were necessary, the main outlines of the modern geographic world had become manifest.

Among other things, the new discoveries and the consequent spread of knowledge resulted in a change in the pattern of world trade. Spices from the Moluccas and elsewhere, required in Europe for the preservation of meat during the winters as well as for providing variety in the

21. On his first voyage he sent an embassy into the interior of Cuba in order to establish contact with the Grand Khan, although not only was Cuba not Cathay, but also there had been no more Khans since the Ming dynasty succeeded the Mongol rulers in 1368, well over a century earlier. On his third voyage Columbus, having discovered the mouth of the Orinoco on the coast of Venezuela, reported to Ferdinand and Isabella that the four mouths of the Orinoco in fact corresponded to the four rivers of Paradise—the Nile, the Euphrates, the Tigris, and the Ganges—and that, furthermore, their waters flowed from the Garden of Eden in the interior of Venezuela, which now formed part of the dominions of Spain. As if this were not startling news enough, he further added that instead of being completely round, the earth was like a round ball "on one part of which is placed something like a woman's breast," at the summit of which stood the Terrestial Paradise. His astral observations led him to the conclusion that he had sailed over this swelling from the Doldrums to Trinidad. At least one contemporary—Las Casas—while not accepting his theories, did not reject them either. Had not Columbus already proved himself right when others had been wrong about the western route to the "Indies"?

diet of the day, had been a highly valuable commodity which had only been obtainable through Cairo via Venice, so that the Arabs and the Venetians between them were able to impose a double monopoly. With the appearance of Portuguese ships in the Indian Ocean, however, the system was undermined, and both Venetian and Arab power began a swift decline. When news arrived in Venice that Cabral had returned to Portugal in 1501 from his voyage to the Indies, his ships laden with spices, the Venetian diarist Priuli recorded that this was "the worst news the Venetian Republic could have had." He was right. Within a short space of time the power of the Arab-Venetian axis was broken. The passing of their monopoly was confirmed by the victory of the Portuguese viceroy, Almeida, off the Indian port of Diu in 1509, over a combined Islamic (Egyptian and Gujerati) fleet that had been assembled with Venetian support. From this time onward the Portuguese were able, for several decades, to retain undisputed mastery of the Eastern trade.

### New Trade Axes

The revision of medieval geographic concepts, and the disintegration of medieval trade patterns which followed, led to the establishment of not one but two new major trade axes. One of these was the Portuguese-controlled trade route to India and the East. The second was the Spanish-controlled transatlantic route to the Americas. It was, however, natural that other European nations, and particularly those such as England, Holland, and France which, no less than Spain and Portugal, had ports on the Atlantic seaboard, should also cast envious eyes at the rich trade advantages being reaped by their Iberian rivals. With the Cape route to the Indies firmly in Portuguese hands, and with the West Indies a Spanish preserve, the would-be rivals had to seek out other means to gain their share of the trade. Despite the incidental discovery of the Americas, the thoughts and dreams of European merchants remained fixed on Cathay and the Indies, as described to them in the pages of Marco Polo. Since the best route—the southeast—was in Portuguese hands, and the southwest in Spanish waters, the possibility of alternative routes—northwest or northeast—should also, perhaps, be explored. In a tentative and unsystematic fashion, and over a period of years as enterprising adventurers appeared and financial backing could be found for them, a number of European ships of various sizes and nationalities therefore sailed in these directions on fresh voyages of discovery. As J. H. Parry has expressed it:

Most sixteenth-century maps show the Arctic as open sea, with large but widely separated islands. Little was then known of the vast extent of the northern ice cap. Seamen argued that the Tropics had proved passable, contrary to all expectations; why not the Arctic?[22]

22. *The Establishment of the European Hegemony: 1415–1715* (1961).

One of the first results of the attempt to find a northeast route to Cathay was—to the surprise of both parties—the establishment of rudimentary Anglo-Russian commercial relations. After two out of an expedition of three English ships which had sailed northeast in 1553 had been frozen in on the northern coast of Norway, and their crews had died of cold and starvation, the third vessel, the *Edward Bonaventura,* under the command of Richard Chancellor, reached Archangel, from where Chancellor reached Moscow by horse-drawn sleigh, and was made welcome at the court of Ivan the Terrible. Ivan lost little time in establishing diplomatic relations with Elizabethan England, which could offer Russia a commercial alternative to the North German Hanseatic League. Subsequent English and Dutch expeditions also sailed northeast, and penetrated considerably further along the northern coast of the Eurasian continent, but none succeeded in establishing any link with far Cathay. Indeed, the northeast passage was never traversed until Nordenskiold, the Swedish explorer, at last made the journey in 1878–79.

The search for the northwest passage was pursued with more perseverance, even though it produced less immediate results. The first attempt to discover it was also English. In 1576 Frobisher made the first of three voyages to North America in search of the passage. Davis, Hudson, and Bylot were later to continue probing for a northern route to the Pacific, but although a profitable fur trade was developed, no route to the Pacific could be found through the maze of straits and islands. It was left to Amundsen to make the journey in 1903–05, by which time interest in the passage had become scientific, and not commercial.

With the search for the northeast and northwest passages proving unsuccessful, the North Atlantic nations were meanwhile seeking to advance their interests by direct competition. On the one hand the union of Portugal and Spain which occurred in 1580[23] aroused fears of Spanish world dominion, while the return of the English adventurer, Sir Francis Drake, from his voyage of circumnavigation of the globe in the same year revealed to other nations the weaknesses in the straggling chain of Portuguese holdings in the Far East.

To begin with this took the form of privateering, especially by English and French ships. Until 1559 letters of marque were issued without undue difficulty by the French government to French privateers who wished to prey upon Spanish shipping.[24] In 1556 Captain le Clerc led a fleet of French ships to sack the Spanish town of Havana, Cuba—also sinking all the shipping in the harbor. The exploits of Drake and other English privateers, often with royal collusion, in the "Spanish Main" are

23. King Sebastian of Portugal dissipated the wealth and manpower of Portugal in an ill-conceived attack upon Morocco in 1578, in which he himself, aged twenty-one, was also killed, at the battle of Alcazar-Kebir. As a result, King Phillip II of Spain annexed Portugal in 1580. In 1640, Portugal seceded from Spain, thus regaining its independence.
24. The privilege, however, was not stretched to include Portuguese shipping, since France had a treaty of alliance with Portugal.

perhaps even better known, although Drake's attacks upon Cadiz and Lisbon in 1587—not to speak of his second attack upon Cadiz in 1596—came after veiled hostility between Spain and England had degenerated into open conflict.

In 1594, when Phillip II of Spain made the mistake of closing the port of Lisbon to Dutch merchants, the Dutch, in revenge, traveled directly to India to conduct their business. In the very next year—1595—Dutch ships first appeared off the West African coast. In 1596 England, France, and Holland, by the Treaty of the Hague, made common cause against Spain, although each later concluded a separate peace: the French by the Treaty of Vervins in 1598, the English by the Treaty of London in 1604, and the Dutch by the Treaty of Antwerp in 1609. Although the French obtained no colonial concessions from Spain in making peace, both the English and the Dutch recognized Spanish claims to all territories effectively occupied by Spain in the Americas, but did not recognize any Spanish rights in regions which remained unoccupied. From this time on the colonizing powers of the North Atlantic watched one another as closely as they watched the Spanish. France and England in particular, beginning their long-drawn-out global struggle for colonial domination, followed each other's maneuvers with the closest attention. Swedes and Danes also formed "East India Companies." All the principalities of Europe that could were entering the newly discovered lands as rivals.

The religious struggle between Islam and Christendom that had marked the character of the Middle Ages had thus undergone a remarkable development. To sum up: the Venetians, having helped to undermine Christian Byzantium, had entered into an alliance with Moslem Egypt to control the spice trade. In order to outflank the Moslems, Portugal had then made her own way to the Indies, and in so doing had not only undermined the economic position of Arabs and Venetians alike, but had also opened new paths to power and fortune not only for Spain, but also for other European powers. The split which at that time divided Christendom into Protestant and Catholic sectors was, while an added irritant to economic quarrels, not the ultimate determinant, by any means. Before long English and Dutch Protestants, no less than French and Spanish Catholics, would be fighting fiercely against one another for the sake of economic advantage in the new lands. Thus, whereas at the outset European fought Arab for religion, at the conclusion European fought European for economics. There could be no clearer sign of the passing of the medieval world.

*First European Contacts with Colored Peoples*

What were the relations between newly arrived Europeans of all nationalities, and the peoples of the lands to which they came? The records of these first contacts, where they are not repetitive, as they often are, make interesting reading today in the light of all that has since occurred.

In West Africa, the Portuguese had made contact first with Berber tribes south of Cape Bojador, and then further south with black West Africans. Relations both hostile and friendly were established, but were sometimes indirectly conditioned by the Islam-Christian struggle. After one Portuguese commander, Nuno Tristao, had been ambushed and killed with poisoned arrows while taking two boats up the Gambia River, Cadamosto, who followed him later, discovered that the reason for local hostility was that the Gambians had been told by the Moslems that the Christians were cannibals. There were, however, other reasons for hostility. The Portuguese may not have been cannibals, but they were slavers. While Prince Henry sanctioned the slave trade as a part of his policy, as contacts with West Africa grew he tended to favor merchant captains who promoted friendly relations with African rulers, thus increasing the volume of trade, rather than bold adventurers whose violent proceedings aroused the West African populations against the white man.

In East Africa, the anonymous chronicler who accompanied Vasco da Gama on his first voyage commented on the people of Delagoa Bay in what is now Mozambique:

The young women are good-looking. . . . These people took much delight in us. . . . Two gentlemen of the country came to see us. They were very haughty and valued nothing that we gave them. . . . A young man in their company had come from a distant country and had already seen big ships like ours.

Some twenty years later, and several degrees further north, another Portuguese observer, Gaspar de Correa, was less complimentary concerning the people of "Ethiopia" (who were in fact probably Somalis) who came to greet the Portuguese Embassy of 1520:

They are a poor civil people with miserable clothes, and they come into the water uncovered, a black tall people with thick matted locks, which from their birth they neither cut nor comb.

Of greater dramatic interest are the first European-American contacts, since neither population had had previous intimations of the existence of the other.[25] Fortunately for us, Columbus's own description of his first meeting with the people of the Americas was preserved by Las Casas, who drew directly from Columbus's original journal (now lost) in writing as follows:

Two hours after midnight land appeared, at a distance of about two leagues from them. They took in all sail . . . waiting for day, a Friday, on which they reached a small island of the Lucayos, which is called in the language of the Indians "Guanahani" [San Salvador]. Immediately they saw naked people, and the admiral [Columbus]

25. Legends, such as those of the Aztecs about the white man, or the possibility of earlier European visits to the Americas, may, in this context, be virtually discounted.

went ashore in the armed boat. . . . Soon many people of the island gathered there. What follows are the actual words of the admiral . . . "I," he says, "in order that they might feel great amity towards us, because I knew that they were a people to be delivered and converted to our holy faith rather by love than by force, gave to some among them some red caps and some glass beads, which they hung round their necks, and many other things of little value. At this they were greatly pleased and became so entirely our friends that it was a wonder to see. Afterwards they came swimming to the ships' boats, where we were, and brought us parrots and cotton thread in balls, and spears and many other things, and we exchanged them for other things, such as small glass beads and hawks' bells, which we gave to them. In fact, they took all and gave all, such as they had, with good will, but it seemed to me that they were a people very deficient in everything. They all go naked as their mothers bore them, and the women also, although I saw only one very young girl. And all those whom I did see were youths, so that I did not see one who was over thirty years of age; they were very well built, with very handsome bodies and very good faces. Their hair is coarse almost like the hairs of a horse's tail and short; they wear their hair down over their eyebrows, except for a few strands behind which they wear long and never cut. Some of them are painted black, and they are the color of the people of the Canaries, neither black nor white, and some of them are painted white and some red and some in any color that they find. Some of them paint their faces, some their whole bodies, some only the eyes, and some only the nose. They do not bear arms or know them, for I showed to them swords and they took them by the blade and cut themselves through ignorance. They have no iron. . . . I saw some who bore marks of wounds on their bodies, and I made signs to them to ask how this came about, and they indicated to me that people came from other islands, which are near, and wished to capture them, and they defended themselves. And I believed and still believe that they come here from the mainland to take them for slaves. They should be good servants and of quick intelligence, since I see that they very soon say all that is said to them, and I believe that they would easily be made Christians, for it appeared to me that they had no creed. Our Lord willing, at the time of my departure I will bring back six of them to Your Highnesses, that they may learn to talk.

In South America, Magellan's encounter with a Patagonian in 1520, during his circumnavigatory voyage, resembled Columbus's experience on "Guanahani" in some respects. One morning, according to Pigafetta, the chronicler of the voyage, a giant appeared on the beach, dressed in skins, and with boots made from skins. The man was so large that "we reached only to his waist." Magellan treated him kindly and ordered that he should be given food. So overcome was he at catching sight of himself in a mirror that he jumped backwards, oversetting four of the men who were standing by. Magellan, like Columbus, wished to take captives, using a stratagem to capture two Patagonians so that he might take them back to Spain as a present to the Emperor.

Whereas some Europeans had traveled East before Marco Polo, and many after him, the arrival of Vasco da Gama's fleet at Calicut in 1498 marked the first occasion since the time of Alexander the Great in the fourth century B.C. that a Western expedition had encountered the populations of India. Unfortunately da Gama's behavior was notoriously undiplomatic, and created considerable ill will towards Europeans.

Some details of the first encounters between the Easterners and the Westerners are revealing. The unknown chronicler of da Gama's voyage was, for example, under some misapprehensions concerning the religion of the Hindus that were as remarkable as those of Columbus concerning American geography:

The city of Calicut is inhabited by Christians. They are of tawny complexion. Some of them have big beards and long hair, merely allowing a tuft to remain on the crown, as a sign that they are Christians. . . . The women of this country as a rule are ugly and of small stature. . . . All these people are well disposed and apparently of mild temper. At first sight they seem covetous and ignorant.

Upon entering Calicut, the Portuguese visited a temple. The Hindus gathered round them and pointed to a statue, crying out "Maria! Maria!"

Many other saints were painted on the walls of the church, wearing crowns. They were painted variously, with teeth protruding an inch from the mouth, and four or five arms.

One of the Portuguese, Joao da Sa, doubted whether the paintings were in fact of Christian saints. As he knelt beside Vasco da Gama to pray he whispered, "If these be devils, I worship the true God."

Despite the tenor of relations between Portuguese and Indians—which varied—there was, at least, no doubt from the outset about the reactions of the Arab merchants whom the Portuguese had come to displace. Upon entering a house belonging to two Arabs from Tunis or Oran, the Arabs greeted them with the words "The devil take you! What brought you here?" With admirable succinctness the Portuguese replied, "We come in search of Christians and spices." Here was a meeting not of new friends, but of old enemies in a new setting.

Europe, which had thus impinged so suddenly upon so many African, Asian, and American peoples—who, "stunned by this strange apparition rising from the pathless ocean, offered no effective opposition"[26]—did not succeed in making the same impact upon China. Christians had been tolerated at the court of Kublai Khan and other Tartar rulers of Cathay —but then the Tartars were themselves regarded as foreigners, and perhaps felt better able to place their trust in Christians such as Marco Polo (who was employed in the Khan's diplomatic service) than in the Chinese over whom they ruled. Contact between China and Christendom had, as we have seen, been broken off as a result of two events, the Black Death, and the emergence of the Ottoman Turks. After this, in the early fifteenth century, the Chinese themselves, for reasons which still remain somewhat obscure, suddenly adopted a policy of isolationism, which lost them the trade of the Indian Ocean to the Arabs, and cut them off from the world at the very moment when Europe's expansion had begun in earnest. Europe, however, had no intention of leaving

26. Theodore Lothrop Stoddard, *The Rising Tide of Color Against White World Supremacy* (1920).

China isolated, and in 1514 the first European to arrive in China for many years—Jorge Alvares, a Portuguese—appeared, although he was only allowed to reach the mouth of the Canton River. Another Portuguese, Raphael Perestrello, later penetrated further, and reported on his return that the Chinese were a good people and were interested in establishing friendly relations with Portugal. Before matters could develop much further, however, the Chinese changed their opinion of the desirability of good relations with Europeans, in view of the kidnaping of Chinese children as slaves by some Portuguese. The Emperor closed China to European traders, and relations did not develop further until the end of the sixteenth century, when the cultivated and devout Italian Jesuit, Matteo Ricci, created a better impression. China, unlike most other lands, succeeded for the time being in keeping Europeans at arm's length.

Nothing succeeds like success. It was, of course, the sudden acquisition of new tools—maps, navigational instruments, improved ships, and more effective armaments—that was responsible for the astonishing rapidity with which Europe was able to impose itself upon non-European peoples. The guns of Almeida at Diu in 1509—outranging the armament of the Islamic fleet, and shooting to sink vessels rather than to kill men —achieved a strategic victory for Christendom over Islam that all the struggles, sacrifices, and cannonades of the Crusaders had failed to do.

And yet, whereas the new tools of European power rapidly converted the medieval age into the Renaissance, the ways and patterns of thinking even of the Europeans themselves were less easily altered. Columbus himself—a symbol in some ways of the new age—remained in other respects medieval in his thought. His metaphysical motive for undertaking the venture that became the discovery of the Americas was to raise funds in order to free the Holy Sepulcher from the Moslems. When, on December 13, 1502, a waterspout threatened his fleet, he took a sword in one hand and a Bible in the other and exorcised it, making a circle with his sword around all his ships as he did so. Sir Francis Drake—another symbol of the new age—in the course of his voyage of circumnavigation had one of the *Golden Hind's* officers, Sir Thomas Doughty, beheaded not only for inciting members of the crew to mutiny and desertion, but also for practicing witchcraft. Later in the sixteenth century the Welshman John Dee, a contemporary of the geographer Hakluyt, an effective advocate of English enterprise overseas, and a supporter of Frobisher's quest for the northwest passage and other ventures, was an avowed wizard. Finally, in 1582, Dee's interest in the occult appears to have surpassed his interest in discovery, for in that year, in company with other necromancers, he left England for Bohemia, a country which, he believed, provided better conditions for his work. The old world was slow in fading, and the new world full of contradictions.

Many of the medieval myths, however, encouraged the adventurers of the new age to pursue their discoveries. Especially in the earlier stages the legends of Prester John, of the Gilded Man,[27] of Monomatapa,[28] of the northwest passage, and of the mysterious southern continent known as Locach, all provided targets at which imaginative adventurers might aim. In retrospect it is also curious to observe how often there remained a kernel of truth to each legend, once the husk of mythology was peeled away. There was a Prester John; there was a Gilded Man; there was even a southern continent—Australia. Knowledge appeared to forerun each discovery, even if it assumed vague and legendary forms. One of the many mysteries of geographical exploration is found in the pages of *The Life, Adventures, and Piracies of the Famous Captain Singleton,* by Daniel Defoe. The book, in part, describes the adventures of a party of sailors, marooned on the coast of Mozambique, who made their way from east to west across the African continent, finally reaching the Atlantic at "one of the Dutch settlements on the Gold Coast." How, it has recently been asked, could Defoe, writing in 1720 well over a century before Livingstone or Stanley ventured into Central Africa, have provided a relatively exact description of the geographical features that would be encountered in such a journey?[29] Defoe's *Robinson Crusoe,* of course, had a real-life counterpart in Andrew Selkirk. Was there also a counterpart to "Captain Singleton"?

27. The Gilded Man was the American equivalent of Prester John. He was reputed to live in the golden city of Mawoa on the shores of a Lake Parima. This original "El Dorado" myth attracted treasure hunters for a hundred years. The factual basis for the myth was that religious rites were practiced by the chief of the Guatavita tribe, who smeared himself with turpentine, rolled in gold dust, and then jumped in the sacred lake of Guatavita, near Bogotá.

28. Monomatapa was an African kingdom, or chieftancy, ruled over by the Monomatapa who lived on a mountain called Faro, identified by some with Ophir. Its wealth was highly exaggerated by fable. Its exact location was finally established by Jesuit missionaries in 1560.

29. Defoe did, however, occasion his voyagers some unnecessary fatigue by causing them to cross a fictitious desert which he situated in the region.

# Chapter 4

# "Black Ivory": The Transatlantic Slave Trade

**AFTER THE** great reformist storm which led to the abolition of the slave trade, it still remains difficult to consider the subject of slavery dispassionately, if only because the transposition of attitudes concerning slavery into the context of the race problems of our own day is so easily made. In fact, this circumstance is not without significance, for a relationship between the slave trade and contemporary race problems does exist. In the earlier phases of the transatlantic slave traffic, before abuses had developed to the point at which they attracted the attention of the abolitionists, no philosophic connection was made between slavery and race. The slave traders themselves regarded the slaves as fellow human beings. Only when abolitionist efforts placed the slave traders on the defensive did they begin to propagate the thesis that Negroes were by their nature inferior, and therefore marked down by destiny to be a subject race. The great debate which opened in the eighteenth century and which raged throughout the nineteenth resulted in the end of the slave trade. The arguments of the proponents of slavery were not, however, without their effects. These effects remain with us today in the form of that racialism which exacerbates so many contemporary problems.

The transatlantic slave trade lasted from 1502, if not earlier, until the 1860s—that is to say, for over 350 years. We cannot doubt that the prosecution of the trade for so long a period made it one of the principal formative influences on the evolution of African, American, and European society.

From the sixteenth century onward, as a result of the slave trade, African society was subjected to a continual drain of its manpower, to the dissipation of its energies in internal conflicts, and to the disruption of normal commercial development. Even when the slave trade was finally abolished, its very abolition—as Sir Harry H. Johnston bluntly phrased it—"furnished the excuse or cause of European intervention in many cases." The slave trade, in other words, was superseded by the European occupation of Africa.

In the Americas, the alienation of American-Indian lands was accompanied by the introduction of African slave labor. The effects throughout the Americas have been profound, and not least in the United States. Although he was writing a generation before the American Civil War, the words of the prophetic Alexis de Tocqueville still remain applicable:

> The most formidable of all the ills which threaten the future existence of the Union, arises from the presence of a black population upon its territory: and in contemplating the cause of the present embarrassments or of the future dangers of the United States, the observer is invariably led to consider this as a primary fact. . . . The negro race will never leave those shores of the American continent, to which it was brought by the passions and vices of Europeans; and it will not disappear from the New World as long as it continues to exist. The inhabitants of the United States may retard the calamities which they apprehend, but they cannot now destroy their efficient cause.[1]

In Western Europe, profits obtained from the slave trade, or from West Indian plantations in which slave labor was used, gave a new impetus to industry. This was particularly true of England, whose virtual monopoly of the transatlantic slave trade followed the signing of the Treaty of Utrecht in 1713. The operation of the "great trade triangle"— by which cheap European manufactures were carried to Africa; African slaves to the Americas; and American sugar, tobacco, and other products to Europe—provided the basis not only for the amassing of private fortunes, but also for capital accumulation that could be used—and was used—for industrial development. The industrial revolution that followed in Britain constituted the first massive and demonstrable breach in the walls of scientific ignorance that permitted society to advance in the direction of a new technological age. The connection between slavery and scientific advance for mankind's benefit, like the connection between good and evil, requires the vision of a Blake (who, incidentally, living from 1757 to 1827, was conscious of such contemporary events as the American and French Revolutions, the practice of slavery, and the rise of industrial society), to be fully comprehended, but we can guess that it exists. Further inklings of the historical implications may be obtained when we consider that it was primarily disputes over the trade in Afri-

---

1. *Democracy in America* (1835–1840 [1961 edition]).

can slaves and West Indian sugar that first brought to a head differences between the English colonists in North America and the most powerful financial interests in London. Slaves and plantation sugar having played a major role in the rise of Western European industrialism, this industrialism then, in due time, demanded European colonial occupation of the tropical regions of the world for the sake of establishing control over markets and sources of raw materials. The slave trade and its effects run like a thread through the fabric of the modern age.

## From Incident to Institution

Technically it may be said that the European slave trade from black Africa began in 1442, when one of Prince Henry's captains, Antao Goncalves, instructed by Henry to bring back some people from the newly discovered lands, brought back "ten blacks, male and female," as well as the first gold dust obtained directly from Africa by Christians, instead of through the agency of the Moors of North Africa. Azurara recounts how Goncalves landed with nine picked men to seize "some man or woman" to take back to show to Henry the Navigator so that he might gain "knowledge by that means of what kind are the other dwellers in this land." They found first a "naked man following a camel with two assegais in his hand," and took him, and then "saw a black Mooress come along," and seized her too. Goncalves was now satisfied, but another Portuguese, Nuno Tristam, arrived and proposed "what is still better, namely for us to carry off many more; for, besides the knowledge which the Lord Infant will gain by their means, profit also will accrue to him by their service or ransom." They accordingly took ten prisoners of the Saharan Azanaghi tribe, later described by Cadamosto as of "deep brown complexion."

One of the captives was a "noble" named Adahu, who having been taken to Portugal, was "very well clad in garments given him by the Infant," and was then returned to his own land against a promise of ransom. Adahu was landed to make the necessary arrangements, but disappeared, not to be seen again. He did, however, cause to be sent by caravan some days later ten adult Negroes, some ostrich eggs, a shield, and some gold dust. These were duly exchanged for two young Berbers, captured at the same time as Adahu and held on board the ship. Goncalves therefore became not only the first European to take black African slaves, but also the first to bring back gold to Europe from the newly discovered lands.

The immediate effect of the return of Goncalves and Tristam with their captives and gold was to produce a change in attitude toward Prince Henry's enterprise among his own people. He had previously been regarded as an eccentric who wasted money. Now, however, that changed. As Azurara wrote:

When [the people] saw the first Moorish captives brought home, and the second cargo that followed these, they became already somewhat doubtful about the opinion they had at first expressed, and altogether renounced it when they saw the third consignment that Nuno Tristam brought home. . . . And so they were forced to turn their blame into public praise; for they said it was plain the Infant was another Alexander; and their covetousness began to wax greater. And, as they saw the houses of others full to overflowing of male and female slaves, and their property increasing, they thought about the whole matter, and began to talk among themselves.

It is somewhat difficult, today, after all that has happened, to enter into the state of mind of the Portuguese of the fifteenth century, and to view the matter of taking slaves through their eyes. They had no foreknowledge of the "immense mass of evil" (as Thomas Clarkson, the English abolitionist, later called it) that the slave trade was to become. They knew nothing of America, and so had no thought of transporting millions of Africans there. They would remember, of course, that slavery as a regular institution among the Christians of Western Europe had been finally eliminated by steady pressure from the Christian Church in the twelfth century—three hundred years earlier. But the Portuguese suffered from a labor shortage, and they would also remember that Moors frequently took Christian prisoners for ransom, or, failing that, to use them for labor. Had not Prince Henrys' own brother, Prince Fernando, been held as a captive by the Moors until he died in prison in Fez in 1443, the price for his ransom—nothing less than the return of Ceuta itself—being too high?

And, at the eastern end of the Mediterranean, slave trading had flourished throughout the preceding two hundred years. The Byzantine Emperor Paleologus had himself authorized the trade. The Egyptian Mamelukes regularly bought slaves from many countries to man their armies and fill their harems. (Circassians were valued the highest and Serbs the lowest in the markets of Alexandria). Genoan and Venetian merchants had long been accustomed to import Tartar, Circassian, Turkish, Russian and other slaves, especially young women for resale throughout Europe, in all countries from the North Sea to the Mediterranean. Marco Polo himself had possessed at least one slave, "Peter the Tartar," who was manumitted upon Polo's death in accordance with the terms of his will. Indeed, were not slaves still very numerous among the population of Venice itself—that city state whose power Portugal sought to rival and surpass?

The taking and sale of slaves, to the men of the fifteenth century, no doubt weighted lightly indeed in the moral scales beside such acts as, for example, the perpetration of a massacre, or the sacking of a town. The Church, the moral arbiter in such questions, laid strong strictures on the sale of Christian slaves to Moorish masters but, while not approving slavery per se, welcomed the conversions to Christianity that resulted from the sale of Moorish slaves to Christian masters. The word "Moor," of course, denoted "Blackamoor"—black African—no less than a white or brown-skinned North African.

A dramatic description, again by Azurara, has come down to us of the scene when the Portuguese divided up their African captives on August 8, 1444, on a field in the port of Lagos, Portugal:

These, placed all together in that field, were a marvelous sight, for amongst them were some white enough, fair to look upon, and well proportioned; others were less white, like mulattoes; others again were as black as Ethiops, and so ugly, both in features and in body, as almost to appear (to those who saw them) the images of a lower hemisphere. But what heart could be so hard as not to be pierced with piteous feeling to see that company? For some kept their heads low and their faces bathed in tears, looking one upon another; others stood groaning very dolorously, looking up to the height of heaven, fixing their eyes upon it, crying out loudly, as if asking help of the Father of Nature; others struck their faces with the palms of their hands, throwing themselves at full length upon the ground; others made their lamentations in the manner of a dirge, after the custom of their country. And though we could not understand the words of their language, the sound of it right well accorded with the measure of their sadness. But to increase their sufferings still more . . . it was needful to part fathers from sons, husbands from wives, brothers from brothers.

The captives were divided into five groups, as earlier agreed upon. Prince Henry was there, "mounted upon a powerful steed, and accompanied by his retinue," and "of the forty-six souls which fell to him as his fifth, he made a very speedy partition [among other people] . . . for he reflected with great pleasure upon the salvation of those souls that before were lost."

Meanwhile, other caravels were questing south, and returning with gold, slaves, and other things. In 1448 a base was established on an island in Arguim Bay, in what is now Mauretania—the first of a series of Portuguese trading forts that were to be strung along the length of the West African coast. A few years later a Portuguese company was established for trading in West African slaves and gold. Sometimes the Portuguese captains traded for the slaves they took, and sometimes they resorted to simple kidnaping. Alvaro Fernandez, for example, as Azurara reports, sailed "to the land of the Negroes," where, after various adventures, the Portuguese landed and espied "some of the wives of the Guineas" going to a creek to collect shellfish, and captured one of them, a woman of about thirty with a son about two years old. "But the strength of the woman was much to be marvelled at, for not one of the three men who came upon her but would have had a great labour in attempting to get her to the boat." Instead, therefore, they "conceived it well to take her son from her and to carry him to the boat; and love of the child compelled the mother to follow after it, without great pressure on the part of the two who were bringing her."

The European demand for African slaves was not insatiable, however, and before long it appeared that, irrespective of whether the captives were bought or seized, the trade was reaching its limits. Those who were taken to Portugal usually became converted to Christianity, and many later obtained their freedom, intermarrying with the Portuguese. The African-European slave trade might well have dwindled and died, were it not for the discovery of the Americas.

Considerable speculation has taken place as to who might have been the first African in the New World. It has been claimed that Pedro Alonso Nino, a member of Columbus's crew, was black. This was quite likely since there were a number of blacks in Spain in the late 1400s, and according to tradition one or two of the crew carried by Columbus were black.

By 1502–3 the first slaves had been taken from Portuguese Africa to the Spanish American colonies—if, indeed, some had not been taken there earlier. There is, however, no record of the trade being conducted in a systematic way at this time, and the authorities were of two minds as to its advisability. Queen Isabella of Spain, acting on the advice of Ovando, Governor of Hispaniola (now Haiti and the Dominican Republic) gave orders that no more African slaves were to be brought to the West Indies. This restriction soon disappeared, however, with Isabella's death in 1504. Qualms were nevertheless experienced by other Christian authorities as to what might be the consequences for the future of Europeans in the New World if Islam were to make its appearance there. Might not the Christian-Moslem struggle that had racked the old world be needlessly resumed in the new as a result of the imprudence of introducing Moslem slaves there? Some Christians appear to have thought so, for the instructions issued to the Governor of Hispaniola permitted him to import African slaves "born in the power of Christians," but not others. In 1506, moreover, he was ordered to expel all Berber and pagan slaves from Hispaniola. The Spanish Crown also strove to ensure that all slave ships bound for the Americas passed through the port of Seville. This was for two reasons —to collect export duty, and to satisfy the authorities that the slaves were all from West Africa, and that none of them, whether black or brown, were North African Moslems who might introduce Islam to the "Indians."

Meanwhile, the trade progressed. In 1510 Ferdinand V of Spain gave orders for 250 Christian Africans to be purchased from the Portuguese and sent to the New World. By 1513 the sale of licenses for trading in slaves to the Americas had become a source of profit to the Spanish government. On Ferdinand's death in 1516 the trade was arrested by Cardinal Ximenes, but the lapse was only temporary, for in 1517 Charles V of Spain authorized its resumption. Pressures of many kinds for its resumption had, indeed, been at work. The colonists demanded labor for the mines. Courtiers wished for income from the sale of licenses. Las Casas, the Spanish bishop, disturbed at the plight of the Indians, recommended in 1517 that Christianized Africans might take the place of the Indians as laborers, and that each Spaniard in the "Indies" be allowed to import twelve slaves. The trade thus became an institution, with licenses being regularly granted, and with attempts being regularly made by one contractor or another to secure monopolies.

By 1542, however, Charles V appeared to have repented of his action in fostering the trade, for in that year he caused to be drawn up a code of laws to ensure the protection of the American Indians, and further ordered that all the slaves in Spain's American possessions should be freed. Pedro de la Gasca was sent to the Americas to implement this decree, but upon his return to Spain, and upon the retreat of Charles to a monastery, slavery was resumed.

Legal doubts about the slave trade appear to have been entertained by many, especially in the earlier days before the slave-trading interests had consolidated their power in courts and chancelleries. Roman law had made a distinction between captives taken in just wars and those taken in unjust wars. Who was to tell which slaves, bought from African chiefs, had been captured in the advancement of a just cause, and which had been wrongfully enslaved? Other misgivings were also reportedly felt. In England Thomas Clarkson said:

The first importation of slaves from Africa, by our countrymen, was in the reign of Elizabeth, in the year 1562. This great princess seems on the very commencement of the trade to have questioned its lawfulness. She seems to have entertained a religious scruple concerning it; and, indeed, to have revolted at the very thought of it. . . . When Captain (afterwards Sir John) Hawkins returned from his first voyage to Africa and Hispaniola, whither he had carried slaves, she sent for him, and, as we learn from Hill's "Naval History" expressed her concern lest any of the Africans should be carried off without their free consent, declaring that "it would be detestable, and call down the vengeance of heaven upon the undertakers."[2]

The Church also reviewed its attitude in the light of events. Whereas Pope Nicholas V in 1452 had granted King Alfonso of Portugal powers to conquer and enslave pagans in the new lands, Pope Leo X, in the first quarter of the sixteenth century, adopted a different view. A dispute having arisen between Dominicans and Franciscans as to slavery in the Americas, with the Dominicans favoring its abolition, the matter was re-

2. *History of the Rise, Progress, and Accomplishment of the Abolition of the African Slave Trade by the British Parliament* (1839).

ferred to Pope Leo X for a decision. He took the position "that not only the Christian religion, but nature itself cried out against a state of slavery." Needless to say, despite this prophetic declaration, the slave trade continued: it had, indeed, hardly yet begun in earnest.

## The Slave Trade in Africa

The design of the slave trade in Africa itself is composed of a mosaic of local history, into which the different patterns of European rivalry interlock. In its initial stages it appears to have been conducted on a relatively small scale, with the various African chiefs and rulers along the coast selling some prisoners of war captured from hostile tribes to the European ship captains, and with some kidnapings of African villagers by European slavers. Toward the end of the sixteenth century, however, a certain event occurred which was indirectly to give a powerful impetus to the development of the slave trade. This was the overthrow of the inland empire of Songhai[3]—last of the ancient kingdoms of the West African Sudan—by an army sent by El-Mansur of Morocco.

The Protestant-Catholic schism that rent Europe during this period not only prevented religious pressure from being exerted against the slave trade from the outset, but also fostered intrigues that helped to spread those anarchic conditions in Africa which permitted the slave trade to develop on the scale that it did. England, at the time when Elizabeth I reigned, was obtaining saltpeter for manufacturing gunpowder from Morocco. This trade was pursued even though trading with Moslems was regarded as a most heinous crime for Christian princes. The King of Portugal had commanded that one Portuguese ship's captain caught selling arms to the Moors should be martyrized "in a cart, and that they should make a furnace of fire and throw him into it with his sword and his gold." But Elizabeth, in order to attain her ends, felt no compunction in sending not only guns to the Moors but also in developing friendly relations still further. She sent timber for Moorish galleys, cannon balls, oars, and even English shipwrights to help the Moors develop their seapower further. The Moorish arms that defeated the Portuguese army so overwhelmingly at Alcazar-Kebir in 1578 were made in England. The pretender to the Portuguese throne, Don Antonio—a thorn in the side of Spain, after the union of the two kingdoms—was financed with Moroccan gold at the instance of Elizabeth of England.

El-Mansur, Shereef of Morocco, who succeeded to the throne in dramatic fashion after his predecessor, Abd-el-Malek, had died at the very moment of victory at Alcazar-Kebir, now found himself a wealthy monarch enjoying international prestige. His two enemies, Turkey and Spain,

3. Sonni Ali, king of Songhai, by the time of his death in 1492, had built up his state to a commanding position in the West African Sudan. Under his successors the power of Songhai was maintained for a century.

were neither of them in a position to pose a serious menace. Much as Elizabeth might have liked to encourage Spanish-Moroccan tension, El-Mansur, no doubt unwilling to resume the long struggle with Christian Iberia which had ended in Morocco's expulsion from Europe, instead let his thoughts turn south, and dreamed of seizing the West African gold mines of Songhai. Morocco would thus control not merely the terminus of the trans-Sahara gold trade, but also the source of production. Among other things this would halt the drain of gold from the West African interior into the holds of the Portuguese ships along the coast. As early as 1481 the Portuguese had begun to build a factory in what is now Ghana at Sao Jorge da Mina—later known as Elmina—and from this base they had succeeded in institutionalizing the gold trade in a manner that had brought great wealth to Portugal, at the expense, as El-Mansur no doubt viewed it, of Morocco.

El-Mansur therefore fitted out an army to cross the Sahara and seize the kingdom of Songhai, which was then ruled over by Askia Ishak, and extended from Tekrur in what is now Senegal to the Hausa states of what is now Northern Nigeria. The Moroccan army was of a somewhat international character. It was led by a young Spaniard named Judar—a eunuch born in Grenada, and captured by the Moors as a child. The official language of the army was Spanish, and while over one-third was Moroccan, the remainder were either Europeans, Turks, or Spanish Moors of Andalusian origin. Leaving Marrakesh on October 16, 1590, the army traversed the Sahara, suffering, it is believed, heavy losses during the journey. In early 1591 Judar's troops defeated a much larger Songhai army at the battle of Tondibi, the Moors' possession of firearms proving decisive.

In the years that followed, the Songhai kingdom disintegrated but without effective Moroccan control becoming established. Factional fighting and tribal revolts were punctuated by massacres and reprisals. Inter-tribal conflicts which had been stilled by Songhai rule before the Moorish invasion now broke out once more. The Tuareg tribes of the Sahara also came in to the attack. In his *Tarikh es-Sudan* the seventeenth-century writer es-Sadi, who had been born in Timbuktu, described these times in the following words:

> Security gave place to danger, wealth to poverty, distress and calamities and violence succeeded tranquillity. Everywhere men destroyed each other; in every place and in every direction there was plundering, and war spared neither life nor property nor persons. Disorder was general and spread everywhere, rising to the highest degree of intensity.

The Tuareg raids were punished, however, by the Moors, who captured so many captives that the price of slaves dropped sharply. The conflicts that continued in the years that followed did not lessen the number of captives, while during the same period the European ships that came and disappeared again on the coast provided a ready market for slaves. The Europeans had discovered the value of African labor to their interests in the New World. All the elements of the great forced migration of Africans to the Americas were now at hand. The inconsequential degree of slave trading that had occurred in the fifteenth century and the experimental slave trading of the sixteenth now gave way to the heyday of the trade in the seventeenth and eighteenth centuries. No accurate computation of the number of slaves thus transported is possible, but the enormous proportions that it reached have never been in doubt. John Hope Franklin cites an estimate that 900,000 Africans were imported to the New World in the sixteenth century, 2,750,000 in the seventeenth, 7,000,000 in the eighteenth, and 4,000,000 in the nineteenth. Few commentators have placed the numbers at so low a level. Some have mentioned the total numbers involved as being in the region of 40 million. R. R. Kuczynski, the noted demographer, concluded that the grant total of Africans landed alive in the Americas might be 15 million, but that this would be "a rather conservative figure." The high mortality which accompanied the conduct of the trade would indicate that the drain on Africa's population would be represented by an even larger number.

Where did the slaves brought to the New World come from? A pattern of considerable complexity emerges if some of the evidence available is studied. In 1854 a member of the British Church Missionary Society, the Reverend S. W. Koelle, who had lived in Sierra Leone for several years, wrote a book called *Polyglotta Africana,* in which he published the results of information that he had collected from freed slaves who had been landed from British cruisers. He noted down over 200 languages, including most West African tongues from Lake Chad to Senegal; South West African languages; South East African languages; and those from the Lake Nyasa vicinity. A great body of cultural evidence also exists. Many Yoruba influences are to be found in Brazil. The Haitian *Voodoo* is clearly derived from the West African Ewe *vudu* or *vodu.* It has been argued that the Jamaican Obeah derives from the Twe word *obayifo,* meaning witchcraft. Ivory Coast captives, shipped through Elmina, were sent to Cuba. The archives of the Mexican Inquisition mentioned members of many West African tribes as having been enslaved and brought to Mexico. They also mentioned some slaves coming from Mozambique and elsewhere in East Africa, even as early as the sixteenth century. An English traveler, writing in 1726, mentioned that the slaves to be bought at Accra included some that were supposed to come from "very remote parts," and added that it was not uncommon to find a Malayan or two among "a Parcel of other Slaves." "They differ much from the Guinea Negroes," he added, "being right East Indians of a tawny Complexion, with long black Hair. They all go clad with long Trowsers and Jackets, and can write and read and speak the Malayan language." Some Malayans, he explained, fleeing from Dutch oppression, had settled in the Red Sea area, on the African coast, from where they engaged in long journeys into the interior for slave trading and other reasons. Sometimes some of them were also taken as slaves. The Mexican records also spoke of slaves coming from Burma, Malaya, Java, and China.

Opinions differed as to the respective quality of slaves taken from different regions. John Atkins, a surgeon in the British Royal Navy who visited the West African coast in 1721, and described his experiences in *A Voyage to Guinea, Brasil, and the West Indies*, published in 1735, commented:

> Slaves differ in their Goodness; those from the Gold Coast are accounted best, being cleanest limbed, and more docible by our Settlements than others; but then they are, for that very reason, more prompt to Revenge, and murder the Instruments of their Slavery, and also apter in the means to compass it. . . . To Windward they approach in Goodness as is the distance from the Gold Coast; so, as at Gambia or Sierraleon, to be much better than at any of the interjacent places. To Leeward from thence, they alter gradually for the worse; an Angolan Negro is a Proverb for worthlessness; and they mend (if we may call it so) in that way, till you come to the Hottentots, that is, to the Southernmost Extremity of Africa.

A London tract, published in 1753, referring to the African trade, held that because Gold Coast, Popo, and Whidah Negroes were born in a part of Africa that was "very barren," they were accustomed to habits of regular cultivation, which enabled them to adapt easily to agricultural labor on the American plantations. On the other hand, it was held, those from Gambia, Calabar, Bonny, and Angola came from areas that were extremely fertile, so that "on that account, the men never work, but lead an indolent life, and are in general of a lazy disposition and tender constitution . . . so that when those people are carried to our sugar islands, they are obliged to be nursed, to be taken great care of, and brought to work by degrees."

A Brazilian military leader, Henrique Dias, writing in 1647 about the quality of the troops in his regiment, reported, however, that the "Angolas are so robust that no labor tires them." Another Brazilian commentator, Gaspar Barleus, writing in 1660, spoke of the "slackness and laziness" of the Negroes of Guinea, Sierra Leone, and Cape Verde, and stated that the most industrious of all were the *Angolenses*, good for labor in the field. Such reputations, good or bad, were frequently based, no doubt, on personal prejudice, or upon myths that gained popular currency.

### The Development of the Slave Trade

The trade itself soon became a competitive struggle between rival European powers for control of the coastal "factories" or trading castles, as well as the carrying trade, on the one hand, and between different African tribes and their leaders for control of the interior, and hence the monopoly of supplying slaves to the Europeans, on the other. Much has been made by Europeans of the fact that Africans sold fellow Africans into slavery, and that therefore they should share the historic blame for participating in the slave trade. The fact remains, however, that individual African chiefs had little choice as to whether to participate in the trade or not. Slaves were exchanged, among other things, for European muskets and guns, and those chiefs who did not engage in the trade in order to obtain such arms would soon find their people enslaved by the guns and muskets of their neighbors. To engage in the slave trade offered the best chance of survival for a West African tribe. Thus, as the commercial and agricultural state of Songhai, last of the great Sudanese kingdoms, was overthrown by European firearms at the service of Morocco, so there then began the rise of new African slave-trading states, such as those of Ashanti and Dahomey, situated midway between the savannah lands and the coast—states whose power was based ultimately upon firearms obtained from Europe in exchange for slaves: the slaves that the Europeans needed to work the plantations of the Americas.

On the European side, the Portuguese may be said to have dominated the trade in the fifteenth century, until the fall of their most powerful base, Elmina, to the Dutch in 1637. In the seventeenth century the Dutch, through their efficiency in financing, shipbuilding, and organization, predominated, although constantly challenged by the English. (Earlier, during what might be called the "experimental stage," both the English and the French had failed to compete effectively with the Portuguese because they had not realized the importance of land bases: any Africans trading—whether in slaves or any other commodities—with English or French ships were left to face the vengeance of the land-based Portuguese after the ships had departed.) During the seventeenth century, indeed, the principle of monopoly broke down, and a remarkable variety of traders of different nationalities appeared on the coast—Danes, Swedes, Brandenbergers, and, no doubt, others. At the outset of the eighteenth century, William Bosman, a Dutchman, the chief factor at Elmina, wrote:

The Negroes of Fantyn [i.e., the Fanti people, who occupy that part of the coast] drive a very great Trade with all sorts of Interlopers, and that freely and boldly in the sight of both Nations; I mean the English and Dutch, neither of them daring to hinder it: For if they should attempt it, 'twould ruine them there, we not having the least Power over this Nation.

It was in the seventeenth century that the trade in slaves had outdistanced that in other "commodities." The reason for this was that the European powers had one by one begun to acquire possessions in the West Indies, and so to enter into the market for slaves. England, which had come to the Bermudas in 1609, settled St. Christopher (together with the French) in 1625, after which the English occupied the other Leeward Islands of Nevis, Antigua, and Montserrat, as well as Barbados and Jamaica. The French took Guadeloupe, Martinique, Marie Galante, St. Lucia, and Grenada; the Dutch, Curaçao, St. Eustatius, and Tobago; and the Danes, in 1671, St. Thomas.

At the beginning of the century, Spain was still considered to be the power responsible for the New World west of the demarcation line drawn at the Treaty of Tordesillas. By 1660, however, interlopers had penetrated so frequently and so successfully that Spain was finally obliged to recognize the principle of the freedom of the seas. The century was the epoch of the buccaneers, and with every nation's hand turned against the other, the Jolly Roger symbolized the age.

Not until the end of the century did national navies begin the task of restoring order, and limiting conflicts to those arising from official disputes between the nations of Europe. Meanwhile wars and rumors of wars had provoked innumerable collisions between men of different European nations on the West African coast, in the Caribbean, and on the high seas. Browsing through the correspondence and lawsuits of that era, one obtains glimpses of the many episodes that occurred, for the most part unrecorded. For example, John Winthrop of Massachusetts, writing in his journal in July, 1645, reported that a Mr. James Smith, who was a "member of the church of Boston," together with his mate Keyser, had been bound "to Guinea to trade for negroes."

But when they arrived there they met some Londoners, with whom they consorted, and the Londoners having been formerly injured by the natives (or at least pretending the same) they invited them aboard one of their ships upon the Lord's day, and such as came they kept prisoners, then they landed men and a murderer [i.e., a small cannon] and assaulted one of their towns and killed many of the people, but the country coming down, they were forced to retire without any booty, divers of their men being wounded with the negroes' arrows, and one killed. . . . For the matter of the negroes, whereof two were brought home in the ship, and near one hundred slain by the confession of some of the mariners, the magistrates took order to have these two set at liberty, and to be sent home; but for the slaughter committed, they were in great doubt what to do in it, seeing it was in another country, and the Londoners pretended a just revenge. So they called the elders; and desired their advice.

In another example, Adriaen Blaes, in 1659, made a deposition that he had been skipper of the Dutch slaver *St. Jan*, which had taken on 219 slaves, "big and little," at Calabar, West Africa. By the time the ship reached Tobago, however, the greater part of the slaves had died "from want and sickness in consequence of such a very long voyage, so that we saved only ninety slaves out of the whole cargo." As the skipper then wrote in the ship's log: "Nov. 1. (1658). Lost our ship on the reef of Rocus [Los Roques, southeast of Curaçao] and all hands immediately took to the boat, as there was no prospect of saving the slaves, for we must abandon the ship in consequence of heavy surf." In returning to the scene of the wreck in another of the company's boats, which they had met at the Dutch island of Aruba, they were overhauled and taken by an English privateer, captained by a Dane. After the privateer had also driven ashore a Spanish ship mounting six guns, and a Spanish periauger (a flat-bottomed sailing barge), it set sail, together with the captured Dutch bark with a prize crew aboard, for Rocus. Arriving there it found yet another Dutch ship. Taking the slaves and "about 70 pounds of elepant's tusks," as well as one of the Dutch ships, the privateer then permitted Blaes and his companions to depart in the other.

While this adventurous Atlantic crossing may not have been typical of a slaving voyage, neither can it be said to have been particularly unusual. For example, in January, 1664, we find the Directors at Amsterdam writing to the Director, Peter Stuyvesant, and Council of New Netherland: "Honorable, Prudent, Worthy, Beloved, Faithful . . . We, likewise, have been not a little astonished at the insufferable and hostile action committed by a certain English privateer in attacking and seizing our ship, *'t Waepen van Amsterdam,* on her way from the coast of Guinea, which he carried, with her cargo of Slaves, into Virginia." No wonder that Director Stuyvesant, writing to Holland on July 30, exclaimed: "On the 24th May, arrived here in safety, God be praised, the Company's ship *Sparrow* . . . The slaves and merchandize arrived safely according to invoice and bill of lading." He went on to ask for more Negroes to be sent, asking that "your Honor will please to bear in mind to have them sent off in time that they may probably arrive here before, or about All Saints, and that they be suitably provided against the cold." Before All Saints arrived, however, not content with merely seizing ships and cargo, the English, on September 8, came and took New Amsterdam itself, freemen, slaves, Stuyvesant, and all, renaming the colony "New York."

Not only the English gained the upper hand during these turbulent years. Sir Henry Morgan, the Welsh-born buccaneer captain, who had been appointed Lieutenant-Governor of Jamaica, wrote to Lord Sutherland from Port Royal:

> There lately arrived here a ketch empty, with only two men on board. Their statement on oath is that they were bound from New England to Guinea, where they loaded with negroes, elephants' teeth, and dust gold, and sailed for Nevis. On their way they called at an island called St. Martin's under the French Government, to wood and water, and were first invited into the harbour with much friendship, but afterwards suddenly seized and the ship unloaded. The master and mate stayed there to obtain redress, but consented that these two men should adventure by stealth to this island.

During these years of anarchy, not only did European fight European, and African fight African, but Africans and Europeans were also in frequent conflict, both on land and on sea. The Earl of Bellomont (who, incidentally, is known to have been in collusion with Captain Kidd of piratical fame), in 1699 wrote from Boston to the English Board of Trade to complain of the deceptions practiced by one Baldridge:

You had directed . . . that I should inquire after some pirates kill'd in St. Maries near Madagascar. I question'd Kidd about it, and he told me Baldridge was the occasion of that Insurrection of the Natives and the death of the pirates, for that having inveigled a great number of the natives of St. Maries, men, women and children on board a ship or ships he carryed and sold them for slaves to a French Island called Mascarine or Mascaron, which treachery of Baldridges the Natives on the Island revenged on those pirates by cutting their throats.

In *An Abstract of a Voyage to Congo River or the Zair, and to Cabinde, in the year 1700,* by James Barbot, Jr., supercargo, and John Casseneuve, first mate of the ship *Don Carlos* of London, we find this account of the events of January 5, 1701, when the ship was five days out from Cabinda on a voyage to Jamaica:

About one in the afternoon, after dinner, we according to custom caused them, the slaves one by one, to go down between decks, to have each his pint of water; most of them were yet above deck, many of them provided with knives, which we had indiscreetly given them two or three days before, as not suspecting the least attempt of this nature from them; others had pieces of iron they had torn off our forecastle door, as having premeditated a revolt, and seeing all the ship's company at best but weak and many quite sick, they had also broken off the shackles from several of their companions feet, which served them, as well as billets they had provided themselves with, and all other things they could lay hands on, which they imagin'd might be of use for their enterprize. Thus arm'd, they fell in crouds and parcels on our men, upon the deck unawares, and stabb'd one of the stoutest of us all, who receiv'd fourteen or fifteen wounds of their knives, and so expir'd. Next they assaulted our boatswain, and cut one of his legs so round the bone, that he could not move, the nerves being cut through; others cut our cook's throat to the pipe, and others wounded three of the sailors, and threw one of them overboard in that condition, from the fore-castle into the sea; who, however, by good providence, got hold of the bowlin of the fore-sail, and sav'd himself, along the lower wale of the quarter-deck, where, (says Casseneuve), we stood in arms, firing on the revolted slaves, of whom we kill'd some, and wounded many: which so terrify'd the rest, that they gave way, dispersing themselves some one way and some another between decks, and under the forecastle; and many of the most mutinous, leapt over board and drown'd themselves in the ocean with much resolution, shewing no manner of concern for life. Thus we lost twenty-seven or twenty-eight slaves, either kill'd by us, or drown'd.

## Pieces of Eight

Just as the capture of Elmina in 1637 had symbolized the transition from Portuguese to Dutch predominance, so the signing of the Treaty of Utrecht in 1713 symbolized the opening of Britain's eighteenth-century ascendancy in the slave trade. One of the principal aims of the British, in the War of the Spanish Succession which preceded the signing of the treaty, had undoubtedly been to prevent Louis XIV or his relations from succeeding to the Spanish throne, which would have meant that the French would have obtained the Asiento, or agreement to supply the Spanish colonies with slaves. Such Asiento contracts had previously been held by the Genoese and the Portuguese, and also—subcontracted —by the Dutch and English. The Spanish themselves, as we have seen, once their European rivals had established bases in the West Indies, no longer had the power of monopolizing the transatlantic slave trade. The Asiento therefore provided them with a means whereby at least some degree of benefit could be derived from and some degree of control maintained over the slave trade. Meanwhile, the responsibility and expense of defending cargoes in transit from the depradations of rival powers devolved upon the nation holding the Asiento. Since English naval supremacy had been asserted by the English[4] defeat of the French fleet in 1704, and was subsequently—although not without challenge—maintained throughout most of the eighteenth century, the granting of the Asiento to the British in 1713 was an act of political realism.

Under the terms of the Asiento it was stated that

> Her Britannick Majesty does oblige herself, or the persons whom she shall appoint, to introduce 144,000 negroes into the Spanish Americas within the space of 30 years, to begin on the 1st day of May, 1713.

Duty on the Negroes was to be paid to the King of Spain at the rate of 33⅓ pieces of eight per head, provided the slaves were not old or defective. The signing of the agreement marked not only Britain's rise as a commercial power, but also the transition of the slave trade from the experimentalism of the sixteenth century and the adventurism of the seventeenth into the commercialism of the eighteenth, at which time the trade reached its zenith. A list of the "Guineamen," (or ships trading with Guinea) belonging to the Port of Liverpool alone in the year 1752 gives the names of eighty-eight ships and their commanders, and mentions them as carrying "upward of 24,730 slaves." More slaves than this may well have been carried by these ships, for company agents on the Guinea coast often engaged in the practice of buying slaves on their own account and then adding them to the cargoes bound "for the Indies" in order to realize, at the risk of further overcrowding, some personal profits in addition to the wages that they received from their employers. With the seas better policed, with trading methods firmly established, and with three continents involved, it was small wonder that the trade reached its apogee.

As it was pursued, the slave trade played its part in promoting the general brutalization of morals that became apparent in the eighteenth century in Western Europe, and particularly in Britain and France. However, toward the close of the century, when new democratic tides

---

4. The adjective "English" is used in referring to the events of 1704, and "British" in referring to 1713 because England and Scotland were joined under the Act of Union of 1707.

began to run, a new phenomenon became apparent. The institution of kingship became endangered. The new commercial class that the kings themselves had often encouraged, in order to offset the power of the aristocracy, became conscious of the dawning of new opportunities, and of the possibility of still greater freedoms for itself. Ironically, the new freedom of the merchant class was based on a system of which slavery formed an integral part. The rum, sugar, molasses, and tobacco fortunes of the Atlantic traders were built upon slave labor. When, therefore, the philosophic spokesmen of the age proclaimed a new dawn of liberty, primarily envisaging thereby the declining power of pope and king, they presumed—as men often do when they aspire to greater freedom for themselves—to speak in the name of all humanity. Thus, whereas many persons of the commercial class understood words like "freedom" in a sense restricted in its application to themselves, other men gave such words a wider connotation. The new social context in Europe, together with the inhumane carrying conditions of the transatlantic slave trade, combined to produce a powerful movement favoring abolition. Moreover, the French Revolution, heavy with threats and promises, gave warning of the need for remedial changes. The independence of Haiti —an event that we shall examine in detail later—was, meanwhile, a visible sign that freedom for slaves was no contradiction in terms.

Carrying conditions had, indeed, become appalling. As early as 1788 King George III of the United Kingdom directed the Privy Council to inquire into the African trade, with particular reference to the slave trade. As a result of cross-examinations, the notorious conditions of the "Middle Passage"—that is, the passage from Africa to America, as distinct from the passage out to Africa, and the passage home from America— were established. To quote Clarkson:

> Every slave, whatever his size might be, was found to have only five feet and six inches in length, and sixteen inches in breadth to lie in. The floor was covered with bodies stowed or packed according to this allowance: but between the floor and the deck or ceiling were often platforms or broad shelves in the mid-way, which were covered with bodies also. The height from the floor to the ceiling, within which space the bodies on the floor and those on the platforms lay, seldom exceeded five feet eight inches, and in some cases it did not exceed four feet.
>
> The men were chained two and two together by their hands and feet, and were chained also by means of ring-bolts, which were fastened to the deck. They were confined in this manner at least all the time they remained upon the coast, which was from six weeks to six months as it might happen.
>
> Their allowance consisted of one pint of water a day to each person, and they were fed twice a day with yams and horsebeans.
>
> After meals they jumped up in their irons for exercise. This was so necessary for their health, that they were whipped if they refused to do it; and this jumping had been termed dancing.
>
> They were usually fifteen and sixteen hours below deck out of the twenty-four. In

rainy weather they could not be brought up for two or three days together. If the ship was full, their situation was then distressing. They sometimes drew their breath with anxious and laborious efforts, and some died of suffocation.

Naturally, the mortality was great among the slaves. Nor were the seamen who sailed in the slavers unaffected. They were also frequent targets for the brutality of those placed over them, apart from the various hazards to which their health was exposed.[5] Analyzing statistics of mortality, Clarkson calculated that "two vessels to Africa would destroy more seamen than eighty-three sailing to Newfoundland." Not only were the incidental physical conditions of the slave trade repulsive—it was said that one could smell a slaver at sea before one could see her—so, often, also was the treatment given to the slaves by their captors. Thumbscrews were used to torture slaves "in case of obstinacy . . . at the discretion of the captain." An instrument called a *speculum oris,* invented for surgical purposes in order to wrench open the mouths of persons suffering from lockjaw, was used in the slave trade to force slaves to eat, because "slaves were frequently so sulky as to shut their mouths against all sustenance, and this with a determination to die."

## The Abolition of the Trade

The rising tide of abolitionist and religious protest coincided with a growing practical realization that enough slaves had been transported to the Americas, and that if more were sent future European control might eventually be jeopardized. The first country to abolish the slave trade was Denmark, and the reasons given by Denmark are revealing. In an ordinance dated March 16, 1792 (a date which is contemporary with the most dramatic events of the French Revolution), and issued from the Danish Palace of Christiansborg (not to be confused with the Danish-built Christiansborg Castle, now called Osu, that still stands in Accra, Ghana), Christian VII of Denmark announced that from the "Commencement of the year 1803, we forbid any of our Subjects to carry on the Slave-Trade, from the Coast of Africa or any other place, except in our West-India Islands." The ordinance, after "considering the Circumstances which occur in the Slave Trade," said that "we are convinced that it is possible, and will be advantageous to our West-India Islands, to desist from the farther Purchase of New Negroes, when once the Plantations are stocked with a sufficient Number for Propagation, and

5. An extraordinary incident occurred, illustrative of one of the hazards of the slave trade, in the year 1819. The French ship *Rodeur* of Le Havre took on a cargo of slaves on the West African coast, at Bonny, and set sail for the West Indies. An epidemic of opthalmia broke out among the slaves, and affected the captain and all the crew except one man with total blindness. The ship drifted, unworkable, until at last, to the great joy of all, the sound of another ship approaching nearby was heard. But the joy was short lived. The ship, the *San Leone* of Spain, was also drifting, her crew likewise stricken blind, and dying of hunger and thirst. Neither ship could help the other. The *Rodeur* finally made port. The *San Leone* was never heard of again.

the Cultivation of the Lands." Mention was also made about "proper Encouragement" being given to marriage amongst the Negroes.

Other nations followed Denmark's lead. On March 2, 1807, the United States, in accordance with its libertarian principles, abolished the slave trade, and less than a month later, on March 25, the United Kingdom did the same. At the Congress of Vienna in 1814 France also agreed in principle that the slave trade should be suppressed, meanwhile attempting to obtain concessions from Britain in return for abolishing it in practice. When Napoleon returned to power in 1815, however, France abolished the slave trade completely and unconditionally.

Prima facie it seems surprising that the United Kingdom, rather than revolutionary France, the United States, or indeed any other country, should have moved to abolish a trade from which it had profited so hugely. In Britain, too, however, great changes had occurred. A new industrial system had come into being, based on coal and iron, and a new technology was being introduced. The West Indian sugar and slaves lobby, however important its role might have been in laying the foundations of industrial expansion, was no longer the cornerstone of Britain's economic power. Indeed, the "West Indian lobby," not content with amassing huge fortunes from the slave trade, had helped to lead Britain into war with its own colonists in the Americas by pushing through Parliament such measures as the Molasses Act of 1733 (which compelled the colonists to buy the lobbyists' sugar, whatever the price, by preventing them from buying cheaper sugar from the French West Indies), or the Stamp Act of 1764 (which laid high duties on all non-British sugar, rum, and molasses imported into the North American colonies). With the total loss of the American colonies to the British Crown, however, the injury that had been inflicted upon the British national interest by the lobby became clear. Not all the arguments of the West India lobby in favor of the continuance of the slave trade—and they were many and ingenious—could henceforth prevail. Britain, too, monarchical and unrevolutionary though she was, was also to abolish the trade. So much, indeed, was the abolition of the slave trade a part of Britain's new liberal thought that the British Prime Minister, Pitt the Younger, asked Wilberforce, an influential British Member of Parliament, to begin a campaign in Parliament against slavery. As C. L. R. James has commented:

Pitt was in a hurry—it was important to bring the trade to a complete stop quickly and suddenly. The French had neither the capital nor the organization to make good the deficiency at once and he would ruin San Domingo at a stroke. In 1787 he warned Wilberforce that if he did not bring the motion in, somebody else would.[6]

6. *The Black Jacobins* (revised edition, 1962), p. 53.

Abolition, however, did not necessarily mean implementation. The passing of a law by the United States Congress, no less than the signing of a bill by George III of the United Kingdom, did not mean that ships, laden with slaves, ceased to cross the Atlantic. Indeed, abolition of the trade increased the demand for new slaves in the Americas, and thus offered tempting profits for those enterprising enough to risk being caught breaking the law. Thus, in its nineteenth-century years, the slave trade flourished with well nigh the same vigor as it had in the eighteenth century.

After the 1807 Act Abolishing the Slave Trade, a further act was passed in Britain in 1811, which declared slave trading to be a felony punishable by transportation for fourteen years, and this in turn was reinforced by another act, passed in 1824, which treated slave trading as piracy, to be punished by death and confiscation of property. These measures exerted a discouraging influence upon British slaving, at least. It was easier, however, for the United Kingdom to adopt a position favoring the active suppression of the slave trade than it was for the United States, if only because the United Kingdom, having lost its North American colonies, no longer needed slaves in quantity, and no longer could hope to monopolize the carrying trade to the English-speaking Americas. The United States, however, having ousted the influence of George III for a variety of reasons, including, as the Declaration of Independence put it, his "cutting off our trade with all parts of the world," now for the first time was in a position to engage in the pursuit of profit from the African slave trade without the interference of British middlemen. When the United Kingdom sensed that a protectionist American policy would place British slaving at a disadvantage, she embarked upon the total suppression of the trade, knowing that this would at once reduce the threat of American competition in Africa to negligible proportions, encourage other forms of African commerce to develop that would also benefit British merchants, and transform national and international criticism directed against the trade into a factor that would strengthen instead of weaken both British policies and Britain's international standing. Expediency and morality, from Britain's point of view, for once went hand in hand.

Taken aback at finding the British Crown more revolutionary that the Jacobins, so to speak, as far as the slave trade was concerned, the United States agreed to suppression in principle, even if it showed little enthusiasm in practice. Indeed, the nineteenth-century slave trade—at least until Lincoln's day—was primarily destined to benefit the United States, just as the three previous centuries had enriched, in turn, Portugal, Holland, and the United Kingdom. Thus from 1807 to 1861 the

Stars and Stripes, despite U.S. presidential censure and national and international criticism from the abolitionists, provided the best protection available to ships engaged in the slave trade. In this way the principles of freedom espoused by the newly born United States were used not only to defend the freedom of the seas for all who sailed upon their lawful occasions, but also to defend the freedom to pursue the slave trade.

In the trade itself Baltimore clippers, famous for their speed, which had proved their worth in the war of 1812–1814, were adapted for illegal use. Few men-of-war could overtake a Baltimore clipper, and, as was observed in a recent study,[7] "The designers of Baltimore studied their market diligently and reaped a golden harvest—but not without resort to sharp practices and even violence." The shanghaiing of crews, the bribing of officials, and murder were the concomitants of Baltimore's participation in the slave trade, in the same way that, in the circumstances of the previous century, they had been concomitants of Liverpool's participation.

Havana, Cuba, was a major slave-trading depot during these years. Here, under the protection of Spanish sovereignty, slaves were disembarked in order that they might later be smuggled into the southern United States, or elsewhere. In 1836, when the American consul in Havana reported that cargoes of slaves fresh from Africa were daily being shipped into Texas, it was estimated that more than one thousand such had been sent within a few months. At times as many as 16,000 Africans were kept on Bay Island in the Gulf of Mexico, ready to be shipped into Florida, Texas, Louisiana, and elsewhere.

The British Royal Navy was not, however, inactive in all these years. They had begun their effort in 1808 when, with 601 ships in commission, the frigate *Solebay* and the sloop *Derwent*, both small and old ships, had been sent to the West African coast to begin the suppression of the slave trade. It was a small beginning, but an auspicious one, for with Britain and France at war, and with the Royal Navy committed to the blockade of Napoleon's Europe, it was surprising that even two ships were spared to chase slavers in tropical waters. The two vessels were harbingers of the fleets that were to follow in their wake.

At the Congress of Vienna of 1814–1815, held at the conclusion of the Napoleonic Wars, the British Prime Minister, Castlereagh, proposed that the five main European powers of the day suppress the slave trade by means of an armed international police force. Such a concept, radical for its day, was not accepted, although a Declaration was made which stated that the powers were "animated with the sincere desire of con-

7. Peter Duignan and Clarence Clendenen, *The United States and the African Slave Trade: 1619–1862* (Hoover Institute Studies, 1963).

curring in the most prompt and effectual execution" of the universal abolition of the slave trade. In 1818 at the Aix-la-Chapelle conference, Castlereagh renewed his proposal. It was, however, a proposal that was relatively easy for the British to make. As the United Kingdom was determined to retain command of the seas, the suppression of the slave trade provided reputable peacetime employment for Britain's idle naval forces. But no other European power wished to enter into such a commitment: nineteenth-century Europe was not ready for the concept of collective security. The United Kingdom, therefore, obtained what amounted to international consent to proceed alone. In policing the seas against the slave trade, and in later providing the naval forces that made the Monroe Doctrine of 1823—originally a British suggestion—practicable, the United Kingdom established what became known as the "Pax Britannica."

British ships, however, could not act against any slavers, other than those that were themselves British, except by virtue of bilateral treaties with the governments of the countries whose flags the slavers flew. Often such treaties—for example, a treaty of 1817 concluded with Spain—were only obtained in return for cash payments. In due course, such treaties were concluded between the United Kingdom and a number of European and Latin-American countries. Britain's great rival, France, was one of those co-operating with her. Agreement between the two nations, however, would have been more complete had it not been for active American lobbying in Paris against the British claim to "Right of Search" of vessels suspected of slaving. An agreement between France and the United Kingdom in 1833 permitted the Right of Search between certain latitudes, but General Cass, U.S. Ambassador in Paris, was instrumental in preventing the conclusion of a "Quintuple Treaty" in 1841. Whatever obstacles there might exist to agreement between the United Kingdom and any European power over the contested Right, they were dwarfed by Anglo-American differences on the subject.

The question of the Right of Search on the high seas had, of course, been the immediate cause of the Anglo-American War of 1812–1814. During the period of the transatlantic slave trade that followed, the question arose within a new context. On the American side it was claimed that the Monroe Doctrine also applied to U.S. shipping at sea, and that if the United Kingdom were granted the Right of Search, American vessels upon their lawful occasions would certainly be detained by the British and sent in for trial upon some excuse in order to handicap American trade. The British view, on the other hand, was that without the Right of Search—which they were prepared to limit to the "Right of Visit"—the slave trade could not be abolished at all, as the American flag would confer immunity upon all slaving vessels which chose to fly it. Faced with this deadlock, relations between the two countries developed a momentum of their own, in which incident succeeded incident. The possibility of a compromise appeared briefly when, in 1840, a working agreement was reached between Lieutenant Paine of the U.S. *Grampus* and Commander Rucker of the British *Wolverine,* according to which naval ships of either nation could detain slavers flying the American flag: if they should prove American they were then to be handed over to the U.S. authorities, and if they should prove otherwise, they should be dealt with by the British. The agreement was, however, declared to be *ultra vires* (exceeding legal authority) by the U.S. government.

By 1841 Anglo-American relations had deteriorated so far that the U.S. Ambassador in London informed Washington that there was a general impression that war had become inevitable. The climate improved after the conclusion in 1842 of the Webster-Ashburton Treaty, in which compromises were reached on a number of questions in dispute between the two countries. Not only was the air thus cleared, but it was also provided that the United States should send out a squadron to West Africa in order—independently of the British—to suppress the slave trade.

A U.S. squadron of from two to four vessels was from 1843 onward stationed at Porto Praya in the Cape Verde Islands. The Cape Verdes were regarded as safe from malaria, but time consumed in sailing from Porto Praya to those parts of West Africa where the trade was rife much reduced the efficiency of the squadron. For example, in 1859 the British complained that although the Congo had become the principal market for the slave trade, no U.S. cruiser had been near it for six months. The squadron was also charged with protecting legitimate U.S. commerce, and at times was specifically entrusted with giving this task precedence over the suppression of the slave trade. In practice this meant that more time was spent in preventing the British from stopping U.S. ships than was spent in stopping slavers.[8] Under these circumstances it was, therefore, small wonder that accusations were made that the squadron was deliberately avoiding the capture of slaving vessels. The fact remains, however, that the U.S. squadron did capture some slavers, although the exact number does not yet appear to have been clearly established.

Despite the fact that the United States adopted various laws and entered into a series of international agreements—for example, Article 10 of the Treaty of Ghent, which ended the Anglo-American War of 1812–1814, according to which both sides were to "use their best endeavours" to suppress the slave trade; the U.S. Congressional Act of 1820, which stated that slave trading should be treated as piracy and punished by death; Article 8 of the Anglo-American Webster-Ashburton Treaty of 1842 that established a naval force on the coast of Africa to enforce "separately and respectively, the laws, rights and obligations of each of

8. The British eventually renounced the Right of Search in the Declaration of Paris of 1856.

the two countries, for the suppression of the slave trade"—the slave trade continued to flourish. The effort to abolish the transatlantic slave trade in the nineteenth century, therefore, despite the involvement of Brazilian, Spanish, and Portuguese nationals, principally took the form of a long duel between the American slaving interests on the one hand, and the British Royal Navy on the other.

In the years immediately before the American Civil War, the trade rose to fresh heights. By 1854 slaving interests had grown confident enough openly to propose that the slave trade should again be officially permitted. Humanitarian arguments, even, were used to support this request. Because the slave trade was illegal, it was claimed, even greater numbers of slaves were crowded into a single ship, so that the conditions which prevailed before, already the target of international abomination, deteriorated still further. Meanwhile, the expense of maintaining the African squadron and the loss of British lives from fever, as well as in action, was frequently leading British officials and politicians to wonder whether it might not be better for all concerned to abandon the attempt to suppress the trade. To the end, however, the work of suppression was maintained, perhaps because the many collisions which occurred between the British Royal Navy and the slavers served to dramatize the larger moral conflict to the public, as well as to engage the emotions of the Lords of the Admiralty, who did not like to admit defeat.

One outcome of the struggle to suppress the trade was the establishment of three settlements for freed slaves on the West African coast. British naval vessels landed cargoes rescued from transatlantic slave ships at Freetown, Sierra Leone, where abolitionists had already established a settlement for freed slaves that became a British Crown Colony in 1808. The French, for their part, founded Libreville, Gabon, by landing a cargo of freed slaves there in 1849, while the U.S. Navy set freed slaves ashore in Liberia, which had been founded in 1822 by the American Colonization Society, a group seeking to return free black Americans to Africa. Although none of these three settlements achieved as much for social advance in Africa as their warmer partisans claimed, they did nevertheless play a necessary role, both in providing a solution to a practical problem, and in providing a basis for the international publicizing of the emancipation thesis.

The deathblow to the transatlantic slave trade was delivered by the Treaty of Washington, concluded between the United States and the United Kingdom in 1862, after President Lincoln had taken office. Already, in March, 1861, Commodore Edmonstone of the Royal Navy, reporting to the Admiralty on the successes scored in the suppression of the slave trade by Commodore Inman of the U.S. Navy, had expressed his conviction that for the first time the Americans were indeed in earnest.

"I have great pleasure," he wrote, "in bringing to your attention the efforts made by the American Squadron to put a check on the Slave Trade carried on under the protection of their flag." Once the cruisers of both nations, under the provisions of the treaty, were permitted to visit and search suspected ships, the American slave trade quickly died. The Cuban trade withered away soon after. Before long all was over: President Lincoln and the British Navy had slammed the door shut.

Particular historic interest attaches to the British effort to suppress the trade. Command of the seas at that time was the touchstone of world power. The British, through the use of this instrument, came closer to achieving world supremacy than any other nation had previously been able to do. This new worldwide power, moreover, was in part used to intervene in what has since become perhaps the most fundamental question confronted by mankind—the question of the relationships that should exist between men of different colors. Thus, for the first time, the question of world power and the question of race impinged upon each other. The puffs of smoke that billowed over the Gulf of Guinea from the guns of Britain's men-of-war represented some of the first shots to be fired in a conflict that was to spread through years and decades—to be fought out later at Shiloh and on many another field, and in many another circumstance. The suppression of the slave trade may therefore be seen as a preliminary struggle in a series of others yet to come.

TWO

*The Age of European Dominion*

"The ancients," wrote J. A. Hobson at the opening of the twentieth century, "carried off the lower races to their own country, because they could use their labor but had little use for their land; we moderns wish the lower races to exploit their own lands for our benefit."

Whatever Hobson may have meant by "the lower races" (and it would be charitable to think that he meant "subjugated peoples" rather than "lesser breeds"), there is no doubt that in that single sentence he defined the similarity as well as the difference between ancient slavery and modern colonialism. Colonialism was, however, merely one facet of the process that began in 1415 with the Portuguese capture of Ceuta on the North African coast, and that may perhaps be said to have reached its apogee almost 500 years later in 1914 when, on the eve of the first world war, the white peoples of Europe had gained control of every other continent. At that time it had become popular for white men to speak of "The Yellow Peril," perhaps because it was sensed that the Chinese, with their great numbers, remained the greatest potential barrier still remaining to white world domination. Had not Napoleon warned against awakening the sleeping Chinese giant? Yet, from the point of view of the American Indian, the black African, the Polynesian, the Hindu, or of the Chinese themselves, there would have been more justification for speaking of a "White Peril," for the process of the white man's seizure of land, whether in Mexico, in East Africa, or from the Maori of New Zealand, was a danger to non-whites that was not potential but manifest.

The European, however, rarely paused to view matters from any standpoint except his own. These were the centuries of adventure or of profit, when with ship or gun he sought conquest and gold; or when, master of oversea estate, he followed his bent, whether for labor or for ease, unchallenged for the most part, except by other Europeans. The white man's destiny was clearly to rule the earth: in the Americas, in Asia, in Africa, in Australia. History carried him toward that goal so implicitly, and the process seemed so evident to all, that it hardly seemed necessary even to speak of it. Europe's expansion was the constant factor of what was sometimes called "the modern age."

# Chapter 5

# "Manifest Destiny":
# The European Occupation of
# the Americas

*. . . our manifest destiny is to overspread the continent allotted by Providence for the free development of our yearly multiplying millions.* —From an editorial by John L. O'Sullivan in *The Democratic Review* (July–August, 1845)

*This land is your land, This land is my land,*
*From California to the New York island;*
*From the red-wood forest to the Gulf Stream waters;*
*This land was made for you and me.*
            —From a song by Woody Guthrie (1956)

THE STORY OF THE European occupation of the Americas is of such relative recent date, and the process has been brought to an apparent conclusion such a short time since, that we still tend to view it as an ongoing process. It has generated a psychological climate that still lives on. The underlying assumptions of the doctrine of "Manifest Destiny," specifically proclaimed by white men in North America in the nineteenth century, still furnish many white-skinned persons with the historic basis for a mystique that can justify if need be an unending forward march of white occupation, just as, to the Spaniards of the sixteenth century, it appeared clear that new-found America, mountain mine and tropical isle, was God's gift to the Spanish Crown.

Upon his return from his first voyage, Columbus brought back with him six or seven American "Red Men"—Taino Indians of the Arawak group—whom he exhibited at the Spanish Court, and who were also led in procession first through Seville, and then through Barcelona, where they were also baptized. All except one of this group sailed with Colum-bus on his second voyage, but only two survived it; the Indian who remained in Spain was "well behaved and circumspect," but died within two years. However, in 1494 about 600 more Indians were brought back to Spain, and more were taken there in subsequent years. In 1502 three American Indians were taken to the court of Henry VII of England, and in 1506 another group was taken to Rouen in France. The sight of these strange new men with horselike hair, unlike any seen before, "possessing speech but no religion," or "clad in beasts' skins, eating raw meat," soon aroused moral, religious, and scholarly interest. Various academic debates, ranging from the theological to the classical and scientific, thereupon ensued, as Europeans attempted to relate the new-found beings to the body of their own past experience.

Peter Martyr, writing in *De Novo Orbe* in 1511, described the Ameri-can Indians in favorable terms:

Among these symple soules, a fewe clothes serve the naked . . . [they] have not the use of pestiferous money . . . they seeme to live in that golden worlde of the whiche the olde wryters speake so muche, wherein men lyved symplye and innocentlye without enforcement of lawes . . . they seeme to lyve in the golden worlde without toyle, lyvynge in open gardens. . . .

Others, however, took a less charitable view. In the first book pub-lished in English on America (also published in 1511, although it had appeared earlier in Dutch), the American Indians were said to be

lyke bestes without any resonableness. . . . And they ete also on[e] a nother. The man eteth his wyf his chylderne . . . they hange also the bodyes or persons fleeshe in the smoke as men do with us swynes fleeshe.

The passage of time did not quickly resolve the mystery. In 1544 Sebastian Muenster of Basle identified the "cannibals" of the Americas with the anthropophagi of antiquity, classifying them with monsters. As late as 1595 Sir Walter Raleigh was reporting the presence in Guiana not only of Amazons but also of a people who had "eyes in their shoulders and their mouths in the middle of their breasts."

While the academic debates proceeded at a leisurely pace, European interests more directly involved were arriving at their own conclusions. To the question "Are the Indians human beings or not?" Spain, with the sanction of the Church, for reasons perhaps as much political as humani-tarian, gave a clear reply. A document known as the *Requerimiento* (the Requirement) was drafted by a Spanish jurist, and was read to the Indians before each Spanish attack in order to validate the legal position of Spain. Of course, the *Requerimiento* was incomprehensible to the Indians, who did not yet speak Spanish. On some occasions, moreover, it was read to them from shipboard, out of earshot of land. The *Requeri-*

*miento,* which demanded that the Indians recognize Spanish dominion over their lands, explained that

> The Lord our God, living and eternal, created the heaven and the earth, and one man and one woman, of whom you and we, and all the men of the world, were and are descendants, and all those who come after us. But, on account of the multitude which has sprung from this man and this woman in the five thousand years since the earth was created, it was necessary that some men should go one way and some another, and that they should be divided into many kingdoms and provinces. . . .

The American Indians, therefore, while subject to Spanish rule through the sanction of God's representative on earth, the Pope, were juridically recognized as being a part of the human race.

At the time of the European discovery of the Americas, the American Indian populations were dispersed over the mainland and the islands in a series of groupings that were for the most part tribal. Cultural diversity among the American Indian peoples was as great as the differing environments to which they had adapted—a diversity which included the nomadic cultures of the hunting tribes of tundra and forest as well as those of the sedentary fishing and agricultural communities of the tropics. Yet, whereas the nations and tribes of the American Indians became, in the course of the following centuries, individually known to European travelers, traders, governments, settlers, and ethnologists, the greatest interest still attaches to the Aztecs of Mexico and the Incas of Peru.

The underlying reason for this interest undoubtedly lies in the fact that the Aztec and Inca societies represent mysteries that, in part at least, will now never be solved. The mystery remains Janus-like, with two faces, pointing to the past as well as to what might have been their future. Concerning the past, we may cite one example from the historian W. H. Prescott:

> A correspondence quite extraordinary is found between the hieroglyphics used by the Aztecs for the signs of the days, and those zodiacal signs which the Eastern Asiatics employed as one of the terms of their series. The symbols in the Mongolian calendar are borrowed from animals. Four of the twelve are the same as the Aztec. Three others are as nearly the same as the different species of animals in the two hemispheres would allow. The remaining five refer to no creature then found in Anahuac. The resemblance went as far as it could. . . . I shall pass over the further resemblance to the Persians, shown in the adjustment of time by a similar system of intercalation; and to the Egyptians, in the celebration of the remarkable festival of the winter solstice; since, although sufficiently curious, the coincidences might be accidental. . . .[1]

The chances of throwing fresh light on the American Indian past have been much reduced by the actions of the Spanish upon their arrival in the New World. Being suspicious of the Mexican picture writing, which they considered to be connected with magic or idolatrous practices,

1. *The Conquest of Mexico* (1843).

the Spanish destroyed great quantities of manuscripts that might have helped to dispel much of the mystery. For example, the first archbishop of Mexico caused manuscripts to be assembled at Tlatelolco, including those from the Aztec national archives of Tezcuco, had them piled in a "mountain heap" in the marketplace, and there had them burned.

Concerning what might have been the future of the Aztec and Inca civilizations, we may cite the words of a contemporary Spanish scholar, Salvador de Madariaga. After mentioning that the American Indians were prone to cannibalism and drunkenness, and after discussing other aspects of the interaction between the Spanish and American Indian cultures, he goes on to say:

> And yet, who doubts but that, looking at things from an adequate distance, these Whites [i.e. the Spanish Conquistadores] were usurpers of destiny, like the Whites in Africa, like the English in India, the French in Indo-China and later, by a curious recoil of history, the English in Spanish Trinidad and Jamaica, the Americans in Spanish New Mexico, Texas and Puerto Rico, usurpers of the land, twisters of the natural course of things, meddlers with an evolution which, to judge by the state of the Inca and Aztec cultures, might and probably would have led the natives of the New World to meet European civilization on a footing of lesser inequality a few centuries later.[2]

The Spanish, however, represented merely the vanguard of the European invasion of the Americas. The occupation itself was accomplished in phases, which we will look into in more detail. By the end of the sixteenth century the initial phase of the occupation was over: the Spanish had overthrown the two main centers of American Indian power in Mexico and in Peru, and Europeans of one nationality or another had penetrated, albeit often in a cursory way, to most parts of the American mainland. The Portuguese had taken possession of Brazil, and French, English, Danish, and Dutch had established their presences in the Caribbean area. A second phase followed in the seventeenth and most of the eighteenth century, in which a great part of the energies of the Europeans were expended in feuding with one another. A third phase opened with the American War of Independence—an event that led, between 1774 and about 1820, to most of the other colonies in America rejecting European rule and declaring themselves independent. Finally there followed a phase during which the world witnessed the phenomenal growth—in territory, in power, and in population—of the United States of America.

*The Conquistadores*

The age of the conquistadores may be said to have lasted from about 1519—when Cortes, having landed on the coast of Mexico, set out with about 400 men and 15 horses to march on the Aztec capital—and 1550,

2. *The Fall of the Spanish American Empire* (1963). Madariaga adds: "No one is at fault. It is all a part of the human tragedy which we call History."

by which time the Spanish had laid the foundations of the first extensive empire of European settlement overseas. For by 1550 not only had the most densely settled areas of population of the American mainland fallen to the conquistadores, they had also passed out of the hands of the conquistadores into those of the duly appointed agents of the Spanish colonial system.

The epoch of the conquistadores remains, however, one of the most extraordinary epochs in all history, combining, as it does, some of the greatest feats of courage in the annals of war with discoveries and situations so unusual as to defy comparison with the most extravagant tales of legend or romance. From the viewpoint of the conquistadores themselves, not the least interest lay in the great treasure of gold and silver that they sought, confidently expected to find, and—some of them—found. Of far greater consequence, however, was the fact that the arrival of those Spaniards in the capital cities of the Aztecs and the Incas marked the first time that the American Indian rulers were confronted with the indubitable fact of the existence of European culture and of European power. The event marked a circumstance even yet more momentous. Fate had at last brought together the three strains—American Indian, black African, and white European—that were henceforward to be blended together throughout the subsequent history of the Americas.

CENTRAL AMERICA

Española (or Hispaniola) was the first Spanish colony in the New World. The party of Spaniards whom Columbus had left there on his first voyage, at a settlement called *La Navidad,* were killed by Indians. Whether they were killed by the initially friendly Indians in whose company they were left, or whether by hostile invaders, could not be decided, although Columbus wrote that "we began to hear complaints that one of the Spaniards had taken three women to himself, and another four; from whence we drew the inference that jealousy was the cause of the misfortune that had occurred." Other Spanish settlements proved more permanent, but Spanish-Indian relations did not improve after this unhappy beginning. Bartolome de las Casas, the Spanish bishop, having described the Indians as "patient, meek, and peaceful," went on to say:

To these quiet Lambs, endued with such blessed qualities, came the Spaniards like most cruel Tygres, Wolves and Lions, enrag'd with a sharp and tedious hunger; for these forty years past, minding nothing else but the slaughter of these unfortunate wretches, whom with divers kinds of torments neither seen nor heard of before, they have so cruelly and inhumanely butchered, that of three millions of people which Hispaniola itself did contain, there are left remaining alive scarce three hundred persons.[3]

3. *Brief Relation of the Destruction of the Indies* (1552). From the English edition of 1656, translated by John Phillips, under the title *The Tears of the Indians: Being an Historical and True Account of the Cruel Massacres and Slaughters of above Twenty Millions of Innocent People*).

In 1511, when it became evident that the mineral resources of Hispaniola were being rapidly exhausted, it was decided to occupy Cuba. The central American isthmus was occupied first under the leadership of Balboa, and then under that of Pedrarias, who, in 1519, founded Panama, the oldest European settlement on the American mainland. Following a voyage of reconnaissance to the Mexican coast by Grijalva, who returned to Cuba with tales of the Aztec empire and of much gold, an expedition was dispatched to Mexico from Cuba under the command of Cortes. Landing on the east coast of Mexico in 1519, Cortes dramatically burned his ships and, after resigning his Cuban commission, founded the municipality of Vera Cruz, thereby placing himself and his followers directly under the authority of the Spanish Crown, rather than under that of the governor of Cuba. He then began his march on the Aztec capital of Tenochtitlan (today Mexico City), defeating large numbers of attackers en route. The first attackers were Tlaxcalans, traditional enemies of the Aztecs, who, being unable to defeat Cortes, came over to his side. Accompanied by his new allies, Cortes, with just under 400 men, then continued his march on the capital.

Bernal Díaz, who served with Cortes, has described, in his vivid memoir, *The Conquest of New Spain,* not only the further adventures of the party, but also the astonishment of the Europeans at the new land in which they found themselves, where volcanoes and pyramid temples dotted the landscape, where strange plants, flowers, and birds, many of astonishingly beautiful color, were to be found, and where even the food and beverages, such as turkey and chocolate, were new and strange. In the city of Iztapalapa, Díaz gazed at the palaces in which they were lodged, "very spacious and wellbuilt, of magnificent stone, cedar wood, and the wood of other sweet-smelling trees, with great rooms and courts"; as well as at the orchard and garden. "I say again," he wrote, "that I stood looking at it, and thought that no other land like it would ever be discovered in the whole world, because at that time Peru was neither known nor thought of. But today all that I then saw is overthrown and destroyed; nothing is left standing."

The wonder of the Europeans had risen to fresh heights when they came to a causeway, eight yards wide.

> When we saw all those cities and villages built in the water, and other great towns on dry land, [and] that straight and level causeway leading to Mexico, we were astounded. Those great towns and pyramid temples and buildings rising from the water seemed like an enchanted vision from the tale of Amadis. Indeed, some of our soldiers asked whether it was not all a dream. . . . It was all so wonderful that I do not know how to describe this first glimpse of things never heard of, seen or dreamed of before.

In such a mood Cortes and his army marched straight forward to Tenochtitlan—once inside which, their friends repeatedly warned them, they would not again be allowed to emerge alive, but would be offered as sacrifices to the Mexican gods. The causeway along which they traveled was thick with people, while other sightseers in canoes covered the lake and other crowds looked on from the temple towers. "No wonder," comments Díaz, "since they had never seen horses or men like us before." Díaz also commented, in a moving statement that nevertheless appears to hold overtones of the later doctrine of "Manifest Destiny":

Now that I am old, I often pause to consider the heroic actions of that time. I seem to see them present before my eyes; and I believe that we performed them not of our own volition but by the guidance of God. . . .

In the city of Tenochtitlan, Cortes and his men met Montezuma, the Aztec emperor, and being well treated by him, later succeeded in taking him prisoner as a hostage for their own safety. The respect and consideration extended to Cortes would seem to have much to do with an ancient legend that held that the future rulers of Mexico would come from the east, as the Spaniards had in fact done. It might also be that Cortes had some certain knowledge of the power of this legend upon the minds of the Mexicans—a knowledge that did not even extend to his followers— and that would, if it were known, explain his incredibly bold and apparently foolhardy actions.

It would also appear that Cortes contemplated the possibility of some form of military alliance, in which the Aztec ruler would become a vassal of the Spanish Crown. According to the Spanish account, however—the only one available to us—the question of religious difference proved insurmountable. Spain was intent upon retaining its position as the accepted leader of Christendom, in purity of faith as well as in feats of arms, and consequently the Spanish had become fanatical in mood, and bigoted in religion. The human sacrifices made by the Aztecs seemed, despite the relatively small strength of the Spaniards, too much to accept, so that, in the absence of Cortes, one Alvarado led what he claimed was a preventive attack upon a group of Mexican chiefs and dignitaries who were engaged in a religious dance. This, together with the demand that the Christian cross be raised in the temple sanctuary of the most important Mexican gods, led to an Aztec uprising aimed at liberating Montezuma and driving the Spanish from the country. Montezuma was killed in the resulting confusion, and Cortes, who had returned from the capital by forced marches, barely succeeded in extricating the Spaniards; in the fighting along the causeways leading from the city the Spanish lost one-third of their number in what has been called *La Noche Triste* (the Sad Night). The following year, however, Cortes returned again, bringing overland with him brigantines to be launched on the lake surrounding Tenochtitlan. At the head of an army of Spaniards and Tlaxcalans, he fought his way over the causeways, and systematically reduced the city, destroying it house by house, until the Aztecs, under Cuauhtemoc, a successor to Montezuma, surrendered.

The years which followed, during which the Spanish consolidated their power, were unhappy ones for Mexico, which suffered much from the oppression of Nuno de Guzmán, one of the members of the first audiencia (court of appeal) sent from Spain, who had succeeded in placing himself in a dominant position. When news of the abuses perpetrated by Guzmán reached Spain, arrangements were made for a viceroy to be appointed. The arrival of the first viceroy, Don Antonio de Mendoza, in 1535, marked the beginning of Mexico's colonial period.

## SOUTH AMERICA

The conquest of the second major center of American Indian power —the Inca empire of Peru—was inspired by and patterned on the action of Cortes in Mexico. Francisco Pizarro, an adventurer, having compacted with two other Spaniards to form a syndicate to conquer the Inca realm, of whose existence Balboa and others had already heard, set forth in 1524 on the first of three expeditions, with about one hundred men. Two years later they returned empty-handed, having suffered from sickness, received wounds from hostile American Indians, and lost a number of their company, all without so much as catching sight of the golden realm that they sought. A second expedition, thanks in part to the skill of Bartolome Ruiz, the navigator, was somewhat more successful, although also attended by great hardship. Members of the expedition returned to Panama for fresh supplies, leaving Pizarro and some of his men on the Pacific island of Gallo. Here, half-naked, plagued by mosquitoes, and drenched by the incessant storms of the rainy season, the party subsisted mostly on crabs and shellfish until, at last, two vessels finally came for them with instructions to take the entire group back to Panama.

At this juncture Pizarro manifested the same spirit that Cortes had exhibited when he burned his boats. With his sword he drew a line in the sand, dividing north from south, and challenging those who would follow him—risking toil, pain, and death—to cross it for the sake of Peru and its riches. Thirteen men, including Ruiz, the pilot, chose to follow him. The commander of the rescuing ships refused, however, to recognize the act as a legal one, much less to leave the little band a ship for their own purposes. He therefore sailed away and left them on the island.

After seven months of waiting, during which the party came close to despair, a ship from Panama eventually returned and placed itself at the disposal of Pizarro for not more than six months. The expedition steered for the port of Tumbez, a part of the Inca realm. The people of Tumbez were much amazed at the sight of Pizarro's vessel, and even more amazed at the fair complexion of the whites, and the dark skin of an African member of the ship's crew, which they took to be caused by dye, and which they tried to rub off with their hands. Swine and poultry were also new to the people of Tumbez, and when a cock, which the Spanish had brought with them, crowed, the Peruvians are reported to have clapped their hands and inquired what he was saying. Iron was also new to them, as also was gunpowder, which the Spanish used to discharge their arquebuses. The Europeans, for their part, were highly impressed by the great quantity of gold and silver in use. The temple at Tumbez was said to be hung with plates of gold and silver.

Pizarro, after coasting further south and receiving other certain evidences of a wealthy civilization, returned to Panama in triumph. But despite the interest created by the return of his expedition, he still did not receive the wholehearted backing that he sought for his conquest. He therefore traveled directly to Spain, where, in 1528, he appeared in Toledo in person before the Emperor Charles V, and was accorded a favorable reception, being appointed Governor of Peru for life. By 1530 he had left Panama at the head of his third expedition.

Once more he landed at Tumbez, near which he founded the town of San Miguel before beginning a daring march over the Andes, at the conclusion of which he arrived at Caxamalca, where the powerful Inca usurper Atahualpa had established his seat. The Europeans now found themselves in a precarious position. At night the watchfires of the Peruvian army which surrounded them lit up the sides of the mountains and sparkled in the darkness "as thick as the stars of heaven." If they showed fear or retreated, all would be lost. They therefore resolved to imitate Cortes' treatment of Montezuma, and to take the Inca prisoner. An occasion presented itself when the Inca came to visit the Spaniards in their quarters. There first occurred a conversation between the Inca and a Spanish friar, in the course of which the friar informed the Inca that the Pope had commissioned the Spanish Emperor to conquer and to convert the western hemisphere. To this the Inca angrily replied that he would be no man's tributary, and added: "As for the Pope of whom you speak, he must be crazy to talk of giving away countries which do not belong to him."

While the Inca was thus visiting them, borne high in a litter, the Spanish soldiery, at a prearranged signal, burst forth and set about slaughtering the Inca's entourage. Only Pizarro's intervention saved the Inca's life in the massacre that followed. The audacity of the Spaniards had been so much greater than the Peruvians could have imagined that, seeing the Inca captive in their hands, the bonds of the realm were effectively dissolved. There was, indeed, another Inca named Huascar, who was the legitimate ruler, but whose weakness of character had placed him a position of inferiority. At the time of the arrival of the Spaniards,

Atahualpa and Huascar had been contesting the realm between them, and it would appear that Atahualpa would have emerged as victor. Huascar had the advantage, however, of occupying the capital city of Cuzco. When Pizarro, having taken Atahualpa prisoner, announced his intention of bringing the two Incas before him to decide the merits of the dispute, Atahualpa, evidently foreseeing that the Spaniards would choose the weak and malleable Huascar as the rightful Inca, secretly gave orders that Huascar be murdered. These orders were carried out. The Spaniards, meanwhile, plundered the realm, finding there gold and silver in quantities that surpassed their highest expectations. The following year, 1533, Atahualpa was strangled, allegedly for plotting an uprising of his countrymen against the Europeans.

In November of 1533 the Spaniards entered the capital, Cuzco, a town with a population of some 200,000 inhabitants, not counting those living in its suburbs. After this, sporadic resistance was encountered from the Peruvian forces, but in the twenty years that followed, the principal hostilities took place between different Spanish factions in the so-called "Peruvian civil wars." Not until 1548 did bloodshed and turbulence come to an end, and the era of the conquistadores give way, as in Mexico, to the colonial era.

Although no more civilizations comparable to the Aztec and Inca empires remained to be discovered, hopeful Spanish expeditions nevertheless traversed other regions of the Americas seeking realms of gold. For example, in 1536 an expedition left Mexico to search for the "Seven Cities of Cibola." Six years later a handful of the original party returned, having suffered great hardships, and penetrated as far as what is now Kansas, without, however, finding the "Seven Cities." Meanwhile Cortes himself, in the 1520s, penetrated, together with others, to Guatemala and Honduras. In the 1530s he had turned his attention to the Pacific Coast and to Lower California, where he founded the town of La Paz.

By 1550 the Spanish had ascertained the lineaments of the New World from 40° North to 40° South—that is to say, from north of what is now San Francisco to south of the River Plate—and had established scores of settlements. Among the many notable exploits which led to this result was that of Quesada, who in 1536–37 struggled through the Venezuelan forests, losing most of his men, and then proceeded to the conquest of the uplands of Colombia, where he founded Bogotá. Spanish arms were everywhere triumphant, save in Chile and, at the outset, Argentina. In central Chile the Araucanian Indians, mastering the art of horsemanship, defeated the Spaniards and executed the Spanish leader, Valdivia. The Araucanians continued to maintain their sovereignty, first against the Spanish, and later against the Chilean government, to whom they did not submit until 1870. In Argentina the American Indians of the pampas drove off Spanish incursions, thus maintaining their autonomy for several decades. Having at first killed Juan Diaz de Solis, upon his "discovery" of the River Plate in 1516, they later, in 1541, forced the Spanish to evacuate a settlement that they had made at Buenos Aires, and to proceed to another region upriver instead. Not until 1580 did the Spanish return to found the present city of Buenos Aires.

The Portuguese, for their part, remained primarily concerned with their African and Asian discoveries, and were consequently slow to occupy Brazil, which had fallen to their lot by the Treaty of Tordesillas. Although Cabral had made his Brazilian landfall in 1500—when, bound for India via the Cape, he had sailed far out into the Atlantic to avoid becoming becalmed—it was not until the 1530s that the Portuguese attempted to colonize the territory, establishing settlements at Bahia and Santos, and dividing the coastline into twelve captaincies. The first Portuguese Governor-General of Brazil was appointed in 1549.

## The Viceroyalties

The era of exploration and conquest in the Americas now gave way to the era of colonial administration. The Spanish possessions were at first administered as two viceroyalties—that of New Spain (Mexico), and that of Peru. Later, in the eighteenth century, when the Bourbons replaced the Hapsburgs on the throne of Spain, and instituted certain colonial reforms, two new viceroyalties, those of New Granada (Colombia) and of La Plata, were detached from Peru. The most popular aspect of these changes was that henceforth trade and communication between Buenos Aires and Spain could take place directly across the Atlantic, instead of being circuitously channeled through Lima and Panama first.

The harsh abuses of the conquered populations by the Spanish having been particularly marked at the outset, attempts were made by the Spanish Crown—following the representations of Las Casas and others—to limit the powers of the colonists, and to provide certain safeguards for the American Indian populations. The first question to be answered, however, was, What was to be Spanish policy toward these populations? It was decided that the viceroyalties should form separate realms from the kingdoms of Spain, and should be governed through a separate royal council, with Chile and Guatemala being governed as provinces of the viceroyalties, under the authority of a captain-general. *Audiencias* (which were partly administrative and partly judicial) and also the Church would act as checks upon the authority of the viceroys themselves.

The American Indian populations were to be converted to Christianity, and were also to be considered as direct subjects of the Spanish Crown, rather than of the Spanish State. American Indians were to be equal with Spaniards in the eyes of the law, and could own land and property. They were also to be permitted to retain their own forms of customary law, except when these forms clashed violently with Spanish law, or were greatly at variance with Spanish morality. Tribute from certain villages, known as *encomienda,* was, however, payable to the conquerors (and in some cases to settlers), and to their descendants. In return the recipient bore the obligation of rendering military service, and of paying the salaries of the parish priests. Under the system known as *repartimiento,* however, forced labor was required of the American Indian population, but this was only to be exacted by public and not by private authorities, and such labor was to be paid at a fixed scale.

In consequence of these arrangements, a society—the Spanish-American Empire—came into being that was to endure for almost three centuries, and that has marked the region in language, religion, architecture, and culture, down to this day. In the new society the ethnic complexities that soon arose were in due course accorded recognized social gradations. Spaniards from Spain (*peninsulares*) held the highest positions and status; *creoles* (Spaniards of American birth) were next in rank; *mestizos* —those of mixed European and American-Indian birth, whose numbers increased as time proceeded—occupied the position of a middle, or trading, class; while the bulk of the American-Indian populations performed the menial tasks. Although slaves from Africa were never brought into the Spanish Americas in the same quantities as into Brazil, a substantial number were nevertheless imported, particularly in the territories closer to the Equator. The mixing of Europeans and Africans produced *mulattoes,* whereas African and American-Indian mixing produced *zambos.* Nor did the mixing stop there. As Salvador de Madariaga has written:

> *Mestizos,* mulattoes and *zambos,* simple mixtures of the three colours two by two, mixed in their turn either with one of the two colours whence they came or with the third colour or with other mixtures. The outcome was a rich palette of human blends, with an equally rich vocabulary to describe them. There was hardly a combination of colours, a mixture of mixtures, without its own name; particularly those which marked the stages in the ladder from black to white: Mulatto, *Terceron* (*Mulatto* and White), *Cuarteron* (*Terceron* and White), *Quinteron* (*Cuarteron* and White). The cause of this wealth of names was the extreme touchiness of the parties concerned with regard to their position in the ladder.[4]

Brazilian society, under the Portuguese, while comparable to that of Spanish America in a number of respects, was nevertheless different both in tenor and in tone—which is to say both in the pace of its development, and in its ethnic composition. The first settlers from Portugal were,

4. *The Fall of the Spanish American Empire* (1963).

for the most part, restless exiles. The Portuguese government, involved as it was with its Eastern trade axis, never put forth the degree of effort exhibited by Spain in the Americas. It was the Jesuit missionaries in Brazil, as much as any other factor, who were responsible for the achievement of the measure of unity that was attained over the vast and disparate region—a region that was enlarged yet further in the seventeenth century by the *bandeirantes*—armed slave raiders, who pushed Portuguese influence to the west of the official demarcation line as far as the present western frontier of Brazil. Instead of shipping a convoy of bullion across the Atlantic to the home country, as Spain did every year, the Portuguese, at the outset, contented themselves with shipping the dye-wood that had given Brazil its name (it was so red that it resembled a glowing coal, "braza"). Later, however, sugar was cultivated in plantations worked primarily by African slaves. Earlier attempts by the Portuguese to enslave American Indians had not met with success, many of the Indians committing suicide rather than submit to labor for the Portuguese. By 1700 the Portuguese had brought so many African slaves into Brazil that they outnumbered the European population by two to one.

The administrative shock that resulted from the union of the Spanish and Portuguese Crowns—a union that lasted from 1580 to 1640—was another factor that inhibited centralization in Brazil. French and Dutch interlopers took advantage of the interlude to establish their presence in the country, but were eventually driven out. The Dutch, however, took with them the knowledge of sugar cultivation, as well as some sugar plants. They used the plants and the knowledge in the islands of the West Indies to obtain results that were not without further consequences. In Brazil itself, however, first gold and then coffee displaced sugar as the primary crop. Sugar, gold, or coffee, it was nonetheless produced by slave labor. The lot of the Brazilian Indians was, however, somewhat improved by the action of the Portuguese Minister Pombal who, directing the affairs of Brazil for a number of years, declared in 1755 that the Brazilian Indians were free citizens and could not be enslaved.

### The Sugar Islands

The islands of the Caribbean were soon colonized by non-Iberian powers. The Spanish, mindful of the reputation of the Carib Indians as ferocious cannibals,[5] had tended to avoid a number of islands on which the Caribs lived, thereby leaving them open for occupation by other European powers. Spain, in any case, did not have sufficient naval power to exclude the other European nations of the Atlantic seaboard from the Americas for an indefinite time. Inter-European rivalries soon found both

5. A possibly apocryphal story, mentioned by Samuel Eliot Morison, states that some Caribs ate a Spanish friar who was so indigestible that he made them all sick. After this, ships watering on that island dressed their landing parties in monks' habits to ensure their safety.

a new theater and also new causes for dispute in American waters, where French, English, Dutch, and Danish interests were not slow to establish land bases. Bases were attacked, landings made, islands taken and retaken in a seemingly endless diplomatic and military game, in which ships, colonies, and colonists were meant to be the pawns, and would have been, had they not frequently taken their destinies into their own hands.

Economic, rather than military, activity in the West Indies was stimulated, however, by the development of sugar cultivation. Sugar had been introduced to the Canary Islands from Sicily by Henry the Navigator, and was later taken to the West Indies by Columbus on his first voyage. It was soon established as a lucrative crop in Spanish and Portuguese possessions on the American mainland. On the first English slaving voyage, Hawkins traded his slaves to the Spanish colonists for cargoes of sugar and hides. It was left to the Dutch, however, to give economic impetus to sugar cultivation by introducing it from Brazil to the non-Spanish islands of the Caribbean. Sugar, molasses, and rum produced in Barbados, Jamaica, and San Domingo (Haiti) were to make many a French and English fortune, were to require yet more slave labor for increased production, and were—together with the slave trade itself, with which they were almost inextricably connected—to provide the economic base for the powerful West Indian lobby that developed in eighteenth-century England. It was this sugar lobby, as we have seen, whose hunger for profit demanded most insistently the continuation of the slave trade, and it was also this sugar lobby whose rigidity of attitude, as expressed in legislation such as the Molasses Act of 1733, was to awaken emotions in the British North American colonies that helped to lead the colonists to the threshold of revolution—and beyond.

For the moment, all this was still to come, and in the meanwhile the tropical colonies of the West Indies, where African slaves worked the sugar, and where sugar made the European masters' fortunes, took on a popularity with which the allurements of New England's stony fields or West Africa's malarial coasts could not compete. Fortune, therefore, beckoned many to the West Indies, and, in waters where for well over a century no one power was dominant, beckoned not only those who sought legitimate awards. Buccaneers—who took their original name from their habit of curing meat over open fires by the *boucan* process— terrorized the Spanish Main, and added new legends to an already violent era. It was, indeed, a party of buccaneers, settling on the island of Tortuga, off the northern coast of San Domingo, that first brought French influence to that island. In 1659 these pirates asked France to appoint a leader over them, to send them some women, and to extend French sovereignty over the area they controlled. France heard their plea, and what they asked for was given them. The western half of San Domingo thus falling under French rule, the division of the island between France and Spain was formalized by the Treaty of Ryswick in 1695.

France had no cause to regret its action, for the prize—the territory which corresponds to modern Haiti—was to prove a rich one. By 1789, according to one authority, French San Domingo had become the most profitable colony the world had ever known, exporting sugar, indigo, cotton, hides, molasses, cocoa, and rum. "If," commented C. L. R. James, "on no earthly spot was so much misery concentrated as on a slave ship, then on no portion of the globe did its surface in proportion to its dimensions yield so much wealth as the colony of San Domingo."[6]

Not that the misery of the slaves ceased upon arrival at San Domingo. The worst excesses of the slave owners were, however, theoretically controlled by the French Crown through the provisions of the *Code Noir* (the "Negro Code") of 1685. Whereas in fact the Code—which, for instance, allowed a slave to be whipped, but limited the number of lashes, and also provided that the lash should not be of such a nature as to cause serious injuries—may have often provided protection for the enslaved Africans, it was also often honored as much in the breach as in the observance, if contemporary reports are to be believed. For example, the Baron de Wimpffen, a traveler who visited San Domingo in 1790, alleged that not a single one of the articles of the *Code Noir* was respected, and said that he had sat at table with a rich and beautiful woman, held in local admiration, who had had her cook thrown into the oven for spoiling a sauce.

Before long, as elsewhere in the Americas where African slaves had been imported, the union of European and African produced the mulatto. With Gallic logic, however, the degree of genetic mixture in the various unions that then occurred was calculated not merely by simple nomenclature, as in the Spanish Americas or Brazil, but mathematically. Individuals were held to be composed of 128 separate units, which is to say that the ethnic admixture was traced to the eighth generation, thus providing a system of classification which permitted no ambiguity, and made possible equations such as the following:

| WHITE | | BLACK | | |
|---|---|---|---|---|
| 64 parts | + | 64 parts | = | *mulattre* |
| 72 parts | + | 56 parts | = | *sacatra* |
| 88 parts | + | 40 parts | = | *marabou* |
| 96 parts | + | 32 parts | = | *quarteron* |
| 127 parts | + | 1 part | = | *sang melée* |

6. *The Black Jacobins* (1963).

One could, however, play with figures. For example, a *quarteron* need not result solely from the union of a "128 per-cent" white mating with a mulatto. The same result could also be obtained as follows:

72 parts white + 56 black mating with 120 parts white + 8 black = *quarteron*

Or again:

88 parts white + 40 black mating with 104 parts white + 24 black = *quarteron*

In practice, however, many persons not sufficiently adept at such calculations took to applying the nomenclature somewhat more loosely, and took, for example, to describing as a *quarteron* not only individuals resulting from the union of pure white with mulatto, or the mathematical equivalent, but also the result of mixing "128 per-cent" white and *sacatra* (that is, darker than a certified *quarteron*), as well as the result of mixing "128 per-cent" white and *marabou* (that is, lighter than a certified *quarteron*). Human nature required quicker terms of reference than the law provided, even at the cost of oversimplification.

Indeed, for methodological reasons alone it was perhaps as well that the original inhabitants of San Domingo, the American Indians, were not present in sufficient numbers to complicate the functioning of the system still further. It was, without doubt, because their numbers were so insignificant that they were not taken into the reckonings. At least virtually never, for on at least one occasion they were invoked in relation to the system. In 1771 a certain Sieur Chapuzet obtained a decree declaring that he was white. Subsequent researches, however, purported to show that one of his ancestors, 150 years earlier, had been an African from St. Kitts. Legally, at least, he finally succeeded in establishing that this ancestor was not, in fact, an African, but a "free born Carib"—an alleged circumstance that enabled him to pass in the eyes of the law as completely white. So strong, however, was the reaction to the incident among the community of mixed blood, who saw in the Chapuzet affair a precedent of hopeful augury for themselves, that the colonial authorities, despite Chapuzet's accepted white status, dared not grant him the appointment that he had been seeking in consequence.

### The North American Colonies

So far as North America was concerned, the Spanish, who were ready to risk their lives for gold, expressed little enthusiasm. After the explorer Gomez had surveyed the east coast of North America in 1524–25, and had reported that he had found the region composed of "agreeable and useful countries," Peter Martyr observed crushingly: "But what need have we of what is found everywhere in Europe?"

In 1578 Sir Humphrey Gilbert, a half-brother of Sir Walter Raleigh, obtained a royal patent "to inhabit and possess at his choice all remote

and heathen lands not in actual possession of any Christian prince."
Gilbert's efforts to establish a North American fishing and fur-trading
colony having failed, Raleigh made his more famous but likewise ill-
starred attempts to found, in 1585 and 1587, a colony at Roanoke in
Virginia. When a relief ship arrived in 1590, the men and women colonists
were nowhere to be found. This unlucky settlement has since been referred to as "Raleigh's Lost Colony." Neither did Raleigh's dream of
another colony in Guiana in South America come true. (Perhaps potential backers believed him when he said that there were people there with
"eyes in their shoulders and their mouths in the middle of their breasts,"
and therefore decided that they wanted no part of the venture.)

By the beginning of the seventeenth century the Spanish monopoly
over most of the Americas was being infringed with relative impunity
by other European nations. Indeed, the failure of Spain itself to ship
adequate supplies of all that was needed to equip the empire in the
"Indies" made the Spanish colonists receptive to interloping trading ships
from other European countries. Thus interlopers, too, became acquainted
with the topography of the New World. Although it was not until after
1660 that Spain was officially to recognize the principle of the freedom
of the high seas, already in 1604 the English, and in 1609 the Dutch,
had declared their adherence to the principle of effective occupation of
territory as the basis for recognizing jurisdiction. Before long French,
English, and Dutch colonies had not only succeeded in establishing
themselves along the eastern American coastline, they had gone further
to the next logical stage, and had come intermittently into conflict with
one another.

Four main motives would appear to have been present in the establishing of the North American colonies. First, mercantile theory of the
day favored trading by the home country with its own dependencies,
rather than with the colonies of others. (As the French statesman Colbert
expressed it: "The colonies are founded by and for the metropolis.")
Second, such colonies, lying athwart Spain's line of communication with
Europe, provided strategic bases from which to attack the Spanish, or
harry their shipping, as occasion warranted. Third, it was believed that
the colonies would drain off the unemployed from the European homeland, and reduce excess of population there. Fourth, there was the religious motive. Other more specific motives often appeared. For example,
the British sought to assure themselves of a supply of fir trees, which they
needed for the masts of their ships. Previously they could obtain such
trees only from the Baltic, but the Baltic could be closed to them in
time of war. New England firs thus came to be of vital interest to the
British.

Styles in colonization also varied. The Dutch ran their colonies with

efficient business acumen, developing them as way-stations in their growing world-wide carrying trade network. Their aim was to promote commerce rather than to occupy land. The English style varied. In New
England, Puritanism set its unique stamp. Despairing of winning over
the American Indians to their type of morality and religion, the Puritans
tended, for the most part, to leave the Indians to their own devices,
persuading them to relocate as need arose, that is, when the colonists
had need of their lands. Tobacco-growing Virginia, however, after the
first few years, became a Crown Colony, and therefore developed certain
royalist and aristocratic features that stood in strong contrast to Puritanism. The French style, again, was different. Far more subject to royal
control than other colonies, the settlements of New France were closely
supervised by Paris, but also enjoyed the advantage of being able to call
upon the home government for a greater degree of support, militarily and
otherwise. Other differences were also in evidence. French Protestants
were strictly barred from emigrating to the French-American colonies,
but French Catholics who did come were not only permitted but sometimes actively encouraged to intermarry with the American Indians.
Jesuit missionaries and French traders (whose interests often clashed)
habitually left the confines of New France itself and ranged deep into
the hinterland of the continent, to the Great Lakes and beyond.

A great struggle between England and France was joined in the early
seventeenth century, and was fought to its conclusion in the eighteenth.
As war and peace alternated, each of the contestants took the measure
of its rival and gauged its actions accordingly. The French formed, at an
early stage, an alliance with the Algonquin Indians of the Northeast,
whereas the English later succeeded in allying themselves with the
Iroquois "Five Nations," who lived to the south of the Algonquins. The
use of Indian allies by both sides—which meant in practice that Europeans promoted Indian attacks, in which Indian methods of warfare were
used, upon other European communities—soon envenomed the struggle.

The French, having extended their influence into the Canadian wilderness, also obtained control of the rivers to the west of the English colonies,
and claimed all the territory down as far as the Gulf of Mexico, thus
completely blocking the westward expansion of the English. A series of
French and English wars, however, finally resulted in the defeat of the
French, following the capture of Quebec and the occupation of Montreal
by the English. By the terms of the Treaty of Paris in 1763, England
obtained the whole of Canada, and all French territory lying to the east
of the Mississippi, Spain obtaining that to the west.

In the selfsame year that the French were thus defeated, two events
occurred. These were the establishment of the Proclamation Line by the
English, dividing the European communities of the Eastern seaboard
from the Indian territories, and the Pontiac uprising.

With regard to the Proclamation Line, the British Cabinet, considering the future of North America from far off, decreed that no settlers should venture beyond this new boundary, which was an imaginary line running down the crest of the Allegheny Mountains, separating the European colonies of the coast from the Indian tribes and nations inhabiting the "wilderness" on the farther side. France, intending to return to North America when the fortunes of war should change in her favor, and Spain, already concerned over the appearance of Russian fur traders on the northwest corner of the continent, both approved of the establishment of the line, because it provided a clear delimitation of the extent of English influence. England, for her part, sought not only to reassure other European powers as to her immediate intentions, but also to avoid the occasion of future conflict between colonists and Indians, thus saving the Treasury the expense of further military operations.

Military operations, however, had nonetheless to be paid for immediately as a result of Pontiac's rebellion, which raged in 1763 and 1764. Pontiac, a chief of the Ottawas, who had already fought with the French and against the British, realizing that the British victory over France presented great dangers for the future of all the Indian peoples, attempted to organize a general uprising. The uprising was put down, and Pontiac himself assassinated a few short years later, in 1769.

British plans for the maintenance of the Proclamation Line, and Indian plans to retain their lands, were alike upset by the emergence of the white American frontiersman, part pioneer, part settler, part hunter. Soon able to live off the land as well as the American Indian himself, skilled in woodcraft, contemptuous of governments and laws, the frontiersman formed the "cutting edge" of the European invasion and occupation of North America by the white man, which now began in earnest, and which was to continue for over a century until the whole continent, from coast to coast, had fallen not only under European occupation, but also to European settlement.

Pressure to move to the West had, indeed, begun to make itself felt years before the American War of Independence which led to the establishment of the United States. Once the way to the West was clear, land speculation provided much of the dynamic of expansion, even while the land itself still remained in Indian possession and occupation. From the outset prominent Americans, such as George Washington and Benjamin Franklin, foreseeing the future trend, became involved in western land schemes, thereby allying themselves with those forces that, resentful of restrictions, wished for white settlement to overleap the Appalachians and break through the Proclamation Line.

In the years to come the American Indians, living in towns and villages in forests and valleys, or carrying on a semi-nomadic existence on the Great Plains, were not to prove a serious obstacle to European advance. The North American Indians, as distinct from those of some other regions of the Americas, were relatively few in number, amounting to perhaps no more than just over a million from the Atlantic to the Pacific. They were, despite campaigns of harassment and attack, and despite some major battles, not numerous enough to offer effective resistance to the incoming tide of immigration from Europe itself. The white population of what was to become the United States numbered, in 1700, merely 250,000 persons. By 1800 the whites numbered, 4,300,000, perhaps four whites to each Indian. This, of course, was merely the beginning. By 1860 the total population of the United States had risen to 31 million, whereas by 1900, some ten years after the western movement had run its course, and the entire continent had come under European occupation, the population of the United States had risen to 76 million. By 1960 the white population of the United States was 158,831,-732, and the Indian population 523,591, with Negroes numbering 18,871,-831.

The struggle was, nevertheless, harder for the Europeans in the earlier stages, when numbers were somewhat more equal, when the American Indians were better adapted to the environment than the settlers, and when certain adjuncts, such the railroad and the telegraph, were not yet available. Even in these earlier days, however, the passing of land from American Indian to European hands continued steadily and systematically—by diplomacy when possible, and by force when, for one reason or another, diplomacy could not be applied. Diplomatically the tactic of division, which played upon traditional rivalries between different tribes or groups of American Indians, was employed again and again with success. For example, at Fort Stanwix in 1768 the Iroquois entered into collusion with the British. They called together the greatest conclave of Indians of that region that had ever been known, supposedly for the purpose of co-ordinating Indian resistance to further European expansion, but in effect to betray the interests of other tribes in order to safeguard their own. As a result of the Treaty of Fort Stanwix the inflowing tide of European settlement was turned away from Iroquois lands and directed to those of their neighbors.

Force was employed on other occasions, sometimes with more and sometimes with less justification. After a British and Indian alliance not only prevented U.S. expansion on the northwest frontier, but also began to threaten recognized U.S. territory, the U.S. Army succeeded in 1794, at the Battle of Fallen Timbers in what is now Ohio, in turning the tide of reverses and winning a decisive victory, which ensured that most of southern Ohio would be surrendered to the whites by the Indians.

War was inevitably followed by settlement, and settlement—when the numbers had grown sufficiently—by the admission of new territories to statehood. The remarkable growth of the United States, a new political and technological phenomenon in world history, is a tale that needs no repetition here. What is of interest, however, in this context are some aspects of its growth that affected or were affected by "race relations."

The war of 1812 between the United States and the United Kingdom, for example, allegedly broke out over the disputed right of the United States to ship its goods to Europe through the British blockade during the Napoleonic wars. The war itself was precipitated, however, not by the New England shipping interests, which were the most directly affected by the circumstances, but instead by communities and interests connected with the western frontier of the United States, who were anxious to take advantage of the opportunity that the war would offer them to seize fresh lands in British Canada to the north and in Spanish Florida to the south. Indeed, western frontiersmen were already embroiled in a war with Chief Tecumseh, leader of an Indian confederation pledged to fight to prevent the alienation of any further Indian lands. The Westerners, however, blamed British intrigue rather than Indian instincts of self-defense for the conflict, and prodded President Madison into a declaration of war against the United Kingdom. In the course of the ensuing hostilities the U.S. forces broke Indian resistance at the Battle of the Thames in 1813, at which Tecumseh himself was killed, and again defeated the Indians at the Battle of Horse Shoe Bend in 1814. The way was now open for a new surge of European expansion and settlement that was to sweep into and fill the entire Mississippi Valley.

## *"Manifest Destiny"*

The next crisis came in the 1840s, when the American people were faced with the question of whether or not to opt for further expansion in general, and whether or not to attempt to annex in particular various Spanish-speaking territories such as Mexico and Texas, which were in effect already Europeanized to some extent. Texas—a province of Mexico that had become infiltrated by American frontiersmen and had then seceded in consequence—was eager to be annexed to the United States, but the question became entangled with the anti-slavery controversy within the United States itself. When, however, the U.S. electorate gave the incoming presidential candidate, James K. Polk, a mandate to implement an expansionist platform, the outgoing President, John Tyler, proceeded with action to annex Texas, which formally entered the Union in 1846, slavery or no slavery.

Already the phrase "manifest destiny" had crept into popular usage, the concept that it represented implying that forces beyond human control—God, destiny, or fate—had decided that the white man, through the agency of the United States of America, would spread his rule from ocean to ocean across the American continent, and (some further held) would then proceed to dominate or to annex the remainder of the North American, and perhaps the South American, continent. Once the basic premise of predestination was accepted, the thesis had the same quality of inevitability about it as, for example, is found in the Marxist view of history. It represented, in terms of the theory, a force with which one could co-operate or refuse to co-operate as one chose, but a force that one could not hope to resist or to hold back. In effect, it was implied, by co-operating with this force one was co-operating with and fulfilling the will of God.

The thesis, one gathers, was assiduously propagated by those who had financial interests to further by the expansion of U.S. governmental responsibilities to fresh territories. For example, Moses Y. Beach, editor of the New York *Sun*, who held that Providence had "willed the Mexican War" to unite and exalt Mexico and the United States, and who wrote on October 22, 1847, that the Mexican race was "perfectly accustomed to being conquered, and the only new lesson we shall teach is that our victories will give liberty, safety, and prosperity to the vanquished," was also interested in obtaining a broker's fee for helping to end the Mexican War, together with the right of transit across the Tehuantepec isthmus, which he would then sell to would-be canal builders. In this instance both Beach's vision of himself helping to end the Mexican War, as well as the vision of a canal across the isthmus, proved illusory. But there were many other supporters of "Manifest Destiny" with comparable schemes, not all of them by any means doomed to disappointment.

The Mexican War itself, which lasted from 1846 to 1848, developed because of American westward expansionism, which had already claimed Texas, and which now threatened the Mexican province of California. U.S. troops were victorious, but peace negotiations dragged on as the United States tried to make up its mind as to the peace price that was to be exacted from Mexico. There were those who favored annexing "all Mexico," and, when it was pointed out to them that out of the Mexican population of some eight million people more than half were Indian, only one-sixth white, and the remainder of mixed origin, replied that a part of the duty laid upon those who upheld "Manifest Destiny" was the regeneration of "lesser breeds." Others, however, were more interested in vacant land or financial profit, but not in accepting responsibility for a large nonwhite population. John C. Calhoun of South Carolina, for example, an upholder of slavery, and an opponent of the war with Mexico, told the U.S. Congress in 1848:

> We have never dreamt of incorporating into our Union any but the Caucasian race —the free white race. To incorporate Mexico, would be the very first instance of the kind, of incorporating an Indian race; for more than half of the Mexicans are Indians,

and the other is composed chiefly of mixed tribes. I protest against such a union as that! Ours, sir, is the Government of a white race. The greatest misfortunes of Spanish America are to be traced to the fatal error of placing these colored races on an equality with the white race.

The admonitions of Calhoun and others bore fruit. The United States, already riven by the passions of the approaching Civil War, kept Texas, and took California and New Mexico. But the more densely inhabited regions of Mexico were not claimed. What remained of Mexico was to remain Mexican.

The tendency, the underlying assumption, whether explicit or implicit, was to see the destiny of the American people, the people for whom the Constitution had been framed, as a white man's destiny. Yet there was always a vocal minority who challenged this assumption, and who pointed, for instance, to the authority of the United States Declaration of Independence, in which it was stated:

We hold these truths to be self-evident, that all men are created equal; that they are endowed by their Creator with certain unalienable rights; that among these, are life, liberty, and the pursuit of happiness. . . .

"All men," clearly, could be interpreted to include such mixed American stocks as those alluded to early in the nineteenth century by Fisher Ames, the Bostonian, when he spoke of "the Gallo-Hispano-Indian *omnium gatherum* of savages and adventurers." "All men" could be—and was—interpreted to include black Africans or those of African descent. The contradiction between the promise "all men" and the interpretation "white men" was to continue, emerging as a major theme of the Civil War era, and echoing on in after years.

The changes that time now brought to the American continent, after the conclusion of the Civil War in the United States, were rarely those of major shock, but rather of slow ineluctability. The United States Army, exploring and campaigning in the Far West, covered ground that had already been penetrated years earlier by white traders, fur-trappers, and frontiersmen. Despite the dramatic interruptions, the outcome was a foregone conclusion. "Custer's Last Stand," in which a white unit was overrun by a surge of aroused Indians, produced a strong emotional effect upon white men, who for once were placed in the position of having to identify themselves with the vanquished. Yet in the historic context the incident was virtually meaningless, representing no more than a local tragedy with elements of human interest, resulting from overconfidence on the part of the white commander. White power, from its European springboard, had leapt the Atlantic and consolidated its hold upon the Americas. The strategic victory of the white man in gaining dominion over North America was merely a part of his conquest of all the Americas. The white-dominated countries of Latin America, too, most of which had long since, in emulation of the United States, shaken off their allegiance to Europe, were also to experience no challenge that was to endanger white hegemony.

By the 1890s, when the westward movement dissolved itself at last into the settled communities of the Pacific coast, and the American frontier was proclaimed closed, white power was strung across the continent by cable, was welded down overland in a network of shining rails, and was manifest in ironclads that were soon to slide from ocean to ocean through the Panama Canal. A mere thirteen years was to pass between the announcement by the U.S. Director of the Census in 1890 that "the unsettled area has been so broken into by isolated bodies of settlement that there can hardly be said to be a frontier line," and 1903, when a white man was to lift the first airplane with a gasoline engine off the ground at Kitty Hawk in North Carolina.

In the new technical age that was dawning, with fresh wonders promised that would outdo those already revealed, the American Indian was no longer viewed by the white European as representing any threat to him. The American Indian, original possessor of the continent, was on his way to becoming reduced, instead, to the status of a tourist attraction, a befeathered mannequin, a butt for wit, a despised tiller of the soil, or a phantom from past legend. It was the white man, now, who had become the American.

In a mere four centuries the white man had seized America, North and South, sweeping the red man from his path, and bringing in the black man to labor for his purposes. The secrets of science were opening to his touch. Now the future appeared to him as a broad road, stretching forward unencumbered into a limitless distance. Destiny, indeed, appeared to be manifest.

# Chapter 6

# "The White Man's Burden":
# The European Occupation of Asia

*Take up the White Man's burden—*
*Send forth the best ye breed—*
*Go bind your sons to exile*
*To serve your captives' need;*
*To wait in heavy harness*
*On fluttered folk and wild*
*Your new-caught, sullen peoples,*
*Half-devil and half-child.*
　　　　—Rudyard Kipling ( 1899 )

THE PATTERN OF EVENTS is most often not discerned in advance, but only when they have moved sufficiently far forward for the design to have become clear, and for the conclusion to be at hand. Thus "manifest destiny" was proclaimed in North America not at the time when the first covered wagons began to roll over the Appalachian barrier, but only when California was about to be added to the Union. Kipling, the poet who proclaimed the White Man's mission in Asia, arose not when Clive was gaining mastery of Bengal, but when the Indian subcontinent was held in firm subjection by the British Crown, and when the United States was enunciating the Open Door doctrine for China.

For about 250 years after Cabral, the Portuguese, made the first commercial voyage "to the Indies" in 1500, it does not appear to have occurred to any European power that there could be any possibility of occupying Asia as a whole, or even any substantial part of it. Individual islands or archipelagoes could, perhaps, be conquered or dominated, but the assumption of rule over the vast populations of the Asian mainland, with their developed military organizations, political systems, and religious creeds, seemed clearly unthinkable. Not until the Frenchman Dupleix discerned that the rule of the Moghul dynasty in India was crumbling to ruin did European dreamers and schemers begin to think in imperial terms. Even then such ventures appeared daring in the extreme. Apart from the utter disparity in numbers between Asians and Europeans, there were such problems as logistics to consider: it took an average of six months to sail a shipload of soldiers from Europe out as far as India.

In opening commercial relations with the East at the beginning of the sixteenth century, the European suffered from two principal drawbacks: first, the fact that the trade of the Indian Ocean was in Muslim hands, and second, the fact that they had little or nothing that was acceptable to offer to the Asians in return for the spices, silks, cloths, medicines, and jewels that they sought. The Zamorin of Calicut, it will be remembered, was markedly unimpressed with the cheap trade goods that Vasco da Gama brought with him on his first voyage. As J. H. Parry has put it:

European manufactures were crude and unattractive in Eastern eyes; and the local rulers could not be expected to see, in the tatterdemalion crews living in crowded squalor in their sea-stained ships, the fore-runners of a power which was to conquer half the East. Momentarily dangerous the Europeans might be; but in the eyes of a cultivated Hindu they were mere desperadoes, few in number, barbarous, truculent and dirty.[1]

What appeared true to the Hindus in the early sixteenth century certainly appeared no less true to the Chinese in the eighteenth, if the statement of the Emperor Chi'en Lung is to be believed. When George III of the United Kingdom proposed to him that Britain and China should open diplomatic and commercial relations, the Emperor, rejecting the request, replied, "I set no value on objects strange or ingenious, and have no use for your country's manufactures."[2]

In establishing their commercial empire, therefore, the Portuguese did not feel able to compete economically. They could, it is true, have traded with gold, which they had in abundance from their West African monopoly, but economists of the day frowned sternly upon any systematic diminution of national reserves of specie. They had, therefore, to rely upon force of arms.

Since any major attack upon the realms of the Asian mainland was out of the question—as an abortive assault upon Calicut, which had cost the life, among others, of a Grand Marshal of Portugal, had proved—the only alternative for a European power was to establish control of the

1. *The Establishment of the European Hegemony: 1415–1715* (1961).
2. He also added that "even if your envoy were able to acquire the rudiments of our civilization, you could not possibly transplant our manners and customs to your alien soil."

Asiatic seas. For a task of such dimensions the Portuguese produced a man great enough to undertake it—Affonso Albuquerque.

Albuquerque has been called "the Portuguese Mars." He was his country's greatest military leader. His vision and courage enabled him, under different circumstances, to accomplish for Portugal in Asia what his fellow Iberian, Cortes, had accomplished for Spain in the Americas—the laying of the foundations of an empire. Daring and, in medieval crusading style, fanatically anti-Muslim, Albuquerque even contemplated, at one time or another, such feats as the ruining of Egypt by diverting the Nile waters into the Red Sea by digging a canal, or marching to the Holy City of Mecca, sacking it, and seizing the coffin of the Prophet Mahomet, in order to use it to ransom back the Holy Land. These dreams were never to be realized, but in other ways Albuquerque proved himself to be a scourge to the Muslim cause. After his second capture of Goa in 1510 he proudly reported that he had put every Moor in the city to the sword, or else had filled the mosques with them and burned them. In Malacca in 1511 he burned the Muslim shipping that he found in the harbor, and later, after the capture of Malacca itself, proceeded to a massacre of Muslims there, selling the survivors into slavery.

Albuquerque himself spoke, in connection with such activities, of "the great service we shall perform to Our Lord in casting the Moors out . . . and of quenching the fire of the Sect of Mahomet so that it may never burst out again hereafter." He also spoke, in the same breath, of taking the Eastern trade away from the Muslims and so ruining Cairo and Mecca, as well as forcing Venice to buy from Portugal. In effect, although—despite Albuquerque—the "fire of the sect of Mahomet" still burns brightly in parts of the East to this day, the "Portuguese Mars" did succeed in wresting the Eastern trade from Arab hands and placing it in those of the Portuguese.

Strategically, Albuquerque planned to dominate the great arc formed by the shoreline of the Indian Ocean—an arc which swings around in a gigantic semicircle from Madagascar north to the Persian Gulf, and then, after the interpolation of the wedge-shaped Indian land mass, from the mouths of the Ganges down to the islands of Indonesia, and—had Albuquerque but known it—Australia. This he planned to do by seizing four key points, and establishing naval bases there. Aden, at the mouth of the Red Sea, and Ormuz, at the mouth of the Persian Gulf, were to dominate the west of the oceanic lake. Goa, on the Indian mainland, was to be the center and pivotal base of the entire Portuguese empire in the Indies. Finally Malacca, dominating the straits which run between Malaya and Sumatra, was to complete the design.

Goa, after changing hands three times within the year, was finally captured in 1510. Malacca was taken from the Sultan of Malaya the following year. Ormuz, situated on an island, had been captured by the Portuguese in 1507 but then abandoned again: now it was retaken. Finally, although Albuquerque, who died in 1515 did not live to see it, Aden became subject to Portugal in 1524. The design was complete.[3] The fact that such East African ports as Sofala, Kilwa, and Mombasa had earlier passed into Portuguese hands, was a final assurance of continued Portuguese control. Even by the time of Albuquerque's death, Muslim shipping had effectively been cleared from the waves of the Indian Ocean and bottled up in the Red Sea. Any ships that did venture forth on the ocean itself did so only by Portuguese permission. A final Muslim attempt in 1528 by the Governor of Egypt, Suleiman Pasha, to join with the Calicut fleet and defeat the Portuguese at sea proved unsuccessful. With the Portuguese ranging as far east as the Moluccas, and with the Spanish appearing in the Spice Islands from their bases in Spanish America, Europeans had clearly seized control of Asian waters.

Within the framework of the Portuguese system, Ceylon fell under Portuguese dominion, and relations, reflecting varying degrees of Portuguese influence, were established with Persia, Bengal, Indochina, China, and Japan—not to speak of the Spice Islands themselves. Many a dramatic tale may be told of these times: the adventures of the Portuguese in the Far East—as, indeed, elsewhere in Africa and Asia—were of the very stuff of which legends are made. Moreover, their adventures took place, so far as Europe's relations with other continents are concerned, "in the beginning of years, when the world was so new and all," as Kipling put it. It was during these years that Camoëns, shipwrecked, swam ashore off the coast of Indochina, with the manuscript of his *Lusiad* held above his head, to wander naked on a foreign shore before finding his way back to Malacca; that de Castro sailed up the Red Sea to Suez, braving the guns of the Islamic fleet; that St. Francis Xavier carried out his extraordinary missionary work in India, Malaya, the Spice Islands, and Japan; that the crew of one of da Gama's ships, sailing out to the Indies on his third voyage, mutinied, and set sail on their own to try their hands at piracy in the vicinity of the Red Sea; and that other Portuguese, known and unknown, sung and unsung, quested in search of trade, conquest, loot, or souls, throughout the Orient.

In seizing Goa, and in holding it, the task of the Portuguese was facilitated at the outset by political circumstance. At the time of da Gama's arrival, and in subsequent years until 1565, when it was conquered by the Muslim sultanates of India, the Hindu kingdom of Vijayanagar in the southern part of India was in its last years of glory. Domingo Paes, a Portuguese who visited it in 1522, described the city of Vijayanagar

---

3. Or almost. Albuquerque had wished also to establish a fortress at Massawa in Eritrea, but died before he could do so. See Chapter 7, p. 152.

(capital of the state of the same name) as being "as large as Rome and very beautiful to the sight." The rulers of Vijayanagar favored the Portuguese hold over Goa, partly because both they and the Portuguese were opposed to the Muslims, and partly because Goa thus provided them with a commercial outlet to the sea. Vijayanagar, therefore, at least until 1565, offset the danger of a Muslim attack on Goa from the landward side.

Throughout the sixteenth century Portugal remained the predominant power in the Indian Ocean. After 1530, however, a slow decline set in that by 1600 had become apparent to all. Portugal was, after all, a country of only some two million people, and the opportunities for fame, fortune, and adventure offered by her Eastern empire led to a constant drain upon her population. Soon Portugal was to find herself short not only of administrators and military leaders, but even of seamen. Nothing could have illustrated this so clearly as the decline in the standard of Portuguese seamanship that resulted. Farm boys had to be engaged in place of sailors, and some of them, we are told, had difficulty in distinguishing port from starboard. One captain is therefore said to have hit upon the expedient of hanging a bunch of garlic over one side of the ship, and a bunch of onions over the other, and to have ordered the helmsman to "Garlic your helm," or "Onion your helm," as the case might be. Furthermore, whereas of the ships that sailed from Portugal to the East in the eighty-odd years that followed Vasco da Gama's first voyage, some 93 percent arrived safely, in the forty-odd years after that only 69 percent reached their destinations.

Moreover, the drain on population was not only caused by overextension, but also by the disappearance or absorption of many of those who sailed East. One observer calculated that of the Portuguese who traveled East during these years, only one in ten ever returned home again. The life led by the Portuguese in Asia was, also, habitually degenerate, so that men were lost to the state in civil as well as in military pursuits. Thus Portuguese who were active soldiers on the one hand often tended eventually to get themselves killed fighting. On the other hand Portuguese who were civil servants often possessed a great degree of local power that was remote from home control. As a result they were susceptible to a degeneration in their way of living that earned for Goa, the central Portuguese base, the title of "Babylon of the East." Speculation, bribery, nepotism, influence-peddling, and other forms of corruption were commonplace. Slavery increased. Debauchery was habitual. Some of the Portuguese took several concubines, whereas the Indian or mixedblood wives of other Portuguese often bought female slaves of their own in order to send them out as prostitutes. One Dutch commentator wrote of the Portuguese in the Indies that "although a man were of iron or steel, their unchaste life with women . . . was able to grind him to powder and sweep him away like dust." Syphilis, dysentery, malaria, and a variety of tropical diseases all combined to lessen the numbers of the Portuguese.

Albuquerque himself, moreover, introduced a policy which encouraged intermarriage between Europeans and Asians, so that as time progressed the original Portuguese stock became slowly absorbed by the Asian populations. To this gradual erosion of the physical Portuguese presence were added other circumstances that contributed to a rejection of Portuguese influence by the Asian peoples. The establishment of the Inquisition in Goa led to a religious persecution that was at variance with tolerant Indian habits. The Church, too, despite the good that it undoubtedly effected in Asia, became involved in the growing corruption that was characteristic of the Portuguese system. The annexation of Portugal itself, as well as its possessions, by Spain in 1580 was a further blow that accelerated the rate of decline. Finally, the fact that the Dutch and the English had turned to Protestanism, and so no longer felt themselves restricted by the papally approved Treaty of Tordesillas, meant that the Portuguese had to meet a growing challenge not only from the Muslim powers of Asia and the Middle East, but from European rivals as well. Voyages such as that of Sir Francis Drake, when he circumnavigated the globe in 1577–1580, revealed to other European nations that Portugal's empire in the Indies was scattered, and highly vulnerable to competition. France was not slow in following Holland and England into the Asian arena.

### "Ginger for Pepper"

As a realization of Portuguese weaknesses in the East grew in Europe, the Dutch decided to contest the Portuguese monopoly of the spice trade. Information on the Indies in general and the Portuguese position there in particular had been given them by Jan Huygen Linschoten, who had served as secretary to the Archbishop of Goa. The decision to compete with Portugal was taken in 1592 by a group of leading Dutch merchants who, in 1595, sent four ships to the Indies under the command of Cornelis de Houtman. The expedition established contact with the Spice Islands of Indonesia, and returned showing a profit, despite many deaths among the crews. Other voyages followed, but the Dutch soon discovered that their merchants were competing not only with the Portuguese but also with one another. As a result, in 1602, they formed the Dutch United East India Company, with powers to conclude treaties and alliances and to conquer territory. Through the instrumentality of the company, the Dutch sought to displace the Portuguese in the East, a purpose that they ultimately accomplished.

In 1605 the Dutch began by taking Amboina in the Spice Islands. Continuing from this base, they expanded their power through the instrumentality of Jan Pieterz Coen. Coen, in 1618, became Governor-General of the Dutch East Indies, in which post he performed for the Dutch the same kind of services that Albuquerque had performed for the Portuguese. In 1619 Coen captured Djakarta—which he renamed Batavia—thus consolidating the hitherto tenuous Dutch hold over the Spice Islands. Unfortunately, despite his military qualities, Coen laid the foundations not only of Dutch predominance but also of Dutch oppression. Claiming that the people of the Indonesian islands were no more than cattle, he declared, "The law of this land is the will of the King, and he is King who is strongest." As an Indian scholar, K. M. Pannikar, has pointed out:

> Neither under Hindu nor under Muslim theory was there ever a claim that the ruler owned the people, but this pernicious doctrine of Coen became the basis of Dutch practice and the theoretical foundation of the planter-coolie relationship which held sway for a hundred years in Inodonesia.[4]

In effect, until the eighteenth century, the Dutch aimed at profit and exploitation, unhampered by either the religious or administrative checks that to some extent characterized, for example, Spanish rule. Dutch officials were primarily commercial agents. Local powers were delegated, where it was judged necessary, to chosen Asian agents, who were assured of complete Dutch support for all that they did. These regents had every opportunity to establish themselves as petty tyrants who did not have to consider the welfare of their compatriots. Only later did the Dutch begin to appoint other officials who were empowered to review the decisions of the regents.

Whereas Coen was the consolidator of Dutch power, it was left to Van Diemen to expand it. In 1641 Van Diemen captured Malacca, one of the four cornerstones of Portuguese power. Having thus established themselves in the eastern part of the Indian Ocean, the Dutch did not, as might have been expected, move directly against Goa. Instead they moved to Ceylon which, they correctly calculated, would provide them with a leverage point from which to complete the downfall of Portuguese power. With the help of the kings of Kandy they ousted the Portuguese from Ceylon in 1658, in order to take their place. A rueful Sinhalese proverb refers to the effects of the change: "We gave pepper and in exchange got ginger."[5] The Dutch then proceeded to the occupation of various Portuguese trading stations on the Malabar coast, such as Cochin; only such ports as Goa, Diu, and the East African coastal possessions remained to Portugal. The power of the Portuguese Catholic conquerors had been dissipated, and in their place came the Protestant Dutch, tidy, efficient, and businesslike.

---

4. *Asia and Western Dominance* (London: 1953).
5. No doubt the Portuguese became identified with pepper by bringing it from West Africa, and the Dutch with ginger by bringing it from the East.

Having established themselves, the Dutch at first determined to avoid the basic mistake that they judged had led to the downfall of the Portuguese—over-extension. They therefore attempted at the outset to confine themselves strictly to trade, and to eschew so far as possible the acquisition of territory. They chose Batavia, situated in the Sunda Straits, as the central entrepôt of their Eastern trading empire, and sought to make it the hub of inter-Asian commerce. They already held Malacca to the north, while to the west the approaches were guarded by their base in Ceylon, as well as by a way station, acquired in 1652, at the Cape of Good Hope. They had expelled the British from Amboina in 1623, and effected the withdrawal of the Spanish from Ternate in 1663. Dutch sway over the Indonesian archipelago was to last, with minor interruptions, for 300 years.

Before long, however, they found themselves repeating that very aspect of Portuguese behavior that they had wished to avoid—the acquisition of territory. To begin with, by extending loans to local farmers, the Dutch obtained control of the land in the Moluccas, Amboina, and the Banda Islands. They then insisted that cloves and cinnamon be cultivated in place of rice, so that rice—required for subsistence itself—had to be bought from the Dutch company at monopoly prices. As a result of this situation the unfortunate populations became reduced not only to poverty but also to economic servitude. The system was later extended to Java and other islands. Dutch power was progressively expanded, despite the resistance of such local authorities as the Susuhunan of Mataram and the Sultan of Bantam, and despite popular uprisings, such as that in Ternate, which were repressed.

The Dutch also made their presence known still further east. For a time they succeeded in holding a fort they had built on Taiwan, although they made no attempt to colonize the island itself. They were, however, driven out by Cheng Cheng-Kung—or Koxinga as he is better known—a partisan of the Ming dynasty which had just been driven from the mainland by the Manchus. Not until the death of Koxinga's son, who held the island after him, did the Manchus succeed in annexing Taiwan.

In 1655 and 1665 the Dutch also sent diplomatic missions to Peking in the hope of trade, but met with scant success. Pieter van Hoorn, the leader of the second embassy, reported on his return that they had been conducted to Peking like spies and sent away like thieves.

They were somewhat more fortunate in Japan, where the authorities had permitted them to establish trade relations as early as 1611. The Japanese, however, were cautious in their dealings with all Europeans—the Dutch no less than the others—having kept themselves fully informed of the effect of European domination on the populations of Asian countries. Realizing that the effects were not necessarily beneficial, but that the Europeans possessed technical knowledge which made them formidable opponents, they proceeded with circumspection. When, however, in 1622, they learned of a projected Spanish invasion of Japan, and being fully apprised of the fate of the rulers of Mexico after the Spanish conquest, the Japanese Shogunate, or military government, immediately ordered the deportation of all the Spaniards in Japan. The suppression of Christianity was also ordered. Some years later, in 1638, all other European communities were likewise deported, with the exception of the Dutch.

It would appear that the Shogunate decided that, rather than sever all connections with Europe, it would be the better part of wisdom to keep Japan informed of European scientific and technical progress. Europe had, after all, already taught them the technique of casting cannon—despite, as it happened, the misgivings expressed by some Europeans as to the wisdom of imparting such knowledge. The Dutch, the Japanese felt, would provide them with an insight into new technical and other developments in Europe. The Dutch, moreover, unlike the Spanish or the Portuguese, had shown themselves to be more concerned with trade than with proselytizing, and so constituted less of a political threat. Consequently they were permitted to remain in Japan, albeit under restricted conditions. The Dutch community was moved from its previous location to the small island of Deshima, near Nagasaki. No individual merchant or sailor was allowed to remain in Deshima for more than one year. No European woman could come there, nor, indeed, any Japanese woman either, unless she was a prostitute. Once a year the Dutch were called into audience with the Shogun, at which time they were also asked questions by Japanese scholars about scientific and other matters. Later, in the eighteenth century, a Japanese group known as the *Rangakusha,* or "Dutch" scholars, translated medical, mathematical, botanical, and other works from Dutch into Japanese. Throughout the period of Japan's seclusion—from 1638 to 1853—the Dutch community at Deshima provided Japan with a window to the West, albeit a window from which they could look out without themselves being seen.

### The English

Although the English were not to acquire sovereignty over any Asian base until 1665, when Bombay was obtained from the Portuguese as dowry, they had already become acquainted with Asia in the second half of the sixteenth century. For a time English agents of the Muscovy Company had traded with Persia via Moscow, until harassment by the Turks and the dangers and distances involved discouraged the merchants. In the same period other English adventurers arrived in India. One English party of six, led by John Newbery, underwent a variety of experiences.[6] Two of the party remained in Basra to trade. The remainder were arrested upon arrival in Ormuz, and were shipped on to Goa, where they were imprisoned. One of the four obtained his freedom there by promising to paint a church, and marry a Eurasian woman. The remaining three fled to the court of the Moghul Emperor near Agra, where one of them accepted an appointment as a court jeweler. The other two decided to return home to England by different routes. Newbery himself, who was to travel overland, vanished forever while traveling across Asia. The last of the party, Fitch, having visited Burma, Malacca, and Ceylon, finally arrived in England to find that his relatives had given him up for dead, and had divided up his estate.

Other Englishmen were soon to follow the party to India, sailing round the Cape, but suffering great hardships on the passage, notably from scurvy. Not until the antiscorbutic properties of citrus fruits were discovered did conditions improve. The Portuguese, thanks to a chain of ports strung out along the African coast, had not encountered the same difficulties, since they had been able to receive fresh vegetables regularly.

At first the English had attempted to establish themselves in the coveted Spice Islands, but having been driven from there by the Dutch, decided to concentrate upon the Indian trade. The instrument of English influence was the East India Company, which had been granted a charter by Queen Elizabeth in 1600. In 1612 the company had opened a post at Surat on the Indian mainland, from where it had obtained the Indian textiles that were so salable in the Spice Islands. Other trading posts in India were later opened, and in 1641 the company obtained permission from the Rajah of Chandragiri to build a fort at Madras. The direction of the company's affairs, however, remained plagued by the ambiguities which characterized English politics during the period of the Civil War and the Commonwealth. Not until the Stuart restoration did consistency return, and the company's affairs take a turn for the better.

In 1665 the English Crown obtained the island of Bombay from the Portuguese, and in 1688 transferred it to the company, which made it its base. There then occurred a curious episode—prophetic of later English attitudes. Whereas one of the presidents of the East India Company, in addressing the Moghul Emperor, had described himself as "the smallest particle of sand, John Russel . . . his forehand at command rubbed on the ground," one of his successors, Sir Josiah Child, was by no means

---

6. They set sail in 1583 on the *Tiger*, bound for Aleppo via Tripoli. A topical connection is suspected between the subsequent account of the journey published by Hakluyt, and the words of Shakespeare's First Witch in *Macbeth*: "Her husband's to Aleppo gone, master o' th' Tiger." (Act I, Sc. iii). *Macbeth* was written in 1605 or 1606.

so accommodating. Aggressive, ambitious, and despising "everything Asian," it was said of him that "his appearance as a city merchant instead of as the Emperor of China or the Great Mogul seems an error of Providence." From his own point of view, however, Providence also erred in not supplying him with the means to support his pretensions. When he declared war upon the Mogul Empire, the East India company's trading posts in Bengal were occupied, and the company's agents evicted. Only after a fine had been exacted and a contrite promise of future good behavior made was the company allowed to return. When they did so they founded Calcutta, on the River Hooghly, in 1690. Madras, Calcutta, and Bombay were to be the springboards from which England would later take over the Indian subcontinent.

For the moment, however, only on the island of Bombay was sovereignty claimed, and the humiliation of Sir Josiah Child appeared to have demonstrated the futility of vaunting ambition. The appearance of the French, however—here, as elsewhere, traditional rivals of the English —soon obliged the English to view matters in a different light. The presence of the French at Pondicherry and other small ports was not, indeed, a matter for undue concern to the English. What did awaken misgivings was the vision and enterprise of an agent of the French East India Company—Dupleix.

Dupleix, indeed, could be said to have been the founder of Britain's Indian empire. For, paradoxically, it was he, a Frenchman, who first had the imagination to envision in practical terms a European imperium that would replace that of the Moghuls. For the Moghul Empire, which had existed since Babar had led his Turco-Mongol followers into India from Central Asia, was in a decline. The effect of the establishment of European trading posts along the Indian coast had been, slowly but inevitably, to produce a change in the functioning of the pattern of India's economic life. An influential class of Indian merchants, working in close association with the Europeans, came into being. In the course of the seventeenth century, European preoccupation with spices had given way to interest in Indian textiles, such as calico, muslin, and silk. The wealth of the Americas was now flowing to Western Europe, so that the populations of the European Atlantic seaboard could now think, for the first time, of clothing themselves in silks, cottons, and other Indian cloths, rather than in the traditional woolens.[7] This new trading pattern—caused indirectly, as we have said, by the discovery of the Americas—raised the Indian

---

7. Indian textiles were popular in Europe because, among other reasons, they were far easier to wash and to dry than woolen clothes. This preference of imported cloth hurt the interests of, among others, English sheep farmers and weavers. One of the protectionary legislative measures they succeeded in having enacted in consequence decreed that all English corpses should be "buried dressed in wool." Parish registers of the period, when they were kept, duly affirm, in recording interments, "buried in wool."

merchant class associated with the Europeans, no less than the European merchants themselves, to a social and financial eminence that was represented, to give one example, by the Marwari millionaires of Bengal.

As a result, in most regions where European companies began to operate, the Moghul influence was weakened, and war lords arose to challenge the authority of the local Moghul governor. One result was that the Moghuls could no longer guarantee protection to the European trading posts, which led the Europeans to begin thinking of ways to establish an Indian polity that would provide them with civil and military protection. Another result was the rise of Maratha power, the Marathas being a Hindu confederacy which came into being in opposition to the rule of the declining Moghuls. Confusion spread, accompanied by intrigue and armed conflicts, until at last, particularly after the death in 1707 of the last great Moghul emperor, the narrow and fanatical Aurangzeb, who alienated much potential support by his religious persecutions, the Moghul authority became patently nominal. Frequent disputes arose as a result of attempts to convert what had been previously official Moghul appointments into family inheritances, and these disputes, in turn, provided an opportunity, which Dupleix was the first to seize on, to intervene on the side of one disputant or the other.

The support which Dupleix gave in 1749 to claimants in Hyderabad and at Arcot attracted the immediate attention of the British East India Company. The British promptly threw their support to an influential regional rival, Mohamed Ali, for whom they obtained the throne of the Carnatic as a result of Robert Clive's military victory at Arcot. Mohamed Ali, as a result, became something of a power in his own right, obtaining extensive credit, which he used, among other things, to seat his agents in the corrupted British Parliament of Georgian days, where, for a time, he personally controlled six seats.

Anglo-French rivalry was also manifest in Bengal, also through rival claimants. On the outbreak of the Seven Years War in 1756, the French-supported claimant, Sirajud Doula, captured Calcutta from the British.[8] The following year, after the British under Robert Clive had prepared the ground in their favor by intrigue, Calcutta was retaken, and Sirajud Doula and his French supporters defeated at Plassey—an engagement that has been called more of a transaction than a battle. The immediate result was to end French influence in Bengal, and to make the new governor a puppet of the British. Shortly after, in 1760, the British, as a

---

8. Holwell's story of the "Black Hole of Calcutta," relating to this period, is now virtually discredited. Holwell, an official of the British East India Company, alleged that after Sirajud Doula's capture of Calcutta in 1756, 146 prisoners were incarcerated for the night in a cell 18 feet long by 14 feet 10 inches wide, only Holwell himself and twenty-two others surviving. Both Asian and European authorities have doubted the tale, and no official report was made to the company's headquarters. The tale has, nevertheless, passed into legend.

result of their control of the sea, also defeated the French at Wandewash in Southern India. The Treaty of Paris in 1763 confirmed the results of the British victories in India, as well as in the Americas.

"The real protagonists for power in India during the eighteenth century," wrote Jawaharlal Nehru, "were four: two of these were Indian and two foreign. The Indians were the Marathas and Haider Ali and his son Tipu Sultan in the south; the foreigners were the British and the French."[9]

The expulsion of the French from India thus reduced the protagonists to three. A crushing defeat of the Marathas by Afghan forces in 1761, however, weakened Maratha power for a number of years. After the death of Haider Ali the British defeated his son, Tipu, the sultan of the state of Mysore, in 1799. Of the four protagonists only two now remained. The British, from representing a foreign trading power precariously established in a few coastal bases, had become in scarcely half a century a principal contender for the domination of the whole of India. Already, in Bengal and Orissa, they had won Moghul recognition for the establishment of a state—albeit a state that, particularly in its first decade, was characterized by its exploitative and extortionate nature. (Only when Warren Hastings, the administrator, introduced radical reforms did it cease to be what Pannikar has called it, "the robber state of Clive.") In a pattern that the British were later to repeat in Asia, the profits of conquest were diverted, at least in part, to further conquest. From Bengal in the north and from Mysore in the south the British were now ready to move against their last remaining rivals—the Maratha state, with Poona as its capital city. Within little more than half a century their aim, the destruction of Maratha power, was to be achieved.

At first, however, success did not come easily. Although a coup d'etat in Hyderabad had reduced the Nizam of that state to British subjection, and although other Indian states were likewise falling away from Maratha influence and coming under British domination, it was still too early for the British to challenge Maratha power decisively. A victory over the Marathas by British forces under the command of Arthur Wellesley (later Duke of Wellington) at Assaye in the Deccan in 1803 was followed by a reverse near Agra in 1804. A further period was to pass, during which the British assiduously forwarded their aims by bribery, espionage, and the encouragement of divisions among the Maratha leaders, before, in 1818, they were able to inflict a decisive defeat upon the Marathas, and occupy Poona itself.

The British now turned their attention to Afghanistan, and to the Sikh Empire in the northwest. The Afghanistan campaign of 1838–1842 was a disastrous failure, but the campaign to reduce the Sikhs—first that

9. *The Discovery of India* (1946).

against their province of Sind in 1844, and then the main attack upon the Sikh stronghold of the Punjab, which culminated with its annexation in 1848—was costly but successful.

It would now appear that the British—or rather their East India Company—had gained ascendancy throughout India, from the Khyber Pass in the north to Cape Cormorin in the south. This was, indeed, the appearance. Yet the Indian tiger still had some fight left in him.

From 1857–1859 there occurred a great uprising, known to the British as the "Indian Mutiny." Essentially the mutiny was a joint Hindu-Muslim revolt against British dominion, in which the remaining elements of both the Maratha and the Moghul systems participated. As the Mutiny is dealt with in a subsequent chapter, it is sufficient at this point to recall that it took on aspects of a popular revolution in Delhi, Agra, Oudh, parts of Central India, and Bihar. An attempt was made to restore the Moghul Empire, and many hundred Europeans were massacred. The British were fortunate in that their erstwhile foes, the Sikhs, remained with them, enabling them to suppress the uprising. The suppression itself was conducted with great brutality. Jawaharlal Nehru quotes British Parliamentary records to show that, in his own district of Allahabad alone, a general massacre was perpetrated against the population, in addition to the official "Bloody Assizes" that were conducted there by a General Neill.

Volunteer hanging parties went into the districts and amateur executioners were not wanting to the occasion. One gentleman boasted of the numbers he had finished off quite "in an artistic manner," with mango trees as gibbets and elephants for drops, the victims of this wild justice being strung up, as though for pastime, in the form of figures of eight.[10]

As a result of the Mutiny, the British reformed their entire administration in India. No longer was coinage issued in the name of the Moghuls. The East India Company was taken over by the British Crown, and the Indian Army was reorganized. Indians were henceforth employed in subordinate positions in the Civil Service. A vast and generally efficient system of government that was to administer India until well into the twentieth century was established—a governmental system, moreover, that was not merely to run India for the benefit of the United Kingdom, but was also itself to assume certain of the attributes of a sovereign entity in its own right.

It was during the nineteenth and early twentieth centuries that the tide of the invasion of Asia by Europeans reached its high watermark. The invasion came from three directions: first, from Europe; second, overland from Russia to the Pacific; third, into the Pacific from North America.

The successes of the British in India, which were evidently to lead to

10. *Ibid.*

complete domination, demonstrated to other European powers the possibilities of expansion in Asia—expansion, moreover, that through the
spoils of conquest would cover its own costs. At the same time improvements in technology gave to all the European powers a sense of strength
and confidence.

The Dutch for their part—venturesome empire builders in the seventeenth century—received a discouraging check during the Napoleonic
Wars, in the course of which they not only lost most of their colonial
empire to the British, but also, for a time, their national independence
to France. Dispossessed of their Indian holdings and ousted both from
Ceylon and from the East Indies by the British, they were glad enough,
when the wars were concluded and the Pax Britannica established, to
make the best of a bad bargain and have the East Indies restored to
their jurisdiction once more. Showing small taste for further adventures,
they set themselves instead to profit from their rich estates in Java,
Sumatra, and other islands.

Britain, until 1914 the undisputed major world power, expanded the
frontiers of her Indian Empire at her leisure. Indeed, Britain's Indian
Empire soon developed a political and diplomatic personality of its own
that was often somewhat at variance with the policies promoted and
tactics chosen by the mother country. An example of such divergence is
to be found in the dispute between the British government and the
government of India as to who should have the responsibility for diplomatic relations with Persia—a dispute that continued for many years until
at last, in 1860, it was settled by a compromise which gave at least titular
supremacy to London rather than to Calcutta.[11]

Like the acolytes of some secret and mystical society, the officials and
agents of the British Raj moved, openly or covertly, over an enormous
expanse of Asia, fulfilling their duties, as they believed, and as no doubt
the sincere servants of all successful imperialist systems have believed,
in the service of a higher cause. Serving Queen and country, they also
saw themselves as preparing the ground for the ultimate introduction of
Christianity and "British justice," which would one day hold sway
throughout the world. Meanwhile, as they saw it, they served in the
"heavy harness" of which Kipling spoke, insulated professionally, at all
events in the later stages of British hegemony in India, from the taint of
commercial relationships. However, Asians who did not view relations
between Indians and British as those between a people who were "half-
devil and half-child" on the one hand, and noble-minded civil servants
on the other, did well, for the most part, to avoid expressing their views
too openly.

The writ of British India, meanwhile, ran ever wider afield, until

11. Calcutta was the capital of British India from 1773 to 1912.

eventually it extended from Suez to Singapore. Singapore, the strategic base in eastern Asia, served the same pivotal role for the British that Malacca had served for the Portuguese, and Batavia for the Dutch. It had been founded in 1819 as the result of the recommendations of a talented English individualist, Sir Stamford Raffles, who spoke several Asian languages. Suez fell under British dominion at a much later date. Until 1869 the maritime link between Britain and India had run round the Cape of Good Hope, where the British had finally displaced the Dutch in 1806. After 1869, however, shipping could pass directly through the Suez Canal.

The building of the canal was, in the last resort, an example of Anglo-French co-operation—a co-operation that was the more remarkable because it occurred at a period when the partnership between the two powers, so far as it went, was riven by traditional jealousies and suspicions. The construction of the canal itself, by shortening the route between Europe and India by a distance that was variously estimated as between 2,000 and 3,000 "leagues," had indeed been advocated previously, as the words of the English Elizabethan playwright Christopher Marlowe in his *Tamburlaine the Great,* published in 1587, testify:

> Whereas the Terrene and the Red Sea meet,
> Being distant less than a full hundred leagues,
> I mean to cut a channel to them both
> That men might quickly sail to India.

Harun al-Rashid and the Venetians were among the other not-so-impractical visionaries who had previously shown interest in such a project—as, indeed, had Napoleon.[12] At the time of the French Revolution a British Consul, George Baldwin, had climbed the Great Pyramid in Egypt, and had poured upon the summit three libations, consisting of the waters of the Thames, the Ganges, and the Nile, thus prefiguring, as it were, their future confluence through the canal—a premature but meaningful gesture. Nevertheless, despite such auguries, the reaching of Anglo-French agreement upon the desirability of the canal's construction still represented, at that epoch, a triumph for common sense over mutual political suspicion. It was said, however, that the argument that carried the most weight with the British was that, had the canal been built in time, troops could have been transported from Britain to India quickly enough to have suppressed the Indian Mutiny.

From its Indian base, British power expanded east into Burma and west into Baluchistan. Burma was absorbed in stages, beginning in 1824–1826 when, as a result of the first Anglo-Burmese war, the British East

---

12. Lepère had prepared a paper for Napoleon on the *Canal des Deux Mers,* which de Lesseps, the builder of the canal, first read in 1832 when, as French Vice-Consul, he was quarantined for cholera in the lazaret of a ship in Alexandria.

India Company took the provinces of Arakan and Tenasserim. (The British had originally launched the campaign for the alleged purpose of recovering a relatively small sum of money claimed by a British captain named Lewis in compensation for slights inflicted and fines levied upon him by the Burmese authorities.) In 1852, after a second outbreak of hostilities, the British annexed the remainder of Lower Burma. Finally, in 1885, partly to forestall the French and partly for the sake of the territory itself, the British decided to take the remainder of the country. An ultimatum was sent to King Theebaw, who rejected it, after which a British expeditionary force marched to Theebaw's capital, Mandalay, and took the king prisoner. Upper Burma was formally annexed on January 1, 1886.

Meanwhile Baluchistan in the west had been annexed in 1887 after a period during which British influence had steadily grown stronger. Britain was, however, as already mentioned, less than successful in its attempts to dominate Afghanistan, which the British feared might fall under Russian domination and thus pose a threat to the British position in India itself. In 1838 the British invaded Afghanistan for the first time, sending the reigning ameer, Dost Mohammed, back to India as a prisoner. In 1841, however, an anti-British uprising occurred in Kabul, the capital, after which the British Army, retreating from Kabul in January, 1842, was annihilated with the exception of one single survivor. Kabul was recaptured by fresh British forces later in the year, after which Dost Mohammed was restored to power. A second Afghan war took place in 1878, after Dost Mohammed's son and successor, Shere Ali, had refused to receive a British mission at a time when Russian power in Central Asia was being extended. Once more a British army marched to Kabul, while the ameer, Shere Ali, fled the capital, dying shortly thereafter.

In 1879 the British concluded the Treaty of Gandamak with Afghanistan, by which Shere Ali's son, Yakub Khan, was recognized as ameer, and it was also agreed that a British Resident should be established in Kabul. Hardly had the Resident, Sir Louis Cavagnari, arrived, however, before he and his staff were assassinated. A British punitive expedition was sent to Afghanistan hanging and burning as it went, but it met with such effective resistance from the Afghans that it was obliged to withdraw after a political settlement had been reached. Under this settlement Abd-ur Rahman Khan, another grandson of Dost Mohammed, replaced Yakub Khan as ameer, and undertook not to enter into relations with other powers. In effect, Afghanistan became a buffer state between Russia and British India—a tacit arrangement that was later formalized by the Anglo-Russian Treaty of 1907.

Afghanistan was by no means the only buffer state between Russia and British India. Writing in the last twilight of British rule in India, one commentator stated:

The most important buffer zone in the world is that dividing Russia from the British Empire. Russia lies in the long curve of the British Empire rather like an egg in a spoon, but the two are separated by a layer of weak states stretching from the Near to the Far East: Turkey, Persia, Afghanistan, and China with its autonomous dependencies, Tibet and Manchuria. . . .[13]

Anglo-Indian relations with these buffer states varied according to time and circumstance. One of the more dramatic, and at times ludicrous, episodes was the British invasion of traditionally isolationist Tibet in 1904. The British had discovered that the Russians were in contact with the Dalai Lama, and were also much exercised about a Russian monk named Dorjieff who periodically visited Lhasa, the Tibetan Holy City, and who, they suspected, might be pursuing political or military, as well as religious, ends. There were even rumors that a Russian munitions factory had been established in Lhasa. Lord Curzon, then the British Viceroy in India, consequently dispatched a British expedition to Tibet, led by Colonel Younghusband. After an adventurous journey, made against stiff resistance, the expedition reached Lhasa, but found it devoid of Russian monks and munition factories alike. The victorious British then intended to make a dignified and impressive entrance into the Potala, or palace of the Dalai Lama, but found the steps as slippery as ice, as they had been polished smooth by the feet of generations of monks, so that ignominiously they had to cling to one another and to the walls while making their entrance. Despite the fact that the Dalai Lama had fled to Mongolia, the British then concluded a trade treaty with the Tibetans, and withdrew. The expedition, motivated by a mixture of unfounded fears and imperial ambitions, had clearly been unnecessary, and was much criticized, even in Britain itself. Subsequently both Russia and the United Kingdom recognized Chinese suzerainty over Tibet, and the matter was ended. The monk Dorjieff subsequently took up residence in Fontainebleau in France, where he established an unusual religious cult.

Under British rule India thus became the dominant power in Asia, with influence extending far beyond its own frontiers. Indian traders settled in Hong Kong and Sinkiang, and Indians emigrated not only to other Asian countries, such as Malaya, but also to South and East Africa, and even to British Guiana and the British West Indies. In lands around

13. Martin Wight of the British Royal Institute of International Affairs, writing in 1945. Another Briton, Guy Wint, has used another image: "The Indian Empire is to be thought of as consisting of a kernel which was the rich lands directly administered and of a protective rind; this rind was made up partly of minor and more or less primitive states, such as Bhutan and Nepal, and partly of mountain and desert territories. . . . Still further afield, and as a sort of open ground in front of the outworks, the Indian Government formed a ring of neutral states, Persia, Arabia, Tibet and Afghanistan, and even for a time a part of Sinkiang." (See *The British in Asia.*) In comparing the two statements, both of which refer to the same situation, a persistent note of ambiguity appears —Mr. Wight speaking of the "British Empire" and Mr. Wint of the "Indian Empire."

the earth, throughout the empire "on which the sun never set," Indian communities were to be found—a new circumstance that was an unforeseen by-product of British imperialism.

*Overland to the Pacific*

At about the time when the Dutch overseas empire was in its heyday, Russia was expanding eastward across Asia to the Pacific. From the early thirteenth century until 1480, when Ivan the Terrible refused to pay tribute to the Khan of the Golden Horde, the Russians had lived under Mongol subjugation. The pagan Mongols had, however, proved tolerant of the Christian religion. There had also been little Russo-Mongol intermarriage. With the waning of Mongol power, the Russians began to expand their frontiers eastward from the Ural mountains, which they crossed in 1581. The eastward movement had a spontaneous character of which the wild and adventurous spirit of the Cossacks provided much of the dynamic, although the enterprise of the Novgorod traders as well as the Russian sense of falling heir to the tradition of the Byzantine Empire provided other elements. Wherever conditions favorable to agriculture were to be found, the Cossacks settled, as they moved across the sparsely inhabited plains of northern Asia. Here intermarriage beween Russians and Mongols did occur to some degree, and it was not long before the Russian element outnumbered the population of the Mongol and other nomadic tribes of these regions. To the south the Russians established a cordon of forts, but to the east no frontier line was drawn until, in 1639, they caught sight of the waters of the Pacific.[14]

Some difficulties arose between Russia and China at this time, as a result of the vacuum left by the decline of Mongol power. Both the Russians and the Chinese appear initially to have underestimated each other's importance, and it was only after some sporadic conflicts that the Treaty of Nertchinsk—the first treaty between China and any European power—was concluded in 1689. Under its terms the boundaries between Russia and China were agreed upon, further Russian expansion to the south limited, and the situation stabilized. The treaty was to remain effectively in force for 150 years.

In 1730, during the reign of Peter the Great, Russia also began to expand its power south into the Central Asia region of Kazakhstan—an expansion that was not completed until 1819. Two principal hordes of Kazakhs lived in this large territory, one of which voluntarily transferred its allegiance from the Mongols to the Russians in 1734, so that, eventually, with relatively little fighting, the entire region became incorporated in Russia. One curious feature of Russo-Kazakh relations was that the

---

14. It was the Cossacks who later penetrated to San Francisco, where, about 1812–1815, they placed landmarks to establish a boundary line with the Spanish.

Russians mistakenly identified the Kazakhs as Tatars, for 120 years insisted on corresponding with them in the Tatar language, and are also said to have built a considerable number of mosques for their benefit, despite the fact that Kazakh notions of Islam remained somewhat vague.

Finally, between 1855 and 1881, the Russians moved south from Kazakhstan to the frontiers of Persia and Afghanistan. This final expansionary movement, which concluded with the battle of Geok-Tepe (at which a Turkoman fortress was captured), led to an oasis region of Muslim culture, containing the cities of Bokhara and Samarkand. The Russians appear to have been somewhat unwilling to assume responsibility for this new region, inhabited by Kirghiz, Uzbek, Turkmens, and Tadzhiks, but found that the southern frontiers of Kazakhstan afforded no protection from attacks against Russian caravans. Contemporary murmurings against Russian involvement in Central Asian affairs must have been loud, however, for Dostoevski, on the occasion of the capture of Geok-Tepe, penned a defense in answer to those Russians who asked the question, What is Asia to us? Proclaiming an Asian destiny, as well as a European one, for Russia, he wrote:

In Europe we were hangers-on and slaves, whereas we shall go to Asia as masters. In Europe we were Asiatics, whereas in Asia we, too, are Europeans. Our civilizing mission in Asia will bribe our spirit and drive us thither.

He then called for the construction of railroads, and—answering imaginary critics who raised the question of expense—exclaimed:

Then you speak about losses. Oh, if instead of us Englishmen or Americans inhabited Russia, they would show you what losses mean! They would certainly discover our America! Do you know that in Asia there are lands which are less explored than the interior of Africa? And do we know what riches are concealed in the bosom of these boundless lands? Oh, they would get at everything—metals and minerals, innumerable coal fields; they would find and discover everything—and they would know how to use these materials.[15]

Tsarist Russia, too, had its prophets of Manifest Destiny.

## The Opium Wars

The European subjugation of China in the nineteenth century was a logical consequence of the subjugation of India in the eighteenth. But here certain geographical and other differences however, produced a different pattern of domination. For one thing two powers and not four confronted each other—the United Kingdom on the one hand, and China on the other. The United Kingdom, after the defeat of Napoleon at Waterloo in 1815, was at the zenith of its powers and wealth, and was profiting already from the first fruits of the industrial revolution.

15. *The Diary of a Writer,* Vol. II.

China, for its part, unlike India, was a centralized state, under the rule of an emperor. Even more than India at the time of the coming of the Europeans, China was uninterested in foreign trade, since, as we noted, the Chinese felt that the Europeans had no commodities that were of value to them. At the beginning of the century what trade there was was carried on by the British East India Company, which gave bullion in exchange for the Chinese tea and silks that they sought. Soon, however, a lucrative alternative to bullion was found—opium. Grown for the most part in India, and smuggled illegally into China, where it was literally imposed by force on certain Chinese coastal regions, through piratical "trading expeditions," the trade in opium was conducted by the British in the face of a categorical ban imposed by the Chinese imperial government with the approval of the emperor himself, who quite naturally had the welfare of his subjects at heart. It was also the impression of the Chinese that the British government was itself also opposed to the opium trade, and that therefore the trade was conducted only by adventurers operating outside governmental control. But the Chinese were mistaken in this assumption.

An attempt by the Chinese to suppress the trade ended disastrously for them. Lin Tse-Hsu, the Viceroy of Hu-Kuang Province, was appointed as a special commissioner with the widest powers to act. Attempting to encourage legitimate trade but to suppress the trade in opium, he confiscated 20,000 chests of opium from the European merchants, and had them publicly destroyed. At this juncture a relatively minor incident—the killing of a Chinese by some British sailors—led to a naval confrontation between the ships of the two powers. The British vessels were the first to attack, sinking the fleet of Chinese war junks, and so firing the opening shots of the first Opium War. The war, which lasted from 1839 to 1842, was won by the British, who occupied Shanghai, reached the Yangtze, and advanced on Nanking. The Treaty of Nanking, signed in August, 1842, set the pattern for the total domination of China that was to follow. Hong Kong, was annexed, and five "treaty ports"—Shanghai, Ning-po, Foo-Chow, Amoy, and Canton—were opened to foreign trade. A warship was to be stationed at each of the ports, consular officers were to reside on shore, and foreign merchants were enabled to trade "without molestation or restraint." A ransom was also exacted by the British as compensation for not plundering certain Chinese towns.

Two years later treaties similar in their main provisions—except, of course, the annexation of Hong Kong—were accorded to the United States, France, Belgium, and Sweden-Norway. In the case of at least one of these powers—the United States, which in 1844 concluded the

Treaty of Wanghia with China—the negotiation "was not unaccompanied by veiled threats."[16] The Treaty of Wanghia also introduced the principle of extraterritorial rights[17]—rights that were specifically defined both in this treaty and in the other treaties between China and the European powers that were subsequently concluded. China's isolation from the world had finally been breached.

One of the provisions of the Treaty of Nanking had particularly far-reaching effects. The Chinese, apparently at the instigation of the United States, had insisted that other European powers besides the United Kingdom should be allowed to trade at the treaty ports. This would appear to give China the chance to play one European power against another, and thus more opportunity to safeguard her own sovereignty. As it transpired, however, the Americo-European powers made common cause against the Chinese, so that any concession made to one was soon demanded by all. Thus were planted the seeds of what was later to be known as the "Open Door" policy. In the years ahead the European powers, acting in concert, were to continue to force China, whether willing or not, to trade with them. Moreover, European nationals were to become a specially privileged group, entitled to exemption from the normal processes of justice to which all others, Chinese or not, were subject. The possibility had now been created, in China as well as in India and elsewhere, that in any dispute between a European and an Asian, it might be decided that the European must automatically be considered right by virtue of the fact that he was a European. Evidently, once such a possibility had been introduced, China was falling under European domination, and losing a part of its sovereignty.

The European merchants were, however, despite their triumphs, somewhat disgruntled. The legendary wealth of Cathay that they were now in a position to tap was failing to materialize. Refusing to admit the possibility that the goods that they had to offer might not be desired by the Chinese, they began to press for fresh concessions to be made to the European powers by the Chinese government. Diplomatic relations must be opened with Peking itself. The European merchants must be permitted to navigate freely on the Yangtze. They must also be allowed free access to every part of the Celestial Empire. Finally, the opium trade and the trade in forced Chinese labor, more generally known as the "pig trade," should be legalized.[18]

Naturally, however, no independent Chinese government could have

16. Samuel Flagg Bemis, *A Diplomatic History of the United States* (third edition, 1950), p. 345.
17. Extraterritoriality is defined as the possession or exercise of political rights by a foreign power within a state.
18. According to K. M. Pannikar, it was the "poison trade" (opium) and the "pig trade" (transportation of forced Chinese labor) that "made the iron enter the soul of the Chinese and made them bitterly anti-foreign." (*Asia and Western Dominance*, 1953).

assented to all these demands, and at best could only have given conditional assent to some of them. When the British authorities began to extend immunity to Chinese nationals whom they took under their protection—and specifically, in 1857, a Chinese pirate named Li Ming-Tai—the Chinese government felt obliged to resist the British demands. The United Kingdom was thereupon joined by its ancient rival, France, in pressing matters further. In the Anglo-French war against China of 1857–1858 which followed, the Chinese, despite a diversion elsewhere of British military strength to deal with the Indian Mutiny, were again defeated. Four new treaties, known collectively as the Treaties of Tientsin, were then, in 1858, concluded between China on the one hand, and the United Kingdom, France, Russia, and the United States on the other. Under the terms of these treaties eleven more ports were opened to foreign trade, and Europeans obtained not only the right to free navigation on the Yangtze, but also to travel and trade throughout China, protected by the principle of extraterritoriality. The traffic in opium was legalized, as also was the trade in Chinese labor. European representation was also to be established in Peking. The Christian religion was to be tolerated, and missionaries and Chinese converts protected. European officials were also permitted, as agents of the Chinese government, to collect customs dues on imports.

But hostilities, were not yet over. Friction developed between the British representative, Lord Elgin, and the Chinese authorities over the implementation of the terms of the treaty, with the result that fighting, in which the French once more joined, was resumed for a further two years. The Anglo-French forces finally succeeded in forcing their way to Peking, but not before the exceptionally beautiful Chinese imperial Summer Place had been burned down on Lord Elgin's orders—an event that, far from impressing the Chinese with the folly of resisting Britain's might, as it was intended to do, instead instilled in them a deep resentment toward a nation that could perform such an insensate act. The Convention of Peking, in which the United Kingdom obtained Kowloon, near Hong Kong, and in which the British and the French also exacted apologies and indemnities from the Chinese imperial government, patched up the peace once more.

The years that followed were marked by considerable confusion. The defeat of the Chinese in the First Opium War had already startled both the Chinese and the Japanese peoples, and the consequent concessions made by the Chinese government to the Europeans had aroused considerable feeling in China—feeling that led to a revolt against the imperial Manchu authority, known as the Taiping Rebellion. The strength of the Europeans had been ascribed by many to Christianity, with the result that, particularly in the south of China, anti-Manchu sentiment combined with a form of Christianity to form a new movement that came near to overthrowing the Manchu dynasty. The Taiping Rebellion was only eventually suppressed when, at the conclusion of the Anglo-French wars against China, or "Foreign Wars" as they were called, the Europeans assisted the Manchus to restore their authority. This was not done, however, before the Taipings had for a time gained control of the Yangtze valley, and, for ten years, had established a "Celestial King" ruling from the city of Nanking. Not until 1864, by which time innumerable lives had been lost, heavy blows dealt to China's cultural heritage, and the Yangtze valley devastated, was peace restored. The Europeans, having first forced the Chinese government to submit to them, had now succeeded in placing their yoke upon the necks of the dissatisfied Chinese populations.

Further troubles were to ensue. No sooner was this fourteen-year rebellion repressed than another fourteen-year rebellion occurred, lasting from 1864 to 1878, in which the province of Sinkiang, under the leadership of the gifted Yakub Beg, attempted to secede in order to form an independent Muslim state. Yakub Beg was relatively successful for a while, and even entered into relations with foreign powers, including the United Kingdom, which at one time suggested to the Chinese that they might accept the existence of an independent Muslim Sinkiang. The suggestion was rejected, however, and after a time the Chinese reasserted their authority, and destroyed the vestiges of Yakub Beg's independent state.

Meanwhile, between the end of the Taiping Rebellion in 1864, and the Sino-Japanese war of 1895, the European powers consolidated their position in China, through settlements, missions, and concessions. First in the treaty ports and then elsewhere European "settlements" were established over which the Chinese had no jurisdiction, and where Europeans had their own law courts and municipalities. Many European missions also infringed further upon Chinese sovereignty. For example, without any legal justification the French erected a cathedral, in Tientsin itself, upon the site of a temple. Difficulties between missionaries and their converts on the one hand, and the Chinese people on the other were, on occasion, "resolved" by the resort of calling upon European military power, in the shape of the gunboats that patrolled the Yangtze. "Concessions"—in effect, small independent states—were established in some of the main treaty ports. The most notable concession was certainly that of Shanghai, where the British concession developed, in the course of time, into a virtual sovereign state with an influence rivaling that of the Chinese government in Peking itself.

As a new trade network, run by a rising Indian middle class, had developed in Calcutta and elsewhere in India, so a new Chinese middle class began to accede to wealth through helping to run the European trading system that extended throughout China from its focal point in Shanghai. While the structure of the Chinese government still appeared sturdy enough to the casual observer, in fact it was being steadily undermined by the military, commercial, political, and religious incursions of the Europeans, while opium was being openly distributed as a commodity like any other, and individual Chinese could be, and were, abducted or kidnaped to be sold abroad in the coolie traffic, in which cheap Chinese labor was shipped to California, Hawaii, the Philippines, Australia, and ports of Latin America, such as Cuba and Peru. China, beaten, occupied, and humiliated, was approaching the point at which the discredited central government—headed, except for a short interval, from 1860 to 1908 by the dowager empress Tzu Hsi—would finally collapse, and the Celestial Empire itself be divided up among rival European imperialisms.

A threatening sign of such a denouement was the stripping away from China of some of the surrounding states that had previously recognized Chinese hegemony in Eastern Asia—Cambodia, which became a French protectorate in 1863; Indo-China, comprising the Annamite kingdom, Cochin-China, and parts of Siam, which all, partly by treaty and partly by conquest, passed under the authority of the French at various dates between 1861 and 1886; and Burma, which, as mentioned earlier, was finally annexed by the British in 1886. Tibet, too, as we have seen, was invaded by the British considerably later on, and assigned the status of a buffer state under Chinese suzerainty. In Manchuria and Korea, Chinese influence was, in due course, to be challenged primarily not by a European but by an Asian power—Japan.

In the Indo-China region, acceptance of the French, who like the British elsewhere in Asia had made a point of attempting to demonstrate their "racial superiority" in many small ways, was less than enthusiastic, and local or regional uprisings against the French were of frequent occurrence. Siam itself, by virtue of its position as a buffer state between British India and French Indo-China, was able to maintain a precarious independence, due in some measure, to able statecraft on the part of King Chulalancorn.

## Japan Reopened

Japan, some years earlier, had, like China, been forced out of her isolation and obliged to open her ports to American and European shipping, and her courts to foreign diplomats. Once the United States had acquired California, which it did in 1844, the Pacific, and Japan in particular, took on a new significance in American diplomacy. The Japanese, meanwhile, were well aware of the Chinese defeat in the

Opium War, as well as of the terms of the Treaty of Nanking that had concluded it, and had understood that their turn must soon come. They had, therefore, to some extent prepared themselves in advance against the event, both by readying their defenses, and by considering the political implications. Unlike the Chinese, the Japanese had some advance knowledge of what was to come, and were therefore in a better position to try to turn the unsought yet seemingly unavoidable experience to national advantage.

On July 8, 1853, four American ships under the command of Commodore Matthew Perry arrived off Uraga on the Japanese island of Honshu with a letter from the United States President, Millard Fillmore. The letter was friendly in tone, but hinted that a larger American naval force was to visit Japan in the following year. The Shogunate decided not only to comply with the desire of the Americans and to open Japanese ports to American and European trade, but also to learn American and European techniques with a view to dealing with the Americans and Europeans on terms of equality at a later date. In 1854 Perry returned as promised with a larger fleet, and demanded a treaty similar to that which the United States had obtained from China. The treaty of friendship which resulted opened two of the smaller Japanese ports—Hakodate and Shimoda—and permitted a U.S. consul to reside at Shimoda. No provision was made for coaling American ships in Japan, but as Perry had used the interval between his two visits to establish a coaling base at Okinawa, after signing an agreement with the ruler of the Lew Chew island group to which it belonged, this did not constitute an immediate problem. Other treaties were shortly after concluded by Japan with the United Kingdom, Holland, and Russia, thus widening the scope of European relations with Japan. It was, however, the first American Consul at Shimoda, Townsend Harris, who concluded in 1858 what may be considered as the definitive agreement that guided Japanese commercial relations with the U.S. (similar treaties applied to relations with European powers) for the rest of the nineteenth century. This "Treaty of Commerce and Navigation" opened further Japanese ports to U.S. trade, imposed a low scale of import duties, provided for Japanese representation in Washington and U.S. representation at Yedo (Tokyo), gave Americans extraterritorial rights in the treaty ports, and increased the number of U.S. consuls in Japan to six. Japan was also invited to study naval construction, and to buy both merchant vessels and warships from the United States. In negotiating this treaty, Harris informed the Japanese that the U.S. was not itself threatening Japan, but that if the treaty were not concluded other powers would exact treaties by force which would contain less favorable terms. The British, he alleged, were even then preparing to send a fifty-ship expedition to

Japan from Hong Kong in order to obtain such a treaty. The Japanese, in agreeing to conclude the treaty, were impressed by these arguments, but were even more decisively influenced by the fact that that same year—1858—China had been forced by European guns to conclude the far more disadvantageous treaties of Tientsin.

The opening of Japan, however, soon produced an intensely strong internal upheaval. Patriotic feeling against the Europeans and Americans ran high, and focused not only against them, but also against the authority—the Shogunate—that had permitted them to enter the country. For almost 700 years the Shogun had ruled at the head of the Bakufu, or "tent government," which was military in form. The Emperor had exercised an authority that was primarily mystical in nature, being consequently unconcerned with military decisions. After the entry of the Europeans and Americans, however, the *daimyos,* or feudal lords, used popular discontent to overthrow the Shogunate and to restore administrative authority to the Emperor. A form of government was instituted which followed a Chinese model first introduced into Japan in A.D. 702, which was based upon Confucian principles. Not surprisingly, the American and European diplomats who had just arrived in Japan, and who had been confidently dealing with the Shogunate as the legitimate authority, did not understand the significance of the revolutionary events that occurred, and for a time became confused.

The period from 1858 to 1868, at which latter date the Emperor's power was finally restored, was punctuated by a series of dramatic and frequently violent events. The Emperor had, at the outset, only placed his signature on the various treaties with the foreigners, or "red-haired barbarians," as they were known, upon the private understanding that they would be driven out of Japan as soon as possible. The Shogunate had, in fact, agreed to fix a precise date for their expulsion—June 24, 1863. A climate of xenophobia spread throughout Japan, and individual Americans and Europeans were subjected to sudden assassination and other types of attack from groups of Japanese patriots who held their own lives cheap. Foreign shipping was attacked, and the British and United States legations burned down. The British Royal Navy thereupon destroyed the city of Kagoshima, and a United States warship sank some hostile Japanese vessels. In 1864 a joint American-European naval force, with the tacit support of the Shogunate, bombarded Shimonoseki, and indemnities were obtained from Japan as compensation for European and American losses. These events, together with the advice of Japanese returning from missions abroad, succeeded in convincing the new authorities that Japan could not now return to its isolation, but must meet the challenge of foreign influence as best it could. Once the Shogunate had been defeated in a brief civil war, the new regime proved to be one of great stability. The Emperor's administration was given the title *Meiji,* or the "Enlightened Government." Under Meiji rule Japan made technical progress at a speed that astonished other nations, and soon emerged as a great power in Eastern Asia.

The story of the consolidation of the final stages of the European domination of Asia is therefore complicated by a paradox: the European states striving to wrest sovereignty and influence from a prostrate China were joined by Japan, a resurgent Asian power seeking to demonstrate to the world its right to be accorded great power status.

## The Open Door Policy

Acting in its new role as a great power, Japan viewed the Korean peninsula as of particular strategic interest, and sought to increase its influence there. Korea, however, only recognized a tenuous bond with Japan, having traditionally accepted the suzerainty of China. Anxious to forestall Russia, which was also showing interest in Korea, Japan pressed the question of Korea's allegiance, and war between China and Japan ensued in 1894. In this war, as in the Russo-Japanese war that took place ten years later, Japan was victorious. However, whereas the later war confirmed Japan's strength and claims to be considered as a world power, the Sino-Japanese war of 1894–1895 was merely taken by the other powers as a final proof of Chinese weakness. Having obtained the surrender of the Chinese fleet (which had not been supplied with enough ammunition to fight effectively), defeated the Chinese forces in Korea, and marched its armies into Manchuria, Japan concluded the Treaty of Shimonoseki in 1895. Korea was recognized as an independent state instead of a Chinese dependency, and China lost Taiwan and the Pescadores to Japan. Japan would also have obtained the Liaotung Peninsula in Manchuria had not Russia, France, and Germany prevented it. (Germany, a new arrival in Asian affairs, was already involved in Samoa, and in 1892 had intervened militarily in China, occupying the port of Tsingtao in Shantung.) A large indemnity was also to be paid by China to Japan, to raise money for which China turned to European powers for loans. China was now under the financial control of Europe, and it became generally felt that the partition of its territory could not now be long delayed.

By 1898, whether by acquisition, leasehold, or the establishment of "spheres of influence," most of China was effectively under foreign domination, and the central government had become more than ever a convenient fiction. In the south and west the French had established themselves in Szechwan, Yunnan, Kwangsi, Kwangtung, and the island of Hainan. The United Kingdom held the Yangtze valley and some large areas in the south, as well as Kowloon, and a naval base at Wei-hai-Wei in the north. The Japanese had Fukien province, opposite Taiwan, which they also held, and the Germans had the province of Shantung. Russian interest in Manchuria was complicated by Japanese aspirations there, although for the moment, with the support given by France and Germany —who obtained European advantages for according it—Russia remained predominant. Special emphasis was placed by each European power on obtaining railway concessions, since railways not only formed highways of trade, but could also be used for swift transport of troops. Soon, in addition to the gunboats on China's rivers, railroad tracks snaked their way over her inland territory, being set down like manacles upon whole provinces. The French, indeed, thought out a doctrine based upon railroad links which was called the doctrine of "soldering"—and foresaw the day when the French-controlled provinces of China would be "soldered" by railroad tracks to French Indochina. All that was now needed was for the partition of China to be formally recognized.

At this moment, when history seemed to hesitate before happening, the United States announced the formulation of an "Open Door" policy for China. The announcement took the form of notes sent by the U.S. Secretary of State John Hay to the United Kingdom, Russia, Germany, France, and Japan at various dates between September and November, 1899. In effect the notes proposed that "spheres of influence" should not affect the treaty rights of other nations, that the Chinese government should collect customs dues, and that harbor and railway dues should not be levied in such a way as to benefit any one power. China was not to be partitioned, but was to remain open to joint competitive exploitation.

The United States, up to this time, had been sufficiently absorbed in its own continental affairs not to have played a principal role in Asian affairs. Before the Spanish-American war of 1898, according to S. F. Bemis, the American historian, "the average American citizen could not have told you whether Filipinos were Far Eastern aborigines or a species of tropical nuts."[19] Whereas the United States had participated in trade and missionary activities in China, its investments in China were smaller than those of any of the other major powers involved, and it had made no demands for either naval bases, or for a "sphere of influence." In 1898, however, during the war with Spain, a U.S. naval force had captured the Philippines with the help, at first, of Philippino patriots led by Emilio Aguinaldo. Under the terms of the peace treaty with Spain, concluded in 1899, the Philippines were annexed by the United States, which, in this acquisition, now felt that it had an Eastern Asian

19. *A Diplomatic History of the United States* (third edition, 1950), p. 469. Finley Peter Dunne, an American humorist of that epoch, made his "Mr. Dooley," a Chicago Irishman, tell a friend apropos of the Philippines in 1899: " 'tis not more than two months since ye larned whether they were islands or canned goods."

base comparable to that of the British in Hong Kong, the Germans in Kiachow, and the Russians in Port Arthur. U.S. Senator Albert J. Beveridge, speaking in the Senate in January, 1900, on a resolution defining U.S. policy toward the Philippines, said:

The Philippines are ours forever. . . And just beyond the Philippines are China's illimitable markets. We will not retreat from either. . . . We will not abandon our opportunity in the Orient. We will not renounce our part in the mission of our race, trustee, under God, of the civilization of the world. . . . Our largest trade henceforth must be with Asia. The Pacific is our ocean. More and more Europe will manufacture the most it needs, secure from its colonies the most it consumes. Where shall we turn for consumers of our surplus? Geography answers the question. China is our natural customer. She is nearer to us than to England, Germany, or Russia, the commercial powers of the present and the future. They have moved nearer China by securing permanent bases on her borders. The Philippines gives us a base at the door of all the East.

Should China now be partitioned, however, the United States would find itself excluded, and the opportunity offered by China's "illimitable markets" would go to others. Under the "Open Door" policy, however, U.S. commercial interests would be safeguarded.

Of even greater weight than U.S. sponsorship in the acceptance of the "Open Door" policy by the powers of Europe was the attitude of the United Kingdom, which was still the major world power, and which still controlled the seas. The United Kingdom, in fact, decided that, being itself able to compete commercially with her European rivals in the China trade, it would be preferable to choose the "Open Door," rather than to acquiese in China's partition—a partition, moreover, that might lead to the formation of new Asian land empires that might one day threaten British India. There are even indications that Hay's "Open Door" letters may perhaps have been originally of British inspiration. Certainly there appears to have been some coincidence of Anglo-American interests, as well as something approaching a tacit understanding whereby the United Kingdom would leave the United States a free hand in the New World (where the possibility of a canal across the isthmus of Panama was then being explored), in return for a joint approach to the China question.

Before the "Open Door" policy was formalized, however, it was to be tested by the reactions of the European powers to the Chinese Boxer[20] uprising of 1900. The Boxer uprising was a powerful anti-European outbreak that had some encouragement from the Dowager Empress of China. European, American, and Japanese troops intervened, and for a time there seemed a possibility that events would precipitate a partition of China. But the uprising was suppressed, punishment and reparations

20. The name "Boxer" came from a loose translation of the Chinese name for the groups that together formed the "Society of Harmonious Fists."

exacted from China, and the matter left there. In 1903 the "Open Door" policy was crystallized in the form of a Chinese-American Treaty of Commerce, which, in addition to the previous proposals, specified that U.S. policy toward China was, among other things, to "preserve Chinese territorial and administrative entity . . . and safeguard for the world the principle of equal and impartial trade with all parts of the Chinese Empire." The policy was supported by the United Kingdom, France, and Germany, although hardly by Russia and Japan, who, in 1904, were to resort to armed conflict against each other for the possession of parts of China's territory.

The white man's domination of Asia had now reached its apogee. The two main events still to occur in the East before the First World War—the Russo-Japanese war of 1904–1905, and the fall of the Manchu dynasty and its replacement by a revolutionary Republic in 1911—were both, in a sense, tremors in advance, proclaiming the great upheavals to come. For the moment, however, Asia appeared more than ever to belong to the white man. The white man's warships ruled the rivers and the seas; his telegraphs linked vast distances; his railroads bound province and region together in a long unending chain. Throughout Asia, in his work as in his play, most of the immediate advantages were in his favor, and the facilities at his disposal. In India the British Raj appeared at the height of its majesty. In China, a vast future was opening. Not those with the sharpest eyes, or those with the most carefully attuned ears, could, in those years before the First World War, have guessed what destiny held in store for Asia in the years to come. To foresee destiny's secret, the gift of prophecy itself was needed.

# Chapter 7

# "The Dark Continent":

# The European Occupation

# of Africa

*Lo! Christian Europe, fair exalted state,*
*Excelling all in might and manners meet,*
*Afric, for worldly wealth insatiate,*
*Incult, and all brutality complete.*
—Camoëns, from *The Lusiad* (1572). Book X, Verse 92

I prefer land to niggers. —Cecil Rhodes (Circa 1894)

WHY WAS AFRICA, which lies so close to Europe, the last of the continents to fall under European dominion? There are a number of reasons for the postponement of any European attempt at political domination—reasons that have varied at different epochs. The fact remains striking, however, that, whereas the Europeans upon arrival in the Americas virtually immediately stormed their way to power, it was not until almost all the rest of the world had become subject to Europe's sway that age-old Africa, too, at last was occupied.

Propinquity had meant that contact between Africa and Europe, in some form, had been a constant factor from the beginning of recorded history. Geography, however, had meant that, except for those who had filtered north or south across the Sahara, or up or down the Nile valley, white Europe and black Africa had remained insulated from one another until the time when the Portuguese caravels had found out the sea road which led past Cape Bojador. Climate had meant that, even after the Portuguese monopoly was broken, and ships of other nationalities came raiding and trading down the African coast, Europeans could not hope to settle in most of the parts of Africa that they knew. In the absence of accurate medical knowledge, malaria alone—apart from yellow fever, sleeping sickness, or the darts and musket balls of hostile Africans— earned the West African coast the name of the "White Man's Grave."

"There is no other region of the world," wrote the English traveler Mary Kingsley in 1897, "that can match West Africa for the steady kill, kill, kill that its malaria works on the white men who come under its influence." Only in the twentieth century can it be said that mortality from malaria has markedly decreased. Before then, the pattern was invariably the same. In 1554 the first Englishmen, Wyndham, to sail to West Africa died of fever on the Benin River with two-thirds of his crews. "Of seven score men, scarce forty returned to Plymouth of whom also many died." In 1825, a detachment of 108 troops landed at the Gambia; four months later only 21 remained alive. In 1832 two British ships sailed up the Niger. On one of them 15 men died of malaria, and 4 men survived; on the other, 24 died, and 5 lived. Writing of her 1895 visit to West Africa, Mary Kingsley reported, "At Accra, after I left it, and all along the Gold Coast, came one of those dreadful epidemic outbursts sweeping away more than half of the white population in a few weeks." She also added: "Do what you may it is almost certain you will get fever during a residence of more than six months on the Coast, and the chances are two to one on the Gold Coast that you will die of it. But, without precautions, you will probably have it within a fortnight of first landing, and your chances of surviving are almost nil."

Why did the Europeans first go to Africa? Why did they then lose interest in it? Why did they later, in the nineteenth century, regain interest to the extent of partitioning in between them? The answers to these questions may be given with some degree of certainty. We have already touched upon some of them. The Europeans first went to Africa to obtain gold for use in the Asian trade, and to find out the sea route around Africa to India, the Spice Islands, and Cathay. The Europeans then lost interest in Africa because they became absorbed in their newly discovered Asian and American empires. The Europeans regained interest in Africa in the nineteenth century because, having consolidated their hold on other continents, they began to jockey for strategic positions in Africa—a land mass that lay athwart the key military-trade axis between Britain and India. This axis in the nineteenth century became the lifeline of British world power, and, after the opening of the Suez Canal in 1869, it ran in a double strand—around the north as well as around the south of Africa.

The history of Europe's relations with Africa up to 1914 therefore falls into three phases: the first, or Portuguese, phase; next, the period when Europe virtually lost interest in Africa, except as a source for slaves; and the final phase, in which Europe explored, scrambled for, and colonized Africa.

## The Portuguese Adventurers

Apart from other intimations of African realities, some Europeans received a firsthand report from a European upon conditions in the hinterland of West Africa as long as thirty-one years before Cape Bojador was rounded. In 1413 a Frenchman named Anselm d'Isalguier had returned to Marseilles from West Africa after an absence of eleven years. It is not clear under what circumstances d'Isalguier, a native of Toulouse, had gone to Africa. He may have formed a part of a Norman experition under the leadership of Jean de Bethencourt which set out to conquer the Canary Islands, and which had included recruits from the Toulouse area. De Bethancourt is also known to have landed on the African mainland. In any event, d'Isalguier spent some years in Gao on the Niger, from where he returned to Europe accompanied by an African wife named Casais, a daughter, and an entourage of three eunuchs and three African women, as well as a dowry of gold and jewels.

The gold in particular must have aroused interest—even more so, perhaps, than the fact that one of the eunuchs set up as a doctor, and numbered the Dauphin Charles among his patients. Europe lacked gold to pay for the produce of Asia that, coming overland, was so much in demand. Although it was not included by Azurara in the six reasons that he cites as motivating Henry the Navigator in his actions,[1] it is known that Henry's imagination had been kindled by what he had heard in Ceuta of the African gold trade, and one may be certain that he, no less than the specie-hungry bankers of Europe, wished to penetrate the secret of where the Barbary Moors obtained their gold. By the middle of the fifteenth century, while Portuguese caravels continued to explore the African coastline, attempts were being made by European merchants to find a trans-Sahara route that would lead them to the source of the gold. One of these merchants, a Genoese named Malfante, penetrated to the middle of the Sahara, from where he sent back a report on his progress which was the last that was heard of him. Another, a Florentine named Benedetto Dei, was the first European known to reach Timbuktu, where he established himself in business, eventually returning home safely.

It was the sea route, however, which led the more surely to the gold. But, although the Portuguese occasionally obtained some gold or gold dust here and there along the West African coast, it was not until they

1. See Chapter 3, p. 42.

reached Elmina in 1471 that they found it regularly obtainable and in quantity. The source of this gold was evidently Ashanti, but the Portuguese were content to trade for it on the coast, and made no attempt to seize the gold fields themselves. The Wangara deposits that were the source of the trans-Sahara trade, and that lay between the sources of the Senegal and the Niger rivers, remained for the moment beyond their reach. In fact, only, in 1550 did a party of Portuguese reach the Bambuk gold mines of Wangara, and even then none of them returned alive.

After some argument in the council of the King of Portugal, it was decided to build a fortress at Mina—the "Mine"—from which the modern Elmina takes its name. This was a stronghold which was to play an important part in the international power struggle to come. One court faction had maintained that to build the fortress would be "very dangerous, and, in fact, impossible, or, even if they allowed it to be built, its upkeep would be very difficult, both on account of the great remoteness of the land and because the climate was very sickening and the Negroes little truthful and less trustworthy." King John II nevertheless overruled these arguments, and sent out an expedition under the command of Diego da Azambuja, one of his knights, carrying with them all the timber and stone necessary for the fortress, ready "cut and shaped" in Portugal so that construction could take place without delay. "And . . . the whole . . . was carried in urcas and great ships with the idea that they might not return or sail any more, and besides these, there went other ships and caravels, strong and sound, with many provisions, medicines, and rich wares."[2] After permission had been obtained from "Caramansa, whom the Negroes called king," San Jorge da Mina was then erected, placed under the command of a royal governor, and manned with a garrison. From this time on the amount of gold obtained by the Portuguese from Elmina has been estimated to have averaged the equivalent of $280,000 a year.

It is a curious fact of history that Christopher Columbus, who had once sailed north to Iceland, had also visited this southerly extremity of the (to him) known world. He was, it appears, much impressed by "Guinea." S. E. Morison comments:

Columbus either took part in d'Azambuja's expedition, or made a voyage to Mina shortly after the castle was built. This is proved by the postils he jotted down on the margins of his favorite books. In his copy of Aeneas Sylvius' "Historia Rerun," opposite a passage where Eratosthenes is quoted as to the climate below the equator being temperate, Columbus writes "Perpendicularly under the equator is the castle of Mina of the most serene King of Portugal, which we have seen.[3]

2. From Ruy de Pina's *Chronicle of John II* (1482), translated by J. W. Blake in *Europeans in West Africa* (1942).
3. *Admiral of the Ocean Sea* (1942).

Because of Columbus's failure to mention da Azambuja, Morison believes that Columbus visited Elmina in 1482–1483, or 1483–1484, "perhaps both years."

On the palimpsest of African history, the story of the Portuguese is written in strongly marked and recognisable characters, showing through the later inscriptions in many places. Relatively few in numbers as the Portuguese were, they affected the course of events in more than one country.

That the Portuguese achieved as much as they did was undoubtedly due to the fact that they did not recognize their own limitations. For example, among the presents taken by an early Portuguese embassy to the Negus of Ethiopia was a *mappamundi*, given to show "Prester John the roundness of the world." The Negus, at that time—in 1523—Lebna Dengel, asked to be shown Portugal on the globe, and when shown it, exclaimed how little it was. How could such a small country prevent the Turks from holding the Red Sea? Should they not call in the Kings of France and Spain to help? The Portuguese were disconcerted: it had never occurred to them that their country would appear to others as small. Like the Spaniards in the New World—Cortes had taken the Mexican capital a mere two years earlier—they had not realized their limitations. (Circumstances in Mexico, however, had differed from those in Ethiopia: Montezuma, unlike the Negus, had not been a Christian, nor had he required help against Muslim attackers). Faced with the Ethiopian's awkward question, the Portuguese dissembled, and the Negus went on to speak of other things. Nevertheless, history answered the question that the Portuguese could not: Portugal was too small a country. In their own interest, as well, perhaps, as in that of beleagured Christian Ethiopia, they should have called in the Kings of France and Spain.

Too few to consolidate their hold on all the territories and oceans to which they penetrated, they nevertheless left their mark behind them. The passage of the Portuguese is to be found, for example, in many a West African place name—Sierra Leone, the lionlike mountains; Cape Palmas, the cape of palms; Cabo Corso (Cape Coast), the cruising cape; Lagos, the lakes; Calabar, "the bar is silent"; Cameroons, prawns; Gabon, "the hooded cloak," from the shape of the estuary. Even the name "Abyssinia" itself owes something to the Portuguese, being a Portuguese version of an Arab and Indian term for "Negro"—*Habesh*. They also introduced new crops and plants into tropical Africa—oranges, lemons, limes, sugar cane, cacao, chili peppers, yams, maize, red wheat, tobacco, tomato, pineapple, rice, beans, guavas, pawpaws, small bananas, and even manioc (cassava), which is now, under various names, a main staple of African diet. In the 1890s the Gallas of Harar were found to be venerating a sixteenth-century Portuguese sword which they said had once belonged to a great hero who had come into the country long ago. In Nigeria, Benin tradition records that in the years 1485–1486 a Portuguese named John Affonso d'Aveiro visited Benin City, and "introduced guns and coconuts."[4]

In West Africa, as they worked their way down the coast, the Portuguese set up a number of bases. Arguin, the first, later dwindled in importance. Santiago, in the Cape Verde Islands, was the next to be established. Here, away from the mosquito-ridden coast, health conditions were better, so that Portuguese colonists came and settled. Agents who were sent from the Cape Verdes to the mainland, and who were expected to forward Portugal's civilizing mission as well as to obtain gold and other commodities, soon settled down, married African wives, and formed a society that as J. D. Fage has expressed it, "was free from the more annoying restrictions of both European and African life." Exiles and criminals were attracted by these libertarian conditions, with the result that the Senegal-Sierra Leone area became a haven for traders of ill-repute from many European countries, who flourished with the slave trade. Their interests, rather than Portugal's, were served by their penetrations into the hinterland, and the rare official Portuguese appearances there—for example, those of the Portuguese embassies that reached Timbuktu and Mali—had little effect.

Moving east, the next base was Elmina. Throughout the Portuguese period the "Mina coast," as it was usually referred to by contemporary writers, was the principal scene of commercial activity, as storms and offshore currents discouraged regular landings on the harborless Grain and Ivory Coasts. Mortality on the coast was so high, however, and John II of Portugal had such difficulty in recruiting men to go to Elmina that he was obliged to ask the Pope to grant the same dispensation that had been accorded to crusaders. In 1481 the request was heard, and Sixtus IV granted "a plenary indulgence for the remission of all the sins of every member of the faithful who should happen to die in the castle already built or about to be built in Mina in Africa." (Less than 40 years earlier, it will be recalled, Henry the Navigator had gained a similar dispensation for his Order of Christ.

Plenary indulgences may have reconciled many to the idea of death, but they did not prevent deaths from taking place. Friendly relations were established with the Kingdom of Benin in 1483, a Benin Ambassador—"a man of good speech and natural wisdom"—was received in Lisbon, and "the first pepper from Guinee" was shipped to Portugal from Benin. After this auspicious beginning, however, the Portuguese trading

4. The coastal cocoanut palm is distributed along tropical coasts from Indonesia to West Africa. It originated in the Pacific. Duarte Lopes, the sixteenth-century Portuguese chronicler, says that the Portuguese found the cocoa-nut palm growing in West Africa when they arrived.

post at Gwato, the port of Benin, which had been opened in 1486, had to be closed about thirty years later "as the land was afterwards found to be very dangerous from sickness." The disappointment of the Portuguese, who used the nearby islands of Sao Tome and Fernando Po instead, was somewhat tempered by the fact that they had meanwhile obtained access to East Indian pepper. From Sao Tome, then, they continued to trade in slaves and other commodities with Benin.

Sao Tome soon became an important factor influencing life on the mainland. Settled by a mixture of convicts, exiles, adventurers, and Jews deported from Portugal, it soon became the principal slaving center for the whole of West Africa. (Only in the Dutch period which followed did Elmina become primarily a slaving as distinct from a gold center.) In the sugar plantations of Sao Tome a way of life was evolved that was soon to be transported to Brazil. Before long the Sao Tome colonists had grown so powerful as a result of the slave trade that they were able to cut off communications between the kings of the Congo and Portugal itself, and, by expanding the slave trade into the Congo on a large scale, to convert that country into their economic dependency.

The tale of Portuguese contact with the Congo is a particularly sad one in the history of Afro-European relations, the more so as it began so hopefully. The mouth of the Congo River, which the Portuguese were to call the Zaire, had first been reached by Diogo Cao in 1482. He landed an embassy of four, who were dispatched into the interior, and who made their way to the court of the Manicongo at Mbanza. As they did not return, Cao kidnaped four Africans, and returned to Portugal. In 1484 or 1485 he returned to the Congo, and exchanged the Africans—who had been handsomely treated in Lisbon—for the members of his embassy. Cao and his men then visited Mbanza themselves, carrying presents to Nzinga Nkuwu, the reigning Manicongo, whom they asked to become a Christian. The Manicongo, having requested the King of Portugal to send him missionaries, builders, and farmers, agreed, and was baptized together with many of his court in 1491. By about 1500, however, Portugal had failed to show sustained interest, and the Sao Tome colonists began to make their influence felt, and to introduce the slave trade. The Manicongo, who had become disillusioned with the Portuguese, then abandoned his new religion, and exiled one of his sons, who had taken the name of Affonso and who remained a Christian, to the provinces. In 1506 or 1507, however, the reigning Manicongo died, and Affonso took his place, perhaps, it is thought, with Portuguese help.

Affonso's reign, which lasted until 1543, was marked to the end by his efforts to ameliorate the lot of his people, who were being increasingly subjected to the depredations of the slave trade. He not only carried on a correspondence with the King of Portugal, in which he pressed for the ending of the slave trade, but also sent three delegations to the Vatican. He also tried to insist that the island of Sao Tome, which had become "a nest of Portuguese pirates," should be annexed to his realm, but without success. Although he had earlier been involved in slave-trafficking himself—the slaves involved were apparently not what he called "freed and exempt men," but were probably those captured in war—he increasingly attempted to stop the trade, which was swallowing up, as he put it, "sons of the land and the sons of our noblemen and vassals and our relatives, because the thieves and men of bad conscience grab them wishing to have the wares of this Kingdom which they are ambitious of; they grab them and get them to be sold; and so great, Sir, is the corruption and licentiousness that our country is being completely depopulated." He therefore informed the King of Portugal most categorically (the words are emphasized in the original letter, written on July 6, 1526), that "it is *our will that in these Kingdoms there should not be any trade of slaves nor outlet for them.*"

A struggle for succession took place on Affonso's death, which was won not by the Portuguese candidate, Pedro, but by Affonso's nephew, Diogo, who reigned from about 1545 to 1561. During his reign the slave trade, which had by now become a Portuguese royal monopoly, waxed ever stronger, and despite the changing of the name of Mbanza to San Salvador, and the dispatch of the Jesuits to the Congo (at least one of them, Father Jorge Vaz, collected sixty slaves for embarkation and sale), Congo-Portuguese relations continued to deteriorate. Another bloody succession struggle after Diogo's death was followed by a brief period of peace, which ended in 1568 when the Congo was invaded by the Jagas and the Anzicos, who were, no doubt, tempted to attack by the growing weakness of the kingdom, caused by slaving and by civil war. The Manicongo, Alvaro, appealed to Portugal for help, and in 1570 received from young Don Sebastian—he who was to lead the Portuguese to disaster in Morocco in 1578—600 Portuguese, who, together with their Congolese allies, drove out the Jagas once more.

After this, Portuguese influence rapidly waned in the Congo, just as it began to wax in neighboring Angola, where Paulo Dias de Novais, having been sent there with the support of the Jesuits, arrived in 1571, and founded the city of Luanda. Portugal's eclipse followed, however, in 1580, when it became temporarily absorbed by Spain. Under these circumstances another Manicongo, Alvaro II, in 1590 attacked the Portuguese and attempted to place the Congo under the tutelage of the Vatican. While he was engaged in this endeavor, the Dutch arrived off the Congo coast. The Portuguese period was over. Since the subsequent history of Angola and the Congo is best dealt with in the context of later periods, we shall return to them later.

Two further episodes of the Portuguese era in Africa remain, however, to be mentioned—the conquest of the South East African coast by the Portuguese, and the astonishing Ethiopian epic.

South East Africa was seen originally by the Portuguese not, as it were, in relation to its African context, but as a Muslim coastline guarding the route to India, which should be seized as soon as possible for strategic reasons. Between 1500 and 1509 Portugal, thanks to its cannon, captured or gained control of the main Arab trading ports on the East African coast—Sofala, Kilwa, Mombasa, Malindi, Mogadishu, and the islands of Pemba and Zanzibar. At Sofala, for example, Joao dos Santos, a Portuguese priest, writing at the end of the sixteenth century, reported that

The Fortresse was built in An. 1505 by Pero da Nhaya, with consent of the Moorish King Zufe, a man blinde of both his eyes (in both senses, externall and internall, religious and politike) who too late repenting, thought to supplent it with trecherie, which they returned upon himselfe and slew him.[5]

The Portuguese also established a new base of their own on a small island known as Mozambique, and later another at Quelimane. Resentment against their sudden and violent arrival ran high, however, and they had to combat frequent uprisings, especially in Mombasa. Apart from such difficulties, their commercial hopes for the region were also disappointed. Knowing that under Arab (i.e. usually Swahili) rule, these coastal cities had been flourishing trade centers, with gold, ivory, and other products arriving from the interior for the India trade, the Portuguese had confidently expected to profit in their turn. In their reports to Lisbon there were allusions to the "gold of Ophir," and "King Solomon's mines." They overlooked the fact, however, that the traditional pattern had been for the "Arabs" of the coastal cities to send regular trading expeditions into the interior, thus assuming responsibility for transport to the coast. The Portuguese made no such efforts, but instead waited for the gold and ivory to be brought to them. They were usually disappointed. Later sporadic, and frenetic, attempts to control the source of the gold supply led them to the Manica gold-bearing area, which they also found disappointing.

The Manica district lay inland from Sofala (the port on which the Portuguese had pinned the greatest hopes for gold accumulation) along the Zambesi valley. Here the dominant African group was the Vakaranga or Makalanga (the name has various spellings), who were ruled by the Monomotapa (or Benametapa) dynasty, which had earlier moved from the Zimbabwe area. The famous stone buildings of Zimbabwe would appear to have been constructed by this people at an earlier period. The Portuguese established trade relations with the Monomatapas, and later

5. *Ethiopia Oriental* (Translated in *Purchas His Pilgrimes*, 1905).

gave them military assistance against the neighboring Changamires. Eventually, weakened by the depredations of the slave trade (for the friendship of the Portuguese could prove more fatal than their enmity in some cases), the Monomatapa kingdom fell under Portuguese domination, and was finally—despite the Portuguese—overrun by the Changamires in the late seventeenth century.

On other parts of the coast the Portuguese failed to establish permanent contacts with the interior, and, indeed, found themselves so little able to suppress clandestine trading from East Africa to India by the "Arabs" that at one time they considered recognizing and licensing it, so as to profit, even to a small extent, from a trade that they could not prevent.

In Madagascar the Portuguese presence was brief: a settlement was made in the southeast of the island in 1540, but nearly all of its members were massacred by the islanders in 1548.

## Prester John

In 1453 Constantinople fell to the Ottoman Turks who, in 1517, proceeded to occupy Egypt. From here the Turks expanded their power in four different directions: west to the Maghreb; southeast down the Arabian peninsula; southeast down the African coast of the Red Sea to Somalia; and south down the Nile valley to the Sudan. Their military strength—they had acquired firearms—much encouraged the Muslim peoples of northern and eastern Africa, who consequently grew bolder in opposing the Portuguese incursions that were then taking place in East Africa, the Red Sea, and elsewhere. Both Turks and Portuguese viewed the conflict as a metaphysical struggle between religions, as well as a physical struggle for trade and political domination. Within this context —and before the defeat of Muslim seapower by the Christian fleets at Lepanto in 1571—a curious drama, which had little strategic bearing on the outcome of the greater conflict, took place in the mountain fastnesses of Ethiopia.

We have already spoken of the legend of Prester John,[6] the Christian priest-king whom medieval Europe believed to be descended from the race of the Three Wise Men, and who, it was also said, would one day deliver Christendom from its Muslim foes. As early as 1340 Prester John was identified with the Negus of Ethiopia. The Portuguese were particularly anxious to establish contact with the semi-mythical monarch, but were not precisely sure where his realm was situated. They therefore inquired diligently about him as they worked their way along the West African coast, where they first received a hint of his existence when they reached Benin. The chiefs of Benin told them of the great King Ogané,

6. Chapter 2, p. 24.

who lived twenty moons journey toward the rising sun. They added that without a brass helmet and a brazen cross received from Ogané, no king of Benin could legitimately rule. With this intelligence, the Portuguese conjectured that Ogané, whom they identified with Prester John, must live to the south of Egypt. They continued their inquiries: a party of Portuguese who were left in the Congo in 1491 had instructions to discover the way to reach Prester John and the Indies. Four years earlier, in 1487, Pero da Covilhan and Afonso da Paiva had been sent out directly, by the King of Portugal, to find Prester John, as well as to get information about the Indies.

It is not known precisely what travels da Paiva made, only that, upon returning from them he died in Cairo. Da Covilhan, having visited the Indies and East Africa, also returned to Cairo where he learned of da Paiva's death. At that time he received fresh instructions to find Prester John before returning home. Thus it was that in 1494 he finally reached Ethiopia, where he was warmly received, but not allowed to leave. A further delegation, landed by Albuquerque in Somalia in 1508, is known to have reached Ethiopia, but then later disappeared. This contact, however, led to the nomination of an Ethiopian representative (thought to have been an Armenian), who, after many difficulties, reached Lisbon. Meanwhile, at the time of his death, Albuquerque, the great Portuguese admiral, was known to wish to complete his strategic plan for the domination of eastern waters not only by capturing Aden, but also by establishing a fortress at Massawa on the coast of Eritrea. Massawa, wrote Albuquerque, "would be a good port for our ships, because it touches the land of Prester John, is the principal port of his country, and replete with provisions, and reinforcements of men if necessary, or any other things that we might need . . ." But Albuquerque's death prevented the realization of this project, or the history of the Red Sea might have taken a different turning, since communications between Ethiopia and Europe, which were later to be cut once more, might have been kept open.

In 1520 a Portuguese delegation arrived at last in Ethiopia, although unfortunately a kingly present and the returning Ethiopian ambassador both failed to survive the journey.[7] The Ethiopian court, as was its custom, was living in tents, and moving from time to time around the country. The Portuguese were able to meet da Covilhan, by then an old man, who shortly thereafter died.[8] In 1526 some members of the delegation, unlike da Covilhan, succeeded in leaving to return to Portugal.

7. The kingly present may have been converted to private uses, and the ambassador—possibly a potentially embarrassing witness—was, some think, eliminated in consequence.
8. Some authorities state that da Covilhan died while returning to Portugal: it would seem that they may refer to Pero da Covilhan's son, by his Ethiopian wife. The son was sent to Portugal, but died en route.

These leisurely contacts between the two countries might have proceeded thus indefinitely were it not for the growing power of the Turks, who encouraged a Somali leader to attack the Ethiopians, which he began to do in 1527. The Somali's name was Ahmed-ibn-Ibrahim el Ghazi, but he was generally known as Granye, meaning "the left-handed," and he soon became the scourge of Ethiopia. Armed with firearms, he pressed Christian Ethiopia so hard that by 1540 the realm was approaching the point of dissolution. Responding to an Ethiopian appeal for help, the Portuguese sent Dom Cristovao da Gama, a son of Vasco da Gama, together with 400 men, to the relief of the beleaguered land. The expedition encountered some astonishing experiences. Between Debaroa and the stronghold of Amba Sanayt they were shown, in a hilltop town, the mummified bodies of 300 white men that, according to tradition, had belonged perhaps to men who had conquered the land in Roman days, or perhaps to saints. "The bodies were almost perfect," it was reported, "with only nose, lips, and some fingers missing." In 1542, after heavy fighting, Dom Cristovao was killed. The following year, however, the surviving Portuguese defeated and killed Granye, thus preserving Ethiopia as a Christian state. Many of the Portuguese were rewarded with estates, married Ethiopian wives, and settled down in the country.

It soon became clear, however, that theological differences existed between the Latin and Ethiopian churches, such as, for example, the definition of the second person of the Trinity. A Jesuit mission was consequently dispatched to Ethiopia, where it was tolerated by one monarch, but ignored by his successor. In 1557, meanwhile, the Turks captured Massawa, and so cut off once more the tenuous link between Ethiopia and Europe. In 1602, however, Father Pero Paez, another Jesuit, and a remarkable individual, succeeded in entering the country. He further succeeded, among his other achievements, in visiting the source of the Blue Nile, and in converting the Emperor to the Church of Rome. As a result a Patriarch was sent from Rome in 1625, but the changes demanded in the Coptic religion proved too much for the nation to accept. Revolts and unrest occurred between 1628 and 1632, with local political issues inflaming the religious question. Finally, when the land was in turmoil, the Emperor, in desperation, restored the national church. Rejoicing, the Ethiopians echoed the couplet:

> The sheep of Ethiopia have escaped
> From the hyenas of the West.

Two years later the Jesuits were expelled from Ethiopia. A remarkable interlude had drawn to a close.

The Portuguese era in Africa is one that still remains, to some extent, cloaked in mystery. Although much is known, much was suppressed by the "conspiracy of silence"—the policy we mentioned earlier under which the Portuguese tended to remain secretive about their African expeditions, so as to keep information from their competitors. Many records, too, that might have thrown much light upon this period were completely destroyed in the great Lisbon earthquake of 1755, which was followed by a tidal wave and then by fire. One example, alone, may suffice to indicate the gap in our knowledge. The source of the Nile—so far as Europe is concerned, for some Africans were already aware of its location—is generally held to have been located in Lake Victoria-Nyanza by John Speke in 1862. Father Paez, the Portuguese priest, had, for his part, already visited the source of the Blue Nile in Ethiopia in 1618. Yet, under these circumstances, how are we to explain the following lines from Camoëns *Lusiad*—published in 1572—unless some Portuguese had already learned the secret?

> Yonder are the lakes, the birth place of the Nile
> Which none among the ancients ever kenned.[9]

## *"The Dance of Death and Trade"*

In Asia, we have seen how the Portuguese had been replaced by the Dutch, and Dutch power, in turn, had given way to that of the British. While some reflections of these changes were to be found in Africa, both geography and the political and social situation in Africa itself produced a less simple pattern. To be sure, the Dutch replaced the Portuguese at Elmina in 1637, as well as elsewhere along the Guinea coast at various dates, and also took possession of the Cape of Good Hope in 1652. But both in East and West Africa the Portuguese clung on. Other European powers also soon arrived to establish themselves at various places on the coast—the French in Senegal, the British in the Gambia, at Sierra Leone, and on the Gold Coast, the Danes, Swedes, and Brandenburgers on the Gold Coast. (The Spanish were not to acquire Fernando Po and Rio Muni until late in the eighteenth century.) Such holdings, however, usually represented no more than tiny enclaves or forts on the coast, subject to a high rate of mortality, and principally concerned with the prosecution of the slave trade. The coastal forts, or "factories," changed hands from time to time in raids or wars, and were passed back and forth like small change at major diplomatic conferences held in Europe. While the slave trade was increasingly throwing the interior of black Africa into social disorder, on the coast what Joseph Conrad was later to call the "merry dance of death and trade" went remorselessly on, decade after decade.

Nevertheless, during the seventeenth and eighteenth centuries, some

9. *The Lusiads,* Book X, Verse 95. (Translated by Leonard Bacon. Hispanic Society of America, 1950).

Europeans did occasionally penetrate into the hinterland of the African continent. Through the unco-ordinated and frequently unrecorded travels of adventurers, missionaries, explorers, sea-captains, and other miscellaneous wanderers, the European presence was taken into many regions of Africa long before Europe itself was generally conscious of the fact. In this way a body of assorted knowledge about Africa, compounded partly of rumor, partly of unverifiable assertion, partly of misinformation, and partly of corroborated fact, became known to the European governments. The governments, however, remained generally indifferent to these distant echoes, seeing no reason why they should be concerned.

Toward the end of the eighteenth century, however, profound changes took place elsewhere that were, slowly but inevitably, to affect the future of Africa, and to lead first to the exploration, and then to the occupation of Africa by the European powers. These changes were partly theoretical, and partly practical. Theoretically, democratic ideals were coming into vogue, creating political pressures for the ending of the slave trade and the extension of the "Rights of Man." Mercantilism was also giving way to *laissez-faire* in economic theory, while the Age of Reason was challenging tradition, and opening up new pragmatic possibilities. In practice, the American Revolution—for a time, at least—broke British confidence in the profitability of the transatlantic trade axis, and led the United Kingdom to place its primary faith instead in the trade axis running from Britain around the Cape of Good Hope to India and beyond. (After earlier attempts had failed, Britain finally seized the Cape from the Dutch in 1806.)

The French Revolution, after a time, produced Napoleon, who embodied both the theoretical changes and the practical spirit of the age. Seeking to challenge Britain's growing world power, Napoleon landed with his army in Egypt in 1798, proposing to dig a Canal at Suez,[10] to threaten the British hold over India, cut the trade axis, and thus, as it were, break the backbone of Britain's economic power in order, no doubt, to replace it with a French backbone.[11] Although the British succeeded first in destroying Napoleon's fleet, and then later in effecting the withdrawal of the French Army from Egypt, the strategic fact that was to prevail in the future had been made clear to all: control over Africa meant control over the world's major trade route. Africa, therefore, massive, partly unexplored, often unhealthy for, and sometimes virtually uninhabitable by, Europeans, had acquired a new significance.

10. Lepère's study on the *Canal des Deux Mers* concluded that the project could not be completed because the Red Sea was, according to his calculations, 33 feet higher than the Mediterranean. (See note in Chapter 6, p. 126). His calculations were wrong: the levels were approximately the same.

11. Leibnitz, the German philosopher, had earlier advised Louis XIV to conquer Egypt as a way station to India. In 1672 Leibnitz wrote a book on the subject, *Consilium Aegyptiacum*. Napoleon probably knew of both the advice and the book.

It took Europe the whole of the nineteenth century, as well as the early years of the twentieth, to explore, partition, "pacify," and colonize Africa. A gigantic effort was required that had to make its way not only against the difficulties of climate and geography and the hostility of many of Africa's inhabitants, but also against indifference and political criticism in Europe itself. The opposition of W. E. Gladstone, the British Prime Minister, and of the anti-imperial "Little England" faction, to further colonial expansion was intense, and other European powers were subjected to similar pressures. As late as 1871 Chancellor Bismarck stated flatly, "For Germany to acquire colonies would be like a poverty-stricken Polish noblemen providing himself with silks and sables when he needed shirts."

We can see Europe's century-long colonizing effort as falling into three phases, which to some extent overlap. First, there was the period of exploration, during which the main geographical facts about the African continent, and in particular the course of the Niger and of the Nile, were ascertained. Second, there was the period in which the European powers jockeyed for strategic advantage—a period which virtually ended with a confrontation at Fashoda in 1898. Finally there followed the period of "pacification" and of colonization.

## The Exploration of Africa

Nothing can demonstrate more clearly the progress of European knowledge about Africa than an examination of European maps of the continent from Napoleonic times onward. To begin with, the words "UNKNOWN INTERIOR" appear over vast areas, and then, as time and discovery progress, rivers, lakes, and mountains are slowly traced in with increasing accuracy, and mythical features are removed. Indeed, early explorers often had as much difficulty in convincing those at home of the truth of what they had found as in making the discoveries themselves. For example, James Bruce's reasonably veracious account of his travels in Ethiopia was covered with scorn, and his book was compared to the fanciful escapades of Baron Munchausen. (Possibly, influential Britons may have wished to discredit Bruce's work because he had imparted his experiences to the French before he returned to London.) Later, the reports of Johan Ludwig Krapf and Johan Rebmann that they had seen snow-covered mountains in East Africa were disbelieved by authorities who had never been to Africa. Indeed, such untraveled authorities often produced African discoveries of their own: Major Rennel, an eighteenth-century English scholar, maintained that the River Niger did not flow into the sea, as some claimed, but instead into what he called "the great sink of Africa," where, he said, it evaporated.

The story of the exploration of Africa contains episodes of a highly dramatic nature, and has been recounted, in part or in whole, many times. At stake, often, was the explorer's life, and often hazardous communications jeopardized the chances of his reports ever being received. Perhaps one of the best known illustrations of this concerns Henry Morton Stanley's correspondence from the court of the Kabaka of Buganda. In 1875 Stanley gave his letters to a Frenchman, Colonel Linant de Bellefonds, to take home for him. Upon reaching the Sudan, de Bellefonds was murdered. When his body was discovered, Stanley's letters were found hidden in his boots. The fate of many other explorers still remains unknown.

The two principal themes which characterized the European exploration of Africa were the search for the Niger's course, which lasted from 1788 to 1830, and the search for the source of the Nile, which began in the obscurity of previous centuries, and which was ended by Speke's journey in 1862, although it was only in 1875 that the last doubts were dispelled by Stanley.

THE SEARCH FOR THE NIGER

The quest for the Niger was undertaken systematically in 1788, when the Association for the Discovery of the Interior Parts of Africa, generally known as the "African Association," was founded in the United Kingdom. The Association aimed not only at discovery, but also at the suppression of the slave trade, and the location of new markets for British goods. It was given "benevolent encouragement" by the government of William Pitt, who permitted it to collect information through the British consular service. Under the association's auspices, a young Scottish surgeon, Mungo Park, was sent to West Africa in 1795, where, leaving the Gambia and Senegal rivers, he made his way to the Niger near Segou, from whence he returned in 1797, having made a remarkable journey and established the fact that the Niger flowed east and not west.

In 1805, together with a party of forty-three, he undertook a second journey to attempt to follow the Niger to the sea. Fever and fighting reduced their numbers until at last Park and four survivors, one of whom had gone mad, were attacked and killed by hostile Africans at Busa, on the Niger. After this, the intensification of the Napoleonic wars delayed further Niger investigation. Fresh information was next obtained indirectly by a British mission which, under the command of T. E. Bowdich, was sent to Ashanti, in what is now Ghana, in 1816, and which returned to give a notable account of Ashanti life and customs. Two Englishmen, Dixon Denham and Hugh Clapperton (a third member of the party, Dr. Walter Oudney, soon died), then crossed the Sahara in 1822–1823, and located Lake Chad, after which, variously, they visited the states of Bornu, Kano, and Sokoto, before arriving back in England in 1825. In the same year Clapperton returned to West Africa with a small party, with which he left the coast at Badagri, in what is now West Nigeria, and struck inland. He reached the Niger at Busa, where Park had been killed, and traveled on to Sokoto, where he himself died. The only surviving member of his party was his English servant, Richard Lander, who wished himself to follow the Niger down to the sea, but was unable to do so, being obliged instead to return to the coast at Badagri. Refusing to be discouraged, Lander obtained some token support from the British government, after which he returned with his brother, and once more traveled from Badagri to Busa, from where the two paddled down the Niger by canoe. Near the mouth of the Niger they were seized by a fleet of Ibo war canoes, but their lives were spared through the intercession of some Muslim teachers. They navigated the Niger delta, emerging at the mouth of the Brass River in 1830. The source of the Niger was now determined. Lander himself, however, was killed in the Niger delta on his return from a third voyage, in which he had been engaged in exploring the course of the Benue, the Niger's main tributary.

With the Niger's source now determined, a wealth of information on the West African hinterland was amassed by a courageous and painstaking German explorer, Dr. Heinrich Barth, who between 1850 and 1855 traveled widely through the Sudanic countries, with the support of the British government, publishing a five-volume work on the territories that he visited which still remains informative.

Sir Harry Johnston, in his comments on Barth, makes an observation that eloquently illustrates the contemporary disregard for Africa. Barth had been employed by the British government—Germany had not yet proclaimed its own colonial policy which, in embryonic form, was being developed in co-operation with the British—and was, according to Johnston, insufficiently rewarded (he was made a Companion of the Order of the Bath), and then ignored. To the British government, said Johnston, "an African explorer, laying bare to our knowledge hundreds of thousands of square miles of valuable territory, was less worthy of remembrance than a Chargé d'Affaires at the court of the Grand Duke of Pumpernickel." In effect, this was because Europeans in general still viewed Africa as an unhealthy wasteland with no function beyond the traditional but discredited one of acting as a slave mine. In the mid-nineteenth century, however, this view began to give way. The change was brought about because the abolitionists, the churches, and the British industrialists of the Manchester school combined to form a powerful political coalition for the triple purpose of ending the slave trade in Africa, Christianizing the continent, and opening it up to commerce.

The man who did the most to publicize these aims was a Scottish missionary, David Livingstone, whose travels and explorations included the search for the Nile sources—still unknown despite Father Paez's travels and Camoëns' mysterious explorer (see p. 154). The quest for the Nile, unlike that for the Niger, was metamorphosed, for some, into a well-nigh mystical search, as if the "fountains" (as Ptolemy had called them) from which the Nile flowed were the wellsprings of the spirit of civilization that, if found, would lead to the regeneration of Africa itself. Livingstone's attitude can be seen in the following excerpt from a letter he wrote to his son Robert on May 31, 1859, shortly after his discovery of Lake Chilwa in Nyasaland. The anti-slavery, missionary, and commercial themes are all intertwined, together with Livingstone's concern for the condition of the working class in Britain:

> The discovery is the chief end in view, although that lies in the way. The great object is the promotion of the welfare of man. . . . We are guilty of keeping up slavery by giving increasing prices for slave-grown cotton and sugar. We are the great supporters of slavery in the world—unwittingly often, but truly. Now I long to see our nation relieved from this guilt and stain, and our Great Father in this fair world has provided ample means for this purpose. We could not only get cotton and sugar in abundance from the region I am opening up, but in doing that by our own people we should be conferring incalculable blessings on our own poor toil-worn fellow-countrymen.

Livingstone, who came from a poor family (at the age of ten he had been put to work in a cotton factory, where he had set up his Latin grammar book so that he could memorize it as he walked to and fro about his work), had gone out to Bechuanaland as a missionary in 1841. He had, however, soon left his mission station and begun his explorations. His saintly character and the drama inherent in his experiences succeeded, over the years, in focusing some degree of European attention upon Africa, and although his actual discoveries—which included the mouth of the Zambesi, and Lake Nyasa—were mostly in southern and eastern Africa, and therefore did not bear directly upon the Nile itself, like Moses he nevertheless pointed out the goal. The explorers who followed him were to receive the full attention of the European public.

THE SEARCH FOR THE NILE

The first systematic attempt to find the source of the Nile during this period was made by Sir Richard Burton and John Speke, two Englishmen, who had previously explored Somalia together in 1854, and who, in 1856, were sent to find the great lakes, of which reports had been received, presumably from the Africans. They traveled under the sponsorship of the British Royal Geographical Society (which, in 1830, had developed from the African Association). Leaving the East African coast in 1857, they went separately, Burton discovering Lake Tanganyika, and Speke reaching the southern shore of Lake Victoria, which he rightly surmised to be the source of the Nile. Both then returned home, and began a public dispute about their discoveries. Speke's surmise did not amount to proof, so in 1862 he returned to Africa, accompanied by James Grant, to continue his investigations. On this journey they located the point—Ripon Falls—at which the White Nile issues from the shore of Lake Victoria. Then they traveled north to Egypt, but, leaving the Nile for a part of the way, missed Lake Albert, which was later discovered by Baker, another Englishman. Confusion about these discoveries, complicated by the quarrel between Speke and Burton (Speke died suddenly from a gunshot accident in 1864, when the public argument was at its height), persisted until 1875, when Stanley removed the last doubts about Speke's discovery.

It is Stanley, indeed, who may be said to represent, in his own person, the transition from the period of Africa's exploration to the period of its annexation by rival European powers. Combining in himself courage, cruelty, imagination, and insecurity, he did much to sway the course of events in his day, with effects that are still apparent.

Henry Morton Stanley, a Welshman, was born "John Rowlands." As an illegitimate child, he was rejected by his family, and placed in a workhouse. Escaping, he ran away to America, where he was adopted by a kindly New Orleans businessman, who gave him some education, as well as the name of "Stanley." After fighting in the American Civil War, Stanley became a war correspondent. Later the New York *Herald Tribune,* a daily newspaper, assigned him to a number of tasks abroad, including that of locating Dr. Livingstone, who was then rumored to be "lost" in Central Africa. After arriving at Zanzibar in January, 1871, Stanley marched inland with a well-equipped expedition, and on November 3, 1871, reached Livingstone, who was then at Ujiji on the shores of Lake Tanganyika.[12] This date may conveniently be taken as marking the watershed between two periods: Livingstone, for his part, represented the period in which the abolitionist-Christian-commercial coalition was backing the exploration of Africa; Stanley represented the next period, that of undisguised governmental interest.

Stanley and Livingstone, having met and communed together, separated, never to meet again. Livingstone, who continued on his unending journey, searching for the Absolute no less than for the Nile waters, died at Lake Bangweulu in 1873, less than two years later. Stanley returned in triumph to London, from where the New York *Herald* and the London *Daily Telegraph* together sent him back to Africa to complete Livingstone's discoveries. He succeeded admirably. Leaving Zanzibar in 1874,

12. Stanley, having become confused in his reckoning during a bout of fever, thought that the date was November 10.

he circumnavigated Lakes Victoria and Tanganyika, marched to the Lualaba, and after a journey of the utmost difficulty which killed all his European fellow travelers and many of his African ones, followed the Congo down toward its mouth, reaching the coast at last in Cabinda in 1877. This journey has been described as "the greatest feat to be found in the annals of African exploration." A recent commentator has said that "neither before nor since has any single African expedition accomplished so much."[13] More than any other white man, Stanley rent aside the veil of secrecy which had obscured the interior of Africa from European eyes.

Until this time, Europe's impingement upon the sovereignty of Africa had been limited to a slow erosion of the African status quo. The sovereignty of the African body politic, already undermined by the slave trade, had been cut into in a desultory fashion in the coastal areas, but elsewhere remained essentially intact. European governments had occasionally shown interest in reducing parts of Africa, but only as mechanics might, who attempt, sporadically, to reduce the bulk of a large lump of metal by cutting off small corners and filing the edges. Or, to use another image, the European invasion had been like the sea beating upon the African coastline, with the French flooding up the Senegal River, the British up the Niger,[14] and one or other of the two powers surging onto the coast to establish enclaves whose confines could often be more appropriately measured in yards than miles. Once the nature of the interior became known, however, there dawned upon European minds an understanding both of Africa's commercial potential and of the world-wide strategic implications of its position. France and Germany, in particular, realized that, prudently handled, the African situation might develop in their favor, and that if once either of them were to succeed in dominating Africa, then they might perhaps proceed to the domination of the main trade routes of the world. The United Kingdom, however, which since 1815 had found itself in precisely this advantageous position through its control over both the overland and the sea route to India, also understood the potential challenge posed by its rivals, and was ready to respond.

From the British point of view, no threat to British world power involving Africa had arisen since the time of the Napoleonic invasion of Egypt, and of the French attacks upon the Cape, which occurred at about the same time. Britain had then checked the French in both places. British exploration in West Africa had had objectives that had been

13. These two comments are cited at random—there must be many others in the same sense. The first quotation is from Johnston's *The Colonization of Africa* (1913 edition); the second from a biography of Stanley, *The Man Who Presumed, by Byron Farwell* (1957).

14. Some Africans also drew a marine connection. In about 1900 the Emir of Kontagora in what is now Northern Nigeria told his people that the British were a species of fish, and would die if they left the banks of the Niger. In those days, no doubt, the allegory held true.

commercial rather than strategic. So long as France and Germany left Africa alone, therefore, Africa remained to British planners a waste space in which individual visionaries saw possibilities of replacing the slave trade with other forms of economic development. Unfortunately for such optimists, however, the disapearance of the slave trade did not always yield, or even seem to promise to yield, the positive results that had been anticipated. Charles Dickens, in *Bleak House*, satirized the impractical utopianism of Mrs. Jellyby and her concern for an industrial settlement at "Borrioboola-Gha" on the banks of the Niger—a fictional enterprise inspired by the facts of life and of death (from malaria) of the Model Farm that was founded at the confluence of the Niger and Benue rivers in 1841.[15]

Abolitionists had convinced themselves that the suppression of slavery would also logically lead to the disappearance of the other ills that Africa was heir to, but this was evidently not so. Nor were there many tempting commercial opportunities in evidence to attract the enterprise that was to bring about the transformation of the continent. The yield of the West African gold-bearing regions was, at this time, insufficient, and the gold of the Transvaal was not to be discovered until 1886. Diamonds, it was true, had been found in quantity near Kimberley in 1870, but while this increased British interest in their settlements at the southern tip of the continent, and attracted a crowd of white immigrants there, it had little effect upon Africa as a whole.

Only when Germany moved, therefore, did the United Kingdom— and France—react, and the "Scramble for Africa" begin. In the meantime, however, British apathy with regard to Africa had permitted a new and unforeseen factor to become injected into the situation in the form of Leopold II, King of the Belgians.

Leopold was, beyond doubt, an unusual man. Even today he is viewed as a hero or as a monster, depending on the standpoint from which he is viewed. A tall man with a long pointed nose, and with his hair parted in the middle, he had a fan-shaped beard that in early life was auburn, and later turned snow white. Interested in geography from an early age, Leopold (known as the Duke of Brabant before his accession to the throne) in his youth was constantly harassing government departments with his endless questions. He traveled to the Dutch East Indies, and also paid a series of visits to the Suez Canal. To his confidants he insisted, "Belgium must have a colony."

Before he became king in 1865, Leopold considered the possibility of establishing Belgian colonies either in West Africa, China, Japan, Borneo,

15. The survivors of the enterprise had been evacuated in 1842, and the official report had suggested that in the future, as the climate was so deadly to the European, such settlements had best consist of "men of colour"; eventually, it was felt, a chain of such colonies might be established at all important ports and riverheads in West Africa.

Indochina, Sarawak, Argentina, or Bolivia. At one time he also explored the possibility of a Belgian annexation of the island of Taiwan. Later, after he had established his Congo Free State, he also showed an interest in many Asian, Middle Eastern, or American countries, and at one time —through the agency of the Congo Free State—offered to buy the Canary Islands from Spain. His aim in these various enterprises was to acquire wealth and power for the Saxe-Coburg dynasty, thus giving to the Belgian monarchy the substance of power that European kings of an earlier day had held. In seeking a colony for Belgium, however, it was not his intention to follow the doctrines of the Manchester school of economists, which held that trade was beneficial to the economies of the two trading partners, and therefore did not necessitate political control of one by the other. Instead he reverted to the mercantilism, or state imperialism, of an earlier period, in which it had been held that colonies existed solely for the benefit of the metropolitan country—that is, quite simply, in order to be exploited. His visit to the Dutch East Indies had provided him with a pattern that he intended to follow.

Leopold was devious by nature. His father, Leopold I, once described him in the following terms:

Leopold is subtle and sly: he never takes a chance. The other day, when I was at Ardenne, I watched a fox which wanted to cross a stream unobserved: first of all he dipped a paw into the water to see how cold it was, then he lowered the paw carefully to see how deep it was, and then with a thousand precautions, very slowly made his way across. That is Leopold's way. . . .

In acquiring his African kingdom, Leopold proceeded with this reynard-like cunning. In 1867 he joined the Société Geographique de Paris, and, after following the course of new explorations with great attention, several years later helped to finance the International Geographic Congress that was held in Paris in 1875. The following year, 1876, he organized a conference in Brussels at which the Association Internationale Africaine was founded. The A.I.A., which brought together distinguished national delegations from France, the United Kingdom, Germany, Austria, Italy, and Russia, as well, of course, as Belgium, aimed specifically to end the slave trade and to open Central Africa "to civilization." After attempting to obtain money from the national contingents, Leopold quietly permitted the A.I.A., of which he was the chairman, to expire, and in its place brought into existence the Association Internationale du Congo (A.I.C.), an organization that he rigidly controlled, and which was to form a springboard for his Congolese adventure. Leopold took some pains to ensure that the defunct A.I.A. and his newborn A.I.C became confused one with another in the mind of the international public.

Meanwhile, in 1877, Stanley had completed his trans-African journey.

Upon his return to Europe, he was met at Marseilles by Leopold's emissaries, one of whom was Henry S. Sanford, formerly U.S. Consul in Brussels. But Stanley was bound for England, and it was only after he had found the British unenthusiastic about the Congo that he returned to Brussels and met with Leopold in person. A Comité d'Etudes was then formed, and it was decided that Stanley should return to the Congo to lay the foundations of Leopold's projected new state there. Leopold chose at this time to confuse international opinion about his true intentions by announcing that his aim was to create in the Congo a Confederation of Free Negro Republics—a convenient myth that was designed to attract for himself and his project the sympathy of liberal-minded people, who felt that Liberia, the Negro state founded in 1847 as a result of American initiative, had not lived up to their expectations.

Meanwhile, Stanley sailed for the Congo in 1879 with secret instructions to found a new political state there, "as big as possible." Leopold himself was to be head of the new state, and his Comité d'Etudes would have provided the legislation, had not Leopold dissolved it the same year. Nothing further was done to create a Confederation of Free Negro Republics, although, allegedly to foster the creation of the confederation, Leopold's political agents signed numerous treaties with Congolese chiefs under the terms of which they yielded up sovereignty to Leopold's new state. By 1883 Stanley with a hundred white mercenaries—Americans, Danes, English, French, and Belgians—supported by African troops, armed with quick-firing rifles, and transported by a fleet of river steamers, had subjugated the Congo up as far as what is now Stanleyville. Much to Leopold's rage, however, Savorgnan de Brazza, in the service of the French, had stolen a march on Stanley by claiming the right bank of the Congo at Stanley Pool, thereby, in effect, founding modern Brazzaville.

Slowly and unobtrusively the European powers, in the years before 1884, had been becoming increasingly interested in Africa—an interest which Leopold, by his actions, did much to stimulate further. Leopold represented, as it were, the first power—albeit actually a quasi-governmental one—to view the domination of Africa as an end in itself, and this encouraged similar thinking in his contemporaries. Until 1884, however, there was a tendency to view African questions in purely regional terms. Up to now European interest had been primarily expressed, therefore, in Africa's Mediterranean coastline, in Egypt; or in East Africa, where Zanzibar was the pivotal point of influence.

After the French invasion of Egypt, the country, still under Turkish hegemony, had fallen victim to internal conflicts, from which Mohammed Ali, an Albanian, emerged as the new ruler. Rejecting Turkish control, and breaking the power of the Mamelukes, the hereditary ruling caste who had governed Egypt on behalf of the Turks, he obtained the support of the Egyptian people, and laid the foundations of a modern state. In his foreign relations, fearing the power of Britain more than that of France, he strove to establish friendship with the French. The British, however, were even more disturbed by his commercial independence from Turkey than by his military ambitions, and would have welcomed a Turkish victory over Egypt in the hostilities that ensued. But they were disappointed in this hope, and instead a compromise settlement was reached in the Treaty of London, signed in 1841, which confirmed a degree of Egyptian independence from Turkey, but which also limited the size of the Egyptian army. Relieved of the burden of maintaining a large army, however, Egypt was able to some extent to develop its internal economy. Cotton-growing was introduced, the port of Alexandria modernized, and the canal system, which had fallen into disuse, reopened. It was also at this time that the overland mail route to India was organized. Mohammed Said Pasha, who came to power in 1854, after the five-year rule of Abbas I, a traditionalist, continued the policy of modernization. Through his friend de Lesseps he committed Egypt to supporting the Suez Canal scheme, but, equally pliant in other respects, he also did much to deliver a degree of control over the country into European hands. Ismail, who acceded in 1863, showed more character. He immediately began to make approaches to the Sultan of Turkey with a view to having some of the provisions of the Treaty of London altered in Egypt's favor, in return for financial inducements. He thus prevailed upon the Sultan to issue a series of firmans, or decrees, of which the most important was that of 1873, which granted Egypt self-government, and virtual independence from Turkey. Ismail—who had already been given the title of Khedive (originally a Persian word meaning "Prince" but in effect signifying "Viceroy")—was also, like Mohammed before him, given the right to rule over the Sudan, as well as Egypt. All restrictions on the size of Egypt's military power were also removed.

By this time the Suez Canal had been completed and opened, and, inside Egypt, a modern transport and communications network laid down. Ismail's habit of indulging in lavish spending had resulted in an Egyptian vogue among European royalty, who were frequent visitors to the country, and who did much to stimulate a tourist industry, as well as other commercial enterprises. But Ismail's heavy expenditure, much of which was represented by the exorbitant interest on loans demanded by European bankers, eventually resulted in Egypt's bankruptcy. When the United Kingdom and France called upon him to abdicate in 1879, he was obliged to do so.

The United Kingdom, which in 1875 had purchased a controlling interest in the Suez Canal, now had an opportunity to move toward con-solidating its position in Egypt. Finances were placed in the hands of an Anglo-French Dual Control, which in effect ruled Egypt through the agency of Ismail's son and successor, Tewfik. But the exploitation of the Egyptians by successive rulers, working in close co-operation with Euro-pean interests, finally resulted in the emergence of a nationalist move-ment of revolt, led by Colonel Ahmed Arabi, in 1882. The United King-dom and France both made clear their support for Tewfik, and sent more forces to Egypt. Tension rose, but at the last moment France desisted from attacking, while Britain proceeded against the nationalists. The British fleet bombarded the Egyptian forts at Alexandria and landed marines there. British forces under General Sir Garnet Wolseley then landed at Ismailia on the Suez Canal, and defeated the Egyptians at the battle of Tel el-Kebir, at which some 10,000 Egyptians were killed. Arabi was exiled, and the effective occupation of Egypt by the United Kingdom began. The Khedive still ruled in name—at first the tractable Tewfik, and then his successors—but in effect the Khedive was no more than a puppet, since all important decisions, including the appointment of cabinet ministers, first had to receive British approval.

As for Germany, in the earlier period of Bismarck's rule, there was not yet an openly declared interest in Africa. Fearing French revanchism after the German victory over the French in 1870, Bismarck encouraged French involvement in North Africa, and, specifically, in Tunisia. At the same time Bismarck also discreetly encouraged both French and British interest in Egypt, hoping that the two countries would before long not only find themselves deeply involved there, but also in conflict with one another—leaving Germany to act as the ultimate arbiter. In effect, the British conquest of Egypt in 1882 was galling to the French, and in the years that followed the French did thwart many of Britain's aims in Egypt's internal administration, through the Dual Control. No open Anglo-French conflict developed, as Bismarck hoped it would, but the form taken by the European occupation and administration of Egypt reflected a compromise that was in differing degrees unsatisfactory to British, French, and Egyptian alike. Still, British pre-eminence in Egypt was later to make possible Britain's strategic predominance on the con-tinent of Africa as a whole.

### The Decline of Turkish Power

A further factor in promoting Europe's sudden interest in Africa was the decline of Turkish power, which was also as suddenly perceived. As recently as 1872 the English writer and explorer, Winwood Reade, apparently still viewing Egypt as a Turkish province, and observing the gradual spread south from Egypt of "Turkish" power toward the interior, could comment:

> Should the Turks be driven out of Europe, they would probably become the Emperors of Africa, which in the interests of civilisation would be a fortunate occurrence.[16]

After the Russo-Turkish war of 1877–1878, few people continued to think of the Turks as the future Emperors of Africa, and although Turkey participated in the Conference of Berlin in 1884–1885, its role remained minimal.

As mentioned earlier, the Turks had captured Egypt in 1517. They had then proceeded to establish Turkish regencies in Algeria, Tripoli, and Tunis; only Morocco failed to recognize the hegemony of the Sultan of Constantinople. But from the outset of the nineteenth century, from the time of Napoleon's invasion of Egypt, scant attention was paid to Turkish claims in North Africa. Turkey's tenuous hold over these distant provinces of her empire was roughly broken, as if the links were no stronger than spider webs. Napoleon himself had, in fact, had plans drawn up for the invasion of Algeria, no less than of Egypt–plans that were only to be put into effect after his death. In 1827 the Dey of Algiers expressed his irritation with the French Consul, who had been making representations over a claim for debt, by striking him with a fly whisk.[17] After three years spent in reflection and preparation, the French landed an army 37,000 strong and captured Algiers. They had originally announced that the occupation would be temporary, but after the fall of Charles X the new government of Louis Philippe did not wish to assume responsibility for a withdrawal. The Algerian people had little sympathy for the Dey, who was Turkish, but the behavior of the French soon alienated their sympathies, and as a result a regional leader, Abd-el-Kader, arose and rallied the population against the Christian invaders. In a campaign which lasted from 1835 to 1837 he inflicted a number of defeats upon the French, after which he was recognized as sultan of a part of what is now Algeria. Hostilities were soon resumed, however, and in 1841 he was driven into Morocco. Periodic fighting between French and Algerians continued throughout most of the remainder of the nineteenth century. Meanwhile, in 1848, Algeria was declared to be a part of France, and was divided into three departments. Military and civil rule alternated thereafter, depending on the attitudes of successive governments in Paris. Under French rule European settle-

16. *The Martyrdom of Man* (1872). Reade went on to say, "The Turkish government is undoubtedly defective in comparison with the governments of Europe; but it is perfection itself in comparison with the governments of Africa."

17. An earlier Dey on occasion expressed his displeasure in stronger terms. In the 1760s James Bruce, then British consul in Algiers, saw the French consul taken away in chains, and witnessed the strangulation of a court official in the Dey's presence.

ment was encouraged, despite many failures, so that by 1900 the European population of Algeria—composed of Spanish, Italians, and Maltese, as well as French—had increased to a quarter of a million.

War by the French against Morocco had resulted in the stabilization of Algeria's western frontier. To the east, however, Tunis, where for some time the Bey had been experiencing increasing financial difficulties, lacked the protection of any one European power, although after 1869 its finances were controlled by a tripartite commission composed of British, French, and Italian representatives. In 1881 Tunis was invaded by France, and Tunisia placed under French protection. This action surprised Italy, which itself had ambitions toward Tunisia, but did not surprise the British who, at the Congress of Berlin in 1878 had intimated to the French that, in view of the decline of the Turkish Empire and the fear that was entertained of the consequent expansion of Russian influence, they were prepared to replace the influence of the Ottoman dynasty with some territorial rearrangements. The French were given to understand that while the United Kingdom—evidently concerned for the security of its Indian empire—claimed a dominant influence in western Asia, and especially in Iraq (Mesopotamia), it had no intention of establishing an exclusive footing in Egypt, while in Tunisia Britain did not wish "to contest the influence which the geographical position of Algeria gave to France." Nor did Germany stand in France's way; the encouragement given by Bismarck to the French regarding Tunisia has already been mentioned.

## The Sudan and Zanzibar

Meanwhile, European influence was spreading into the heart of the continent through the medium of two agencies—the Egyptian government, and the Sultanate of Zanzibar. These two authorities, both of which were or had been involved in the slave trade, employed Europeans as administrators of African territories, thereby providing them with preparatory experience that was to influence the forms of European colonial rule soon to follow. Both authorities likewise relied, to some extent, upon European support, although they were not yet dependencies.

The armies of Mohammed Ali of Egypt had first conquered the Sudan as far as Gondokoro in 1819. In 1841 Mohammed was recognized as Viceroy of the Sudan as well as of Egypt. In 1869 the Khedive Ismail persuaded Baker, the British explorer, to lead a military expedition to the Sudan in order to annex the Upper Nile to Egypt, and to suppress the slave trade. The new region was given the name of Equatoria, and Baker was appointed as its Governor-General. No precise frontiers were defined, and although Baker established Egyptian authority over vast areas, he was driven from the Ugandan kingdom of Bunyoro after attempting to annex it in 1872. In 1874 Baker retired, and was replaced by another Briton, General Gordon, who administered Equatoria until 1876, when he resigned, only to find himself appointed as Governor of the entire Sudan in 1877, with a German, Emin Pasha, serving under him as Governor-General of Equatoria. The deposition of Khedive Ismail, however, led to Gordon's resignation in 1879. He was succeeded by Raouf Pasha.

By 1882, when the British attack on Egypt was in progress, the Sudan was in full revolt. Mohammed Ahmed, who took the title of the Mahdi, or rightly guided one, led an uprising in the Northern Sudan, in the name of the Muslim religion, against Turk, Egyptian, and European alike. From 1881 on Egyptian forces sent against him were defeated. The United Kingdom, primarily concerned with the occupation of Egypt, could spare little time for Sudanese problems until, at last, they became unmanageable. In 1883 a large Egyptian force under the command of Colonel Hicks of the Indian Army was destroyed by the Mahdists. General Gordon, with wide public support in Britain, was then sent back to the Sudan to arrange for the evacuation of the remaining beleaguered Egyptian garrisons there. Upon arrival, however, Gordon, an unusual and eccentric man who followed his own ideas rather than his instructions, established his headquarters in Khartoum, and refused to abandon the Sudan—which, from past experience, he had become accustomed to govern. By the time a slow-moving British relief force arrived in Khartoum in 1885, Gordon had also been killed by the Mahdists, and Khartoum overrun. The British relief force had no alternative but to evacuate the city once more, particularly in view of the fact that a Russian threat to India was then foreseen, so that the troops were required elsewhere. In Britain the public outcry against the Gladstone government of the day at this "betrayal" of Gordon was very great, and did much to create a climate in which a commitment to an imperial policy in Africa in general, and to the administration of the Sudan in particular, eventually became possible. General Sir Herbert Kitchener, who had served with the British force which had relieved Khartoum in 1885, finally obtained authority to return to wrest the Sudan from the Mahdists in 1896. His campaign culminated in a decisive victory over the Mahdists in 1898 at the battle of Omdurman.

European relations with Zanzibar had sprung from different roots. During the Napoleonic wars the Imam of Oman, Seyyid Said, had co-operated with the British against the Wahabi tribes of the desert and the Jawasmi pirates of the Persian Gulf, thus founding an alliance that was to endure throughout the century. The alliance did not, however, only involve Oman, since in 1832 Sayyid Said, who also laid claim to possessions on the East African coast, moved his capital from Muscat to the island of Zanzibar. Here he introduced the cultivation of cloves, and built a commercial empire, based on the ivory and slave trades, which reached out to the Great Lakes and beyond for its "commodities," and which found markets in India, the United Kingdom, and the United States. British, French, and American consulates were opened, and by the time the Sultan died in 1865 his new empire was flourishing, despite abolitionist disapproval of the slave trade in general, and of the famous Zanzibar slave mart in particular. In 1862 both France and the United Kingdom recognized the Sultan's claims on the East African mainland. British influence grew strong primarily through the work of Dr. John Kirk, the British Consul and political agent in Zanzibar, who developed a close relationship with the Sultan Seyid Barghash. So close, indeed, was this relationship that from 1873 on, when the British finally succeeded in persuading the Sultan to abolish the slave trade, Kirk was virtually co-ruler with Barghash of Zanzibar's mainland dominions. From 1881 on, at Kirk's suggestion, the Sultan employed Britons, such as the explorer Joseph Thomson, to help him administer and develop his East African possessions.

## The Congress of Berlin

This nascent system, together with much else in Africa, was changed by the Berlin Conference, which was held from November, 1884, to February, 1885, and which was concluded by the Berlin Act of February 26, 1885.

Of the German penchant for launching a sudden and dramatic assault after a long period of silent preparation, history provides several examples; of which Bismarck's entry into the colonial field in 1884 is one. After the German defeat of the French in the war of 1870, expanding German trade, it was felt, had required naval protection, and in 1871 Wilhelmshafen on the North Sea became a naval base, and the Imperial Admiralty was founded. Without a navy it had been unthinkable for Germany to acquire colonies in Africa or anywhere else. However, for over a decade thereafter, fearing the frictions and the cost involved in maintaining colonies, Bismarck had sacrificed German colonial interests to German goals in Europe, such as the establishment of the Triple Alliance. By 1883 Bismarck felt secure enough in Europe to risk affronting the British in Africa by openly seeking a colony there. He inquired of the United Kingdom whether there would be any objection to the placing of the settlements in the bay of Angra Pequena in South West Africa under German protection. The United Kingdom, which had itself declined to take responsibility for the entire coast of South West Africa, prevaricated, until finally, with the support of an aroused German public opinion, Bismarck acted. On April 24, 1884, he declared the settlements of Herr Luderitz—a Bremen merchant—in Angra Pequena Bay to be under German protection.[18] Germany, too, had now become a colonial power in Africa.

Moving speedily Germany then also proceeded to place the coastal regions of Togo and the Cameroons under her protection, which was done in July, 1884, through the agency of Dr. Gustav Nachtigal, the German explorer, who signed treaties with the local chiefs. The British, had accepted German interest in South West Africa (one British official was quoted as remarking tactfully that he "did not even know where Angra Pequena was") but were intensely irritated by Nachtigal's actions. This was for two reasons. First, it had been the British intention to conclude treaties with the Cameroonian chiefs within a matter of days after Nachtigal's coup. Second, the German government had originally asked the United Kingdom to facilitate Nachtigal's journey to West Africa on what had been represented as a purely commercial mission, and the request had been granted. The British therefore felt themselves to have been doubly deceived.

In the same year, 1884, the British—realizing at last that the King of the Belgians was working in his own interest, and not, as they had believed, in theirs—attempted to lay claim to the Lower Congo region by drawing up a treaty relating to that region with Portugal. France and Germany, reacting against this agreement (which was, in fact, never ratified), called for an international conference to be held on African affairs—the Conference of Berlin.

This Berlin Conference, whose terms were subsequently violated by King Leopold and, no doubt, other signatories, nevertheless provided the basis for the subsequent partition of Africa, since it agreed to the division of the coasts of Africa among rival European powers. The subsequent occupation of the interior, and the subsequent agreements on colonial African frontiers, were merely logical developments growing out of the terms of the Berlin Act.

Agreement on certain other matters was also reached at Berlin. Both the Congo and the Niger were to become international waterways "to assure to all nations the advantages of free navigation on the two chief rivers of Africa flowing into the Atlantic Ocean." The Congo basin was to be neutral, and its boundaries established. A declaration was made against the slave trade.

It was King Leopold who emerged as the principal beneficiary of the conference. He had indeed gained advantages so great that five years later, in 1890, he was able to comment that, "In the recent scramble we

18. The German flag had been hoisted there almost a year earlier, on May 2, 1883, after which a British gunboat had confronted a German gunboat, and the matter had been taken up on the diplomatic level. Luderitz had earlier received assurances from his government that he would eventually receive German protection.

have drawn the winning ticket."[19] It was in fact at the conclusion of the conference that he had the satisfaction of seeing the participating powers formally welcome the birth of his "Etat Indépendent du Congo," as it was officially called, or "Congo Free State" as it was generally known in English. The campaign for recognition, stage-managed by Leopold, had begun earlier when the United States Congress had recommended recognition. Leopold had apparently promoted the U.S. initiative by organizing a lobby in Washington which included Sanford, the ex-U.S. consul, and which had as its main target Senator John T. Morgan, who had been asked by the U.S. Secretary of State to investigate the question of whether or not to recognize Leopold's state. Leopold also had the further advantage of a "friend" on the U.S. delegation—no less a person than his former employee Stanley, who had the title of adviser. Thus U.S. support for Leopold appears to have given further substance to what might otherwise have initially seemed somewhat flimsy claims to consideration. France was also committed to the new state by a clever maneuver of Leopold's by which the Association Internationale du Congo (A.I.C.) and the French made a joint statement according to which the Congo would be ceded to no other power, but if the Association Internationale du Congo should relinquish its "estates," then France should have the first option on them. This ensured that the French would prevent other powers from annexing the Congo while at the same time the French were to obtain nothing in return.

### The Scramble for Africa

The Berlin Conference had set down the rules for the "Scramble for Africa," and the scramble itself soon followed. Italy, perhaps the least significant of the participants, had taken possession of parts of the Red Sea coast of Eritrea in 1882, and had then extended its hold to include the port of Massawa. In 1889 Italy acquired parts of the Somali coast, later extending its influence to include the port of Mogadiscio. In 1896 the Italians attempted to seize Ethiopia itself, but were resoundingly defeated at the battle of Adowa. Not until 1911 did Italy land troops in North Africa for the occupation of Tripolitania.

The main contestants in the scramble, however, were France, Germany, and the United Kingdom. The contest between the three powers took place on two levels. First, there were attempts by France and Germany to place themselves athwart Britain's Suez lifeline to India, or else, by establishing themselves either in the Sudan or in East Africa, to place themselves in a position from which they could threaten it. Second, there were attempts by each of the three powers to obtain profitable or

19. He was, no doubt, using the royal "we."

potentially profitable territories, while at the same time establishing a favorable strategic position for themselves on the African continent, irrespective of Suez and intercontinental strategy. Thus France sought, at the height of the scramble, to found a new empire that would stretch from the Mediterranean in the north to the Atlantic in the west and to the Indian Ocean in the east. Germany, more modestly, wished to create a *Mittel-Afrika* that would stretch from the Cameroons through the Congo to German East Africa. (Some German visionaries later expanded the Mittel-Afrika dream to include all the territory south of the Sahara and north of the Zambezi). It was, however, ultimately the United Kingdom which succeeded in gaining the dominant political control in Africa, winning, as it were, the continental game of noughts and crosses by linking up the Nile valley in the north with the Cape Colony in the south, through a long and tortuous line of territory that included veldt and desert, mountain and swamp, and that, despite dreams of a Cape-to-Cairo railway, was never effectively joined by any means of regular communication until the day of the airplane.[20]

Yet even although Britain achieved a dominant strategic position vis-à-vis her European rivals, no one European state ever succeeded in dominating the entire continent. This was because the Congo, the heartland of Africa, remained "neutralized." The main European powers tolerated first Leopoldian and then Belgian rule over the Congo in order to prevent this key territory from passing into the hands of one of their rivals.

As already mentioned, Germany's strategy was to encourage France in Africa, so as to draw her into conflict with the United Kingdom there, thus eventually permitting Germany to become the arbiter. Even Germany's own acquisition of colonies is viewed by some as a ploy to rouse the French into hastening the pace of their own involvement. In fact two Anglo-French confrontations did occur in 1898, of which the first was over the northern limits of Nigeria, and the second, and ultimate one, was at Fashoda in the Sudan. It would appear, however, that despite an aroused and nationalistic public opinion in both countries, the British and French governments became sufficiently aware of the German intent and were able to avoid open conflict by delimiting their respective spheres of influence.

To understand the events that led up to these two confrontations, we need some background. To begin with, France, which already had

20. Sir George Goldie of the Niger Company was critical of the Cape-to-Cairo link advocated by Cecil Rhodes. Goldie pointed out that "trade seeks the sea by the shortest route," and added that in Africa the natural lines of intercourse ran across and not lengthwise. Africa, taken crosswise, was homogeneous, whereas lengthwise it was heterogeneous..The relative transience of the European grip upon Africa may have been due in part to the fact that it was Rhodes' concept, and not Goldie's, that prevailed.

footholds in Algeria, in Gabon (occupied in 1844), in French Somalia (where earlier interests had been consolidated by occupation in 1883), and in Madagascar (where a French protectorate was established in 1885 after a two-year war against the Malagasy government), had begun to expand inland from its Senegal settlements in the direction of the Niger. As early as the 1850s the French general Faidherbe had secured the Senegambia area and had pursued campaigns against the Fula leader Omar, who headed the *Toucouleur* forces. Faidherbe had also annexed some coastal areas before 1865, a year before Omar's death, when he returned to France. In the years that followed, France, involved in its quarrel with Germany, became inactive in West Africa until at last a new wave of expansion began with the arrival of Captain Gallieni in 1880. Pursuing a campaign against Ahmadu, a nephew of Omar, Gallieni, in 1883, founded and fortified Bamako, in what is now Mali. He also surveyed a railroad route between the Senegal and Niger rivers, the railroad itself being completed in 1888. Between 1888 and 1890 a French explorer, Captain Louis Binger, made a remarkable journey from Senegal down to the Ivory Coast, signing treaties with local chiefs as he went, and thus limiting further expansion inland of Portuguese Guinea, Sierra Leone, or Liberia. In 1890 a further diplomatic point was won by the French when the British conceded the area between the French North and West African holdings to be entirely their zone of influence. French fears that some other power might drive a wedge between the two were thus allayed. After this date, the French continued to expand. In 1893, advancing along the Niger, they reached Timbuktu, and in the same year, driving inland from their Port Novo settlement, defeated King Behanzin of Dahomey, deposed him, and occupied his country. By 1896 they had marched through Upper Volta to link their Niger possessions with Dahomey, thus cutting off further inland expansion of the British Gold Coast and of German Togo.

Limited in West Africa, Germany had nevertheless gained fresh territory in the east. In 1884–1885 Dr. Carl Peters and two companions had arrived in Zanzibar in disguise, and had then traveled through East Africa, signing treaties as they went. The treaty rights were transferred to a newly founded German East African Company and the territory placed under the protection of the German Emperor. While the Sultan of Zanzibar protested at this invasion of territory that had previously been subject to him, his allies the British meanwhile plunged into the hinterland on their own account to lodge territorial claims. By 1886 Germany and the United Kingdom had partitioned East Africa into their respective spheres of influence, while the Sultan was permitted to retain control of Zanzibar itself, together with a titular claim to certain

territories on the coast. In 1890 the British recognized the French position in Madagascar in return for French recognition of the British
position in Zanzibar. France then formally annexed Madagascar in 1896.

For some time the progress of the French in West Africa was impeded
by wars against such African leaders as Ahmadu, Behanzin, or Samory,
but not by opposition from any other European power. Between 1896
and 1898, however, a period of extreme tension occurred between France
and the United Kingdom as a result of their conflicting interests on the
Niger. The French were attempting not only to limit the northern expansion of British Nigeria, but also to travel down the Niger far enough
to establish themselves on waters navigable by ocean-going shipping.
The British, however, had their own ambitions for the Niger, which
they saw as a potential African Ganges, on whose banks, one day,
crowded cities would arise, with markets clamoring for British-made
manufactured goods. In 1890 Britain and France had agreed that
neither the British from the south nor the French from the north would
cross the Say-Barruwa line, which ran approximately from west to east
in the region where there now runs the northern frontier of Nigeria.
However, the French—expanding more speedily and systematically in
West Africa than the British—interpreted the agreement in a manner that
the British considered to be jesuitical; that is, arguing that although they
might not *cross* the line from the north, they might nevertheless go
round it, or approach the territory to the south of the line from any
other direction, and thus establish that "effective occupation" which was
recognized as the final confirmation of any colonial claim.

Against this tactic the British opposed another—that of the "chessboard." Wherever French forces appeared, British forces were sent to
occupy adjacent villages. Within a short time tension grew as platoons
became scattered behind one another's lines like pieces on a chessboard.
The officers on the spot often believed that this deployment was the
preliminary to a general war between the French and the United
Kingdom, but it was designed to be a confrontation to test French will,
and not a war. War did not result, and agreement was reached in the
Niger Convention of 1898, whereby the limits of French and British
rule in West Africa were decided.

The confrontation on the Niger was preliminary, however, to the
more serious Anglo-French confrontation at Fashoda in 1898. It was,
indeed, at Fashoda that the decision was made which determined
whether the French dream of an empire stretching from Senegal to
Somalia, or the British Cape-to-Cairo plan, would prevail. In the incident
General Sir Herbert (later Lord) Kitchener with a British-led army
of 20,000 at his disposal, fresh from his victory over the Mahdist forces

at Omdurman, came face to face with Colonel Marchand, commanding about nine Frenchmen and 150 Senegalese. Another French party had a short time earlier been to Ethiopia, where they had presented the Emperor Menelik with 10,000 rifles in the hope that he would extend the Ethiopian frontier to Fashoda, thus forestalling the British. Menelik, however, failed to move, and Marchand was left to face Kitchener alone. Upon meeting, both forces awaited further instructions from their respective capitals. The brief but sharp crisis that ensued menaced for a moment the peace of Europe—after which the French bowed to *force majeure* in the Sudan. Marchand proceeded to Somalia, but no longer, as it were, in his capacity as a representative of French expansionism. Cape-to-Cairo had won the day. The main lines of the pattern of Africa's partition among the European powers had been decided.

Yet another force had been scheduled to rendezvous at Fashoda in support of Marchand against the British. This force was to have been provided by none other than Leopold II, who, having established himself as King of the Congo, had begun to conceive designs on the Upper Nile, and to indulge himself in Pharaonic moods.[21] In collusion with the French, therefore, a force under the command of Dhanis had been dispatched from Stanleyville in the Congo Free State, bound for Fashoda. Unfortunately for Leopold and the French, this force included members of the Batetela tribe. The Batetela had combined with the Belgians some years earlier to help drive the Arabs from the Congo, but the Belgians had repaid them by treacherously executing their leader, Ngongo Lutete. The Batetela had not forgiven or forgotten this act. When the Dhanis expedition was far on its way, the Batetela led an uprising that destroyed the force from within. Dhanis himself was fortunate to be able to reach Stanleyville alive.

The Cape-to-Cairo design might have prevailed, but, politically, the line was not yet clear, since the Boer republics stood in the way. In Southern Africa, tension had grown between two differing types of European society—the Boer republics on the one hand, and Britain's Cape Colony on the other. The Boers were the descendants of the Dutch immigrants who had settled at the Cape in 1652. When the Cape had finally been seized by the British in 1806,[22] the Boers had begun to move inland. Gradually they moved beyond the purview of the British until at last they consolidated their own forms of government in the interior. It was at this time that the personality of the Boer settler, whose Calvinism and independence were represented by his Bible and

21. A suggestion had appeared in the Belgian press in 1897, perhaps at Leopold's instigation, that the Nile might be made an international waterway, as the Congo had been, and placed under the care of some disinterested power, neither Britain nor France. The implied invitation to hand over Egypt to Leopold was not, however, accepted.
22. It was ceded to the United Kingdom by the Dutch government in 1814.

his gun, emerged. To escape British governmental control such settlers trekked north into the interior. After coming into conflict with the Zulus, led by Chaka, the Boers attempted to settle in Natal, but had been prevented from doing so by the British. It was therefore above all in the Transvaal and north of the Orange River that they settled, and here they founded two republics—the South African Republic (in the Transvaal) in 1852, and the Orange Free State in 1854. These republics were both self-governing and were to some extent independent of the United Kingdom in their foreign relations.

In the years that followed the Boers were frequently harried by the British, who nevertheless refrained from asserting themselves fully to the south of the Zambezi when it would have been relatively easy for them to do so. Dutch settlers in the Boer Republics also did much to mobilize Dutch and German opinion against Britain's South African policies, which were not made easier to defend by reason of their ambiguity.[23]

The discovery of diamonds in the Cape Colony and then of gold in the Transvaal attracted a flood of adventurers, many of them British, to South Africa. Before long these "Outlanders" (as the Boers called them) outnumbered the Boers in the Transvaal itself by five to one. The Boers maintained their autocratic governmental tradition intact, while at the same time imposing a high tariff on imported goods, so as to discourage economic dependence upon the Cape, but thereby substantially raising the cost of European living until it was several times higher than at the Cape. A conflict was brewing that has justly been described as a collision between the customs and Puritanism of the seventeenth century and the impatient commercialism of the nineteenth.

Ready to stop at nothing to ensure the emergence of their brave new world, the captains of the expansionist wave of British imperialism, such as Cecil Rhodes (who, having made a fortune in diamonds, had risen to become Prime Minister of the Cape Colony), and Joseph Chamberlain, the British Secretary of State for the Colonies, worked in collusion to launch what became known as the Jameson Raid. Directed against the Transvaal Republic in 1895, the raid was an attempt by a band of adventurers, headed by a British doctor named Leander Starr Jameson, who was an intimate of Rhodes, to overthrow the Transvaal government of Paul Kruger, and then, in the resulting confusion, to impose British control. The raid failed pitiably; the adventurers were captured by the Boers without reaching their first objective—Johannesburg. Subsequent denials of complicity by the British government did

---

23. For example, at an earlier stage (in the 1840s)—to quote Sir Harry Johnston—"The usual shilly-shally on the part of the British Government misled the Boers into thinking that they could maintain themselves in Natal against our wishes."

nothing to improve the situation, but, on the contrary, led to a hardening of attitudes on both the Boer and the British side, thus helping to prepare the way for the Boer War which followed in 1899.[24]

Thoroughly alarmed by the Jameson Raid, the two Boer republics had concluded a military alliance in 1896, after which they had imported large quantities of arms and ammunition via Mozambique. It was the belief of the Boers that in the event of war between themselves and the British one or more European powers would come to their support, thus diverting Britain's attention from South Africa, after which the Dutch living in the Cape Colony would also rise to help the Boer cause. They therefore declared war on Britain on October 11, 1899. But, despite pronounced military successes by the Boers in the early stages of the war, no European power, as it happened, came to their help, nor did the Cape Dutch rise. The Boers were defeated. President Kruger sought political asylum in Holland, and Britain annexed the two republics. The war was concluded by the Peace of Vereeniging in 1902. In order to seek to heal the breach between white and white in South Africa, a degree of self-government was then restored to the two states, and when the Union of South Africa was formed in 1910—joining together the Cape Colony, Natal, the Transvaal, and the Orange Free State— the first Prime Minister of the bilingual Union, Louis Botha, was one of the Boer generals. A semblance of harmony was thus given to a country so deeply divided that not only white and black sought different destinies, but white and white were separated by the memory of bloodshed and injustice. Joseph Chamberlain's policy of risk-taking, which had worked on the Niger, helped to lead South Africa toward rancorous social division.

The ending of the independence of the Boer republics was followed, in 1908, by another rectification—the transfer of the Congo from the control of King Leopold II to the Belgian government. Rumors of the abuses perpetrated by Leopold's agents had long been circulating. An Englishman, E. D. Morel, struck by inconsistencies in the official statistics provided by the Congo Free State, had discovered the degree of suffering caused by the compulsory collection of rubber quotas from the Congolese, and in his book *Red Rubber* and other writings exposed the workings of the system. The substance of his allegations was confirmed by an official British report made in 1904 by Roger Casement, a British consul who had verified conditions in the Congo Free State at

24. "One of my most dramatic moments as a historian," writes C. W. de Kiewit, "came when I first saw the almost blank sheet of paper which is part of the evidence of the complicity of Joseph Chamberlain and the Colonial Office in this unworthy effort of the government of a great Empire to solve its problems by rapine and then to hide its complicity by helping to engineer a lie which no later generosity or statesmanship could wholly purge." (*The Anatomy of South African Misery*, 1956, p. 12.)

first hand.[25] The attitude of Casement toward Leopold's Congo is clear from the following excerpt from a letter that he later wrote to Morel:

> For my part, I said . . . that if I got home again I should go to all lengths to let my countrymen know what a hell upon earth our own white race has made, and was daily making, of the homes of the black people it was our duty to protect.

After the publication of Casement's report, public feeling in Europe against Leopold became pronounced. In Belgium, too, the public became disturbed at the degree of extraconstitutional power that Leopold had accumulated for himself by means of his Congo holdings. In 1908 the Belgian government voted to annex the Congo as a colony, and on November 15, 1908, the flag of the Congo Free State was lowered. Leopold died the following year.

By treaty and agreement almost all of Africa had now been partitioned between the European powers, bilateral agreements completing the details left unattended to by earlier conferences. There remained, however, one corner of Africa where inter-European friction had not yet been resolved—Morocco. It is a curious irony of history that it should be the very country where the European invasion of Africa began, with the Portuguese attack upon Ceuta in 1415, that was also the last to fall to European domination.

The rise of German power had led France and the United Kingdom to draw together and, in 1904, to form a new alliance, the Entente Cordiale. Within the framework of the Entente, general agreement was reached on African questions. More specifically, the United Kingdom gave France a free hand in Morocco (except for certain areas that were to be reserved for Spain) in return for a free hand for Britain in Egypt. Germany, however, in 1905, decided to assert itself about Morocco in opposition to this understanding, and therefore made approaches to the United States, Russia, and the Sultan of Morocco, receiving varying degrees of support from each. In order to resolve the situation, the conference of Algeciras, in Spain, was called in 1906, at which France and Spain each obtained a privileged position in Morocco. In 1908, however, increasing European influence in Morocco led to internal disorders which culminated in civil war. In 1911 France intervened in support of the then reigning sultan and to protect the local European community, as both the sultan and the Europeans were threatened by the insurgents. Fearing the establishment of an outright French protectorate, the Germans then sent a warship—the *Panther*—to Agadir in Morocco, where they cherished hopes of establishing a naval base that would

25. Joseph Conrad, who had met Casement in the Congo, wrote of him in 1903: "I always thought some particle of Las Casas' soul had found refuge in his indomitable body." Casement, it will be recalled, was subsequently executed in the First World War by the British government for high treason, having accepted German support for an Irish insurrection against British rule.

make Germany an Atlantic power to reckon with. In the resulting crisis the United Kingdom, which saw its command of the seas threatened, strongly supported France, and Germany was obliged to be content with the transfer of some of the territory of the French Congo to German Kamerun, by way of compensation for Germany's disappointed hopes in Morocco. This transaction having been completed, the Sultan of Morocco, in 1912, accepted French protection. In the same year a Franco-Spanish Treaty placed certain parts of Morocco under Spanish administration. In addition, the port of Tangier was given a special status as internationalized territory.

So ended the partition of Africa among the European powers. The partition was virtually bloodless. No major European conflict arose over the occupation of Africa, despite the fact that such conflicts had at times seemed imminent. But the occupation, as distinct from the partition of Africa, was not bloodless. Every colonizing power engaged in hostilities against the African peoples. The place, time, and circumstance may have varied, but the tale of African dead, burned huts, and destroyed crops was dismally the same. Power, through quick-firing rifles and punitive expeditions, was made manifest to all. Nor, so far as Europe was concerned, was much doubt entertained as to the natural justification for such a process. Europe had a mission to civilize Africa, and to use its wealth for the benefit of the world. So ran the argument.

### The "Pacification" of Africa

To African rulers of various degrees it was not always clear that the European newcomers were divided among themselves—or, if it was clear, it was not apparent which one of them was in fact the stronger. Such was the situation of the King of Kiama in what is now Nigeria, who wrote to Lugard, the British colonizer who was the first white man he had seen and with whom he had concluded an agreement:

> The French came to me three times after your visit. . . . I do not know what country they came from, or what people they are; they are too strong for me and I pray that you will come between me and them; this is what I want to say to you.

Sometimes African rulers accepted European domination, and sometimes they did not, and sometimes when the rulers accepted it, the people did not. Resistance, however, was everywhere overcome, even when it was long drawn out. For Africa fought back, and did not automatically accept the imposition of the new alien rule. The forcible repression of African attempts to retain independence was referred to by the Europeans by the euphemistic term of "pacification."

A number of punitive expeditions were launched against various regions of Africa at various times in the nineteenth century before the

Berlin Conference of 1884–1885. The United Kingdom, for example, fought a number of wars against the Ashanti of the Gold Coast hinterland.[26] It was not until after the Berlin Conference, however, that military operations were begun throughout Africa to end resistance to European occupation. In the twenty years that followed, such operations, in one part of Africa or another, were the rule rather than the exception.

German rule appears to have been particularly characterized by African uprisings. In 1888–1889 the Germans found themselves combating an uprising in East Africa led by Bushiri. In 1891–1893 they were fighting the Wahehe in the same region. In 1903 an uprising in German South West Africa by the Bondelswarts (a people of mixed Boer and Hottentot ancestry) was repressed only to be followed by another uprising—also in South West Africa—of the Herero people, who were so decimated by General von Trotha that they came close to being totally exterminated. Earlier the Germans had repressed an uprising in Kamerun in 1895, only to have another occur in the western region of the same country in 1905. Most grievous of all was the great *Maji-Maji* uprising of 1905–1907 in German East Africa. The word *maji* means "water," and the rising was so called because the African religious leaders averred to their people that they were immune to German bullets, which would have no more effect upon them than if they were made of water. The Germans suffered considerable losses, but in revenge devastated a large region in the south of the territory. Altogether an estimated 120,000 Africans were either killed or starved to death. Parts of the area still remain depopulated and uncultivated to this day.

As we have already seen, the British achieved their most dramatic military victory over African resistance in the reconquest of the Sudan, culminating in the battle of Omdurman in 1898, at which Kitchener's forces, in what was little more than a mechanical slaughter, killed an estimated 20,000 Sudanese partisans of the Mahdist movement. Elsewhere, the British marched once more on the Ashanti capital of Kumasi in 1896, in order to depose the Asantehene, and in 1900 fought a final, and difficult, campaign against the Ashanti, after having inadvertently offended the religious and cultural traditions of that nation by demanding the surrender of their golden stool. In Nigeria, too, a number of campaigns were fought, of which that against Benin in 1897 was only one example. Other parts of British-dominated Africa saw comparable actions.

26. At least one of these—the Ashanti war of 1824—was notably unsuccessful from the British standpoint. The British Governor, Sir Charles MacCarthy, at a critical moment in the battle of Asamankow, had the Royal Africa Corps play "God Save the King" in the belief that this would lead the greater part of the Ashantis to come over to his side. Not only did the Ashantis not join the British, but they also defeated Sir Charles, and cut off his head. His skull was converted into a drinking cup which may still be viewed in Kumasi.

In what was to become Rhodesia, war was waged against the Matabele in 1893, and against both the Matabele and the Mashona in 1896–1897. Even in the model colony of Sierra Leone an uprising was caused by taxation and was suppressed.

African resistance to French occupation was symbolized by the remarkable Samory, a Mandingo leader who defied French efforts to apprehend him. In the 1890s, moving freely throughout West Africa, he almost succeeded in embroiling the French in a clash with the British, and was able to launch repeated attacks upon French outposts. Not until 1898 was Samory finally captured, to be exiled to Gabon.

Not all repression was instigated by the European governments. Often European officers, thinking themselves free from administrative control, would indulge in cruel excesses for which one could find no justification in their instructions. Perhaps the most striking example of this was the Voulet-Chanoine expedition of 1898. These two French officers commanded an expedition that left Senegal with the purpose of converging with two other French expeditions—one from Algeria and one from the Congo—upon Lake Chad, in order to take effective possession of newly acquired French territory. En route, Voulet ordered the burning of villages and the massacre of villagers in the Niger Bend area. When the French learned of this, they sent another officer to take command. Voulet had his replacement shot down—an event that occurred on Bastille Day, in the sultanate of Sokoto, which was then technically British territory. Voulet then proposed to his Senegalese troops that they should march on with him in order to establish a new independent African state of their own, since they and he had now become outlaws. But the Senegalese preferred to return home to Senegal. They shot down Voulet and Chanoine, and placed themselves under the command of another French officer, after which the expedition proceeded to its Lake Chad rendezvous.

The rendezvous was kept, but this was not the end of military operations. The combined French forces then attacked and defeated Rabah Zobeir, a former slave who had succeeded in becoming Sultan of Bornu, after which he had attempted to form a buffer state between the zones of French and British influence—a well-conceived plan which had one fatal defect: neither the British nor the French intended to permit such a buffer state to exist. Rabah Zobeir was defeated and killed.

One remarkable phenomenon that characterized the occupation of Africa was, indeed, the degree of European solidarity that persisted, despite conflicts of interest between different European nations. Evidence of this is to be found, for example, in the Anglo-French conflict over Borgu. Before the matter was decided, the British general, Sir James Willcox, called upon the King of Borgu to discuss the matter. In

Margery Perham's words, "Willcox refused even to listen to his talk of a ruse by which the French might be evicted. His code of loyalty to his own race, even in the circumstances, was inviolable."[27]

Once the pacification was completed, numbers of other Europeans began to arrive in Africa to play various roles—as administrators, missionaries, traders, miners, and, in some cases, settlers. Whether they were called "Master," *Baas*, or *Bwana*, their social position as superior beings to the Africans among whom they lived appeared manifest. The immediate effect of their arrival may be symbolized by the awe and wonder with which, while watching the Swiss missionary and anthropologist Henri Junod play the organ, a little Bathonga boy whispered to himself, "White people are only overcome by death." For so, indeed, it did then seem.

27. *Lugard: The Years of Adventure: 1858–1898*, p. 692.

# Chapter 8

# To the Antipodes:

# The European Occupation

# of Australasia

*We mean to travel to the antarctic pole,*
*Conquering the people underneath our feet,*
*And be renowned as never emperors were.*
—Christopher Marlowe, *Tamburlaine the Great* ( 1587 )

*We whites have signally failed to populate New Zealand, where we number*
*only a million and a half instead of tens of millions in each of the two islands.*
*. . . We have given up Australia as uninhabitable except in a few corners.*
—George Bernard Shaw ( 1944 )

THE PEOPLING of Australasia by Europeans was a process
that lacked the dramatic dimensions of the European epic
in other continents. No Congo, no Amazon flowed out to wash with its
waters the keels of the early voyagers. The wild wastelands that lay behind the Gulf of Carpentaria did not lead on to any court of a Kublai
Khan. In place of the kingdom of Prester John, or of the realm of Montezuma, was only to be found an unforgiving land that was described in
the report of the first European ship known to have visited Australia—the
*Dufyken*, commanded by Willem Janzsoon of Amsterdam—in the following terms:

They found this extensive country for the greatest part desert, but in some places
inhabited by wild, cruel, black savages, by whom some of the crew were murdered.

The unfolding of the subsequent tale of settlement contains almost
always the same harsh climatic theme, in which the triumphs, being
those of endurance rather than of conquest, were necessarily muted.

The *Dufyken* had sailed from Bantam in Java in November, 1605, unaware that the following month a Spanish expedition, headed by a Portuguese, Quiros, was also to set sail for Australasian waters. The Dutch intention was to investigate the southern coast of New Guinea for gold: the aim of Quiros was to discover the great southern continent, lying somewhere to the south of Java, that Marco Polo had perhaps referred to as Locach, and which was later sometimes known as Beach.[1] Quiros, who had sailed on an earlier voyage of Pacific discovery with Alvaro de Mendana de Neyra, had spoken to the Pope, and, Columbus-like, yearned to find new lands and save souls for Christ. Sailing from Peru in December, 1605, he arrived in the New Hebrides in May, 1606, mistaking an island—which he named Austrialia del Espiritu Santo[2]— for the continent that he sought. Firm in his belief that the new land stretched all the way to the South Pole, he proceeded to create a Ministry of War and Marine, a new religious Order—the Knights of the Holy Ghost, and a civil administration. He also named a local river the Jordan, and chose a site for the construction of "New Jerusalem." During the next month, June, 1606 (in which the *Dufyken* returned home to Bantam), some form of dissension arose within the Quiros expedition, as a result of which Quiros' own ship sailed back to Peru,[3] while the other ships sailed on westward under the titular command of Diego de Prado, but in effect under that of another Portuguese, Torres. Between mid-July and September, 1606, Torres cruised along the southern coast of New Guinea, passing through the Strait which now bears his name. What is somewhat surprising, however, is that Torres did not refer to his Strait as a new discovery, but speaks of it as something that he already knew to exist. This leads one to ask, Had the Portuguese already sailed through the Strait? In other words, did the "conspiracy of silence" with which the Portuguese had enshrouded their West African discoveries, and which may have been extended to Brazil, also extend to Australia? The question may be asked, but we cannot answer it. Torres himself was a Portuguese, even though in the service of Spain. (The two realms were at that time united.) Furthermore, French maps made between 1530 and 1550 show a large land in the South Pacific which is roughly in the position of Australia. If these maps portrayed contemporary discovery, and were not based upon guesswork, that discovery would necessarily have been made by the Portuguese. A second question

1. Marco Polo reported that "Gold is abundant to a degree scarcely credible: elephants are found there. . . . The country is wild and mountainous." J. A. Williamson states, apropos of Locach and other lands, "Marco Polo made some statements about the Malay peninsula and the adjacent islands, but these were garbled by transcribers of his manuscript and made to refer to great lands as yet undiscovered by Europeans, regions of the southern continent rich in gold, spices, and aromatic drugs."

2. The spelling, it may be noted, is "Austrialia" and not "Australia."

3. Quiros, a good pilot, had by 1605 become a mystic. On one occasion when asked by the helmsman what course to steer, he replied that the ships might go where they would, for God would guide them right. Some have hinted that Quiros' crew declined to follow such a captain further, and sailed the ship back to Peru. A discovery by the expedition of the true dimensions of Austrialia del Espiritu Santo could also, if it occurred, have contributed to the undermining of Quiros' authority.

also remains unanswered: Did Torres and his companions realize that the tip of the Cape York Peninsula was, in fact, part of a great southern continent? What is certain, however, is that they did realize that they had overtly established the southern limits of New Guinea. Their discovery—if discovery it was—remained nevertheless little publicized. Ambiguity about the geographical relationship between Australia and New Guinea persisted for over a century and a half longer, for Torres' account of his voyage was only published in the eighteenth century.

The day of Spanish and Portuguese discovery was fading, and now the Dutch were to predominate in Pacific waters. In 1611 a Dutch captain made a time-saving discovery: by sailing due east from the Cape of Good Hope, and then turning north when the longitude of Batavia was reached (instead of using the seasonal monsoon to travel via East Africa and India), the passage time was reduced by more than half. After 1614, the route became mandatory for Dutch East Indiamen, and it was not long before Dutch ships began to make occasional landfalls on the west coast of Australia.

The first of these ships was commanded by Dirck Hartog of Amsterdam, and it reached the Australian coast in 1616, anchoring in the shelter of what is now Hartog's Island. Later another Dutch captain, Houtman, after narrowly escaping shipwreck on some reefs in 1619, suggested that a Dutch way station between the Cape and Batavia might be established on the new-found coast. The Dutch, however, were on the whole, as we have noted, more interested in pursuing their regular commerce than in making new discoveries, so that the knowledge of the coast of Australia was but intermittently acquired. Coen, the Governor-General of the Dutch East Indies, outlined a plan for discovery, but circumstance prevented its being followed. In 1627 part of the south coast was discovered and named Peter de Nuyts Land. Thus, in haphazard ways, all the west coast and parts of the north and south coasts became known to navigators. It was a long time, however, before assurance was gained that the Gulf of Carpentaria in the north was not, in fact, the entrance to a north-south channel splitting Australia into two separate islands.

One of Coen's successors in Batavia, Governor-General Van Diemen, finally resolved to pursue a systematic scheme of exploration. As one of his agents he was fortunate to obtain Abel Tasman, a competent captain. On his famous voyage, which began in 1642, Tasman sailed due east along the southern side of Australia, although out of sight of land. He thus became the discoverer of Tasmania (he himself called it Van Diemen's Land), which he reported to be probably inhabited by a race of giants. He then continued and came upon New Zealand, although here again he made a quantitative error, as he apparently concluded that it consisted of one large island instead of two.

As in other continents, the Iberians (although in this instance they had merely brushed by) were to be followed by the Dutch, and the Dutch, in turn, were to be followed by the French and the British. Competition between the European nations, however, was hardly intense so far as Australia was concerned. Australia, if it was indeed Locach, was more visibly characterized by its "wild and mountainous" nature than by its hypothetical elephants, or its still-hidden reserves of gold. It was, moreover, exceedingly remote. A country named Locach, hypothetical or not, in which even its Asian neighbors did not exhibit interest, was hardly likely to hold for long the interest of men who searched for rivers of gold and fountains of youth. In 1577 the promoters of the voyage of Sir Francis Drake to the Pacific planned that he should found an empire in *Terra Australis*. In practice, however, Drake, with royal support, attacked Spanish treasure ships instead, and thought no more about searching for southern continents.

It was not until the seventeenth century that European interest in the South Pacific was aroused—by another buccaneer, William Dampier, who was the first Englishman to visit Australia. Sailing on board the *Cygnet*, he was one of a group of buccaneers who, while in the Pacific, casually decided to visit Australia in 1688. Upon his return to England, after many more adventures, Dampier published his *New Voyage Around the World* in 1697, thus creating interest not only in himself but also in the lands that he had visited. In consequence the British Admiralty sent him out once more to "New Holland" (as Australia was then known) as captain of the *Roebuck*, engaged on a voyage of discovery. He had intended to explore the south and east coasts of Australia, but circumstances prevented him from doing more than adding to the knowledge of the environs of New Guinea. (The *Roebuck* was ill-equipped and so rotten that on the return voyage she foundered off the island of Ascenscion in the Atlantic "thro' perfect Age." Luckily the crew was saved.)

The South Pacific appears to have entered into vogue in Britain in the earlier years of the eighteenth century. The South Sea Company, while its operations were conducted on paper in London rather than in the Pacific itself, came to symbolize a feverish spirit of speculation that disintegrated in the financial disaster of 1721, known as the "South Sea Bubble." Five years later Swift's Gulliver, in recounting his travels, alluded to "my cousin Dampier," and reported that he had landed in Lilliput after being shipwrecked "north west of Van Diemen's Land."

## Terra Australis Incognita

By the sixteenth century enough had become known of the Pacific for theories to be formulated about it. Some theorists held, in a concept that could be traced back to Ptolemaic times, that a large land mass—

*Terra Australis Incognita*—must exist in the southern hemisphere in order to balance Europe and Asia in the north, since otherwise the world would be too top-heavy. On the basis of a little knowledge, therefore, a theory came into being which held that a large southern continent, this same Australis, did in fact stretch for thousands of miles from the known parts of Australia to Tierra del Fuego in South America. This was the land that Quiros sought (and thought that he had found), and that Drake was meant to colonize. From about 1570 until 1775, belief in the southern continent flourished in various forms, even though it became clear that the hypothetical land mass did not, as was first thought, extend into the tropics. Tasman had also proved that "it" was unconnected with Australia, although he believed that New Zealand must constitute a part of it. By 1763, when the Seven Years War with France had ended, the British Admiralty had time for peaceable pursuits once more. In 1768 it was decided to send a ship to observe the transit of the planet Venus across the face of the sun from Tahiti,[4] after which the expedition could make a voyage of discovery. It was generally expected that Alexander Dalrymple, a firm believer in the southern continent, would be placed in command of the expedition. Instead the Admiralty chose Captain James Cook, a competent navigator with no preconceived ideas. Upon leaving Tahiti, Cook's secret Admiralty instructions ordered him to proceed southward, where "there is reason to imagine that a continent, or land of great extent, may be found." If the continent was populated, the friendship of its inhabitants was to be cultivated, and trade with them begun.

Cook was not only an able navigator, he was also an outstanding leader. He was of humble origin, and his science was self-taught. His qualities had first attracted notice when he served under Wolfe in Canada. The last eleven years of Cook's life were to be spent mainly in the exploration of the Pacific. By the time he was killed on the beach at Hawaii in 1779, in a fracas with the islanders that was not of his seeking, he had provided an answer to every major question concerning the geography of the Pacific. Above all he had shown that, apart from Australia and Antarctica, no great southern continent existed. This knowledge was welcome news to the Lords of the Admiralty. Had such a continent existed, Britain would have had to attempt to occupy it, if only to deny it to the French or to any other European nation. Such a commitment on the other side of the globe would have strained British power, already overextended, still further. As it was, at the time of Cook's first voyage the British were experiencing difficulties in controlling their own North American colonies.

4. It was believed that observation of the transit of Venus from various points on the globe might help to determine the distance of the sun from the earth. As it happened, the problem was solved otherwise.

Although parts of both Australia and New Zealand had been discovered, both territories awaited identification in their totality. To both
lands it was Cook, on his first voyage of 1768–1771, who gave positive
geographic identity.[5] Having rounded Cape Horn and visited Tahiti, he
sailed south and then headed west, where he made his landfall on the
east coast of New Zealand, which he proceeded to circumnavigate and
chart. Still sailing west, his next discovery was the east coast of Australia, which he was the first European explorer known to have visited.
Accompanied by Sir Joseph Banks, a botanist and a member of the
Royal Society, Cook went ashore at "Botany Bay," the first landing
place that he could find after coasting north for over a week. Botany
Bay later became the name around which the concept, if not the reality,
of British colonization in Australia was to coalesce. The British settlement was in fact to take root at Sydney Cove.

Sailing north, Cook's voyage of discovery along the eastern coast
of the continent was nothing less than epic. His ship, the *Endeavour*,
was badly holed on a coral reef and had to be beached for repairs.
Then he found himself entrapped in coral shoals inside the Great
Barrier Reef. When he moved outside the shelter of the reef, he was
driven back by the ocean swell. Only after a narrow escape from disaster
was he able to resume his slow journey within the reef until, at last, he
reached the Cape York Peninsula, from where he passed through Torres
Strait, and so, by stages, home to England. Before leaving the Australian
coast Cook landed, just before sunset, at Possession Island, and formally
took possession of Eastern Australia under the name of "New Wales,"
and in the name of King George III.

Cook's second voyage—from 1772 to 1775—dissolved the last doubts
concerning Terra Australis Incognita. Sailing south from the Cape of
Good Hope until he arrived within the Arctic Circle, he followed a
zigzag course eastward until he reached New Zealand. He then sailed
the South Pacific Ocean in two great circles, traversing the area in such
a manner as to leave no doubt that, from the Marquesas to the Antarctic, no great continent remained to be discovered. Belief in Terra
Australis Incognita vanished quickly, like smoke in a strong wind.
Cook's third voyage, in which he met his death, was devoted to the
problems of the North Pacific, and, in particular, to an attempt to find
the eastern entry to the Northwest Passage.

## Australasians and Europeans

Who were the original inhabitants of Australasia? Australia, before
the Europeans came, appears to have been populated by three migra-

5. He did not, however, discover that Tasmania, instead of being the southern tip of Australia,
was a separate island. This fact was established in 1798 by Mathew Flinders, who sailed through
Bass's Strait.

tions—that of the Negritos from Southeast Asia; of the Murrayans, who were related to the Ainu of Japan; and of the Carpentarians, related to the Vedda of Ceylon. New Zealand was populated by the Maori people, who were of Polynesian stock. Tradition held that they had arrived there in war canoes in about 1350 A.D., mingling with an earlier population of Papuan origin.

From the outset the European newcomers, possessing firearms and other accessories, found themselves in an advantageous position compared to the often nomadic inhabitants of these remoter regions of the world. Only in numbers did the Australasians, for some years yet, find themselves the stronger.

The first seventeenth-century encounters between Australasians and Europeans were few and haphazard. For example, Carstenz, commander of the *Pera,* a Dutch vessel which visited the Cape York Peninsula in 1623, reported that the inhabitants were black and barbarous, "poor and abject wretches, caring mainly for bits of iron and strings of beads." A Dutch attempt to kidnap an unarmed man on this occasion resulted in a fight, in which the Dutch killed a man. After this Carstenz and his companions were treated as enemies: at one place they were assailed by no less than 200 attackers.

Tasman, on his visit to Tasmania in 1642, had heard human sounds and the noise of an instrument like a small gong, but he had seen no human beings. His impression that the land was inhabited by giants was apparently due to the fact that he had seen two great trees with notches up the trunks five feet apart, from which he had deduced that a race of giants went climbing after birds' nests in this way—unless normal-sized inhabitants used some other device of which this formed a part.

Upon reaching New Zealand, Tasman's ship was approached by two Maori war canoes, the crews of which blew upon an instrument that the Dutch described as sounding like a Moorish trumpet. In reply, the Dutch sailors played upon European musical instruments. Other canoes then approached, but attacked a small cockboat that was maintaining communication between Tasman's ships, killing several members of its crew. The Dutch fired upon the Maoris, but without effect, then weighed anchor and left what they could only regard as a hostile coast.

Dampier, visiting western Australia in 1699, judged the inhabitants to have "the most unpleasant looks and the worst Features of any People that I ever saw, though," he added, "I have seen great variety of Savages."

Cook, in the eighteenth century, was more charitable; in Australasia as elsewhere in the Pacific he sought to avoid conflict and to promote friendship. He also frequently held the peoples among whom he traveled in respect, unlike some other European voyagers. In New Zealand, however, Cook's first appearance caused alarums and excursions. An attempt to stop a Maori war canoe in order to obtain information by firing over the heads of its crew merely provoked them to launch an immediate attack. The children of the Maori, who also witnessed Cook's arrival, years later told Europeans that his ship had, at first, been mistaken for a large bird, and the boat that put off from its side for an unfledged one. Cook's crew were clearly goblins, they said, for they rowed ashore facing backwards, presumably having eyes in the backs of their heads; moreover, when they looked fixedly at a normal mortal it made him feel ill. The Maori elders, however, were not intimidated by such phenomena.

In the coastal region where Tasman's boat had been attacked, Cook, after a few stones had been thrown at his ship, established friendship with the people, although he reported them to be cannibals. He judged the Maori to be of fine appearance, warlike, and of high intelligence. He was, however, interested in their land as well as in themselves, and thought that the northern island would prove the more suitable for European settlement, should the British ever decide to colonize it.

In Australia his arrival created less of a sensation than in New Zealand. Some of the inhabitants were so busy fishing that they hardly seemed to notice the sight presented by his *Endeavour*, though to them it certainly must have been a novel one. When a delegation set out to go ashore, however, two men came to contest the landing of over thirty Europeans, but retreated after small shot was fired. Further north, Cook's expedition encountered a people who were straight-haired and chocolate in color, being, unlike those of Dampier's description, neither disagreeable in feature, nor unpleasant in voice.

## The Settlement of Australia

The precisions which Cook's discoveries added to British knowledge of Australasia led to a new interest in the area—an interest that was not diminished by signs of increasing French concern with the South Pacific. In 1768 Bougainville, on his circumnavigatory voyage, had encountered Australia's Great Barrier Reef, upon which the thunder of the surf appeared to him to sound "as the voice of God," to which he was obedient, changing course to the northwest toward New Guinea. The following year, 1769, de Surville, another Frenchman, arriving on the New Zealand coast shortly after Cook, had just missed meeting the *Endeavour,* the two ships passing each other unawares during a spell of bad weather.

Positive considerations were, before long, to be added to the fear of French rivalry as an impetus for settlement. Following the loss of most of Britain's American colonies, the proposal was made, in 1780, that the British Loyalists who had fought for George III during the American War of Independence might find a new home in Australia. The proposal was dropped, but only to be replaced by another. For some time the British had been accustomed to transport many of their convicts to their American colonies, particularly those in the south, such as Georgia. The American Revolution ended this practice. In consequence, British prisons soon became crowded, and even the use of prison hulks did not solve the problem, since these also were soon filled. In 1779 consideration was given to resuming the transportation of convicted criminals overseas, and the botanist Sir Joseph Banks—the same who had accompanied Captain Cook on his first voyage—urged that a convict settlement be established at Botany Bay. Among the reasons that he gave for choosing this site was that he did not anticipate "any Opposition from the Natives." He "did not think there were above Fifty in all the Neighbourhood and had Reason to believe the Country was very thinly peopled;" those he saw were "naked, treacherous, and armed with Lances, but extremely cowardly, and constantly retired from our People when they made the least Appearance of Resistance." The climate, he added, was similar to that of Toulouse in the south of France. The committee before which he spoke viewed the suggestion with favor, but no immediate action was taken. Then in 1784 the Transportation Act was adopted, which authorized the resumption of the practice of deporting convicts, but opinions differed as to which country they should be sent to. Some favored Africa, and the advantages of the island of Lemane up the Gambia River were pressed. However, in 1785 a Mr. Smeatham, who had spent four years there, told a committee of inquiry that "if 200 convicts were left on an Island in the River Gambia, without any Medical Assistance than what they might give to each other, not One in 100 would survive the first Six Months."

It was Sir Joseph Banks' suggestion which gained favor. In 1786 the decision was taken to begin the transportation of convicts to "the eastern coast of New South Wales." On January 20, 1788, the first convoy of transports, under the command of Captain Phillip, arrived in Botany Bay to found a settlement. A few days later, on January 26, they moved to Sydney Cove, where they found "the finest harbour in the world." The British flag was raised, and the convicts were landed. The European colonization of Australia had begun.

The early days were hard. One convict wrote home:

> To give a just description of the hardships that the meanest of us endure, and the anxieties suffered by the rest, is more than I can pretend to. In all the Crusoe-like adventures I ever read or heard of, I do not recollect anything like it.

To begin with the new settlers, both convicts and troops, had to be "hutted"; then crops were to be planted. Only eight acres could be cleared and sown the first year. Some of the convicts worked more willingly than had been anticipated, whereas others, according to the Governor, dreaded punishment less than they feared labor. However, the consciousness of the immense distance between the penal colony of New South Wales and the English homeland afflicted the spirits of all. The same convict quoted above, writing home in 1790, said:

> We have heard that some convicts at home, who might have been pardoned for capital crimes, have chosen their former sentence rather than come here; and which, though it was contradicted, we cannot help thinking is true.

The arrival of a ship from England, bringing requirements of every shape and size, from cows to needles, occasioned the deepest emotions. Above all it brought news from Europe. After the arrival of one such ship in 1790, a Mr. Tench commented:

> News burst upon us like meridian splendor on a blind man. We were overwhelmed with it; public, private, general, and particular. Nor was it until some days had elapsed, that we were able to methodize it, or reduce it into form.

The news, on this occasion, was, it must be admitted, of more than everyday interest. Not only did it tell of the illness and subsequent recovery of George III, but also included "all the attendant circumstances of that wonderful and unexpected event" the French Revolution of 1789, which, said Mr. Tench, "amazed us."

Relations with the aborigines did not, despite the efforts of Governor Philips, develop favorably. Thefts by both aborigines and settlers led to retaliatory violence by both. On one occasion, in 1788, two convicts who had tried to steal a canoe were found dead, the head of one being beaten to a jelly. Of contacts between Europeans and aborigines at the outset, the best that could be said was that they were "neither frequent nor cordial."

Slowly the colony established itself. When, in 1792, the first Governor, Philips, returned to England (taking with him "natives of the country, Bennilong and Yem-mer-ra-wan-nie, two men who were much attached to his person," as well as plants, birds, and animals, including four kangaroos), he left behind him 1,700 acres under cultivation. It was also found that settlers labored more diligently on the land when they worked for themselves instead of for the common good.

In 1802–1803 an event occurred which affected the future development of the colony of New South Wales: Mathew Flinders, a British hydrographer, circumnavigated the continent for the first time; demonstrated that New South Wales in the east, and New Holland in the west formed parts of a single territorial unity; and suggested that this unity be named "Australia." His suggestion was eventually adopted. Nevertheless, not until the land mass as a whole had been occupied by European settlers did the name "Australia" acquire a constitutional, as distinct from a geographic, meaning.

British keels were not the only ones to furrow Australia's coastal waters. French ships were seen in the vicinity of "Van Diemen's Land," as Tasmania was called until 1853, and it was learned that the French were investigating the island in order to find a place suitable for establishing a settlement. In order to forestall the French, the New South Wales authorities hastily established a British colony in Tasmania in 1803–1804. By 1814 there were almost 1,900 settlers there, of whom almost a quarter were convicts. Ten years later, in 1824, the settlement had grown to 12,000, of whom almost half were convicts. The population continued to grow steadily thereafter until it reached over 40,000 in the 1830s, and over 70,000 in the 1840s. As the numbers of European settlers grew, so the numbers of the original inhabitants diminished. Hostilities between the two groups occurred from the outset. By 1830, when Governor Arthur held a "Black Drive" to attempt to drive the Tasmanians into the neck of East Bay, the island's inhabitants, who originally had numbered several thousand, had been reduced to 360. This remnant was gathered together and taken to Flinders Island in Bass Strait, where they soon became extinct, the last male dying in 1869.

On the Australian mainland the original inhabitants are estimated to have numbered about 300,000 at the time of the Europeans' arrival. The introduction of drink and of disease, together with the alienation of tribes from their familiar territories, resulted in progressive depopulation. Even in the first year of the arrival of the Europeans disease appears to have struck the aborigines. As Tench wrote in 1788:

> An extraordinary calamity was now observed among the natives. Repeated accounts brought by our boats of finding bodies of the Indians in all the coves and inlets of the harbour, caused the gentlemen of our hospital to procure some of them for the purposes of examination and anatomy. On inspection it appeared that all the parties had died a natural death: pustules, similar to those occasioned by the small pox, were thickly spread on the bodies; but how a disease, to which our former observations had led us to suppose them strangers, could at once have introduced itself, and have spread so widely, seemed inexplicable.

It was, however, the alienation of tribal land which seems to have produced the most harm. The original inhabitants of Australia were divided into some four or five hundred tribes, each of which appears to have possessed its own traditional territory, or hunting ground, delimited by well-known geographic features, and upon which other tribes were forbidden to trespass. As a result, an intimate relationship between tribe and land existed, which had a religious as well as a practical significance. The slaughtering of game by the incoming Europeans, and the alienation of tribal lands, produced a disturbance throughout the Australian body politic. Tribes, driven from their traditional homes, found themselves in conflict with neighboring tribes, and these, in turn, with others. Nor was there any question of successfully resisting the white invaders, armed as they were with superior weapons. The numbers of the invaders, moreover, steadily increased. By 1851 the total European population of the Australian colonies amounted to over 437,000. Even had the aborigines maintained the strength of their original numbers, they still would have become a minority in their own land.

With increasing numbers among the Europeans, the loneliness of the first settlers of New South Wales became somewhat mitigated. Some disturbance was caused in the early years by the appointment of William Bligh as Governor. Bligh's autocratic personality had already led him—and others—into difficulties. As captain of the *Bounty* he had provoked his crew to undertake the most notorious mutiny on a single ship known to British naval history. Similiar arrogant conduct on his part as Governor of New South Wales—a post to which he was appointed in 1806—led to a similar result. In 1808 the local military deposed him as Governor, holding him as a prisoner until such time as he could be sent back to England. He was replaced by Lachlan Macquarie who, between 1810 and 1821, did much to conciliate some of the colony's internal political divisions. Even Governor Macquarie, however, was unable to bridge the social division between the convicts (or "emancipists," as they became known when their sentences had expired) and the free settlers. Some conception of the problem may be gained from the fact that in 1821, the last year of his governorship, out of a European population of nearly 30,000, some 12,000—about 41 percent—were convicts.

The colony's economy, at first unpromising, was much helped by the introduction of sheep farming. John Macarthur, a local settler of substance, took the initiative of crossing Calcutta ewes with merino sheep from South Africa. The resulting stock produced fine wool that was exported to British factories, where it soon began to compete with woolen exports from Spain and Germany. The sheep-grazing proved well suited to the Australian climate, and, once the Blue Mountains were crossed in 1813, the graziers were able to spread out in the well-watered country beyond. Writing in 1840 one commentator observed:

> As well it might be attempted to confine the Arabs of the Desert within a circle traced upon their sands, as to confine the Graziers or Woolgrowers of New South Wales within any bounds that can possibly be assigned to them.[6]

6. Gipp's "Memorandum on Disposal of Lands in the Australian Colonies" (19th December, 1840).

From the New South Wales colony, European settlement spread through Australasia. Founded as a prison, New South Wales changed its essential character at the earliest opportunity. Indeed, no sooner did the first Governor leave, than an individualistic group of officials and settlers, later joined by emancipated convicts, began trading and farming for themselves, often using unpaid convict labor to accumulate capital. It was this group, or their descendants, who financed the enterprises which took white traders to New Zealand in 1810, which led to the expansion of New South Wales itself into what were later to become the separate colonies of Victoria and Queensland, and which sent settlers to South and Western Australia. The establishment of new colonies thus gave form to a dynamic process. Tasmania ("Van Diemen's Land") was given a separate status in 1825; Western Australia was founded in 1829; South Australia in 1834; New Zealand in 1840; Victoria in 1851; and Queensland in 1859.

The expansion of white Australasian power led, in turn, to demands for greater local control. As early as 1823 the New South Wales Act had created in the colony a Legislative Council of appointed members with powers that were largely advisory. As time passed by, and the emancipists grew in number and became reconciled with other settler groups, a demand rose for the ending of the transportation system. Other powers, too, were demanded, such as local control over taxation and customs duties. The reaction of the British government, with respect to transportation, was to move toward the abolition of the system in principle although not in practice. For example, although the admission of convicts to South Australia was forbidden in 1834, and although transportation to New South Wales was abolished in 1840, the effect of these measures was negated by the disembarkation of felons from Britain in Tasmania, from where, as the Australian Anti-Transportation League expressed it in 1851, "the avowed object of Her Majesty's Secretary of State is to transfuse the convicts throughout the Australasian Colonies, and thus to evade the spirit of the promises and Act of Parliament so made." Finally, after the discovery of gold in Australia in 1851, the transportation system was ended, except in Western Australia, where it continued until 1868. Whatever the immediate reasons given, it may be said that, in a deeper sense, transportation ended because it had fulfilled its function—that of providing forced labor to lay the foundations of a new European society overseas. Viewed in this light the parallel between the transportation of British convicts to Australia and the transportation of African slaves to the Americas will be evident.

### The Gold Rush

Until 1851 the ancient legends of the gold of Locach, spoken of by Marco Polo, by whomsoever they may have been credited had received little credit from the settlers of New South Wales, despite the fact that from 1823 on individual discoveries of gold had been made in the colony. The principal discoverer of Australia's gold, E. H. Hargraves, was in fact much mocked at when he landed in 1851 and announced his purpose. Although not a trained geologist, he had visited Australia eighteen years before, and had since been struck by the similarity of the land formation in parts of Australia and in the gold-bearing regions of California. At the first attempt he found gold where he had expected to find it, in the Bathurst district of New South Wales.

What I said on the instant [he later wrote] has since been much laughed at. And though my readers may renew the laugh, I shall not hesitate to repeat it. . . . "This," I exclaimed to my guide, "is a memorable day in the history of New South Wales. I shall be a baronet, you will be knighted, and my old horse will be stuffed, put into a glass case, and sent to the British Museum."[7]

The day was, indeed, a memorable one, for the discovery of gold marked the end of an epoch in Australia's history, and the opening of a new one. The change was attended by unparalleled excitement. Employers were deserted by their laborers, ships by their crews, wives by their husbands, pupils by their teachers—all who could, or would, were off to the diggings. Prices rose, business came to a standstill, and normal life appeared, for the time being, to have been suspended. One of the immediate effects of the discovery was, as we have already mentioned, the ending of the system of transportation, at least to the greater part of Australia. As one contemporary wrote in 1852:

It would appear a solecism to convey offenders, at the public expense, with the intention of at no distant time setting them free, to the immediate vicinity of those very goldfields which thousands of honest labourers are trying in vain to reach.[8]

Another effect was the granting by Britain of a greater degree of self-government to New South Wales than had hitherto seemed possible. As the British Secretary of State observed in 1852, the British government had been influenced by "those extraordinary discoveries of gold," and had now to take into consideration the wishes of the settlers "with reference to a state of affairs which has no parallel in human history, and which must, in all probability, stimulate the advance of population, wealth, and material prosperity with a rapidity alike unparalleled."

The most profound effect of all was indeed seen in the "advance of population." In the ten years from 1851 to 1861 the population doubled, rising from less than 450,000 to over a million. After this the rate of increase, however, became less dramatically rapid, rising to over two

7. "At that instant," he added, "I felt myself to be a great man. I was as mad, perhaps, at the moment, as Don Quixote was his life through; and, assuredly, my companion was as simple as Sancho Panza—for the good youth afterwards told me, he expected I should obtain for him the honour I had promised." (E. H. Hargraves, *Australia and its Gold Field*, London, 1855).

8. Pakington to Denison, 14th December, 1852, "Further Correspondence on the Subject of Convict Discipline and Transportation," *Parliamentary Papers*, 1853, LXXXII, 1601.

million in 1877, and to over three million in 1889. Nevertheless, from the time of the discovery of gold in 1851 the surge in numbers of the Europeans ensured that the original inhabitants of the continent were less than ever taken into account in any consideration of Australia's future. From this time on it was clearly felt that it was the white man who had the right to call himself an Australian.

In effect, a new name now came into vogue for the original inhabitants of the continent—the "aborigine." The name was, of course, not a new one, and had previously been used to designate a people who were believed to have originated in the country in which they still dwell. At different times British writers used it to refer to inhabitants of Asia, Africa, and America. The first Governor referred to the people of Australia as "natives," and other Europeans called them, variously, "natives," "Indians," "savages," or "blacks." By 1835 the New South Wales *Government Gazette* was, however, referring to "the aboriginal natives," in order, no doubt, to distinguish them on paper from native-born Australian whites. As the novelist Anthony Trollope, in writing of the original Australians, later explained to his British readers: "It will be as well to call the race by the name officially given to it. The government styles them 'aboriginals' . . . the word 'native' is almost universally applied to white colonists born in Australia."[9] By whatever name they were called, the aborigines were clearly diminishing in number. The London *Spectator* was unduly pessimistic for their future when, in 1864, it commented: "It seems probable that in half a century there will not be one aborigine left in Australia," but it nevertheless had grounds for making such a mistake.

The adoption of the name "aborigine," however, in conjunction with the dispossession of the aboriginal tribes and their diminution in numbers, soon led to the name acquiring a pejorative connotation. Restricted to reserves, regarded (after being subjected to well-intentioned but ill-conceived social experiments) as incapable of adapting to European ways, and often the victims of injustice, the aborigines were progressively driven toward the arid wastes of the north, and left to their own devices. Elsewhere, detribalization and discouragement led to the slow dissolution of the race.

### "A Long Black Mark"

The Europeans were not, however, the only newcomers to the Australian continent. Chinese and Polynesians were also to arrive in the second half of the nineteenth century. The Chinese came into Australia in the early 1850s, soon after the discovery of gold, and made their way to the diggings. They arrived in hundreds with the intention of digging

9. *Australia* (1893).

enough gold to return home again with a modest profit. Almost all were Cantonese from the Kwantung province, and almost without exception were male. One parliamentarian in the colony of Victoria proposed that a committee be appointed "to frame a Bill to control the flood of Chinese immigration . . . and effectually prevent the Gold Fields of Australia Felix from becoming the property of the Emperor of China and the Tartar hordes of Asia." The committee reported, in 1857, that the Chinese numbered over 40,000, "of which there are not more than four or five females, and those are of inferior class." An attempt had already been made to limit the numbers arriving by the introduction of a poll tax, but it was very frequently evaded by the stratagem of the new arrivals disembarking where the tax was not collected. Whether the Chinese themselves were responsible for this evasion, or whether unscrupulous ships' captains collected the poll tax from their passengers in advance but hit on this method to avoid paying it to the Australian authorities was a question to which the answer was frequently lost in the equivocal perplexities of Anglo-Chinese communication. One white Australian vividly described an encounter with the newcomers in 1854:

> I met between six and seven hundred coming overland from Adelaide. They had four wagons carrying their sick, lame, and provisions. They were all walking single file, each one with a pole and two baskets. They stretched for over two miles in procession. I was half-an-hour passing them. As I stood on a hill when I first came in sight of them, I could not make out what it was coming. They were winding across the plain like a long black mark, and as I passed them, every one behind seemed to be yabbering to his mate in front in a sing-song tone. It was a beautiful morning, so I did not feel very much against them, although they were defrauding the revenue. . . . They nearly all had hats like the top of a haystack, nearly a yard across.[10]

On a beautiful morning a single white Australian traveler may not have felt "very much against them," but there were other white Australians, and other mornings, when the climate was less propitious. In 1861 a serious riot occurred at Lambing Flat on the gold fields, in which some 3,000 white Australians attacked several hundred Chinese with unexpected brutality. The original attacks appear to have been concerted, for they took place to the accompaniment of music from a brass band. The unfortunate Chinese were mobbed and bludgeoned, few escaping uninjured. Almost all also had their pigtails cut off, in some cases the pigtails being taken with the scalps still attached. Any property the Chinese had that was not plundered was burned. After a delay of several days the police arrived upon the scene to restore order. The principal result of the riot was, however, the adoption by the various Australian parliaments of legislation that restricted further Chinese immigration and that discriminated against the Chinese already in the country.

10. J. Chandler, *Forty Years in the Wilderness* (1893).

The Polynesians, or *Kanakas*,[11] who arrived in Australia from Fiji, Noumea, and other islands were brought in from 1860 on as cheap labor to work on the Queensland sugar plantations. The system amounted in practice, however, to a form of semi-slavery, the methods being used to recruit the Kanakas being often dubious and at times nothing less than outright kidnaping. But the Kanakas were never so numerous as the Chinese, and Australian public opinion was consequently less exercised about them. Eventually most of the Kanakas returned home after the mechanization of many phases of sugar production had reduced the demand for their labor. Another factor which promoted their departure was the introduction by the Australian government of controls against abuses—a reform which raised the price of Kanaka labor, thereby making it less profitable for white employers to use.

The anti-Chinese riots had reflected one aspect of a new spirit that was abroad in Australia, and that had become manifest after the discovery of gold and the resulting social changes. Anthony Trollope compared Australia during this period to a young whale that had risen at last from the depths and was beginning to blow. Democratic and nationalistic, the new Australia was also brash and xenophobic. The spirit of the age may, perhaps, be summed up by the following extract from the Sydney *Bulletin* of July 2, 1887:

> All men who leave the tyrant-ridden lands of Europe for freedom of speech and right of personal liberty are Australians before they set foot on the ship which brings them hither. Those who fly from odious military conscription; those who leave their fatherlands because they cannot swallow the worm-eaten lie of the divine right of kings to murder peasants, are Australians by instinct—Australian and Republican are synonymous. No nigger, no Chinaman, no lascar, no kanaka, no purveyor of cheap coloured labour is an Australian. True to his grovelling and lickspittle nature, the Chinaman in Australia is a toady and a "loyalist."

The same spirit was echoed three years later, in 1890, by R. Thomson, in his book *Australian Nationalism: An Earnest Appeal to the Sons of Australia in Favour of the Federation and Independence of the States of our Country:*

> So far from thinking a Chinese war would be a calamity to Australia I fervently believe it would be the greatest blessing we could possibly receive. For it would give us an excuse to clear out every yellow alien from our midst; and there would be such an uprising of patriotism in Australia as has seldom been seen in Anglo-Saxon annals; for the Australian is more enthusiastic and excitable than his fathers.

## The "White Australia" Policy

The new spirit abroad constituted, in effect, the birth of an Australian national consciousness, and led to an increasing demand for the federa-

---

11. The word *Kanaka* is Polynesian and means "man." It also became applied to the inhabitants of Melanesia and of Micronesia.

tion of the separate Australian colonies. The demand for federation was stimulated by the awareness of a latent threat to Australia's national identity. This threat, it was felt, lay in part in the growth, in the 1880s and 1890s, of French and German interest in the Pacific, and in part in the possibility of an Asian immigration that would eventually undermine white predominance in Australia. Writing a report in 1889 a member of a Royal Commission stated:

> Federation of the colonies means the exclusion of all Asiatic and coloured races from Australia, except to a very inappreciable extent. The public men of the larger colonies . . . have already intimated in their several addresses at the recent general elections in those colonies their belief in federation, and their intention at the same time to keep Australia free from all Asiatic or coloured races.

After some years of discussion, in which the local interests of the different Australian colonies were reconciled, they were constitutionally transformed into states, and federated on January 1, 1901, under the name of the "Commonwealth of Australia."

One of the first legal instruments adopted by the new Commonwealth was the Immigration Restriction Act of 1901, which legalized what was popularly known as the "White Australia Policy." Under the provisions of the Act any person who failed to pass a dictation test of fifty words in a European language might be declared a prohibited immigrant. Other racially discriminatory legislation ensured that no aborigine, Pacific Islander, Asian, or African could vote, that almost all the same groups were denied the right to old-age pensions, that Chinese still living within the country were to live apart from white Australians, and that the Kanakas—with certain exceptions that were permitted on humanitarian grounds—were to be deported from Australia before December 31, 1906. In law as in fact Australia had become the white man's preserve.

## "The Land of the Long White Cloud"

Meanwhile, New Zealand—*Aotearoa,* or "The Land of the Long White Cloud," as the Maoris called it—had also undergone the experience of European occupation.

"We are, I think, going to colonize New Zealand," an Englishman had told a committee of the British House of Commons in 1836. "Though," he had added, "we be doing so in a most slovenly and scrambling and disgraceful manner."

The Englishman in question, Edward Gibbon Wakefield, was an admirer of orderly procedure, although it must be admitted that his early life had not been entirely orderly. Having run away with and married one heiress, he later—after her death—attempted to abduct yet another, being sent to prison in consequence. Of Quaker and radical antecedents, he believed that the European colonization of North America and Australia had had undesirable results, not so much concerning the fate of the original inhabitants of these territories (to which he was indifferent) as concerning the character of the European society that had developed there. The shipping of paupers to America and of convicts to Australia had resulted, Wakefield felt, in the evolution of a degraded type of society lacking the traditional English virtues. The answer to the problem, he believed, lay in the selection of future colonists, so that a new colony would reflect a vertical section of English society, in which only the lowest elements would not be represented. Colonizing would thus be pursued as an art in itself, aiming at the systematic re-creation of English civilization overseas. The concept was viewed, in its day, as a radical one, and yet, paradoxically, its aim was essentially conservative.

A further advantage that Wakefield claimed for his concept—and in his eyes by no means the least important—was that it would siphon off from England honest laborers who would otherwise be liable to join the growing ranks of the discontented. For, under the first shock of industrialism, social conditions in many parts of England had deteriorated to such an appalling extent that hunger and unemployment were rife, and mass discontent was manifest. The possibility of the eruption of an English Revolution as alarmingly historic as the French was by no means discounted. Wakefield's New Zealand plan was, indeed, one of a number of the solutions proposed by thinking men to the problems of the day. Yet Wakefield's vision, like that of the Pre-Raphaelite Brotherhood of artists, and like that of William Morris, drew inspiration from the past. Wakefield did not, like the Chartists, or Engels, or Marx, all of whom were also preoccupied with the condition of the British working class, propose radical political solutions. The controversies and intrigues in which Wakefield and his supporters soon found themselves engaged were not, therefore, with political factions, but with religious and humanitarian ones. Since his scheme paid scant attention to Maori interests, he soon found himself at odds with the missionary societies, and with an assortment of other forces that had already found a common cause in working together for the abolition of slavery. As the instrument of his policy Wakefield had formed a "New Zealand Association," and both the association and its founder soon came under attack from the Church Missionary Society, which aimed not at colonization but at converting New Zealand into a Christian Maori state.

While these as yet theoretical wrangles were in progress in London, the Maori, on the other side of the world, were being disturbed by white intruders who were interested neither in orderly colonization, nor in Christian evangelism. Even in the late eighteenth century sealing and whaling ships from Australia had begun to visit New Zealand, to be joined later by others from Britain, France, and the United States. Australian interest in New Zealand also developed until, in the early nineteenth century, the two islands virtually became a sphere of influence for Sydney-backed enterprise. By the 1830s colonists had acquired land and had become prosperous farmers, while both Maoris and Europeans were engaged in the victualing of ships, especially at the Bay of Islands on North Island, where in 1838 alone about 130 ships of various nationalities called. In addition to whaling and sealing, lumbering and flax-growing also engaged both Maoris and Europeans.

European relations with the Maoris were not, however, developing satisfactorily. Before the arrival of the Europeans the Maori had called themselves by no generic name. The very meaning of the word that they now began to use to distinguish themselves from the intruders—*Maori*, or "normal"—implicitly revealed their view of the newcomers. Actually, the Maoris more often than not found themselves confronted with men who were far from typical of European society. Some were convicts or ex-convicts from New South Wales. Others were deserters from whalers —ships which, being engaged in unusually long voyages, recruited their crews from those seamen who felt themselves the most alienated from life on land.[12] Others, again, were runaway sailors or unprincipled adventurers of all kinds. Charles Darwin, on his visit to New Zealand in 1835, commented that "of the English the greater part are the very refuse of society." Debauchery was habitual, at first on shipboard but, in later years, on shore, where the beachcombers of Kororareka on the North Island made themselves notorious. Among the initial benefits introduced by the Europeans were prostitution, venereal disease, firearms, alcohol, typhoid, tuberculosis, epidemic influenza, and measles, none of them known to the Maoris before. Small wonder that, as Keith Sinclair has written, "Europe came to New Zealand like nothing so much as a plague."[13] The structure of traditional life tottered under the impact, and the Maori population—perhaps 200,000 at the time of the coming of the Europeans—began to fall.[14]

The combination of old and new ways also frequently worked to the Maoris' detriment. For example, a feature of traditional Maori life had been the obligation of *utu*, or revenge. The introduction of the European musket led to more deaths in battle, and this in turn led to further conflicts necessitated by the demands of *utu*—conflicts, needless to say, in which muskets were again used. One Maori chief, Hongi, visited London

---

12. In 1809 a Maori who had sailed on a whaler, the *Boyd*, had been treated in such a fashion that when the ship took him home the crew were killed and eaten by his compatriots. Maori diet, it may be added, usually consisted of fern-root, birds, shellfish, dogs, rats, and other foods. Te Rangi Hiroa (also known as Sir Peter Buck), the famous Maori scholar, stated that "human flesh was eaten when procurable."

13. *A History of New Zealand* (London, 1959).

14. Captain Cook, whose charts must have been more accurate than his demography, estimated the Maori to have numbered 100,000. Te Rangi Hiroa (Sir Peter Buck) took the view that the Maori in Cook's time numbered approximately 400,000.

and returned in 1821 laden with presents, which he exchanged for muskets. With these arms he attacked his enemies, killing them by the hundreds, and thus initiating a series of ferocious civil wars which raged in both islands in the 1820s and 1830s.

Missionaries and Wakefieldians alike pressed for British government intervention to end the growing chaos, but the government was in no haste to become involved. A British Resident had, however, been appointed in 1833, and later, in 1838, a U.S. Consul was also to arrive. A diversion had also occurred when, in 1835, a certain Charles Philip Hippolytus de Thierry, who was of Anglo-French provenance, had informed the British Consul that he was the King of Nukuheva, and sovereign chief of New Zealand, and that he would shortly arrive in his realm. He also intimated that he was about to cut the Panama Canal, which would then become New Zealand property for fifty years. The British Resident, alarmed at this news, feared that a serious French purpose might underlie these farcical claims. He accordingly persuaded thirty-five Maori chiefs to declare independence, and to form the "United Tribes of New Zealand," in the name of which they claimed sovereignty. But the Resident need not have been perturbed: the eccentric de Thierry was not a threat. When he finally landed in New Zealand he soon ran into debt, and was forced to subsist on Maori charity.

Unwilling to hasten to assume responsibility for New Zealand, the British Colonial Office was nevertheless apparently in the process of accustoming itself to the prospect when, in 1839, the Wakefield faction, which had organized itself into the New Zealand Company, sent a ship, the *Tory*, under the command of Wakefield's brother, to buy land and prepare for settlement. The New Zealand Company later claimed that it had acted solely for patriotic reasons in order to forestall a French occupation of the islands. It appears more likely, however, that in fact the company acted to forestall the British government itself, which, the company feared, would act on the advice of the missionaries and protect Maori interests when it came to questions of the purchase of land.

Faced with the Wakefieldian fait accompli, the British government acted at last. In August, 1839, William Hobson, formerly the captain of H.M.S. *Rattlesnake*, which had visited New Zealand two years earlier to protect British settlers during a Maori war, was sent by the British government to negotiate with the Maoris for the establishment of Queen Victoria's sovereignty in New Zealand. He was also permitted to acquire the whole of the South Island by what the British somewhat dubiously claimed was "the right of discovery." The annexed territories of New Zealand were to be dependencies of New South Wales. Hobson was instructed to deal fairly with the Maoris, and to guarantee their land rights. In both the spirit and the letter of his instructions the missionary and abolitionist spirit of the day was implicit, and sometimes explicit. Britain, the custodian of world peace, was to rule supreme, dispensing justice, acknowledging right, protecting the weak, and upholding Christianity. New Zealand was to be annexed to palliate "the process of War and Spoliation, under which uncivilized Tribes have invariably disappeared as often as they have been brought into the immediate vicinity of Emigrants from the Nations of Christendom."

Relations between the Maori, the New Zealand Company settlers, and the British government were clarified early in 1840. In January the first settlement of Company colonists was established at Port Nicholson, where later Wellington was to be built. This event was quickly followed by the landing of Hobson and a governmental entourage at the Bay of Islands. In February the Maori chiefs met at "The Waters of Lamentation"— Waitangi—to discuss the British proposal of annexation, which necessarily required their consent. After a debate in which profound uneasiness was expressed concerning the amount of Maori land that had already been sold to Europeans, fifty of the Maori chiefs—the majority—agreed to cede their sovereignty to Queen Victoria. In the Queen was vested the sole right of purchasing their land. In return the chiefs were given the rights and privileges of British subjects. But meanwhile, as Hobson learned, the New Zealand Company was making its own laws—a development that he could not tolerate. He acted rapidly. On May 21, 1840, he proclaimed British sovereignty over both islands—in the north by virtue of the Treaty of Waitangi that he had signed with the Maori, and in the south by "right of discovery." New Zealand had become British territory. A boatload of French colonists who arrived in New Zealand shortly thereafter found that they had come too late. One year later, in 1841, the administrative link with New South Wales was broken, and New Zealand became a British colony in its own right.

The establishment of British sovereignty did not, however, mean the immediate establishment of order. If anything confusion, at first, became worse confounded. Relations between Maoris, settlers, and government alike were strained. The Maoris, the dominant power in New Zealand, resented growing settler encroachment on their lands, and often contested the legality of land titles claimed by the settlers. The settlers, meanwhile, established themselves on both islands, the New Zealand Company having founded settlements at Wellington in the north and at Nelson in the south, and the Plymouth Company having founded a settlement at Taranaki in the north. Constantly in dispute with the Maoris, the settlers rancorously accused the government of siding with the Maoris against them when it refused to sanction the more dubious examples of European alienation of Maori land. But the Maoris, for their part, did not feel themselves under any debt of gratitude to the government.

In attempting to raise revenue the government had introduced customs dues that had driven shipping away from New Zealand to find other Pacific ports, thereby depriving the Maoris of lucrative income. The government, meanwhile, had so few resources that it was virtually powerless. The impotency of the government to deal with the attacks, made in 1843, of a Maori chieftain, Hone Heke, revealed humiliatingly the extent of its weakness.

To bring order out of chaos the British, in 1845, sent a new governor, George Grey, furnished with adequate funds. Grey ended hostilities, and conciliated, to some extent, both Maoris and settlers. Thanks to the funds at his disposal he was able to help Maori agriculture with loans, and to subsidize Maori education. So far did he progress in gaining Maori confidence that, as a result, he was able to purchase more lands from them, which he then made available to the settlers with clear title, and at lower prices than they had paid in the past. Having thus introduced a degree of stability, he then took a further step that was to have a profound effect on New Zealand's future. He established provincial boundaries, thereby permitting the provincial councils to organize themselves before the colonial legislature was convened, and thus strengthening their powers at the expense of that of the central government. By the end of his term of governorship in 1853 there had also been established three final Wakefieldian settlements, at Otago and at Canterbury in the South Island, and at Wanganui in the North.

The most significant occurrence of these years remained, however, the separation of the Maoris from more of their lands. Much land was thus alienated in the North Island, where the greater number of Maoris lived, while almost the entire South Island passed from Maori to European possession in a few huge blocks. The process of the transfer of land to the Europeans was perhaps occurring in a more gentlemanly fashion than it had in other parts of the world, but it was occurring nonetheless. As the implications became apparent, the Maoris became increasingly disturbed. Increasingly, also, they became convinced that a halt to land sales must be called. This conviction brought them into direct conflict with the interests of the settlers, who had begun to make money from sheep-grazing. Casting covetous eyes on the valley lands of the Maoris, the settlers insisted that the government obtain more acres for their use, by foul means if fair would not suffice. Meanwhile, the discovery of gold in Australia had an effect on New Zealand agriculture. As labor grew scarce as a result of the rush to the diggings, the price of agricultural produce rose. Both Maori and European farmers alike reaped benefits. But, while the Europeans wished to use some of their profits to invest in further land purchases, the Maoris used theirs to purchase firearms, the better to defend their lands when the time came.

In 1854 a meeting of Maori leaders took place at Manawapou to discuss what was to be done about the loss of Maori lands. One faction favored driving out the Europeans by force from the lands they had already occupied. The prevailing view at what appears to have been a somewhat confused gathering was, however, that the land which had been sold had been sold, but that no further land sales should take place. This intertribal meeting, disorganized as it may have been, was the first of a series that marked the rising temper of Maori nationalism—itself a new phenomenon. Until now the Maori had thought primarily in tribal terms. Now they began to draw together in the face of a common threat. The European rat, they reminded one another, had "eaten" the Maori rat, and the European dog had driven out the Maori dog. If the Maoris themselves lost their lands to the Europeans, inevitably they too would become extinct.

Another step toward unity among the Maori occurred a few years later. In 1858 the Maori elected a king. The concept, previously unknown, had been introduced by a Maori chief, Tamihana Te Rauparaha, who had visited Britain and had been presented to Queen Victoria. The first king elected, Wherowhero, having assumed the title of Potatau I, appointed a Council of State and adopted a flag. The King movement, as it became known, gave the Maoris a rallying point against the Europeans which tribalism, with its separatist tendencies, had been unable to do.

The temper of the times was changing for the worse. In 1858, the year of the King's election, the number of Europeans in New Zealand for the first time exceeded the number of Maoris—a fact that was noted by both groups. Governor Grey, whose reputation with the Maori had stood high, was no longer there, and the growing number of settlers were more easily able to exert their influence on the colonial government, demanding more Maori land. Among both Maoris and settlers war factions arose, and the feeling grew that war itself was becoming inevitable. In the opinion of the government the only way to avoid a conflict was for land sales to be resumed—that is to say, for the Maoris to give in. Incidents between Maoris and settlers proliferated, while the settlers began to supply the Maori minority known as the "land-sellers" with ammunition and supplies, so that they might defend themselves against the "land-holding" majority. They also called upon the government to confiscate the lands of the Maori "land-holders."

Hostilities developed after an attempt by the government to purchase some land at Waitara without the consent of the chief living on it, Wiremu Kingi. In the emotional climate of the moment, the Governor, Gore Browne, persuaded himself that he was acting correctly: it soon became apparent to all except the settlers that he was not. Meanwhile the damage had been done. Waitara had become a *casus belli*. In taking up arms Wiremu Kingi proudly declared, "What though my people and I may die, we die for New Zealand." The fighting had at last begun.

## The Maori Wars

The Maori wars that followed lasted from 1860 until about 1872. The hostilities themselves were confined to the North Island, and were for the most part sporadic. To begin with the Taranaki region in the west was the heartland of Maori resistance. At first hostilities did not involve the Maori king, but later, after a period of armed truce had ended, he and his followers were also drawn into the fighting. British regiments soon arrived to take part in the war, which they found to be a strange one. Had the Maori employed guerrilla tactics at the outset, instead of in the final stages, the task of the Europeans might have been difficult indeed. As it was, however, their favorite method of fighting was to occupy a *pa*, or fortified village, and then fight off any attackers that appeared. Before long the British troops began to wonder why they were fighting at all, and at one point their general openly accused the settlers of using the British Army to help them rob the Maori of their lands. In 1865 and 1866, after an influential Maori chief, Wiremu Tamihana, had made peace with the government, all the British regiments except one were withdrawn from New Zealand. The settlers, with some Maori allies, were obliged henceforth to bear the brunt of the fighting.

By this time a new element had been introduced in the appearance of a new and militant religious movement among the Maoris known as *Hau Hau*. The Hau Hau sect regarded themselves as a chosen people, and believed that they would return from the wilderness to reoccupy their hereditary lands. Sir William Fox, a New Zealand premier of the day, who was hardly a detached observer, described Hau Hau as "a large infusion of Judaism, some leading features of Mormonism, a little mesmerism, a touch of spiritualism, occasional ventriloquism, and a large amount of cannibalism."

Meanwhile Grey had been sent back to try to pacify the country once more. This time the task was beyond his powers. His suggestion that the land of the rebels might be confiscated was taken up greedily by settler interests, and he soon found himself embroiled in bitter disputes as to which land was to be confiscated. Before long the crown monopoly of land purchases was suspended, and the "free sale" principle adopted. The settlers might have to do the fighting, but at least they could now do as they pleased in land questions, without what they regarded as "interference" from the British government. Over three million acres of Maori land was confiscated, and, fed by Maori resentment, the war increased in ferocity, with brutal excesses being committed by both sides. In 1868 a new Maori leader, Te Kooti, arose, who founded yet another religion, *Ringatu,* and who effectively employed guerrilla tactics. At last, however, the Europeans began to gain the upper hand. In 1872 Wiremu Kingi himself submitted, while Te Kooti and the Maori king both retired, together with their followers, into the central highlands of the North Island, known to this day as the "King country." Here, until the 1880s, no European dared to enter. Thus, slowly, the Maori wars ended.

The best Maori lands were now there for the taking. About seven million acres in the North Island had been sold to the government before the wars began, and another three million confiscated. By 1892 another seven million acres were sold, leaving the Maoris with eleven million of the poorest acres for themselves, of which two and a half million were leased to Europeans. Under the brunt of defeat and demoralization, Maori numbers dropped until in 1871 they amounted to no more than some 37,000. Writing in 1872 Anthony Trollope commented, "There is scope for poetry in their past history. . . . But in regard to their future— there is hardly a place for hope." It is a testament to the Maori will to survive that to some extent they belied this observation. By 1914, instead of disappearing, they had increased their numbers to about 50,000. Nevertheless, they remained a remnant, a minority in their own land.

Meanwhile, the Europeans had flourished in the South Island. Gold had been discovered there in 1857, and a gold rush had followed in 1861. The gold itself was soon worked out, but the economic stimulus and the increase in population that had also resulted produced more lasting effects. The fact that the South Island was spared the alarms and expenses of the Maori Wars also led to a faster rate of development. Only in 1901 did the population of the North Island again exceed that of the South.

The years that followed the Maori Wars saw the consolidation of Europe's hold over New Zealand. Slowly a transport network was developed that linked the various settlements more closely together. The introduction of refrigerated shipping gave further impetus to the expansion of sheep-herding. New Zealand mutton became a familiar commodity on the London market, and by 1914 the sheep population of the country had grown to about 24 million. The economic problems of the "new" country were thus overcome, despite New Zealand's isolated position in the watery vastness of the South Pacific.

Thus the white New Zealand nation came into being. More egalitarian than Wakefield would have wished, it nevertheless bore its own individual stamp, the result of the historic and geographic factors that had molded it—the latest in a series of new European societies that, in the space of less than 300 years, had come into being in different parts of the world.

Indeed New Zealand represented, in a sense, the final stage in the fulfillment of Europe's expansionary drive. For, with the birth of a white New Zealand, it could truly be said that, at last, the white man's power encircled the globe. Like the British Empire, the white man's communities, varied in language and in culture, and yet resembling one another in many essential ways, formed a chain around the world on which the sun never set—a chain in which Australia and New Zealand, the white bastions of the southern seas, formed the final connecting link.

# THREE

*The Rise of the Colored World*

# Chapter 9

# The Revolution Comes:
# The Rights of Man Are Proclaimed

*All the symptoms which I have ever met within History, previous to great Changes and Revolutions in Governments, now exist and daily increase in France.* —Lord Chesterfield (December 25, 1753)

*Bless, citizen, bless the National Assembly, which, by overthrowing the thrones of kings, has founded the happiness of the human race upon equality and liberty. Remember that the distinctions of color are no more: that a negro is as good as a white man; a white as good as a black.* —Letter written to Toussaint Louverture by the French Civil Commissioners in San Domingo (June, 1794)

*It was the French and not the American Revolution that set the world on fire.* —Hannah Arendt. *On Revolution* (1963)

IT WAS THE French Revolution and no other during which there first came into general view those opposing ideological poles of progress and of conservation which have governed the magnetic force field of politics ever since. The French Revolution, moreover, was no mere local or even national phenomenon: France had struggled with England on every major continent, and had become used to exerting an influence on a world scene. The French Revolution, like the Declaration of the Rights of Man which it produced, was proclaimed to be for the benefit of humanity at large. Concepts such as "the left," and "the right"; adjectives such as "counter-revolutionary"; terms such as *ancien régime,* or *bourgeoisie*—all came into general use during the French Revolution.

One has only to realize the extent to which these terms form a part of the political vocabulary of the twentieth century to appreciate the seminal influence of the Revolution of 1789 and the strength of the ideas which inspired it.

At the time that the Revolution began, the foundations of European world dominion had been firmly laid, even though many of the African, Asian, Australasian, and American populations who were to be directly affected had yet to recognize the fact.[1] European methods of communication and of weaponry, both constantly being improved, ensured that the non-European populations could ultimately have no hope of openly opposing Europe's expanding power, so long as the Europeans remained united. In racial confrontations—in Asia, in Africa, in the Americas, and in Australasia—the Europeans, at first by diplomacy, and then, if necessary, by force, could overwhelm any opposition, once they set their minds to it.

Once this realization had dawned—as it did, slowly and gradually, first in one region and then in another—it also became evident that, at that time, it was the social ideology of the Europeans that would determine the future of the peoples who had now become dependent on them. For the subject peoples overseas could only hope for any amelioration of their lot—sometimes, indeed, could only hope for survival—by forming an alliance with the Europeans whose social opinions would favor their progress.

The social classes in Europe had, in fact, established an equilibrium among themselves during the period that is now called the Middle Ages. Birth determined an individual's social status. Social mobility was discouraged—a circumstance that, in consequence, encouraged the perfection of specialist skills, whether in building, in the arts, or in warfare. Whereas, on occasion, a beggarmaid might perhaps become a queen, such a turn of fortune's wheel was sufficiently exceptional to border on the miraculous. When, after unprecedented sufferings, the peasant uprising called the Jacquerie took place in 1358 in Beauvais and other regions of France, the nobility were shocked and outraged not so much by the danger to themselves as by the fact that the peasantry had forgotten their place in medieval society, and were thus deemed to be acting "against nature" itself.

Nevertheless, two factors ran counter to the prevailing tendency of

1. One individual concerned who did, however, grasp the situation was a San Domingan slave named Toussaint Breda (later known as Toussaint Louverture). This was largely due to the fact that he had read and reread the Abbe Raynal's *Histoire Philosophique et Politique des Etablissements et du Commerce Européens Dans les Deux Indes* (1770), a book which was at the time banned in France and also placed on the Catholic Index. Despite the fact that the book was held to be impious and blasphemous, and also tended to stir up peoples against sovereign authority, and was torn up and burned in consequence, it nevertheless ran into twenty editions, apart from many more pirated versions.

European society to rigidify its class structure and institutions: the Plague—that Black Death whose influence we have noted in so many aspects of history—and the discovery of the new lands overseas. The Plague, by depopulating much of Europe, disrupted the normal operation of feudalism by creating a labor shortage, thus encouraging the introduction of wage labor in place of feudal servitude. The discovery of new lands overseas opened a thousand new paths to individual advancement, thus producing social transformations that had been previously thought of only as the stuff of which legends are made. In this connection it will be sufficient to mention two illustrative examples—one legendary, and one factual.

The legendary example is that of Dick Whittington, a starving orphan who had been granted a place in a London merchant's house, and who was then called upon to make a token investment in a commercial venture to the Barbary Coast. He had nothing to give but his cat, which, however, fetched such a high price in mice-troubled Barbary that it laid the foundation of Dick's fortune. He later became three times Mayor of London, and was so rich that he was able to lend money to the King. There was, in fact, a real Dick Whittington (1358?–1423), who did become Mayor of London three times, and who made frequent loans to both Henry IV and Henry V. However, he was not a starving orphan, but the son of a Gloucestershire knight, and a merchant by trade. The legend of Whittington and his cat seems first to have appeared two centuries later in a play, now unfortunately lost, which was licensed in London in 1605, and which was entitled *The History of Richard Whittington, of His Lowe Byrth, His Great Fortune*. Despite its fourteenth-century setting, the English legend[2], with its hint of easy wealth to be gained by voyages overseas, evidently owes more to the Elizabethan age than to any other.

The factual example is that of Hernando Cortes, who sailed at the age of nineteen to seek his fortune in the New World, and whose parents, although esteemed, were not rich. Upon his return to Spain in 1528, having completed his conquest of Mexico, he "came in the pomp and glory not so much of a great vassal, as of an independent monarch."

Such dramatic changes of fortune, whether real or hypothetical, could not fail to make a profound impression on the bulk of the population. The examples before their eyes, moreover, soon became numerous. Cabin boys no less than captains were wont to return home with their fortunes made. Others, in their turn, left to adventure abroad. But not everyone, evidently, was going to become rich, and those who decided

---

2. Other versions of the story have been traced by Thomas Keightley as far back as the thirteenth century, and appear in Persian, Danish, and Italian folklore.

to stay behind in Europe must have had matter to reflect upon. The effect of witnessing a few, thanks more often perhaps to luck than to talent or to virtue, vaulting high in rank as a result of their newly gained riches must inevitably have led many to question the justice of the social system that countenanced such unorthodox transformations. Traditional habits of mind must also, inevitably, have been challenged; unsuspected desires must have been awakened, and dreams of better things have been born. Why only a better life for the few? Could not society itself be fashioned so that it was just? Could it not be made so that all might benefit? Perhaps once, at the beginning, in the early days of antiquity, it had been so. Had there not once been a Golden Age? If one could but return to those just and virtuous days, the world could perhaps be made new again. What a revolution[3] that would be! What a thing to dream about!

The dream of a return to the social origins of things arose most potently in France. For it was in autocratic France, above all, that the dreamers were denied the possibility of action. A French bourgeois litterateur had little chance, under the monarchy, of holding a responsible public position comparable to those held in England, for example, by Milton as foreign secretary, or by Pepys as secretary to the Admiralty. Set aside from public life, therefore, French writers and propagandists dreamed of a new dawn. Nor were they able to test their lucubrations in the light of practical experience. Slowly the conviction of a coming change spread through France as the eighteenth century progressed. Even some of the nobles fell under the spell of the times, and on occasion, together with their ladies, waxed enthusiastic about the great age of equality, the great revolution to come.[4]

Writers and publicists, such as Diderot with his *Encyclopedia,* or Rousseau with his *Contrat Social* and other books, spread the message.

In Diderot's *Encyclopedia,* for example, published in 1755, we find

---

3. The original meaning of the word "revolution" as applied to politics was borrowed from the circular movements of planets and other astral bodies and implied not, as some today think, a movement forward, but rather a turning back—that is, a complete revolution of a society back to its point of departure. See Hannah Arendt, *On Revolution* (1963).

4. Jacques Cazotte, author of *Le Diable Amoureux,* is credited by La Harpe with making some remarkable prophecies about the coming revolution at a dinner party held in Paris in 1788. "It seems to me only yesterday," wrote La Harpe, ". . . we were at table." Chamfort, Condorcet, and many other distinguished persons were there. Chamfort was mocking religion, and so were some others. Cazotte, a member of the Society of *Illuminés* then began to prophesy. "You will all see this great and sublime revolution that you want so much. . . . YOU WILL SEE IT. . . ." "You, Monsieur de Condorcet, you will die stretched out on a dungeon floor. . . . You, Monsieur de Chamfort, will cut your veins with 22 strokes of a razor. . . . You, Monsieur de Nicolai, will die on the scaffold. You, Monsieur Bailly, on the scaffold." Finally the company broke up in confusion when he said that the only one to have a confessor before dying would be the King of France.

Cazotte himself was executed during the Revolution on September 25, 1792. He had been sentenced by Lavau, a former fellow member of the Society of *Illuminés.* It is alleged that La Harpe left among his papers a note declaring that Cazotte's prophecy was his own invention, and that he had composed it with the intention of preparing a "poetic fiction" on the subject. According to Gerard de Nerval, however, a number of people present confirmed the authenticity of the event.

the following comments appearing in the article entitled "Slavery," written by M. le Chevalier de Jaucourt:

> All men are born free; in the beginning they had only one name, and only one status; in the time of Saturn and of Rhea[5] there were, according to Plutarch, neither masters nor slaves: nature had made all equal. . . .

The entry went on to say—and we must note the paradox that the *Encyclopedia* bore on its title pages the information that it was published "With the Approbation and by Privilege of the King":

> The natural liberty of man is not to know any sovereign power on earth, and not to be subjected to any legislative authority whatsoever, but only to follow the laws of Nature."

Small wonder that, when such ideas were freely circulated and taken up with enthusiasm by some members of the nobility and the church, no less than by the commonality, a great Revolution soon thereafter occurred. Lord Chesterfield had no need of unusual prescience in the comment quoted at the beginning of this chapter—the Revolution was generally awaited on every hand. No more would Frenchmen be divided, as monarchy had long succeeded in dividing them,[6] into jealous social factions—the nation would, at last, be one. Equality would reign, with the sanction of Reason, and Nature would be the lawgiver.

## The Revolution

The Revolution, when it came, broke the power of the King of France, and in its place put that of the Nation—that is to say, of the French people.

Dramatic in the extreme, the Revolution began a chain of events that, in turn, destroyed the power of the French monarchy, opened a bitter class struggle, plunged Europe into war, and, eventually, developed into the ultimate phase of the long-drawn-out struggle between France and Britain for world hegemony—a struggle that fostered the emergence of Napoleon Bonaparte as the leader of France, and that ended with Waterloo and a British victory in 1815.

The revolutionary process, so long awaited, began with the summoning in 1789 of the Estates-General of France for the purpose of dis-

5. Saturn, or Cronos, reputedly the father of Zeus, was an ancient king of Latium. Rhea, his wife, was a goddess of nature and fertility. The reign of Saturn is identified with the classic Golden Age.

6. ". . . It was the desire of preventing the nation whose money was being asked for from asking back its freedom that led the government to spare no pains in maintaining the barriers between the various classes, which were thus unable to join forces and put up an organized resistance. This ensured the safety of the central power, which had to deal only with small, isolated groups of malcontents. Though in the long history of the French kingdom so many admirable monarchs occupied the throne at various periods . . . not one of them ever made an attempt to unite classes and obliterate distinctions otherwise than by reducing them all to a common state of dependence on the Crown." (Alexis de Tocqueville, *L'Ancien Régime et la Révolution*, 1856).

cussing the national financial crisis that had grown to unmanageable proportions. In the Estates-General, held at Versailles near Paris, a struggle was soon joined between the three Estates—the nobility, the clergy, and the commonality. First by taking the Oath of the Tennis Court on June 20, 1789, and then in the days that followed, the Third Estate, or commons, successfully resisted menaces from the other two Estates, as well as from the throne itself. The revolutionary sentiment which had seized the representatives of the third estate, however, unexpectedly spread to the people of Paris. Fearing aristocratic intrigues, the Parisians arose spontaneously and, on July 14, 1789, seized and destroyed the Bastille, the symbol of monarchical power in Paris. Although, as was later said, the Bastille was taken "chiefly by infinite noise," it was through this single symbolic event that the opening of the French Revolution was signaled to Europe and to the world. In effect, July 14, 1789—which is, despite all subsequent changes, still celebrated in France as the national day—is also the birth-date of the international era in which we, today, are still living. The forces which appeared into general view on that date are those that are still in motion. They also were, and are, the forces that have since permitted the subjugated peoples of Asia, Africa, and the Americas to move toward those same goals for which the sans-culottes of eighteenth-century France were striving.

The third estate having triumphed, it was rejoined by the two other Estates, and French history next noted the famous night of August 4, 1789, in the course of which serfdom and seignorial dues were abolished, the clergy renounced their tithes, the nobility their special privileges, and the middle classes their special exemptions.[7] "Before dawn", as the historian Albert Mathiez has put it, "a new France had come into being under the urgent pressure of the poorest classes."[8] Of greater international fame, however, was the adoption on August 26, 1789, by the French National Assembly (into which the Estates-General had now been transformed) of the Declaration of the Rights of Man and the Citizen —a document which was soon to carry the democratic message throughout the world, and produce widespread repercussions. As Thomas Carlyle, writing in his extraordinary high-flown style, expressed it:

Rights of Man, printed on Cotton Handkerchiefs, in various dialects of human speech, pass over to the Frankfort Fair. What saw we, Frankfort Fair? They have crossed the Euphrates, and the fabulous Hydaspes; wafted themselves beyond the Ural, Altai, Himmalayah; struck off from wooden stereotypes, in angular Picture-writing, they are jabbered and jingled of in China and Japan. Where will it stop? Kien-lung smells mischief; not the remotest Dalai-Lama shall now knead his dough-pills in peace.[9]

7. All personal bonds were thus abolished outright, but title deeds were made redeemable for a money payment. Men were thus set free but property rights remained.
8. *The French Revolution* (1962).
9. *The French Revolution* (1837).

The Declaration itself, however, was a document that, in contemporary terms, has marked limitations—notably in respect to the right of association, to the liberty of the press, and to freedom of religion. However, to quote Mathiez once more:

Born in the heat of conflict, it sanctioned "resistance to oppression"—in other words, it justified the revolt which had just triumphed, heedless of the fact hat it justified other revolts in advance.[10]

Regardless of the finer shades of meaning, the essence of the Declaration was contained in the first three paragraphs, which read as follows:

1) Men are born, and always continue, free and equal in respect of their rights. Civil distinctions, therefore, can only be founded on public utility.

2) The end of all political associations is the preservation of the natural and imprescriptible rights of man; and these rights are liberty, property, security, and resistance to oppression.

3) The nation is essentially the source of all sovereignty; nor can ANY INDIVIDUAL or ANY BODY OF MEN, be entitled to any authority which is not expressly derived from it.

In sanctioning the shifting of power from King to Nation, the Declaration called for the basic change from autocracy to democracy that was later to produce effects not only in Europe but also in the other continents. Nevertheless, how far, at first, the democratic message was from being understood by certain uneducated persons abroad is revealed by a statement made in 1793 by a rebel Negro leader in San Domingo, named Mayaca. Mayaca had at first been converted to republicanism, but later reverted to monarchism, explaining his action to the French Commissioner in the following terms:

I am the subject of three kings—the King of the Congo, lord of all the blacks; the King of France, who represents my father; the King of Spain, who represents my mother. These three kings are descended from those who, led by a star, went to adore the Man-God. If I passed into the Republic's service, I should perhaps be forced to make war on my brothers, the subjects of these three kings to whom I have sworn fidelity.

In October, 1789, both the royal family and the National Assembly were moved from Versailles to Paris, after which the National Assembly began to prepare a Constitution. The monarchy and the nobles, however, feeling themselves losing control of the situation in France, began to prepare a counter-revolution with help from abroad. For some time the French public did not realize this, believing, instead, that the King had indeed, as he pretended, accepted the Revolution. The abortive attempt of the King and Queen to flee and to join the Austrian army

10. *The French Revolution*, p. 59.

was prevented by their arrest at Varennes[11] on June 20, 1791, after which they were brought back to Paris as virtual prisoners. With the Constitution completed, elections were held, and the new Legislative Assembly took the place of the National Assembly on October 1, 1791, remaining in power for almost a year.

On April 20, 1792, France declared war on Hungary and Bohemia. Prussia entered into the war against France in July. Following reverses and governmental indecision, the Parisian populace, suspecting treachery,[12] rose in insurrection on August 10, 1792, and stormed the Tuileries, the King's residence, obliging him to seek shelter in the Legislative Assembly, from whence, in due course, he and his Queen were taken to the Temple as "hostages." August 10, 1792, signaled the emergence of revolutionary power in place of the legal power deriving from the old regime. On that same date it was declared that the Legislative Assembly should be replaced by a Convention, following national elections. On September 20, 1792, the French Revolutionary Army gained its first victory at Valmy, and on September 21, 1792, the Convention met in Paris for the first time. The Republic was declared, Royalty abolished, and the Revolutionary Calendar adopted.

King Louis XVI—now called Louis Capet—was executed on January 21, 1793, and war with England and Holland ensued in February. Military reverses and food shortages resulted in a general discontent that led to increased support for the Jacobin faction,[13] who were under the inspiration of Robespierre. After the overthrow of the Girondin faction,[14] Robespierre and the Jacobins proceeded to institute a Reign of Terror, with the aim of holding the Republic together. The guillotining of the Girondins was followed by the execution of the Hébertist faction, and then that of Danton and his followers. Finally, however, the remaining deputies of the Convention came to fear for their own heads, and on the 9th Thermidor of the Year Two of the Revolutionary Calen-

11. Cazotte's alleged prophecy is not the only one associated with the French Revolution, which appears to have attracted the attention of various prophets. One of the best known quatrains of Nostradamus, published in 1555, mentions Varennes—a town which has only this once figured in history, in 1791—and concludes with the interesting line: *Esleu cap. cause tempeste, feu, sang tranche.* If by *Esleu cap.* Nostradamus did indeed mean the Elected Capet—Louis XVI was the first constitutional king of France—then the co-incidence is remarkable. To our hindsight the word *tranche* may also seem evocative of the guillotine. Nostradamus, elsewhere, referred, in dealing with this period, to something that he called *le Commun Advenement* (the Advent of the Commons). Another line of his, also referring to this period, is striking: *Les rouges rouges le rouge assommeront*—"The red reds will slaughter the red"—a line which at once brings to mind Robespierre and the Committee of Public Safety. According to James Laver, "Even the most sceptical writers on Nostradamus have been compelled to admit that he knew something about the French Revolution." (*Nostradamus,* 1952, p. 39). However, Nostradamus, like the subject of prophecy, raises questions that require consideration in their own right.

12. They were right. Among other things, Marie Antoinette had, in fact, communicated the French plan of campaign to the enemy.

13. The Jacobin Club was a Parisian political society which took its name from the Jacobin convent in which its meetings were held. Jacobinism became synonymous with extreme and uncompromising republicanism.

14. The Girondins, mostly men of wealth and property, supported the Revolution provided it maintained a bourgeois character. They were named "Girondins" because their political strength was drawn from the Gironde region.

dar (July 27, 1794), Robespierre himself was overthrown; he was guillotined the next day, and the Jacobin Clubs in France were closed soon thereafter. The coalition which had overthrown Robespierre, the Thermidoreans, concluded peace with Prussia, Spain, and some other European states in 1795, and, toward the end of the same year, the Directoire was established.

The Directoire, a five-man executive supported by a bicameral legislature (owning, it is said, at its beginning an "old table, a sheet of paper, and an inkbottle"), was short of funds, and not noticeably efficient. Its rule provided an interregnum before the rise to power of Napoleon, and the development of that ultimate stage of the duel between France and England known as the Napoleonic Wars. During this great power struggle the international content of the French Revolution, which had been at first so much in evidence, became supplanted by the rampant nationalism of a France committed to a war for total world supremacy. Commentators and historians differ as to the exact date when the French Revolution may be considered to have ended. It may be argued, with good reason, that in a sense it has not ended yet.

## San Domingo

The doors of the Jacobin Club in Paris may well have been closed, but the spirit which had inspired the Jacobins and the emotions engendered by the Revolution itself continued to work as a leaven throughout the world. Pandora's Box some might say, had been flung open. Others, on the contrary, saw in the phenomenon the birth pangs of a new world.

The strongest immediate effect of the French Revolution, outside the confines of France, was felt in the French colony of San Domingo. For in San Domingo an entirely unforeseen situation arose, which soon developed into a successful rebellion by the black and mulatto population against white colonial rule. The San Domingan Revolution may, indeed, be considered as the precursor of all subsequent successful colonial rebellions.

In 1789 San Domingo—called *Saint Domingue* by the French, and today known as Haiti—was not only the richest colony possessed by France, but was also the richest colony possessed by any European power. Although it consisted of merely the western half of the island known to Columbus as Hispaniola, its plantations were estimated as supplying half of Europe with sugar, coffee, and cotton. Its prosperity was also increasing at a remarkable rate, which made all the more apparent the economic stagnation of the eastern or Spanish half of the island. Not only was San Domingo France's most valuable overseas possession, but, strategically, it was evidently an important base whose value would be realized when (as then felt) the inevitable day would come for France to reclaim its former colonies on the North American mainland.

The administration of San Domingo was, after the King of France, ultimately the responsibility of the French Ministry of the Marine, although locally power was vested in a governor, and in an *intendant*. The governor and the intendant (the latter a bureaucrat), and their respective administrative hierarchies inevitably engaged in interminable bickering. In the last year that any population census was taken, 1783, it was reported that there were in the colony slightly less than 28,000 whites, 22,000 free mulattoes and freed Negroes, and some 405,000 slaves. The colony itself was divided into three provinces, the North, the West, and the South, which had been colonized in that order, so that the North was thus the most economically developed, and the South the least. The main port and metropolis, Cap Francais, was in the North, while the administrative capital, Port-au-Prince—which was likened by one contemporary to a Tartar camp in appearance—was in the West.

The whites of San Domingo were composed of Europeans, and of Creoles—the Creoles being those who had been born and bred in the colony. Since the colony had originally been founded by adventurers, it differed from most other French colonies, where, on the contrary, the pioneering had usually been done by aristocrats with government backing. This gave to San Domingan society a libertarian flavor that contrasted with the conditions prevailing in other French colonies. Members of the nobility had, nevertheless, later come to San Domingo and become resident planters. In the towns lived a number of what were called *petits blancs*—white town-dwellers who were drawn from many European countries, and who later adopted the vocabulary of Jacobinism. Among the white population as a whole, men outnumbered women by more than two to one—a factor that, doubtless, did not discourage a constant increase in the number of mulattoes. In effect, many white planters used their mulatto mistresses to manage their households and to warn them of impending plots among the slaves.

The mulattoes were almost all free men, only a small number of them being slaves. Many were property-owners and slave-holders, particularly in the Western and Southern provinces. Some mulattoes were entirely white in appearance, but a strict color line was nevertheless kept, with infinite gradations.[15] The number of mulattoes showed a steady increase despite strong social strictures, such as that enjoined by the Superior of Missions in his report for 1722 who, after noting the increase in the number of mulattoes, both legitimate and illegitimate, added that

15. See Chapter 5, pp. 101–102.

the mingling of the races was "a criminal coupling of men and women of different species, whence comes a fruit which is one of Nature's monsters."

The Negro and slave populations were virtually identical, although there were a small number of free Negroes, just as there were a small number of mulatto slaves. The slaves were frequently worked to death, for many plantation-owners held that it was cheaper to buy slaves than to breed them. Consequently most of the Negro slaves had been born in Africa. By 1789 African slaves were being imported into the colony at the rate of about 40,000 a year, mostly from the Congo-Angola region. The slaves were often cruelly treated, being whipped, subjected to tortures, or to having their ears cut off, and other similar punishments. They were barely protected by the Code Noir, as we said in Chapter 5. Small wonder that, being so ill treated, some slaves declared themselves happy to die, believing that after death they would return to their own country, Africa.

The slaves were, however, by no means docile. From time to time leaders arose among them who attempted to free them from bondage. The first such incident occurred in 1679, when the Negro population numbered only 2,000, and the white population 5,000. Led by a "Spanish Negro" the rebels tried "to massacre all the French." The French had been obliged to fight a regular campaign before order was restored. In 1691 a similar uprising had occurred in the Port-de-Paix district, and in 1704 the Negroes of Le Cap had conspired to kill all the whites of the city by night. Indeed, in the first decade of the eighteenth century another Negro leader had waged a type of guerrilla warfare for seven years, attacking plantations and conducting a campaign of terror. When, at last, he was killed, a successor arose and flourished for a further twelve years. In about 1750 there appeared the formidable figure of Macandal, an African from the Senegal-Guinea region of Africa, who claimed to be a black Messiah sent to drive the whites from the island. Having consolidated his hold over the Negro population, in 1758 he prepared to poison the water supply of Le Cap, intending then to attack the town while the whites were in convulsions. But the plot was discovered and he was captured and executed.

The first signs of the storm that was to break over San Domingo were not, however, to be seen in the colony itself, but in Europe. They took the form of the creation of certain organizations that were, in the earlier stages, to have some influence on developments in San Domingo. In 1787 Thomas Clarkson, whom we have already noted, founded the Anti-Slavery Society in London. This was followed by the formation in 1788 in Paris of an organization known as *Les Amis des Noirs*. *Les Amis des Noirs* soon achieved a strength and an influence to which the

Anti-Slavery Society was never able to aspire. Clarkson's group, limited in influence, nonconformist and Quaker in tone, sought to achieve its ends by quiet persuasion, careful documentation, and reformist parliamentary action, drawing its strength from the efforts of a handful of modest but dedicated individuals. *Les Amis des Noirs*, on the other hand, grouped together among its supporters some of the great names of the age—Brissot, Condorcet, Lafayette, Robespierre, and, above all, Mirabeau. Unlike its English counterpart, it quickly founded a chain of affiliated secret revolutionary groups throughout France—groups whose adherents held views that were later to be identified with the doctrines of Jacobinism. Preaching the Rights of Man, *Les Amis des Noirs* advocated the abolition of both slavery and the color line.

Meanwhile, in San Domingo plantation owners sought to organize themselves to defend their interests. In 1788 a movement began among them which sought to gain representation for San Domingo at the forthcoming Estates-General in France in order to counteract anti-slavery and anti-color-line sentiment. The partisans of this movement argued that whereas San Domingo had of course not been represented at the previous Estates-General in 1614, since it was then unknown, neither had such regions as Franche-Comte or Lorraine. Now, all regions should be included. On July 15, 1788, the French branch of this movement formed itself into the "Colonial Committee" under the patronage of the Duke of Orleans, with the Chamber of Commerce of Cap Francais in San Domingo itself acting as the steering committee. Its first petition for representation was, however, refused by the King's Council.

Details of the aims and activities of *Les Amis des Noirs* had arrived in San Domingo in 1788, where they caused a sensation. It was then realized by some whites that the representation of San Domingo in the Estates-General might provide insufficient protection for the slave-owners, since the colony's representatives would inevitably find themselves to be a minority, and, furthermore, representation would place the colony's affairs under the direct jurisdiction of the Estates-General. These whites therefore decided, instead, to send agents who would strive to prevent public controversy from developing in France over the colony's affairs, and who would seek changes directly from the Crown with a view to placing control of the colony in the hands of the local whites, rather than of the Ministry of the Marine.

Oblivious to this view, certain other white planters nevertheless continued to seek representation. Elections were held among the San Domingan whites, as a result of which thirty-seven delegates, some of them already living in France, were sent to the Estates-General, where they made clear that their aim was to have the colony ruled by the white planters. It was, incidentally, as a result of the holding of these elections, as well as of an acute phase developing in the interminable Governor-Intendant quarrel, that the Governor of San Domingo was recalled to France. Thus the government of the colony was virtually paralyzed when the first news arrived in the island of the fall of the Bastille and other revolutionary events.

Earlier in 1789 the Colonial Committee, which attracted primarily royalist supporters, had clashed openly in France in debate with *Les Amis des Noirs.* Meanwhile other colonists in France, sensing the danger to their interests in such open controversies, grouped themselves around the Club Massiac, and strove to lobby behind the scenes, achieving considerable success in their efforts. Supported by the wealthy merchants of Bordeaux and other ports, whose prosperity depended primarily on San Domingo, they were sympathetic to the aristocratic Colonial Committee, but with one vital difference. The Club Massiac was in favor of the *Pacte Coloniale*—a trade arrangement that restricted San Domingo's trade to France, and that was primarily of advantage to French merchants. The Colonial Committee, on the other hand, sought the abolition of the *Pacte* and freedom for the privileged San Domingan planters to trade with whomsoever they chose—which, in practice, often proved to be the British or the Americans, who could often offer them more favorable terms than the French merchants.

The Colonial Committee's attempts to achieve representation for San Domingo met with sudden success on "The Day of the Tennis Court"—June 20, 1789. At the height of the crisis, the Committee's spokesman, Gouy d'Arcy, lent his faction to the support of the beleaguered Third Estate, which, thereupon, spontaneously and immediately, granted San Domingo the right of representation in the Estates-General. However, in the discussions that subsequently took place in the National Assembly on the number of seats to be granted to the San Domingan delegates, the question of democratic principle was raised. *Les Amis des Noirs* attacked the lack of African or mulatto representation, and even the Club Massiac—albeit from very different motives—lodged a protest concerning San Domingan representation.

It was, however, Mirabeau himself who led the attack against the white San Domingan representatives, and who most effectively made French opinion conscious of the issue. He pointed out that the "free colored" (that is, mulattoes and free Negroes) were land-owners and tax-payers, but had no vote. As for the slaves, he said, either they were or were not men. If they were men, the colonists should free them, give them the vote, and permit them to send representatives of their own. It they were not, then he asked the question, "Have we counted in the population of France the number of our horses and mules?" Finally the Assembly agreed to admit six San Domingan deputies, instead of the twenty that the colonists had hoped for. Representation had been gained, but it had been a Pyrrhic victory, since French opinion had begun to turn against the colonists. Gouy d'Arcy and his confrères now at last realized the superiority of the strategy that had been proposed by the Club Massiac; it was, however, too late. They themselves had created a situation whereby not they but the French National Assembly was ultimately empowered to legislate on the destiny of San Domingo. They had also created a situation whereby the libertarian ideas of revolutionary France were now to become generally known in San Domingo, and in which the colony was to follow closely and react violently to each turn in the destinies of the French Revolution itself. Too late the Colonial Committee joined forces with the Club Massiac to try to disentangle their fortunes from those of revolutionary France. On August 12, 1789, the new San Domingan deputies wrote home as follow:

The colony is in the most imminent peril. People here are trying to raise a revolt among our Negroes, and the danger is such as to cause us the most horrible alarm. We see the danger—and yet are forced to keep silence. Gentlemen, these people are drunk with liberty. A society of enthusiasts who style themselves "Les Amis des Noirs" is writing openly against us; it is watching eagerly for the favorable moment to explode the mine against slavery; and should we have the tactlessness to but utter that word, its members might make it the occasion to demand the enfranchiasement of our Negroes.

The colonists determined to attempt to free themselves from the web in which they found themselves caught. Realizing that the old regime was sinking, they sought to act before the National Assembly had consolidated its power. They asked the Ministry of the Marine for royal authorization to convoke a colonial assembly in San Domingo itself. The request was favorably received, and as a result the necessary orders were sent to San Domingo on Sunday, September 27, 1789. The colonists had acted just in time, for the following Sunday there occurred the Women's March on Versailles, as a result of which the King (as well as the National Assembly) was taken to Paris, after which all his actions were subject to close scrutiny.

On October 22, 1789, representatives of the *Colons Americains*—a society of wealthy Parisian mulattoes with San Domingan connections—obtained a hearing before the National Assembly, asking for mulatto representation in the Assembly not as a favor but as a natural right. After a protracted debate with intensive lobbying by all factions the request was rejected. But, again, the colonists' victory was obtained at a cost: the cost of the further crystallization of French opinion on the issue of equal rights for all the inhabitants of San Domingo, whether white, black, or mulatto.

Meanwhile the doctrines of the Revolution were beginning to take effect overseas. In February, 1790, came news of some disturbances in San Domingo, as well as of rebellion among the Negroes of Martinique and Guadeloupe, who were seeking liberty. The news shocked the National Assembly which had, no doubt, not envisioned the immediate violence that would be engendered by the generous principles it had espoused. As a result the Assembly bowed to colonial pressure, and formulated the Decree of March 8, 1790, which categorized as "criminal against the nation" whomsoever should seek to foment uprisings against colonial assemblies. For the moment *Les Amis des Noirs* had received a setback.

The struggle between the colonial lobby and *Les Amis des Noirs* was soon resumed, however, over the question of the implementation of the Decree of 8th March. The struggle crystallized around Article Four of the measure proposed, which, as the draft text stood, would grant the franchise to "all persons" over twenty-five who were property-owners or tax-payers. The wording did not specifically exclude mulattoes. Did it tacitly include or exclude them? The Assembly could not make up its mind. Being unable to reject either the universal principles of the Declaration of the Rights of Man and of the Citizen on the one hand, or the interests of the white commercial lobby on the other, it therefore simply perpetuated the ambiguity by voting Article Four as it stood, with both sides claiming that this result favored their cause.

*Inter-white Rivalries*

Meanwhile, in San Domingo itself, political changes had taken place among the whites. The *petits blancs* in the towns had not profited from the results of the elections of January, 1789, which had, instead, benefited the planter aristocracy. When news had come of the fall of the Bastille, the *petits blancs* had vociferously rallied to republicanism, donning the tricolor cockade. All whites were to participate in the elections which were to be held to the provincial assemblies of the North, the West, and the South. They were held at a time when anti-royalist sentiment was running so strongly, particularly in the more economically developed North, that many royalists, among them even the Intendant of the colony, were obliged to leave the island and to return to France. When details arrived from France of the proposed (but not yet approved) measures for the establishment of a Colonial Assembly, the three provincial assemblies convened a colonial assembly to meet at Saint-Marc in the western province on March 25, 1790. Before it could meet, however, a mulatto uprising took place in the West.

The mulattoes living in San Domingo, encouraged by reports of the debates in the French National Assembly, had demanded political rights, but instead of having their demands met with sympathy, let alone acceptance, they were subjected to lynchings and persecution—a persecution that was the more virulent because many of the *petits blancs* were jealous of the mulattoes' wealth, and found a political justification for their hostility in the mulattoes' traditional pro-royalism. Consequently, the mulattoes found themselves both encouraged and suppressed at the same time and, with their emotions thus worked upon, rose up in anger. The uprising was dispelled without undue difficulty, and, for the sake of future stability, the whites were preparing to conduct themselves in a somewhat more equitable manner toward the mulattoes in the future, when news arrived of the March decrees adopted by the French National Assembly, including Article Four with its ambiguity on the question of the mulatto vote. White fears regarding the mulattoes were at once revived, and attitudes of outright hostility were resumed.

The new colonial assembly of Saint Marc succeeded in meeting on April 15, 1790. Anti-royalist in sentiment, it also showed strong secessionist tendencies, constituting itself as a General Assembly instead of a colonial one, and proclaiming itself to be the sovereign authority in the colony—actions that were condemned in France as amounting to an attempted declaration of independence. The assembly was then embarking on the task of constitution-making when its critics—who included the governor and his royalist supporters, as well as the French commercial lobby and its agents in San Domingo—claimed that the Assembly was illegally constituted because it had been elected before, and not after, the official promulgation of the March decrees. Elections were again held, and a new assembly, even more republican and independent than its predecessor, was returned. The Assembly then attempted to seize the local arsenals, but open fighting between royalists and republicans ensued. Triumphant at Port-au-Prince in the West, the royalist forces were proceeding to march on the Assembly itself at Saint-Marc when the deputies escaped by boarding a French naval vessel, the *Leopard*, whose republican crew had mutinied. The Assemblymen then sailed for France to seek support from the same French National Assembly whose authority they had, so short a time before, been prepared to challenge. The royalists, alarmed by the possible consequences of this last act, made a truce with the remaining republicans, and awaited further developments. In time, the appeal of the fugitive assembly was rejected, and the colonial assembly was declared to be dissolved—a ruling which, however, the San Domingan republican whites refused to accept.

Before this outcome could be known, another development that was quite unexpected—at least to the San Domingan whites, whether royalist or republican—occurred. This took the form of a far more serious mulatto uprising, which developed in October, 1790.

Thomas Clarkson, visiting Paris in 1789 to seek to advance the cause of the abolition of slavery, had, while dining one day at the house of Lafayette, met six "Deputies of Color" who had arrived the day before from San Domingo, seeking representation for mulattoes in the French National Assembly. Later the deputies began to visit him at his hotel, but, said Clarkson, showed themselves disheartened at their lack of success, and began to be convinced that they would make no headway against the intrigues of the white colonists. One of them, named Ogé, could not contain himself, but broke out hotly as follows:

I begin not to care whether the National Assembly will admit us or not. But let it beware of the consequences. We will no longer continue to be beheld in a degraded light. Dispatches shall go directly to San Domingo; and we will soon follow them. We can produce as good soldiers on our estates as those in France. Our own arms shall make us independent and respectable. If we are once forced to desperate measures, it will be in vain that thousands will be sent across the Atlantic to bring us back to our former state.

Later Ogé went secretly to London, where he met Clarkson again, and, allegedly, also obtained there money and letters of credit to purchase arms in the United States. He returned to San Domingo where, on October 28, 1790, he led a revolt, attacking Le Cap with a few hundred men. Defeated, he fled to the Spanish part of the island, from where he was extradited, being handed over by the Spanish to the mercies of the local whites. After a trial lasting two months, he and his principal lieutenant, a mulatto named Chavannes who had fought in the American War of Independence, were condemned to death, together with others. In the presence of the entire provincial assembly of the North they were broken on the wheel, after which their heads were cut off.

The effect of the uprising was considerable on both whites and mulattoes. The mulattoes were filled with bitterness at the tragic death of one of whom they had been most proud. The whites were disturbed by the fact that the rising had received encouragement from abroad, and that large numbers of mulattoes had taken up arms. When news of Ogé's death reached Paris in April, 1791, the response was also considerable. His agony was re-enacted on the Paris stage, and public opinion became fiercely anti-colonial, much sympathy being shown for the mulatto cause. The effect of a decree adopted by the National Assembly on October 12, 1790, which had reasserted the provisions of the decree of March 8, 1790, was completely negated.

Indeed, Paris was becoming more revolutionary in spirit, and, as a result, all that came from France seemed to be harmful to the interests of the colonial aristocracy. De Tocqueville's general declaration that "the various occurrences of national existence have everywhere turned to the advantage of democracy" was amply illustrated by the arrival in Port-au-Prince, in the West, of two regiments of French troops on March 2, 1791. The troops, already indoctrinated with republicanism, fraternized with the *petits blancs* of Port-au-Prince, mutinied, and expelled the royalists, including the Governor, from the West, obliging them to seek sanctuary in the North. In the evolution toward the predominance of the majority that had now begun on the island, already the former masters, the privileged whites, were being driven from the West and the South.

In France, meanwhile, the French National Assembly—in which, whatever emotions might periodically sweep over it, the entrenched commercial interests remained powerful—began to debate the colonial question once more, with traditional and revolutionary attitudes toward the colonial question coming into sharp conflict. The result was a compromise which took the form of the National Decree of May 15, 1791, which stated that the French National Assembly would never deliberate upon the political status of people of color *who were not born of free father and mother,* without the previous free and spontaneous desire of the colonies. It was also provided that the colonial assemblies should continue, and that people of color born of free father and mother should be admitted to all future colonial assemblies if in other respects they possessed the necessary qualifications. The "compromise" was, however, unacceptable to the colonial faction in the Paris Assembly, which feared the symbolic effect of this breach of the color line, even although only 400 mulattoes were affected. To mark their repudiation of the measure, the colonial deputies walked out of the Assembly.

The reaction of the colonials in San Domingo was far stronger. When news of the decree arrived in Le Cap on June 30, 1791 it provoked such an outburst of anger that the Governor himself, reporting to Paris, wrote that even "the most loyal hearts are estranged," adding that he dared not report most comments, and stating that if the decree were enforced, the colony was resolved to secede. So deep was the impression made by the decree that the whites could talk of nothing else, and could attend to no other business. In this atmosphere a new colonial assembly was elected, and met at Léogane in the West on August 9, 1791. It was decided that the Assembly would convene in regular session at Le Cap in the North on the 25th of the same month. Before it could do so, however, not only the mulattoes but also the African slaves on the northern plantations rose in revolt. San Domingo's own revolution had begun.

## The Northern Plain Aflame

Throughout the summer of 1791 there had been increasing signs that the Negro population was becoming disaffected. One correspondent had written "The negroes are stirring in an astonishing fashion." The ideas of the French Revolution had spread to the farthest plantations, and, no doubt, in the most unpredictable ways. When the mutinous French soldiers had landed at Port-au-Prince earlier in the year, they had given the fraternal embrace to all the Negroes and mulattoes that they met, and had told them that the French National Assembly had declared them free and equal to the whites. The report of these and other incidents could not fail to travel fast, or to produce effects.

At first, seeing the whites declare themselves for liberty and equality, the Negroes had wanted to rise and obtain freedom too. Some of them resorted to armed rebellion, but exemplary executions had dissuaded them for the moment. Slave mutinies had also occurred on a number of plantations, but these, too, had been quelled. However, through the medium of the prevailing African religious cult of Vaudoux, or Vaudon which combined African metaphysics with sorcery, and which had resisted every attempt by the French authorities to stamp it out, the means of attempting to gain liberty for the slaves were decided upon, and an uprising organized. Details of the preparation of this uprising, which was to take the whites almost completely by surprise, are not known, but there was a report of a secret meeting that was held on August 14, 1791, and which was attended by Negroes from most parishes of the North Plain "to fix the day for the outbreak of the insurrection decided upon long before." Apart from this, however, the whites would seem to have remained almost completely in ignorance of what was coming. Only in Le Cap itself had some inkling been gleaned. On the very eve of the 23rd of August, the Governor became convinced that some conspiracy was being prepared, as a result of which he took certain precautions that saved the town. He could not, however, tell in advance whether the danger came from the Negroes, the mulattoes, or even from the white revolutionaries.

The rising began during the night of August 22. Before first light on the morning of the 23rd the whites, fleeing from the plantations on the Northern Plain, began to arrive in Le Cap, bringing news of a terrible massacre. On the plantations the slaves had killed white men and violated white women, and had set fire to houses and cane fields alike. A great glow in the sky behind the backs of the distraught survivors confirmed their words. "For three weeks," wrote one white eyewitness later, "we could barely distinguish between night and day, for so long as the rebels found anything to feed the flames, they never ceased to burn, resolved as they were to leave not a cane nor a house behind."

The strength of the uprising was soon demonstrated. A party of French National Guards who went out to reconnoitre was suddenly overwhelmed in the early dawn by a group of Negroes who bore as a standard the impaled body of a white child. Only two or three of the guardsmen succeeded in escaping. Later in the day a strong column of French troops which tried to leave Le Cap to enter the plain beat a retreat before swarming crowds of Negroes.

A terrible racial struggle then ensued in the North. The whites fortified Le Cap, and also the hill country that divided the North from the West. The Negroes, led by one Boukman, who was allegedly high in the Vaudoux hierarchy, and by another named Jeannot, used guerrilla tactics. Neither side showed any mercy to captives. Negroes were tortured to death in public in Le Cap, while approaches to the white camps in the hills were marked by clusters of the bodies of Negroes who had been hanged on the trees. The Negro camps for their part were decorated with the skulls of white prisoners who had been tortured to death. After a time Boukman was killed by the whites, and Jeannot by his own followers. Other leaders, however, arose to take their places.

In the West and the South, meanwhile, other events were occurring. The whites had also gathered themselves into fortified camps in these regions, but still remained bitterly divided into royalist and revolutionary factions. The royalists however, had formed a tactical alliance with the mulattoes, which was formally concluded, and was called the Confederation of La-Crois-des-Bouquets. The confederation inflicted a defeat upon the white revolutionaries, after which they surrendered the capital, Port-au-Prince.

But the Confederation was built on a fragile foundation. The royalists had entered into it merely for the sake of crushing the white revolutionaries. Although they had agreed not to oppose the mulatto rights accorded in the Decree of May 15, 1791, they had done so in the belief that in the near future Prussian troops would march into Paris, and the days of the National Assembly would be ended, for, as one of them put it, "50,000 Germans will have thrown out of the windows this legislative canaille." When that moment came there would clearly no longer be any necessity for compromising with mulattoes about the terms of the Decree of May 15, or anything else.

The royalists' hopes were soon to be dashed, however, and it was, ironically, the question of the May 15th Decree that helped to undo them. Word had arrived in Paris of the uprising in the North, and the National Assembly, horrified, had hastened to reverse its position on the May 15th Decree, which had not yet been officially communicated to

San Domingo. Instead, the Assembly enacted a new Decree—that of September 24, 1791—according to which the status of both mulattoes and slaves was to be fixed by the colonial assemblies, whose decisions were then to be ratified by the King. To prevent further changes, the provisions of the new decree were made articles of the French Constitution itself.

When news of the latest *volte-face* of the National Assembly reached San Domingo in November, 1791, the alliance between whites and mulattoes, already strained, broke down completely. In the fighting that soon began between whites and mulattoes, most of Port-au-Prince was burned down, and the mulattoes driven out. The mulattoes then attacked whites on the plantations in the West, and in the South succeeded in driving them out to a last stronghold on the tip of the peninsula, known as *Le Grande Anse*. Here the whites rallied, and prepared to attempt the reconquest of their lost lands.

*The Civil Commissioners*

Before the great uprising of August, 1791, the French National Assembly had appointed three Civil Commissioners to visit San Domingo. Despite later developments, the original appointments remained unchanged. Espousing a generous but flexible liberalism, the three Commissioners (one of whom, Mirbeck, was said to have "unedifying habits") were stricken with horror when, landing at Le Cap on November 29, 1791, they found racial passions inflamed to the highest degree, with actions suited to the cruel words that were spoken. Treated, at the outset, with marks of respect by the whites, the Commissioners announced that military forces were soon to arrive from France. They then attempted to act as peacemakers, establishing contact with the Negro leaders. The leaders proposed to them that they would attempt to restore peace in return for liberty for themselves and for their principal followers. The white colonial assembly rejected this proposal out of hand saying that it would place a premium on rebellion, and reminding the Commissioners that the recent decree vested power for legislating on the status of persons in the Colonial Assembly alone. The Commissioners, they declared, were only "intercessors"—a statement that destroyed the prestige of the Commissioners in the eyes of the Negroes. The Commissioners, angry at seeing their hopes dashed and their prestige shattered, strongly declared that their powers had no limits, and claimed that their authority was "a veritable dictatorship."

Once more the representatives of the French National Assembly and of the whites of San Domingo found themselves at loggerheads. Matters were not improved by the visit to the West of one of the Commissioners, Saint-Leger, who witnessed not only the horrors of the white-mulatto struggle there, but also further complications resulting from a local Negro uprising with religious overtones, headed by a man calling himself Romaine the Prophetess. Saint-Leger's attempts at reconciliation aroused white suspicions against him, with the result that he took refuge with the mulattoes, whom he persuaded to crush Romaine's uprising. When the white attack upon the mulattoes grew more intense, however, the mulattoes summoned the Negroes to their assistance, and the entire region fell into a state of disastrous anarchy, with whites and mulattoes both striving to exterminate the others. On April 9, 1792, in a state of fear and despair, Saint-Leger sailed for France.

Even before he sailed, another of the three Commissioners, Mirbeck, having, together with his remaining colleague, Roume, narrowly escaped being drowned in an attempted coup against them at Le Cap, had decided that he too had had enough of San Domingo, and sailed for France on March 30, 1792. The last Commissioner, Roume, a revolutionary of character and principle, remained only for one reason—because he believed that only his continued presence prevented the Governor from joining the royalist cause, thus placing the whole island at the disposal of the counter-revolution.

Meanwhile the white colonists were asking why the French troops whose arrival had been promised by the commissioners had not come. The answer was that, with revolutionary sentiment growing stronger in France, and with the expulsion from the National Assembly of certain deputies who defended the colonists' interests, the impression had spread in Paris that the events in San Domingo formed part of a royalist plot against the revolution, and that the troubles there had been fomented with the aim of depriving France of troops at a time when she found herself at war with some of the European monarchies. As a result, almost no troops at all were dispatched to the island; the few who did arrive produced little effect on the situation.

### The Second Civil Commissioners

The mood of Paris had changed to such an extent since the previous September that even conservatives with commercial interests in San Domingo were asking one another why the colonists should demonstrate such fanaticism in opposing the principle of equal rights for mulattoes. As Lothrop Stoddard expressed it: "What appeared to the colonists a vital principle, seemed to Frenchmen a foolish prejudice, and the whites of San Domingo were more and more regarded as a stiff-necked generation in a great part responsible for the woes which overwhelmed them."

On March 10, 1792, the Feuillant ministry had fallen, and, as a result, the Jacobin campaign against the colonial system gained in momentum and scope. The immediate result was the National Law of April 4, 1792, in which, once more, the National Assembly reversed its position, by completely nullifying the Decree of September 24, 1791, whether it formed a part of the Constitution or not. New elections were to be held to choose colonial and provincial assemblies, and in these elections mulattoes and free Negroes were to be allowed to vote, as well as to stand as candidates for election. Only the institution of slavery remained, for the moment, unchallenged. Once again three Civil Commissioners were to be appointed, but this time the powers of the Commissioners were to be made dictatorial, and, in order that the new law should be enforced, they were to be given the backing of an army. Even as the two first Civil Commissioners were dejectedly making their way home to France, news was traveling in the opposite direction of the new decisions of the National Assembly. The news reached San Domingo on May 11, 1792. When it was received the whites were plunged into rage and utter despair, while the mulattoes rejoiced. The whites would have liked to oppose the provisions of the new law, but, rather than attack the army that was being sent from France, were obliged to decide to submit.

Until the new Commissioners and the army arrived, confusion continued to prevail. In the West the mulattoes, who still tended toward royalism, once more joined the royalist whites, forming an alliance which, in July, 1792, obliged the *petits blancs* of Port-au-Prince to surrender the town to them. The remaining commissioner, Roume, had meanwhile traveled to the West, and was attempting to persuade the mulattoes to abandon the royalists and throw in their lot with the National Assembly, which had now given them the vote. Roume hoped to persuade them to join him in crushing the Negro revolt in the North, but the mulattoes instead demanded help against both whites and blacks in the South. There was no end in sight, it seemed, to the conflicts that had been engendered.

Meanwhile, in Paris, one Cougnac-Mion, the representative in that city of the San Domingan Colonial Assembly, had got wind, he averred, of a secret that filled him with the darkest foreboding. There was, he said, a plot to end all slavery in the colonies, and then to use emancipation and revolutionary subversion as weapons in pursuance of a strategy that would attempt to give France supremacy in the New World, if not around the globe.

> I send you, gentlemen [he wrote to the San Domingan Colonial Assembly on July 20, 1792], a decree of the National Assembly which will give you the key to the operations by which its Commissioners are to bring about the general enfranchisement of the negroes. Do not doubt these words, gentlemen. I know whereof I speak; and I swear upon my honour that my words are true. The plot is already hatched within the National Assembly and will be carried out the moment the Commissioners have attained complete authority. The plan is to enfranchise all the negroes in all the French colonies; then, with these first freedmen, to bring about enfranchisement in all

the foreign colonies; and thus to carry revolt and independence throughout the New World—a thing which, according to its authors, will give them supremacy over all the Powers of Europe. And this atrocious plan producing such torrents of blood will certainly be executed if you do not join haste to resolution, concord to preparation, and to your resistance the courage of despair. Gentlemen, beat off these tigers athirst for blood; crush in these wretches' hearts their barbarous projects; and thereby earn the love of your countrymen and the blessings of an entire world saved by your courage from the atrocious convulsions which these madmen have in store.

If you are sufficiently united to follow my counsel, I guarantee the salvation of San Domingo. But, in any case, let no one cherish the hope of mercy from these men, let no one be deluded by their sly tricks of policy; the negroes alone find room in their affections, and all the whites without distinction, all the mulattoes as well, are doomed; all alike are dangerous to their projects, all alike will be sacrificed as soon as these men shall have disposed of the officers, gotten rid of the troops of the line, and become at last the undisputed masters.

This letter must certainly have aroused the gravest apprehension in San Domingo. However, when the French fleet, bearing the three new commissioners and 6,000 French troops, sailed into Le Cap on September 18, 1792, no attempt was made to "beat off these tigers athirst for blood." Instead, an impressive reception was accorded them, while at the same time the colonists expressed the deepest concern as to the possibility that the institution of slavery might be threatened.

The immediate effect of the arrival of the commissioners and the troops was to encourage the *petits blancs* of Le Cap at the expense of the royalists. The royalist Governor was shipped back to France, where he was later guillotined. Commissioner Roume was also sent home, although with less fatal consequences. The Colonial Assembly was dissolved, but no new elections were held. Instead the commissioners appointed an advisory council, composed of six whites, five mulattoes, and one free Negro. All these measures were, however, overshadowed by momentous news from France—the news of the storming of the Tuileries on August 10, 1792, of the King's fall, and of the summoning of the Convention. The Jacobins were, at last, coming to power in Paris, and would clearly soon try to do so in San Domingo as well. Alarmed, the royalists of Le Cap prepared a military coup in October, 1792, but it miscarried, and those involved were shipped back to France. The place of the military leaders involved was, however, soon thereafter filled by the opportune arrival of General Rochambeau who, together with 2,000 troops, sought refuge in San Domingo after having been driven off from royalist Martinique.

Two of the Commissioners—Polverel and Ailhaud—left Le Cap for Port-au-Prince by sea at about this time to see what could be done to discourage royalism in the West. The third Commissioner, Sonthonax, remained at Le Cap, where his actions soon led to a sharp rise in tension among the whites. If there was indeed a Jacobin conspiracy to carry "revolt and independence" throughout the New World, then Sonthonax must certainly have been a part of it. His tactical moves would seem to have been directed toward the ultimate aim of transferring power to the majority—the Negroes of San Domingo. To begin with, he had disposed of the royalists in the North by favoring the white "patriots," the *petits blancs*. Finding himself alone at Le Cap, he now ceased to favor Europeans of whatever social status, and began instead to favor the mulattoes. All who surrounded Sonthonax—counselors, mistresses, friends—were now seen to be mulattoes. The whites, who had earlier rallied to the French republican cause, now found themselves called by a new and pejorative name—*Aristocrates de la Peau,* "aristocrats of the skin."

As if this was not enough to set the whites quarreling among themselves, white opposition to Sonthonax was strengthened by his decision to levy a forced loan. Dissatisfaction was rife, and Sonthonax found himself obliged to send white dissidents back to France by the shipload. When, in addition, Sonthonax began to appoint mulatto officers to the regiment of Le Cap, a mutiny broke out, in December, 1792. The mutiny failed, however, since the white mutineers suddenly found themselves confronted with mulatto troops who Sonthonax had had recruited for him. The humiliated whites, powerless, abandoned their trust in France, and prayed only for a war which would lead to their deliverance by the British fleet. Meanwhile these internal dissensions prevented either whites or mulattoes from making any progress in crushing the Negro insurgents in the Northern Plain, who, Sonthonax reported, were "aided by the perfidious Spaniards" from their colony in the western half of the island. Only the abolition of slavery, he hinted, could end the revolt.

In the West, the two Commissioners had at first been welcomed at Port-au-Prince, which was controlled by the republican whites, while the royalist whites, now allied with the mulattoes, predominated in the countryside. This situation soon changed, however. One of the Commissioners, Ailhaud, sent to investigate the situation in the South, tired of San Domingo and its broils, and sailed instead for France. While his colleague, Polverel, was visiting the South in his place, the Port-au-Prince whites and the mulattoes of the West alike got wind of the developments in the North, and realigned themselves accordingly. The mulattoes once more broke off their alliance with the royalist whites, and rallied instead to the support of Sonthonax, who seemed to them so clearly pro-mulatto. All the whites of the West, however, whether royalist or republican, now buried their differences and made common cause against the mulattoes and the Commissioners.

At this juncture both Commissioners rejoined each other in the West, and proceeded to blockade Port-au-Prince by sea, while mulatto forces besieged it by land. Port-au-Prince surrendered to the Commissioners on

April 13, 1793, after some whites had fought their way out of the trap and had rejoined the white royalists still holding out in the South. Numbers of the remaining whites were sent back to France. "Should we dare make a murmur," complained one white republican, "we are thrown aboard ship like bags of dirty linen and sent to France without a word to those left behind."

News had meanwhile come to the North of the execution of Louis XVI, and of the outbreak of the war with England—news which aroused the strongest emotions. Soon after, in view of the state of war, Paris dispatched to San Domingo a new Governor-General with military experience, one General Galbaud. When the two Commissioners returned to Le Cap in June, surrounded by mulatto troops, they found the whites seething with hostility toward them, and ready to rally to Galbaud as their savior—Galbaud being popular first because he was known to disapprove of the Commissioners' actions, and second because he was married to a white creole San Domingan. But the commissioners declared that Galbaud's credentials were invalid and announced that he was deposed. Galbaud, trained to soldierly obedience, accepted their ruling, and re-embarked on one of the ships of the French fleet anchored at Le Cap. Racial tension between mulattoes and whites in the port ran so high, however, that before long French sailors became involved in incidents, and the fleet demanded intervention. On June 20, 1793, Galbaud decided to act against both Commissioners and mulattoes, and landed at Le Cap with 2,000 sailors, being supported also by the local whites. Fierce fighting between the whites on the one side and the mulattoes and Negroes on the other then ensued. Galbaud's forces began to gain ground, and the situation of the Commissioners became precarious. They then took the one step left to them to take. On June 21, 1793, they came to terms with the Negro insurgents on the Northern Plain, proclaiming the liberty of all Negroes who would join them. The Negroes responded in force. Le Cap was set on fire, and overrun by thousands of insurgents from the Plain. Fifteen thousand more came pouring in the following day. The whites were driven back to the ships. Galbaud and the French fleet, loaded with a freight of 10,000 refugee whites, set sail for the United States, leaving Le Cap in flames and with corpse-covered streets behind them. After a calm passage the fleet anchored in Chesapeake Bay. The condition of the refugees aroused great sympathy in the United States, where both private and public resources were mobilized to assist them. The news that they brought of developments in San Domingo also created a sensation, and, for the first time, some white slave-owners in the southern states began to ponder about the dangers to their own security arising from the importation of too many slaves.

*The Abolition of Slavery*

Polverel now returned to the West, leaving Sonthonax in control of the North. Sonthonax began the next phase of his policy—the replacement of the mulattoes in his entourage with Negroes, just as previously the mulattoes had replaced the whites. On August 29, 1793, he officially proclaimed the emancipation of all the slaves in the North. The proclamation opened with a quotation from the Declaration of the Rights of Man and of the Citizen: "All men are born and remain free and equal." "Behold, citizens," added Sonthonax, "the evangel of France!" Polverel was alarmed by this unexpected event, but, finding himself before a fait accompli, soon was obliged to follow suit and proclaim the emancipation of the slaves in the West and the South as well. At least one of the results was, however, unforeseen: in many places the Negroes equated slavery with labor, and now refused to work, beginning, instead, a life of idleness. Other paradoxes, similarly arising from a lack of education, were also evident: for example, some of the Negro leaders had still not fully seized the meaning of the French Revolution and demanded a king to serve. Failing to find one exercising authority over French San Domingo, they went to the western half of the island to serve the King of Spain, being, no doubt, recompensed by him accordingly.

Meanwhile the white royalist Confederation of the Grande Anse, holding out on the tip of the southern peninsula, placed itself under British protection, leaving the future status of San Domingo to be decided when peace was eventually concluded. As a result of this pact with the British, British troops landed on the island on September 19, 1793. Three days later a single British ship arrived off the northwest tip of the island, where the heavily fortified stronghold of the Môle Saint-Nicholas still remained in French hands. Upon catching sight of a British sail, the French garrison immediately, and presumably enthusiastically, surrendered. The white counter-revolutionary forces on the western extremities of the island, and the Spanish forces in the East, now formed a giant vise—which began slowly but surely to close in upon Sonthonax and his Negro soldiery. His situation was not improved by his new pro-Negro policy, for this created discontent among the mulattoes, who now began to turn against him. Sonthonax wept with rage, and wrote letters to his colleagues that were barely comprehensible. By early 1794 his situation had deteriorated so far that it seemed it must soon become untenable.

In Paris, meanwhile, events had also moved forward. As a result of the great number of complaints lodged against the Civil Commissioners by the deportees and refugees from San Domingo, the Convention passed a decree of accusation against them. This action did not, however, mean that the Convention was becoming pro-colonist in sentiment. Quite the contrary. The calling in of the British by the French colonists in the South had raised public opinion against them to a new pitch. Any colonists who found themselves in France became the targets of abuse, and did not dare to risk replying for fear of being guillotined. "From Toulon to my journey's end," wrote one, "in coach or barge, in public house or private home, at cross-road or in city square—everywhere I found the same prejudice, the same virulence against the colonist." He added that he had met many persons "so touched by the unhappy lot of the slaves that they had long since ceased to take coffee, thinking that they swallowed only blood and sweat in this sugared drink." With such a general opinion prevailing, it was hardly surprising that on February 4, 1794, the Convention announced the abolition of slavery in all the colonies. Sonthonax's action had now received official sanction. The greatest effect in San Domingo was, however, finally to alienate the mulattoes, many of whom were slave-owners, from the Commissioners' cause, thus facilitating the fall of Port-au-Prince to the British troops. The Commissioners then fled to the South where, fortunately for them, a fast French corvette hove into view, sent especially to arrest them and to take them home for trial. They left behind them the British victorious in the South and in the West. Only in the North did the British writ not run, for here the Negroes had found a new and remarkable leader, Toussaint Louverture.

# Chapter 10

# Toussaint Louverture and
# the Black Republic

*Nations of Europe, your slaves will break the yoke that weighs upon them. The Negroes only lack a leader. Where is that great man to be found? He will appear, we cannot doubt it; he will show himself to raise the sacred standard of liberty and to gather around him his companions in misfortune. More impetuous than the mountain torrents, they will leave behind them on all sides the ineffaceable signs of their resentment. The old world as well as the new will applaud him. The name of the hero who will have re-established the rights of the human species will be blessed forever.* —The Abbé Raynal, *Histoire Philosophique et Politique des Etablissements et du Commerce des Europeéns dans les Deux Indes* (1770)

*I take up arms for the liberty of my color, that France alone has proclaimed; she has not the right to enslave us; our liberty does not belong to her any more. It is ours; we shall know how to defend it or die.* —Toussaint Louverture, upon hearing that Bonaparte was sending an invasion fleet to San Domingo to restore slavery in the year X of the revolutionary calendar (1801–1802)

*I have to reproach myself with an attempt against this colony [San Domingo] at the time of the Consulate; it was a great fault to have wished to subject it by force. I should have contented myself with governing it through the intermediary of Toussaint.* —Napoleon in exile on St. Helena

TOUISSAINT LOUVERTURE was a black slave from the Bréda plantation near Le Cap in San Domingo, who rose to power in his country late in life. Enlightened and humane, Toussaint exercised such influence over the blacks of San Domingo, and showed such acumen in government and statecraft that Napoleon himself began to fear that unless he were overthrown "the scepter of the New World would sooner or later pass into the hands of the blacks." In an age of remarkable men, he was remarkable.

Much and little is known about him. "Men of genius," as a Haitian writer has expressed it, "have the rare privilege of writing their history themselves by heroic deeds, and of entering alive into immortality."[1] Toussaint's great deeds are known to all, but much else remains obscure. Uncertainty surrounds the date of his birth; there is uncertainty as to who was his father; it is uncertain how he got the name of "Louverture"; there are controversies on many points of fact and of motive in his career. Lothrop Stoddard has written:

It seems improbable that the mists enveloping his personality will ever be cleared away. Extremely little first-class material exists, and practically everything written about him is of such doubtful value that his figure seems destined to remain forever shrouded in the haze of legend and tradition.

Yet behind the mists he stands like a mountain, clear in the main outline: a great historic figure who understood the needs and potentialities of both European colonist and emancipated African slave; who sought to found a free society to which both would contribute, and which would become the keystone of the New World. It was, perhaps, only due to the ignorance and the prejudices of another great man, Napoleon, that Toussaint's dream was not consummated.

François-Dominique Toussaint, later known as Toussaint Louverture, and popularly known in his earlier years as Toussaint Bréda, was born on the Bréda plantation in the village of Haut-du-Cap. His son Isaac later said that Toussaint was born on May 20, 1746. Other historians have said that he was born in May, 1743. He himself claimed to be fifty years old when the French Revolution occurred, which would place his birth date in 1739. The prison register of Fort de Joux, France, where he was incarcerated in August, 1802, gave his age—presumably on the basis of Toussaint's own statement—as fifty-eight, which would mean that he was born in 1745. Other indications would support the thesis that he was born in 1745 or 1746, but the doubt remains.

Toussaint's father—again according to his son Isaac—was the son of a chieftain of the Arada[2] tribe of Dahomey named Gaou Ginou, who was captured in war and sent to San Domingo as a slave. With humanitarian attitudes prevailing on the Bréda plantation, and in consideration of his former social rank, the chief's son was allegedly given *la liberté de savane*—a special status which permitted the slave virtual freedom, but which still left him under the protection of his master. Toussaint's father,

1. H. Pauléus Sannon, *Histoire de Toussaint Louverture* (Port-au-Prince, 1920).
2. *Arada* is the San Domingan version of the Dahomeyan *Allada* tribe. *Rada,* the name for the voudun religion, derives from the same origin.

who had five sons and three daughters, knew much about herbs and medicinal plants, and passed on his knowledge to his eldest son, Toussaint. Toussaint himself, in his correspondence, never referred, however, to any relationship to this man, but twice mentions Pierre Baptiste as being his father. Pierre Baptiste, also of the Arada tribe, was an elderly man who lived in the village of Haut-du-Cap, and who taught Toussaint to read and write. Pierre Baptiste, who had himself been taught what he knew by a missionary, was certainly Toussaint's godfather, if not his true father. Speaking of the relationship between Toussaint and Pierre Baptiste, Pauléus Sannon writes:

> Toussaint-Louverture perfected himself by his own efforts, in turning his leisure time to advantage. He achieved this through reading, meditation, and, later, by contact with men of distinction with whom his high position put him in contact, often under his orders. He was avid for knowledge.

Pierre Baptiste also knew some Latin, and, like the son of Gaou Ginou, plant lore, both of which he transmitted to Toussaint. Years later, when Toussaint had risen to power, it was said that he liked to approach a group of his black officers and cry out to them as a greeting: *Dominus tecum, salve Domino, tibi gratias!* When they looked at him nonplussed, he would shake his head and say: "You don't know Latin? Too bad! Too bad! You will never amount to much."

An Englishman named Marcus Rainsford, who was shipwrecked on the island during the time of Toussaint's rule and who met him, saw the following books among those in Toussaint's library, mostly in French translations: Caesar's *Commentaries*; *The History of Alexander and of Caesar*, by Declaison; *Rêveries Militaires*—Marshal de Saxe's book on tactics; *Military Memoirs of the Greeks and the Romans*, by Guischard; *History of the Spanish and English Revolutions*, by d'Orléans; *Mémoires de l'Académie des Inscriptions et des Belles-Lettres*, by Le Beau; *Military and Political Memoirs*, by Lloyd; and works by Herodotus, Plutarch, and Cornelius Nepos. It is known that Toussaint read—and it is quite clear that he was influenced by—the writings of Epictetus, a philosopher with whom he may well have felt an affinity in view of the fact that he too had been a slave. It is also generally accepted that during the earlier part of his life he had read and reread the work by the Abbé Raynal on the European colonies in the "two Indies" to which we have already alluded, and of which the most famous extract appears at the head of this chapter: "The Negroes only lack a leader. Where is that great man to be found? He will appear, we cannot doubt it. . . ."

It was in the Creole language—of which the vocabulary is based mainly upon French and the grammar upon African languages—that Toussaint expressed himself most easily. In French itself he was less proficient. From his justificatory memoir to Napoleon, and in other letters that came directly from his own hand without benefit of correction or rewriting by others, it is clear that he wrote phonetically and that his turns of phrase were sometimes incorrect. In his spelling, for example, instead of asking Napoleon to *jeter un coup d'oeil*—that is, "to glance"— he asked him to *jai té un cou deuille*. It is also clear, however, that he wrote with dignity, good sense, and eloquence, citing classical examples, and showing nobility of thought.

Toussaint was throughout his life thin in body. As a boy his playmates nicknamed him *fatras-baton*—a thrashing stick. In the last year of his life the prison register of Fort de Joux described him as follows:

> Five feet two inches tall; bust lean and slight; eyes lively and large, nose flattened and turned up. Large lips, chin long and rather pointed; teeth long and covered with tartar, those in the middle, upper and lower, missing; the last joint of the little finger of the right hand bent upward into a semi-circle as a result of a wound; finally Negro, extremely black.

According to Toussaint himself he lost his middle teeth after receiving a blow in the mouth from a spent cannon ball during a siege of Saint Marc. A fall from a horse in early youth had caused his broken finger, which had then been poorly set.[3]

It has been claimed that Toussaint was given the name of *Louverture* ("the opening") because of the gap in his teeth. This would seem un-likely, since the first time he is known to have signed his name *Toussaint Louverture* was in August, 1793, while in his memoirs, written in prison during the last months of his life, he says that it was while fighting against the English, which he did not begin to do until 1794, that he was hit by the cannon ball, which shook his jaw so much that, as he put it, "the greater part of my teeth fell out, and those which remained are still very shaky." His son Isaac stated that he received the name of *Louverture* after the French Commissioner, Polverel, hearing that Toussaint had left the service of Spain and fought his way through to the French, capturing the towns of Dondon and Marmelade in the process, cried out: "What! That man makes an opening (*ouverture*) everywhere!" However, again, this incident did not occur until 1794. It has also been suggested, without any supporting evidence whatsoever, that Toussaint had once been the property of a man named Louverture. Another suggestion[4] is that the choice of name was made deliberately to link Toussaint in the popular mind with the voudun deity Legba,[5] the opener of the gate of destiny.

3. When Toussaint was the de facto ruler of San Domingo, he sent for his sister Geneviève, who had been sold to a planter when he was a child, and whom he had not seen since. Upon receiving the news, Geneviève found it difficult to believe that "that little boy" had since become a great man. Only after she had been reassured that one of his fingers curled upwards did she allow the affectionate reunion to take place.

4. See Ralph Korngold, *Citizen Toussaint* (1944).

5. Legba, like Toussaint himself, derives from Dahomeyan origins.

Certainly the populace spoke of "Papa Louverture" just as they spoke of "Papa Legba," and a Haitian chant, still current, runs *Papa Legba,* ouvri *barriére pour moins!* ("Papa Legba, open the gate for me!")

Possibly Toussaint was nicknamed *Louverture* after he had first captured the garrison of Dondon for Spain in the summer of 1793, since this victory made a breach, or opening, in the mountain defenses of Le Cap, thus causing much chagrin to the French. If so, the name would have became sufficiently current for him to use it, as he first did, in August of that year, perhaps for purposes of identification in making his appeal to the black populace at large. This, in turn, would have been consistent with Polverel's exclamation the following year (which, literally, was *ce bougre-là se fait donc ouverture partout!*), in which he said, in effect, that Toussaint had not merely made one opening, but was making openings everywhere. Isaac Louverture may have remembered the Commissioner's exclamation, to the exclusion of earlier circumstances, because it would tend to give an official French sanction to the name. All this, however, remains conjectural. As with Toussaint's exact age, and the exact name of his father, the facts have now been obscured.

In his earlier years Toussaint was put to minding cattle. His skill in horsemanship and his way with horses soon led, however, to his being made a stable boy. The Bréda plantation was the property of the Comte de Noë, a member of the Bréda family. He was, however, an absentee landlord, and the management of the plantation eventually devolved upon a M. Bayou de Libertat, who was struck by Toussaint's capacities, and made him first a coachman, and then his confidential agent. He had married, relatively early, another Bréda slave named Suzanne Simon— a woman of sense and character, whom he chose in preference to one of the "frisky negresses" that his masters advised him to take. Suzanne had a four-year-old mulatto son, Placide, whom Toussaint also adopted. Placide repaid this act of kindness on Toussaint's part with a lifelong devotion which the vicissitudes of fortune left unchanged.

To the casual observer it would appear, at this late date, that Toussaint only emerged in the later stages of the San Domingan revolution. He himself, however, claimed to have been the one to organize the slave uprising of 1791 on the Northern Plain. In a sense this was true, although an even stronger claimant of that honor might have been—paradoxically —none other than Governor Blanchelande himself.

It appears that in the summer of 1791 the Governor and the royalist party, wishing to paralyze the Colonial Assembly and to prevent it from obtaining control over the colony, hit on the idea of organizing a slave revolt—a staged event that would, it was calculated, make the colonists aware of their ultimate dependence on France and the Crown. A member of the royalist party, visiting the Bréda plantation, spoke of the project in Toussaint's hearing. Toussaint was bold enough to express approval of the plan, and to advance some suggestions of his own. By promising the slaves three days off a week,[6] and by abolishing the penalty of whipping, their co-operation could, he said, be easily obtained. He also proposed that the main organizers might be granted their freedom. In making this proposal—which was virtually the same as proposing himself as the principal organizer—Toussaint realized that although the royalists did not have the interests of the slaves at heart, his African brothers might nevertheless benefit from the circumstances that had arisen. His suggestions were approved, and he himself was given a safe-conduct, guaranteeing him against any eventual prosecution.

Toussaint then immediately made contact with certain friends of his —Boukman, Biassou, Jeannot, and Jean-François—all of whom were to become prominent in the earlier stages of the Domingan revolution. Toussaint, meanwhile, was not to put himself forward, but was to remain the secret intermediary between the royalist party and the rebels. Boukman and the others then told the slaves that the King and the French National Assembly wished to abolish whipping as well as to give them three days off a week, but that this was opposed by the local Colonial Assembly. As proof of this allegation a forged gazette was manufactured and shown to them at a secret meeting held at the Lenormand plantation at Morne Rouge,[7] at which they were also told that troops were soon to arrive from France to help them. After the meeting the participants were led into the woods to Bois Caïman, where certain voudun rites were performed.

On the night of August 16, 1791, one of the members of the conspiracy, apparently as a result of a misunderstanding, took premature action by setting fire to a building. Under interrogation by the colonists he revealed further details of the planned uprising. The Municipality of Le Cap became concerned, and, on the night of August 21, the arrest of some of the Negro leaders was ordered. The wanted men, however, fled in time, and on that same night of August 21–22, 1791, began the uprising. The uprising, however, apparently soon assumed proportions far greater than those envisaged by its instigators.[8] Governor Blanchelande proved either unable or unwilling to control what he had begun. Plantation after plantation was set on fire; men, women, and children were massacred; and the horrified and terror-stricken whites were driven to seek refuge in Le Cap.

The original agreement had stipulated that the government troops

6. The slaves had one day a week to work on their own plots of land, and also had their Sundays free. Another day to work for themselves was thus proposed.
7. See Chapter 9, p. 231.
8. Unless, that is, the royalist party, in collaboration with the French Court, had wished the uprising to be as large as possible, in order that the greatest possible number of troops be dispatched to quell it, thus weakening the resistance of France to the anticipated counter-revolutionary attack by Prussia and Austria.

were only to feign an attack on the Negroes. What was to have been a stage revolt, however, soon became a revolt in earnest, and the fighting that ensued was by no means feigned. Toussaint and the royalists, however, still planned to negotiate peace. Toussaint had succeeded in saving the Bréda plantation from the flames, but, after a month had elapsed, he saw that he could no longer guarantee the safety of Madame de Libertat, who had stayed at home while her husband had gone to Le Cap. Toussaint himself helped her to pack, after which his brother Paul drove the carriage taking her and her belongings to Le Cap to rejoin her husband. When she had left, Toussaint went to the Gallifet plantation, and joined the guerrilla headquarters of Jean-François and Biassou. His life as a slave was over.

By virtue of his knowledge of herbs, Toussaint, at first, was given the title of "Physician to the Armies of the King." It was at about this time that the first Civil Commissioners entered into contact with the Negro rebels, and Toussaint, in view of his education and character, became involved in the negotiations, such as they were. At one stage, when the Colonial Assembly had rejected what were evidently the comparatively reasonable terms offered by the Negro leaders, Biassou wished to kill all the white prisoners. Toussaint, however, who acted as Biassou's secretary, dissuaded him from doing so. The granting of liberty to some of the Negro leaders—a proposal that had originally formed part of the agreement between Toussaint and the royalists—also figured in the negotiations. After Toussaint and the others had offered to try to induce the rebels to return to their work on the planations in return for the granting of freedom to 400 Negro leaders and their friends, and the offer had been refused, Toussaint secretly reduced the number to 60 men—his final offer. This proposal was also rejected by the enraged colonists. Toussaint then came to a decision which he never altered as long as he lived, and which provided the key to all his subsequent actions: *all the blacks living in San Domingo must become free.* This personal decision to assume responsibility for the abolition of slavery in San Domingo was reflected in a change of title, for now, instead of physician, he took the rank of brigadier-general.

In the months that followed he distinguished himself in combat on several occasions, notably in the defense of Morne Pélé on October 7, 1792. His growing reputation made him the target of the jealousy of one of the Negro leaders, Jean-François, who had him put in prison—a predicament from which he was extricated by Biassou.

### The Question of Allegiance

In early 1793 war was declared between revolutionary France and royalist Spain, both of whom then began to vie for the allegiance of the Negro chiefs of San Domingo. By this time Toussaint personally commanded a group of 600 Negroes, and paid only nominal allegiance to Biassou. He had made considerable efforts to train and to discipline his troops, and had received advice in so doing from two white prisoners who were versed in military matters. Realizing that classical military techniques were ill adapted to San Domingan circumstance, he modified traditional methods, and evolved guerrilla tactics, as well as methods of mass attack. He achieved considerable success, both in the field, as well as in establishing strict discipline among his troops, and in exacting obedience from them. Thus, though he had only a small force at his command, it was nevertheless a tight-knit one.

The French Commissioners offered Toussaint and the other leaders freedom for themselves and their followers if they would fight for France. But Toussaint had already witnessed the weakness of the Commissioners when it came to attempting to fulfill their promises. The Spanish, on the other hand, offered not only freedom, but also land concessions for all in both the French and the Spanish part of the island, as well as subsidies and supplies for Toussaint and the other leaders. Under these circumstances, as we noted in the preceding chapter, Toussaint, as well as Biassou and Jean-François, chose to fight for Spain rather than for France. Toussaint appears also to have believed that the royalist cause would finally triumph, and that the royalist offer of liberty gave better guarantees for eventual freedom.

Toussaint and his colleagues therefore placed themselves under the orders of the Spanish, who thereupon found their territory correspondingly expanded. In the summer of 1793 Toussaint further proved his worth to the Spanish by capturing the French commandant of the garrison of Dondon, whom he then prevailed upon to induce the whole garrison to surrender, thus effecting a breach (the famous *ouverture*), in the Cordon of the West. When the surrendering French garrison marched into Toussaint's camp with flags flying, drums beating, and even the gunners' matches alight, Toussaint's troops are said to have been so overwhelmed by the sight that they would have fled on the spot had not Toussaint prevailed upon them to stay and to receive the submission of the French. In this instance, as in others, surrendering to Toussaint was a much more acceptable prospect than surrendering to Jean-François or to Biassou, since Toussaint was renowned for his common-sense humanity toward prisoners, while his colleagues had established very different reputations. This was, however, merely one of the reasons contributing to his success. The degree of that success was demonstrated by the fact that whereas he began his campaign against the French with 600 men, he ended it with 5,000—a circumstance which justified him in his assumption of the title of general.

The Negro leaders having been won over by Spain, and the French suffering reverses, the French Commissioners, whose support was crumbling on all sides, attempted to win over the Negro masses by ending slavery. On August 29, 1793, as described in the preceding chapter, one of the French Commissioners, Sonthonax, decreed the abolition of slavery. But Toussaint, who knew about this in advance, did not feel that he could permit a European official to claim the honor of granting his people liberty—the very aim for which he himself was struggling so hard and so single-mindedly. Four days before the proclamation, on August 25, 1793, Toussaint issued a proclamation of his own—nominally directed to the Negroes fighting on the French side. The immediate purpose was clearly to counteract the effect of Sonthonax's impending action, but the following words which appeared in it equally clearly demonstrated Toussaint's view that to accept freedom from the hands of others would be demeaning:

Who has laid the foundations for this idea of general liberty, in which cause you are fighting against your friends? Are we not the first authors of it? . . . liberty is a right given by Nature; equality follows from this liberty . . . I am the one who must work for it, as being the first to join the cause that I have always upheld; I cannot yield on this; having begun, I shall finish. . . .

For the first time, so far as is known, he signed himself "Toussaint Louverture," adding the words "General of the Armies of the King." It was evidently only fitting that, when the abolition of slavery was about to be proclaimed in San Domingo by a white man, a black man should place himself on record beforehand by pointing out that it was the blacks themselves who had, by their own efforts, regained their freedom —a freedom which, moreover, was no more than their inherent right.

On the day of the proclamation itself, August 29, Toussaint issued another short appeal, which said:

I am Toussaint Louverture. My name is perhaps known to you. I have undertaken vengeance. I want Liberty and Equality to reign in San Domingo. I am working to bring them into existence. Unite with us, brothers, and fight with us for the same cause.

Toussaint was becoming uneasy, however, about the prospects of achieving liberty and equality by continuing to serve the royalist cause. After the French Commissioners had abolished slavery, the French colonists, appalled at what they regarded as a mortal blow to their interests, called in the English, who landed in San Domingo in the month which followed Sonthonax's proclamation. The English, moreover, were reintroducing slavery in all the regions that they occupied. The Spanish, too, though they had originally promised Toussaint that they would grant freedom, now insisted that they had only meant this promise to apply to Toussaint and the other leaders, and to their armies. But every time Toussaint captured a parish, he would free all the slaves in it, maintaining that this had been the original understanding. Not only the Spanish disagreed with him on this, but so did Jean-François and Biassou, who, accepting the Spanish interpretation of the agreement, were receiving money by selling Negroes to Spanish slave traders. The confirmation of Sonthonax's proclamation by the French National Assembly, which abolished slavery by its decree of 16 Pluviose of the Year II (February 4, 1794), was the final straw. Toussaint, seeing not merely one colonial official on his own responsibility but France itself abolish slavery, resolved that he must change sides. As always, however, he made haste slowly, and did not yet show his hand.

Toussaint's Spanish superior, the Marquis d'Hermona, had full trust in Toussaint. After confirming his promotion to the rank of general, he exclaimed, upon seeing him praying in church: "If God descended upon earth he could inhabit no purer heart than that of Toussaint Louverture!" Other Spaniards, however, perhaps less spiritually minded than the Marquis, were becomingly increasingly suspicious of Toussaint, as also were Biassou and Jean-François. Finally Jean-François arrested some of Toussaint's officers. Toussaint, with his youngest brother, Jean-Pierre, hastened to the camp where they were detained. They were met with a volley of musketry, and Jean-Pierre, riding on horseback at Toussaint's side, was shot dead in the saddle.

Toussaint then made final preparations for a break. Having made clear to the Spanish that he had served them in his own right, and not as a dependent of Biassou, he entered secretly into contact with General Laveaux, then the interim French Governor in San Domingo. Laveaux later described Toussaint's action as follows:

He [Toussaint] fought against us until 6 April, 1794. He fought only for the freedom of the blacks; he had been told that only a king could give this freedom. When, at this epoch, I was able to prove to him that republican France was granting this freedom, he rallied to the tricolor flag.

Publicly, however, Toussaint only made his break with Spain in May, 1794. In that month he passed over to the service of France, taking all his troops and the territory he controlled with him. He also attacked and destroyed the camp of Biassou, who was obliged to fly for his life—Toussaint, with his customary gallantry, sending his carriage, his watch, and his tobacco box on to him. Toussaint then attacked the forces of both the Spanish, and of Jean-François, obliging them to withdraw, and wresting from Spain the town of Gonaives. The French then named him commandant of the Cordon of the West—an appropriate act, since he had already conquered all the territory that it comprised.

In the next two months he fought over 200 engagements, large and small, moving rapidly and unexpectedly to many different places, and attacking the Spanish and British forces, as well as their black allies.

To Laveaux he must have appeared as a heaven-sent ally, emerging at the precise moment when all seemed lost. Between Toussaint and Laveaux a close friendship sprang up. Upon one occasion, when Toussaint had captured two towns from the Spanish, Laveaux rewarded him with a grenadier's plume that he wore on his three-cornered hat for the rest of his life.

The period of conflict which began with Toussaint's change of side lasted until July 22, 1795, when France and Spain concluded the Peace of Basle, under the terms of which the Spanish part of the island was ceded to France, on the understanding that the Spanish troops could remain there until a French garrison could be sent from Europe to relieve them. The armies of Biassou and of Jean-François were disbanded, with most of the troops rallying to Toussaint. Jean-François retired to Spain, where, with the rank of lieutenant-general, he became a wealthy citizen of Cadiz. Eloquent and handsome, he received the attentions of a number of Spanish ladies. Biassou went to Saint Augustine, Florida—then Spanish territory—where he was killed in a brawl. Toussaint, with his customary large-heartedness, granted Biassou's widow a pension.

It was indeed the mark of Toussaint's greatness that he would ever seek to show clemency or generosity to an opponent, thereby often turning enemies into friends, strengthening his own position, and restoring harmony. Realism, not vengefulness, was his characteristic, and thus peace was his goal. During this period he went to extraordinary lengths to conciliate the white colonists, both republican and royalist. Upon one occasion his troops intercepted a fleeing column of white plantation owners, loaded with bullion and valuables. Toussaint, having interviewed them, sent them on to Port-au-Prince, then British-occupied, with an armed escort to ensure their safety. Small wonder that his black rivals accused him of favoring the whites. Yet he knew the strength of the whites, and of his country's continuing need for them. He therefore sought to conciliate them and to allot them a recognized place in the nation he was building. But that the interests of the majority—the blacks —must be recognized was never in question.

Many obstacles nevertheless remained to be overcome. For one thing there were the British, who had been on the island since 1793, and for another there were the mulattoes. The British had long had their eye on San Domingo, which represented a strategic foothold for France in the New World, as well as a source of wealth. Seeing the French in difficulties there, the British Prime Minister, Pitt, became persuaded that the moment to seize the whole island had arrived, and in October, 1795, sent General Howe and 7,000 troops to take it. Toussaint in the North, and Rigaud, a mulatto leader who had emerged in the South, both defended the territories that they controlled against the invaders. They were helped in their task by the climate: yellow fever struck the British troops, and before long Howe's army had "wasted to a shadow." The most that the British could do was to hold certain coastal areas, and the city of Port-au-Prince. So severe were the losses in men, and so costly their endeavors in money, that they soon ceased to put forward any major military efforts. Between 1793 and 1795 the British had lost 40,000 men altogether—both in battle and from yellow fever.[9]

For long the mulattoes had determined that, when the status quo in San Domingo should at last be re-established, they would become the rulers. Before the French National Assembly itself they had offered to co-operate with the white colonists in reducing the blacks to slavery once more. The abolition of slavery and the rise of Toussaint had caused them serious concern. In November, 1795, the British had given them encouragement by promising them equal treatment with the whites. Again and again they had intrigued against Toussaint and the blacks, both by suddenly changing sides on the field of battle, and otherwise. Speaking of the "perfidy of the men of color," Toussaint reported: "Never have I experienced so many treasons. . . . Whenever I have made them prisoners, I have treated them like a good father. The ungrateful wretches have replied by seeking to deliver me to our enemies." Laveaux, reporting to the French Ministry of the Marine, wrote: "Citizen Mulatto is resolved to govern this country. He cannot bring himself to be the equal of a black, and wishes to be more than a white."

As tension rose between blacks and mulattoes, the French government —witnessing the increasing friendliness of the mulattoes with the British, and no longer itself hostile to the blacks—began to regard the mulattoes as the major threat to their interests. The tension polarized around Le Cap itself. A mulatto general named Villate was commandant there, and was beginning to show signs of ambition. The French government therefore ordered Laveaux to move his headquarters—which had been temporarily at Port-de-Paix—to Le Cap. Meanwhile Rigaud, the mulatto leader in the South, had established contact with Villate, and—evidently in collusion with the British, who sought to wrest Le Cap from the French—prepared an intrigue against Laveaux. Laveaux found himself obliged to appeal to Toussaint for protection. Finally, on March 20, 1796, while twelve British and two American vessels blockaded Le Cap, Laveaux was seized by the mulattoes and cast into jail. The mulattoes had calculated that Toussaint, whose troops were encamped on the heights around Le Cap, would not risk a civil war to save the French Governor. Toussaint, however, did not hesitate. Prominent mulattoes throughout the North were arrested, and black plantation workers were

9. The British forces included not only British troops, but also French emigrés and colonists, mulattoes, and specially imported African slaves trained as soldiers.

armed and sent into the streets of Le Cap, while Toussaint ordered the immediate release of Laveaux. After Laveaux had been released, and the mulatto conspirators given time to flee, Toussaint rode into Le Cap at the head of 10,000 troops. It was the first time he had been to the city since the days when, still a slave, he had driven a coach through its streets. He was received by a cheering populace, black and white. Toussaint and Laveaux, standing side by side, reviewed the troops. Overcome with emotion, Laveaux pointed to Toussaint and cried before the assembled crowds: "There stands that black Spartacus whose coming Raynal prophesied, whose destiny it is to avenge the outrages against his race." Toussaint, in reply, raised his sword and cried: "After God— Laveaux!"

Toussaint was proclaimed the Lieutenant-Governor of San Domingo; Laveaux's power had become merely titular. The blacks, under Toussaint's leadership, were now the strongest power on the island. Toussaint's remaining years were to be devoted to a struggle, waged by intrigue and by combat, to consolidate that power in order to guarantee the liberty of the blacks.

## The Third Civil Commissioners

Although evidently pleased with the role that Toussaint had played, the French were nevertheless becoming uneasy about his growing authority. On May 11, 1796, the third Civil Commissioners arrived from France. They were five in number, and included some who had served in the previous Civil Commissions—notably Roume, and Sonthonax. Sonthonax, having successfully defended himself against the charges lodged against him at the time of his arrest and deportation to France, was now, however, a servant of the Directoire, rather than of the Jacobins, whose day was done. With the Commissioners came General Rochambeau and 3,000 troops. The misgivings of the French government about the degree of Toussaint's power found ample confirmation. Reporting to the Directoire in this connection, one of the Commissioners stated:

> To speak of laws to the Negroes is to burden them with things too metaphysical for their understanding. To these people the man is everything. . . . The regime which we found established upon our arrival in San Domingo was exactly similar to the feudal system of the eighth century.

A struggle for power now ensued among the leading French officials. Some of them appeared inclined to support the mulattoes as a counterforce to Toussaint and the blacks. Sonthonax—adept, experienced, and as ruthless as ever—soon emerged as the most forceful personality among the whites. Forming an alliance with Toussaint, the better to rid himself of his rivals, he began by deporting Rochambeau, who was opposed to Toussaint. The mulattoes grew alarmed, and, seeking to divide their opponents, successfully incited some of the blacks to massacre a number of whites. One of the Commissioners then suffered a nervous collapse, returning to France of his own volition. Another Commissioner died suddenly, not without suspicions of poisoning. Yet another—Roume— went to the Spanish part of the island, thus removing himself from the center of the conflict. Apart from Sonthonax, the only Commissioner remaining was Raimond, a pliable mulatto who was friendly to Toussaint, and so involved in his own private business that he was left undisturbed. Sonthonax and Toussaint together then persuaded Laveaux to become one of the deputies for San Domingo in the French National Assembly[10] —a post that necessitated his returning to France. Toussaint wrote him a firm but cordial note which invited him, in effect, to leave the island with honor—which he did. It is notable that, in later years, he continued to speak of Toussaint with affection and respect.

There now remained only Toussaint and Sonthonax. Sonthonax attempted to undercut Toussaint's support by making himself popular with the black army by increasing their pay, while at the same time holding back supplies and permitting Toussaint to take the blame. To Sonthonax's immense surprise, however, Toussaint now invited him also to return to France as a deputy from San Domingo—an invitation that he found hard to refuse as Toussaint suddenly appeared backed by thousands of troops, and issued him an ultimatum, after which he was escorted on shipboard. Sonthonax, waxing bitter upon his return to France, claimed that Toussaint aimed at independence from France, and said that his whole political life had been "one long revolt against France." He added that "Toussaint has fooled two kings; he may well end by betraying the Republic." Toussaint, for his part, wrote a report to the Directoire in which he gave a verbatim version of the dramatic conversations which had taken place between himself and Sonthonax, and according to which Sonthonax had repeatedly urged him to massacre the white colonists and to secede from France. In reply he had told Sonthonax that "Whenever scoundrels, be they mulatto, white, or black, want to commit some stupidity, they use the blacks to do it for them." He also accused Sonthonax not only of turning the blacks against the whites, but also "the reds against the blacks," as well as of sowing dissension in his army.

If the Directoire had harbored any doubts as to the dangers to French authority posed by Toussaint, they were now reinforced by Sonthonax's expulsion, despite the official explanations that Toussaint gave. They therefore sent General Hédouville to the island—a man who had acquired fame for his successful conciliation of the warring factions in the Vendée

---

10. Under the Constitution of the Year III (1795), San Domingo had been declared an integral part of France, and therefore required representation in the French National Assembly.

rebellion in France. Upon his arrival in March 1798, Hédouville landed in Spanish San Domingo to confer with Roume.

Toussaint had by now grown so powerful that it was evident that he could expel the British from San Domingo whenever he wished. Seeing him prepare to do so, the British entered into negotiations with him on the terms of their withdrawal—a development that caused Hédouville concern, since he was not privy to the proceedings. Having surrendered the capital, Port-au-Prince, to Toussaint, the British then made other proposals. Instead of fighting to maintain such bases on the island as those at the Môle St. Nicholas and at Jérémie, they saw a way, by diplomacy, to advance their interests—that is to say, by injuring those of the French. While agreeing to abandon all their defenses, they secretly proposed to Toussaint that they recognize him as King of Haiti (*Haiti* being the old Indian name for San Domingo), and that he be given the protection of a British naval squadron. In return he would agree to a commercial treaty. Toussaint judged, however, that France might successfully invade England at any time, and he therefore rejected the proposals, with the exception of the commercial treaty, to which he secretly consented. He wished to create a peaceful and prosperous San Domingo, and with a British blockade in force this would be difficult indeed.

Toussaint continued, nevertheless, to pay allegiance to France. In view of this, in negotiating with the British at all, let alone in entering into secret agreements with them, he was clearly stepping beyond any French-derived authority he possessed. He had, however, already in 1797 got wind of the probability that the French would eventually seek to restore slavery in San Domingo, and considered therefore that his responsibilities to the Negroes outweighed considerations of how much power his official mandate gave him. But in moving beyond his authority, he moved with care. The Creole proverb *Doucement allé loin* ("He who moves slowly goes far")[11] was always on his lips—and in his mind.

Hédouville was far from content—particularly since the British had not maintained the same discretion that Toussaint himself had shown, but had leaked news of the treaty to the British press, which was, to say the least, attentively read in Paris. Toussaint became so angry when he learned of this indiscretion that he wished to break with the British and to sign instead a treaty with the United States. When the British envoy next visited Toussaint, Commissioner Roume ordered Toussaint to arrest him—an order with which, despite his anger, Toussaint did not comply. Finally, in the course of 1799, the treaty was concluded between Toussaint on the one hand, and the British and the United States on the

---

11. Cf. the Italian proverb, "Chi va piano va sano e va lontano" ("He who goes slowly goes safely and goes far"), and similar proverbs in many other languages.

other.[12] It resulted in an immediate amelioration of the island's economic plight, and won Toussaint plaudits from his foes as well as his friends.

Since, with the British controlling the seas, the French could not hope to exert force against Toussaint, Hédouville attempted the classic policy of "divide and rule"—in this instance by dividing the mulattoes and the blacks. This was, moreover, not hard to do, as the blacks were already hostile to the mulattoes for having reintroduced slavery in the southern part of San Domingo, which they controlled. Rigaud, the mulatto leader in the South, was told to report directly to Hédouville, and not to Toussaint. Hédouville also appears to have contemplated kidnaping Toussaint, although Toussaint did not allow himself to be taken, and declined an invitation to dine on the French flagship, as well as a suggested visit to France. Relations between Hédouville and Toussaint were also not improved by Hédouville's decree that black cultivators should enter into three-year work contracts—a decree that the blacks felt to be a partial return to slavery. Hédouville's attempt to introduce himself into the negotiations with the British, which was unsuccessful, also further strained relations between the two men. The French felt that they admittedly were in a difficult situation on the island, but with Toussaint and his army in control there, and with the British in control of the seas, they could see no immediate way to improve their position.

At last, however, the Directoire hit upon a possible expedient to rid itself of both Toussaint and his army—an expedient that was remarkably similar to that whereby it also, although temporarily, rid itself of Napoleon Bonaparte and his army by sending them to Egypt: Toussaint might be encouraged to embroil himself in a foreign adventure that, if successful, would serve France. A French officer named Debuisson was accordingly sent to San Domingo with the proposal that Toussaint and his army should invade Jamaica and the southern United States with the avowed aim of abolishing slavery in those territories. In this enterprise Toussaint would receive the aid of the French fleet. But Toussaint showed no enthusiasm for the proposal. He recognized that with himself and his soldiers out of the way, slavery could easily be restored in San Domingo itself. As one Frenchman had informed Hédouville when enquiry was made about Toussaint's character and personality, Toussaint appeared to possess the faculty of reading the secret thoughts of those with whom he had dealings. When the French made the invasion proposal to him a second time, Toussaint got in touch with the U.S. Consul-General in Le Cap, Stevens, informed him about the invasion plan, and asked him to communicate it to the British. The U.S. Consul-General naturally informed not only the British, but also the U.S. Secretary of State, Timothy

12. When the treaty was concluded, Toussaint himself no longer attempted to deny the existence of the secret clauses which, he said with perfect truth, were in the interests of San Domingo.

Pickering. Pickering was also told, by Stevens, that Toussaint, and not the French, wielded power on the island, and that Toussaint had at his disposal 55,000 men, of whom 30,000 were disciplined troops.

The British and the Americans were both concerned at the possibility of such an invasion—the more so as they would have to contend not only with the invading army, but also with their own insurgent slaves, many of whom had heard of the successful slave uprising in San Domingo. They need not have worried themselves, however. Toussaint had no intention of allowing himself and his army to be diverted into adventures of uncertain outcome, however convenient they might prove to France. He intended to remain in San Domingo to prevent the restoration of slavery there.

Hédouville now attempted yet another method of ridding himself of Toussaint. On the grounds that the British had now left the island, he attempted to disband a large part of Toussaint's army, and to disperse the remainder to different parts of the island. He began by attempting to disband the regiment commanded by Toussaint's nephew, Moyse. Meanwhile, Toussaint was to be lulled by envoys, while Rigaud would march swiftly at the head of a large mulatto force to form a junction with Hédouville's whites. Toussaint would then find himself confronted by a considerable force. As it turned out, Moyse's regiment was indeed disbanded, with Moyse himself fleeing to safety; but Rigaud hesitated to move. Toussaint arrested the envoys sent to lull him, and raised the blacks of the Northern Plain with the cry "Hédouville wants to restore slavery!" Thousands upon thousands of blacks, armed with any weapons they could find, then poured into Le Cap, obliging Hédouville and his officers to seek refuge on shipboard. When Toussaint arrived, riding slowly through the crowds to the accompaniment of cries of "Papa Toussaint! Save us!" he invited Hédouville and his entourage to return to their posts on shore again, as they would now be completely safe. Hédouville, knowing he was beaten, chose instead to sail for France. He who had conciliated the Vendéean aristocrats had been defeated by the former slaves of San Domingo. Members of his entourage who, earlier, had laughed at Toussaint's appearance, because he sometimes wore a yellow Madras handkerchief tied round his head, which, they said, made him look like "a monkey in a linen head-dress," and who had felt that four bold men sent to arrest him would be enough to dispose of the problem of Toussaint Louverture, were now presumably obliged to revise their estimation of the black leader. Hédouville's own failure was undoubtedly due to his refusal to listen to the advice of another French officer, General Kerverseau, who, speaking of Toussaint, had told Hédouville upon his arrival, "With him you can do everything; without him, nothing."

Hédouville's final act had been to send a secret message to Rigaud, in which he had relieved him of any obligation to recognize Toussaint as his commander-in-chief, and in which he had also increased the southern territory under Rigaud's jurisdiction at the expense of the area under Toussaint's command. This evidently further aggravated the differences between the two men, and hastened the conflict between black and mulatto that was, it seemed, inevitably approaching. Toussaint, however, strengthened his position by establishing good relations with Commissioner Roume, who now represented French authority on the island. (The remaining Commissioner, Raimond, the mulatto, was at about this time "elected" a deputy by Toussaint, and sent off to Paris—as much for his own safety in the coming conflict as, no doubt, for any other reason.) Toussaint then prevailed upon Roume to sponsor a reconciliatory meeting between himself and Rigaud—a meeting which Rigaud, who was of a choleric character, left in a rage, thereby placing himself in the wrong. When Toussaint and Rigaud then publicly exchanged reproaches, and Rigaud published Hédouville's secret instructions to him, Roume, at Toussaint's instigation, in the name of France proclaimed Rigaud guilty of treason and rebellion.

Among the charges made by Rigaud against Toussaint was the allegation, for which he quoted Hédouville as authority, that Toussaint was in the pay of the British. It was an old charge, to which Toussaint had previously replied in public. "Hédouville would have you believe," he had told his listeners, "that I am the enemy of liberty, that I have sold myself to the English, that I am striving for independence. Who is likely to value liberty more—Toussaint Louverture, the slave of the Bréda plantation, or General Hédouville, former Marquis and Chevalier of the Order of Saint Louis? If I had wished to hand the colony over to the English I would not have driven them out."

### "The War of the Knives"

Bitter fighting between black and mulatto soon broke out on the island. So bitter, indeed, was the struggle that it later received the name of "the War of the Knives." Combatants were seen to throw away their muskets in order to cut one another's throats, or to attack them with their teeth. Massacres occurred, the countryside was ravaged, and famine ensued. At the outset Rigaud had some initial success, but Toussaint first regained control of the northern territory, and then carried the war into Rigaud's homeland, the South. Rigaud's resistance was prolonged as a result of the seige of Jacmel, a mulatto stronghold which held out longer than it might otherwise have done as a result of the action of the British fleet, which confiscated the seige guns that Toussaint was sending there by sea. The British had grown uneasy about Toussaint, as Roume had secretly sent agents to Jamaica to raise an anti-slavery revolt there,[13] and the British suspected that Toussaint might have been party to the plot.

On March 11, 1800, Jacmel fell. The event was followed by a terrible conflict on the southern peninsula, representing an intensification of the war. At last, on July 5, 1800, Rigaud's army was defeated at Acquin, shortly after which, at the end of the month, Rigaud and his officers quit San Domingo to take refuge on the Danish island of St. Thomas. The elite of his mulatto soldiery fled to Cuba. A general pardon in the South was proclaimed by Toussaint on August 1, 1800. Any ameliorative effect it might have had was, however, negated by the action of one of Toussaint's generals, Dessalines, who had, incidentally, not been born in San Domingo, but in the Congo. When ordered to "pacify" the region he did so with the great brutality, torturing many mulattoes to death, and massacring others. When Toussaint, heard of Dessalines' actions, he exclaimed "I told him to prune the tree—not to uproot it."

Toussaint was now the uncontested master of the former colony. He had sent an official representative—a Frenchman, General Vincent—to Paris to explain his actions to the French government. No sooner had he arrived, however, than he witnessed Napoleon Bonaparte's seizure of power. Toussaint realized at once that this development meant that, as soon as peace was restored between France and England, Bonaparte would almost certainly try to restore slavery in San Domingo.[14] This view was supported by the first message sent to Toussaint by Bonaparte, which announced "a new social pact." The new French Constitution of the Year VIII (which was ratified by referendum in February, 1800) would not apply to the French colonies in America, Asia, or Africa, which would henceforth be governed by special laws—an arrangement, it was explained, that was necessitated by the differences in climate, customs, morals, interest, cultural diversity, and products. Reassurances were added that the "sacred principles of liberty and the equality of the blacks" would never be harmed or modified. Upon receiving the message from the Consulate, Toussaint stated, "We are free today because we are strong. The First Consul maintains slavery in Martinique, which means that he will make us slaves when he feels strong enough to do so."

Among the black population the "new social pact" was decidedly unpopular. The protection of the old French Constitution, of the Year III, had been removed, and now it would be possible for slavery to be

13. Debuisson, one of the agents, was pardoned in return for denouncing the other, Sasportas. Sasportas, a Jew, refused to denounce others involved, and died on the scaffold, calling on the blacks of Jamaica to imitate those of San Domingo, and to end slavery by rising and killing their masters.

14. Toussaint always kept himself well informed about developments in Paris. Two Frenchmen, Huin and d'Hébecourt, are known to have acted as secret agents for him there; he also had other sources of information.

restored by simple decree. Toussaint declined to comply with the instruction which would have had him inscribe upon the flags of his army in letters of gold the following words, taken from the Consulate's message: "Brave blacks, remember the French people alone recognize your liberty and the equality of your rights.[15] General Dessalines, who was certainly privy to Toussaint's inner counsel, went even further. On the defeat of Rigaud and the mulattoes he told his troops, "The war that you have just ended was a little war. There still remains two more important ones to fight—one against the Spanish who have insulted our brave commanding general, the other against France which, when rid of its enemies, will attempt to put you back into slavery."

Toussaint realized that when Bonaparte's army came, it would logically land in Spanish San Domingo, which had been ceded to France by the Treaty of Basle in 1795. He quickly saw that he must assert his control over this part of the island. As usual, however, he was not precipitate, and first began by establishing a legal basis for his intended action. For this he required a decree from Roume, authorizing him in the name of France to take possession of the territory. But Roume, realizing at last that Toussaint was moving in the direction of independence, ever though he never mentioned that to be his aim, was unwilling to sign such a decree. However, public emotions were stirred up against Roume, and demonstrations were organized—evidently at Toussaint's wish. Finally Roume and his officers were locked up in a chicken coop for nine days—to be rescued by a supposedly neutral Toussaint who, with a diplomatic admixture of sympathy and indirect threats concerning the impossibility of controlling the populace in the future, quickly obtained the required decree from him. Roume was soon after relieved of his functions by Toussaint, who sent him to a pleasant country estate, while writing to Bonaparte, "Citizen Roume . . . is at your disposal. When you want him, I will send him to you." When Bonaparte did not reply, Toussaint sent Roume back to France, allegedly for the sake of his health.

Meanwhile, both the Spanish and the British showed themselves opposed to the occupation of Spanish San Domingo. The U.S. Consul-General reported to his government that, in view of this, he did not believe that Toussaint dared to move. But Toussaint wrote to the Spanish Governor that he was sending his nephew, General Moyse, to take over the government. When the Governor replied that he protested "one thousand and one times," Toussaint replied, "Your thousand and one protestations are futile. . . I will hold you responsible one thousand and

15. It was not the first occasion upon which the regimental flags had figured in politics. In 1791 when tension was rising among the blacks, before the August uprising, the French regiments were ordered to remove the words "Liberty or Death" from their flags, lest the message be taken literally by the slave population.

one times for any untoward incident that may result from your intran-
sigence." When Moyse marched into the Spanish territory with 10,000
troops he was opposed by Spanish forces, which he defeated. Meanwhile
Toussaint with an additional 4,000 men, followed by a different route,
defeating another contingent of troops sent against him. He then released
the Spanish prisoners he had taken, and, on January 26, 1801, received
the keys to San Domingo City from the hands of the Spanish Governor.
He then unified and made himself master of the entire island.

*Toussaint's Rule*

Already in French San Domingo, Toussaint had been working to lay
the foundations for prosperity. The commercial treaty with the United
Kingdom and the United States had been merely the first step in this
policy. But prosperity was not a goal in itself. Prosperity meant money
to buy guns from Britain and the United States so that Toussaint's
armies might resist those of Napoleon Bonaparte when at last they came
to reimpose slavery. Yet, at the same time, if all was not to be lost,
Toussaint had to ensure prosperity by emergency measures that themselves involved a degree of compulsion. On October 12, 1800, he had
issued a decree that placed the black cultivators on the same basis as
soldiers in the army—a decree that in effect introduced a system of
peonage or forced labor on the island. In principle it differed from the
old system of slavery only in that the cultivators were paid for their
labors, and were under ultimate black authority. In practice there were
other differences as well: whipping was prohibited, no longer did
slavers bring Africans to the island to replace the ninth of the total labor
force that had died each year from maltreatment or overwork, the birth
rate among the black population increased. Toussaint, however, needed
not only money for guns, but also more soldiers than he had. Foreseeing
a French attack, Toussaint did, in fact, make an effort to buy some
African slaves from the British in order to swell the ranks of his army.
For better or for worse, the deal was not consummated.

Whatever the means employed, San Domingo, after ten years of
warfare, began to return to a condition somewhat comparable to its
former prosperity. The U.S. Consul-General reported that agriculture
and commerce were beginning to revive, and that "the most perfect
tranquillity" had been restored. General de Lacroix stated that in Le
Cap and throughout the North buildings were springing up "like toad-
stools after rain," and that the colony was regaining "all its old-time
splendor." An English observer wrote that there was a large increase
in the number of blacks, and that the progress of agriculture was rapid.
Anxious to convince the white planters that they had more to gain
under the new regime than by attempting to restore slavery, Toussaint

encouraged as many of them as he could to return to the island. This part of the policy, however, was one with which Toussaint's nephew, Moyse, disagreed. He also showed dissatisfaction with Toussaint in several other ways. That region of the northern plain for which Moyse was responsible was the only one that failed to compare with other regions in its economic recovery. Finally Moyse organized a local uprising, massacring a number of whites. Toussaint had the incipient revolt suppressed, after which Moyse was executed. A curious fact which has never been explained satisfactorily was that, as a result of Toussaint's intercession, Moyse was condemned without being allowed to defend himself publicly—possibly because, knowing all to be lost, he might have taken the occasion to strike at Toussaint by revealing state secrets. He died bravely, giving the order himself for the troops to fire upon him.

Toussaint, meanwhile, was secretly importing large quantities of arms from the United States, where, also in secret, he had placed a large amount of money in Philadelphia banks.[16] Fearing the trend of events General Vincent warned him against the direction in which he was proceeding. Toussaint told him, in reply, that it was impossible for him to "slow down his gigantic momentum," and that he was being "carried forward by an occult force that he could not resist." It was also reported that, at about this time, he exclaimed, "I have taken my flight in the realm of eagles; I must be prudent and return to earth once more; I can only alight upon rock, and this rock must be the constitutional institution that will guarantee me power so long as I shall be among men."

The constitutional foundation for his power that he envisaged was soon thereafter drafted. It made him Governor-General for life, and gave him the right to appoint a successor. Taking Bonaparte's new constitution literally, it agreed that conditions in San Domingo differed from those in France, and therefore proceeded to weaken the links uniting the island to the mother country, without, however, breaking them. Catholicism was made the state religion.[17] Slavery was abolished forever. All citizens, white, black, or mulatto, were able to hold public office. Immigration from Africa was encouraged.

General Vincent was appalled by the introduction of the Constitution, which was locally enacted and applied without having first received the approval of the French government. When Toussaint asked Vincent to take the Constitution to Paris for approval, Vincent replied that it gave the French representative on the island no greater status or influ-

---

16. At the time of Toussaint's death there was over six million francs on deposit.

17. Toussaint attempted to enforce this provision by suppressing the practice of voudun. Upon one occasion Dessalines' soldiers attacked a voudun assembly, bayonetting fifty people. Voudun, nevertheless, continued to survive.

ence than that of the ambassador or envoy of any foreign power. Then Toussaint told him that he would be asked to take the Constitution to Paris not merely in draft, but in its final printed version, his horror was unbounded. He was only prevented from expressing himself more strongly by the great emotion shown by Toussaint himself, who maintained that he was obliged to act as he did. Finally Vincent carried the controversial document together with other missives to Paris, via the United States. En route he wrote to Toussaint from Alexandria, Virginia: "Here they talk of nothing else but your declared independence: they openly call you the King of San Domingo." Whatever the general talk, the United States well knew that San Domingan independence had not yet been declared, although it might be in the future. Foreseeing such an eventuality, Alexander Hamilton himself, one of the drafters of the United States Constitution, drafted another for an independent San Domingo, which he forwarded to the U.S. Consul-General at Le Cap, recommending that he submit it to Toussaint. Whether Toussaint ever saw this document is not known.

Toussaint's new constitution had been proclaimed on July 7, 1801; Vincent's arrival in Paris was noted in the *Moniteur* on October 14, which also mentioned that he had come officially to present the San Domingan constitution for French approval. It has been claimed that it was Vincent's message that resulted in Bonaparte's decision to attempt to reconquer the island. Yet it was on October 6 that the preliminary articles of the Peace of Amiens between France and the United Kingdom were signed, on October 7 that Bonaparte allotted the regiments for service in San Domingo, and on October 8 that Bonaparte issued secret instructions to the French Ministry of the Marine to prepare an expedition to San Domingo—an expedition whose avowed object, as General Vincent later admitted, and as was common knowledge in Paris, was the restoration of slavery.

### Bonaparte's Decision

"Sire, leave it alone! It is the happiest spot in your dominions. God meant this man to govern. Races melt beneath his hand. He has saved this island for you."

So wrote Vincent in a memorandum to the Minister of the Marine, with a request that the document be shown to the First Consul. His voice, however, was but one among many—and other voices prevailed with Bonaparte. The Minister of the Marine himself, Decrès, was a strong believer in the restoration of slavery, and his arguments were backed by appeals from powerful commercial and colonial interests. Active and vociferous, the pro-slavery lobby advanced arguments that appealed to Bonaparte's pride. Much had been made of *Africains dorés,* or *Negres dorés*—"gilded Africans, "gilded blacks"—phrases which sounded in contemporary ears as echoes of the *Jeunesse Dorée*, the bedizened youths of the Directoire period who had not hesitated to bring their lead-filled canes down on the heads of the Jacobins in the Paris streets. The implication was clear. Toussaint and his officers were undisciplined popinjays who, having got themselves military uniforms, had become strangers to any form of control. A good lesson, evidently, was needed. Bonaparte himself told Vincent in a personal interview, "I shall not leave a single epaulette on the shoulder of a black." He had also told his Council of State, "I am for whites because I am white. I have no other reason. That one suffices." Vincent, an honorable man who had not hesitated to express contrary views when he felt it his duty to do so, to both Toussaint and to Bonaparte, was removed from Domingan affairs, and was sent to serve his country on a smaller island —Elba, where Bonaparte (who had, meanwhile, been crowned Napoleon I in 1804) re-encountered him when he himself was sent there in exile in 1814.

At an earlier stage, when he was formulating his colonial policy, Bonaparte had asked his advisers what colonial system had proved most financially beneficial to France. They had told him that it was the system prevailing before the Revolution. "Then the sooner we return to it the better," said Bonaparte.

Further information on San Domingo had, however, later made him hesitate, if not change his mind altogether. He wished to regain Louisiana for France, and—being Bonaparte—probably to establish French supremacy in North America. By placing himself in accord with Toussaint, the San Domingan springboard for an invasion of the mainland would be available to him. On March 4, 1801, he wrote to Toussaint that he was commissioning him as Captain-General of the French part of San Domingo, adding, "The Government could hardly offer you greater proof of its confidence in you . . . I hope the time is not far distant when an Army from San Domingo will be able to contribute to the extension of French possessions and glory in your part of the world." The letter, however, was never sent. Bonaparte changed his mind again.

Why did he do so? A number of reasons have been adduced. The influence of the vocal *ci-devant* colonists was certainly extremely strong in the French government. Many of the colonists were bitter at their losses, and contemptuous of the blacks whom they looked upon as unpunished slaves in revolt, rather than as men entitled to freedom. The French historian Thiers later wrote that Bonaparte sought to compensate a number of Vendéean aristocrats for the loss of their French estates by restoring to them their San Domingan plantations. It has also been said that Bonaparte's wife, Josephine—a Creole from Martinique, one of the Windward Islands to the south of San Domingo, where as we have noted slavery had already been restored—used her influence with him to have the expedition sent to San Domingo. In her memoirs, Josephine later confirmed that Bonaparte had indeed consulted her, but said that she had advised him to uphold Toussaint.[18] (She herself owned the Beauharnais plantation in San Domingo—which Toussaint arranged to have run at government expense, then sending the revenues on to her).

It has also been pointed out that Bonaparte wished to send the republican element in his armies out of France, in order the more easily to make himself Emperor. Fouché, his Minister of Police, said that he wanted to send a great number of regiments, as well as officers insufficiently devoted to him, to a remote part of the world. One of his Ministers of the Marine, Forait, alleged that Bonaparte said to him, "There are 60,000 men whom I want to send as far away as possible." This would appear likely—yet why were these men sent to overthrow Toussaint rather than to ally themselves with him? Possibly Bonaparte was not yet ready to fight the Anglo-Americans—he had, after all, just concluded peace with the British. Moreover Toussaint might rise to power in North America as he had in San Domingo. There was no more lack of slave plantations on the mainland than there had been in San Domingo, and those returning to France from the island were constantly reminding Bonaparte what a remarkable man Toussaint was. Perhaps it would be better to use the 60,000 men to dispose of Toussaint at the outset of the American adventure, while France was still at peace with Britain. The affair might prove profitable too—it was said that Toussaint had had his treasure, which according to various reports amounted to between 40 million and 250 million francs, hidden in a great vault in the Cahos Mountains.

And then—again—there were the colonists and their friends in France to think of, not to speak of the commercial interests. Two-thirds of France's entire "foreign" trade had previously been with San Domingo. Now Toussaint was trading with whomsoever he chose, and no longer exclusively with France. Bonaparte said to his Council, "Do you think that if the majority in the Convention had known what it was doing and had any acquaintance with the colonies it would have freed the blacks? To maintain that policy now would be hypocritical." There remained only the problem of the attitude that might be taken by the British toward a reconquest of San Domingo by France. This, however, was soon settled. "I merely notified them," said Bonaparte, "that if

18. Josephine's sister-in-law, Countess Françoise-Marie de Beauharnais, married a mulatto named Castaigns.

they did not consent, I would give Toussaint unlimited power and recognize the colony's independence." They consented.

The force that Bonaparte sent against San Domingo was enormous. It was headed by General Leclerc (accompanied by his wife Pauline, who was Bonaparte's favorite sister). Twenty thousand men were to sail in the first contingent, to be followed soon thereafter by 20,000 more, followed by monthly reinforcements. Thirteen generals were to be included, numbering among them several, such as Rochambeau, whose names were known throughout Europe. Spain and the Netherlands were to assist in the transportation of the army, and the British promised to provide some of the supplies. Leclerc had secret and confidential instructions, written in Napoleon's own hand. Upon arrival in San Domingo he was to divide his action into three phases. In the first phase, which was to last not more than fifteen to twenty days, he was to reassure Toussaint and his followers, occupy the coast towns, and reorganize his forces. In the second phase he was to revoke the powers of the Negro leaders, and disband their armies. Should, as was expected, he meet with opposition over this, he was to smash organized resistance by a quick converging movement. In the third phase, Toussaint, his generals, and chief supporters were to be deported to France, and the population disarmed. No black above the rank of captain was to remain on the island. Scattered black bands were to be hunted down by mobile columns. No fourth, or final, phase was mentioned in the instructions, although it had in effect been decided upon. Slavery and the French commercial monopoly were to be restored.[19]

Other provisions were also made. All white women who had "prostituted themselves with Negroes" were to be sent back to France,[20] as well as Frenchmen, whatever their rank, who spoke of or showed sympathy for Negro rights. Bonaparte's educational policy was to be one of retrogression. "No public instruction of any kind shall exist in San Domingo. All the [white] Creoles shall be required to send their children to France to be educated." This provision was, no doubt, intended to ensure that no further Toussaints, either white, mulatto, or black, should arise.

Both the black population of the island and the revolutionary-minded French troops were to be kept in ignorance of Bonaparte's intentions for as long as possible. To this end handbills were printed for the benefit of the blacks, assuring them of French attachment to liberty and equality. The French troops, for their part, were given the impression that Tous-

19. The United States appears tentatively to have agreed to co-operate by blockading Toussaint and aiding Leclerc. The arrangement seems quickly to have broken down, possibly when President Jefferson realized that a French victory would mean the end of U.S. trade with the island.
20. Leclerc found that so many white women cohabited with blacks that it would be quite impractical to carry out this part of his instructions.

saint was a traitor, in the pay of the British, and of reactionary French émigrés and priests.

With the fleet sailed certain personalities associated with San Domingo. These included Rigaud and other mulatto leaders hostile to Toussaint, as well as Toussaint's son Isaac, and his adopted son Placide, both of whom had been receiving a Parisian education. In the event of Toussaint's failing to offer resistance to Leclerc, Rigaud and his colleagues were to be shipped to Madagascar. As it turned out, Rigaud remained for a time in San Domingo, but was then deported to France. Isaac and Placide were later unsuccessfully offered to Toussaint as bait in exchange for his surrender to the French, adding that whatever to choose between San Domingo and France, adding that whatever their choice he would not blame them for it. Isaac chose France, while Placide, whom Toussaint had adopted out of kindness, opted for San Domingo. Toussaint placed Placide in command of a battalion, which he soon thereafter led into battle. Toussaint intended to return Isaac to the French, but Isaac's mother refused to let her son leave.

On December 14, 1801, Leclerc himself set sail from Brest to take command of the expedition. The fleet had a rendezvous at Cape Samana on the eastern tip of the island, and on January 19, 1802, a first contingent bearing about 11,900 troops, assembled there. Bonaparte had attempted to keep both the peace with the British and the sending of the fleet a secret, so that the invasion might appear as a bolt from the blue, but Toussaint had got to know of both events.

As the French fleet gathered at the Samana rendezvous, Toussaint himself gazed down at the spectacle from a high promontory. It was an awe-inspiring sight. "We must perish," he told his entourage, "the whole of France is coming to San Domingo." He then began to make his way back to the French-speaking part of the island to prepare his defence. As he was doing so, he received word from General Christophe that a French squadron had appeared off Le Cap on February 2, 1802. The French were following a plan worked out by General Kerverseau the previous September, according to which they would land at different points on the island. Toussaint himself wished to use a "scorched earth" policy, and to keep his troops together, and then wipe out the separated French forces at their landing points one at a time. But his subordinates refused to agree to this strategy, apparently because they were both loath to abandon personal command over their troops, or to leave the territories for which they were immediately responsible. The French general de Lacroix and the black general Christophe, discussing the campaign afterwards, admitted that Toussaint had been right. Christophe said, "Old Toussaint kept dinning it into our ears, but we would not listen to him."

General Rochambeau was the first to land; on February 4 he captured Fort Dauphin in the North. Enraged at the loss of fourteen of his men in battle, he massacred a part of the defending garrison as a reprisal. This was the beginning of a policy of bloodshed and atrocity associated with his name that was to increase in horror as the two-year struggle developed.

On February 3, 1802, Leclerc himself had appeared off Le Cap, and had demanded that the town submit to him. Christophe had refused to accede to his demand without Toussaint's authorization. When the first French frigate attempted to approach the roadstead, a warning shot was fired from the shore, at the sound of which Christophe and his men immediately set the town on fire. Many buildings, particularly the public ones, had been spared the conflagration of 1793, and these were now set ablaze—Christophe himself setting an example by firing his own handsome residence with his own hands. Toussaint, returning from the East, caught sight of the town just as the flames were leaping skyward. Abandoning Le Cap in cinders to the French—less than fifty-nine of its 2,000 buildings were left standing—he then fell back upon Gonaives on the west coast. Most of the news that he received was bad. The French had already taken Port-au-Prince, while the Spanish part of the island had welcomed them with open arms after Paul Louverture, Toussaint's brother, who had been charged with its defense, had been duped by a French stratagem. One of Toussaint's generals, a white man named Agé to whom he had accorded signal honors in the past, had gone over to the French—an action that, together with the abandonment of his cause by most of the white planters whom Toussaint had tried so hard and so unremittingly to conciliate, plunged Toussaint into an unwonted mood of bitterness. Writing to a subordinate at Jérémie, he said,

The whites of France have united with those of the colony to deprive us of our liberty. . . . Don't trust the whites. They will betray you if they can. Consequently I give you carte blanche. Whatever you do will be well done.

A full-fledged Napoleonic campaign was now opened against Toussaint, with the French seeking to cut him off from the Spanish border and to drive him south over the mountains to be crushed by French troops marching up from Port-au-Prince. On February 23, 1802, his main position was stormed, and he was obliged to retreat, leaving 1,000 dead. The French troops from Port-au-Prince failed to appear, however, and Toussaint and his men took refuge in the mountains. In March, Leclerc attempted a converging movement against Toussaint's new position. Heavy fighting took place as 12,000 of Bonaparte's veterans tried to storm the Crête-a-Pierrot, a mountain bastion near Saint Marc, defended by 1,200 blacks under the command of Dessalines—a man who bore the marks of the whip beneath his general's uniform. Standing near an open powder barrel with a lighted brand in his hand, Dessalines told the defenders that those who wished to be slaves might leave, but that he and those who were brave would remain. If the French set foot inside the fort, he would blow it to smithereens. "We will die for liberty", he said. On the other side the French troops, loyal to the revolutionary principles of republicanism, were bewildered and disturbed by the fact that, in intervals of the fighting, they heard the defenders singing the *Marseillaise* and the *Ça Ira.* By the time that the French had taken the fortress they had lost 2,000 men, and had seen the defenders cut their way out to freedom. Ashamed of his losses, Leclerc reported to Bonaparte that he had lost only 500 men in combat, and swore his officers to secrecy about the true casualty figures, ascribing other losses to sickness. But Bonaparte appears to have learned the truth. Leclerc was told that the wounding of four French generals in the fighting, and the loss of "so many brave men . . . affected the First Consul painfully."

Fighting also took place at many other points. The armies of Toussaint and of Rochambeau came into direct conflict, with the French being thrown across the Lacroix River, leaving many prisoners behind. Before setting out from France Leclerc had imperiously told a critic that when the blacks saw the French armies arrive, "they will lower their arms; they will be only too happy to be forgiven." He was now obliged to think otherwise. So, too, was Rochambeau—who had told his troops that they had only slaves to fight against, "men who dare not look you in the face and who will flee in every direction." The French commanders had believed these things, which had been told them by the former colonists, remembering the days of slavery. But both colonists and commanders had been the victims of wishful thinking. Times had changed. The slaves, in their own minds, had now become free men. Even the French reinforcements now arriving were insufficient to give Leclerc victory, and, meanwhile, the number of French soldiers falling sick was constantly increasing. Even though the Northern Plain had now once again been cleared of organized defenders, the French were anxious and concerned. Matters were not going according to plan. They would have been even more concerned had they known that the yellow fever epidemic which was to break out at La Cap and at Port-au-Prince in mid-May, 1802, would be the worst ever known in the history of the West Indies.

### Toussaint's Decision

At this moment, after a hard-fought three-month campaign, Toussaint decided to make peace. The move would appear to have been a tactical one. The season of sickness was coming, and if an armistice were to be concluded now, by the time fighting was resumed later in the year the number of French troops would certainly be considerably reduced. Already the French had lost 5,000 men in battle, while 5,000 more were sick or wounded. It may also have seemed to Toussaint that a respite might give the French a chance to reassess the situation, and to profit from their mistake in thinking that the blacks would not oppose them. Perhaps, even, they might realize that they had more to gain by co-operating with the blacks than by seeking to crush them. The peace negotiations were, however, hastened to a premature conclusion by the sudden submission to the French of Christophe, who told his comrades that he was "tired of living in the woods like a brigand." On May 6, 1802, Toussaint and Leclerc made a peace treaty, after which Toussaint retired to private life.

But Toussaint's powerful enemies did not intend that he should be left in peace. The French military authorities were constantly pillaging his property, and his complaints to the authorities appeared to be disregarded. When he threatened to move to the Spanish part of the island to escape from this harassment, Leclerc took the occasion secretly to order his arrest. The order could not have been given if some of Toussaint's own generals, motivated by unprincipled and shortsighted self-interest, had not promised the French that they would stand aside.

Toussaint was taken by treachery. Although he had been warned that Leclerc had ordered General Brunet to arrest him, he believed the assurances of Leclerc to the contrary, placing his faith in the military code of honor. When Brunet wrote to him inviting him to his house for a talk, assuring him that he would find there "the frankness of a gallant man who has no other desire than the prosperity of the colony and your personal happiness," and inquiring after Madame Toussaint, Toussaint went to see him, on June 7, 1802. After greeting him, his host left him, seemingly for a short time. Soldiers with fixed bayonets then rushed into the room. Toussaint drew his sword. The officer in charge told him that they had come to arrest him, and not to make an attempt upon his life. Toussaint put his sword back in the scabbard, and demanded to see his host, General Brunet, who had pledged his word of honor. Brunet, however, remained out of sight—"probably," said Toussaint later, "to avoid the merited approaches that I could have made to him." Toussaint was then dragged off, his hands bound behind his back "like a criminal," and placed on board ship. His family and intimates were arrested the next day, and also placed on shipboard, while his home was plundered by soldiers. The ship took him to France, leaving San Domingo on June 15 and arriving at Brest on July 9, 1802. Leclerc had advised that Toussaint be sent to a fortress in the interior of France, far from the sea, "so that he will never have the opportunity to escape and return to San Domingo, where his authority is that of a religious chief." Separated from his family, he was sent to the medieval Fort de Joux in the Jura mountains, near Switzerland, traveling in a closed carriage.

Toussaint arrived at the Fort on August 24, 1802. He was locked in a room 20 feet by 12, to which access could only be had down a corridor flooded with six inches of water. Three small glass panes, embrasured and covered with mesh, showed a little sky. The general's uniform that he had worn with distinction (he had been wounded seventeen times) was taken from him, and he was given second-hand soldier's clothes. For a short time he was allowed the company of a personal servant, Mars Plaisir, but soon he too was sent away.

During his imprisonment three things of note occurred. He wrote his memoirs—a justificatory document intended for Bonaparte's eyes; he received a mysterious visit from a man named Dormoy, formerly mayor of Dijon; and he was interviewed several times by General Caffarelli, one of Bonaparte's aides-de-camp. Bonaparte did not respond to his memoirs; after Dormoy's visit—which was reported to Bonaparte, but the purpose of which still remains unknown—he was guarded much more closely, even his watch being taken from him; Caffarelli was unable to extract from him certain admissions that Bonaparte wanted. Above all Bonaparte wanted an admission that Toussaint had sought independence, but he also wanted to know any secrets about his relations with the British, and where he had hidden his "treasure." Toussaint denied that he had ever sought independence, and said that he had no secrets to reveal, either relating to the British, or to money. He did not tell Caffarelli about the six million francs that he had deposited in the United States.

Toussaint's health did not prosper in the cold climate of the Jura Mountains. He constantly shook from ague, although he usually kept a wood fire burning in his room. Even in November, 1802, the commandant had reported that Toussaint "pretended" to be in bad health, adding that he did not know if this was true. Indeed, the commandant had no way of knowing, for he himself, on October 30, had reported on Toussaint's health to the Minister of the Marine as follows: "The constitution of Negroes in no respect resembling that of Europeans, I dispense with giving him either physician or surgeon, who would be useless for him." Small wonder that the following week the commandant had to report that when he made "observations" to Toussaint concerning his "complaints of want of justice which he pretends to suffer here, he stamps his feet, and strikes his head with his two fists. When he is in this state, which seems to me a sort of delirium, he says the most indecent things of General Leclerc . . . Three days ago, my General, he was impudent enough to tell me that in France there were none but men wicked, unjust, calumniators (those were his terms), from whom justice could not be had."

Between April 3 and April 7, 1803, the commandant of the prison visited Neufchatel, refusing to turn the keys of Toussaint's room over to any other person. It is not known whether or not he left Toussaint supplied with food. On April 7 he returned, and entered the room with a tray of food, finding Toussaint dead beside a burned-out grate—"seated on a chair, near the fire, his head leaning against the chimney." There were few witnesses to events in the ninth-century Fort de Joux. Everyday a soldier had closed the shutter to Toussaint's window from the outside, half an hour before sunset. The autopsy stated that he had died from apoplexy and pleuro-pneumonia, but could give no explanation for his frequent stomach pains. He was buried in an unmarked grave in the vault of the chapel. In the last quarter of the nineteenth century, during structural alterations, all the skeletons found beneath the chapel vault floor were thrown in with rubble used in the construction of new buildings there.

On February 2, 1803, two months before Toussaint's death, the English poet William Wordsworth published a poem addressed to him, which had probably been composed the previous August:

> Toussaint, the most unhappy of men!
> Whether the whistling Rustic tend his plough
> Within thy hearing, or thy head be now
> Pillowed in some deep dungeon's earless den;—
> O miserable chieftain! Where and when
> Wilt thou find patience! Yet die not; do thou
> Wear rather in thy bonds a cheerful brow;
> Though fallen thyself, never to rise again,
> Live, and take comfort, Thou hast left behind
> Powers that will work for thee; air, earth, and skies;
> There's not a breathing of the common wind
> That will forget thee; thou hast great allies;
> Thy friends are exultations, agonies,
> And love, and man's unconquerable mind.

### Leclerc Pays the Reckoning

According to his custodian, General Severin, when Toussaint boarded the frigate *Heros* that was to take him to France, he uttered the following prophecy: "In overthrowing me they have only felled the tree of Negro liberty in San Domingo. It will shoot up again, for it is deeply rooted, and its roots are many."

To Bonaparte, however, it was merely Toussaint and the other black leaders that stood in the way of his purpose—not Negro liberty. Hundreds of less important black leaders had been deported and sent to French seaport prisons or to the galleys—to such an extent that municipalities were beginning to complain. But it was the quality and not the quantity of those deported that concerned Bonaparte. Not yet having heard that Toussaint had been arrested, he wrote to Leclerc on July 1, 1802:

I count that before the end of September, you will have sent here all the black generals; without that we shall have done nothing, and an immense and beautiful colony would always be a volcano, and would inspire no confidence in capitalists, colonists, or in commerce.

Leclerc, however, attempting to fulfill his instructions in the face of intractable circumstances, was finding that he had other problems beside Toussaint to think of. As early as February 17, 1802, he had written to Decrès, the Minister of the Marine, "Our hospital effects were disembarked today. . . . They are all damaged. I know not how we shall manage. Come quickly to our aid. We are barefoot. Send me 30,000 pairs of shoes."

Leclerc did not, however, underestimate the significance of Toussaint, whom he took to calling "this man." "This man," he wrote, "has so fanaticized the country that his presence would suffice to set it on fire again." And on another occasion: "If this man were to return after three years, he could still undo all that has been accomplished." But sickness among his troops was beginning to cause him concern. As early as May 8, 1802, he wrote to France: "Sickness makes frightful ravages in the army. . . . You will see that the army which you calculated at 26,000 men is reduced at this moment to 12,000." On June 6, the day before Toussaint's arrest, he wrote, "Germinal [March 21–April 19] cost me 1,200 men dead in hospital. Floreal [April 20–May 19] cost me 1,800, and I fear much that this month will cost me 2,000. . . . Every day the blacks recover audacity."

On June 11, after reporting Toussaint's arrest, he urged, "Sickness makes frightful progress here, and it is impossible to calculate when it will stop. Possibly less than 4,000 French troops will remain . . . by October. Judge then what will be my position. . . . I have taken from the blacks their rallying point [i.e., Toussaint], but I am very weak. . . . For pity's sake send me aid."

His problems, however, were about to grow worse rather than better On the 30th Floréal (May 20, 1802), slavery was in principle re-established in the French colonies by Bonaparte's own decree, after the French Legislative Corps had voted, by 211 to 60, to approve the measure. San Domingo and Guadeloupe were supposedly exempted from the new law. After Toussaint's arrest, Bonaparte had sent the decree to General Richepanse, commander of Guadeloupe, explaining that it had not been applied either to that island or to San Domingo because of the recent troubles there, and leaving it to his discretion as to when he would proclaim the restoration of slavery in Guadeloupe. A similar communication was sent to Leclerc concerning San Domingo. Leclerc did not publish the decree, saying that the task of restoring slavery to San Domingo would be left to his successor. Richepanse, however, did not hesitate to proclaim slavery re-established.

Leclerc had the progress of yellow fever to concern him. On July 6 he wrote, "Prairial [May 20–June 18] may have cost me 3,000 men; . . . Messidor [June 19–July 18] will cost me more; till now it has cost me 160 men a day. . . . I have hardly more than 8,500 men under arms, not counting the 2,000 I have just received." And on July 23: "It is impossible for me to make the European troops march. They break down on the way."

Leclerc's troops had, moreover, someone to march against. Many of the blacks had immediately understood the implications of Toussaint's arrest in June. The act had profoundly alarmed them, and a local uprising, led by a man named Sylla, broke out, soon assuming proportions that disturbed Leclerc. The efforts of General Brunet, supported now by Dessalines and the mulatto leader Pétion, succeeded, however, in restoring a tentative calm by August. Dessalines had been ordered to disarm the black population, yet as soon as he disarmed one district, new armed bands sprang up elsewhere, each with a new leader—a Jean Panier, a Samedi Smith, a Sans Souci, a Janvier. The fighting between these bands and the French-supported troops was, moreover, a war to the death, with no prisoners being taken on either side. Leclerc was beginning to hope that he might end by gaining the upper hand—a hope that compensated him to some extent for the heavy losses he was suffering from yellow fever, when another event occurred. News of General Richepanse's action in Guadeloupe arrived.

Writing on August 9, 1802, Leclerc reported, "The decrees of General Richepanse circulate here and cause much evil. That which re-establishes slavery, on account of having been published three months too soon, will cost many lives to the army and colony of San Domingo. I learn news of a bloody combat. . . . The rebels have been exterminated; 50 prisoners have been hung. These men die with an incredible fanaticism; they laugh at death; it is the same with the women. . . . This fury is the work of General Richepanse's proclamation and the inconsiderate talk of the colonists." And, on August 25: "It is not everything to have removed Toussaint; there are 2,000 chiefs here to be removed; there is not an overseer but has influence enough to raise his work gang at will."

September was worse. A plaintive note began to creep into Leclerc's reports. He needed 10,000 men, apart from the reinforcements already sent. He needed more money. If the men and the money were not sent the colony might be lost. The news of the restoration of slavery in Guadeloupe had lost him his influence with the blacks. He was thinking of resigning. His successor should come at the latest by January. He was returning to his bed now, and wished the Minister better health and gayer thoughts than those he himself now enjoyed.

September 13: "With the exception of the Polish Legion, all the reinforcements yet arrived are destroyed. . . . I cannot give you an exact idea of my position. Each day makes it worse. . . . The Seventh of the line arrived here 1,395 strong; it has now 83 sickly men, and 107 in the hospitals; the rest have perished. . . . The Seventy-First, which has received about 1,000 men, has 19 men with the flags and 133 in the hospital. It is the same with the rest of the army."

September 16: "Immediately on arrival of the news of the re-establishment of slavery at Guadeloupe, the insurrection which till then had been only partial became general."

September 17: "I shall have to wage a war of extermination, and it will cost me many men."

September 26: "All my army is destroyed, even the reinforcements. . . . Every day the blacks quit me. The unfortunate decree of General Richepanse, which restored slavery in Guadeloupe, is the cause of our evils."

At about the same time, writing directly to Bonaparte, he reported that he had lost 4,000 men from fever in Fructidor (August 18–September 16) alone, while now the fever, far from abating, was growing stronger. If it went on the colony would be lost. Dessalines himself was now thinking of rejoining the insurgents. He, Leclerc, was playing the three black generals, Dessalines, Christophe, and Morpas,[21] one against the other. But the troops sent him a month ago were no longer in existence. Every day the insurgents were attacking and burning, and the sound of musketry could be heard in Le Cap itself. He was too helpless to counterattack. "I depict my situation to you as black," he said, "for so it is in truth, and I owe you the truth, the whole truth; unfortunately the situation in the colonies is not known in France, where they do not have a very exact conception of the blacks, and that is why I send you an . . . officer who knows the country and who has fought there. The colonists and the commercial interests thought that a decree from the French Government would be sufficient to re-establish slavery. I don't know what steps I shall take, for every day my means diminish and my position alters." He added that if he did not receive more troops and

21. Morpas and his wife were drowned by Rochambeau in November, 1802, as soon as he took over from Leclerc.

money by the end of Nivose (i.e., in January), he could not promise to hold the colony. Altogether it was a painful communication for the First Consul, accustomed to receiving reports of victory upon victory.

On October 7, in one of his last reports, Leclerc wrote, "The sickness continues . . . and I estimate my loss every day at 130 men. . . . No blame can be attached here to anything except the sickness that destroyed my army, the premature re-establishment of slavery in Guadeloupe, and the journals and letters from France, which talked only of slavery."

As the insurrection had grown, Leclerc had withdrawn his forces from the northern coastal towns and concentrated them in Le Cap. Rochambeau fought hard in the West, but the situation grew more desperate. As it did so Rochambeau resorted increasingly to atrocities in an attempt to terrorize the insurgents into submission. At Jacmel he took 100 of his own black troops, whose loyalty he doubted, and had them suffocated by sulphur fires in the hold of a ship, after which they were thrown to the sharks. Soon, at his orders, French troops were daily conducting mass hangings or drownings. The black population became so horror-stricken at this persistent conduct that before long even some blacks and mulattoes who had hoped for a French victory began to turn against France. Already, in August, 1802, when they had been fighting against Sylla, Dessalines and Pétion had formed an alliance that united many of the blacks with many of the mulattoes. Now, on October 12, the mulatto leader Pétion changed sides, and took up arms against the French.

Dessalines was hesitating when an incident occurred which obliged him, too, to burn his bridges: he barely escaped being taken much as Toussaint himself had been taken. Dessalines was invited to dine at the home of an Abbé Videau, cure of Petite Rivière. When the table was set, a mulatto lady, Madame Pageot, brought Dessalines water to wash his hands. Looking him full in the face as she offered the water to him, she showed him by an expressive gesture—pressing her elbows to her sides, and then forcing them back—that he was on the point of being seized and bound. Dessalines understood, rushed immediately out of the house, and leaped on his horse, galloping off at once, followed by his small entourage. He was just in time. Soldiers had already surrounded the house and had been making preparations to capture him. As he rode Dessalines discharged his pistol three times in the air, calling the black population to arms against the French. His troops soon captured Petite Rivière and Gonaïves, and tried to take Saint Marc. The French at Saint Marc, doubting the loyalty of the black troops among the defenders, called on these troops—a battalion of the 12th colonials—to lay down their arms, and, when they refused, massacred them on the spot. This was an act that Dessalines never forgave or forgot. Throughout his life he had had difficulty in dissociating his emotions against slavery from his emotions about whites, and this act, together with others, served only to confirm his view of all whites as monsters. He made an exception, however. Polish troops, remembering their own traditional national struggle for liberation, objected to assisting in the massacre at Saint Marc, and this, too, Dessalines always remembered. When forming his army—for the ranks of the black and mulatto forces were swelling as those of the French were diminishing—he named one section "the Polish Corps."

Meanwhile, Christophe was fighting in the immediate vicinity of Le Cap. Between his attacks on Le Cap on October 27 and November 4, 1802, Leclerc, aged only thirty, died. He had fallen ill of the fever on October 21, and had died on November 1, naming Rochambeau as his successor. At the time of Leclerc's death some of the troops he had requested—an army 16,000 strong—were on their way to San Domingo. Their arrival would be timely, for 6,445 combatants, only 3,100 of them regular troops, were all that remained for Rochambeau to command.

Rochambeau, who had fought in the American War of Independence, was described by the American writer Henry Adams as "an incompetent officer, who began his administration . . . by writing a demand for 35,000 men, and then introduced a period of senseless and debauched cruelty and violence without a parallel even in the history of the Empire." The sending of 35,000 men, the destruction of black and mulatto officers, and the immediate re-establishment of slavery—this was Rochambeau's program. Meanwhile the insurrection spread from the West to the South, where the efforts of Pétion, working in conjunction with Dessalines, did much to reconcile the mulattoes with the blacks, and to lead them to make common cause against the whites. This was made all the easier by the actions of the French, who now initiated a policy toward both black and mulatto that seemed to verge on the genocidal. At Cayes in the South, for example, hangings and drownings were carried out daily. Many French were horrified by the turn that events were taking, but did not themselves know how to halt the killings. A Monsieur Ludot, High Judge, reported to the Minister of the Marine in May, 1803,

> Terror is such everywhere, the abuse of armed force is pushed so far, one is so much persuaded that the number of the pillaged, the jailed, the deported, the drowned, and the assassinated is considerable; the blows that are struck are so unforeseen and so rapidly executed, finally there are so few means to secure oneself against them, that mouths and pens are mute.

At these atrocities, the southern population arose in wrath to join the insurgents, who defeated fresh troops sent against them by Rochambeau, and soon controlled the whole region, with the exception of the towns of Les Cayes and Jérémie, both of which were placed on the defensive. Meanwhile, at Le Cap, Rochambeau continued to exhibit new aspects of his personality. Followed on some public occasions by a cortège of mistresses, he extended his persecution to some whites, as well as to blacks and mulattoes, seeking each day to think of some new spectacle to satisfy his jaded sense of depravity. On one occasion he held an "emblematic ball," from which some badly frightened mulatto ladies fled, after he had sprung on them a death's head spectacle which represented the funeral ceremony of their husbands and brothers. On another occasion he ordered at considerable expense[22] 400 bulldogs to be sent from Cuba for the purpose of devouring the blacks. When the first consignment arrived, Rochambeau sent twenty-eight of them to one of his officers, saying that he was sending him no money for their upkeep as "you must give them Negroes to eat." The bulldogs proved an unsatisfactory substitute for troops, however, as they were useless against armed men, and anyway refused to bite. Rochambeau therefore had them put on a special regime to make them ferocious. As a first test of their efficacy he organized a circus, in the ancient Roman mode, in an amphitheater, to which his military staff and the white ladies of Le Cap were invited. There the hungry dogs were loosed upon a black youth, tied to a post. When they failed to attack him, however, General Boyer leapt into the arena and laid open the youth's stomach with his sword, whereupon the dogs flung themselves upon the young man and, to the cheers of the crowd and the sound of military music, devoured him in an instant.

Rochambeau also turned the buildings of Le Cap into gibbets, hanging numbers of blacks upon them, and also continuing mass drownings. So many bodies were washed ashore by the tide that the people of Le Cap, for a long time thereafter, refused to eat fish. So common, indeed, did death become to the blacks and mulattoes that, when faced with it, they often met it gladly. A Madame Charlier, condemned to death with her husband, cried out to him, on seeing him flinch at the moment of execution: "Are you not glad to die for liberty?"

On another occasion three blacks were burned alive in public at Le Cap. The wind caught the flames, and two of them perished in the most spectacular and sickening manner in less than two minutes, uttering atrocious cries that transfixed the spectators with horror. The third, whom the flames were slower to reach, upon hearing his comrade's cries shouted out in Creole: "You don't know how to die: watch how one should die!" He then twisted himself free from his bonds, sat down, and put his legs in the fire, letting himself be burned without a sound. A Frenchman present, Lemmonier-Delafosse, later commented that the death of this young man was braver than the feat of the Roman, Mucius Scaevola, who had put his hand in the fire to show his courage. "Such are the men," said Delafosse, "that we have to fight!"

22. 660 francs per head. Toussaint Louverture's allowance for food and upkeep in the Fort de Joux was four francs a day—approximately twice the amount upon which a Parisian student then subsisted.

Meanwhile, Rochambeau, on April 14, 1803, was writing to the Ministry of the Marine: "Slavery must again be proclaimed. The sending back of Toussaint, Rigaud, Pinchinat, Martial Besse, Pascal, Bellegarde, etc., will have a very good effect here. I will have them hanged on the very highest scaffold."

Ambiguity, however, reigned as to the precise aims of the insurgents. At times both the French and the insurgent troops were fighting under identical tricolor flags bearing the letters "R.F." for "République Française." To clarify this situation, and other points, a military congress was held by the insurgents at Arcahaye in May, 1803, presided over by Dessalines, whose authority was, on this occasion, recognized by all present. Dessalines, as general-in-chief, then took the tricolor and solemnly ripped out of it its white center stripe, joining together the remaining red and blue stripes to form a new flag. By this action he symbolized the unity of black and mulatto, and the elimination of the whites from any share in the country's future destiny. In place of the letters "R.F." on the flag there were inscribed the words "Liberty or Death."[23] The new flag was flown for the first time on May 18, 1803, after which the congress participants returned to war—to a war which had entered its final phase, and which, for them, had become a war in which victory meant independence, and defeat meant death or slavery.

In Europe the Peace of Amiens was soon broken by Bonaparte in May, 1803. According to Henry Adams, "The First Consul suddenly began a new war with England, which served the double purpose of hiding from France the loss of St. Domingo and Louisiana, and of restoring to Bonaparte his freedom of action on the only field where he could display his true instincts without restraint." On July 4, 1803, as a result, a British squadron anchored off Le Cap to blockade it.[24] The French population there was not slow to realize that the loss of the freedom of the seas at this juncture inevitably spelled the final loss of San Domingo. In effect, the British blockade hastened the fall of the French. Deprived of supplies by sea, Jérémie and Saint Marc fell to the insurgents in August, while in October both Les Cayes and Port-au-Prince also surrendered. By November, 1803, the French held only the Môle St. Nicholas in the northwest, and Le Cap itself. The conflict for Le Cap took place in the grand style of warfare. Delafosse later commented:

What men these blacks are! How they fight and how they die! One has to make war against them to know their reckless courage. . . . I have seen a solid column, torn by grape-shot from our pieces of cannon, advance without making a retrograde step. . . . They advanced singing. . . One must have seen this bravery to have any conception of it. Those songs shouted into the sky in unison by 2,000 voices to which the cannon

23. In 1810 Pétion placed the red and blue stripes horizontally, instead of vertically. He also designed the coat of arms that was placed in the center.
24. The British nevertheless permitted some U.S. ships to deliver various supplies to Le Cap.

formed the bass, produced a thrilling effect. . . . For many a day that massed square which marched singing to its death, lighted by a magnificent sun, remained in my thoughts, and even today, after more than 40 years, this majestic and glorious spectacle still lives as vividly in my imagination as in the moments when I saw it.

On one occasion Rochambeau halted the fighting to compliment an insurgent officer on his bravery. The insurgents marched into battle singing a Creole song that, said Delafosse, was "worth all our republican songs": *Grenadiers, a l'assaut! ça qui mouri, zaffaire à yo! Nan point manmans! Nan point papas. Grenadiers a l'assaut!* ("Grenadiers, to the assault! He who dies, that's his affair! No more mothers! No more fathers! Grenadiers, to the assault!")

The net around Le Cap was slowly drawn tighter. When, after heavy French losses, Christophe at last succeeded in placing artillery on the heights looking down on the town, panic threatened to break loose. On November 19, 1803, Rochambeau and Dessalines signed a truce, by the terms of which the French were given time to evacuate the city. By the end of the month Rochambeau and all his men had withdrawn, having separately surrendered to the British fleet, which carried them captive to Jamaica.[25] The Môle St. Nicholas had also surrendered.

On November 29, 1803, at Fort Liberté near Le Cap, Dessalines and his colleagues signed a preliminary Declaration of Independence for San Domingo. On December 31 it was decided to draft a final Act of Independence. The country was no longer to be called San Domingo, but was henceforth to be known as Haiti. The first draft of the Act was not approved by Dessalines, who felt that it lacked the appropriate spirit. His secretary, Boisrond-Tonnerre (so called because the lightning had played around his cradle just after his birth) proposed that the Act of Independence could only be appropriately drawn up with "the skin of a white for parchment, his skull for an inkwell, his blood for ink, and a bayonet for a pen." Boisrond-Tonnerre evidently knew the mind of his chief. "That is positively what is required," cried Dessalines, "and it is what I want. I entrust you with drafting these acts." Boisrond-Tonnerre stayed awake until the early hours of the next morning, drafting a spirited Act of Independence for Haiti—but using ordinary writing materials. Independence was then officially proclaimed at Gonaïves on January 1, 1804.

Dessalines then attempted to take the Spanish-speaking part of the island—still nominally French—but failed. As he was besieging the city of Santo Domingo in the early part of 1804, a French squadron appeared. Erroneously believing that a second squadron had appeared off Gonaïves, Dessalines returned to Haiti. The mere rumor of another French attack was sufficient, however, to cause a general massacre of all the whites who

25. Later repatriated, Rochambeau was killed at the Battle of Leipzig on October 18, 1813.

could be found in the eastern part of the island. Many, however, had escaped by remaining in hiding. For the benefit of these Dessalines issued a proclamation, promising security. They emerged, and were at once slaughtered in their turn.

Dessalines was bitterly anti-white. He had earlier broken a provision of his treaty with Rochambeau by causing the murder of those sick whites at Le Cap whom he had undertaken to have repatriated in neutral ships. Even after his own personal experiences under slavery, and the sufferings of the blacks at the hands of Rochambeau and others, are taken into consideration, he has been condemned for his duplicity and his inhumanity. It is also of interest, however, that his massacre of the last of the French left in San Domingo did not occur without encouragement from abroad. Three Britons were present at Haiti's independence ceremonies on January 1, 1804—one of them a British agent named Cathcart. They swore that only when the last of the French had been killed would the British trade with San Domingo and guarantee protection of its independence. When, less than six months after the massacre, Dessalines had himself crowned Emperor of Haiti, his ceremonial robes were sent to him from London, while his imperial crown was a gift from the merchants of Philadelphia.

The French could only lick their wounds. Their effort to recapture San Domingo and to reimpose slavery there had cost them the lives of 63,000 Frenchmen—10,000 of whom were sailors, who were badly missed at the battle of Trafalgar in 1805, when the French challenge to British naval supremacy was defeated. All these lives and hundreds of millions of francs had gone for naught. It was not until 1825 that the French could bring themselves to recognize Haiti's independence—the first country to do so. The United Kingdom recognized Haiti in 1833—the same year that the Emancipation Act ended slavery in the British Empire. Southern slave-owners prevented United States recognition until 1862, after the southern states had seceded.

British control of the sea, won in 1805, was confirmed in 1815 after the battle of Waterloo. Under the Pax Britannica which prevailed unchallenged until 1914, Haiti remained outside the mainstream of world politics. At the time of the first world war, however, both French and German interest in a debt-ridden Haiti increased sharply. At this juncture the U.S. Marines landed at Port-au-Prince in 1915. It is not without significance that the whites thus returned to Haiti at precisely the moment when, for the first time for a century, the balance of world power was in question.

The despotism of Dessalines led to his assassination in 1806, after which Haiti was divided into two separate states—a northern kingdom, ruled by King Henri Christophe, and a southern republic under Pétion.

After Christophe's death in 1820, Jean Pierre Boyer, a mulatto, succeeded in uniting not merely these two territories but the entire island into a single republic. His attempt to "Africanize" the eastern part of the island was, however, unsuccessful, and in 1844 it seceded, to form an independent Santo Domingo, later to become the Dominican Republic.

It only remains to mention some of Bonaparte's motives for attempting to restore control in San Domingo. The French historian Thiers stated in 1884 that after the British had thwarted his Egyptian and Oriental plans for conquest, "the First Consul wished to have done something for the colonial greatness of France," and accordingly turned his thoughts from the East to the West—that is, to say to Louisiana. According to Henry Adams, however, Bonaparte's purpose in seeking to acquire Louisiana—which, although he nominally obtained it from Spain in 1800, he in fact only held under French occupation for twenty days before selling it to the United States—was to make it a source for supply for San Domingo itself. In the event of war, San Domingo might be cut off from France, and would therefore become dependent on supplies from the United States, whereas if the French held Louisiana, it would become independent of English-speaking America. Bonaparte evidently knew that his acquisition of Louisiana would greatly increase Franco-American tension, but this was not a prospect that caused him alarm.

In ensuring British neutrality in his projected attack on San Domingo, Bonaparte said, in issuing the appropriate instructions to Talleyrand, that "the interests of civilization" required him "to destroy the new Algier which had organized itself in the middle of America." Bonaparte perhaps mentioned "Algier" because he had recently mooted the idea of forming a league of European maritime powers—specifically those which had signed the Peace of Amiens—for the purpose of "driving the Barbary people from the coast of Africa, their lands to be afterwards used for planting sugar, coffee, cotton, and produce which had to be drawn from remote colonies." It is evident that the products mentioned were precisely those which San Domingo had previously yielded for France. Their production in North Africa would place them within easy reach of France, and, logistically, would make it far more difficult for the British navy to deny them to her in time of war. Justification for the proposed league, which was originally suggested by Joseph Bonaparte, was found in the allegation that Algiers was a nest of pirates who blackmailed and enslaved Europeans and who, in the words of de Méneval, Bonaparte's private secretary, "it was useless to hope to bring . . . to accept the relations and conventions by which international rights are established between civilized states." De Méneval also stated that "If the plan of this league could have been carried though, it might have diverted him [Bonaparte] from the expedition intended for the reconquest of the island of San

Domingo." As it was, a plan of conquest of Algeria was carefully studied by the French Ministry of the Marine, and a first step was made toward putting it into effect. British knowledge of French ambitions in North Africa may have been, in the opinion of contemporaries, one of the reasons for the rupture of the Peace of Amiens, a rupture which ended France's last hope for holding San Domingo.

It is also of interest that Bonaparte also told Talleyrand, on November 13, 1801, to inform the British that

> In the resolution I have taken to annihilate the government of the blacks at San Domingo, I have been guided less by considerations of commerce and finance than by the necessity of stifling in all parts of the world every sort of germ of disquietude and trouble; but I am aware that San Domingo, if reconquered by the whites, would be during many years a weak point, needing the support of peace and the parent country, while the liberty of the blacks, if recognized at San Domingo, would be at all times a point of support for the French republic in the New World.

In other words, in diplomatic language, he was supposedly attempting to convince the British that his main interest was neither economic nor military, but lay merely in ensuring white supremacy in San Domingo, as elsewhere in the world. His message also conveyed a veiled and discreetly worded threat. If the British should find his projected overthrow of Toussaint Louverture unacceptable, then he might perhaps not seek to stifle "every sort of germ of disquietude and trouble" in all parts of the world, but might embark upon a contrary policy. That is to say, he might well foster the revolutionary liberation of peoples under British domination—supporting other Toussaint Louvertures not only in the Americas, but also in India and elsewhere. This was a sugestion that must surely have made the British shiver in their boots.

Even when Napoleon was in exile on St. Helena, in his last years, there was heard an echo of the fears that he, and the French, had aroused in the British. When Napoleon was walking, he frequently encountered a Malayan slave, who had been given the name of Tobias, and who was employed as a gardener. Lacking other matter for thought, Napoleon became preoccupied to some extent with Tobias's lot, which he could not avoid comparing to his own. "Poor devil!" he commented to a companion, "Snatched from his family, torn from his home, robbed of himself, sold into slavery!" Napoleon had also been reading the writings of Pamphile de Lacroix, the French general who had served in San Domingo, and had admitted to himself that he had made a mistake in seeking to overthrow Toussaint. Perhaps, also, he may have realized that his fundamental mistake had been to try to reimpose slavery on the blacks. This would appear likely, for, already, in 1815, after his return from Elba, he had in the name of France abolished the slave trade. Now, either in an attempt to rehabilitate his historic reputation with respect to slavery, or out of genuine sympathy for the man, he himself bought the slave Tobias, and asked for permission to send him home to his family. The British Governor of St. Helena forbade it, however. "It is plain to me," he said, "that General Bonaparte is trying to win the hearts of the colored population, in the hope of setting up a second Negro empire, as in San Domingo."

It would be many years before a non-white people would wage a struggle comparable to that of the people of San Domingo in order to win their freedom. The example of San Domingo was not, however, to be forgotten in the meantime—least of all by the powers of Europe. The black and mulatto population of San Domingo had proved beyond the shadow of a doubt that soldiers of African descent were in every way the equals of whites, both in skill and in courage. They had also proved that men of every color, once roused, were prepared to die rather than to live as slaves. By their courage and sacrifice, the slaves of San Domingo not only provided the world with an object lesson, they also won the first half of the battle to end slavery, in the New World no less than in the Old.

# Chapter 11

# Slave or Free: The Struggle to End American Slavery

*Negro slavery, which the Constitution has vainly attempted to blink by not using the term . . . is a thing which cannot be hid; it is not a dry rot, which you can cover with the carpet until the house tumbles about your ears; you might as well try to hide a volcano in full eruption.* —John Randolph, in the U.S. Senate (1824)

*A house divided against itself cannot stand. I believe this government cannot endure permanently half slave and half free.* —Abraham Lincoln, Springfield, Illinois (1858)

FROM THE MOMENT of its birth, the principal power on the North American mainland, the United States of America, had been haunted by the ambiguities resulting from the existence of slavery within its borders. For the United States was a nation that proclaimed the equality of all men and their right to liberty, while at the same time it upheld in law and in fact the existence of the institution of slavery. In consequence, the Continental Congress of the United States had tended, out of shame, to use euphemisms for such words as "slave" or "slavery." The Constitutional Convention, meeting in Philadelphia in 1787, had likewise avoided the term, although its underlying importance at that time was clearly indicated by James Madison's subsequent comment that any allusion to emancipation at the Convention would have been "a spark to a mass of gunpowder."

The first Africans had been imported into the English colony of Virginia in 1619. Sixty years later slavery had become an institution, which spread from settlement to settlement. By 1790—fourteen years after the Declaration of Independence—out of the total United States population of 3,929,000, no less than 697,681 were slaves,[1] most of them living on Southern plantations, where they were principally engaged in the cultivation of tobacco and cotton. Negro slaves had also been introduced into the New England colonies, but there, as de Tocqueville put it, "the legislation and manners of the people were opposed to slavery from the first."

At the Constitutional Convention of 1787, which was engaged in drafting the Constitution of the United States, discussions proceeded smoothly until the question of slavery was raised in connection with representation in the national legislature. It had already been decided that, so far as national taxes were concerned, a slave would be taxable at three-fifths of the rate due from each free man.[2] This, evidently, was a measure which tended to discourage slavery. At the convention itself, however, it was proposed that a slave should also count as three-fifths of a person in the census that was to be taken for the apportioning of representation among the states. This, then, would give greater political strength to the states where slave-holding was widespread. Conflict over this point, pitting the Northern states against the Southern, became so pronounced that, as one of the participants, Gouverneur Morris of Pennsylvania, later said, the fate of America was suspended by a hair. Unity was only preserved—and the Constitution adopted—by a Northern concession to the Southern view. Further concessions were also obtained by the South in the clauses which provided that for at least twenty years there would be no ban on the importation of slaves, and that fugitive slaves who fled to the free states would be returned to their owners.

The new nation still remained loosely knit: North and South, while differing in their customs and their economies, had not yet evolved into consciously differing regions, each with a developed and articulate public opinion. A number of Northern states still countenanced slavery. Gradual abolition—which meant that children of slave parents were born free—had been introduced in Vermont in 1777, in Massachusetts (including Maine) and in Pennsylvania in 1780, in New Hampshire in 1783, and in Connecticut in 1784. New York was not to introduce it until 1799, or New Jersey until 1804. Most crucial, however, was the adoption of the Ordinance of 1787, which abolished slavery in the territories that had not yet attained statehood to the north of the Ohio River and to the east of the Mississippi. It was eventually to be the conflict over the free or slave status of the westward territories into which the United States was

1. Population statistics in this chapter are taken from the *Statistical History of the United States* (1965).
2. When Southerners in Congress asked why Northern sheep should not also be considered taxable in the same way, Benjamin Franklin replied that "sheep will never make any insurrections."

expanding that was to provoke the ultimate crisis between the two systems.

To begin with the Southern states felt far from secure. Already, during the French and Indian wars, some states had evidenced concern at the possibility of their enemies provoking a slave uprising. In 1755, for example, the Lieutenant-Governor of Virginia had taken certain military measures to protect the whites from "combinations of the Negro slaves," since, he said, "These poor creatures imagine the French will give them their freedom." During the War of Independence, Southerners also expressed fears lest not the French but the British might wage an anti-slavery war in the South.

Fears of Negro insurrection grew more acute after the San Domingo uprising. As early as 1793 a Mr. Randolph of Richmond, Virginia, reported being awakened at night by the voices of Negroes planning a massacre of the whites of the town, and said that one such voice had spoken of the "French Island" where the blacks had killed the whites and taken the country. From 1797 to 1800 fears of a French-supported anti-slavery invasion that would sweep inland like a hurricane from the Caribbean, destroying lives and property and perhaps establishing French hegemony on the mainland, rose to a climax. Such fears were at least partially responsible for the federal rearmament program that was undertaken from 1797 to 1799. Agreements reached with the new regime in San Domingo, however, served to reassure the American authorities, as also did the subsequent British naval victory at Trafalgar which denied the Atlantic to the French. Nevertheless, the knowledge of the events that had occurred in San Domingo continued, like a recurrent nightmare, to haunt the imagination of Southern slave-holders throughout the years that followed.

At the time of the American Revolution, it had seemed for a moment as if the institution of slavery itself—the root cause of the pervasive sense of insecurity—might be terminated. During the war the British had prevented the importation of more slaves to North America, and in South Carolina and Georgia slaves were being turned into soldiers to fight the British in return for their eventual freedom. Furthermore, in 1784 only a single vote had prevented Congress from abolishing slavery in all the Western territories. As the struggle in San Domingo was proceeding, a number of the border states, such as Maryland, Kentucky, and Tennessee, passed laws making manumission easier. It has since been suggested that a single further "impulse" would have sufficed to alter the course of history. Certainly, during these years, the slave system would appear to have faltered, and, momentarily, to have almost lost conviction in its own sense of destiny. Such moments, however, passed. The assurances provided at the Constitutional Convention, the resumption of the transatlantic slave trade, the neutralization of the San Domingan threat, and the growing expectation of a great accession of power and wealth when the Western territories would have become linked to the slave system, all eventually combined to restore the slave-holders' confidence in themselves and their powers. By 1810, when the population of the United States had risen to 7,224,000, the slave population had grown to 1,191,362—an increase of almost half a million in the twenty years since the census of 1790. The rate of increase was, moreover, to be maintained. By the time of the 1830 census, when the U.S. population numbered 12,901,000, the slave population had increased to 2,300,388—over a million more.

*The Missouri Compromise*

In the admission of new states to the Union, a balance between the North and the South had been carefully preserved. Thus the admission of the Northern states of Indiana in 1816 and of Illinois in 1818 had been balanced by that of the Southern states of Mississippi in 1817, and of Alabama in 1819. However, the application of Missouri for admission, also in 1819, precipitated a crisis. No provision had been made by Congress concerning the future slave or free status of the Louisiana Purchase territories of which Missouri formed a part. Southerners had presumed that when the population had increased to the point at which it could qualify for statehood, Missouri, like Louisiana itself, would become a slave state. But the assumption was challenged by a New York Congressman, who proposed that slavery be prohibited in Missouri. A fierce national debate ensued that stirred political passions, and led to Southern threats of secession should the South not get its way. By 1820, however, a compromise was arranged. Missouri was to be admitted to the Union as a slave state, being balanced by the admission of the sparsely settled Northern state of Maine. At the same time it was agreed that in the remainder of the Louisiana Purchase territory north of the 36° 30' line slavery was to be banned. Although the Missouri Compromise applied only to the Louisiana Purchase, many interpreted it as a tacit understanding that the 36° 30' line would eventually be prolonged westward as the future boundary between slave and free territory.

The physical arrangements that were arrived at, however, did not hide the irreconcilable division in the nation which had suddenly been revealed to all Americans. "This momentous question, like a fire-bell in the night, awakened and filled me with terror," commented Thomas Jefferson. John Quincy Adams, later to be President, wrote in his diary, "I take it for granted that the present question is a mere preamble—a title-page to a great tragic volume."

## Slave Revolts

Ambiguity characterized the self-description that the American Southland presented to the world. On the one hand it was maintained that conditions in the South left nothing to be desired, and that both masters and slaves were happy in their appointed social positions—the Negroes, for their part, exhibiting a docile acceptance of their position, which was based on their natural inferiority. In 1861 Jefferson Davis told the U.S. Senate: "Bad men have gone among the ignorant and credulous people, and incited them to murder and arson; but of themselves—moving by themselves—I say history does not chronicle a case of Negro insurrection." Earlier, in a pamphlet published in 1850, George Fitzhugh announced: "At the slaveholding South all is peace, quiet, plenty and contentment." On the other hand, however, it was also held that the Negro was cunning and rebellious, constituting a constant threat to the established order. "We regard our Negroes as the '*Jacobins*' of the country, against whom we should be always upon our guard," wrote a South Carolinian in the 1820s. The matter was further complicated by the pride felt by the state of Virginia in the role it had played in the American Revolution, in which the Virginia patriot, Patrick Henry, had proclaimed, at a delicate moment in the Virginia legislature, the proud words: "Give me Liberty, or give me Death!" In 1800 an American envoy abroad, in a letter to John Quincy Adams, referred to the "eternal clamour about liberty" in Virginia and South Carolina as contributing to slave insurrection.

Actually, it would appear that the African slave in the Southern states was no less ready to attempt to throw off his shackles, when the chance offered itself, than he had been on the slave ships which brought him from Africa. The spirit of revolt which had turned San Domingan society upside down was also seen to be alive in the American South. Yet whereas numbers had favored the Africans in San Domingo, in the South the proportion of black to white was very different. San Domingo, moreover, was an island, so that the changing circumstances of sea control had also influenced events to the advantage of the Africans. But in the South, an insurrection in any one state could be crushed by the introduction of further white forces from neighboring states. White control over the slaves was therefore assured so long as there were only two parties to any conflict—the slave-holders and the slaves.

It was true, stability was maintained at the cost of the virtual militarization of Southern life. In the late eighteenth century an eminent Briton remarked of the Southern white men: "The fact is, they are all soldiers." Later visitors made similar comments. In an account published in 1860, Frederick L. Olmstead, commenting on conditions in the city of

Charleston as well as in other Southern cities, said that there one may see "police machinery such as you never find in towns under free government: citadels, sentries, passports, grapeshotted cannon, and daily public whippings of the subjects for accidental infractions of police ceremonies. I happened myself to see more direct expression of tyranny in a single day and night in Charleston, than at Naples in a week."

While stability, under these conditions, might ultimately be assured, it evidently did not go unchallenged. Even when the word "uprising" is narrowly defined, it would appear that no less than 250 occasions are recorded on which either Negro slaves, or else Negro slaves and whites together, resorted to arms in attempts to gain freedom. The most significant among these many uprisings, which occurred from the seventeenth century on, were the Gabriel uprising of 1800, the attempted Vesey uprising of 1822, and the Nat Turner rebellion of 1831.

The Gabriel uprising took place in Virginia when American concern about the effect of revolutionary ideals upon the slave population was at its height. Throughout the latter part of the 1790s, public opinion had been agitated by a series of mysterious fires that had broken out throughout the major cities of the Eastern seaboard, from Georgia to New York. These fires were generally ascribed to slaves, although some attributed them to the influence of Quakers upon the slaves. To this day the precise origin of these fires remains obscure. The Gabriel revolt of 1800 nevertheless appeared to some as the materialization of the fears that the fires had caused.

Gabriel, who was six foot two inches tall, was twenty-four at the time of the uprising, and was described as being intelligent and courageous "above his rank in life." He had been the property of a local slave-holder and tavern-owner named Prosser, who lived a few miles outside Richmond, and who was notorious for ill-treating his slaves. Helped by his wife, his two brothers, and others, Gabriel succeeded in organizing an insurgent movement of considerable scope. On August 30, 1800, about a thousand slaves rallied a few miles outside Richmond, and armed with homemade weapons, farm implements, and a few guns, took the local authorities virtually by surprise. Had the insurgents been successful, it is believed that many more in other parts of Virginia would have joined them. They had planned to march on Richmond, but that evening there occurred what one contemporary called "the most terrible thunder accompanied with an enormous rain, that I ever witnessed in this State." The heavy rain apparently washed out the route over which the slaves were to pass. The delay permitted the whites to mobilize their forces, the slave army was disbanded, and the revolt was crushed.

Gabriel was captured, after attempting to escape by sea, and he, with at least thirty-four others, was tried and hanged. He died silent. Other leaders of the revolt also went to their deaths with dignity. Four years later an English traveler who visited Virginia was told that one of the slaves before his execution had told the court,

> I have nothing more to offer in my own defense than what General Washington would have had to offer had he been taken by the British and put to trial by them. I have ventured my life endeavouring to obtain the liberty of my countrymen, and am a willing sacrifice to their cause: and I beg, as a favour, that I may be immediately led to execution. I know that you have pre-determined to shed my blood, why then all this mockery of a trial.

It was also learned that Gabriel had intended to procure a piece of silk to make a flag for the rebels, on which he would have inscribed the words "Death or Liberty."[3] Such circumstances caused qualms of conscience both to James Monroe, then Governor of Virginia, and later President of the United States, and to Thomas Jefferson, then on the threshold of the presidency, with whom Monroe corresponded on the subject.

It is also of interest that the Gabriel insurgents had planned not to harm Frenchmen, Quakers, or Methodists. From the French they had hoped for assistance once the revolt had begun. Quakers and Methodists were viewed with favor by them because of their egalitarian and emancipist tendencies. Some slave-holders, indeed, accused the Methodists of organizing the revolt. Methodism appealed to many Negroes, and after the Vesey plot was discovered in 1822 the Bishop of the African Methodist Church in Charleston was obliged to leave South Carolina.

The Gabriel revolt had occurred at a time of economic depression, which inevitably resulted in increased hardships for the slaves. An economic recession also seems to have been a contributory cause of the Vesey plot in South Carolina in 1822. Denmark Vesey, the leader, had been born in Africa, and had served for several years on a slave ship, purchasing his freedom in 1800. At the time of the conspiracy he was bearded, and in his late fifties. He spoke several languages, and worked in Charleston as an artisan. He was, also, the only free Negro involved in the planned uprising. Vesey told the slaves of the discussion in Congress about the Missouri Compromise, as well as about the events in Haiti, and read to them from the Bible about "how the children of Israel were delivered out of Egypt from bondage." He also twice wrote to Haiti to tell of his plans and to ask for help. Apparently the Vesey group, in the event of success, also counted upon some support from Africa.[4]

"Considerable numbers" outside of Charleston itself—one witness estimated the figure to be 6,600, while another said it was 9,000—were involved in the planned uprising, and slaves even beyond the state bor-

---

3. It will be recalled that in 1791 the French troops in San Domingo had been obliged to remove the words "Liberty or Death" from their regimental flags for fear of the effect on the slaves. Dessalines—another insurgent slave—had the words inscribed on the 1803 flag of Haiti.

4. This circumstance would appear to be unique in the history of American slave revolts. (See Herbert Aptheker, *American Slave Revolts*, 1963, p. 98).

der, in North Carolina, were contacted. Numbers of simple arms, such as pike-heads and daggers, had been manufactured, and it was planned that simultaneous revolts were to take place at five separate points, while a sixth force, on horseback, would patrol the streets of Charleston itself. The uprising was to take place in July, a month during which many whites would be absent on their annual vacations. In May, however, an informer revealed some of the plans to the authorities, with the result that the extent of the conspiracy was eventually uncovered and the main organizers arrested before the uprising could take place. Thirty-seven of the conspirators, including Vesey himself, were hanged, and widespread repression followed. Laws were passed in South Carolina which, among other things, forbade the hiring out of slaves for labor, provided that every free Negro should have a guardian to control his conduct, and made it a crime to teach slaves to read and write.

Economic depression would appear to have been a contributory cause of the Nat Turner uprising, as it had been of the Gabriel uprising and of the Vesey plot. The Turner uprising, which took place in Southampton County in the state of Virginia in 1831, had, however, religious undertones that had been lacking from both the Vesey and the Gabriel disturbances. It was later pointed out that many Quakers had been active in the county, but Turner himself, insofar as he could be classified, was a Baptist. Born in 1800, and of a religious bent, he was steeped in the Bible, and was regarded as a local religious leader. Having become convinced that he was "ordained for some great purpose," in 1828 he experienced a revelation while working in the fields. In this revelation he was informed that the time was approaching when "the first should be last and the last should be first." He waited for a sign. The eclipse of the sun of February 12, 1831—which, incidentally, also convinced some New Yorkers that cataclysmic events were at hand—led him to decide to act, and, with four others, he planned an uprising for July 4 of that year. On the appointed day Turner was ill, so action was postponed until another sign had been vouchsafed—an event which was held to have occurred on August 13, when the sun was a "greenish blue color." The revolt itself began on the evening of Sunday, August 21, when Turner attacked and killed his master and his master's family, after which he and five companions attacked other whites. Less than forty-eight hours later about seventy insurgent slaves had rallied to Turner, and fifty-seven whites had been killed, while Turner's force was marching on the Southampton County seat of Jerusalem[5] in order to seize arms stored there. Progress was delayed, however, when some of the slaves stopped at a plantation about three miles from the town, where they raided the

5. One commentator has suggested that Turner may have read and been impressed by a sentence in his Bible: "From that time began Jesus to show unto his disciples, that he must go unto Jerusalem, and suffer many things of the elders and chief priests, and scribes, and be killed."

wine cellar, and rested. This delay gave the whites time to gather enough forces to counterattack, which they did successfully. Sporadic fighting followed, ending in the final suppression of the revolt.

Cruel vengeance was then taken upon the Negro population of the area. Many nonparticipants in the revolt were massacred in addition to the insurgents. After a search of two months Nat Turner himself was caught and, in addition to nineteen others, hanged. The reign of terror that was established at this time was accompanied, however, by feelings of panic among many whites, who feared further uprisings. George Washington's niece, writing to a Boston correspondent, said, "It is like a smothered volcano—we know not when, or where, the flame will burst forth." Further repressive legislation was enacted in many Southern states; further restrictions were placed upon free Negroes as well as upon slaves; and emigration of free Negroes to Liberia was encouraged. There was even some discussion in Virginia itself of the advantages that might be gained from introducing a policy of gradual emancipation. The talk, however, died down, and opinion in Virginia, no less than in the South as a whole, soon opted firmly for the retention and the strengthening of the system of slavery.

## The Slave System in the South

With the annexation of Texas in 1845 the number of slave states in the Union was brought to fifteen—the other fourteen being Alabama, Arkansas, Delaware, Florida, Georgia, Kentucky, Louisiana, Maryland, Mississippi, Missouri, North Carolina, South Carolina, Tennessee, and Virginia. The characteristics of servitude were, however, far from uniform in the various regions. Virginia, for example, a state which could lay claim to being the cradle of the Union itself, no less than to being the first slave state,[6] assumed a distinctive character of its own. In Virginia, tradition to some extent softened the harshest aspects of the system, and on occasion semi-emancipist attitudes could be discerned. Virginia was also the "breeding state," where large numbers of slaves were bred for sale elsewhere, particularly in the "Deep South." In the seven states of the "Deep South" (South Carolina, Georgia, Florida, Alabama, Mississippi, Louisiana, and Texas) lived the majority of the slaves on the North American continent, clustered together on the larger plantations, and producing such crops as, for example, sugar on the river banks and

---

6. Virginians have claimed that it had nevertheless unwillingly so become. Early colonial efforts, they have said, to end both the slave trade as well as slavery in Virginia itself were overridden by the British Crown. However, Elizabeth Donnan in her introduction to the fourth volume of *Documents Illustrative of the History of the Slave Trade to America*, published in 1935, writes "The unsupported statement that thirty-three Virginia acts intended to put a stop to the importation of negroes were disallowed in England, once made has been often repeated, but no careful study of the circumstances under which these acts were passed, the purpose or purposes which lay behind them, the conflict of interests which they represented, or even the motives of the British government has ever been made."

bayous of Louisiana, rice in Georgia or South Carolina, or cotton in Alabama or on the alluvial Mississippi river bottoms. In the Upper South, including the border states, such as Kentucky, Missouri, or Maryland, the pattern of slave ownership was different, and more crop diversification was noticeable. The proportion of slaves to the total population was far less in these states. In 1860, for example, only 1.5 percent of the population of Delaware were slaves, whereas in Mississippi the proportion was as high as 55 percent.

The proportion of slave-owners also varied widely. Kenneth Stampp indicates that

In South Carolina and Mississippi, approximately half of the families owned slaves; in Georgia two-fifths; in Alabama, Louisiana, and Florida, one-third; in Virginia, North Carolina, Kentucky, Tennessee, and Texas, one-fourth; in Arkansas one-fifth; in Maryland and Missouri, one-eighth; and in Delaware, one-thirtieth.[7]

## The Origins of Servitude

Servitude in North America, at the time when the English colonies were established there, was first introduced in the form of indentured service. An indentured servant bound himself for a given number of years, usually varying between two and seven, to serve his master. The practice was firmly established in Europe, and was extended to North America when men bound themselves to service to others in return for payment of their passages. When African labor was introduced in the seventeenth century, the African servants were regarded as bound by much the same conditions as white servants were. Many were freed by their masters after serving a term of years, or after conversion to Christianity. The fact, however, that the Africans, unlike the whites, did not have written indentures, deprived them of the guarantees which protected the interests of the white servants. Without any limitation upon the authority of employers, masters gradually became slave-masters, and servants became slaves. Many of the main features of the system of slavery were thus sanctioned by custom long before they passed into law. The first cargo of Africans was landed in Virginia from a Dutch ship in 1619, but it was only in the 1660s that Virginia and Maryland began to make any legal distinctions between European and African labor. It was only many years later that the principle that the laborer of African descent could be held as property, rather than as a person, was clearly established, or that interracial marriage was prohibited. Not until the eighteenth century was the process of degrading laborers of African descent to the status of slaves completed. From that time on, however, Africans brought to North America by European ships were sold as slaves, and were no longer

7.  *The Peculiar Institution: Slavery in the Ante-Bellum South* (1956).

regarded as merely servants. Temporary servitude had given way to the institution of chattel slavery.

Slavery in North America was essentially rural. Perhaps not more than 10 percent of the slaves lived or worked in the towns or cities. Except for New Orleans and Baltimore—the latter in a border state with few slaves—there were no large cities in the slave states, and few with a population of even 15,000.[8] On the farms and plantations of the South most of the slaves worked throughout the daylight hours, except on Sundays, and sometimes Saturday afternoons. On the smaller farms slaves would work beside their owners, whereas on the larger farms and plantations they habitually worked in gangs under the supervision of an overseer, or—more often—in the charge of a slave-driver, or drivers, responsible to an overseer. Most slave-owners were dissatisfied with their overseers, one planter exclaiming, "They are as a class a worthless set of vagabonds." Few overseers held one job long, and many were licentious and cruel, being given to excessive use of the whip.

Supporters and opponents of slavery disagreed about the amount of cruelty and hardship that the slaves had to endure, but that there was much of it there seems little doubt. "I'd rather be dead than be a nigger on one of those big plantations," a white Mississippian told a traveler in the 1850s. Artisans and house servants were those who received the best treatment. Acting as estate-agents, bookkeepers, carpenters, blacksmiths, physicians, body servants, butlers, nurses, seamstresses, and cooks, they were brought into frequent contact with members of the owner's family, and in consequence often came to enjoy special favors and advantages,[9] advantages that eased for them somewhat the burden of servitude which weighed so heavily upon the majority.

Alexis de Tocqueville, writing in the early 1830s, described the contrast which presented itself to a traveler who "floats down the current of the Ohio," with the slave state of Kentucky to the left, and the free state of Ohio to the right:

> Upon the left bank of the stream the population is rare: from time to time one descries a troop of slaves loitering in the half-desert fields; the primeval forest recurs at every turn; society seems to be asleep, man to be idle, and nature alone offers a scene of activity and of life.
>
> From the right bank, on the contrary, a confused hum is heard which proclaims the presence of industry; the fields are covered with abundant harvests; the elegance of the dwellings announces the taste and activity of the labourer; and man appears to be in the enjoyment of that wealth and contentment which is the reward of labour.

8. Eugene D. Genovese, *The Political Economy of Slavery: Studies in the Economy and Society of the Slave South* (1965), p. 171.
9. The difference in condition thus divided house slaves from field slaves. During the Vesey conspiracy of 1822, one of the organizers warned others against trusting "those waiting men who receive presents of old coats, etc., from their masters."

In this contrast, felt de Tocqueville, the "opposite consequences of slavery and freedom may be readily understood; and they suffice to explain many of the differences which we remark between the civilization of antiquity, and that of our own time."

In effect, as an economic system, slavery was inefficient and wasteful. The slaves, having no incentive to produce, worked indifferently or unwillingly, often feigning stupidity, breaking tools, and always requiring supervision. Labor-saving machinery was being steadily introduced in the Northern states, but in the South relatively few changes were made, and few new inventions introduced.[10] The difference in approach between South and North in this respect were vividly expressed by Frederick Douglass, who had himself escaped from slavery in Maryland, and who later found work in New England:

> On the wharves of New Bedford, I received my first light. I saw there industry without bustle, labor without noise, toil—honest, earnest, and exhaustive—without the whip. There was no loud singing or hallooing, as at the wharves of southern ports when ships were loading or unloading, no loud cursing or quarrelling; everything went on as smoothly as well-oiled machinery. One of the first incidents which impressed me with the superior mental character of labor in the North over that of the South, was the manner of loading and unloading vessels. In a southern port twenty or thirty hands would be employed to do what five or six men, with the help of one ox, would do at the wharf in New Bedford. Main strength—human muscle—unassisted by intelligent skill, was slavery's method of labor. With a capital of about sixty dollars in the shape of a good-natured old ox attached to the end of a stout rope, New Bedford did the work of ten or twelve thousand dollars, represented in the bones and muscles of slaves, and did it far better. In a word, I found everything managed with a much more scrupulous regard to economy, both of men and things, time and strength, than in the country from which I had come. Instead of going a hundred yards to the spring, the maidservant had a well or pump at her elbow. The wood used for fuel was kept dry and snugly piled away for winter. Here were sinks, drains, self-shutting gates, pounding-barrels, washing-machines, wringing machines, and a hundred other contrivances for saving time and money.[11]

Slaves would soon have broken most machinery, and labor-saving, in a slave society, was not regarded as necessarily desirable. Thus, for example, the "nigger hoe" used in Virginia and elsewhere was much heavier and more inefficient than the light "Yankee hoe" that would have been quickly broken in slave hands. Southern agriculturists therefore invested little in equipment, and spent little time worrying about improvements or reforms. Time and energy that in the North was devoted to improvement, in the South was often absorbed by the exigencies of slave supervision or discipline, while money that in the North was

---

10. Paradoxically the cotton gin, whose introduction gave a fresh impetus to the cotton industry, thus increasing the demand for slaves, was invented, in 1793, by Eli Whitney, a Massachusetts man then working in the South.

11. *Life and Times of Frederick Douglass, Written by Himself* (1892 edition).

often invested in increasing production, in the South was more often expended on the conspicuous consumption which was a feature of plantation life from the owner's point of view—or else on the purchase of more slaves. John E. Cairnes, an English economist, said that the possession of slaves in the South had become a symbol of success and of social position, "like the possession of a horse among Arabs." The system consequently became wasteful not only of human resources—the unused potential of both masters and slaves—but also of the land itself. Poor agricultural methods, and the necessity of exploiting the land to the utmost to wring a profit from it, resulted in widespread soil exhaustion. The same land was used again and again for the most profitable crop, while the extensive system of farming that was practiced discouraged fertilization. By 1859 it was reported that soil exhaustion was far advanced in Mississippi and Alabama, while in Texas, in the same decade, Olmstead commented on the appearance of "that spectacle so familiar and so melancholy in all the older Slave States," the abandoned plantation with worn-out fields.

The system thus contained elements that were essentially self-destructive. It discouraged capital formation. As Edmund Ruffin, a Southern agriculturist, who was also a dedicated protagonist of slavery, observed in 1859, without slaves' sales to the Lower South the principal source of capital accumulation in the Upper South would be cut off. Southern slaveocracy, to continue to survive in an unfriendly world, was thus driven to expand by two forces—the necessity of finding fresh lands to work in place of those already exhausted, and the necessity faced by the older states of selling slaves to new states in order to continue to raise capital. Southern thinkers thus began to dream of a great slave empire, stretching not only from the Atlantic to the Pacific, but also embracing the shores of the Caribbean, and extending into Latin America. These dreams alarmed Northern capitalists, who themselves had begun to dream dreams in which slavery had no part. As the United States expanded westward, and as both capital and labor moved into the newly opened lands, conflicts between the proponents of slavery on the one hand, and the emissaries of Northern-style development on the other, became increasingly frequent. As a result the anti-slavery movement, which earlier had been regarded as a faction supported by a small minority, grew steadily stronger until at last, with the organization of the Republican Party in 1854, it became a powerful movement in the North, claiming allegiance from thousands who were at least opposed to the extension of slavery, and providing a moral dimension to the Northern cause in the war between North and South that eventually began in 1861.

*The Early Abolitionists*

The Napoleonic wars had produced for a time in the United Kingdom a spirit of resistance not only to France, but also to the ideas associated with the French Revolution. British conservatism, however, was, throughout the 1820s, being steadily undermined by the growth of an industrialism which, by its nature, necessitated radical social changes. Political barriers to change in the country were removed, at last, by the passage of the Reform Bill of 1832, which tripled the size of the British electorate, thus permitting the introduction of many other reformist measures— among them the Emancipation Act of 1833. This act provided for the abolition of slavery in the British colonies at midnight on July 31, 1834, thus freeing three-quarters of a million slaves in the Caribbean islands, in return for the payment of £20 million compensation to the slave-owners. The former slaves continued, however, as temporary bondsmen, being apprenticed for periods of from four to six years to their former masters, after which they were free to dispose of themselves as they wished. This historic British measure, apart from its direct results, also raised the hopes and gave fresh impetus to the efforts of the small anti-slavery faction in the United States.

The American abolitionist movement, while it may be said to have entered onto the historical stage at this moment, nevertheless had roots that stretched back to the previous century. Both in style and in ethos it differed from its French counterpart. Whereas the French anti-slavery movement had derived its justification essentially from the doctrine of natural rights, anti-slavery in the United States,[12] as in Britain, had primarily based itself upon religion. As the prevailing religion was Protestant Christianity, this meant that ultimate sanction for abolition was sought in a basic text—the King James version of the English Bible of 1611. The peculiar power of "The Book," as it was called, lay in the historical circumstance that some Englishmen had earlier shown themselves ready to be burned to death—and had, in fact, sometimes been burned to death—in order to win the privilege of obtaining access to the Bible in the English language. The abolitionists, by attempting to associate the cause of anti-slavery with the Bible, were thus seeking to identify themselves with the earlier moral struggle to establish a principle. Thus, for example, Elizur Wright, Jr., an early abolitionist, wrote in 1833, "The doctrine of the immediate abolition of slavery asks no better authority than is offered by scripture. It is in perfect harmony with the letter and spirit of God's word."

The same religious spirit was evident in most other abolitionists,

12. The doctrine of natural rights was also, however, frequently appealed to in the United States by invoking the Declaration of Independence.

including the most famous of them, John Brown, who, when told by a Southern clergyman that slavery was "a Christian institution," replied tartly, "My dear sir, you know nothing about Christianity; you will have to learn its A, B, C; I find you quite ignorant of what the word Christianity means . . . I respect you as a gentleman, of course; but it is as a heathen gentleman." Unfortunately for the abolitionists, however, "The Book" provided a mine of useful quotations not only for anti-slavery partisans, but also for those supporting the pro-slavery cause. This circumstance, nevertheless, did little to diminish the ardor of either faction.

From its inception the Quakers were particularly active in the anti-slavery movement. Even in the seventeenth century they had cautioned against "buying or keeping of Negroes."[13] As a sect which rejected external authority and sought guidance from the "Inner Light," which, they believed, represented that part of God which is found in every man, they devoted themselves to meditation, and acted out of personal revelation or conviction. In the eighteenth century one of them, John Woolman, had achieved wide renown and had influenced many with his pious and eloquent rejection of slavery. Other Quakers had acted in more spectacular ways, although not always with as satisfactory results. For example, another eighteenth century Quaker, Benjamin Lay, a hunch-back and himself a former slave-trader, had taken a bladder filled with blood to Quaker meeting, where he had sprayed his co-religionists and caused several ladies present to swoon when he had suddenly drawn his sword and run the bladder through, exclaiming as he did so, "Thus shall God shed the blood of those persons who enslave their fellow creatures."[14] Upon another occasion he had kidnaped Quaker children in order that their parents could sympathize with the situation of slaves whose children were taken from them. For such acts Lay was finally barred from attending Quaker meetings.

An equally convinced abolitionist was the nineteenth century Quaker Isaac Hopper, who was active in Negro education, and who gave aid to runaway slaves. Upon one occasion, when Hopper was remonstrating with slave-holders, they threw him from a second-story window—where-upon, to their intense astonishment, he immediately returned, despite his injuries, to the room from which they had thrown him, cut the bonds of the slave that they were holding there, and ran him down the street to safety. John Greenleaf Whittier, the anti-slavery poet, was also a Quaker, as was the most eminent of pioneer abolitionists, Benjamin Lundy, who traveled widely in the United States, and edited a publication called *The*

13. Henry J. Cadbury, "Colonial Quaker Antecedents to the British Abolition of Slavery," *Friends' Quarterly Examiner* (London, seventh month, 1933).
14. Quoted in *Freedom's Ferment*, by Elis Felt Tyler (1944).

*Genius of Universal Emancipation.* Although Quakers ceased to hold slaves in the eighteenth century, not all nineteenth-century Quakers were abolitionists, and in the 1820's the issue led to schisms in the sect. Nevertheless, when the American Anti-Slavery Society was first formed in Philadelphia in 1833, in an atmosphere of public hostility, of the sixty-two persons who convened, twenty-one were Quakers.

The nineteenth-century United States abounded in reformers, and abolitionism soon became associated with many other reform movements, such as those for women's rights, temperance, pacifism, education, and prison reform, all of which were supported with religious zeal. Although it would appear difficult to see how either phrenology or free love could, of themselves, forward the emancipation of the slaves, even the partisans of these causes gave welcome support to the anti-slavery cause. From many diverse sources, both religious and lay, currents flowed which helped to broaden the course of the great anti-slavery stream which, in the Northern states, increased with each decade.

It was, however, with the appearance of William Lloyd Garrison that abolitionism became an organized force. As a young Massachusetts printer, Garrison joined, in 1829, with Benjamin Lundy in editing *The Genius of Universal Emancipation.* In 1830 he was imprisoned in Baltimore for libeling a slave carrier, after which, in 1831, he founded the most famous of abolitionist publications, *The Liberator.* While its circulation was small, it became nationally known following the Turner uprising in Virginia in the same year, an event with which at first the public incorrectly associated it. Garrison's views caused little stir at the outset in the North, but the emotions they aroused in the South attracted attention to his efforts and made him famous. A visit that he made to the United Kingdom in 1833 had the effect of confirming his position as the main abolitionist spokesman in the United States. Throughout the years that followed he continued to write and speak against slavery, together with other abolitionist personalities, such as Wendell Phillips and Theodore Weld. The cause that they made their own aroused some strong opposition in the North as well as in the South—an opposition that found expression, for example, in the murder in 1837 by a mob in Altona, Illinois, of another abolitionist editor, Elijah Lovejoy.[15] This event gave abolitionism its first martyr, linked the cause of abolition with that of the freedom of the press, and, in the words of John Quincy Adams, sent "a shock as of an earthquake throughout this continent."

Apart from reformers of various persuasions, the significance of the abolitionist movement soon came to be realized by ordinary citizens across the nation. Indeed, the struggle for abolition, linked as it was

15. Elijah Lovejoy was as strongly anti-Catholic as he was anti-slavery—a circumstance that is rarely recalled.

with the concept of a religious quest for a "New Jerusalem" that was to be built in the New World, gave a meaning to the lives of many humble folk which transcended the details of their daily existence. The faith they placed in the abolitionist cause was hardly different in quality to that which their forebears in Europe had placed at the service of the Church after Urban II had preached the First Crusade at Clermont in 1095. The slave-owners, however, finding themselves cast in the role previously reserved for the pagan followers of "Mahound," were less than enthusiastic. Their reactions varied from the peevishness of one Southern planter, who complained that everything seemed "to be against Cotton, not only the Abolitionists: but frost, snow, worms, and water," to that of Southern Congressmen, who proposed hanging certain abolitionists "as high as Haman" if they should venture South.

## Colonization

One solution that was proposed at this time was "colonization," or the sending of free blacks and emancipated slaves to Africa, from where either they or their forebears had come. A pioneer in this movement had been yet another Quaker, Paul Cuffe, a Negro captain and ship-owner from Massachusetts who, in 1815, had taken thirty-eight Negroes to Africa at his own expense. His action had aroused interest, and in 1816 the Virginia legislature had proposed that territory "on the coast of Africa, or at some other place not within any of the states or territorial governments of the United States" be acquired, in order that free or emancipated Negroes might be sent there. As a result, the American Society for Colonizing the Free People of Colour of the United States was established. Composed mainly of white Southerners, it obtained an appropriation from the federal government of $100,000, and, in 1819, was granted a charter giving it the right to set up a state for free Negroes in West Africa. The Society's agents first obtained land on Sherbro Island off the coast of Sierra Leone, and in 1820 eighty-eight Negroes were shipped there. Most of them died, however, and a second colonization attempt was made in 1821 at Cape Montserrado on the mainland. Despite mortality the colony survived, being accorded protection by President Monroe, in gratitude for which its first major village—later to become the capital of the Republic of Liberia—was named "Monrovia."

To begin with the colonization enterprise met with general approval in the United States, but this situation changed with the publication in 1832 of a pamphlet written by Garrison entitled *Thoughts on African Colonization*. In the pamphlet Garrison revealed that the main supporters of colonization were Southerners who upheld that the black man was basically inferior to the white, and that most American Negroes had no wish to be transported to a continent that few of them had ever seen. Until the organization of the New England Anti-Slavery Society in 1832, claimed one abolitionist source, "there was scarcely a rill of pity for the slave which was not diverted to the EXPATRIATION OF THE FREE."

Despite the rejection of colonization by the leading abolitionists, the concept, as well as the Colonization Society, remained alive. From time to time white Americans, both Northern and Southern, advocated colonization as a policy for solving the race problems of the United States. President Lincoln was later to show great interest in colonization, and it was not without significance that Harriet Beecher Stowe, in her famous novel *Uncle Tom's Cabin*, dispatched her leading Negro protagonists to Liberia. It has been argued that this conclusion was reassuring to her white readers, since it implied that emancipation of slaves in the United States need not necessarily mean they would remain in the country with equal status to whites.

Indeed, not only the concept of colonization remained alive. The Cape Montserrado settlement had joined together with other similar settlements in the vicinity to form, in 1839, the "Commonwealth of Liberia." Liberia declared its independence on July 26, 1847, adopting both a constitution and a flag that resembled those of the United States.

### Texas and Mexico

Meanwhile Southern pressure for the acquisition of more slave territory was rising. The immediate goal was Texas, the Mexican province which had seceded in 1836 after having been infiltrated by American frontiersmen from the Southern states, and which was soon to demand admission to the Union.[16] The Southerners who sought the annexation of Texas calculated—correctly, as it transpired—that the appeal of the expansionist doctrine of Manifest Destiny would outweigh any reservations about slavery that the North might harbor. Although they won the victory they sought with the admission of Texas to the Union in 1845, as a slave state, they paid a heavy price for it. The political controversy that raged throughout the North before the decision was reached engaged popular opinion to a far greater extent than had the Missouri controversy of 1820. Benjamin Lundy, the veteran Quaker abolitionist, who had visited Texas several times, wielded considerable influence over opinion by publishing in 1836, as the last political act of his career, a pamphlet providing data on the question, entitled in part *The War in Texas . . . Showing That This Contest Is . . . a . . . Crusade Against the Government, set on Foot by Slaveholders*. The fact that war with Mexico, and perhaps also with the United Kingdom, might ensue

16. Mexico had ended slavery in 1829, and the Southern settlers in the province of Texas had become concerned with the preservation of their slave property.

over the annexation of Texas added further fuel to the flames of debate. Further enlightenment on the question was given in Congress itself by John Quincy Adams, who, from 1836 on, helped to make the public conscious of the implications of the Texas controversy by his stalwart defense of the right of petition. In so doing he also thwarted Southern efforts to prevent abolitionists from making their views known, even in the North. The bitter attacks to which he was subjected in Congress signaled the growing division that was developing within the nation itself.

The annexation of Texas, which led Mexico to break off diplomatic relations with the United States, also led rapidly to war with Mexico. Although the Republic of Texas, during its nine years of independent existence, had not exercised effective jurisdiction over that region, the United States nevertheless assumed Texan claims for Mexican territory stretching down to the Rio Grande. When Mexico refused to concede the territory, and also declined to sell California to the United States, tension rose, a minor clash of arms took place, and war was declared. As we saw in Chapter 5, the United States emerged as victor from the war of 1846–1848, and, by the treaty of Guadeloupe Hidalgo of February 2, 1848, obtained both the territory it claimed, as well as the right to purchase California. California was acquired by the United States in return for a payment of $15 million, and the assumption of certain minor financial responsibilities.

The settlement, however, created at least as many problems as it solved. Even while the war was still in progress, abolitionists and the supporters of slavery were disputing whether Mexican territory should become slave or free. David Wilmot, a Pennsylvania Representative, attempted to introduce the "Wilmot Proviso" in the United States Congress to prevent slavery in the new territories—a proviso which the President, James K. Polk, described as "mischievous and foolish." Although the proviso was defeated, an angry internal debate was begun that soon became a dispute as to whether Congress had or had not the right to proscribe slavery in a specific territory. After a hot debate over abstract principles, the dispute, by 1848, had transformed itself into a controversy as to whether or not the Missouri Compromise line dividing slave from free territory, and running along latitude 36° 30′ North, was to be extended westward into the new territories. By August 1848, the Southern faction had reluctantly agreed that Oregon should become free territory. It was, however, an election year in 1848, and out of the heat of debate the Free Soil Party, a new political phenomenon, came into being. Although the "Free Soilers" were defeated, and Zachary Taylor, a Southerner who had been a general in the Mexican War, became President, the election campaign fanned yet higher the flames of the controversy that, cutting across previous party allegiances, was beginning to divide Northerners from Southerners.

President Taylor, although a Southerner, nevertheless began to follow a policy which tended toward excluding slavery from the new territories. As an atmosphere of impending crisis gathered, Southerners began to talk of secession, and emotions ran high. Henry Clay, a veteran politician, averted the threatened collision by proposing a compromise that was eventually agreed to. The measures comprising what subsequently became known as the Compromise of 1850 provided that California be admitted to the Union as a free state; that the new territorial governments of Utah and New Mexico decide for themselves, at the time of their admission to the Union as states, whether or not they would abolish slavery; that the western boundary of slave-holding Texas be fixed; that slave-trading in the nation's capital, Washington, D.C., be prohibited[17]; and that a stricter fugitive slave law be enacted.

### The North Star

The question of the territorial limits of slavery was temporarily settled, but the question of fugitive slaves continued to agitate opinion. Runaway slaves had, from the beginning, represented to slave-owners one of the hazards of their enterprise. George Washington, in the 1780s, had complained to his friends about escaping slaves. In 1793 the federal government had passed the Fugitive Slave Act in an attempt to safeguard, as far as possible, the right of slave-owners to their human "property" by providing for the return of runaway slaves. Bad treatment, love of liberty, or both—although also on occasion, no doubt, some less worthy motive, such as the commission of a crime—had been persuading slaves to attempt to abscond. From the first, escaping slaves received aid and comfort from abolitionists. In the earlier years this was not on an organized basis; the individual escapes were separately planned and executed. But as the anti-slavery movement grew, the so-called "Underground Railroad" began to function, systematically smuggling slaves along regular escape routes, which terminated in the free states of the North. After 1850, however, when the stronger provisions of a new Fugitive Slave Act made even the Northern states unsafe for escaped slaves, the escapees had to be taken on beyond the limits of the United States to Canada.

Slave-owners were by no means content to see the cash value represented by their slave "investment" disappear literally overnight, and

17. Abolitionists had long decried the practice of slave-trading even in the very capital of a nation that was supposedly founded upon the principles of freedom. The banning of slave-trading in Washington thus removed the basis of their argument while leaving the situation virtually unchanged, as slave-dealers, in order to comply with the law, had merely to move their marts from the northern to the southern bank of the Potomac River—a minor inconvenience.

frequently made efforts to recover the runaways from the North. Sometimes they were successful, but on other occasions, even when a runaway slave had been located and recaptured in some Northern city, popular opinion in the North effected the captive's release. Southern resentment ran high at what was regarded as a co-ordinated attempt to undermine the institution of slavery by systematic theft, just as Southern efforts to limit the expression of abolitionist views, even in the North itself, were resented by Northerners, who considered that such efforts posed a threat to the personal liberties Americans had won through struggle and sacrifice at the time of the Revolution. Thus the question of fugitive slaves, in one form or another, continued to exacerbate North-South relations even when no immediate territorial dispute was being argued.

Above all the fugitive slave question served to focus attention, in human terms, on the plight of the Negroes themselves. It also drew attention to individual Negro personalities. Among the runaway slaves there were some who were sufficiently outstanding to play an active role in the shaping of future events. The names of two of these in particular, are associated with this period—Harriet Tubman, and Frederick Douglass, whom we have mentioned. Both had escaped from plantations in Maryland—a state from which, because of its proximity to the North, escape was not as difficult as it was from the states of the Deep South. Both, too, were motivated by a strong love of freedom, combined with a strong sense of responsibility for the lot of their fellow Negro Americans.

Harriet Tubman, after early sufferings, had escaped on foot in 1849, traveling mostly by night, through forest and field, following the North Star that had guided so many other fugitives along the countless uncharted routes to freedom. When she found that she had arrived in Pennsylvania, and was at last in a free state, she stood on a hill and looked about her. She later described her feelings in the following words:

> When I found that I had crossed that line, I looked at my hands to see if I was the same person. There was such a glory over everything. The sun came like gold through the trees, and I felt like I was in heaven.

In the North, Harriet Tubman was "a stranger in a strange land," and so determined to help others that she knew to escape as she had done. Working as a domestic in Northern hotels, she saved enough money to return again to the South to lead other members of her family North out of bondage. In this way she became a regular "conductor" on the "Underground Railroad." Showing remarkable resourcefulness and bravery she returned South, it has been estimated, no less than nineteen times in the next decade, piloting hundreds of slaves to freedom. She became known by the name of "Moses," and Southerners, believing "Moses"

to be a man, offered large rewards—one of them, for example, for $40,000
—for "his" capture. But Harriet Tubman nevertheless continued her dangerous work without detection until the American Civil War ended the
necessity for it. Nor did she confine her anti-slavery work to the "Railroad" alone. On one occasion, in Troy, New York, learning that a fugitive
slave had been recaptured and was to be taken South, she raised and led
a large mob to free him, after which he was secretly sent on to Canada. As
a result of these and other exploits, Harriet Tubman's name became famous in anti-slavery circles on both sides of the Atlantic.

Frederick Douglass's escape preceded Harriet Tubman's by more than
a decade. Born in 1817 or 1818, his original name was Frederick Bailey.
He, too, had known ill usage and all the attendant humiliations and
circumstances of the slave condition. Combining sensitivity and imagination with a strong practical sense, he learned to read and write in
Baltimore, in the shipyards of which he worked as a caulker. In 1838
he escaped to New York, traveling by train and carrying borrowed papers
which identified him as a free Negro sailor—relying, in doing so, on the
"kind feeling that prevailed in Baltimore and other seaports at the time
towards 'those who go down to the sea in ships.' 'Free trade and sailor's
rights' expressed the feeling of the country just then." He described his
experience in the following words:

> I was well on the way to Havre de Grace before the conductor came into the
> Negro car to collect tickets and examine the papers of his black passengers. This was
> a critical moment in the drama. My whole future depended upon the decision of this
> conductor. Agitated I was while this ceremony was proceeding, but still, externally
> at least, I was apparently calm and self-possessed. . . . He was somewhat harsh in
> tone and peremptory in manner until he reached me, when, strangely enough . . . his
> whole manner changed. . . . He said to me in a friendly contrast with that observed
> towards the others, "I suppose you have got your free papers? . . . you have something
> to show that you are a free man, have you not?" "Yes sir," I answered; "I have a paper
> with the American eagle on it, that will carry me round the world. . . ." The merest
> glance at the paper satisfied him, and he took my fare and went on about his business.

Arriving safely in New York, Douglass eventually made contact with
abolitionists. They advised him to move on to Massachusetts, where he
settled and engaged in various odd jobs. In 1841 he addressed a convention of the Massachusetts Anti-Slavery Society. The society was in
need of speakers who could tell at first hand what it felt like to be a slave
and they offered him a job. As a speaker and editor Douglass was so
effective that he quickly became the leading Negro figure in the anti-
slavery struggle. As the quality of his personality became apparent both
to himself and to others, there were those abolitionists who sought to
limit his rapid development so that it might conform to their own ideas
of what his "place" in society should be. "Better have a little of the

plantation speech than not," one of these friends told him, "it is not best that you seem too learned."

Douglass nevertheless went on to become the most prominent American Negro personality of the nineteenth century. In an age in which slave-holders were assiduously propagating the myth of the inferiority of the black man, Douglass demonstrated in his person the falsity of the myth. Politically, also, he played a role that was of importance in the development of the American constitutional tradition. It came about in this way: Garrison, and many of his followers, held that the American Constitution was "a covenant with death and an agreement with hell," and called for the dissolution of the union with the South. But Douglass disagreed. The Constitution, he said, was ambiguous. "If we adopt the preamble, with Liberty and Justice, we must repudiate the enacting clauses, with Kidnapping and Slaveholding."[18] Consequently, he argued, an oath to support the enacting clauses, as distinct from the preamble, was an oath to perform "that which God has made impossible." Thus, whereas Garrison's slogan became "no union with slave-holders," Douglass, who at first also subscribed to this position, after "careful reconsideration" came to the conclusion that an abolitionist, such as himself, could in all good faith support the Constitution. For this the Garrisonians impugned his motives. Douglass's decision to found his own publication— symbolically to be named *The North Star*—did nothing to heal the rift, even though, to avoid competing with Garrison's *Liberator*, Douglass moved from New England to Rochester, New York. (Among other things, this resulted in Rochester becoming a stop on one of the lines of the Underground Railroad.)

After 1850 the division between North and South grew greater as abolitionist sentiment gained ground in the North, and as resentment hardened in the South. In the North the abolitionist lobby became more powerful as its different currents converged into one broad stream. The Transcendentalist romantics of New England, evangelical Protestants of many sects, and rationalists of every stamp were all united by the common denominator of adherence to egalitarianism. Whether or not they, as individuals, had liking or sympathy for Negroes, all agreed that the institution of slavery must go. Northern politicians, too, sensitive as always to public opinion, began to reflect that the abolition of slavery would mean increased political power for themselves, since the constitutional compromise which apportioned representation to Southern politicians not only on the basis of their voters, but also on that of three-fifths of the slave population, would no longer apply. Other Northerners were also meditating upon the implications of the extension of slavery to the

18. Article IV, Section 2, of the Constitution provided for the return of fugitive slaves.

new territories in the West. Not only would this mean that the rapid development associated with free labor would not take place in these territories, it would also mean that the ethnic composition of these territories would contain a much higher proportion of Negroes. As one Northern newspaper was to express it on the eve of the Civil War:

> Is it not notorious that the existence of Slavery in a State tends to keep and to drive the white race out of it, both by closing up a thousand avenues to profitable employment which might otherwise successively spring into existence, and by affixing to all manual labor a certain badge of degradation? . . . Could anything be more in the interest of the men of the white Caucasian race, than to secure to them the quiet possession of the new Territories, and thus to put an end to that dogging of their steps by gangs of negro slaves by which they have been pursued and driven from one new State to another?[19]

Public opinion in the North crystallized with the publication in 1852 of *Uncle Tom's Cabin,* by a New England author, Harriet Beecher Stowe. Subtitled *Life Among the Lowly,* the story told the tale of the vicissitudes of fortune suffered by a Negro slave, Uncle Tom, and his fellows. Imbued with Christian and egalitarian sentiments, the book was a powerful propaganda tract that had an immediate and phenomenal success. The first American novel to sell over a million copies, it gained renown for Harriet Beecher Stowe not only in the United States, but also in Britain, France, Germany, and Russia. The book, however, caused great bitterness in the Southern states. One Southern reader cut off a slave's ear and sent it through the mail to Mrs. Stowe. A Southern editor asked a reviewer to write a review of the book "as hot as hell fire, blasting and searing the reputation of the vile wretch in petticoats who could write such a volume." The reviewer subsequently wrote, in part,

> Fiction is its form and falsehood is its end. . . . The fundamental position, then, of these dangerous and dirty little volumes is a deadly blow to all the interests and duties of humanity, and is utterly impotent to show any inherent vice in the institution of slavery which does not appertain to all other existing institutions whatsoever.[20]

Years later, during the American Civil War, testimony to the effect of the book upon the course of events in the United States was paid, albeit no doubt half-jokingly, by President Abraham Lincoln. When Harriet Beecher Stowe was presented to him, he took her hands and said, "So this is the little lady who made this big war." His statement was, however, half true. In effect, through her book she helped to focus many previously unspoken Northern feelings and misgivings about slavery, creating thereby a common consciousness of an opinion shared. *Uncle Tom's Cabin* created and perpetuated a potent myth, while at the same time its reception signaled that an irreversible change had

---

19. New York *Daily Tribune,* December 17, 1860.
20. George Frederick Holmes, *Southern Literary Messenger,* December, 1852.

occurred in the thermodynamic evolution then taking place within the American body politic.

Another sign of increasing entropy was the growing militancy of the South. This took the form of renewed demands for more territory not only in the West, but also to the South, in Cuba. In 1848 Spain had refused an American offer to purchase Cuba for $100 million. Subsequently, in 1850 and 1851, two unsuccessful filibustering expeditions were launched against Cuba from the American mainland.[21] After Spain had rejected a further offer, it seemed for a time that a Spanish-American war might develop over the question. As the American Secretary of State, William R. Marcy, wished to sound out possible British and French reactions to an American attack upon Cuba, representatives of the three countries met in Belgium in 1854 for secret discussions. They drew up what became known as the Ostend Declaration, which recommended that the United States should offer Spain $120 million for Cuba, and that if this offer were rejected, the United States should then seize Cuba by force. But the document, intended to be secret, was published at the insistence of the United States opposition. The resulting outcry from the Free Soil Party demonstrated to the United States administration that it did not have sufficient support to wage a war against Cuba for the benefit of Southern slave-holders. The proposal was therefore dropped.

## The Kansas-Nebraska Act

Meanwhile, however, the 1850 Compromise concerning the Western territories had broken down. It was a time when technology had already begun its quick-paced evolution, and the railroad system was threading its way westward, hastening the pace of settlement as it did so. The United States Congress was called upon to support the development of a transcontinental railroad, and there was debate as to the course the railroad should take. In order, it would appear, to secure the interests of Chicago as a terminus, as well as to advance his political career, Senator Stephen A. Douglas of Illinois proposed legislation that would organize the separate territories of Kansas and Nebraska, the two being divided by the 40th parallel. His purpose, in part, was apparently to prevent the railroad from running through the part of Kansas that was Southern-controlled. However, in order to carry the Southerners with him, he also proposed that at the same time the Missouri Compromise should be repealed. The residents of Kansas and Nebraska would then decide for themselves as to whether or not their future states would be slave or free.

21. Pro-slavery groups in the United States, without official government backing, sought to acquire Cuba to offset growing anti-slavery influence in the U.S. Senate.

No express provision was made, however, as to the moment at which this important decision was to be taken. Douglas anticipated that his proposal would raise what he called "one hell of a storm," but its dimensions were larger than he had calculated. Northern feeling against the measure was particularly strong, and Douglas stated that he could have traveled from Boston to Chicago by the light of his burning effigies. Ultimately, the Kansas-Nebraska Act of 1854 was adopted with Southern support, but by a narrow margin. The political conflict over this act was so intense, however, that both parties of the day—the Democrats in office, and the Whigs in opposition—were split, largely along lines of North-South allegiance. At the same time the Republican Party, dedicated to opposing the extension of slavery, came into existence, absorbing into its ranks not only the "Free Soilers," but also many Northern Whigs and some Northern Democrats.

The Kansas-Nebraska Act, which precipitated this important political change, also led to events in Kansas itself. The slave-holders there had little interest in Nebraska, which lay too far to the North for their purposes, but intended to gain Kansas as a slave state, even though it lay to the north of the old Missouri Compromise line. While the majority of the settlers moving into the territory were from the North, some being sent in by the New England Emigrant Aid Society, others also came. So-called "border ruffians" from Missouri began to raid the homesteads of known anti-slavery settlers, and came pouring across the border in 1855 to elect a pro-slavery legislature by casting over 6,000 votes, although there were only slightly more than 2,000 registered voters. Repressive legislation against opponents of slavery was then enacted, and would-be dissidents found themselves menaced, if not attacked, by groups armed with pistols and bowie knives. But the majority of the settlers in the territory were anti-slavery, and later in the same year they met together in Topeka, Kansas, to draw up their own constitution, under the terms of which they elected their own legislature and Governor in 1856. Kansas now had two separate governments.

As might be expected, disorders increased in Kansas. Both Missourians and "free staters" armed themselves. The Missourians raided the town of Lawrence, burning down buildings and attacking "free staters" living there. The following day pro-slavery violence erupted in the United States Senate itself. Charles Sumner, a Massachusetts Senator, had been criticizing the actions of the partisans of the slavery cause in Kansas, singling out one of its Senate defenders, Andrew P. Butler of South Carolina, who, he said, 'with incoherent phrases, discharged the loose expectoration of his speech." As he sat at his desk in the Senate, Sumner was attacked by Butler's nephew, Preston Brooks, who beat him over the head with a cane until it broke, injuring him so badly that he remained an invalid for years, and, indeed, never fully recovered from the assault. The attack on Lawrence, followed by the assault in the Senate, further divided the nation along regional lines, with Southern and Northern press responding accordingly. The North had expected that it could win its way in the new territories by legal methods instead of force. One Kansas settler, however, named John Brown, had already sensed that the slavery partisans intended to gain their cause by violence, and had judged that they could only be discouraged by counterviolence.

John Brown had been born in Connecticut in 1800. His family had been strongly religious, with the direct wholeheartedness of simple pioneer folk who had had little time for theological subtleties. As a child he had met a slave boy, had seen him mistreated, and had come to the conclusion that slavery was evil. Grown-up, he worked first as a tanner, and then as a sheep farmer, raising a family but being denied great financial success, in part because of his moral rectitude. Frederick Douglass, who visited him in 1847, commented: "I never felt myself in the presence of a stronger religious influence than while in this man's house." It was earlier, in 1839, that Brown had taken the decision which shaped his life, and which, in due course, was also to affect the lives of many others. A Negro preacher named Fayette had visited him, and had related a story of injustice. John Brown then told his family of his purpose to wage active war on slavery, and bound his family in secret compact to work for abolition, calling down God's blessing on the enterprise as he did so.

In 1854 five of Brown's sons had gone to Kansas as free-state settlers, making part of their journey there by Missouri river steamer. Brown's eldest son wrote to his father that their fellow passengers had been

mostly men from the South bound for Kansas . . . their drinking, profanity, and display of revolvers and bowie-knives—openly worn as an essential part of their make-up—clearly showed the class to which they belonged, and that their mission was to aid in establishing slavery in Kansas. A box of fruit trees and grape-vines which my brother Jason had brought from Ohio, our plough, and the few agricultural implements we had on the deck of that steamer looked lonesome; for these were all we could see which were adapted to the occupation of peace.

Upon arrival, the Brown brothers began to farm, but as disorder and warfare spread, they wrote to their father to send them arms, so that they could defend themselves and their neighbors. Instead of sending arms, however, John Brown brought them himself, arriving in October, 1855. The following year the Browns were deeply involved in local developments. Then, when a group of nearby "border ruffians" began a terrorist campaign against the Browns and their neighbors,

Brown and his sons, with a few others, "condemned" them to death, seized them by night, and, taking them into the woods, hacked them to death with broadswords. This deed, known as the "Massacre of Potta-watomie," aroused Kansas. Some have since held that John Brown's action resulted in Kansas becoming a free state, whereas others have maintained that it brought on a civil war there.

John Brown was proclaimed an outlaw, after which he withdrew to the forests and organized a band of thirty-five followers, who lived by the terms of a covenant, pledging themselves to be of good conduct and to serve the free-state cause. In the hostilities which followed, Brown's men took part in military operations. When a new Governor was appointed, and attempted to restore peace, Brown and his sons were persuaded to leave the state, although Brown later returned for a time to fight again when the course of events was not proceeding entirely favorably for the free-state cause.

In the 1856 elections, in which the slavery issue received further publicity, the faction-ridden Democratic party nevertheless succeeded in having its candidate, James Buchanan, elected with a clear majority over his principal opponent, the Republican candidate, a soldier and explorer named John C. Frémont. For a time, however, according to press reports from the South, at least some of the slaves believed that Frémont might be coming to deliver them from bondage. In Memphis, Tennessee, to cite only a single example, one slave cook told her mistress, "When Frémont's elected, you'll have to sling them pots yourself." Buchanan was not only to disappoint the Memphis cook, but also many anti-slavery Northerners. Although from Pennsylvania, he tended to defend Southern interests. The anti-slavery tide was, nevertheless, rising fast, and his four-year administration was to prove to be one in which Southerners and their Northern sympathizers were to be placed increasingly on the defensive.

### The Dred Scott Case

Hardly had Buchanan taken office, when the controversial Dred Scott decision was handed down by the United States Supreme Court in March, 1857. Dred Scott was a fugitive slave who, after spending time in the North, had returned to the border state of Missouri, where he presented a suit for his freedom on the grounds that his stay in the North had made him free. The case was evidently a test concerning the territorial status of slavery. The decision handed down asserted, first, that since Negroes had been viewed as inferior at the time the Constitution was adopted, the Founding Fathers had not intended them to become American citizens; second, any mention of the Missouri Compromise, which had drawn a line between slave and free territory, did not apply, as the Missouri Compromise was unconstitutional; third, the Supreme Court had no jurisdiction in the Dred Scott case, which must be decided by Missouri laws, since that was the state to which Scott had returned.

Buchanan had personally intervened with some of the Supreme Court justices, even while the case was still pending, to ensure a decision satisfactory to the South. The decision, consequently—and in particular that section of it which ruled the Missouri Compromise to be unconstitutional —came as a direct challenge to the Republican Party, which had dedicated itself to opposing the extension of slavery to the Western territories. If accepted, the decision, in effect, weakened resistance to the extension of slavery anywhere in the United States. As it was, it had the effect of making the question of the extension of slavery the central issue of the next presidential election, which fell due in 1860.

Before the nation had time to reflect upon abstract principles, however, its attention was caught by further events in Kansas. The pro-slavery faction in that state had obliged the Governor, who had pressed for the repeal of certain anti-democratic statutes, to fly for his life. His successor was not able to prevent the slavery men from holding a rigged election, and from adopting a state constitution which guaranteed slavery. This they did at Lecompton, Kansas, in October, 1857. The Governor recommended that the Lecompton constitution be submitted to the Kansas electorate, but President Buchanan, instead, chose to admit Kansas to the Union under that constitution. The Governor thereupon resigned, and the Democratic Party was riven by further internal disputes. In 1858 the United States Congress finally passed an act which provided that Kansas would be admitted to the Union forthwith if the state's electorate would accept the Lecompton constitution, but that if they rejected it, territorial status would be continued. The Kansans decisively rejected the Lecompton constitution by seven to one. Subsequently, in 1861, after the Civil War had begun, Kansas was to enter the Union as a free state.

### A Man "Built for Times of Trouble"

While the abolitionists labored at realizing their dream by alchemy, the chemistry of politics continued to operate. In 1858 the Republican Party of Illinois considered a cavernous-looking lawyer named Abraham Lincoln as their Senatorial candidate. Much more was to be heard of him. Cut from the same cloth as the then relatively little-known John Brown, although with different quirks of character, he did not at first impress his contemporaries. Like Brown he was hardened by experience, and largely self-educated, but he had a worldly tolerance of men and manners that was broader than Brown's. The merciful spirit of the New Testament was closer to his own than John Brown's Old Testament zeal,[22] yet, when it came to ultimate principle, the same quality of granite had, in the last resort, gone into the making of them both.

If Lincoln's name was known to relatively few before 1858, so too, apart from the Kansas episode, was John Brown's before 1859. In that year, however, Brown undertook a deed so daring that it stunned friend and foe alike. Leading a small group of men, he began in insurrection in Virginia with the intention of seizing a federal arsenal and then ending slavery by force of arms. He and others were captured, however, virtually at the outset. Frederick Douglass later wrote:

> On the evening when the news came that John Brown had taken and was then holding the town of Harper's Ferry, it so happened that I was speaking to a large audience in National Hall, Philadelphia. The announcement came upon us with the startling effect of an earthquake. It was something to make the boldest hold his breath.[23]

For many years John Brown had meditated upon God's purpose for him in life, and he had become convinced that the Allegheny Mountains, which stretch from Maine to Georgia, parallel to the eastern seacoast of the United States, were destined to serve the overthrow of slavery in America. Thomas Wentworth Higginson, a contemporary, later commented, "I shall never forget the quiet way in which he once told me that 'God had established the Allegheny Mountains from the foundation of the world that they might one day be a refuge for fugitive slaves.'" To Douglass he said even more:

> These mountains are the basis of my plan. God has given the strength of the hills to freedom; they were placed here for the emancipation of the Negro race; they are full of natural forts, where one man for defense will be equal to a hundred for attack; they are also full of good hiding-places, where large numbers of brave men could be concealed, and baffle and elude pursuit for a long time. I know these mountains well, and could take a body of men into them and keep them there despite all efforts of Virginia to dislodge them. The true object to be sought is first of all to destroy the money value of slavery property; and that can only be done by rendering such property insecure.[24]

Specifically, Brown planned to seize Harper's Ferry, not to hold it long, but long enough to carry off the contents of the arsenal there to the Blue Ridge Mountains to be distributed to white-officered guerrilla bands, composed mainly of escaped slaves. The guerrilla campaign was intended slowly to gather strength so that, appearing at the outset as little more than a local phenomenon, it would eventually develop until organized warfare was being waged all the way from Virginia, through Tennessee and North Carolina, to the swamps of South Carolina. In this

22. Lincoln was versed in the New Testament; Brown had pored over the Old.
23. *Life and Times of Frederick Douglass.*
24. *Ibid.*

way slavery was to be drained of its strength until the forcible efforts of the slaves themselves would discourage slave-owners from investing any more money in such an uncertain form of property as human beings.

"In person," wrote Douglass, John Brown "was lean, strong, and sinewy, of the best New England mould, built for times of trouble and fitted to grapple with the flintiest hardships." To carry out his purpose, Brown and his associates rented a farm near Harper's Ferry, and passed as farmers until they had collected the arms and recruits that they needed. Then, on October 16, 1859, the group of about twenty-two men, the majority white, and six or seven black, took up their arms and left the farm to begin their personal attack upon slavery.[25] Brown had earlier asked Douglass to accompany him, saying, "When I strike the bees will begin to swarm, and I shall want you to help hive them." Douglass, however, later confessed, "My discretion or my cowardice made me proof against the dear old man's eloquence—perhaps it was something of both which determined my course." Harriet Tubman, too, was approached, and she was willing to join him, but was prevented by sickness.

On the night of October 16, the abolitionists seized the arsenal, and took hostages, including a Colonel Lewis Washington, a local slave-owner, and a relative of George Washington, the first President of the United States. A number of slaves having been armed, John Brown made the engine-house in the arsenal his headquarters. At first, not realizing as yet the relatively small dimensions of the insurgent force, the local white populace was thrown into a state of panic. But delays in bringing up by wagon the quantity of arms and ammunition kept at the farm gave the local whites and the Virginia authorities time to mobilize their forces. Soon Brown and the others were surrounded, and an attack was made upon his engine-house fortress. In the fighting Brown was wounded, and ten of his followers, including two of his own sons, killed. Another of his sons, and others, escaped, but Brown himself and six others were captured.

Knowing that Brown had received money and arms from eminent Northerners, the reaction of the Southern states was of the utmost fury. At first prominent Northerners, even some famous for their abolitionist sentiment, denounced Brown's action. Some of his close friends and associates went into hiding for fear of arrest. Douglass, for example, felt obliged to leave the country and to visit the United Kingdom—where he found the British almost as interested in the Harper's Ferry raid as were the Americans. When Brown was brought to trial by the state of Virginia, however, and his own words became known, Northern sympathy set

25. In the famous song, John Brown captured Harper's Ferry "with his 19 men so true." W. E. B. Du Bois writes, "The number of those who took part in the Harper's Ferry raid is not known. Perhaps, including active slave helpers, there were about fifty. Seventeen Negroes, reported as probably killed, are wholly unknown, and those slaves who helped and escaped are also unknown. This leaves the 22 men usually regarded as making the raid. . . . Six or seven of the twenty-two were Negroes." (*John Brown*, 1962 edition, pp. 279–280.)

strongly in his favor. While in prison he came to understand the new and quasi-Socratic role he was now in a position to play, for, rejecting suggestions that he attempt to save his life, he said, "I think I cannot now better serve the cause I love so much than to die for it; and in my death I may do more than in my life." He was indeed, with his comrades, condemned to death, and hanged on December 2, 1859. In the weeks before his death he spoke and wrote many moving words, but among the most penetrating were those he uttered to his captors when being interrogated after his arrest. "You may dispose of me very easily," he said, "—I am nearly disposed of already[26]—but this question is still to be settled; this Negro question, I mean; the end of that is not yet."

Speaking many years later in 1882, Frederick Douglass commented, concerning the influence of the Harper's Ferry episode upon subsequent events, "When John Brown stretched forth his arm the sky was cleared— the armed hosts of freedom stood face to face over the chasm of a broken Union, and the clash of arms was at hand."

Less than two years after his death, in the spring of 1861, the Boston Light Infantry composed a marching song, set to an old camp-meeting tune called "Say, Brother Will You Meet Us." The chorus ran:

> John Brown's body lies a-mouldering in the grave,
> But his soul goes marching on.

It was a song that was to be sung not only by Northerners in the Civil War which began that year,[27] but, for the sake of its inherent inspirational quality, by people in countries around the world—even though singers often had but the faintest conception of who John Brown was, or why he had died. But, even to the most alien, that John Brown's death had been of historic significance was manifest.

The last written words of John Brown were the following:

> I, John Brown, am quite certain that the crimes of this guilty land will never be purged away but with blood. I had, as I now think vainly, flattered myself that without very much bloodshed that it might be done.

It was true that blood was to be shed, and Thoreau's comment that, after his execution, old John Brown "became more alive than he ever was," was also true.

### The Election of 1860

After Brown's death the nation, fully engaged at last in the political debate over slavery that many had hitherto striven to avoid, began to prepare for the elections that were to be held in November, 1860. The party in power, the Democrats, with supporters in both North and South,

---

26. He had been wounded in the storming of the engine-house by his captors.
27. They called it, simply, "The John Brown Song."

would be challenged by the anti-slavery Republican Party, to which Free Soil Party members had also now rallied. In April, 1860, the Democrats met in convention in Charleston, South Carolina, to choose a presidential candidate. Northern Democrats felt that Senator Douglas, who supported the doctrine of "popular sovereignty" in the Western territories—a doctrine which held that the populations of those territories should pronounce themselves for or against slavery as they best saw fit—was the only candidate who could hope to defeat the Republicans at the polls. But when Douglas refused to promise federal protection for slavery in the territories, the convention adjourned without reaching a decision. The same difficulties arose when it convened once more at Baltimore in June, with the result that the party split in two. The Northerners chose Douglas, and the Southerners their own candidate, John C. Breckinridge of Kentucky. Meanwhile, meeting in Chicago in May, the Republican Party had chosen Abraham Lincoln as their candidate. Southerners warned that if Lincoln were to be elected, the Southern states would secede.

Lincoln had already found himself in opposition to Douglas in the 1858 Senatorial election in Illinois. Although on that occasion Douglas had won, the debates they had held during the election campaign had gone far to clarify the differences between the two men. The debates were reprinted and widely distributed, to be pondered over throughout the nation.

Could the Union continue to contain both slave and free states? "Let each State mind its own business and let its neighbors alone!" said Douglas. "If we will stand by that principle, then Mr. Lincoln will find that this republic can exist forever divided into free and slave States." Lincoln disagreed. "A house divided against itself cannot stand," he said. "I believe this government cannot endure, permanently half slave and half free. . . . I do not expect the house to fall—but I do expect it will cease to be divided. It will become all one thing or all the other."

On the meaning of the Declaration of Independence, too, they were opposed. Douglas held that the signers of the Declaration, when they declared all men to have been created equal, "referred to the white race alone, and not to the African." Lincoln, for his part, stated, "I believe the entire records of the world, from the date of the Declaration of Independence up to within three years ago, may be searched in vain for one single affirmation, from one single man, that the Negro was not included in the Declaration of Independence." On the racial issue thus raised, Douglas expressed himself by saying, "When the struggle is between the white man and the Negro, I am for the white man; when it is between the Negro and the crocodile, I am for the Negro." He appears to have said still more, for on one occasion Lincoln told his hearers, "Douglas will have it that I want a Negro wife. He can never be brought to understand that there is any middle ground on this subject. I have lived until my fiftieth year, and have never had a Negro woman either for a slave or a wife, and I think I can live fifty centuries, for that matter, without having had one for either."

Thus Douglas believed that the Union was meant for free white men, and that what he called the "inferior races"—Negro, American Indian, and Chinese—should be denied citizenship. Lincoln held that the Declaration of Independence meant what it said, that "all men are created equal." The struggle between this principle and the opposing one he saw as an eternal one. "The one is the common right of humanity," he said, "and the other the divine right of kings. It is the same . . . spirit that says, 'You work and toil and earn bread, and I'll eat it.' No matter in what shape it comes, whether from the mouth of a king who seeks to bestride the people of his own nation and live by the fruit of their labor, or from one race of men as an apology for enslaving another race, it is the same tyrannical principle."

Apart from differences of abstract principle, immediate decisions facing the Union held the attention of the debaters. Lincoln's most telling point was gained by a shrewd question that he put to Douglas: "Can the people of a United States Territory, in any lawful way, against the wish of any citizen of the United States, exclude slavery from its limits prior to the formation of a State Constitution?" The question placed Douglas on the horns of a dilemma. If he were to answer "No," he would seem to sanction the extension of slavery, and so lose support throughout the North. If he were to answer "Yes," he would alienate his Southern supporters. In effect he answered "Yes," and, as a result, lost not only much Southern support, but also in consequence the presidency. Abraham Lincoln was inaugurated as President of the United States on March 4, 1861.

### Secession

As soon as the election results became known, Southern spokesmen began to speak of secession. An Atlanta newspaper, entitled *The Confederacy*, announced, for example, that "the South will never submit to such humiliation and degradation as the inauguration of Abraham Lincoln." In Alabama the slogan was proclaimed that "Resistance to Lincoln is Obedience to God!" In the weeks that followed the U.S. government was made aware by unmistakable signs that the split in the nation had become indeed a reality. Despite the fact that Lincoln had stated—and was to restate at his inauguration—that he had "no purpose, directly or indirectly, to interfere with the institution of slavery in the States where it exists," and that he upheld the practice of returning runaway slaves to their owners, most of the slave-holding states had determined to leave the Union. The first to go was South Carolina, which, on December 20,

1860, voted to secede from the Union with effect from December 24. Mississippi, Florida, Alabama, Georgia, and Louisiana followed in January, and Texas in February, 1861. Senator John J. Crittenden of Kentucky had attempted to hold the Union together with compromise proposals, put forward in December, but these proved unacceptable.

The spirit of the South had been expressed earlier by a Mr. Ireson of Georgia, who had told Northern peacemakers that if the people of the South were given a blank sheet of paper upon which to write their own terms, they would not remain in the Union. They had come to hate everything which had the prefix "Free"—free soil, free states, free territories, free schools, free speech, and freedom generally, and they would have no more such prefixes. Nevertheless, the key state of Virginia had also made an attempt to maintain the peace by adjusting what were described as "the present unhappy controversies" by having all states send commissioners to Washington on February 4, 1861. Twenty-one states responded, but failed to achieve a compromise. Indeed, on that very day some of the seceding states met in convention at Montgomery, Alabama, to found a Confederacy. At the convention North Carolina pleaded for conciliation, but this effort also failed. Patience, North and South, was exhausted, and the nation was driving toward civil war. Southern Senators and Congressmen were bidding farewell to Washington, while Southern officers were resigning their commissions, and federal office-holders their posts. As the whirlwind gathered, Lincoln, while admitting the continued existence of slavery, stood firm on a single point—there would be no extension of slavery to the new territories in the West. It now needed only a spark to begin the conflagration.

The spark was provided by the dispute between the federal government and the state of South Carolina over the possession of Fort Sumter, which stood on a small island at the entrance to the Charleston harbor. The Confederacy demanded the evacuation of the fort, eventually issuing an ultimatum that was refused. Local Southern forces consequently began a bombardment of the fort on April 12, 1861. The surrender which soon followed, was, however, of minor significance. For the guns which fired on Fort Sumter announced the opening of the American Civil War.

### The Civil War

Three days after the firing on Fort Sumter, Virginia seceded. Arkansas and North Carolina followed in May, and Tennessee in June. In Missouri secession was prevented until the arrival of Confederate troops, after which, in October, 1861, representatives were sent from the state to the Confederate Congress. Kentucky, Maryland, and Delaware, all slave-holding states, remained in the Union, although after Confederate troops seized a part of Kentucky, representatives from this state were also sent to the Confederate Congress. The Congress itself, which in February, 1861, had chosen Jefferson Davis of Mississippi as its provisional president, adopted a permanent constitution in March. The Congress also abolished the African slave trade, and moved to Richmond, Virginia, which was to be the Confederate capital until its fall in the last days of the Civil War.

Meanwhile Lincoln, after taking office, had issued a call for troops, and had ordered a naval blockade of Southern ports. Embarrassment was caused to the North, however, by the attitude of the United Kingdom, which, while not recognizing the Confederacy as independent, nevertheless declared British neutrality, thereby extending recognition to the Confederacy as a belligerent power. In effect, throughout the war British governmental and financial circles tended to sympathize with the Confederacy, while the British working class tended to sympathize with the North. The France of Napoleon III, for its part, attempted to profit from United States preoccupation with the Civil War by establishing the Maximilian monarchy in Mexico in 1863—a venture which, however, came to a disastrous conclusion in 1867. Imperial Russia, meanwhile, which freed its own serfs in 1861, demonstrated its diplomatic sympathy with the North.

The eventual outcome of the Civil War, which lasted from April 14, 1861, to April 14, 1865, could not be in doubt once the two opposing forces became fully engaged. In numbers alone the North, in April, 1861, had a population of about 22 million persons living in the twenty-three states which adhered to the Union at that time, whereas only about 9 million lived in the seceding states. In industrial organization, output, and potential, the North was clearly superior to the South. The problem was, however, to mobilize Northern sentiment and resources, and, at the same time, to induce Northern generals to take the offensive—processes which took time, and which permitted the South meanwhile to gain some victories. Eventually, however, the North placed itself upon a war footing, and in such great engagements as Shiloh and Gettysburg drained the South of its strength and exposed its weaknesses. The Confederate capital of Richmond fell to the Union forces on April 3, 1865. After General Lee had surrendered at Appomattox, in Virginia, on April 9, the war was ended by proclamation on April 14, 1865—even though it was several weeks later before all the Southern forces yielded.

The waging of the Civil War provides, indeed, a theme in itself, representing among other things a transformation in methods of warfare as a result of developments in industrial technology. It was during the Civil War that the ironclad battleship proved its indisputable superiority, that mass production methods were first applied to the manufacture of arms, and that the telegraph was used by armies at war to send and to receive information and instructions. Because of these and other innovations, the Civil War prefigured the great conflicts of the twentieth century. That it was also concerned with the freedom of black men provided it with a dimension which was to make it akin to the conflicts and controversies of the future, rather than to those of the past.

The war had been understood by all, at the outset, to have broken out over the question of slavery. There were, however, many in the North who felt that, apart from questions of abstract principle, the status of the Negro provided an insufficient reason for white men of the same nation to kill one another. This sentiment, indeed, was to find its apogee in the New York Draft Riots of July, 1863. In these protests, which occurred barely two weeks after the battle of Gettysburg had been fought, white mobs opposing military conscription seized control of New York for three days, drove out the Negro population, after killing about thirty Negroes, and destroyed property.

Aware from the outset of the existence of anti-Negro, if not pro-South, sentiment in the North, the federal government at an early stage, with the intention of preserving unity during the coming conflict, announced that the cause for which the war was being waged was that of the preservation of the Union, rather than of the abolition of slavery. In the spring of 1861 Secretary of State Seward advised Lincoln to "change the question before the public from one upon slavery or about slavery for a question upon union or disunion, in other words, from what would be regarded as a party question, to one of patriotism, or union." Lincoln appears to have had the intention of so doing in any event. Eighteen months later, writing to Horace Greeley, editor of the New York *Tribune,* Lincoln expressed himself on the subject in unmistakable terms:

> My paramount object in this struggle is to save the Union, and is not either to save or to destroy slavery. If I could save the Union without freeing *any* slave I would do it, and if I could save it by freeing *all* the slaves, I would do it; and if I could save it by freeing some and leaving others alone I would also do that. What I do about slavery, and the colored race, I do because I believe it helps to save the Union; and what I forbear, I forbear because I do *not* believe it would help to save the Union.

Lincoln's own feelings were, however, indisputably anti-slavery. Writing on April 4, 1864, he publicly declared, "I am naturally anti-slavery. If slavery is not wrong, nothing is wrong. I can not remember when I did not so think, and feel." Yet, on the other hand, Frederick Douglass had been hurt when Lincoln, no doubt in a dispirited moment, had remarked to him privately that the Negro "was the cause of the war"—a remark that Douglass felt to be unjust, since Negroes could hardly be blamed for their own enslavement. Earlier, too, Lincoln had spoken of the problems that would arise from striking the shackles from the slaves. "What next?" he had asked an Illinois crowd on October 3, 1854. "Free them, and make them politically and socially our equals? My own feelings will not admit of this, and if mine would, we well know that those of the great mass of white people will not. Whether this feeling accords with justice and sound judgment, is not the sole question, if indeed, it is any part of it. A universal feeling, whether well or ill-founded, can not be safely disregarded."

These words had, of course, been spoken in a time of peace, before Harper's Ferry had brought opinions and emotions on slavery into sharp focus. Yet they represented, nevertheless, one aspect of Lincoln's attitude. As Frederick Douglass, speaking years later in 1876, at the unveiling of a monument in memory of Lincoln, was, together with high praise, also to say, "He was pre-eminently the white man's President, entirely devoted to the welfare of white men. The race to which we belong were not the special objects of his consideration. You [my white fellow citizens] are the children of Abraham Lincoln. We are at best only his step-children."

The same ambiguity that characterized Lincoln's attitude to the Negro was noticeable throughout the North both before, during, and after the Civil War. As Lincoln himself told some anti-slavery clergymen who visited him during the war, in 1862, "The position in which I am placed brings me into some knowledge of opinion in all parts of the country and of many different kinds of people; and it appears to me that the great masses of this country care comparatively little about the Negro, and are anxious only for military successes."

Yet, when all was said, it was also clear that slavery—Negro slavery—was ultimately the root cause of the war. Lincoln told the United States Congress on December 1, 1862, "Without slavery the rebellion could not have existed; without slavery it could not continue." Nor was he alone in this opinion. As one Southern leader among others, General Bedford Forrest, a former slave-trader, said at the height of the war, "If we are not fighting for slavery, then what are we fighting for?"

### Emancipation

To begin with Lincoln hesitated to move against slavery lest he lose the border states whose loyalties to the Union were still undependable. Army officers, such as Frémont and Hunter, who took action to emancipate slaves in territories under martial law, or who tried to enlist them as troops, found their orders countermanded by Lincoln. When Charles Sumner of Massachusetts urged Lincoln to abolish slavery on July 4, 1862, he replied, "I would do it if I were not afraid that half the officers would fling down their arms and three more states would rise." Instead, Lincoln pleaded for a gradual program of emancipation under which all states that abolished slavery before January 1, 1900, would receive compensation. The freed Negroes would be encouraged to settle in Africa or elsewhere. Lincoln had little success with these proposals. The border states were too divided to give Lincoln a mandate for compensated emancipation, while the free Negroes showed little enthusiasm for re-settling abroad, even though Lincoln made arrangements for any who wished to obtain free tickets either to Haiti, or to Liberia—the two black Republics which were at last recognized in 1862 by Act of Congress.

Nevertheless, as the war progressed, pressure on the federal government to abolish slavery grew stronger. There were difficulties in raising troops, and some urged that the slaves be freed and enlisted in the Union ranks, thus doubly discomfiting the South. The abolitionists, also, began to attack the administration for inaction. The weightiest consideration of all, however, was the effect of abolition on foreign powers. Above all the South sought diplomatic recognition by European states—a development that would multiply the difficulties which the Union faced, and might well result in the success of secession. Diplomatic reports from such capitals as Vienna and Madrid stated that European recognition of the Confederacy could only be prevented by one of three things—first, a con-clusive Union victory in the field; second, the capture of the cotton ports, such as Charleston, South Carolina, which would release supplies of cotton for European factories; or third, the emancipation of the slaves by the Union government. Such difficulties had arisen in achieving either of the first two conditions that a decision on the third point could not long be delayed.

The way to emancipation was paved by the Confiscation Act of July, 1862. The act provided that slaves owned by persons convicted of treason or rebellion should be emancipated, and that runaway slaves of rebels, slaves whose masters had run away, or slaves found in places formerly occupied by the rebels, should be declared prisoners of war, and freed. The Fugitive Slave Law continued, however, to protect the slave property of slave-owners who remained loyal to the Union. By another measure slavery was ended in the nation's capital, the District of Columbia.

A short time after the Confiscation Act had been promulgated, Lincoln called his Cabinet together on July 22, 1862, and read to them his draft of an emancipation act. It was decided that it would not be advisable to publicize the proposed act at a time when the war was not going well for the Union. General McClellan's attempted march on Richmond was a failure, and, as one Cabinet member, Seward, expressed it, the issuing of an emancipation proclamation "may be viewed as the last measure of an exhausted government, a cry for help," a last "shriek." The matter was therefore postponed until the next favorable opportunity. That came with the news of the battle of Antietam, fought on September 15, 1862, at which the Union army halted the forces of the Confederate general,

Robert E. Lee. On September 22, 1862, Lincoln drew up a preliminary emancipation, the text of which was published two days later, in which he announced that the war would continue, that the policy of buying and freeing slaves in the border states would continue, together with efforts to "colonize" them abroad, and that on January 1, 1863, all slaves in states or parts of states in rebellion "shall be then, thenceforth, and forever free."

The proclamation produced a confused murmuring, but no disastrous counteraction. In the army General McClellan, in whose camp treasonable talk was not discouraged, wrote to his wife that because of the proclamation it had become almost impossible for him to retain his commission and his self-respect at the same time. However, he took no action. In Europe the response of many to Lincoln's action was one of approval. It had become much harder, now, for the European governments to think of recognizing the Confederacy. Aware of this, the South was seized by an emotion of fury. The Richmond *Enquirer* wrote, "What shall we call him? Coward, assassin, savage, murderer of women and babies? Or shall we consider them all as embodied in the word fiend, and call him Lincoln, the Fiend?"

Until the last moment it was uncertain whether or not the final Emancipation Proclamation would indeed be published on January 1, 1863. Frederick Douglass, on the evening of that day, was at "an immense meeting" in Boston, convened to await the news.

> Every moment of waiting [he later wrote] chilled our hopes, and strengthened our fears. A line of messengers was established between the telegraph office and the platform. . . . The time of argument was passed. It was not logic, but the trump of jubilee, which everyone wanted to hear. We were waiting and listening as for a bolt from the sky, which should rend the fetters of four millions of slaves[28]; we were watching, as it were, by the dim light of the stars, for the dawn of a new day; we were longing for the answer to the agonizing prayers of centuries. . . . Eight, nine, ten o'clock came and went, and still no word. A visible shadow seemed falling on the expecting throng. . . . At last, when patience was well-nigh exhausted, and suspense was becoming an agony, a man . . . with hasty step alvanced through the crowd and with a face fairly illumined with the news he bore, exclaimed in tones that thrilled all hearts, "It is coming! It is on the wires!!" The effect of this announcement was startling beyond description, and the scene was wild and grand. Joy and gladness exhausted all forms of expression, from shouts of praise to sobs and tears. My old friend Rue, a colored preacher . . . led all voices in the anthem, "Sound the loud timbrel o'er Egypt's dark sea, Jehovah hath triumphed, his people are free."

General emancipation was not, however, the immediate consequence. Many slaves in the South—a proportion of whom, for reasons of personal loyalty, had enthusiastically contributed services to the Confederate cause —continued to serve their masters. Not until Union troops entered the South toward the end of the war, and not until the Thirteenth Amend-

28. In 1860 the population of the United States totaled some 31,513,000, of whom 3,953,760 were slaves.

ment to the U.S. Constitution, prohibiting slavery or involuntary servitude within the United States, was adopted on January 31, 1865, and declared ratified on December 18, 1865, was slavery utterly abolished. The Emancipation Proclamation was nevertheless recognized at home and abroad as the deathblow to the slave system. Henry Adams, private secretary to his father, the United States Minister in London, wrote from that city, "The Emancipation Proclamation has done more for us here than all our former victories and all our diplomacy. It is creating an almost convulsive reaction in our favor all over this country. . . . Public opinion is very deeply stirred."

### Arming the Freedman

With emancipation proclaimed, the next step was clearly to enlist Negro troops in the Union armies to help to bring the war to a conclusion. Although there was considerable opposition among whites to any proposal to put Negroes in uniform and to arm them, this was nevertheless eventually done. Already in 1861 General Butler, commanding Fort Monroe in Virginia, had not only preceded the Emancipation Proclamation, but had also cut through legal niceties by declaring the slaves who rallied to him to be "contraband," then putting them to use for the Union cause.

On March 2, 1863, scarcely two months after the Emancipation Proclamation, Frederick Douglass, the acknowledged Negro leader, began publicly to urge free Negroes throughout the North to enlist in the 54th and 55th Massachusetts—two Negro regiments whose formation had just been authorized. Two of Douglass's own sons set an example by enlisting.

Many arguments were used to discourage the use of Negroes as soldiers. It was said that America was a white man's country, and that the war, too, was a white man's war. It was also said that the Negro's courage was doubtful: "A crack of his old master's whip will send him scampering in terror from the field." After the 54th Massachusetts had distinguished itself in its desperate assault on Fort Wagner in July, 1863, in which it suffered heavy casualties, no more was heard of this argument. Douglass himself commented that in that single battle "more cavils in respect of the quality of Negro manhood were set to rest than could have been during a century of ordinary life." Harriet Tubman was present at Fort Wagner as an army nurse. Asked to describe the battle later, she said,

And then we saw the lightning, and that was the guns; and then we heard the thunder, and that was the big guns; and then we heard the rain falling, and that was the drops of blood falling; and when we came to get in the crops, it was dead men that we reaped.

In May, 1863, the U.S. War Department opened a new bureau to recruit Negro troops. The Confederate government grew alarmed, and issued an order that white officers commanding Negro troops should not be captured, but put to death. It also became a practice for Confederates to take no Negro prisoners,[29] while on some occasions Negro prisoners were taken only to be sold into slavery. By August, 1863, Douglass had become disturbed, and declined to urge any more Negroes to enlist. Earlier he had told Negroes that he was authorized to assure them the same wages, the same rations, the same protection, and the same treatment as white soldiers. But promises made to him had not been kept. The same wages had not been paid, Negro soldiers had not been protected as whites had been when taken prisoner, and, after performing acts of valor in battle, had not been decorated or promoted as whites had been. Lincoln, hearing of these circumstances, agreed to improve conditions—and conditions were improved thereafter—and persuaded Douglass to continue his recruiting activities. Altogether about 179,000 Negro troops saw service in the Union cause during the war, over 30,000 of them dying, mostly from disease, since it was a frequent practice to send Negro forces to man unhealthy posts.

On the Confederate side Negro troops were also used toward the end of the war. In 1864 when it was evident that Southern manpower was becoming depleted, Jefferson Davis recommended to the Confederate Congress that slaves be drafted into the army. The proposal was controversial, and not until 1865 did the Congress decide, by a majority of a single vote, to arm the slaves. It was a counsel of last resort—the last "shriek" of the old South—for the war was almost over.

As we have said, Lee surrendered at Appomattox on April 9, 1865. Five days later, on the very day that the Proclamation ending the war was published, President Abraham Lincoln was assassinated by a Southern sympathizer at Ford's Theater in Washington. These two events coming together like a clap of thunder signaled the ending of the American crusade against slavery.

### Reconstruction

The crusade was over, and slavery was at last abolished—but what was to be the fate of the mass of newly liberated freedmen in the former slave states? A decade of civil struggle was to ensue before the question was to receive the dusty answer that it finally obtained.

Lincoln had proposed to follow a conciliatory policy toward the defeated Southern states, and his successor, Andrew Johnson, a North Carolinian by birth, who represented the border state of Tennessee, adopted, after a short pause, a similar policy. General Republican sentiment in Congress, however, favored treating the South as a conquered country. As controversy sharpened between Congress and President John-

29. In April, 1864, for example, at Fort Pillow on the Mississippi, Confederate troops under General Nathan B. Forrest, later to become Grand Wizard of the Ku Klux Klan, massacred the Negro garrison and their white officers.

son, Johnson took advantage of a Congressional recess in late 1865 to arrange for the establishment of state governments throughout the South. These governments were not slow to enact what became known as the "Black Codes"—discriminatory legislative measures so harsh that they not only prohibited Negroes from enjoying most civil rights, but also often virtually obliged them to return to work for their former masters under conditions little different from slavery.

The Black Codes aroused a revulsion of opinion in the North. The editor of the *Tribune*, for example, apropos of the Mississippi Black Code, declared, "We tell the white men of Mississippi that the men of the North will convert the state of Mississippi into a frog pond before they will allow any such laws to disgrace one foot of soil in which the bones of our soldiers sleep and over which the flag of freedom waves." When Representatives from the Southern states came to Washington hoping to resume their seats in Congress, that body, dominated by the Republicans, refused to seat them, and instead set up a committee to scan the credentials of Southern Representatives, and to review the President's Southern policies.

Republican irritation at Johnson's attempt to rehabilitate the Southern states so rapidly stemmed, however, not only from revulsion at the provisions of the Black Codes and from the passions that the war had stirred, but also from practical considerations. Under the Thirteenth Amendment to the Constitution, which abolished slavery, any former slave, for representative purposes, was now to be counted as a whole man instead of as three-fifths of one. The number of Representatives of former slave states in Congress would thus be increased from 70 to 82—a prospect displeasing to Republicans, since, under the electoral arrangements made by Johnson, Negroes, the main Republican hope in the South, were excluded. But the Republicans were hindered from simply demanding that Southern states give the Negro the right to vote by the fact that at that time only six Northern states granted Negroes that right. An increase in Southern representation was also distasteful to Northern industrialists and financiers, who were interested in public money being used to develop the West, rather than to reconstruct the South.

In 1866 the struggle between President Johnson and Congress continued. Johnson, having vetoed a bill continuing the Freedmen's Bureau —an agency established during the war to deal with the problems of emancipated slaves—attempted also to veto a civil rights bill which forbade states to discriminate among their citizens on the basis of color, as had been done in the Black Codes. Congress, however, overrode Johnson and adopted the civil rights legislation, then proceeded to reintroduce and to pass a measure continuing the Freedmen's Bureau. Congress was concerned lest the Civil Rights Act be later repealed, and therefore enacted the Fourteenth Amendment to the Constitution to make repeal more difficult. The Fourteenth Amendment, adopted in June, 1866, which effectively declared that Negroes were citizens, provided that no State should abridge the privileges or immunities of citizens, and penalized states for withholding the vote from Negroes by reducing Congressional representation if the Negro vote should be withheld. This arrangement thus reduced Southern representation to 45 seats, at such time as Southerners were readmitted to Congress, yet left Northern states virtually unaffected, since their Negro populations were relatively so small. Congress demanded that the Southern states ratify the amendment before they could be represented in Washington once more, but President Johnson actively intervened by advising them not to ratify. By February, 1867, ten of the former eleven Confederate states had rejected ratification —enough to prevent the Fourteenth Amendment from entering into force.

Meanwhile, however, the elections of 1866 had returned the Radical wing of the Republican Party to Congress greatly strengthened. In 1867 they were then able to pass a series of "Reconstruction Acts"[30] of far-reaching import for the South. The state civil governments established by Johnson were dissolved, and instead the South was divided into five military districts, each placed under the command of a brigadier-general with federal troops at his disposal. The general was to supervise the holding of elections for delegates to a new constitutional convention in each state, the delegates being elected by all adult male voters, both Negro and white. Confederates who had taken a federal oath of office before the war were, however, disenfranchised. Further legislation limited the powers of President Johnson—who, indeed, would have been impeached the following year for exceeding his powers, had not Congress failed by one vote to secure the two-thirds majority required to do so. The mood of Congress at this time was represented by Thaddeus Stevens of Philadelphia. Called an American "Jacobin" by his opponents, Stevens had consistently advocated treating the South as a conquered country. "The whole fabric of Southern society *must* be changed," he had declared, "and never can it be done if this opportunity is lost."

### "Forty Acres and a Mule"

Some 700,000 Negroes in the South were enfranchised by the Reconstruction Acts. The primary demand of this electorate was, however, not so much for the vote as for land—enough land on which to live, now that the slave masters were no longer responsible for the livelihood, and now that the vagrancy clauses of the Black Codes drove the mass of those who had nowhere to go first to prison and then to forced labor.[31] Indeed, from the moment that federal troops had arrived, the emancipated slaves had

---

30. The exact title of the First Reconstruction Act (March 2, 1867) was "An Act to Provide for the More Efficient Government of the Rebel States."
31. The Freedmen's Bureau reported that the Black Codes "actually served to secure to the former slave-holding class the unpaid labor which they had been accustomed to enjoy before the war."

made it clear that their primary need was land—in some instance slaves had immediately divided up among themselves the plantations where they worked. Their need became crystallized in the slogan "Forty Acres and a Mule."

Thaddeus Stevens, the "Jacobin," openly advocated confiscation of the big plantations after which he proposed dividing them up among the landless, thus creating a yeomanry, black and white, which would provide the basis for democracy in the South. He calculated that in the Southern states about 70,000 landowners held 394,000,000 acres, the remaining 71,000,000 being held by persons owning less than 200 acres each. A redivision of land which would break up the large estates by giving 40 acres to each freedman, and by putting up the rest for sale, would at the same time solve the most pressing aspect of the Negro question, reduce the national debt, and strengthen democracy. But Stevens' proposal was rejected. Negro hopes of such a land division, which ran high indeed at first, were postponed again and again, until at last it was clear that, except in a few instances, notably in the Sea Islands, where estates were reapportioned, nothing was going to be done. In 1865 it appeared that the defeated South would have been prepared to accept even such a radical program, but by 1867, thanks to the respite provided by President Johnson, the moment for such a solution had passed. Instead a system of sharecropping became the most general practice. Under this system the freedman received tools and seed from the landowner on credit, sharing with him the profit of the ensuing crop. The landowner himself habitually received credit from suppliers who, in return, charged high interest rates, and usually insisted that nothing but the great cash crop, cotton, be grown. As, over the year, cotton prices fell and debts rose, so the economic independence of both owner and sharecropper became more circumscribed. For the freedman, working without wages, conditions remained, indeed, but a step away from slavery. The French Revolution had resulted, in France, in many of the big estates being divided up among those who worked the land. In the 1860s, the decade in which both Russian serfs and American slaves were emancipated, no such development took place.

## The "Carpetbag" Administrations

The "black and tan" conventions, as the Reconstruction assemblies convened in the South were called, on account of their racially mixed composition, completed the work of drawing up state constitutions in time to participate in the 1868 elections. The Fourteenth Amendment was ratified by all the Southern states but three—Mississippi, Texas, and Virginia—after which their Representatives were accepted by Congress.[32]

32. Mississippi, Texas, and Virginia were readmitted in 1870. Georgia, which had lost representation in Washington after expelling Negroes from its state legislature, was also admitted for the second time in that year.

In the 1868 elections the Republicans were again returned to power, under the leadership of President, formerly General, Ulysses S. Grant. One of the first acts of the new Congress was to adopt, early in 1869, the Fifteenth Amendment. More specific than the Fourteenth, it provided that "The right of citizens of the United States to vote shall not be denied or abridged by the United States or by any State on account of race, color, or previous condition of servitude." It was declared ratified in March, 1870.

The power of the Republican-backed Reconstruction state legislatures depended on three factors—the Negro vote, continuing control of the federal government, and the presence of federal troops in the South. Temporarily effective, the power of the legislatures was, nevertheless, fragile, since, as they did not have the wholehearted backing of the populations, the elimination of any one of the three factors could end that power. Southern white dissatisfaction with the Reconstruction legislatures, meanwhile, found an outlet in the formation of secret terrorist organizations. One of the first of these organizations was the "Black Cavalry," formed by the planters to protect their land from reapportionment. Other such groups were the Knights of the White Camelia in Louisiana, the Knights of the Rising Sun in Texas, and the White Brotherhood in North Carolina. The most famous, however, was the Ku Klux Klan, first formed in Pulaski, Tennessee, in 1865, and which, by 1867, had been organized in several states, being federated under the command of a "Grand Wizard." Using guerrilla tactics, these groups sought by murders and burnings of property to terrorize Republican whites, and to discourage Negroes from exercising their political rights.

These white terrorist organizations remained, however, only of secondary importance at this stage, since their activities were counterbalanced by those of the Negro militias and rifle clubs, organized either openly or covertly, depending on local conditions. Throughout the South, also, the Negroes organized "Union Leagues," or "Loyal Leagues," which were comparable, in some respects, to the Jacobin Clubs that sprang up throughout France at the time of the French Revolution. Local branches took such names as the "Grant Rangers," and the "Heroes of America," while the Negro militias that were often closely associated with them also adopted local names, such as the "Wide-Awakers," or the "Neagle Rifles." In effect the subdued and intermittent struggle between these groups and their Ku Klux Klan and other opponents constituted a species of underground and intermittent continuation of the Civil War itself.

The new state legislatures became, themselves, the object of the most violent verbal attacks by leading white Southerners. White Republicans from the North, whom the war or its aftermath had brought to the South, and some of whom ran for office and were elected, were nicknamed "carpetbaggers," to suggest that they had originally come to the state in question with all their belongings contained in a single carpetbag. White Southerners who supported the Republicans were given the name of "scalawags." For the Negroes names enough were found, but white Southern outrage was based primarily on the fact that they should presume to sit in legislatures at all. A South Carolina newspaper, for example, the Fairfield *Herald,* in 1872 attacked the

hell-born policy which has trampled the fairest and noblest of states . . . beneath the unholy hoofs of African savages and shoulder-strapped brigands—the policy which has given up millions of our free-born high-souled brothers and sisters . . . to the rule of gibbering, louse-eaten, devil-worshipping barbarians, from the jungles of Dahomey, and peripatetic buccaneers from Cape Cod, Memphremagog, Hell and Boston.

The ignorance and rough, torn clothes of some of the Negro legislators were held up to ridicule, and the strongest objections made to the taxes levied on the public by the legislatures in which they sat. The legislatures were, at that time, regarded as curiosities, being visited as such by travelers from abroad, since it was the first time in the history of English-speaking countries that Negroes were known to have participated in such institutions, and the circumstance was one that caused surprise.

For all the ridicule and malice that was directed at them, the legislatures were, nonetheless, not ineffective or irresponsible bodies. They showed a keen concern with education, as well as with equal rights. Negroes did not, as their critics alleged, dominate any of the state governments, even in those states where Negroes were in the majority. In Mississippi, for example, where the Negro population was in the majority, only 55 out of 115 members of the Lower House and only 9 out of the 35 Senators were Negroes. Allegations of corruption and of excessive taxation were also exaggerated. Whereas corruption did, no doubt, exist, in extent it can never have begun to approach the proportions that it was assuming at that time in the Northern states. The great increase in expenditure, also, was not due solely to irresponsible extravagance, but to the fact that no such items as provision for a public-school system had ever appeared in the budgets of Southern states in the days of slavery. Much of the malice that was aimed at the legislatures, no doubt, was stimulated by the corresponding malice which must, almost inevitably, have entered into the legislative proceedings after such an unprecedented reversal of fortune as that which enabled former slaves to help impose taxes on their former masters. There are at least two sides to every controversy, and about the rights and wrongs of the Reconstruction era emotions are still exacerbated, and historians even yet by no means in agreement.

To begin with, however, the "Bourbons"—as their critics, again drawing upon the French Revolutionary experience for a descriptive term, called the former slave-holding whites of the South—considered forming a political alliance with the Negroes in order to counteract the power of the "small" whites, and of the Republican party. Encountering well-nigh insuperable difficulties, however, in weaning the Negroes from a Republican party which had abolished slavery, the "Bourbon" planters abandoned these attempts, and adopted a new tactic. This was to break the alliance of the "small" whites and the Negroes by making a direct appeal to racism and to white solidarity. By 1868 this new approach was accompanied by an increase in a campaign of "White Terror," which assumed such proportions that in 1870 and 1871 Congress adopted Enforcement Acts, aimed at the suppression of the Ku Klux Klan, and also designed to protect Negro rights. But the North was becoming more conciliatory as the emotions aroused by the Civil War subsided, and the opportunity to act against the secret white terrorist organizations was therefore not energetically pursued. Instead, in 1872, Congress also adopted the Amnesty Act, which permitted the return to office of the former Confederates. Slavery was overthrown, but otherwise the way was being cleared for the re-establishment of the pre-war status quo.

Rapidly, in the years that followed, the "Bourbons" captured power in state after state. "Home rule," as it has been termed, was re-established in Texas in 1872, after the Ku Klux Klan had been successful in preventing Negroes from voting, and the Democrats in consequence had won the election. In Alabama in 1874 the Ku Klux Klan launched a reign of terror. Republican and Negro leaders were murdered, and the Democrats were returned to power. With variations the same story was repeated in other states. When, in 1874, the Republican Governor of Mississippi, Adelbert Ames, called upon President Grant to send federal troops because illegal infantry and cavalry organizations had been formed in the state, and had acquired artillery, Grant replied,

> The whole public are tired out with these autumnal outbreaks in the South, and the great majority are ready now to condemn any interference on the part of the Government.

After this, Southern white conservatives gained both in strength and in confidence. More leading Negroes and Republicans were murdered, and anti-Negro violence spread increasingly unchecked.

The final Southern victory was, however, gained in Washington. Samuel J. Tilden, the Democratic candidate for the Presidency in the 1876 elections, was opposing the Republican candidate, Rutherford B. Hayes. After the elections were held, electoral ambiguities in several states placed the outcome in doubt. As tension rose, Grant brought troops to the vicinity of Washington, and there was even talk of a resumption of the Civil War. Secret negotiations were then begun, which resulted in a private understanding being reached between Hayes and the Democrats. In February, 1877, Hayes, in return for the presidency, undertook to restore South Carolina and Louisiana to Democratic control. Hayes became President, and kept his word. In April, 1877, federal troops were withdrawn from both these states. The Democrats, as the party of white supremacy, had returned to power throughout the South. In the years that followed, state after state would disenfranchise the Negroes, and later, in the twentieth century, introduce discriminatory legislation against them. The Negro minority, effectively deprived of the vote, and largely landless, would remain—slaves no longer, but strangers, nevertheless, in the land of their birth.

# Chapter 12

# The White Civil War

*While co-existent nationalities are capable of mutual aid involving no direct antagonism of interests, co-existent empires following each its own imperial career of territorial and industrial aggrandisement are natural necessary enemies.* —J. A. Hobson (1902)

*To me the Great War was from the first the White Civil War, which, whatever its outcome, must gravely compromise the course of racial relations.* —Lothrop Stoddard (1920)

*World War I was a war over spheres of influence in Asia and colonies in Africa.* —W. E. B. Du Bois (1946)

ON NOVEMBER 24, 1859—eight days before John Brown's execution in Virginia—a book was published by an English naturalist that effected a revolution in contemporary thinking, changing the contours of social philosophy as thoroughly as if the landscape had been struck by an earthquake.

The book was Charles Darwin's *The Origin of Species by Means of Natural Selection, or the Preservation of Favoured Races in the Struggle for Life.* In this book Darwin advanced the theory of the survival of the fittest, according to which those organic beings best able to adapt to the various conditions of life were the most likely to produce the species which survived in what he termed "the struggle for existence." Darwin's theory captured the imagination of thinking people in Europe and America, among many of whom it carried immediate conviction. Lest there be any mistake about its implications, another English writer,

Herbert Spencer, propagated the theory of "Social Darwinism," applying the principle of the "survival of the fittest in the struggle for existence" to the evolution of human society.

Although Darwin himself would appear not to have sought to reduce standards of human behavior to the bestial level, but rather, if anything, to ennoble animals, the general effect of his theory was to sweep aside moral restraints upon those who held power. The ideas of the French Revolution, written also into the American Declaration of Independence, which proclaimed that "All Men Are Created Equal," received a stunning blow, as also did the related Biblical theme that "All Men Are Brothers." Now Science and Reason appeared to unite to declare, instead, that "The Strong Shall Inherit the Earth!" John Brown, and the ideas that he stood for, were relegated to the past, his symbolic act the postscript to a bygone time, rather than the prelude to a new age.

The spirit of the new Darwinian era was reflected in many ways, not least strikingly by the German imaginative writer Friedrich Nietzsche, who published the first part of his *Thus Spake Zarathustra* in 1883. In *Zarathustra*, Nietzsche adopted a Biblical stance to announce that "God Is Dead!" and then proceeded to lay down new commandments and to reveal new "truths." In order that a "Superman" might emerge, pity must be crushed, danger courted, struggle rejoiced in, and a "will to power" fostered. "Ye say a good cause will hallow even war?" wrote Nietzsche. "I say unto you: a good war halloweth every cause." Such sentiments were not at variance with the mood of nineteenth-century imperialism. Darwinism needed, indeed, but only the slightest degree of reinterpretation to transform it into a justification for either racism or nationalism. In every European country proponents of both appeared. Cecil Rhodes was merely one individual speaking on behalf of merely one European country when he told his intimates:

> I contend that we are the first race in the world, and that the more of the world we inhabit the better it is for the human race. I contend that every acre added to our territory means the birth of more of the English race who otherwise would not be brought into existence. . . . The objects one should work for are first the furtherance of the British Empire, the bringing of the whole uncivilized world under British rule, the recovery of the United States, the making of the Anglo-Saxon race but one Empire.[1]

Christianity, with its universalism, remained a potential barrier to the Darwinian advance. Christian principles were clearly in conflict with such adaptations of Darwinian theory, yet, while religious fundamentalists on the one hand and supporters of Social Darwinism on the other remained locked in furious debate, nationalists and empire-builders wove a new synthesis from the two themes. Lord Hugh Cecil, for example, in 1900 told the British Society for the Propagation of the Gospel that mis-

1. Felix Gross, *Rhodes of Africa* (1957), p. 61.

sionary work might "to some extent sanctify the spirit of Imperialism"—
a statement that illustrated J. A. Hobson's observation on imperialism
that "out of a medley of mixed motives, the least potent is selected for
public prominence because it is the most presentable."[2] Most Christian
missionaries, rather than opposing imperialism, attempted to use the
facilities it provided for their work, just as imperialism attempted to use
them both to cloak and to forward its material aims.

By the turn of the century, nationalism, flourishing in a favorable
Darwinian atmosphere, had reached extraordinary proportions. Originally it had been a revolutionary force, directed primarily against the
old European oligarchies. The third paragraph of the Declaration of the
Rights of Man and the Citizen had in 1793 declared, for example, that
"The nation is essentially the source of all sovereignty; nor can ANY
INDIVIDUAL, or ANY BODY OF MEN, be entitled to any authority which is
not expressly derived from it." By the early 1900s, however, nationalism
had ceased to be a primarily democratic force, but expressed itself instead in demands for the complete subordination of the individual to
the sovereign nation-state, even although in practice these nation-states
were frequently still directed by representatives of the old oligarchy.
While nationalism never went to the extent of applying one of the suggestions of Johann Fichte—a German contemporary of Napoleon I—that
children be removed from the home to prevent their national development from being undermined by countercurrents, it sometimes acted on
his other suggestion that gold and silver be replaced by paper money so
that the citizen would be obliged to maintain social relationships only
with his fellows, thus leaving the prerogative of dealing with those abroad
to the nation-state alone.

So strong, indeed, did nationalism become that it obscured the tacit
racism that sprang up in its shadow. The beliefs of such writers as the
French diplomat Comte Joseph Arthur de Gobineau, who vaunted the
superiority of the European over the African or the Chinese, were regarded by many Europeans as too self-evident to arouse great interest.
Emotions ran high only when national, rather than racial, rivalries were
involved.

Circumstances seemed to combine to stimulate national pride, and
to encourage delusions of virtual omnipotence among European rulers.
The nationalist press of the various countries, strengthened by the newly
literate readership that the spread of education had brought it, fed
national vanities, and preached contempt of other nations. The steady
introduction of new technical developments, which proceeded unchecked,
added to the general impression of waxing strength and of accelerating
progress. The holding of various "international exhibitions" at home, and

2. *Imperialism: A Study* (London, 1902).

the news of colonial acquisitions abroad, brought added proof to each country that distant lands, with their peoples and products, were falling beneath the sway of the major power. Each European nation thus came to feel that it was called to a higher destiny—a destiny which was challenged only by the rivalry of jealous neighbors. Each became possessed by the desire to dominate.

The United Kingdom was the dominating European—and world— power, with Germany, under Kaiser Wilhelm II, who came to the throne in 1888, its principal challenger. For example, between 1901–1905 the United Kingdom was responsible for an annual average of 29.4 percent of world trade in manufactures, as compared with Germany's share of 20 percent. The growing rivalry between these two powers constituted the most dangerous threat to the peace of Europe in the early years of the twentieth century. France, meanwhile, which had been defeated by Germany in 1870, had since then abandoned dreams of European predominance, and sought, instead, an imperial destiny in Africa—a course, as we have seen, in which it was encouraged by Germany, which hoped to see Franco-British collisions ensue in consequence. Russia, meanwhile, had formed an alliance with France in order to counterbalance the Central European coalition of Germany and Austria-Hungary. However, after the Russians had suffered defeat at the hands of the Japanese in 1905, losing their fleet in the naval battle of Tsushima,[3] Russian prestige was correspondingly lowered, and Germany's expansionist plans encouraged. These plans, however, received an unexpected check when the United Kingdom, reversing its traditional policy of hostility to France, sealed the *entente cordiale* by concluding the Anglo-French Treaty of 1904. As a result, two great coalitions came into being in the years that followed —the Triple Entente, allying France, Russia, and the United Kingdom on the one hand, and the Triple Alliance, allying Germany, Austria-Hungary, and Italy on the other. The stage was set for a gigantic "civil war" between the white nations of Europe.

## "A Place in the Sun"

From 1904 on tension between Germany and the United Kingdom rose steadily. As early as 1897 Prince von Bulow, later to be Chancellor of Germany, had told the Reichstag, "We do not wish to put anyone in the shadow, but we demand our place in the sun." The German demand for

3. On February 17, 1916, U.S. President Woodrow Wilson's emissary, Colonel House, sat next to the British admiral Lord Fisher at a London dinner. Fisher was the advocate of speedy and heavily armed battleships. House recorded in his diary: "Fisher claims to have told the Japanese how to destroy the first Russian fleet in the Russo-Japanese War. The Russian Admiral, he thought, would do the stupid thing. His ships were three knots slower than the Japanese to start with; they were loaded with coal, which reduced their speed another knot or two. Fisher advised the Japanese to coal as lightly as possible; just enough, in fact, to reach the Russian fleet and then manoeuver. The result was that the Japanese were able to steam in front of the advancing Russians and pick them off one by one." (*Intimate Papers of Colonel House,* 1926, p. 191.)

"a place in the sun" was to be repeated ever more insistently. By 1911 the Kaiser himself was speaking of the need "to strengthen our fleet further so as to make sure that nobody will dispute the place in the sun to which we are entitled." The very phrase "a place in the sun" conjured up visions of tropical colonies—colonies, moreover, which would supply Germany's developing industries with the cotton, rubber, and other commodities that they required. To secure and defend such colonies, and the maritime trade that they would sustain, a substantial fleet was evidently necessary, and this meant making a direct challenge to Britain's naval supremacy—a supremacy which had provided the peace-keeping machinery of the Pax Britannica since Napoleonic times. Only British battleships, in other words, stood in the way of German determination to bid for world supremacy—a supremacy in which control of colonies and continents would be based on control of the seas.

Until 1906 the British had followed the practice of maintaining a navy that would be stronger than the fleets of any other two powers combined. Thus in 1896, for example, the British had possessed 33 battleships compared to Germany's 6, and had had 130 cruisers to Germany's 4. The German authorities, having fostered a national demand for a large navy, were beginning to build up their forces when the British placed the rivalry on a new basis by putting into service the "Dreadnought," a new type of heavy battleship with greater speed and fire-power than any existing vessel. The naval arms race that followed placed a strain on British and German finances and emotions alike. There was continued talk of establishing a ratio between the two fleets. In the meantime, however, the British, outraged at the growing threat to their predominance, began to talk of the possibility of a German invasion of their coasts, and the British Admiral Fisher, the First Sea Lord, openly advocated "Copenhagening" the German Fleet—that is to say, launching a preventive attack upon it, as the British Admiral Nelson had done to the Danish fleet at Copenhagen in 1801.

In such an atmosphere, even the family relations which existed between the British, Russian, and German royal families could not smooth over the inevitable collisions that occurred, each threatening to precipitate war between the two rival European blocs. The 1905 crisis over Morocco that terminated in the Algeciras Conference was followed by a further crisis over Bosnia in 1908, and this, in turn, by the Agadir incident of 1911, again concerning Morocco. By 1912 it would appear that the German General Staff had decided that war had become inevitable—and most of the chancelleries of Europe were of the same opinion. Even when, after this date, provisional agreement was reached between Germany and the United Kingdom on the future partition of the Portuguese colonies, the German Kaiser, Wilhelm II, commented sardonically, "No!

We have enough colonies! If I want any more, I will buy them or take them without England's help. . . . The idea is to dazzle us with the idea of a 'Colonial Empire' in Africa . . . and so to distract our attention from world politics." The American envoy, Colonel House, visiting Berlin on a peace mission in 1914, reported, "The whole of Germany is charged with electricity. Everybody's nerves are tense. It only needs a spark to set the thing off."

The spark came that year. It was provided by the assassination on June 28, 1914, at Sarajevo, in Bosnia, then a province of Austria-Hungary, of the Archduke Franz Ferdinand, heir to the throne. The assassination was blamed on neighboring Serbia, of which Russia was considered to be the patron if not the protector. At the end of July Austria-Hungary declared war on Serbia. Russia then gave the order to mobilize her army. This was the true signal for the war that followed. Germany's war plan had been drawn up by Field Marshal Alfred von Schlieffen, Chief of the German General Staff until 1906, who had subsequently died. Under Schlieffen's plan, German mobilization and war were synonymous. To avoid fighting a war on two fronts, according to the plan, the German Army would first be thrown against France, and, with France disposed of, the army would then be deployed against Russia in the East. Since the Russians, with great distances to contend with, were expected to take some time to concentrate their strength, speedy action was called for if the Germans were to carry out the Schlieffen plan—the only one they had—before Russia had completed its mobilization. The plan also called for the passage of the German Army through Belgium, so that the heavily fortified Franco-German frontier might be outflanked. Having declared war on Russia on August 1, and France on August 3, Germany demanded that Belgium permit the passage of German troops through that country. When the demand was refused, the United Kingdom supported Belgium, and entered the war against Germany at midnight on August 4, 1914. Italy, pursuing a policy that her Prime Minister described as one of "sacred egoism," entered the war in the spring of 1915 with a view to acquiring those parts of the Austrian Empire in which the majority of the population was Italian.

The outbreak of war was greeted with scenes of enthusiasm in London, Paris, and Berlin. Eventually, however, it was to dawn on the combatant nations—first the soldiers and later the civilians—that the war was to provide no cause for rejoicing, but was, on the contrary, to result in senseless massacres that would constitute the greatest catastrophe Europe had suffered since it had been struck by epidemics of the Plague in the Middle Ages.

In the west of Europe, the "war of movement" lasted scarcely a month, after which the use of machine guns brought movement to a virtual halt, with the contesting armies digging themselves into trenches for protection. Caught in a deadlock, they remained facing one another for the next four years. The commanding generals, used to cavalry charges, and convinced that offense was the best form of attack, remained at a loss, not yet understanding that the advantage now lay with the defense. From a safe distance in the rear they therefore ordered a series of gigantic attacks, in each of which the overwhelming losses suffered by the attackers in no way compensated for the small amounts of churned-up shell-scarred ground that was wrung from the opponent. On July 1, 1916, for example, in a single day of the Battle of the Somme, the British suffered 60,000 casualties, of whom 20,000 were killed. Between February and June 1916, at the Battle of Verdun, the French lost 315,000 casualties, and the Germans 281,000. Slaughter on such a scale had never been known before in the history of warfare. In the east of Europe, where Germans, Austrians, Russians, and other nationalities were similarly locked in combat, equally appalling casualties were recorded. To explain the results of their actions the generals evolved a new theory: the war was a "war of attrition," in which the aim was not so much to gain territory as to wear down the strength of the enemy by massacring his troops. As each side was engaged in massacring the other, however, it was difficult to see who was to benefit from this mutual attrition.

The deadlock was not to be broken at sea. The rival fleets of Germany and the United Kingdom, apart from their partial and indecisive clash at the Battle of Jutland, never came to grips with each other. For the most part the German fleet remained in port. The Kaiser, reportedly, felt that more than one "Punic War" would be required to destroy the United Kingdom, and therefore wished to keep the fleet intact for future use—or else as a bargaining pawn to be employed in peace negotiations. Instead of surface action, therefore, the Germans waged submarine warfare—a new innovation—in an attempt to starve the British Isles into submission. In 1917, however, their efforts to reach this goal were checked by the introduction of the convoy system, which reduced the rate of sinkings of ships sailing to or from British ports from one in every four to one in a hundred.

So great a war in Europe could not fail to produce repercussions on other continents. The heavy casualties on the Western front led to increasing demands for more troops, with the result that African and Asian troops were brought in by the French and the British to offset their own losses. As early as 1914 British officers had led Indian troops into action in the Battle of the Marne, while laborers from Indo-China and other Asian countries were also brought to Europe to aid the war effort. Troops also came from French West Africa, following the election of the first African representative from Senegal to the French Chamber of Deputies.[4]

Whereas in the past it had always been Europeans who had represented Senegal in the Chamber, in the 1914 election Blaise Diagne, an African, won a seat, partly because his six European opponents were divided among themselves, and party because the African Senegalese voters supported his demand for complete equality between black and white—a demand which took the form of a call for a law to make obligatory military service applicable to black persons as well as to whites. After the law was adopted, Diagne, partly on the basis of his friendship with Clemenceau, then Premier of France, was in 1917 appointed Commissaire-General for French West Africa, charged with the responsibility of recruiting further African troops for the Western front. Diagne was given a rank equal to that of the French Governor-General, Van Vollenhoven—a circumstance which led Van Vollenhoven to resign in protest. As a result of Diagne's recruiting efforts, French-administered Africa sent 680,000 soldiers and 238,000 laborers to France during the First World War. This contribution was later to have an influence upon the development of Africa's destiny. The Germans, meanwhile, however, complained bitterly at finding themselves obliged to fight the Africans, who often inspired them with fear. One German officer, who fought against Senegalese troops, later described their attack upon his position as follows:

They came. First singly, at wide intervals. Feeling their way, like the arms of a horrible cuttlefish. Eager, grasping, like the claws of a mighty monster. . . . Strong, wild fellows, their log-like, fat, black skulls wrapped in pieces of dirty rags. Showing their grinning teeth like panthers, with their bellies drawn in and their necks stretched forward. Some with bayonets on their rifles. Many only armed with knives. Monsters all, in their confused hatred. Frightful their distorted, dark grimaces. Horrible their unnaturally wide-opened, burning, bloodshot eyes. Eyes that seemed like terrible beings in themselves. Like unearthly, hell-born beings. Eyes that seemed to run ahead of their owners, lashed, unchained, no longer to be restrained. . . . Behind them came the first wave of the attackers, in close order, a solid, rolling black wall, rising and falling, swaying and heaving, impenetrable, endless.[5]

The use of African and Asian troops against Germany helped to shatter the concept of "white solidarity," and thus produced a change in German attitudes toward the non-European world. Earlier, German planners and romantics had tended to see Germany as the potential leader of Europe in a new crusade against the "Yellow Peril" in China. (The Kaiser, himself a romantic, had even commissioned an allegorical paint-

---

4. The French Revolutionary Decree of 16 Pluviose of the Year II (1792) had founded the principle of seeking to establish institutions in the colonies similar to those existing in France. As a result, from 1848 on the African inhabitants of the original four communes of Senegal had the right to elect a deputy to the French National Assembly.

5. Captain Rheinhold Eichacker, "The Blacks Attack!" *New York Times Current History.* Vol. XI (April–June 1917), pp. 110–112.

ing on the subject.) The doctrine of the "mailed fist" had been propounded in relation to China.[6] Now, however, German enthusiasm for "white solidarity" having disappeared, a search was begun for a new approach. Some planners, seeking to promote Germany's *Drang Nach Osten* ("Drive to the East") policy, saw the German role as that of the "liberator of Asia" from Anglo-Russian domination. Germany, it was felt, might create a vast Central Asian bloc, stretching from Turkey through Iran and Afghanistan to China, the whole possibly being welded together by a "Pan-Asian Railroad" running from Constantinople to Peking. Even if the initial efforts to form such a bloc did not bring immediate results, it was nevertheless felt that they might not be altogether wasted, since they would contribute toward the accomplishment of such an aim in time for the "Second Punic War" against the United Kingdom.

Meanwhile, Turkey had entered the war in October, 1914, on the German side. In addition to its military commitments in the Balkans, it was also prevailed upon to send some divisions to fight on the Western front. However, German attempts, made in 1915, to encourage Moslems under British rule to join a Holy War under Turkish leadership failed to produce any noticeable results. Instead it was the British, through their agent, Colonel Lawrence, who encouraged an Arab revolt in the Hejaz against Turkish rule.

Not only by land, however, did Germany have to reckon with non-European forces. A source of wonder to many was the appearance of the Japanese fleet in the Mediterranean, where it was sent to help the Anglo-French naval forces combatting the German submarine campaign launched in February, 1917. It was the first time since the sixteenth century that an Asian fleet had sailed into what had virtually constituted Europe's largest inland sea.[7]

The war also resulted in armed conflicts in Africa and Asia. As W. E. B. Du Bois has written, "When Germany invaded Belgium, and with that invasion brought war with England, it must be remembered that by the same token Germany was invading the Belgian Congo and laying claim to the ownership of Central Africa."

While the British fleet denied the seas to Germany in Africa, British, French, and Belgian forces took over the German colonies. At the outset of the war Anglo-French forces quickly moved into Togoland from the Gold Coast and Dahomey, and compelled a German surrender. Similar operations in the Cameroons, with the British moving in from Nigeria,

---

6. In a speech delivered in Hamburg, Germany, in 1897 the Kaiser, Wilhelm II, made the bombastic statement that "The German Michael has firmly planted his shield with the device of the German Eagle upon the soil of China. Should anyone essay to detract from our just rights or to injure us, then up and at him with your mailed fist."

7. Previously the Turkish Navy, considered by some as "Levantine" rather than "Asian," had for a time dominated the Mediterranean, until its defeat at Lepanto in 1571 led to the decline of Turkish naval power.

and the French from Equatorial Africa, resulted, after some fighting, in an Allied victory in 1916, with the main German forces retreating into Spanish Rio Muni, where they were interned. German South West Africa, after some skirmishing, was occupied by Allied forces under the leadership of the South African generals Botha and Smuts. In East and Central Africa the German forces, under the capable leadership of von Lettow-Vorbeck, maintained hostilities until the end of the war. After the German attack upon the Congo had been repulsed, the Belgians joined the British and Allied forces in operations against German East Africa. An Allied attack, launched in 1916, had by 1917 driven the Germans into Portuguese Mozambique—Portugal having entered the war on the Allied side in March, 1916. British forces then advanced against the Germans from Nyasaland, but von Lettow-Vorbeck turned their attack, and had advanced into Northern Rhodesia when the Armistice ended the war in November, 1918. Liberia, meanwhile, had declared war on Germany on August 7, 1917, the main consequence of this being the elimination of German commerce in that country. The Liberian government's preoccupations during this period were, however, less with the European war than with internal uprisings, which were suppressed with American assistance.

## The Chilembwe Uprising

Apart from Allied and German actions in Africa during the war, there also occurred a separate but related phenomenon which was long to be remembered by the populations of Central Africa, and which also indicated that beneath the surface of European rule other forces possibly smoldered. This was the Chilembwe uprising that took place in Nyasaland in 1915.

John Chilembwe, having learned to speak and write a few words of English at a mission school, had sought employment in 1892 with an unconventional English missionary named John Booth. Later, Booth's daughter remembered their first contact with Chilembwe:

> On a scrap of paper he brought to Father a pencilled note. There could be no misunderstanding of either his hopes or his motives. "Dear Mr. Booth," the note read, "you please carry me for God. I like to be your cook boy." Thus did our dear black boy John come into our lives.

Booth, a pacifist and the author of a book called *Africa for the African*, found Chilembwe intelligent and dependable. Seeking to disprove a local tradition which held that the Africans taken away years before to slavery in America had been eaten by the whites, Booth himself partly financed the sending of Chilembwe to the United States in 1897. There were further purposes for the journey. Booth wished Chilembwe to obtain education, and the local Africans wished to discover if the descendants of the long-forgotten folk were in fact still alive, as the white men claimed. So Chilembwe traveled to America. He went to Virginia—the state which, sixty-six years before, had been the scene of the Nat Turner uprising, which had also had religious overtones. In Richmond, Booth, who visited the city together with Chilembwe, reported that Chilembwe "found hosts of educated black ministers and others: but mobs of white young men followed us and frequently stoned us for walking together, sitting on the same public seats in the park and for living in the same Negro house."

Chilembwe studied for two years at a seminary in Lynchburg, Virginia, where he was ordained as a pastor, after which he returned home to Nyasaland to carry on mission work with the help of American Negro missionaries. His American helpers appear to have returned to the States, however, by the time of the outbreak of the First World War. At this time the circumstances of the war, the question of the alienation of African lands by white planters in Nyasaland, and the attitude of the British authorities all combined to make Chilembwe decide to lead a revolt, which he did in 1915, with a view to transforming the country into an independent black theocracy. This uprising gave the local British authorities a severe scare, particularly as they had reason to believe that Chilembwe might have been in contact with the Germans in East Africa.

The revolt broke out on January 23, but was of short duration. In its religious overtones it was not dissimilar to the Nat Turner uprising of 1831 in the United States. Taken by surprise, some of the Nyasaland whites were killed. One of them, W. J. Livingstone, a coffee planter, and a distant relative of the explorer, David Livingstone, was decapitated in the presence of his wife and family, after which his head was stuck on a pole and taken to Chilembwe's church, where it was exhibited to the congregation during the regular Sunday service, at which Chilembwe preached the sermon. But soon thereafter the white planters and the British authorities mobilized their forces and closed in on the dissidents. After a number of rebels had been killed in scattered skirmishes, Chilembwe himself was shot dead on February 3 while attempting to cross the border into Portuguese Mozambique. By the next day the uprising was over.

## "The Twenty-one Demands"

In Asia, the principal consequence of the war was the appropriation by Japan of Germany's Chinese foothold, and of most of her Pacific island possessions. Japan had not forgotten that in 1895 Germany, at Russia's instigation, had helped to oblige her to yield up Port Arthur as well as the territory that she had leased in the Kwantung province of China. An Anglo-Japanese alliance had come into being in the early years of the twentieth century, based on a British desire to check possible Russian designs upon India, and on Japanese anxiety about the possibility of Russia's launching a war of revenge for her defeat in 1905. After Japan, in August, 1914, had entered the war against Germany, therefore, a Japanese land and sea attack, which was given token British support, was launched against Shantung, Germany's foothold in China. A Chinese request, made on August 3, 1914, that her neutrality should be respected, and that no fighting should take place in Chinese territories leased to foreigners, was disregarded. By November, 1914, the Japanese had achieved their aims by capturing Tsingtao, and taking the Kiaochow peninsula. Japan also took over some German islands in the Pacific—the Caroline, Pelew, Marshall, and Mariana groups—Australian and New Zealand forces, meanwhile, seizing the German colonies in New Guinea, the Solomons, and Samoa. In this way Japan not only paid off her old score against Germany in connection with the Port Arthur affair, but also demonstrated that an Asian power was capable of driving a European power out of Asia.

Japan, indeed, was participating in the war in her own interest, rather than in that of the Allies. Her subsequent actions in Asia, therefore, had little direct effect upon the course of the struggle in Europe. In November, 1914, the Japanese Premier, Marquis Okuma, had stated that the day would come when the world would be divided up among a few strong nations, and had urged that Japan prepare herself to become one of these nations. When China in 1915 urged that Japan return the former German-leased territory in Shantung to her, Japan replied by presenting "Twenty-One Demands," the acceptance of which would have transformed not merely Shantung Province but the whole of China into a Japanese zone of influence. Allied pressure resulted in radical modifications of the Japanese demands, although Japan did retain the German rights in Shantung, and also increased her influence elsewhere in China. Indeed, the main long-term effect of the war in the Far East was to enable Japan to increase her commercial, economic, and military standing, at the expense of the European powers, who were then straining all their resources to fight one another. Throughout Asia, in India and China no less than in Japan, little sympathy was shown for the Allies. If anything, some sympathy was shown for Germany, mainly because Germany no longer represented any immediate threat to Asians.

Another, and more intangible, result of the war in both Asia and Africa was the effect that it had on numbers of African and Asian soldiers and laborers, who were enabled for the first time to visit the European heartland. Through them was disseminated a less glamorous and more realistic impression of Europe. Europeans, it became clear, were not necessarily invincible beings destined to rule, but were as liable to suffer adversity and to make mistakes as the inhabitants of other continents. One has only to reflect, for example, that Chou En-lai, one of the future leaders of China, was politically active among members of the Chinese Labour Corps in France at this time to realize the way in which there began the first stirrings in the womb of history of future events.

## The United States Enters the War

By 1917 the vortex of war in Europe had created eddies that drew in new forces. In April, the United States, casting aside its traditional policy of isolation, entered the war on the side of the Allies. After the collapse of the Czarist regime in Russia in the earlier part of the year, a revolution in November brought the Communist Party of the Soviet Union (Bolsheviks) to power in that country. As a result, as A. J. P. Taylor has commented, "In 1917 European history, in the old sense, came to an end. World history began."

Although the United States declared war on April 2, 1917, it had earlier passed over the indeterminate frontier that separated neutrality from commitment.[8] The replacement of William Jennings Bryan by Robert Lansing as U.S. Secretary of State in 1915 signaled the vital change from a policy of strict neutrality to a policy that underwrote the Allied cause with loans for war supplies. The Morgan syndicate—the largest financial group in the United States—extended $2,500,000,000 of credit to the Allies. Repayment depended on an Allied victory—or, at least, on the Allies avoiding defeat. With the United States attempts at conciliating the belligerents having failed, and American public opinion having been agitated both by submarine action and by British interference with American passage on the high seas, the United States gradually drew nearer to war. Germany realized that the American position was ultimately inimical, and informed the United States on January 31, 1917, that it was about to introduce a rigorous submarine blockade of the Allies—an action that made war imminent. One of the last actions that helped to confirm the United States' decision to declare war was the discovery that Germany was attempting to stir up Mexico against the United States in return for the restoration to Mexico of territories lost to the United States in the nineteenth century. The consequent entry of the United States into the war was to tip the balance, saving the Allies from disaster, and resulting in the defeat of Germany.

Heavy losses in the war, and privation at home, had meanwhile led to a popular uprising in Russia, where the people of Petrograd, the capital, demanding peace and bread, obliged the Czar to abdicate on March

---

8. The precise moment would appear to have been October 23, 1914, when President Woodrow Wilson agreed to "look the other way" when war credit was extended by Morgan and Company and the National City Bank to the French and British governments. (See Matthew Josephson, *The President-Makers*, 1940, p. 513.)

15, 1917. Shortly thereafter a provisional government was formed, headed by a socialist, Aleksandr Kerenski, which attempted to continue the war. As a result of further defeats at the front, and unrest at home, however, Kerenski lost control of the situation, and, under the leadership of a revolutionary named Lenin, the Bolshevik, or Communist, Party seized power in Petrograd on November 6 and 7, 1917.[9] This event represented the culmination of a new type of revolutionary movement which had been developing since the mid-nineteenth century—a movement, moreover, which, whether they happened to be in agreement with it or not, was profoundly to affect the subsequent destinies of African and Asian peoples.

Essentiailly egalitarian in character, the movement, which was loosely described as "socialist"—a word that had first come into use in the 1830s—had abandoned the old battlefield of religion to move to the new terrain of economics. The text from which it came to draw its primary inspiration was a book entitled *Das Kapital*, published in 1867 by Karl Marx, a German exile living in England. *Das Kapital* analyzed the workings of the capitalist system, and argued that since wealth was produced—or value created—by labor, workers were being exploited by capitalists and property-holders. In other words, most of the poor of the earth were unjustly kept in poverty by the rich. Marx and his colleague, Engels, had earlier, in 1848, written a "Communist Manifesto," in which they had proclaimed that "the history of all hitherto existing society is the history of class struggles."

In addition to the Marxists, other socialists dreamed of establishing new utopias by radically refashioning the economic and governmental systems then in operation. Mikhail Bakunin, a renegade Russian nobleman, believed, for example, in anarchism, or the abolition of the state, in which he saw the root of all evil. Marxism remained, however, the primary current of radical thought. By studying the French Revolution of 1789, and the various European revolts up to 1848, the Marxists came to the conclusion that it was a law of history that feudal or absolute monarchist systems would inevitably give way to "bourgeois" forms of government, such as had been established in France, the United Kingdom, the United States, and elsewhere. Initially creative, the bourgeois class—in the words of the "Communist Manifesto"—"by the rapid improvement of all instruments of production, by the immensely facilitated means of communication, draws all nations, even the most barbarian, into civilisation." However, as the bourgeoisie, representing the power of capital, developed, so, too, there inevitably developed the proletariat, or the urban working class. Society would therefore increasingly split into

9. Since Russia was then still employing the Julian calendar, according to which October 24 and 25 (Julian) corresponded to November 6 and 7 (Gregorian), the Bolshevik Revolution is habitually referred to as the "October Revolution."

"two great classes directly facing each other—bourgeoisie and proletariat." The struggle between the two would eventually be ended by the forcible overthrow of "all existing social conditions." In the concluding words of the "Manifesto,"

Let the ruling classes tremble at a Communist revolution. The proletarians have nothing to lose but their chains. They have a world to win. Workingmen of all countries, unite!

As a result of the short-lived and ill-fated attempt to establish proletarian rule in the Paris Commune of 1870–1871, the Marxists also came to the conclusion that future attempts at seizing power must be carried out with the utmost ruthlessness if they were to succeed.

In essence, in the nineteenth century, the socialists and their sympathizers were criticizing the functioning of the economic system in Europe and America, and, as few of them indeed had traveled further abroad, they spared little thought for conditions in Africa or Asia. Sometimes, however, a passing comment was made. Karl Marx, for example, writing about India in 1853, commented:

The Indians will not reap the fruits of the new elements of society scattered among them by the British bourgeoisie, till in Great Britain itself the now ruling classes shall have been supplanted by the industrial proletariat, or till the Hindoos themselves shall have grown strong enough to throw off the English yoke altogether. At all events, we may safely expect to see, at a more or less remote period, the regeneration of that great and interesting country.[10]

Marx himself, indeed, held that the proletarian revolution would naturally occur first in the industrial countries of Europe, such as Germany or Austria, rather than among the peoples of Africa or Asia, where industry was still largely lacking.

Increasing attention was, however, paid to African and Asian countries as the twentieth century dawned, and as the European colonial powers became more intimately acquainted with the overseas territories that they had subjected. One result of this growing interest was the publication in 1902 of the first edition[11] of *Imperialism: A Study*, by J. A. Hobson, an English writer, quoted above, who described himself as an "economic humanist," and whose critique exercised a seminal influence upon socialists of many nationalities.

Hobson differentiated imperialism from colonialism. Colonialism he saw as the colonization of sparsely settled regions, such as North America and Australia—a process that, he felt, constituted an ultimate asset both to the country of origin as well as to the world community. Imperialism, however, was a parasitical policy that, despite providing short-term benefits to a few private interests, constituted a liability to the

10. "The Future Results of British Rule in India," New York *Daily Tribune*, August 8, 1853.
11. A revised edition was published in 1905.

country of origin and a menace to the progress of civilization. Of imperialism he wrote:

> It is a constant menace to peace, by furnishing continual temptations to further aggression upon lands occupied by lower races and by embroiling our nation [*i.e.*, the United Kingdom] with other nations of rival imperial ambitions; to the sharp peril of war it adds the chronic danger and degradation of militarism, which not merely wastes the current physical and moral resources of the nations, but checks the very course of civilization. It consumes to an illimitable and incalculable extent the financial resources of a nation by military preparation, stopping the expenditure of the current income of the State upon productive public projects and burdening posterity with heavy loads of debt. Absorbing the public money, time, interest and energy on costly and unprofitable work of territorial aggrandisement, it thus wastes those energies of public life in the governing classes and the nations which are needed for internal reforms and for the cultivation of the arts of material and intellectual progress at home. Finally, the spirit, the policy, and the methods of Imperialism are hostile to the institutions of popular self-government, favouring forms of political tyranny and social authority which are the deadly enemies of effective liberty and equality.[12]

Among those influenced by Hobson was Vladimir Ilyich Lenin, a Marxist, who emerged as the leader of the Bolshevik party which seized power in Russia in November 1917. Lenin—whose original name had been Ulyanov—was a Russian revolutionary who had spent several years abroad in Western Europe. In Zurich in 1916, a year before he attained power in Russia, Lenin completed a book entitled *Imperialism, the Highest Stage of Capitalism,* which was to become the most authoritative text on the subject not only for the new Communist government in Russia, but also for the international revolutionary Communist movement, which found itself immeasurably strengthened in consequence of the success of the Russian revolution.

Lenin concentrated on the economic aspect of Hobson's argument, and developed it further. Unlike Hobson he was not a reformist, but advocated the overthrow of capitalism. As the title of his book indicated, he believed that capitalism had passed into its highest and final stage—the stage of imperialism. In the imperial phase, he held, monopoly capital, or finance capital, had become dominant. Large business having scored victories over small businesses, capital had become concentrated and had entered an epoch in which, working in conjunction with state machinery, it could compel the division of the world among a handful of great powers. Imperialism contained parasitic tendencies, however, as well as fatal contradictions, and therefore was moribund.

> Capitalism [Lenin wrote in his preface to the French and German editions of his book] has grown into a world system of colonial oppression and of the financial strangulation of the overwhelming majority of the people of the world by a handful

12. (1965) edition, p. 152.

of "advanced" countries. And this "booty" is shared between two or three powerful marauders, armed to the teeth (America, Great Britain, Japan)[13] who involve the whole world in THEIR war over the sharing of THEIR booty.

The war itself he described as

imperialistic (that is, an annexationist, predatory, plunderous war) on the part of both sides; it was a war for the division of the world, for the partition and repartition of colonies, "spheres of influence" of finance capital, etc.

The answer to imperialism, Lenin held, was world revolution by the "productive forces," which he identified as the urban proletariat. Less than two years after his book was published in Zurich, Lenin found himself at the head of a revolutionary government in Russia, and therefore in an infinitely stronger position to forward his ideas. Having mastered the revolution which began in Petrograd, he later moved the seat of government to Moscow, where it was installed in that city's ancient citadel, the Kremlin.

### The Decree on Peace

One of the first acts of Lenin's government upon coming to power was to issue, on November 8, 1917, a "Decree on Peace," in which it called upon all belligerent countries and their governments to open negotiations for "a just and democratic peace." By such a peace, it was proclaimed, was meant

an immediate peace without annexations (i.e., the seizure of foreign lands, or the forcible incorporation of foreign nations), and indemnities. . . . The government interprets the annexation, or seizure, of foreign lands as meaning the incorporation into a large and powerful state of a small or feeble nation, irrespective of the time such forcible incorporation took place, irrespective of the degree of development or backwardness of the nation forcibly annexed to, and forcibly retained, within the frontiers of a given state, and finally, irrespective of whether the nation inhabits Europe or distant, overseas countries.

The decree, in effect, called for the ending of annexations in Europe, and the freeing of African and Asian colonies—a radical program calculated to produce immeasurable repercussions throughout the world. After declaring secret diplomacy to be abolished, the decree continued:

The government proposes . . . the conclusion of negotiations for peace with the participation of the representatives of all peoples and nations involved in or compelled to take part in the war, without exception, and the summoning of plenipotentiary assemblies of the representatives of the peoples of all countries for the final ratification of the terms of peace.

13. It is curious that Germany is omitted from the countries named. Possibly this was because the "marriage of convenience" that was later consummated between Lenin and the German government had already begun. The German government facilitated Lenin's return to Russia and encouraged his revolutionary activity with a view to stimulating internal dissension in that country so that its participation in the war might end. They succeeded beyond their wildest dreams.

The government then appealed in particular to the "class-conscious workers" of Great Britain, France, and Germany, because

these workers, by a comprehensive, determined, and supremely energetic action, can help us to bring to a successful conclusion the cause of peace, and at the same time the cause of the emancipation of the toiling and exploited masses of the population from all forms of slavery and all forms of exploitation.

Saying that "three years of war had been a good lesson to the masses," it then concluded somewhat quaintly: "Finally we must remember that we are not living in the wilds of Africa, but in Europe, where news can spread quickly."

Here was a suggested outcome to the war that neither the United Kingdom, France, or Germany—or, indeed, any other belligerent—had foreseen as possible. By this time, however, the main European belligerents were at once too involved in the war and too exhausted to make the imaginative effort that was required to rise to the new Communist challenge of world revolution. The new thinking that the situation demanded came, therefore, from the United States, where for some time certain people had been giving serious thought to the apparent breakdown in world order which had occurred, and to the possible remedies that might be applied.

One of the most notable Americans doing the thinking was a short, slight Texan named E. M. House, who had no official position, lived on a private income, and held the title of a Colonel of militia. By nature a thoughtful man, he was from an early age interested in the functioning of government, and determined that his best course was to translate his ideas into practice by influencing events from behind the scenes. Having played a key role in Texas politics, he moved to the national level, where he effectively aided Woodrow Wilson to become President in 1912, after which he became Wilson's close friend and adviser. The degree of his influence was testified to by such observations as that of Lord Northcliffe, then head of the British War Mission to the United States, who, speaking of Wilson and House, informed Winston Churchill, who that year became a member of the British Cabinet, "The administration is entirely run by these two men."

Earlier, in 1911, a political colleague of House—D. F. Houston, later to be U.S. Secretary of Agriculture—wrote of him in a private letter: "He has a *vision. I should like to make him Dictator for a while.*" Some insight into the nature of House's vision—which many of his contemporaries agreed that he beheld—is provided by a Utopian novel that he published anonymously in 1912 under the title of *Philip Dru: Administrator.* The book was dedicated to the unhappy masses "who have lived and died lacking opportunity, because in the starting, the world-wide social structure was wrongly begun." It used as an epigraph the following words of Giuseppe Mazzini, the Italian patriot who was a precursor of the doctrine of self-determination:

No war of classes, no hostility to existing wealth, no wanton or unjust violation of the rights of property, but a constant disposition to ameliorate the condition of the classes least favored by fortune.

The hero of the novel, Philip Dru, is a West Point graduate who, in the future year 1920, by participating in a popular uprising in a United States oppressed by the tyranny of corporate wealth, becomes dictator. Seeking a solution "not in the socialism dreamed of by Karl Marx," but in a return to a pure and unselfish Christian ethic, he introduces a series of reforms before renouncing power in his own country, and setting sail for Europe to found a "League of Nations"—a League, however, that is to be founded upon Anglo-Saxon solidarity.

Five years after the book's publication it was noticed that many of the reforms introduced by the fictitious hero had in fact become the laws of the United States—from which circumstances it was correctly deduced that the anonymous author might be the President's adviser, Colonel House.

Much of House's success in diplomacy was due to his approach which, indeed, resembled that advocated by his hero, Dru:

Do your work gently and with moderation, so that some at least may listen. If we would convince and convert, we must veil our thoughts and curb our enthusiasm, so that those we would influence will think us reasonable.

With President Wilson's support, House at first, among other tasks, strove to promote a Pan-American Pact which, in language and intent, was the prototype of the League of Nations Covenant. It was felt that the conclusion of such a pact for assuring peace in the Americas would place the United States in a stronger position when the time came to seek to persuade the European countries of the value of a permanent peace-keeping organization. House then began to travel to European capitals, seeking to reconcile the rival European nations by encouraging them not only to co-operate in preserving the peace, but also in "the proper development of the waste places of the earth." The U.S. Ambassador to London, Walter Page, catching sight of the potentialities of such a policy, commented enthusiastically: "If the great world forces could . . . be united and led to clean up the tropics, the great armies might gradually become sanitary police, as in Panama,[14] and finally forget the fighting idea and at last dissolve." House also advocated the establishment of a plan according to which money would be lent to underdeveloped countries at reasonable rates and under conditions by which such

14. Evidently a reference to the work of the U.S. Army in Panama in combatting yellow fever, malaria, etc.

loans would be safeguarded. "Usurious interest and concessions which involve the undoing of weak and debt-involved countries would no longer be countenanced; . . . that same rule must hereafter prevail in such investments as is now maintained in all civilized lands in regard to private loans." This idea, which House discussed with both the British and the Germans, constituted in embryo form the concept that was later to find expression in the mandatory system of the League of Nations.

Even after the outbreak of the European war in 1914 House continued to talk to both the British and the Germans, traveling to Europe on peace missions as the emissary of President Wilson. These missions helped to stimulate Wilson's interest in international affairs, and led him to prepare to play a major role in them. Events were to some extent to be molded by Wilson's character, however—and in that character the virtues had their matching defects. Originally a professor—he had been president of Princeton University—he was austere in habit, idealistic in thought, and strong in conviction. On the other hand, his temperament was coldly puritanical, he sometimes remained oblivious to inconvenient facts, and he was inclined to harbor personal prejudice against those opposed to his views. Above all he was inclined to rigidity, and lacked the adaptability that might best have advanced his cause. As the writer Lincoln Steffens commented, his ideals "were so high that he did not expect to realize them"—and as long as he could feel that he had done his best for them, he was content. The unprecedented triumphs that he was to achieve were to be undermined as much by his own personality defects as by his opponents and by ill-luck. For the moment, however, he had become the first President since the Republic was founded to lead the United States away from the traditional Washingtonian policy of avoiding embroilment in foreign quarrels.

*The Fourteen Points*

The Bolshevik Peace Decree of November 8, 1917, was followed by the publication by the Bolsheviks of the full text of various secret treaties concluded among the Allies, copies of which had been found in the archives of the Russian Ministry of Foreign Affairs. The revelation of the treaties—which were published in the British *Manchester Guardian* on December 13, 1917—caused a sensation, and seriously embarrassed the Allied governments. The Allies had condemned Germany as an aggressive and annexationist power, and had presented themselves to the populations of Europe and the world as being motivated in the war primarily by concern for freedom, justice, democracy, and the preservation of civilization. Now the world learned that under the secret treaties—such as the Treaty of London, the Sazonoff-Paléologue Agreement, the Sykes-Picot Treaty, and the Treaty of Saint-Jean de Maurienne, concluded variously in 1915, 1916, and 1917—some German territory was to be given to France, some Austrian territory to Italy, and Constantinople to Russia, while Turkish territory was to be parceled out among the Allies, the German colonies in Africa were to be divided primarily between France and the United Kingdom, and Japan was to be given the Chinese province of Shantung. The only possible conclusion the international public could draw from these revelations was that the accusation made by the Bolsheviks that the Allied governments, like the Germans, were conducting what Lenin had called "an imperialistic, that is annexationist, predatory, plunderous war," was not entirely without foundation in fact. It was not for this that the peoples of Europe had consented to send their young men to die by the hundreds of thousands, and by the million. Clearly something had to be said—and perhaps done—and clearly the United States, which had not shared in the complicity, was in the best position to say it. President Wilson and his advisers began to consider precisely what United States war aims should be.

On January 3, 1918, Edgar Sisson, a member of the American Mission to Russia which was vainly attempting to prevent the Russians from dropping out of the war against Germany, cabled Washington to urge that President Wilson "re-state the anti-imperialistic war aims and democratic peace requisites of America, thousand words or less, short, almost placard paragraphs, short sentences." These, he felt, would be effective in inspiring some confidence in the United States, if not in the Allies,[15] on the part of Germany as well as of anti-Czarist Russia. Five days later, on January 8, 1918, President Wilson, in a speech to the United States Congress, proclaimed "Fourteen Points," which constituted the war aims of the United States.

The first point called—as had the Bolshevik Peace Decree—for an end to secret diplomacy. Instead there must be, said Wilson, "Open covenants of peace, openly arrived at." The fourteenth point called for the formation of a "general association of nations ... for the purpose of affording mutual guarantees of political independence and territorial integrity to great and small states alike"—a proposition that was to find its realization in the Covenant of the League of Nations. Point Two dealt with the freedom of the seas, Point Three with trade, Point Four with disarmament, and Points Six to Thirteen with the settlement of various territorial questions in Europe and the Middle East. Point Five dealt with colonial questions. It proclaimed the aim of the United States to be

a free, open-minded, and absolutely impartial adjustment of all colonial claims, based upon a strict observance of the principle that in determining all such questions of sovereignty, the interests of the populations concerned must have equal weight with the equitable claims of the government whose title is to be determined.

15. The United States did not have the status of an Ally, but was an Associate Power, thus maintaining its freedom to take such independent action as it saw fit.

From the point of view of the populations concerned, this was clearly not absolute self-determination, but half a cake—half a cake, however, that was very much better than none. Of the drafting of this point, Colonel House, who had worked with President Wilson in the preparation of the speech on January 5, noted in his diary for that day:

> We had less trouble with the colonial question [*i.e.*, after considering disarmament]. At first it was thought he might have to evade this entirely, but the President began to try his hand on it and presently the paragraph which was adopted was acceptable to us both, and we hoped would be to Great Britain.

Further points were later added to the fourteen by President Wilson —for example, the four additional points enumerated in his speech of February 11, 1918, and his five supplementary points mentioned in his speech of September 27, 1918. Although these were not included in the official American commentary later published, they did provide further insights into Wilson's thinking and policy. For example, on February 11, he made the point that "Peoples and provinces are not to be bartered about from sovereignty to sovereignty as if they were mere chattels and pawns in a game, even the great game, now forever discredited, of the balance of power." Territorial settlements should also be made in the interests of and for the benefit of the populations concerned. All well-defined national aspirations should also be accorded the utmost satisfaction—subject to not encouraging threats to world peace. In his speech of September 27, 1918, he made the point that special combinations should not be formed within the projected League of Nations for the purpose of exerting economic pressures. The right to impose economic boycotts should be vested only in the League.

By August, 1918, the last great offensive launched by the German army had been halted, and the French and the British had taken the initiative on the Western front. With American men and supplies arriving in increasing volume, the Germans for the first time were obliged to admit that, in the words of the German general Ludendorff, "It was no longer possible by an offensive to force the enemy to sue for peace. Defense alone could hardly achieve this objective, and so the termination of the war would have to be brought about by diplomacy." The situation of Germany was not improved by the collapse of its ally Bulgaria in September, after which Austria-Hungary, already war-weary, was threatened by the Allied advance. In the Middle East, too, Turkish troops were retreating as the Allies advanced into Syria. The end could not be long delayed. On October 5, 1918, a new German government sent a note to President Wilson, through the Swiss government, urging him to invite the belligerents to enter peace negotiations on the basis of the Fourteen Points, and to conclude an armistice immediately. This set in motion a train of events that was to end with the signing of an armistice on November 11, 1918.

These developments led not only to the urgent consideration of the peace aims sought by the various belligerents, but also to the focusing of attention on the Fourteen Points themselves. On October 30, 1918, President Wilson approved an official American commentary on the Fourteen Points which provided a specific interpretation of them that did much to dispel the vagueness which had hitherto lain behind their "short almost placard-like paragraphs." On Point Five—about which only Belgium expressed reservations of principle, insisting that the integrity of Belgium's colonies be preserved—the American commentary said:

> Some fear is expressed in France and England that this involves the re-opening of all colonial questions. Obviously it is not so intended. It applies clearly to those colonial claims which have been created by the war. That means the German colonies.

The commentary went on to note that title to the German colonies was to be decided, at the end of the war, by "impartial adjustment," based on the observation of the principles first of equitable claims, and second of the interests of the populations concerned. With regard to equitable claims it noted that, according to Britain and Japan, "the two chief heirs of the German colonial empire," the colonies could not be returned to Germany because she would use them as submarine bases and would "arm the blacks," and because Germany already used the colonies as bases for intrigue, as well as oppressing "the natives." Germany, for her part, argued that she needed access to tropical raw materials, that she needed a field for the expansion of her population, and that, under the principles of peace proposed (that is, the Fourteen Points), conquest gave her enemies no title to colonies. As for the interests of populations, the commentary held that this meant that the colonies should not be militarized; that "exploitation should be conducted on the principle of the open door," that labor conditions, profits, and taxes should be strictly controlled; that local custom should be respected; that the protecting authority be stable and experienced enough to thwart intrigue and corruption; and that the "protecting power" have adequate resources in money and competent administrators to act successfully. The commentary then drew the conclusion that it would seem that the principle involved was that the colonial power acts not as the owner of its colonies, but as trustee for the "natives" and for the "society of nations"; that the terms of the colonial administration were "a matter for international concern and may legitimately be the subject of international inquiry and that the peace conference may, therefore, write a code of colonial conduct binding upon all colonial powers."

Less than two weeks after the American commentary was published, the First World War came to an end. The German delegation negotiating the provisions of the armistice had informed Marshal Foch, the French head of the inter-allied forces, that Germany would be overwhelmed by Bolshevism if the Allies did not help them to resist it, and that if they did not, they themselves would afterwards be invaded by the same plague. They agreed to enter into peace negotiations on the understanding that the peace that would follow would be in accordance with the Fourteen Points. The Armistice was accordingly signed on November 11, 1918.

Emotions had run so high in Europe, however, that, while the guns were silent, the psychological change from war to peace could not be made by merely placing signatures on paper. When in April, 1919, at the Paris peace conference that followed the armistice, the German delegation was at last permitted to appear, the hotel in which it was lodged had to be protected by barbed wire, and two delegates were sent back home to a hospital in Germany after being injured by rocks that had been thrown at them.

All belligerents had suffered immeasurable losses. Attempts made to measure them inevitably varied, and inevitably could not achieve great accuracy. In dead alone, and without counting those wounded or missing, estimates now place the French losses at 1,350,000 men, those of the British Empire at over 900,000, those of Germany at 1,770,000, and those of Russia at 1,700,000. Other European belligerents, such as Belgium, Austria-Hungary, and Italy had also suffered, not to speak of Turkey, which adjoined Europe. Lothrop Stoddard, writing in 1920, two years after the war ended, commented:

> Apart from the heavy loss of life in the war, it was the bravest and therefore the best, who were killed. The birth-rate dropped. Among those killed were the youngest, those who had not yet had families. The whole process was life-diminishing.
>
> The war was nothing short of a headlong plunge into white race-suicide. It was essentially a civil war between closely related white stocks; a war wherein every physical and mental effective was gathered up and hurled into a hell of lethal machinery which killed out unerringly the bravest and the best. . . .
>
> And Europe is the white homeland, the heart of the white world. It is Europe that has suffered practically all the losses of Armageddon, which may be considered the white civil war. The colored world remains virtually unscathed.

Two countries—Japan and the United States—emerged from the war with substantial gains to help outweigh the losses they suffered. Japan, at the cost of 300 casualties in battle, and in return for sending a naval force to the Mediterranean, found herself able to take great economic strides forward, to displace European competition in China to a considerable extent, and to make substantial territorial gains. The United States —a country with a predominantly white population—lost 116,000 dead, but gained commercially and economically. As a result of the four years of war the United States was transformed from a debtor to a creditor country, new American industries had been created and scores of new plants built, and the number of millionaires had more than doubled, rising to over 15,000. As one commentator later observed, "Out of the war came the international financial supremacy of the United States: the dream of 1900, of making New York the world's chief money market, was now reality."[16] No doubt this economic development would have taken place in any event, eventually, but certainly the First World War hastened the process.

Subtle, and to some extent deceptive, adjustments had also taken place in the relationship between the white and colored worlds. Whereas in 1914 the only countries in the world not ruled by whites who were either European or of European origin were Afghanistan, China, Ethiopia, Haiti, Japan, Liberia, Persia, Siam, and Turkey, by the end of the war Turkey's provinces had been stripped away from her and placed under European rule; Persia had virtually become a British protectorate; and Haiti had been occupied by the United States. Paradoxically, however, Haiti, despite the fact that it was under the military and financial protection of the United States, had technically the status of a belligerent on the Allied side, and was later, on the strength of this, to become a founding member of the League of Nations. Yet, despite this apparent further extension of white power in the direction of world supremacy, white rule felt itself for the first time threatened—and threatened, moreover, not so much by any external force as by a sensation of internal weakness. It had previously been realized that as time progressed the proportion of white to non-white populations in the world would change to the disadvantage of the whites, not only because there were more non-whites, but also because the non-white birth rate was higher. It was also understood that at some point this would necessitate some power adjustments. Now, however, four years of bloodletting on a scale unprecedented in history left Europe suffering from anemia, unable to face the burden. For the first time a sensation of weakness stole over the old European empires, as the loss of a generation—a generation of youth and, it was felt, of potential genius—made itself felt. Speaking of the decline of European faith in an imperial mission in Asia at this time, K. M. Pannikar commented:

> With the solitary exception of Churchill, there was not one major figure in any of the British parties who confessed to a faith in the white man's mission to rule. Successive Viceroys of India, Liberal, Conservative, and non-party, professed publicly their adherence to the cause of Indian freedom. Secretaries of State . . . claimed that they were working for the freedom of the Indian people and not for the maintenance of British rule. The French were no doubt more brave in their words, but the faith had gone out of them also.[17]

16. Lewis Corey, *The House of Morgan* (1930), p. 428.
17. *Asia and Western Dominance* (London, 1953), p. 201.

### The Peace Treaty

The Peace Conference which assembled in Paris on January 18, 1919, functioned first of all as a "preliminary conference," only changing its status to that of a conference proper in March, 1919. Thirty-two states, comprising those who had fought against or had broken off relations with Germany and the other Central Powers, attended. Ambiguity at first prevailed as to whether Germany was to participate, and the German delegates were not invited until April, 1919, by which time the thirty-two states, dominated primarily by France, the United Kingdom, the United States, Italy, and to a lesser extent Japan, had drawn up the terms of the peace treaty to present to them. Among the thirty-two there were, apart from Japan, a small number of non-white states—China, Haiti, the Hejaz (which was to be renamed Saudi-Arabia in 1932), Liberia, and Siam. White-ruled India and South Africa were also included among the participants.

President Wilson, as the author of the Fourteen Points, and as leader of the United States, the country whose resources in men and material had saved the Allies from defeat, came to Paris with unequaled prestige. Not even the defeat of his party, the Democrats, by their Republican opponents in the 1918 mid-term elections could immediately dim the aura with which he was surrounded. In December, 1918, he visited London, where the premiers of the British Dominions were gathered, waiting for the U.S. confirmation of their claims to the German possessions that their forces had taken during the war. The British Prime Minister, Lloyd George—who a year before, on November 20, 1917, had privately enumerated British war aims to Colonel House, beginning with Germany's African colonies "East and West"—approached Wilson on the subject but was given scant attention. In the forefront of Wilson's mind was the necessity of establishing the League of Nations. While still crossing the Atlantic on a U.S. ship, the *George Washington*, he had briefed his advisers on various problems the U.S. delegation might expect to encounter. Concerning colonies he had said that "He thought that the German colonies should be declared the common property of the League of Nations and administered by small nations. The resources of each colony should be available to all members of the League."[18] Viewing the League that was to be as the "residuary trustee" of the German and Turkish colonial empires, Wilson commented that "nothing stabilizes an institution so well as the possession of property." Wilson apparently envisaged that the colonies might be administered by small nations with no previous

---

18. From a memorandum taken down by Dr. Isaiah Bowman on board the *George Washington* on December 10, 1918. (See *The Intimate Papers of Colonel House*, Vol. 4, pp. 281–2.)

colonial record, such as the Scandinavian countries, or Haiti.[19] His colonial expert, George L. Beer, who had previously, on January 1, 1918, proposed in connection with Mesopotamia that a trusteeship or mandatory system might be considered, disagreed, however, with the handing over of colonial territories to inexperienced administering powers.

Other persons, meanwhile, had also been considering the possibility of a mandatory system. On December 16, 1918, the South African general Jan Smuts, in a pamphlet entitled *The League of Nations: A Practical Suggestion,* proposed that such a system be applied to the "territories formerly belonging to Russia, Austria-Hungary, and Turkey." Smuts hoped, however, that German South West Africa would be annexed by South Africa, just as the Australian premier, William M. Hughes, hoped that the Pacific islands captured from Germany by Australian and New Zealand forces could be annexed outright, without international interference. The British and the French, meanwhile, as early as 1916, had exchanged notes concerning the annexation of other German colonies in Africa. Despite these circumstances, Smuts' pamphlet appeared so opportunely that it resulted in his name being thereafter associated with the mandatory system which was to be adopted by the League.

When the question of African and Asian colonies was raised at the Peace Conference—which was done earlier than had been expected, because of the insistence of those states that sought territories—it was decided first of all that the colonies should not revert to Germany. Lloyd George, on behalf of the British Dominions, then proposed that the colonies be annexed outright by the various occupying powers. Japan then made claims to the Pacific island that she had captured, as well—despite Chinese remonstrances—as claims to Shantung province. France also supported annexation, and there were other territory-seekers as well. As an American writer, Ray S. Baker, put it,

> It also developed presently that the Belgians expected a piece of German East Africa, and that Italy had certain other provisional claims based upon the secret treaty of London. A little later, when she discovered what was going on, Portugal also lifted a piping treble, but no one paid any attention.[20]

President Wilson objected strenuously to outright annexations, evocative as they were of the Old Order which he was attempting to supplant with the New. The resulting deadlock was broken when Smuts once more sponsored suggestions for mandates, with Wilson extending the principle to include the African and Asian territories. The mandatory principle was subsequently incorporated in Article 22 of the Covenant of the

19. As Haiti was then under U.S. occupation, in practice this would have amounted to a form of indirect U.S. administration.
20. *Woodrow Wilson and World Settlement,* Vol. 3 (1922), p. 255.

League of Nations, which was finally approved by the peace conference on April 28, 1919, and which stated, in part, that the colonies and territories

which as a consequence of the late war have ceased to be under the sovereignty of the States which formerly governed them and which are inhabited by peoples not yet able to stand by themselves under the strenuous conditions of the modern world, there should be applied the principle that the well-being and development of such peoples form a sacred trust of civilization.

The mandates were then divided into three categories—A, B, and C. Category A mandates, applicable to Middle Eastern territories, such as Palestine and Iraq, provisionally recognized them as independent, although requiring the temporary assistance of a mandatory administration. Independence was not envisaged for category B and C mandates. The bulk of such mandates fell into Category B, with Category C including only South West Africa and certain Pacific islands—territories in which the populations were so sparse that they were to be administered under the laws of each mandatory as an integral part of its territory. Annual reports were to be submitted by the mandatories to the League of Nations, where they would be received by the body that was to be known as the Permanent Mandates Commission. A certain degree of international accountability was thus introduced. Although the mandates were to be awarded to the different mandatories by the Supreme Allied War Council—the awards being decided in April, 1919—in the future the mandatories had to answer for the "sacred trust of civilization" placed in them, and answer for it to the League, not to the Allies.

The division of the spoils of war was made as follows: Togoland and the Cameroons were each divided between France and the United Kingdom, with most of former German East Africa going to the United Kingdom under the name of Tanganyika. The remainder of German East Africa, consisting of the territories of Rwanda and Burundi, went to Belgium. South Africa obtained South West Africa. Australia obtained German New Guinea. New Zealand obtained Samoa. Japan obtained various Pacific islands. Of the former Ottoman Empire, only the relatively small territory of the Turkish Republic remained as an independent state. Of its former provinces, the United Kingdom obtained Iraq, France obtained Syria, and the United Kingdom—which had agreed to supervise the creation of a national home for the Jews there—obtained Palestine. The Austria-Hungarian Empire, being entirely in Europe, did not fall under the mandatory system, but was divided up into a series of new European states. After the awarding of the mandates was concluded, the British Prime Minister, Lloyd George, who had frequently found himself opposed to President Wilson, walked away from the meeting saying,

"Well, he has saved his precious principles, but we got our colonies."

The greatest difficulties over territories arose concerning the Japanese claims to certain rights in Shantung. Shantung was already experiencing a Japanese occupation which, it was claimed, was from the Chinese viewpoint more oppressive than the German occupation it replaced. Nor did China place much faith in Japanese assurances that Shantung would eventually be returned to her. Japan, in effect, saw not only the port of Kiaochow and Shantung Province as its sphere, but harbored designs upon the whole of China—as it had made clear in its "Twenty-One Demands" of 1915. Impressed by the example of British rule over India, Japan saw China as its natural field for imperial expansion. Pointing out that Japan, after all, was an Asian power, the Japanese government saw a parallel, too, between the situation of the United States, which had kept interlopers out of the Americas by means of the Monroe Doctrine, and its own situation with regard to Eastern Asia in general, and China in particular. Apart from such long-term dreams, Japan's immediate claims to a foothold in Shantung were favored by the secret treaties (now public), concluded with France and the United Kingdom. But President Wilson—aware of feeling in the United States, which viewed China as a future field for American enterprise—strongly opposed the Japanese claim. He urged instead an Open Door policy for the whole of China, with no special spheres of influence being recognized for any power. Japan was willing to agree to this for the same reason that France and the United Kingdom were not—that is, because such a policy would enable Japan to compete effectively against her European rivals. With the Open Door policy thus closed to him by the British and the French, Wilson found himself defending China against Japan and her European treaty partners.

The root of American-Japanese difficulties, in fact, went back to the wartime visit to Washington of a special Japanese mission headed by Viscount Ishii. Japan had then just secured support for her actions in Shantung from her European allies, and sought also to gain the approval of the United States. An agreement had then been concluded which, because of the ambiguity of its wording—which at the same time sanctioned the Open Door policy and recognized Japan's special interests in China— was a constant source of subsequent misunderstanding. This agreement, indeed, was the first cause of all the bitter hostility which in the years that followed was to develop between the United States and Japan. At Versailles, however, rather than oppose the United Kingdom and France, and risk jeopardizing the creation of the League of Nations in consequence, Wilson was finally obliged to bend to the view of the other major powers and to permit Japan to obtain the sanction they sought for their action in Shantung. This circumstance did much to arouse public opinion against the Versailles peace treaty in the United States. The United States government, meanwhile, encouraged China to oppose the terms adopted by the conference. As a result China left the conference and refused to sign the Treaty of Versailles—thus giving clear notice to Japan that, so far as China and the United States were concerned, the matter was by no means closed.

Japan's imperial policies at Versailles stood, meanwhile, in sharp contrast with the Japanese attitude to human rights. When the Covenant was being discussed, President Wilson wished to include an article on nondiscrimination on the grounds of religion. To this the Japanese proposed to add a clause reading as follows:

The equality of nations being a basic principle of the League of Nations, the High Contracting Parties agree to accord, as soon as possible, to all alien nationals of States members of the League, equal and just treatment in every respect, making no distinction, either in law or in fact, on account of their race or nationality.

In introducing the proposal—which clearly had a bearing upon the situation of Japanese in the United States, where they were subject to discriminatory laws and practices—the Japanese representative, Baron Makino, added:

As a result of this war, the wave of national and democratic spirit has extended to remote corners of the world, and has given additional impulse to the aspirations of all peoples; this impulse, once set in motion . . . cannot be stifled, and it would be imprudent to treat this symptom lightly.

In the end the entire article, relating to religion as well as to race, had to dropped. The Japanese had insisted on the racial clause being included if the religious clause was adopted. The Japanese and U.S. delegations agreed on a wording which was acceptable to both, but the British—reflecting the strong objections of Prime Minister Hughes, who was a proponent of the "White Australia" policy—opposed it.

One further attempt was, nevertheless, made by the Japanese to raise the matter. Without mentioning the word "race" they proposed that the preamble to the Covenant of the League recognize "the principle of equality of nations and the just treatment of their nationals." President Wilson, embarrassed both by Australian opposition to the Japanese suggestion, as well as by the effect it would produce on the Pacific coast of the United States, told the League of Nations Commission which was engaged in drafting the Covenant that such suggestions had "set burning flames of prejudice, which it would be very unwise to allow to flare out in the public view." The matter was brought to a vote, and the Japanese proposal, which had gained considerable sympathy from other commission members, received a majority. But President Wilson ruled that a unanimous vote was required for its adoption, and the British and the Americans thus succeeded in blocking the suggestion, although it was generally felt that, as with the question of Sino-Japanese relations, the matter was by no means closed.

The peace treaty drawn up by the conference was now ready for presentation to Germany. Apart from disposing of the German colonial empire, it also changed Germany's European frontiers, and imposed gigantic reparations upon her. Even some of those who had been engaged in working on the various sections of the treaty, when they saw the printed version in its entirety were overcome by the severity of its terms, and sensed the ambiguity of purpose which led them at once to seek to found a new and better international order, and at the same time to punish Germany. A member of the U.S. delegation, Herbert Hoover, presented with the final text, later recalled:

> While I had known many of the ideas . . . I had not before envisaged it as a whole. I was greatly disturbed. In it hate and revenge ran through the political and economic passages.[21]

Confronted with the text of the treaty, together with a time limit for its signature, the Germans balked, and their government fell. However, three hours before Allied troops were to end the Armistice by crossing the Rhine, the German government received the consent of the Reichstag to sign the treaty "under duress." The Treaty of Versailles was accordingly signed on June 28, 1919, and the League of Nations was inaugurated in January, 1920. Meantime, however, China had refused to sign, and the United States Senate, reflecting both isolationist sentiment and a distaste for the treaty terms, had refused to support President Wilson by ratifying the treaty. A final effort to obtain Senate ratification failed on March 19, 1920. The United States therefore did not become a member of the League of Nations, signing a separate peace treaty with Germany on October 18, 1921.

In the midst of his efforts to obtain U.S. ratification of the treaty, President Wilson's health had collapsed. He left office in March, 1921, and died, an invalid, in 1924. He had failed to establish the effective peace-keeping system that he had striven for, but he had made possible a giant step forward toward its realization.

The word now entered into a period of haunted peace—a peace in which the new hopes that had been born struggled to find expression, while the passions stirred by the "Great War," as it was then called, and by the unsatisfactory compromises and accommodations of Versailles, ran strongly beneath the surface, creating a sense of insubstantiality

21. *Years of Adventure* (1951), p. 461.

which affected even the oldest institutions. The old world appeared to have lost its own self-confidence; the new world that struggled to be born, plagued by hopes and fears alike, looked for certainties in an age in which there seemed none to be found. To many the landscape of life appeared to be a wasteland, in which authority was paralyzed, and no man appeared to set things right.

# Chapter 13

# The Awakening Begins

*Let us today, before China's development begins, pledge ourselves to lift up the fallen and to aid the weak; then when we become strong and look back upon our own sufferings under the political and economic domination of the powers and see weaker and smaller people undergoing similar treatment, we will rise and smite that imperialism.* —Sun Yat-sen

*I shall work for an India in which the poorest shall feel that it is their country, in whose making they have an effective voice, an India in which there shall be no high class or low class of people. . . . This is the India of my dreams.* —Mahatma Gandhi

*My people of Africa, we were created in the image of God, but men have made us think that we are chickens, and we still think we are; but we are eagles. Stretch forth your wings and fly!* —Dr. J. E. K. Aggrey

AFTER VERSAILLES, the world entered into twenty years of misbegotten peace. Even as the League of Nations began to function in 1920, three of its most powerful members, who according to the League Covenant had accepted obligations "not to resort to war," had sent troops to fight against the Bolsheviks in Russia. The Bolshevik government, meanwhile, called upon the workers of the world to arise against imperialism, and, having failed to create the Revolution in Europe, called upon the subject peoples of Asia and Africa to rally, in their own interest, to the Communist cause. Meanwhile, the vanquished nations had not all accepted the peace terms that had been imposed upon them. Both Germany and Turkey had been willing to negotiate for peace on the basis of Wilson's Fourteen Points. Some of the terms that they were obliged to sign contradicted the Fourteen Points, and both nations were, in consequence, to continue the war. Germany, exhausted, was not to do so for another twenty years, but Turkey was to do so almost at once. The "war to end war," as it had been called, had failed, it seemed, and after the bitterness of struggle and sacrifice, a pervasive sense of frustration made itself felt. Never, it seemed, had the world been so divided, or had high hopes been so irremediably dashed.

Yet, despite the bleak contours of the age, other aspects sometimes came into view. New men with new ideas were emerging on the political stage, and were, in time, to set new forces in motion. There was, for example, a Macedonian of humble origin who had become a Turkish general—Mustafa Kemal; there was a Hindu lawyer, born in Porbandar, India, who created a new method of political action—Gandhi; there was a Fanti educator from a West African fishing village who dreamed of an Africa redeemed—Aggrey. Then, again, there was the League of Nations, representing in embryonic form a new influence in world affairs. Down to the nineteenth century international conferences had limited their membership to members of Christendom. After the Crimean War, Turkey had also been admitted and, still later, Japan. Now states from every continent were participating in a permanent conference—an innovation indeed, even if the League's achievements lagged behind the hopes that had at first been placed in it by some.

Turkey, as we have said, rebelled against the Allied peace terms almost at once. By the terms of the Treaty of Sèvres, signed on August 10, 1920, by the governments of the Sultan of Turkey on the one hand and by the Allies on the other, the Ottoman Empire was stripped of all its provinces. Only the Turkish heartland of Anatolia remained, and even this did not remain integrally Turkish. The western part of Anatolia, including the port of Smyrna and its hinterland, was given to Greece, while in part of the east an independent Armenian state was to be created, and there was to be an autonomous Kurdistan. The Straits of the Dardanelles were to be internationalized, Turkey's finances were to Western-controlled, and other internal concessions were imposed. Against these terms a section of Turkish opinion, led by Mustafa Kemal, an army officer with a distinguished war record, who was later to take the name of Kemal Ataturk, rallied. In 1920 Kemal formed a new nationalist government, based in the inland Anatolian town of Ankara. Thus for the first time in 470 years Constantinople ceased to be the capital of Turkey—not to speak of the 1,100 years before that during which it had been the capital of the Byzantine Empire. Meanwhile, however, the Greeks, with British support, had taken up arms against Kemal, but found themselves unable to crush him. In the course of the "War of Independence" that followed, Kemal, in order to secure his Eastern frontiers, reached agreement first on March 16, 1921, with the new Bolshevik government in Moscow, and then, on October 20, 1921, with the French.

Kemal and the Bolsheviks, by the Treaty of Moscow, partitioned between them what was to have been the new Armenian state, thus drawing a frontier which has remained stable ever since. The French, for their part—anxious lest Kemal's overthrow would increase British influence, thus jeopardizing their hold on their newly gained territory of Syria—signed the Treaty of Angora, in which they reached agreement with him concerning his southeastern frontier, after which they provided him with some arms. Kemal proceeded to defeat the Greeks in battle, recapturing Smyrna and its hinterland from them in 1922, and making himself the master of Anatolia. He then concluded a fresh agreement with the Allies—the Treaty of Lausanne, signed on July 24, 1923—by the terms of which the integrity of Anatolia, now called the Republic of Turkey, was maintained, foreign troops withdrawn, and other harsh terms revised in Turkey's favor. As a result of Kemal's success, he had the satisfaction of witnessing the downfall of the pro-Greek government of the British wartime leader, Lloyd George. Kemal then embarked on a policy of westernizing his country. Among the reforms he initiated were the abolition of the traditional Turkish headgear, the fez,[1] the emancipation of women from restrictive Ottoman custom, and the introduction of the Latin alphabet and of universal literacy.

The successful Turkish revolt against Western domination produced repercussions throughout Asia. Almost symbolically, the European war into which Turkey had been drawn had ended, for Turkey, with a national rebirth. Furthermore, although white-skinned, the Turks were of Asian origin, and by custom and religion were differentiated from Europeans. As one of Kemal's biographers, Lord Kinross, has put it,

> The East, with its dawning nationalist movements, had indeed begun to look to Nationalist Turkey for example and leadership. Here was the first oriental country to make a stand against Western imperialism and fight to throw off its yoke. The name of Mustafa Kemal spread throughout Asia, as that of Garibaldi had once spread throughout Europe, firing the imagination of all those peoples in whom the First World War had kindled a spark of national consciousness and awakened the desire for freedom. The news of his struggle had its repercussions throughout Syria and Egypt, as far as Persia, India, and even China. Here, surely, was the prototype, for others to emulate, of the Eastern nationalist revolution.[2]

1. The fez itself had been introduced into the Ottoman Empire only in the early nineteenth century, when it had displaced the old-fashioned turban. The fez originated with the Barbary corsairs, but became fashionable among Greek Christians living on the Greek islands, after which the Ottoman Empire adopted it. It was manufactured in Austria for the Ottoman market.

2. *Ataturk: A Biography of Mustafa Kemal, Father of Modern Turkey* (1965). During the Turkish War of Independence, Indian Muslims sent money to Kemal to aid him in the national struggle. Kemal used it to establish the first Turkish bank.

At first the Western European powers, noting Kemal's treaty with the Bolsheviks, had presumed that the Turkish national renascence must be a phenomenon similar in character to Communism. As events developed, however, they came to understand the distinction between Turkish nationalism and Communism, coming to terms with the first, if not with the second. Indeed, in time Turkey served for the Allied powers as a barrier preventing the spread of Communism toward the Mediterranean and the Middle East—thus becoming one of a number of buffer states that insulated the Soviet Union from the rest of the world. For while Czarist Russia had similarly posed a potential threat to Western domination in Asia, the Soviet Union, by reason of the appeal of its doctrine of colonial emancipation to the subject peoples of Asia and Africa, posed an infinitely greater one.

## The Soviet Union and the "National Question"

In the period immediately following the October Revolution of 1917, Lenin and his lieutenant, Leon Trotsky, had confidently awaited an uprising of workers in a war-weary Europe—an uprising that would result in the downfall of capitalism and the establishment of the Revolution first in Europe and then in the rest of the world. When these expectations failed to materialize, however, and the Bolshevik regime found itself attacked and later isolated by the Western nations, new policies were adopted.

As early as 1898 the Social Democrats—who were later to split into the Bolshevik and Menshevik factions[3]—had proclaimed adherence to the principle of self-determination. Various interpretations were given to the term "self-determination," but the Bolsheviks finally specified that it meant the political right of nations freely to secede. Joseph Stalin (Iosiph Dzhugashvili), who was later to become People's Commissar for Nationalities in the first Bolshevik government, before succeeding Lenin in 1924 as the leader of world Communism, made clear, however, that he regarded this right as secondary to the higher right of the proletariat to consolidate the revolution. In an article published in 1913 Stalin wrote that secession might occur under undesirable circumstances. The Transcaucasian Tatars, he said, for example, might assemble as a nation and "succumbing to the influence of their beys and mullahs, decide to restore the old order of things." As this would be disadvantageous to the "toiling strata," it should be opposed, even although the Tatar right of secession—under other circumstances—could later be exercised.

Other aspects of the question of nationalism were also considered at this time. The Austrian Social-Democrats, for example, coming from a

3. The term "Bolshevik" originated in the Russian word for "majority," and "Menshevik" in the word for "minority." The Bolsheviks, however, constituted only a temporary majority.

state which contained many nationalities, had advanced the concept of "national autonomy." According to this concept, the state would remain intact, but individuals within its borders would be granted the status of the nationality they possessed—whether Czech, Polish, or German, etc. Institutions would be established to guarantee complete freedom of cultural development, so that the national peculiarities of the peoples would be preserved and developed. Stalin, who was to become the Communist authority on the national question, attacked these ideas. National autonomy so defined, he said, would "mechanically squeeze nations into the Procrustes bed of an integral state." State boundaries should, where necessary, be redrawn along ethnic lines, and then regional, rather than national, autonomy should be the active principle. Territory would then become the basis for nationality. The encouragement of nationality as envisaged by the Austrian Social-Democrats would, he argued, tend to divide workers by accentuating the differences between them, whereas it was, on the contrary, desirable to promote internationalism among the working class by stressing similarities, thereby promoting unity against the oppressing classes. On the subject of preserving and developing "national peculiarities," he became ironical. "Just think," he observed, "to 'preserve' such 'national peculiarities' of the Transcaucasian Tatars as self-flagellation at the festival of *Shakhsei-Vakhsei*; or to 'develop' such 'national peculiarities' of the Georgians as the vendetta!" Thus, ultimately, Communist policy was to permit each nationality the privilege of self-assertion, of identifying itself, so that it might later become an authentic, rather than an artificial, component part of a greater whole, a whole that was to be formalized, in 1922, in the Union of Soviet Socialist Republics.

Communist policy on nationalities was soon to be tested. From 1917 to 1921 the Bolshevik regime in Russia was fighting for its life. After the German attack ended, counterrevolutionary leaders, such as Kolchak, Wrangel, and Denikin, arose in Russia itself. Obtaining support from the Allies—Kolchak was recognized as Regent of Russia by the Allied powers—they attacked the Bolsheviks. Furthermore, between 1918 and 1921 British, French, American, and Japanese troops intervened in Russia in order to overthrow the Bolsheviks. But they were all unsuccessful, as a result not only of direct military action against them by the Red Army, but also of the Bolshevik policy on nationality. The population of the former Russian Empire at that time was about 140 million, being composed of about 75 million Russians, and about 65 million non-Russians. The Russian population rallied against foreign intervention, while the non-Russian population, which favored the Bolshevik policy of self-determination and feared a return to the imperial status quo, opposed the Russian counterrevolutionaries. As Stalin was to put it in 1923, when criticizing those Communists who advocated a return to what he termed "Great Russian chauvinism" at the expense of the non-Russian peoples,

> Do not forget, comrades, that we advanced against Kerensky with flying colours and overthrew the Provisional Government partly because we were backed by the confidence of those oppressed peoples which were expecting liberation at the hands of the Russian proletarians. Do not forget such reserves as those constituted by the oppressed peoples, who remain silent, but whose very silence exerts pressure and decides much. This is not often felt, but these peoples live, they exist, and they must not be forgotten. Yes, comrades, it is dangerous to forget them. Do not forget that if in the rear of Kolchak, Denikin, Wrangel and Yudenich we had not had the so-called "aliens," the oppressed peoples, who disorganised the rear of these generals by their tacit sympathy for the Russian proletarians . . . we would not have nailed a single one of these generals. While we were advancing on them, their rear was disintegrating. Why? Because these generals depended on the colonising elements among the Cossacks, they held out to the oppressed peoples the prospect of further oppression, and the oppressed peoples were therefore forced into our arms, while we held aloft the banner of the liberation of these oppressed peoples.[4]

Not everywhere, however, was the policy of self-determination favorable to the Bolsheviks. Whereas the Bolshevik government, in accordance with its emancipation policy, renounced claims to Finland, Poland, and parts of Mongolia and China, and also withdrew troops from Northern Persia, difficulties developed with the new Polish government headed by Pilsudski. The Pilsudski government, with British and French support, declared itself dissatisfied with the frontiers proposed by the Bolsheviks, claimed the frontiers Poland had possessed in 1772, and, after refusing to negotiate, attacked the Bolsheviks in the spring of 1920. The Bolshevik counterattack carried the Red Army almost to the gates of Warsaw, and, for a moment, with Germany on the brink of civil war, it seemed that the Revolution might indeed overwhelm Europe. The moment passed, however. Civil war was avoided in Germany, and the tide of battle turned once more in favor of the Poles, who, as a result, gained a settlement that gave them at least a part of their claims.[5] Other nationalist movements that the Bolsheviks regarded as menacing rather than strengthening the Revolution, such as that in Georgia in the Caucasus, were quickly suppressed. In general, however, Asian and colonial peoples tended to react favorably to Bolshevik Russia and its policies. As K. M. Pannikar has put it:

> The Revolution had a well-defined national policy which had an irresistible appeal to the struggling dependencies, colonies, and semi-colonial countries in Asia. The Declaration of the Rights of the Peoples of Russia, over the joint signatures of Lenin

---

4. "Report on National Factors in Party and State" delivered at the Twelfth Congress of the Russian Communist Party, April 23, 1923.

5. Lord Curzon of the United Kingdom proposed a frontier—subsequently known as the "Curzon Line"—that would have separated Poles from Ukranians along ethnic lines. Although this was later approved by the League of Nations, it was rejected by the Polish government of the day. After the Second World War, however, the Soviet-Polish frontier ran roughly along the line suggested by Curzon and approved by the League.

and Stalin, proclaimed the equality and sovereignty of the peoples of Russia, and the right of the peoples of Russia to freedom of development of national minorities. This was indeed an explosive statement and all the nations of Asia, struggling for freedom, heard it with a new hope. The emphasis on national self-determination and ethnic separateness of minorities had an immense effect in shaping opinion in Asia during the next quarter of a century.

During the crisis years of war and famine, which lasted from 1917 to 1921, the Bolsheviks—or Communists, as they now called themselves— had had little time or energy to spare for promoting the struggle against imperialism as defined by Lenin very far beyond the territory that they controlled, despite the fact that, with the founding of the Comintern, or Third International,[6] in Moscow in 1919, Moscow had now replaced Paris as the revolutionary capital of the world. When the crisis years had been weathered, however, the question of the peoples subjected to imperial domination became of increasing importance to the Communists. As Stalin put it in 1921:

> If Europe and America may be called the front, the scene of the main engagements between socialism and imperialism, the non-sovereign nations and the colonies, with their raw materials, fuels, food and vast store of human material, should be regarded as the rear, the reserve of imperialism. In order to win a war one must not only triumph at the front but also revolutionise the enemy's rear, his reserves.[7]

The Soviet Union's African and Asian policies were reflected by those of the Comintern. Students from African and Asian countries received political and other education at such Comintern-sponsored institutions as K.U.T.V.U. (the University of the Toilers of the East) which trained students from Southeast Asia, India, and Africa, and the Sun Yat-sen University, which trained Chinese students. American Negroes, however, were trained at Lenin University, together with Europeans and other Americans. Meanwhile, Communist Parties were established in various Afro-Asian countries—in Turkey, Iran, and the Dutch East Indies in 1920; in China, India, Mongolia, and South Africa in 1921; and in Japan in 1922. Later, Communist Parties were to be formed in Korea in 1925, in Indo-China in 1930, in Algeria in 1934,[8] and in Ceylon and Morocco in 1943. From the outset, however, particular attention was paid to China which, since the fall of the Manchus in 1912, had become an arena in which many different local and international interests were in conflict.

## Sun Yat-sen

The principal Chinese revolutionary leader at the time that the First World War ended was Sun Yat-sen,[9] who was then approaching the final

6. The First International had been founded in London under the leadership of Karl Marx in 1864. It was dissolved in 1876. The Second International, which had been founded in Paris in 1889, was still in existence when the Third International came into being.
7. "The National Question Presented," *Pravda* No. 98, May 8, 1921.
8. Before 1934 the French Communist Party, formed in 1920, had been active in Algeria as well as in France itself.
9. The name of "Sun Yat-sen" is that under which the revolutionary was known abroad. "Chungshan" is the name under which he was and is known in China.

years of his dramatic life. Sun Yat-sen had been born in 1866 in the Kwantung Province of Southern China. In 1879 at the age of fourteen he sailed to Honolulu in Hawaii, where his eldest brother was a farmer. When Sun returned to China in 1883, he had received some Western schooling, and had been converted to Christianity. One of his first acts on his return was publicly to mutilate the village idols—an act of rebellion against tradition that resulted in his being banished to Hong Kong, where he continued his studies. The Franco-Chinese war of 1884–1885, however, which resulted in the loss of Annam to the French, provided him with such a striking demonstration of the ineffectiveness of the Manchus in ruling China that he decided to become a revolutionary. After a further visit to Honolulu, he plunged simultaneously into revolutionary work and medical studies, qualifying as a doctor in 1892, and practicing surgery in Macao until the Portuguese obliged him to leave the colony. He and a friend then traveled to North China, to Tientsin, where they presented the viceroy there with a memorandum urging reforms in education, agriculture, and the Chinese economy. But the memorandum produced no result. After the Sino-Japanese war of 1894–1895, which resulted in the loss of Korea and confirmed his low opinion of the Manchus, Sun founded new branches of a secret organization, the Hsing Chung Hui, or "Revive China Society," in Hawaii. When the society's representations to Peking went unanswered, Sun came at last to the conclusion that there was no hope for peaceful change under Manchu rule. It must be overthrown by revolution.

His first attempt was to try to seize the city of Canton on September 9, 1895. The plan was discovered, however, and the seizure of some of the arms by the Hong Kong Customs authorities led to the failure of the conspiracy. Sun succeeded in escaping, but some of his colleagues were caught and executed. He then traveled to Japan, Hawaii, the United States, the United Kingdom, and several European countries, seeking to gain support from expatriate Chinese, many of whom were wealthy and influential. Before leaving Japan he cut off his queue—a symbolic rejection of Manchu domination which was followed by many other Chinese,[10] and which parallels Mustafa Kemal's subsequent rejection of the fez as a symbol of Ottoman rule. In London Sun was kidnaped on October 11, 1896, while on his way to church, by members of the Chinese legation who held him prisoner for twelve days before a public outcry which followed reports of the incident in the British press forced his release—a fortunate outcome, since arrangements had been made to ship him back to China where, presumably, he was to be executed. It was also in London, probably at this time, that he met some Russian revolutionaries with whom he held discussions. During his subse-

---

10. Opposition to the queue was particularly strong in Southern China. Many members of the secret societies opposing Manchu rule wore false queues in public, which they removed in private.

quent travels in Europe in 1897, he first enunciated the "Three Principles of the People" that were to be associated with his name—principles that were, in essence, nationalism, democracy, and economic welfare. The application of these principles, said Sun, implied three separate yet simultaneous revolutions—national, political, and social.

During the Boxer uprising of 1910,[11] and throughout its harsh aftermath, Sun Yat-sen maintained the same stoic detachment that he had shown during the Sino-Japanese war. Such events, he felt, like the Japanese incursion into Manchuria which followed the Russo-Japanese war of 1905, were an inevitable consequence of Manchu rule. He was, during this period, attempting to unify all the Chinese secret societies into a single movement. Despite his personal differences with the anti-Christian and anti-foreign Society of Harmonious Fists, throughout his career he worked with and often through the various secret societies, which played such an important role in Chinese political life.

From 1900 to 1911 Sun was engaged in organizing various revolutionary attempts, none of which was ultimately successful, but which nevertheless bore testimony to growing Chinese discontent with the Manchu Empire, while at the same time increasing Manchu demoralization. After the 1905 war he and others formed the Tung Meng Hui, or Chinese Revolutionary Alliance. "On the day when the 'Tung Meng Hui' was inaugurated in Tokyo by intellectuals representing the whole of China," he later wrote, "I began for the first time to believe that my revolutionary work might be completed during my lifetime." The movement spread throughout China with astonishing speed.

In April, 1911, the organization launched the largest of a series of revolts but, like those of its predecessors, it was unsuccessful. Taking place in Canton, it resulted in the deaths of a number of the leading spirits of the Tung Meng Hui who, in later years, were celebrated as the "Seventy-two Martyrs of the Yellow Flower Mound." Sun Yat-sen had frequently traveled abroad during these years, and, after the failure of the April uprising, he again set out for the United States and Europe. In Denver, Colorado, he was surprised to read newspaper headlines which announced "Wuchang Occupied by Revolutionaries." He continued his journey to London, however, where he reached a provisional agreement with the International Banking Consortium that no further loans should be made to the Manchu government, after which he concluded a similar agreement in Paris with the French government. He then returned home to Shanghai.

Events had moved fast in his absence. From October on revolution had spread, with some of the military siding with the rebels. Seeking to save itself, the Manchu regime had in November, 1911, appointed as Premier the popular Yuan Shih-kai, a military leader who had formerly

11. See Chapter 6, p. 140.

been dismissed. China was thus split into two separate camps—the revolutionary South, based in Nanking, and the imperial North, based in Peking. On December 29, 1911, representatives of all the provinces which had declared their independence from Manchu rule met at Nanking and elected Sun Yat-sen as Provisional President of China. The Republic of China was inaugurated in the same city on January 1, 1912.

In order to preserve national unity, Sun then proposed to renounce the Presidency in favor of Yuan Shih-kai, on condition that he would formally accept the Republic, and that the Emperor abdicate. The terms were accepted. On February 12, 1912, the Dowager Empress, and the child Emperor in whose name she had ruled, abdicated. The Dragon Throne of the Manchus in Peking had given place to Nanking republican rule, with Yuan Shih-kai becoming President in place of Sun Yat-sen.

Sun was appointed Director-General of Railway Development. Railways had always appealed symbolically to his imagination. He dreamed of covering China with a rail network, just as Lenin dreamed of bringing electric light to every Soviet village. Sun strove to establish a rail system that would bind the nation into one, transform the national psychology, and invigorate economic life. Railways, in a certain sense, represented his "Three Principles of the People" in material form. His dream, however, made no immediate progress. As Sun drafted plans and sought financial backing, Yuan Shih-kai was dreaming another dream—that of making himself Emperor in place of the Manchus. With the republic established, the Tung Meng Hui had been transformed into the ineffective Kuomintang party, which was inaugurated in August, 1912. Its candidate for the premiership, Sun Chiao-Jen, was assassinated in March, 1913, at the instigation, it was strongly suspected, of Yuan Shih-kai, who, meanwhile, was declining to move the seat of government from Peking to Nanking.

When Yuan negotiated a loan with a foreign banking consortium with terms so exacting that President Wilson withdrew U.S. participation from it, on the grounds that it compromised China's independence, Sun felt obliged to break with Yuan. In July, 1913, as one Southern province after another declared its independence of Yuan, and as Nanking broke with Peking, fighting flared up between Northern and Southern forces, and Sun was dismissed from his post at the Railway Development Board. The disorganization of the Southern faction and the lack of military training resulted, however, in the collapse of what had hopefully been called "The Second Revolution." Everyone, Sun complained, talked about their personal liberty and their rights, and thus failed to co-operate effectively. Sun himself was once more obliged to flee abroad in exile to Japan. In November, 1913, the Kuomintang was declared dissolved, while the republican National Assembly was permitted to lapse completely.

Yuan, meanwhile, made himself President for life, expanded the army, and placed his own appointees in key positions. Sun Yat-sen's star seemed at last to be on the wane. Once more, however, his cause was forwarded more by the Chinese government's betrayal of the national interest than by his own efforts, persistent as they were. Following the Japanese seizure of Shantung from Germany, Japan, on January 18, 1915, presented China with its Twenty-One Demands, which Yuan Shih-kai, after vainly prevaricating for five months, felt at last obliged to sign. When the truth was to emerge, Yuan Shih-kai was undone in the eyes of China. It was in vain that, still pursuing his private fantasy, he appointed himself Emperor, ascending the Dragon Throne on January 1, 1916. Province after province rose against Yuan Shih-kai, so that before long he was obliged to abandon his imperial dream. Demoralized, he died in June, 1916.

## The Era of the War Lords

Sun Yat-sen returned from exile in Japan, and sought to revive constitutional government. China was more divided than before, however, with provinces controlled by individual military governors—the "war lords" as they came to be known—whose powers usually depended on their own armed forces rather than on the central government. The North and South also continued at odds, with the North possessing the advantage of organized military forces. It was at the instigation of the North, and in the face of the opposition of Sun Yat-sen and the South, that China, on August 14, 1917, declared war on Germany and Austria— an act, as we have seen, that was primarily inspired by the hope of regaining the Japanese-occupied province of Shantung.

The ten years between 1917 and 1927 were, indeed, those of a bewildering internal dissension, marked by coup and counter-coup, and by fighting in province after province, with the fortunes of civil war swaying now in one direction, now in another. At intervals one leader or another would seek sanctuary in one of the international settlements in the port cities, such as Shanghai or Canton. "China," Sun Yat-sen had commented after the failure of the "Second Revolution," "is a sheet of scattering sand." Never, as he now surveyed the turbulent destinies of the nation from Canton, had his words seemed more apt. Only through the functioning of such services as the post and the customs did China appear to exercise, at least in name, the attributes of an integral sovereign state.

Despite internal anarchy, China nevertheless participated in the Versailles peace conference, even though the inclusion of the clause favoring Japanese claims to Shantung caused China to withdraw from the proceedings. Despite the Chinese refusal to sign the Treaty of Versailles, China's membership in the League of Nations was nevertheless assured by her signature with Austria,[12] on September 10, 1919, of the Peace Treaty of Saint Germain—a treaty which did not include the objectionable Shantung clause among its provisions.

The publication of the proposed terms of the Versailles Treaty, recognizing Japanese claims to Shantung, produced in China, in May, 1919, severe demonstrations against the betrayal of the national interest. It was in this context that on July 25 Sun Yat-sen issued a manifesto to the Chinese people in which he proclaimed his conviction that the Russian people would be "the only ally and brother" of the Chinese in their struggle against imperial domination. It was the first sign of the entente that was soon to develop between Sun and the Bolsheviks. In the following year, 1920, Sun announced the reorganization of the revolutionary movement in the form of the Chung Kuo Kuomintang—the Chinese Nationalist Party. The new party bore no relation to the earlier Kuomintang except by name—the name being used again to avoid reregistration of branches of the party formed by members of the Chinese community in Malaya and the Philippines. In 1921, following the establishment of a constitutional government in Kwantung province, Sun Yat-sen was once more elected President of the Chinese Republic as established in the South. The military government in Peking continued, nevertheless, to exist. By 1922 dissension over the presidency of the Peking government had reached such proportions that Sun, feeling that the moment for vigorous action had come, led a military expedition against the North. He was betrayed, however, by a powerful adherent, Chen Chiung-ming, who had remained with his army in the vicinity of Canton. Supported by Cantonese merchants, who disliked Kuomintang encouragement of trade unionism, Chen began an anti-Kuomintang revolt. When Sun returned to Canton he barely escaped with his life, taking refuge on a gunboat. As it was, his personal bodyguard was massacred. Sun found himself obliged to move from Canton to Shanghai.

Meanwhile, the Northern government had won a diplomatic victory at the 1922 Washington Conference on the limitations of naval armaments in the Pacific. While China had little direct interest in the subject of the conference, she nevertheless was able, with U.S. support, to raise the question of the Japanese occupation of Shantung at the conference. As a result, in return for the payment of compensation, Japanese soldiers left Shantung in December, 1922, and the former German concessions there reverted to China. China also demanded the complete removal of the limits of her sovereignty represented by the special tariff and jurisdictional privileges granted to the Western powers in her territory. While Chinese demands were not all immediately met, China did receive favorable assurances in principle—assurances that were later to be invoked.

12. China also concluded a separate peace treaty with Germany.

The participating powers also agreed on a treaty which ensured that a joint Open Door economic and commercial policy would be followed toward China—an agreement that was concluded more to safeguard Western interests from Japanese competition than to protect China, even though a degree of protection for China did in fact result. As Japan was one of the signatories of this treaty, it was also clear that no more was to be heard of the Twenty-One Demands. The first step in China's national resurgence had, paradoxically, occurred thanks to Western fears of growing Asian power as represented by Japan. Of particular significance, meanwhile, was the new spirit manifested by the Western powers in their dealings with China. Here was imperialism, chastened by the losses of the "Great War," and experiencing an unwonted lack of inner confidence, taking its first step backwards. The steam had gone out of it.

The Soviet Union, evidently, was not one of the powers participating in the Washington conference. Nevertheless, the Soviets, too, were concerned with China's future. After Adolph Joffe, an important Soviet diplomat, had been sent to China, he made contact with Sun Yat-sen and continued to recognize him as the President of the Provisional Government. On January 26, 1923, Joffe signed an agreement with him that included the following:

> Dr. Sun Yat-sen holds that the communistic order, or even the Soviet system, cannot actually be introduced into China because there do not exist the conditions for the successful establishment of either communism or Sovietism. This view is shared by Mr. Joffe, who is further of the opinion that China's paramount and most pressing problem is to achieve national unification and attain full national independence; and regarding this great task he has assured Dr. Sun Yat-sen that China has the warmest sympathy for the Russian people and can count on the support of Russia.

It was at this time, too, that military fortune turned in favor of Sun. Troops supporting his cause recaptured Canton, enabling him to return there once more. Soviet money and supplies also began to flow to him, and Michael Borodin, a Comintern official, was appointed as his adviser. At the same time Sun's chief of staff, an officer named Chiang Kai-shek, later to become his successor, was sent to the Soviet Union, returning in 1924 to establish a Kuomintang military academy at Whampoa in the Canton area. At the end of the year the government in Peking invited him to discuss differences between the Northern and Southern regimes. Sun permitted himself to hope that perhaps the time was approaching when Chinese unity could at last be re-established. He had, however, grown old, was in poor health, and was not to live to see the united China of which he dreamed. After traveling to Peking he fell ill, and died on March 12, 1925, at the age of sixty. Although his life's task had not been accomplished, his constant efforts had helped to promote national consciousness throughout China, and had gained him the affection of his countrymen, who named him the Father of the Chinese Revolution.

## Chiang Kai-shek and the Kuomintang

Sun Yat-sen's death ended whatever chance might have existed of a union between North and South at that time. Overcoming opposition, however, Chiang Kai-shek soon showed himself to be the successor of Sun. One of the differences between the two men was that Chiang favored the United States, and not the Soviet Union. Chiang's visit to Moscow in 1923 had taught him much, but had also alienated him from Communism. Continuing for the moment, however, to work closely with Borodin and to accept Russian support, he planned a new march against the North, meanwhile seizing Hankow, Shanghai, and Nanking. Anti-Western riots coincided with the capture of Hankow and Nanking—those in Hankow resulted in the relinquishing of British rights there—so that in consequence mutual recriminations were exchanged between Chiang and the Communist faction within the Kuomintang, with the Kuomintang taking the Communist side and depriving Chiang of his various posts. But Chiang struck back by organizing a massacre, on April 12, 1927, of all the Communists and Communist sympathizers that his special squads could find in Shanghai and other cities.

The Communist-supported Kuomintang, which was by now based in Hankow, expelled Chiang Kai-shek from the party. They were, however, much weakened by the loss of Chiang and his forces, and were also divided among themselves. Chiang Kai-shek, for his part, proceeded to march to the North, openly repudiating the views of his predecessor, Sun Yat-sen, on the Soviet Union by declaring, "Russia has now betrayed us, and we must look to America as our only real friend among the nations." Shortly afterwards he succeeded in re-establishing his control over the Kuomintang, repressing a Soviet-backed rising of the "Canton commune" in December, 1927, with great bloodshed. Chiang then continued his northward advance—carefully avoiding Japanese forces that, despite treaty obligations, still occupied certain areas—to enter Peking at last in July, 1928. While he still had the problem of Japanese forces to consider, as well as the internal threat to his authority posed variously by the Communists and by the remaining dissident war lords, he could, nevertheless, claim to have united North and South into a single national government in the name of the Kuomintang.

With unity, albeit a qualified unity, restored, it became possible to strengthen sovereignty further. Already, at a conference held in Peking in 1925, revised tariff rates favoring China had been accepted by other powers, and it had also been agreed "in principle" that all tariff restrictions should end by January 1, 1929. Now, by removing the seat of government to Nanking, Chiang, at a stroke, diminished the prestige of the foreign powers—who, in Peking, possessed a "legation quarter" with gardens and palaces, and with its own defense arrangements. In Nanking there was none of this. In 1929 Chiang's government then raised the question of extraterritorial rights enjoyed by foreign powers, and it was agreed that "January 1, 1930 should be treated as the date from which the process of the gradual abolition of extra-territoriality should have regarded as having commenced in principle." The British, who had already left Hankow and Kukiang, also agreed at about this time to permit their concessions in Chinkiang and Amoy to revert to China, also withdrawing from the port of Wei-hai-wei. Slowly but surely China was recovering its sovereignty. There remained the international concessions at Shanghai and Tientsin, and the Peking legation quarter—now, so to speak, functioning out of context—as well as the question of the free use by foreign vessels of China's inland waterways, and in particular the Yangtze, which was patrolled by warships. Before Chiang could raise these questions, however, his attention was diverted by China's deteriorating relations with Japan, which, instead of permitting him to exert further pressure upon the Western powers, obliged him to turn to them for support.

## The Manchurian "Incident"

At the end of the First World War, when the European powers were again in a position to give their attention to Asian affairs, they became concerned over the rapid growth in Japanese power. The Twenty-One Demands upon China had alarmed them, while at the same time demonstrating where Japanese ambitions lay. They had also been concerned when Japan had not limited her military efforts to China and the North Pacific, but had also crossed the Equator southwards, against Allied wishes. Both the United States and Canada felt particularly strongly that Japan's ambitions should be curbed, and prevailed upon the United Kingdom, which was linked to Japan by the Anglo-Japanese Alliance, to permit the alliance to lapse when it expired in 1921. The alliance was replaced by an innocuous Four Power Pacific Treaty, signed by the United Kingdom, the United States, France, and Japan, but this did little to alleviate Japanese feeling, which held that Japan had been sacrificed by the United Kingdom for the sake of the United States. Furthermore, at the Washington Conference of 1922, global naval armament had been apportioned in a ratio of 5: 5: 3 between the United States, the United Kingdom, and Japan, thus ending the Japanese dream of building the most powerful navy in the world. Naval fortification in the Pacific was also limited, although the United Kingdom was permitted a naval base at Singapore—a development that, to the Japanese strategists, brought home not only that the United Kingdom was no longer linked to Japan by alliance, but had now become actively distrustful of Japanese intentions.

Japan felt that it had other reasons for resentment. United States hostility to Japan had been clearly expressed at the Washington Conference, which had resulted in Japan's withdrawal from Shantung. The U.S. Immigration Law of 1924 ended the flow of Japanese immigrants to the United States, and as Japan had hitherto observed a "Gentleman's Agreement" by which, since 1908, such immigration had been restricted to avoid creating economic dislocation in the United States, the Japanese felt that, apart from the injury inflicted upon them by blocking part of the outflow of the rising Japanese population, the new law could be no more than an expression of racial discrimination against them. Following the rejection of Japanese proposals at Versailles for the inclusion of a nondiscrimination clause in the League of Nations Covenant, the enactment of this law did much to stimulate the growth of a nationalist sentiment in Japan that found expression in such slogans as "Asia for the Asians," as well as in warnings against the "White Peril." The Europeans and Americans, clearly, had formed a bloc against Japan, and Japan would have to find a way to respond effectively.

Japan determined to develop by every possible means both her military power and her economy. She would have to become self-sufficient if she were not to be vulnerable. At least some of the things that she required—iron, coal, and a guaranteed food supply—could be obtained from Manchuria, where the war lord, Marshal Chang Tso-lin, with Japanese support, ruled over what had become, like Inner Mongolia, a virtual Japanese protectorate. Manchuria would also provide a satisfactory outlet for colonization, thus relieving the internal pressure of Japan's rising population, which stood at 59,700,000 in 1925, having almost doubled in half a century, and which was to rise to 64,450,000 by 1930.

The population problem was not the only one to produce internal pressures in Japanese society. Rapid industrialization had created many new social tensions and upheavals, which were reflected by changes in the wielding of power. It was in this atmosphere of growing resentment against foreign powers, and growing internal tensions, that there occurred the sudden and dramatic collapse in prices on the New York Stock Exchange which became known as the "Wall Street Crash" of October 24, 1929. The event, which was completely unforeseen, produced devastating economic consequences throughout the world. In the Depression that followed, not only did individuals often lose all their savings, but whole cities, industries, and even countries were stricken with unemployment. The event was seen by many as a vindication of the claim that the Communist economic system was superior to capitalism —a conclusion that the Communists did nothing to dispel. Japan was among the countries deeply affected by the Depression. Many Japanese farmers, for example, had depended on silk exports to the United States, and these were now drastically reduced. The inability of Japanese politicians and businessmen to solve the problems that arose led to the diminution of popular confidence in the parliamentary regime—a diminution that led to politicians being held in widespread contempt. It was the Japanese military who benefited from these circumstances, since, being schooled in the samurai tradition of despising wealth and corruption, and being known for their patriotism, they were held in respect by the farmers and peasants. The situation produced by the Depression, in sum, so aggravated the existing tensions in Japanese society, that it became clear that some form of explosion was inevitable. It only remained to be seen whether this explosion would occur internally or externally.

The explosion was external, and took the form of the invasion of Manchuria on September 18, 1931. Earlier, certain elements in Japan had striven to apply the "Shidehara policy," which took its name from a Japanese Minister of Foreign Affairs, and which aimed at fostering friendship with China and the Soviet Union. However, after the London Naval Conference of 1930 had imposed further restrictions on Japan, which the Japanese government accepted, the resentment of the Japanese military reached new heights. It was in this atmosphere that, in November, 1930, the Japanese premier, Hamaguchi Yuko, was attacked by an assassin, dying of his wounds the following May. Other assassination attempts and murders followed, as the ultra-nationalist movement grew stronger, until a system that became styled "government by assassination" had in fact been instituted. Meanwhile, in Manchuria, a pro-Chinese Nationalist "Rights Recovery Movement" had been established. Paradoxically this did not lead at first to a clash with Japan, but, in 1929, to one with the Soviet Union. When the Chinese Nationalists seized the Chinese Eastern Railway in North Manchuria, the Soviet successfully replied with armed force. The conclusions drawn from the incident by the Japanese military faction were first that China was in no mood to respond favorably to the Shidehara policy, and second that the Chinese forces were unable to resist a well-armed modern force. When it was further realized that the Soviets were double-tracking the Trans-Siberia Railroad, Japan became increasingly concerned lest she be forestalled in Manchuria. Nor, it was felt, was there much time to lose, since China herself was quickly regaining strength. Furthermore, yet another train of events had been set in motion when, in 1928, Marshal Chang Tso-lin, the war lord controlling Manchuria, who had shown signs of becoming increasingly involved in Chinese affairs, was assassinated by a bomb placed in his railway carriage in a conspiracy organized by a small group of Japanese army officers acting on their own initiative. When, in 1930, his anti-Japanese son and successor, Marshal Chang Hsueh-liang, rallied openly to Chiang Kai-shek's cause, the Japanese felt that they should wait no longer, and prepared their invasion of Manchuria. The immediate justification given for their attack was an explosion on the railway line near Mukden, which resulted in a minor clash between Chinese and Japanese troops. Moving in with overwhelming force, Japan occupied Manchuria by January, 1932. Claiming that Manchuria had previously conquered China, and not vice versa, Japan revived Manchurian—as opposed to Chinese—claims to the region, and, on February 18, 1932, countenanced the proclamation of Manchuria as an independent state under the name of "Manchukuo" (Land of the Manchus). Manchukuo was placed under the regency of Pu Yi, last of the Manchu emperors who, as a child, had abdicated his throne in Peking in 1912, nevertheless retaining the title of Emperor of Manchuria.

The invasion of Manchuria was immediately raised by China at the Council of the League of Nations, with the result that a committee of inquiry was established—Japan's action meanwhile being held up to international obloquy. When, more than a year later, the committee published a report adverse to the Japanese, Japan gave notice that it would withdraw from the League, which it did in due course. Beyond publishing a committee report, however, the League did nothing. One contemporary historian described the League's reaction as follows:

> The principle of the Hue and Cry[13] was tacitly abandoned. None of the Great Powers was willing to take the lead in taking action against the aggressor. None was even willing publicly to promise co-operation if and when others took action. Each, like the wedding guests in the parable, pleaded other preoccupations. The "anonymous" aggressor of the Geneva Protocol orations turned out to be an abstract and purely theoretical personage, with no connexion in real politics with the power which on September 18, 1931, violated the Covenant, the Kellogg Pact[14] and the Nine-Power Washington Treaty. Never was it so forcibly demonstrated that "there is safety in numbers."[15]

At least one of the Great Powers had indeed had "other preoccupations." The United Kingdom, passing like other European states through

---

13. According to the principle of Hue and Cry—a concept taken from English common law—every man's hand is raised against a wrongdoer, thus deterring crime. Many supporters of the League had hoped that this principle might be developed among nations by organizing an international "hue and cry" under Article XI of the League Covenant. The word "hue" (from the Old French *heu*, meaning a hunting cry), meant a vociferous clamor. Originally individuals who knew that a felony had been committed were bound to raise a hue and cry under pain of fine or imprisonment.

14. The Kellogg Pact, which took its name from the U.S. Secretary of State, renounced war as an instrument of national policy. It was signed in Paris by fifteen nations, including Japan, on August 27, 1928.

15. George Slocombe, *Mirror to Geneva* (1938), p. 279.

a financial crisis, was already attempting to cut back its armed forces when on September 16, 1931—two days before the Manchurian invasion —a Communist-inspired mutiny had broken out in the British Royal Navy at Invergordon, a naval base in Scotland. The incident had been widely publicized abroad, and appears to have presented the Japanese military authorities with an ideal occasion to set their prepared operations in motion. Finding itself placed at a military and financial disadvantage, and also aware of widespread pacifist sentiment in Britain, the British government apparently tried to make a virtue of necessity by taking the position that the best way to deal with Japan would be to encourage it to find its destiny in China. "After all," said Sir John Simon, the British Foreign Minister, "What is China? A geographic expression." The United Kingdom, like the other League members, thus effectively washed its hands of the affair—a circumstance of which other nations with expansionist plans for the future took careful note.

Divergence between the U.S. attitude and that of the League,[16] which showed itself at the outset, also led to an immediate hardening of the Japanese position. On January 7, 1932, however, U.S. Secretary of State Stimson proclaimed the "Stimson Doctrine," which denied diplomatic recognition of territorial conquest in Asia. The doctrine had no more than moral force at its disposal, and on January 28, 1932, Japan, allegedly to protect Japanese nationals but in fact as a reprisal against economic boycotts, landed marines in Shanghai and attacked Chinese troops, despite Western protests. After a U.S. attempt to invoke the Nine Power Treaty had failed, U.S. warships were moved into the vicinity and the U.S. fleet was concentrated at Hawaii. Japan withdrew her forces from Shanghai in March.

Japan still aimed not at the conquest of China but at bringing China under her control piecemeal, in the same way that the United Kingdom had established its sway over India, by subjecting one region after another to its control, and then ruling through puppet regimes. But now Japan faced world-wide opposition organized by the Western powers. For this reason the appearance of Nazism in Germany appeared to offer her an opportunity of escaping from the isolation that was being imposed on her. When, on November 25, 1936, Germany, Italy, and Spain concluded the Anti-Comintern Pact, Japan decided that she now had powerful and united allies in Europe, and would therefore be free to continue with the subjection of China, a task which clearly had to be undertaken, if it was to be done at all, before China had gained much more strength. A clash between Chinese and Japanese troops near Peking—the latter stationed there in accordance with the Protocol of

16. The U.S. favored direct negotiations between the parties, whereas the League wished to send a commission of inquiry immediately. The outcome was a delay in the sending of the commission.

1901 concluded at the time of the Boxer Rising—and which occurred on July 7, 1937, soon led to general hostilities. An undeclared war between China and Japan thus broke out—a war that was later to merge into the Second World War.

### The "Long March"

Meanwhile, in China itself a development had occurred that, although it had apparently minor significance at the time, was to have far-reaching repercussions. This was the removal between 1934 and 1936 of Communist troops, estimated as numbering some 120,000, from Kiangsi province in the southeast of China to Shensi province in the north, after an extensive two-year journey across the country that is known as the "Long March." Earlier, on November 7, 1931, Mao Tse-tung, the Chinese Communist leader, had proclaimed the foundation of the "Chinese Soviet Republic" at Juichin, a village in Kiangsi province. When Chinese Nationalist forces began to press the Communists too closely, Mao, on instructions from Moscow, began to lead his troops in the direction of Russian-occupied Outer Mongolia. On their way they gained recruits, while their new position brought them greatly increased security. The long and epic journey coincided with an important change in the fortunes of the Chinese Communists. Having declared war against Japan in 1932, they increasingly drew supporters to their cause from 1934 on, when they emphasized resistance to the foreign invader rather than the achievement of internal social goals. Within China there was increasing criticism of Chiang Kai-shek for attacking the Communists rather than the Japanese, and, after Chiang himself had been temporarily kidnaped in December, 1936, during which time he was apparently persuaded to discontinue his opposition to the Communists for the time being, the united Chinese front against Japan for which the Communists had been calling was in fact formed. The identification of nationalism and Communism that was achieved during these years thus brought a great access of strength to the Communist cause in China.

### Mohandas Gandhi

As Chinese national resurgence was initially represented by Sun Yat-sen, so India's resurgence was represented by another strong personality, Mohandas Gandhi.

In part because of the hold that the British Raj had obtained over the country, and in part because of the particular imprint of Gandhi's personality, India's struggle for freedom from Western domination was not to be decided by armed uprisings, civil wars, and foreign interventions, but by new, unprecedented, and more pacific methods. Whether or not the claim is true that Gandhi was the most illustrious Indian to appear since Gautama Buddha was born in the sixth century B.C., there is no doubt that Gandhi's moral influence was a decisive determinant in India's struggle for independence.

Gandhi was born on October 2, 1869, at Porbandar in Gujarat. His patriotism, his readiness to innovate, and his preoccupation with diet— all of which were character traits that were later to remain in evidence —were all demonstrated in his childhood attempt to break with Hindu tradition by eating meat. He and a school friend had been impressed by some lines of doggerel then current in Gujarat:

> Behold the mighty Englishman
> He rules the Indian small
> Because being a meat-eater
> He is five cubits tall.

The experiment was discontinued after Gandhi's revulsion for meat became too strong—after his first taste of goat's meat he suffered nightmares in which it seemed as though a live goat were bleating inside him.

Betrothed at seven, Gandhi was married at the age of thirteen to a wife of the same age. He traveled to England in 1888 to study law, after which he returned to India in 1891 as a qualified barrister. In 1893 he went to South Africa as a lawyer for an Indian firm, allowing himself to be persuaded to remain to help the Indian community fight racial discrimination, thus becoming involved for the first time in public work. In this way what was to have been a visit of one year was extended for two decades. In 1894 he founded the Natal Indian Congress. It was also during his years in South Africa that his personality, formerly uncertain, defined itself under the stimulus of new tasks.

From his Indian upbringing and family life he drew upon tradition, studying the Gita, the Shastras, and other religious writings. He was also deeply impressed by the writings of Tolstoy, Thoreau, Ruskin, and others. As a result, he adopted as simple a life as possible, espoused the ideal of self-help, and strove to realize the possibilities of universal love. Identifying himself with the poorest, he founded *ashrams* (co-operative communities), in which he and other "truth-seekers," both Indian and European, sought to lead lives of poverty and renunciation, the better to practice *ahimsa* (nonviolence), and *satyagraha* (firmness in the truth). During these years Gandhi and his followers inspired the Indian community in South Africa with a new spirit of self-reliance and self-respect. By applying the principle of *satyagraha* to political action, Gandhi, in 1906, organized nonviolent resistance to injustice, thus introducing a new technique.

In pursuance of his ideals, and for conducting civil disobedience campaigns, Gandhi was frequently imprisoned during these years, thus drawing fresh prestige and influence from the circumstance, and attracting sympathy to his cause. In times of adversity, both when the plague broke out in South Africa and when the Boer War occurred, Gandhi helped to organize medical relief, and served as a nurse as well. When the First World War broke out he was returning home to India via England, and, still holding views, as he himself put it, "favourable to the British connection," helped organize a volunteer Indian ambulance corps. Because of illness, however, he soon returned to India, where the tasks that awaited him were to bring him his greatest fame. Already, he found, he had been given the name of "Mahatma"—meaning "Great-Souled"—while his South African work had made him known to Indians and Europeans alike throughout the subcontinent. Indeed, upon his arrival the British Governor of Bombay asked Gandhi to see him whenever he contemplated action which affected the government—an arrangement he willingly agreed to.

Having founded an ashram in Ahmedabad, breaking with tradition by accepting members of the "untouchable" caste into it, Gandhi then revived the use of the hand loom and the spinning wheel—"self-help" weapons which, he felt, would accomplish more than guns in rendering India economically independent of foreign manufactures, and hence of foreign control. He then launched a campaign against the indentured labor system under which Indians were sent to South Africa—a system which, he felt, constituted semislavery. The campaign was successful, and the system was abolished by the Indian government in 1917. Gandhi also conducted an investigation into grievances among the sharecropping indigo workers in Bihar, in the course of which he introduced civil disobedience techniques into India for the first time. Again he was successful, obtaining reforms. The first of his fasts occurred at Ahmedabad, when he swore not to touch food until the striking mill-workers adhered to their promise to remain nonviolent, and until the strike reached a settlement.

At this time Gandhi was reiterating his support for the recruiting of Indians to help Britain in the war, while also urging the British to pledge *swaraj* (home rule) for India, and also to listen to Muslim demands. In the Montagu Declaration of 1917 the British had stated their Indian policy to be "the gradual development of self-governing institutions with a view to the progressive realization of responsible government in India as an integral part of the British Empire." This policy found expression in the Montagu-Chelmsford constitutional reforms of 1918, which introduced partial self-government for the provinces—a system known as "dyarchy," representing a dual form of government which gave a degree of responsibility to Indians, but kept control of key functions in British hands. The system did not satisfy Indian nationalists, who demanded that the term "self-government" be given greater substance than this.

Matters had reached this point when three factors combined to stimulate Indian nationalism to unprecedented heights, and to place Gandhi's footsteps, no less than those of the Indian nation, on the path leading toward the goal of ultimate independence. The first of these factors was the ending of the war and the return of Indians from Europe with the demand that the ideals of liberty for which they had supposedly fought be translated into reality for Indians as well as for Europeans. The second factor was the powerful sympathy felt among India's Muslim population for the Ottoman Empire—a sympathy which became transformed into anti-British sentiment when the existence of the secret treaties dismembering the Ottoman Empire for the benefit of the European powers became known. The third factor was the repression begun by the British in 1919 of which the Rowlatt Act was the symbol. The act—which took its name from Sir Sidney Rowlatt, chairman of a committee that had investigated revolutionary conspiracies in India—struck at the basis of civil liberties, and effaced what limited good will had been created by the Montagu-Chelmsford reforms.

Gandhi had earlier asked the Viceroy of India to withhold his assent from the "black bills," as the Rowlatt measures were known before they were enacted. When his appeal was not heard, he formed a *satyagraha* society, and proclaimed April 6, 1919, as a day of national fasting—actions which drew a response throughout India, and which mobilized opinion against the British. It was in this atmosphere that a week later, on April 13, the Hindu New Year, that the Indian National Congress, despite a ban on public gatherings, organized a meeting attended by 20,000 people in the Jallianwalla Bagh, or public park, at Amritsar in the Punjab. British troops appeared and, blocking the only exit, opened fire on the crowd, killing close to 400 people. The "Amritsar Massacre," as it became known, occurring at a time when the form of the future was in doubt, crystallized Indian opinion against British rule, and made independence inevitable. Anti-British sentiment found confirmation in the wave of repression which followed the massacre, in which, in addition to arrests, jailings, and floggings, humiliations were inflicted upon the Indian populace that aroused resentment throughout India. For example, during the disturbances in Amritsar a British woman medical missionary had been assaulted, and as a collective expiation all Indians passing down a narrow lane where the event had occurred were obliged to crawl on all fours.

Gandhi himself was horrified by the turn that events had taken. When he realized that *satyagraha* was as yet insufficiently understood by his countrymen, and that the movement that he had called into being was tending toward violence, he called it off, admitting that he had made what he referred to as a "Himalayan mistake." He also fasted to express repentance for the violence that Indians had committed. Meanwhile, however, he also began to co-operate more closely with the Indian National Congress than he had previously done, rapidly coming to exercise political power over it.

The Indian National Congress had been created in 1885—paradoxically at the suggestion of a Briton who had retired from the Indian civil service, and who had called for fifty Indians to come forward to found an organization representative of Indian interests. The proposal had been approved by the Viceroy of the day, the liberal-minded Lord Dufferin. For the first twenty years of its existence the Congress had co-operated with the British, until at length a more radical nationalist faction had risen within it, demanding greater Indian control over public affairs. Clearly pursuing a policy of "divide and rule," Lord Curzon, then Viceroy, knowing that the Bengalis represented the spearhead of Indian nationalism, had in 1905 partitioned Bengal, thus pleasing Bengali Muslims, and displeasing Bengali Hindus. Muslim-Hindu relations deteriorated, and in 1906 a Muslim political organization independent of Congress, the Muslim League, was founded. The breach was to some extent healed in 1916, however, when Muslims and Hindus joined together to sign the "Lucknow Pact," demanding early self-government.

Gandhi now further reunified Hindu-Muslim sentiment by supporting the Khilafat movement among the Muslims—a movement which called for the restoration of the Ottoman caliphate—while at the same time uniting Muslims and Hindus alike against the Rowlatt Act, as well as the Amritsar massacre and its aftermath. At a special session of Congress held in Calcutta in 1920, and at the annual meeting at Nagpur which followed in 1921, it was decided to endorse *swaraj* (home rule) as an objective, as well as such other objectives as the redress of wrongs in the Punjab, the attainment of Hindu-Muslim unity, the settlement of the caliphate question in a manner acceptable to India's Muslims, the abolition of untouchability, and the introduction of homespun cloth. The last two objectives were clearly adopted at Gandhi's behest, and it was a testimony to the moral authority he wielded that from this time on Congress members clad themselves in homespun. Gandhi himself continued to exhort Indians to study *satyagraha*, to refuse to accept government posts or decorations, and to be prepared, should the need arise, to refuse to pay taxes.

By 1922 the British, who had for some time been uncertain what attitude to adopt toward Gandhi, arrested him for "exciting disaffection," and placed him on trial. At his trial Gandhi stressed once more his abhorrence of violence, and called upon the presiding judge, an Englishman, either to resign at once to dissociate himself "from evil," or, if he believed that British rule was good for India, to inflict upon him the heaviest penalty under the law. The embarrassed judge stated publicly that Gandhi was "in a different category from any person I have ever tried or am likely to have to try," and sentenced him to six years imprisonment, hoping that this period might be reduced. Gandhi was released from prison in 1924, having spent his time spinning and reading religious books, activities in which he felt, as he himself put it, "happy as a bird." From 1924 to 1929 Gandhi then pursued what he termed his "constructive program"—advocating hygiene, self-help, and the attainment of other special goals—a program that absorbed his energies during the years when he was not actively promoting *satyagraha* campaigns.

Indian national consciousness was now awakened, however, and British authority had begun its slow but certain retreat. Knowing that their rule was now fatally undermined, the British could therefore only contemplate delaying action to prolong their presence. This action took two forms—the granting of a series of concessions to nationalism, and the strengthening by the British of their links with the Indian princes, through whom they might hope to continue to rule indirectly.

The concessions to nationalism were granted intermittently. First fiscal autonomy was granted to India on the condition that the central legislature and the Indian government were in agreement on measures to be taken. Then Britain, which had itself moved away from a policy of free trade toward one of protection, permitted India to introduce a tariff policy protecting its own manufactures, thus encouraging the development of Indian industry. The progressive nationalization of the Indian railroads was also permitted, and the rupee was slowly freed from London's control. The Indianization of the army was begun, with Indian cadets being sent to Sandhurst in England for training. In 1924 the Royal Indian Navy was established, and an air force was also founded. In the civil service it was agreed that up to 50 percent of the higher posts should be held by Indians—about the same proportion that held posts in the Central Cabinet. Meanwhile, as these far-reaching innovations were introduced, and slowly made their effect felt, the princely states, which constituted two-fifths of India's area, were made directly subject to the British Crown. A number of the Indian princes, however, came to realize the danger in which they would place themselves by acting for the United Kingdom and against Indian nationalism, and consequently declined to play the roles that the British intended them to play. Instead, therefore, the concept of a central federal government, formed of a union of provinces and of princely states alike, gained ground.

During this time, Indian opinion was becoming increasingly restless and impatient, and Gandhi once more became politically active. It was decided that if Dominion status within the British Empire had not been granted by the end of 1929, Congress would advocate independence as India's goal. Consequently, on January 26, 1930—a date since celebrated as India's independence day—millions of Indians took a pledge to work for *Purna Swaraj*, complete independence. On March 12, 1930, Gandhi began his March to the Sea—also known as his Salt March—walking 200 miles to Port Dandi, where he arrived on April 6 to make a handful of salt out of sea water, thus symbolically breaking the government's salt monopoly. Throughout the march, in which he was accompanied by vast crowds, mass meetings supporting him took place in Indian cities; *satyagrahis*—those dedicated to the principles of *satyagraha*—became active; the Indian nation was stirred to its depths; and international interest was awakened. Despite the arrest of over 100,000 people, including Gandhi himself and other leaders, the British administration, faced with an aroused India, was virtually paralyzed. India had made a decisive demonstration of its latent strength.

In June, 1930, a few weeks after Gandhi's arrest, the Simon Commission—which, named after Sir John Simon, had been appointed in 1926 to examine the question of the constitution in India—published its report, proposing a federal constitution with full self-government for the provinces. A Round Table Conference, to which Congress sent leaders when the British agreed to release them from prison, was then held in London toward the end of 1931. Even before it opened Gandhi had come to an agreement with the British, an agreement by which he would halt the civil disobedience movement if the British would abolish the salt monopoly, end emergency measures, and declare a general amnesty. From this time on, despite intermittent disturbances, India's advance toward independence was to assume a primarily constitutional character.

At an earlier Round Table Conference, in which Congress had refused to participate, India's Muslims had agreed to accept a federal state, while the Indian princes had agreed that their states should enter such federation. The second Round Table Conference, in which Congress participated, ended, however, in deadlock on December 1, 1931, after Gandhi, on behalf of Congress, had expressed willingness to agree to any solution acceptable to Hindus, Muslims, and Sikhs—who together composed 90 percent of India's population—but had rejected the proposal that separate electorates be established for the smaller minority groups. When Gandhi returned to India the British had once more begun a campaign of repression, and Gandhi himself, when he protested, was soon rearrested. When the British Prime Minister, Ramsay MacDonald, announced a "communal award," providing for separate electorates for, among other groups, the Untouchables—whom Gandhi considered to form a part of the Hindu community—Gandhi announced that he would "fast unto death" rather than accept such an arrangement. He began his fast on September 18, 1932. It resulted not in Gandhi's death but in the "Poona Pact," in which the leader of the Untouchables, Dr. Ambedkar, abandoned his claim to separate representation. Gandhi's attitude on this occasion also evoked widespread and unprecedented sympathy for the 50 million Untouchables living in India.

Eventually, after further negotiations, the British adopted the Government of India Act in 1935. While the act was, as Jawaharlal Nehru expressed it, "bitterly opposed by all sections of British opinion," the Indian National Congress ultimately agreed to participate in the new provincial system of government that it proposed, with the result that in 1937 Congress, without abandoning its demand for Indian independence, obtained control of eight out of eleven provincial governments. Thus between 1937 and the outbreak of the Second World War in 1939, India experienced a period of partial democracy that, again to quote Nehru, was "always on the verge of conflict."

## The Smaller Asian Territories

Inevitably, the weakening of European control over Asia and India produced repercussions in other Asian territories, such as Burma, Ceylon, Afghanistan, Siam, Indochina, and Indonesia.

Until 1937 Burma was annexed to India, with the result that Burmese nationalists waged a double struggle for independence not only against the British, but also against Indian influence, since some Indian financiers had been able to alienate land and to lend money at exorbitant rates with the result that, in certain districts, some Burmese were virtually reduced to peonage. This situation led to a rebellion against both the British and the Indian connection which lasted from 1930 to 1932. Earlier, in 1921, the dyarchy had also been introduced into Burma. But when the Simon Committee presented its report, it recommended that Burma be administered separately from India. The Burmese feared, however, that the separation from India might result in Burma remaining a colony indefinitely, while India itself advanced toward independence. A Burmese Anti-Separation League was consequently formed, but disintegrated when the United Kingdom refused to countenance its arguments. Subsequently, as a result of the adoption of the Government of Burma Act in 1935, the connection between India and Burma was broken in 1937, and a system of provincial autonomy resembling that prevailing in India was introduced.

Ceylon's constitutional evolution had begun as early as 1833, when a Legislative Council had been established, although it had, during the nineteenth century, generally reflected the views of the British administration. By 1912, however, its composition had been changed to make it somewhat more representative of the Ceylonese. Following disturbances during the First World War which sprang partly from religious and partly from political causes, the Ceylon National Congress was formed in 1919. Its membership was drawn from among all groups on the island, but before long the Tamils withdrew from it to form their own minority party. Further constitutional changes had followed, of which the most far-reaching took place after the Donoughmore Commission, which had arrived in Ceylon in 1927, had presented its report in 1931. As a result of its recommendations communal representation was abolished, and direct adult suffrage introduced instead, with eight representatives being nominated to protect minority interests. Although this constitutional arrangement was the subject of strong local controversies, it nevertheless represented perhaps the most democratic system then permitted to operate in any comparable British dependency. By 1936, in consequence, the entire membership of the Ceylon Cabinet was Sinhalese.

Afghanistan, following its nineteenth-century conflicts with the British government in India, had undertaken not to enter into relations with other powers, thus becoming an independent buffer state between India and Russia. Perceiving the weakness of the British after the First World War, however, King Amanullah of Afghanistan had in 1919 launched an attack against India. Hostilities did not last long, and by the Treaty of Rawalpindi, which was concluded in the same year, Afghanistan was permitted to open relations with other countries. After being recognized by the Soviet Union and other major powers, Afghanistan was subsequently admitted to the League of Nations.

Another buffer state, Siam, had strengthened its international position by declaring war on the Central Powers in 1917, after which it sent a small Siamese expeditionary force to France. This action enabled Siam to sign the Treaty of Versailles and to join the League of Nations. During the interwar years any Western control that existed was partially reduced. A coup d'etat in 1932 having transformed the country's absolute monarchy into a constitutional monarchy, the nationalist spirit, already stimulated, grew stronger. One indication of this was the change of name from "Siam" to "Thailand," which took place in June, 1939.[17]

In Indochina—divided into the colony of Cochin-China, with Saigon as its capital, and the four protectorates of Annam, Cambodia, Laos, and Tonkin—nationalism, which had always been strong, asserted itself after the First World War. Wartime promises made by the French had not been kept, and there had been resentment at the forcible recruitment of 100,000 Vietnamese—the Vietnamese constituting about 75 percent of the population of Indochina—for war service in Europe. In addition colonial

17. From 1945 to 1948 use of the name "Siam" was again resumed, after which "Thailand" became once more the official designation.

exploitation constituted a fundamental reason for nationalist condemnation of French rule. The ideas of Wilsonian self-determination, of Gandhian *swaraj*, and of the Chinese revolution all gave inspiration to Indochinese nationalists. The French, however, rejected even moderate proposals for reform, and thus tended by their actions to confirm the interpretation of events provided by the Marxist faction among the nationalists, who drew inspiration from the Russian revolution. The Marxists were led by Nguyen-Ai-Quoc (Ho Chi Minh), who had joined the Communist Party in France before the First World War, and who had subsequently studied revolutionary techniques in the Soviet Union. Nguyen-Ai-Quoc proclaimed national independence as his aim, indicating nevertheless that such independence would best be attained through what he termed a "bourgeois-democratic" regime. Indochinese discontents culminated in an uprising in 1930, which was suppressed with great severity by the French. It was, nevertheless, the Communist faction led by Nguyen-Ai-Quoc which best endured the hazards of the time, and which consequently came to be identified with nationalism in the eyes of the Vietnamese and other peoples of Indochina. The French, in the meantime, continued to exercise control over the region by ruling indirectly through such French-educated personalities as Bao Dai, who had succeeded to the throne of Annam and Tonkin in 1925 at the age of twelve.

In Indonesia the practical Dutch, as we have noted before, had not wasted energy on justifying their domination, but had concentrated their efforts on conducting economic exploitation as scientifically as possible. Nationalism, principally in Java, one of the large Indonesian islands, had first found organized expression in 1908 by the formation of *Budi Utomo* ("High Endeavor"), a group which drew inspiration from the Indian poet Rabindranath Tagore, as well as from Gandhi. In 1911 a Muslim nationalist group, *Sarekat Islam*, was formed, which, while pledging itself to work by constitutional methods, was at first directed not so much against Dutch rule as against the Dutch-encouraged Chinese influence on the islands. After the Russian revolution Marxist ideas were introduced, and a Comintern-backed organization, the *Perserikatan Komunist India* (P.K.I.) was formed—an organization which opposed religion, and hence came into conflict with Sarekat Islam. While Sarekat Islam became increasingly anti-Dutch as a result of the example set by nationalist advance in other Muslim countries, such as Turkey and Egypt, and strove to apply Gandhian doctrines of non-co-operation, the P.K.I., at first small, became increasingly aggressive, and thus attracted growing support. Between 1923 and 1926, however, a series of revolutionary attempts were made by the P.K.I., all of which were suppressed by the Dutch, after which the Communist movement was banned and driven underground. In 1927 a new party, the Perserikatan National Indonesia, was formed, seeking to unite all tendencies. However, when it showed signs of acquiring a revolutionary character, its leaders (among whom Sukarno was prominent) were imprisoned. After this the Depression struck Indonesian rubber production, creating widespread economic and political discontent—a discontent that led, in turn, to further Dutch repression. Requests subsequently made for a form of self-government, however, met with little response from the Dutch. For example, the Indonesia Volksraad (Legislative Council) which had been introduced during the First World War, and which tended to reflect administration rather than nationalist attitudes, in 1936 adopted a motion asking the Netherlands government to summon an imperial conference to discuss the method by which self-government should come into effect, and to establish a time limit for this. The motion was treated in so dilatory a fashion by the Dutch, however, that no reply was made to it until five years later, by which time the Germans, during the Second World War, had driven the Dutch government out of the Netherlands and into exile in London.

## Africa's New Dawn

While the Asian awakening took place during the interwar years, the populations of Africa remained as yet largely unaffected. Only in the Muslim countries of the Mediterranean seaboard and in the industrialized Union of South Africa was nationalist consciousness manifest. In most of the territories between these two northern and southern latitudes, colonial life pursued its regular tenor, if not completely insulated from world events, at least for the moment unaffected by major cataclysms. And yet, for those who looked for portents, there were signs that even in what the 1917 Bolshevik Decree on Peace had termed "the wilds of Africa," a nationalist awakening could not be indefinitely delayed, but must surely come.

If there was any country in which the United Kingdom, still the world's principal imperialist power, could ill afford to make concessions to the rising tide of nationalism, it was in Egypt. The principal imperial sea lane to India and the East still ran through the Suez Canal, and the control of Egypt still insulated the African continent from many forms of intervention, political if not military, that the British would have found unwelcome.

Lord Cromer, a British pro-Consul, had virtually ruled Egypt from 1883 to 1907, providing in those twenty-five years an administration which, while alien, had nevertheless possessed the virtue of stability. Nationalist discontent had, however, grown in the final years of his tenure, and in the period which followed. This discontent had only been partially alleviated by the introduction in 1913 by Lord Kitchener of a new Egyptian constitution. When, after the outbreak of the First World War, the United Kingdom in December, 1914, made good its long-standing threat to convert Egypt into a British Protectorate, nationalist dissatisfaction became pronounced. Under wartime conditions, however, the Egyptians could take no effective counteraction, and therefore instead made preparations to do so when the war ended.

In January, 1919, Saad Zaghloul, a former Minister of Education, assumed leadership of the nationalist party, the Wafd, calling for complete independence, and demanding the right to send a delegation to London, as well as to the Peace Conference at Versailles. These demands were refused, and when the nationalists, who were outraged to see Ethiopia and the Hejaz participating in the Versailles conference, whereas Egypt was excluded, began to express their bitterness, Zaghloul and other leaders were deported to Malta by the British. The result of this action was a rebellion, in part spontaneous and in part directed by a Committee of Independence established in Cairo. The British, who had large numbers of troops stationed in Egypt, were nevertheless able to maintain their authority, although they released Zaghloul and permitted him to travel to Paris. In Paris, however, he was unable to prevent the Allies from agreeing to maintain the British protectorate over Egypt, or from confirming this decision in Article 147 of the Treaty of Versailles.

The United Kingdom, aware of the depth of Egyptian feeling, nevertheless felt that protectorate status was not a permanent solution, and therefore hesitated between either annexing Egypt outright to the British Empire, or else protecting British interests by treaty. An investigating mission headed by Lord Milner, which was boycotted by the nationalists, recommended that relations between Egypt and the United Kingdom be established by agreement. It also made proposals envisaging Egypt as a constitutional monarchy enjoying the shadow of independence while Britain retained the substance of control. Zaghloul, for his part, asked for amendments to the Milner proposals which would have limited the number of British troops in Egypt and confined them to the Suez Canal area, and have given Egypt an equal share with the United Kingdom in the administration of the Sudan. But the United Kingdom rejected Zaghloul's amendments, and during the ensuing deadlock new disorders took place in 1921.

A calmer atmosphere ensued in 1922 when the United Kingdom announced unilaterally that the protectorate was terminated, and that Egypt was to be an independent sovereign state with King Fuad as constitutional monarch. Independence was, nevertheless, to be qualified by a far-reaching degree of British control over both foreign and internal affairs. The question of the status and the administration of the Sudan, which proved to be a bone of contention between the British and the

Egyptians, was left in abeyance. The new constitution was enacted in 1923. In the elections which followed the Wafd obtained an overwhelming majority, and Zaghloul took office as Prime Minister in January, 1924. His representations for more independence proved fruitless, however. The Anglo-Egyptian struggle was soon transferred to the Sudan, where Egyptian troops mutinied. In November, 1924, nationalist terrorists assassinated Sir Lee Stack, the British Commander-in-Chief of Egypt's armed forces who also held the position of Sirdar of the Sudan. This act led to a hardening of the British position, after which Zaghloul resigned as Prime Minister; the British after further fighting suppressed the dissident Egyptian troops in the Sudan; parliament dissolved, and new elections were held in 1925.

The death of Sir Lee Stack in effect marked the ending of the revolutionary period that had begun in 1919. From 1925 on, until the time of the Second World War, Egypt was composed of a triangle of forces in which the Egyptian monarchy and the British represented two elements which combined were stronger than the third, the Wafd. The Wafd was further handicapped by the fact that it was a republican movement that relied on middle-class support, and did not represent the mass of the population. The true awakening of Egyptian nationalism was yet to come.

The Italian invasion of Ethiopia in 1935 alarmed both the United Kingdom and Egypt, and led to the conclusion of the Anglo-Egyptian Treaty of 1936. By the terms of the treaty the United Kingdom agreed to several long-standing Egyptian claims. Egypt was to be admitted to the League of Nations—an event that took place on May 26, 1937. The Egyptian position in the Sudan was also strengthened, and the system of capitulations—an anachronism whereby Egypt's judicial sovereignty was restricted because of the chaotic conditions that had prevailed under Ottoman rule—was to be ended. Furthermore, the British military occupation of Egypt was to end, with the United Kingdom retaining responsibility for the defense of the Suez Canal, as well as the right to station troops in a special canal zone. British air force overflights of Egypt were also to be permitted, and certain areas were also reserved for British army training. The nationalists, naturally, were dissatisfied with the restrictions which remained, but that the 1936 treaty represented, however cautiously, a further imperial retreat could not be doubted. Before the terms of the treaty could make themselves felt, however, the Second World War transformed the situation once more.

In the other North African countries, independence movements took varying forms. The French, Spanish, and Italians were all obliged to fight to retain the hold over the territories they claimed, and the principal power in the Maghreb—France—also found itself faced with constitutional movements seeking progress toward independent sovereignty, if not sovereignty itself.

Resistance to French rule was particularly marked in the mountainous regions of Morocco and Algeria. At the time of the First World War, according to 'Alal al-Fasi,[18] "the entire Maghrib, except the largest towns and ports, was in full fledged rebellion against foreign occupation." The French forces in Morocco, commanded by Lyautey, had consequently suffered 56,000 casualties in 1912; 70,000 in 1913; and had 63,000 in 1914. There was also resistance to enlistment in the French Army, from which 120,000 North Africans deserted, many of them making their way to the mountains. There was widespread sympathy, and some contact, with the Ottoman Turks, and in 1917 the Tuareg tribes of the Sahara began an uprising which led to conflict in the southern regions of Algeria and Tunisia, where fighting lasted until 1921. In Libya the Italians fought the Senussi of Cyrenaica from 1911 to 1917, when the Italians, driven back to their coastal garrisons, were obliged to admit Senussi independence in the interior by the Treaty of Acroma. Hostilities were resumed, however, from 1923 to 1932 as the Italians sought to gain control. In the course of the fighting they captured Omar Al Mukhtar, a famed Senussi leader, hanging him in public before the eyes of his followers. These efforts, however, while costly, brought Italy little profit, for by 1930, despite further heavy expenditures on roads and irrigation, only about 2,000 Italians had settled in the whole of Libya.

By all means the most pronounced nationalist manifestation in Northern Africa between the two world wars was the Moroccan Riff Rebellion of 1921–1926. Under the leadership of Abd al-Karim (Abdel Krim), a guerrilla uprising took place first in Spanish and then in French Morocco. The fighting was heavy. For example, in March, 1922, the Moroccan forces defeated a Spanish army of 50,000 troops, led by General Berenguer, after a week's battle in which 5,000 Spanish troops were killed and 3,000 taken prisoner. A Riff government was established which proclaimed that it was founded on "modern ideas, laws, and civilization," and which stated that "we are privileged to enjoy our freedom, as we have enjoyed it for centuries, and to live freely as other peoples live. . . . We desire to be our own rulers and to maintain and preserve our indisputable rights and unequivocal independence." Meanwhile Marshal Lyautey in French Morocco had expressed fears to his government that the establishment of a free Moroccan state in Spanish Morocco might imperil the entire French position in North Africa. By May, 1925, in consequence, the French and Riffian forces were at war, with increasing numbers of Moroccan tribesmen rallying to Abd al-Karim's banner. By

---

18. *The Independence Movements in Arab North Africa* (Cairo, 1948. Translated from the Arabic by Hazem Zaki Nuseibeh, American Council of Learned Societies, 1954).

May, 1926, however, combined French and Spanish forces obliged Abd al-Karim to surrender, after which he was sent into exile on the island of Réunion in the Indian Ocean.[19]

Nonviolent efforts were also made to advance the cause of North African independence. Both Algerian and Tunisian delegations attended the Versailles peace conference, and submitted memorandums to President Wilson asking for independence—requests that, like so many others made at Versailles, went unheard. In 1925 an Algerian organization, *Najm Shamal Ifriqia*, known in French as the *Etoile Nord-Africaine* (E.N.A.), was formed in Paris with Messali Hadj, a militant nationalist who had served in the French army, being elected as its president in 1926. Campaigning against the French presence in the Maghreb, he appealed to the League of Nations in 1930 for the establishment of an independent Algeria. After the foundation of the Algerian Communist Party in 1934, however, the E.N.A. in 1936 came into collision with the Communists and their allies in the French Popular Front. As a result the E.N.A. was dissolved by decree of the French government on March 26, 1937.

In 1907 the Young Tunisia party had been formed, under the leadership of Ali Bash Hambah, with a view to opposing French rule and seeking the restoration of the sovereignty of the Ottoman caliphate over Tunisia. The movement was active until 1911. After the First World War a new group, the Destour (Constitution) party, was formed, seeking the introduction of a constitutional system to Tunisia, rather than independence, which they felt was not attainable at that time. By 1934, however, the Destour had lost its fervor, with the result that a younger generation of nationalists, represented by Habib Bourguiba, broke away to form the Neo-Destour party. When the French restricted the Neo-Destour leaders to the south of the country, the movement grew rapidly in popularity, and, when they were released in 1936, they launched a campaign for the ending of the French protectorate. In 1938, however, following a severe riot, Bourguiba and other Neo-Destourian leaders were imprisoned in France, where they remained until the Second World War.

### African Advancement

Meanwhile, as we noted earlier, in the remainder of Africa no major nationalist awakening occurred, even though significant stirrings indicated that such an awakening would eventually take place. The stirrings, however, were themselves of considerable interest. Three types of approach to the question of African advancement were in evidence, and not the least interesting fact concerning them was that all three were associ-

19. In being transferred from Réunion to France after the Second World War, Abd al-Karim managed to escape his captors while passing through the Suez Canal, after which he made Cairo his home.

ated, in one form or another, with the United States of America. It was as if history, before enacting itself, were hinting that the nineteenth-century struggle for the advancement of the peoples of African descent in the New World was now in the twentieth-century to be resumed in new forms in the original home continent.

The three types of approach to Africa's progress were the following. First, it was held that Africa could best advance by Africans obtaining Western education, becoming Christian, co-operating with white men and winning their respect, and practicing self-help and self-reliance. Second, it was held that Africa was a continent destined to be occupied by black peoples, and that therefore the peoples of African descent should leave the Americas, and return to Africa to lead a crusade that would end white rule and drive white men from the continent. Third, there was the revolutionary approach, which held that the workers and peasants of Africa should organize in order to launch a revolution that would end the stranglehold of imperialism over Africa—an imperialism that, circumstantially, happened to be white. Each of these approaches to the question of Africa's progress were represented by a different personality.

The principal representative of the first approach—that of self-help and co-operation with Europeans—was James E. Kwegyir Aggrey, a Fanti, who was born at Anamabu, a fishing village on the West African Gold Coast, on October 18, 1875. At the age of eight he was baptized a Christian. Aggrey was educated at a Methodist school at nearby Cape Coast, after which he became an assistant teacher. In 1896 he served as an interpreter with the British expedition against the Ashanti. Two years later he traveled to the United States, where he studied the classics at Livingstone College[20] in Salisbury, South Carolina, from which he graduated in 1902. Aggrey then became a registrar and professor at Livingstone. In 1905 he married an American Negro woman and settled, until 1920, in the United States. During these years, in addition to his academic work, he continued his studies, in part at Columbia University. He also lectured, wrote, became a Freemason, and undertook without fee much educational and social work. He was a follower of the self-help doctrines of the American Negro educator Booker T. Washington, and was active in urging the local black community in South Carolina to improve their condition by studying Christianity, education, and agriculture. In 1920, and again in 1924, he served as a member of commissions sent by the Phelps Stokes Fund to survey education in Africa. In 1924 he was appointed to the staff of Achimota, a new educational enterprise in the

20. The college took its name from the fact that Robert Livingstone, aged nineteen, and son of Livingstone the explorer, had died in a Confederate prison camp in Salisbury, South Carolina, during the American Civil War. According to tradition he was then buried at Gettysburg under his assumed name of "R. Vincent."

Gold Coast which was the expression of a new educational policy that sought to achieve a synthesis of African and European culture. However, in 1927, while in New York on a visit to the United States, Aggrey suddenly died of meningitis.

Aggrey's significance cannot be measured by the bare outline of his biography. That he was most unusual those who met him repeatedly testified. His unique faculty appears to have been a gift for conciliation. Thus he was able at the same time to take up the cause of the poorest, while gaining the co-operation of the traditional authorities, both African and European. In the same way in South Carolina he was able to forward the cause of the blacks, while winning the co-operation of the local whites. A great deal of his time, throughout his productive years, was spent in exercising his gift for conciliating quarrels and thus enabling people to work harmoniously together. His achievement was to win the co-operation of black and white for the seminal Achimota endeavor which was to create the image of a new Africa—an image that would contrast, in the minds of Africans and Europeans alike, with that of the old Africa of bloodshed, malaria, and slavery. The harder part of his task was undoubtedly to win European support for African advancement, but the extent to which he did this, and lived up to the expectations of his sympathetic European friends, is shown by the undoubted friendship and admiration in which he was held by the Governor of the Gold Coast at this time, the liberal-minded Sir Gordon Guggisberg, as well as by the principal of Achimota, the Rev. A. G. Fraser. These three men together, it has often been said, opened a new door to the future. Even Aggrey's early death could not prevent the outreach of the work that had been done. The shock produced in the Gold Coast by the news of his death was overwhelming. One of Aggrey's students, Kwame Nkrumah, later President of the Republic of Ghana (as the Gold Coast became known after independence), who said of Aggrey "It was through him that my nationalism was first aroused," described his reactions as follows:

> The sudden shock of this news, followed by the gradual realization that I had lost for ever the guidance of this great man, sapped everything for me, and I was quite unable to eat for at least three days. . . . It was because of my great admiration for Aggrey, both as a man and a scholar, that I first formed the idea of furthering my studies in the United States of America.[21]

The exact quality which Aggrey possessed, and which individuals found so striking, still remains, however, to some extent elusive and indefinable. In part it was because he represented in his person what the new Africa could be. But there was also something else, some quality of commitment to the constructive and positive side of life which produced

21. *Ghana: The Autobiography of Kwame Nkrumah* (1957), p. 17.

unforeseen and unforeseeable reactions in others. In a letter to a white friend, Mr. A. L. Smoot of Salisbury, dated July 10, 1926, he recalled an incident, known to them both, which illustrates this:

> You understood me so well and I understood you so well that it was the love I had for you that made me consent to allow the chain gang on my farm to get the rocks to macadamise three miles of the old Statesville Road from Jump and Run stream to the city limits of Salisbury. Do you recollect, Mr. Smoot?—You were then Clerk of Court, or Registrar, or Secretary of the Board of Aldermen or County Commissioner. Anyway, they sent you, and at that time I was the only one who had a place near with rocks on it. I was to charge by the square yard, you remember, after they had finished. I had thought of building a stone house and did not care to part with the rocks, but your speech, your plea, won me, and I consented. At the completion of the road, you came to my house again in a horse-and-buggy—I remember distinctly. You pled that I should not ask too much because the county was poor. But I had decided what I was going to do. You had won me for the county. I shall never forget the sparkle in your eye when I told you to tell the county officials that I would not charge anything for the rocks that macadamised three miles: it was my contribution to the improvement of the county. . . . And, by the way, it is unwritten history, but true—that the night those Lyerlys were lynched at Henderson Grove, a white friend of mine told me a few days after that he went to see what the crowd was doing. After the lynching, someone, obviously a farmer or country folk, said, "Now let us go and burn up the nigger college," and they might have done so, but, this friend whom you know very well told me, one man said: "No, let's don't, because one of the professors there gave us rocks to macadamise the road from here up to Jump and Run and wouldn't charge a cent." "Is that so?" they asked. "Sure, because I know." And the College was saved, because you had won me, and I had not refused to be won. I have never repeated this openly, but I thank God you won me.[22]

## "Back to Africa"

The "Back to Africa" approach was advocated by a totally different type of personality, Marcus Aurelius Garvey. Garvey, who was born in 1887 in Jamaica in the West Indies, was completely black. The fact of his color was of importance, for, reflecting some local Caribbean attitudes, he distrusted those of mixed blood even more than the whites, whom he regarded as his open, and therefore less dangerous, enemies. This attitude of his later alienated much potential support for him on the American mainland, where—as he never fully understood—the division between those with black skins and those with skin of a lighter color did not possess the degree of political and social significance that it did in some parts of the West Indies.

Having traveled in Central and South America, Garvey visited London, where for several years he worked closely with an Egyptian nationalist of Sudanese origin, who was a supporter of Zaghloul and the Wafd. As a result Garvey became a convinced "black nationalist," and in 1916 established himself in New York, from where he began to promote

22. See Edwin W. Smith, *Aggrey of Africa: A Study in Black and White* (1929), p. 98.

the independence of a black Africa. Like Moses he would lead the black people of the Americas out of bondage and home to the Promised Land. Before long his plans had matured. As George Padmore was later to write, "Marcus Garvey founded his Negro Empire in New York in the year 1920. Territory it had none; but its subjects were counted by the millions and scattered throughout the world."[23] The founding of the empire took place at a convention summoned on August 1, and here Marcus Garvey's instrument, the Universal Negro Improvement and African Communities League (U.N.I.A.) was born. With thundering rhetoric Garvey impressed himself and his idea upon the consciousness of black America more firmly than any other Negro leader had yet been able to do. Likening himself to Napoleon—the only white man whom he conceded to be his equal—Garvey launched his "Back to Africa" crusade:

> Up you Mighty Race. You can accomplish what you will. It is only a question of a few more years when Africa will be completely colonized by Negroes, as Europe is by the white race. No one knows when the hour of Africa's redemption cometh. It is in the wind. It is coming. One day, like a storm, it will be here.

Pledged to work for the uplift of the Negro peoples of the world, the U.N.I.A. also proclaimed its belief in the "Brotherhood of Man and the Fatherhood of God." Among its aims were the establishment of a "central nation" for the black "race," the civilizing of "the backward tribes of Africa," and the founding of commissaries or agencies in different countries to represent Negro interests. Garvey himself was elected Provisional President of Africa by the convention he had convoked, as well as President-General and Administrator of the U.N.I.A. He was officially to be addressed as "His Highness the Potentate," and was aided by an eighteen-person "High Executive Council," the members of which were given resounding titles, such as Earl of the Congo, Viscount Niger, Duke of the Nile, and Baron Zambezi. Dress, titles, and insignia were based on those of the English chivalric orders. Garvey himself wore a striking uniform with a white-plumed hat. Money came pouring into the U.N.I.A. headquarters from Negro supporters whose imaginations had been stirred, and, for a moment, much began to seem possible. Garvey, formerly a Catholic, founded his own African Orthodox Church, which worshipped a black Christ and a black Madonna, and which was headed by a West Indian Patriarch. A weekly newspaper, the *Negro World,* was also founded, as well as the Black Eagle Flying Corps, and a steamship company, the Black Star Line.

The European colonial powers became seriously concerned at the possible consequences of Garvey's interest in Africa. The French, for example, meted out sentences of life imprisonment to Dahomeyans caught reading the *Negro World.* Nevertheless, in Africa itself reactions began

23. *Pan-Africanism or Communism? The Coming Struggle for Africa* (London, 1956), p. 92.

to be observed. "Even in the remote corners of the Ciskei, illiterate peasants suddenly became wildly excited over the anticipated advent of Garvey to liberate them."[24] When Aggrey visited the Transkei in South Africa in 1921, he was accorded an enthusiastic reception by Africans who believed that all Americans were black, that they intended to drive Europeans out of the country, and that Aggrey was their emissary. At one point, seeking to place matters in perspective, Aggrey told a South African audience, "Everywhere I have gone they have asked me about the fleet that is coming from America. I have told them that I know those two ships, and one of them is leaking." The rumors nevertheless died hard. Five years later in 1926 a Zulu posing as a American Negro and calling himself Doctor Wellington was to receive some credence in the Transkei when he announced that America was sending warplanes to drive the Europeans from South Africa and to establish African rule.

Garvey chose Liberia as the most promising territory for his African base of operations, and for political support he chose white Southern leaders who were in favor of Negroes leaving the United States. Earlier he had openly co-operated with the leaders of the Ku Klux Klan and the Anglo-Saxon Clubs who had praised his campaign for "racial purity," and Garvey, in return, had praised them, saying that the Klan was fighting to make America a white man's country and that he was fighting to make Africa a black man's country. For this he was attacked by his critics, who called him a Fascist—an appelation that he did not reject. Indeed, later he was proudly to claim, "We were the first Fascists . . . Mussolini copied Fascism from me." Meanwhile he pressed for U.S. and Liberian governmental backing for his schemes. A resolution was introduced in the Mississippi Legislature petitioning the U.S. Congress and the President to use their influence to obtain African territory from the Allies in liquidation of their war debts, and to permit an independent nation for American 'Negroes to be established in Africa. Garvey himself suggested that the former German colonies in Africa be turned over to American Negroes, and also that Sierra Leone and the Ivory Coast be surrendered by the United Kingdom and France respectively and added to Liberia to form a new and greater Liberian state. While awaiting United States reactions to these proposals, Garvey sent a mission to Liberia in 1920 to obtain from the Liberian government land upon which to establish U.N.I.A. community settlements. By 1924 provisional agreement had been reached. Fertile land was to be provided and in the first two years between 20,000 and 30,000 Negro families would leave America for Africa at a cost to the U.N.I.A. of about $2 million.

24. Mary Benson, *The African Patriots: The Story of the African National Congress of South Africa* (London, 1963), p. 57.

It had been understood, however, that Garvey and the new immigrants would not threaten the power of the Liberian True Whig party, then led by President Charles King. But Garvey appears to have laid plans to challenge the True Whig direction of affairs with a view to assuming power himself. While in public the U.N.I.A. praised the True Whigs, in private it circulated a damning report accusing the Liberian government of corruption and slavery. The Liberian government had already received indications that Garvey was harboring political ambitions. When a copy of the secret report came into their hands, their suspicions were confirmed, and they did not hesitate to act. The concession granted to U.N.I.A. was canceled, and the goods and construction materials that had already been shipped to Liberia were seized and put up for sale, all U.N.I.A. personnel being deported.

Garvey's "Back to Africa" movement had come to grief. Nor did his other enterprises fare better. Two of the Black Star Line ships confirmed the accuracy of Aggrey's words by sinking, and others were sold at heavy loss. The S.S. *Frederick Douglas,* for example, was bought for $165,000 and sold for junk at $1,600. Many of Garvey's associates similarly proved to be fair-weather friends, who turned against him when hard times came. In 1925 Garvey was sentenced to jail for using the U.S. mails to defraud; he was deported to Jamaica two years later, after which his political activity there earned him a three-month sentence for contempt of court. His organization disintegrated, and he spent his last years in London, trying to rebuild his movement. He died in 1940. Despite his lack of organizational and diplomatic ability, Garvey had passed like a meteor across the sky of Negro consciousness; he had dreamed a dream and made others share it with him, even though he could not make it come true.

### Pan-Africanism

The third approach, that of Pan-Africanism, was represented by yet another personality, a light-skinned Negro scholar from Massachusetts, Dr. W. E. Burghardt Du Bois. In Africa, as in America, he stood for the equality of all men, of whatever coloration. His efforts, which were carried on throughout a long life—he was born in 1868—came near to universality in their scope, but in the evolution of the Pan-African concept in particular he played a leading part. In spirit he was militant, and he proclaimed a battle cry:

The problem of the twentieth century is the problem of the color line,—the relation of the darker to the lighter races of men in Asia and Africa, in America and the islands of the sea.[25]

25. *The Souls of Black Folk* (1903).

His personal attitude to race relations had first been formed when, as a child at school in New England, he had for a game taken part with others in an exchange of visiting cards. One girl, "a tall newcomer," had refused his card "peremptorily, with a glance." Then he suddenly realized that he was "different," and from that moment decided that he would not try to cross through or creep through the veil that separated him from others, but would hold all beyond that veil "in common contempt." It was a decision from which, throughout his long life, he never retreated, and although it often lent a certain cantankerousness to his nature, at least he never had to suffer the life-diminishing price that hypocrisy exacts.

After graduating from Fisk University in Nashville, he studied for four years at Harvard, and for two years in Berlin. In Berlin, encouraged by the economic historian Gustav Schmoller, he became convinced that color prejudice was caused by ignorance and that scientific knowledge would dispel it. Having obtained his doctorate from Harvard University for his work, *The Suppression of the African Slave Trade*—the first of many volumes that he was to author—he joined the faculty of Atlanta University, where he was Professor of Economics and History from 1897 to 1910. He came to feel, however, that scientific inquiry was not enough to solve the problem of color prejudice, and that further commitment was called for. He drew attention to himself by rejecting the approach to race relations in the United States advocated by the well-known Negro leader Booker T. Washington.

Booker Washington, the founder of Tuskegee Institute, had come into prominence after the Reconstruction era. He had advocated a new formula for Negro advancement that was, he felt, adapted to the temper of the times. According to his formula, which later became known as the "Atlanta Compromise," he proposed a new guideline for relations between black- and white-skinned persons: "In all things purely social we can be as separate as the five fingers, and yet one as the hand in all things essential to mutual progress." To his Negro listeners he proposed that they abandon for the time being any aspiration toward political power, civil rights, or higher education, and instead concentrate their energies upon work, thrift, and industrial education. This doctrine, which was well adapted to the commercial spirit of the age, won him the enthusiastic backing of influential Southern whites, and the more dubious adherence of many Negroes. At a time when, following the ending of Reconstruction, the struggle for Negro rights had reached its nadir, Booker Washington provided a formula which at least made survival more feasible.

It was not, however, a doctrine for all seasons, and to a man of the caliber of Dr. Du Bois it was not acceptable. While paying courteous respect to Washington's positive contribution, he nevertheless challenged his approach as one which led to the disfranchisement of the Negro, the legal creation of a distinct status of civil inferiority for him, and the lessening of opportunities for higher learning. In 1905 Du Bois organized a conference to develop another approach, out of which grew a protest organization known as the "Niagara Movement," a movement which called for the full extension to the American Negro of the rights provided by the United States Constitution, including those mentioned in the 14th and 15th Amendments; the ending of discrimination; and higher education for Negroes. The new movement, although small, attracted widespread attention and five years later, in 1910, led to the founding of another organization, the National Association for the Advancement of Colored People (N.A.A.C.P.), with Dr. Du Bois as editor of its organ, *The Crisis*. Under his editorship it soon became the most influential Negro publication in the United States. It was at this juncture in his life that Du Bois began to devote his attention to Pan-Africanism.

Pan-Africanism's first advocate had been a barrister from Trinidad, Henry Sylvester-Williams, who was active in the United Kingdom, where he gave legal advice to African delegations from colonial countries when they visited London. In 1900 Sylvester-Williams had convened a Pan-African conference in London in order to uphold African rights, to protest against their violation by white colonizers, and to obtain sympathy and support from British liberals. As a result of this conference, which made the expression "Pan-Africanism" generally known for the first time, Queen Victoria committed herself not to "overlook the interests and welfare of the native races" of Africa. Mr. Sylvester-Williams' subsequent death, however, prevented the concept from developing further in the context of that time.

Du Bois had attended the 1900 Pan-African Congress in London, and, between 1919 and 1927, he himself organized four more such congresses.[26] By all means the most effective of these was the first, held in Paris in 1919 at the same time that the Versailles Peace Conference was meeting. Du Bois had arrived in Paris from the United States in December, 1918, with the tacit approval of the U.S. government for the purpose of organizing such a congress, and had obtained a hearing from Colonel House, who was "sympathetic but noncommittal." Du Bois advocated the application of the Wilsonian principle of self-determination to African territories, arguing that in settling what was to be done with the German colonies, the wishes of Africans in other colonies might also be considered. From the consultation of African wishes, it was thought, an internationalized Africa might emerge. The holding of the Pan-African Congress

26. Colin Legum in *Pan-Africanism: A Short Political Guide* (revised edition, 1965), numbers the Pan-African Congresses in sequence from the First in London in 1900 to the Sixth in Manchester in 1945. The practice followed by Du Bois, Padmore, Nkrumah and others, however, was to number the congresses from the First in 1919, thus regarding the 1900 Congress as precursory in character.

on French soil remained, however, in doubt until Du Bois secured the support of Blaise Diagne, the deputy from Senegal who had so successfully recruited soldiers from French West Africa to fight on the Western front. Through Diagne's intercession the French Prime Minister, Clemenceau, gave a qualified approval to the Congress: "Don't advertise it," he said, "but go ahead."

The Congress accordingly met in February, 1919, being composed of 57 delegates—12 African, 16 from the United States, and 21 from the West Indies. More would undoubtedly have attended had not transport and visa problems existing at the conclusion of the war prevented them from doing so. The fact that some of the American Negro delegates were officers in U.S. Army uniforms did not, however, pass unremarked. The Congress asked specifically that the former German colonies be administered by an international organization rather than by the colonial powers themselves. It also called for a permanent bureau to ensure that a new code of law designed to protect African rights and welfare be applied. The recommendations of the Congress were subsequently reflected in attenuated form in the establishment of the League of Nations Mandates system for the former German colonies, and in the Mandates Commission.

In 1921 Du Bois' Second Pan-African Congress met in London and Brussels. Its activities were, at first, confused by some Belgians with those of the Garvey movement. The Congress called for racial equality and local self-government among the world's suppressed peoples. A petition was also presented to the League of Nations, asking it to appoint a Negro representative to the Mandates Commission, and to give attention to the "condition of civilized persons of Negro descent throughout the world." The guiding idea of the 1921 Congress, as well as of the following one, which was held in 1923 in London and Lisbon, was that democracy should, in Du Bois' words, "be made to encircle the world." The 1923 Congress asked that Africa be developed for the benefit of Africans "and not merely for the profit of Europeans," that free education and trial by jury be introduced into Africa, and that "in fine, we ask in all the world, that black folk be treated as men." The Lisbon meeting was strengthened by the support of the Liga Africana, an association of Portuguese Negroes with headquarters in Lisbon. A further congress was planned to be held in the West Indies in 1925, with a chartered ship sailing from island to island. The shipping companies proved unaccommodating, however, and the next Pan-African Congress—Du Bois' Fourth— was held in New York in 1927. In New York, where American Negro representation was extensive but African delegates were few, demands similar to those made in the past were put forward. An attempt in 1929 to hold a Pan-African congress on African soil, in Tunis, came to grief in part because of the refusal of the French government to countenance the project, and in part because of the disruptive effect of the Depression. No further Pan-African Congresses were to be held until the end of the Second World War.

Relations between Aggrey, Garvey, and Du Bois were often acerbic. Du Bois, for example, ridiculed Aggrey's emphasis on sound agriculture as a basis for African progress. "Of course the white world wants the black world to study agriculture," he said. "It is not only easier to lynch Negroes and keep them in ignorance and peonage in country districts, but it is also easier to cheat them out of a decent income."[27] Ideological differences separated the capitalist-minded Garvey from the socialist Du Bois, not to speak of the differences of approach between them stemming from their differences in skin color. Also, as Padmore expressed it, "Garvey appealed to the Negro's emotions; Du Bois to his intellect."[28] Yet, seen in perspective, the self-help, the "Back to Africa," and the democratic approaches often overlapped. When the differences in dogma were permitted to become blurred, the effect of all three approaches, none of which met with the degree of success that, for example, Gandhi achieved in India, was to stimulate fresh efforts toward Africa's regeneration. That progress was disappointing and that setbacks occurred was, under the circumstances, only to be expected. The dream was kept alive; the soil was prepared for the generation that was to follow.

## The African National Congress

Meanwhile, in South Africa, Africans had formed an organization to protect their interests and to forward their aims—the African National Congress of South Africa.

During the Boer War of 1899–1902 the British had assured the Africans that in return for their support they would be granted the same privileges as whites when peace was made. But when the Treaty of Vereeniging was signed in 1902, no such privileges were accorded. The Africans were now faced not only with British indifference, but with the active hostility of the Boers, who had not forgotten the Africans' wartime actions. At first, however, the Africans lacked such leadership as, for example, was given to the Indian community by Gandhi. This situation changed with the return from abroad of a young Zulu lawyer, P. ka Izaka Seme, who had studied in New York and at Oxford. Under his inspiration, African tribal chiefs gathered together at Bloemfontein in January, 1912, to "form a federation of one Pan-African association," an

27. *Aggrey of Africa*, p. 255.
28. *Pan-Africanism or Communism*, p. 138.

organization that took the name of the South African Native National Congress,[29] and that modeled itself on the American Congress. The first President-General was another Zulu who had studied in the United States, J. L. Dube, while the Secretary-General was S. T. Plaatje, a journalist. The Congress aimed at the advancement of Africans through constitutional means, and through the encouragement of self-help and of higher education.

The Congress had hopefully expected quick progress, but it soon discovered that it would have to devote more of its energies to defending African rights in South Africa than to advancing them. On June 20, 1913, despite strong opposition from the Congress and its friends, the Native Land Act came into force, forbidding Africans from buying land in the country of their birth. The act also provided for the eviction of African squatters on white farms, squatters who numbered nearly a million. As a result large numbers of African families wandered homeless throughout the land, looking for a place to live. A Congress delegation was sent to London to try to have legislation changed, but although it gained the sympathy of the British press and public, it received little from the British Colonial Secretary, who told the delegates that the Africans had too much land already.

Pass laws had been enacted in South Africa restricting African freedom of movement and inspiring protests in the form of passive resistance by African women. The end of the First World War—in which Africans in South Africa had again rallied to the British cause but had been refused the right to bear arms, although they were given noncombatant duties—saw no improvement in the situation. On the contrary, the Masters and Servants Act made it a criminal offense for an African to refuse to obey an employer's order. African strikes were also held to be illegal —a regulation that was soon put to the test. The years from 1918 to 1924 were years of increasing industrial unrest. The Congress supported strikes for higher wages, organized mass demonstrations against the pass laws, and founded a women's section, led by Charlotte Maxcke, who had studied in the United States before the war. Encouraged by President Wilson's pronouncements on self-determination, the Congress also sent a delegation to the Versailles Peace Conference to oppose the granting of control over South West Africa to the South African government. The delegation was led by J. T. Gumede, and also included S. T. Plaatje. While Plaatje participated in Du Bois' Pan-African Congress, the delegation made little progress in putting its views before the Peace Conference itself, as they found themselves opposed not only by the official South African delegation led by General Smuts, but also by an unofficial Afri-

---

29. In 1925 the words "South" and "Native" were dropped from the title, which thus became the African National Congress (A.N.C.).

kaaner Nationalist delegation which, better supplied with funds than the Congress, was able to continue its representations in the United States after the conference had ended. Eventually the Congress delegation, after one more vain attempt to influence the British government by visiting London, returned home disillusioned.

African discontent was increasing in the Union, but the African National Congress, lacking organizational experience, laid emphasis on the attainment of dignity rather than on achieving material gains in the form of higher wages and better living conditions. The Congress, moreover, not only failed to organize a mass movement in consequence, but also found itself still opposed by Smuts, who had become Prime Minister in 1919, and who showed no qualms about using military force against Africans. This he did to crush strikes, as, for example at Port Elizabeth in 1920, as well as to compel compliance, as in South West Africa in 1922, when Smuts authorized bombing attacks by aircraft upon the Bondelswarts, a Hottentot tribe who had refused to pay a heavy tax on dogs, and who were punished by the loss of over 100 dead tribesmen in consequence.

In 1922, however, a situation developed that was to weaken Smuts' position. The South African Chamber of Mines proposed to permit nonwhites to perform some semi-skilled work previously reserved for whites. The white miners on the Rand struck, and violence followed. Paradoxically, the South African Communist Party, which was supporting the white miners against the employers, in a moment of ideological aberration raised a banner reading "Workers of the World Fight and Unite for a White South Africa"—a slogan that it was later to regret. Smuts personally directed the repression of the white miners—a circumstance that cost him popularity with his electorate, and led to the return to power in the 1924 elections of an anti-capitalist coalition government composed of his rivals, the Afrikaaner Nationalists and the Labour Party, with General J. B. M. Hertzog as Prime Minister. Hertzog, after threatening to enforce complete segregation of the races, then embarked on a program of legal and economic repression of the non-white inhabitants of South Africa. At this point, however, a new factor entered into the situation in the form of an organized African trade union movement, led by Clements Kadalie from Nyasaland.

Kadalie had a charismatic personality, and starting in 1919 soon built up the Industrial and Commercial Workers Union (I.C.U.) until it had a membership of 20,000. The I.C.U. brought renewed hope to the African populations, eclipsed for the time being the A.N.C., and made Kadalie a power to be reckoned with, capable of exerting pressure on the government. In the later twenties, however, organizational quarrels and misuse of funds led to the I.C.U.'s decline. At the height of his power Kadalie had been the most popular African leader to emerge in South Africa for generations.

After the deterioration of Kadalie's union, no comparably effective movement appeared. The A.N.C. continued its activities, but did not succeed in obtaining wide popular support. In 1928 the President-General of the A.N.C., J. T. Gumede, returned from the Soviet Union saying that he had visited "the new Jerusalem"—an interpretation that led to an upheaval within the A.N.C. and the eventual replacement of Gumede by P. ka Izaka Seme. The South African Communist Party itself never succeeded in generating mass support. After its early tactical mistake in supporting the white miners' interests at the expense of the Africans, it began to establish a reputation among Africans because alone among South African political parties it treated its members of all races on a basis of equality.[30] The white-skinned Communist the most widely admired as an individual by the Africans was S. P. Bunting, who founded a League of African Rights. However, in 1929 the League was ordered dissolved by the Comintern, and in 1931 Bunting, together with others, was expelled from the party as a "right-wing deviationist." As a result of this internal dissension, by 1933 the membership of the South African Communist Party had fallen to an estimated 150, most of whom were white.

Meanwhile the A.N.C. continued its efforts with limited success. The Depression of 1929 affected South Africa deeply, particularly after the United Kingdom abandoned the gold standard in 1931. The outcome of the resulting crisis was a coalition government, formed in 1933, led by Hertzog and supported by Smuts. The Depression had resulted in many non-whites being dismissed from their jobs, and to this economic deprivation adverse political discrimination was later added. In 1935 an All-African Convention was called at Bloemfontein to organize opposition to the removal of African voters from the common roll in the Cape, to the establishment of separate white representation in Parliament, and to the creation of a Native Representative Council as an outlet for African complaints. However, the only result of the Bloemfontein meeting was that a deputation was sent to Hertzog. Hertzog, who claimed that joint voting paved the way to miscegenation, was not impressed by African arguments, however, and instead succeeded in obtaining the support of Smuts for the disenfranchisement of the Africans, which took place in 1936. Frustration and increasing segregation were to be the lot of the non-white populations of South Africa between the two world wars and after.

30. C. F. Andrews, the English Anglican who was an associate of Gandhi, and had been a member of his ashram, said that "his whole heart went out" to the European Communists in South Africa because of their readiness to admit racial equality for Africans, Indians, and Cape Colored alike.

## The Kimbanguist Movement

Further to the north the African populations of Central and Eastern Africa continued to live under colonial administration while remaining virtually untouched, as yet, by any hopes of change or signs of political awakening. Occasionally, however, a movement would suddenly arise, as the Chilembwe movement had done during the First World War, which would challenge the assumptions on which colonial rule was based, only to find itself quickly suppressed. Such a manifestation was the Kimbanguist movement which arose in the Congo in 1921.

Simon Kimbangu was a carpenter at Stanley Pool who began to prophesy and to perform "miracles" which attracted thousands of people. As the movement gained strength, tension arose between the African and European communities. Not only did the Europeans fear the veiled threat that the movement came to constitute, but also European employers became uneasy, complaining, for example, that the Kimbanguists were disrupting the work week by celebrating their day of rest on Wednesday instead of Sunday. At length the Belgians ordered Kimbangu's arrest, after which, in a disturbed atmosphere, he was brought to trial. After he was sentenced to death, the sentence was commuted to one of life imprisonment. His movement, after an interval, was permitted to resume some of its activities, but was kept under surveillance by the Belgian authorities.

Another movement, with points of resemblance to that founded by Kimbangu was the Watchtower movement, which appeared sporadically in Central African territories from 1906. In 1925 a Watchtower leader in Northern Rhodesia began to preach that in order to gain eternal life man must first die—a doctrine that led to 170 persons deliberately drowning themselves. Movements such as those of Chilembwe, Kimbangu, and the Watchtower appear in their manifestations like sudden flashes of tropical lightning, which reveal in a sudden blinding yet eerie light the features of a hidden political landscape—a sight that appears only to be effaced a moment later by total darkness.

## Italy Attacks Ethiopia

In 1935 the Fascist government in Italy headed by Benito Mussolini successfully attacked and later occupied Ethiopia.[31] The Italo-Ethiopian war appeared anachronistic to some at the time, since the era of colonial conquest was felt to have ended before the First World War. In fact, however, the basis for the Italian action was dissatisfaction with the

---

31. Ethiopia, and not Abyssinia, is the correct name of the country. "Abyssinia" appears to derive from the Arabic *habesh*; it has sometimes been used by non-Ethiopians to describe the country. Lord Avon, in his memoirs published in 1962, was still referring to Abyssinia rather than Ethiopia, and the name "Abyssinia" even crept occasionally into official League of Nations usage.

terms of the Paris peace settlement which had left Italy empty-handed. It also demonstrated to the world the breakdown of the collective security system envisaged in the League of Nations Covenant, and thus signaled the opening of a period in which the European nations hastily began to rearm in preparation for the war which was to follow.

Strategically Italy had long contemplated the advantages of obtaining a predominant position in Ethiopia so as to link the Italian colony of Libya with those of Eritrea and Somaliland. Italy also sought land in which to settle some of her growing population—and Ethiopian land, it was felt, would prove more welcoming and less expensive to colonize than the hostile and arid wastes of Libya. Ethiopia's independence had previously been protected by its difficult terrain. With the advent of the airplane, however, new possibilities lay open to an invading force. Reconnaissance was now possible beyond the highest mountain ranges, and enemy troops could now be suddenly and unexpectedly attacked wherever they were.

Ethiopia's isolation, breached by the British punitive expedition of 1867 against the Emperor Theodore, had begun to some extent to be eroded after the First World War. This development, historically inevitable, was facilitated by the personality of Tafari Makonnon, a Provincial Governor who, unlike most of his contemporaries, favored the introduction of certain Western innovations and reforms. After the deposition of Lij Yasu in 1916, the Princess Zauditu had become Empress of Ethiopia, with Tafari Makonnon, who was given the title of *Ras*, being recognized as heir to the throne. Ras Tafari wielded considerable influence thereafter, particularly in foreign policy, and was able to secure Ethiopia's admission to the League of Nations in 1923—an admission that only took place, however, after guarantees were given that slavery in Ethiopia would be prohibited.[32] By 1926 Tafari had consolidated his position in the country, ruling in all but name. In 1928 he was crowned Negus (King), and in 1930, on the death of the Empress Zauditu, he became Emperor, taking the title of *Haile Selassie* ("Might of the Trinity").

Ethiopian efforts to introduce reforms under Haile Selassie's rule were, however, to be interrupted by the Italian intervention. Since Italy's reverses at the battle of Adowa in 1896, the Italians had not forgotten Ethiopia. In 1906 Italy, France, and the United Kingdom had signed a Three Power Treaty by the terms of which Ethiopia was to be divided into respective zones of influence—an arrangement which, however, Ethiopia upset by failing to approve. After the accession of Mussolini to

---

32. Ironically Italy, as well as France, supported Ethiopia's admission at this time. The United Kingdom, Australia, and others, had advised delaying admission because of the allegations of slavery. France and Italy intimated, however, that they believed that the British position was taken because of a British desire to annex the sources of the Blue Nile.

power in 1922, Italian interest in Ethiopia was renewed. On August 2, 1928, a Treaty of Friendship, Conciliation, and Arbitration was signed between the two countries in Addis Ababa. But, when the treaty failed to result in the Italian economic expansion in Ethiopia that Mussolini doubtless had hoped would be the prelude to political annexation, he decided, in 1933,[33] to achieve Italian aims by war. The first steps were made in secret. Italian political bureaus were established to incite subversion inside Ethiopia, military plans were perfected, and, as a prelude to invasion, roads were constructed in Eritrea.

A serious frontier clash at Wal-Wal in a disputed area between Italian Somaliland and the Ethiopian province of Ogaden resulted in a formal Italian claim to Wal-Wal. In response Haile Selassie proposed that the problem be settled by arbitration and, on December 15, 1934, notified the Council of the League of Nations of the situation that had arisen. When the Council considered the matter in January, 1935, however, both France and the United Kingdom, concerned about the rising threat posed by Nazi Germany, showed themselves unwilling to offend Italy. The Allies reminded themselves hopefully that Mussolini had sent troops to the Italian-Austrian frontier in July, 1934, at the time the Austrian Chancellor, Dollfuss, had been murdered, thus checking Hitler's threatened invasion of Austria at that juncture. Ethiopia's independence was now to be sacrificed to Allied hopefulness—a hopefulness that was to continue to persist long after any reasonable basis for it had disappeared. At first, however, the Italians appeared to agree to resort to peaceful methods of settlement, although from March, 1935, it was clear from the military preparations that were taking place that Mussolini contemplated an attack on Ethiopia and that his supposedly peaceful gestures were only intended to gain time. Haile Selassie appealed to the League to settle the dispute by arbitration under Article 15 of the Covenant. Italy argued that the League need not occupy itself with the matter as it was Italy's intention to have the dispute arbitrated under the appropriate provision of the 1928 Italo-Ethiopian Treaty. The Allies, concerned by Hitler's increasing militarism, hastened to accept the Italian view of the matter. Seeing this the Italians stiffened their position, and continued to use delaying tactics. Three times Italy rejected suggested settlements that would have resulted in substantial concessions by Ethiopia—for example the settlement proposed by Anthony Eden to Mussolini in Rome in June, 1935.[34]

33. Marshal de Bono wrote in 1933: "The Duce [Mussolini] had spoken to no one of the coming operations in East Africa: *only he and I knew* [de Bono's italics] what was going to happen and no indiscretion occurred by which the news could reach the public." Emilio de Bono, (*Anno XIII. The Conquest of an Empire*).

34. See *The Memoirs of Anthony Eden, Earl of Avon: Facing the Dictators. 1923–1938* (1962), pp. 247–252.

World public opinion, meanwhile, continued to count on the League to find a just settlement to the dispute, feeling—rightly, as it proved—that if the League could not provide security for an independent state in Africa, then it would not be able to guarantee the peace of Europe either. The failure of the League to safeguard Ethiopia would also signal its failure to protect colored nations from colonial aggression. The League itself, however, while continuing to consider the dispute periodically, took no diplomatic initiative in the course of 1935, while the Italians were energetically interceding on their own behalf with other governments, notably the French and the British. An appeal to the United States government by Haile Selassie to avert the impending violation of the Kellogg Pact resulted, moreover, in a weakening of the Ethiopian position, since it stimulated United States isolationist sentiment, with the result that the United States Congress adopted the first Neutrality Act of August 31, 1935. Under the terms of this act the United States President was obliged, so long as the United States remained neutral in any war, to place an embargo on the export of arms or ammunition to any belligerent. The effect of the act was to render it impossible for President Roosevelt to take indirect action in support of Ethiopia or the League once hostilities had begun, and thus to encourage Mussolini, not to mention Hitler, to proceed more confidently with military preparations. Meanwhile, Italy had put pressure on other countries not to supply arms to Ethiopia—France, for example, embargoed arms to Ethiopia, and the United Kingdom embargoed them both to Ethiopia and to Italy. As, however, Italy was manufacturing arms for herself, which Ethiopia was unable to do, the result of the British action, no less than that of other countries, was to help to prevent Ethiopia from defending herself when the attack came.

The attack itself began on October 3, 1935. The Italian army crossed the Ethiopian frontier, and Italian planes began bombing Ethiopian towns. In Geneva the League decided that Italy "had resorted to war in disregard of its covenants," and fifty nations agreed to impose sanctions against the aggressor nation. The sanctions were only partial, however, and did not produce the desired effect, in part because the Italians won the war more quickly than had been anticipated. Had the British taken resolute action by closing the Suez Canal with the League's approval, Mussolini's Ethiopian venture would quickly have ended. This, however, together with many other actions which might have been taken, such as refusing Italian airplanes on regular flights between Eritrea and Italian Somaliland permission to land and refuel in British Somaliland, was not done. As A. J. P. Taylor, writing of the Ethiopian war, put it:

> The British generals and admirals at this time were mostly elderly; they were all Conservatives of an extreme cast. They admired Mussolini. They found in Fascism a

display of all the military virtues. On the other hand they detested the League of Nations and everything associated with it. . . . Those who were clamoring for sanctions against Italy had spent earlier years denouncing British armaments and British military experts. It was hardly to be expected that these experts should now wish to fight a war as the agent of the League of Nations Union.[35]

A world-wide wave of sympathy for Ethiopia meanwhile arose. At the League of Nations itself most national representatives refrained from criticizing Italy openly, though their governments were to varying degrees critical of the Italian aggression. Even before the invasion had begun the South African representative had appealed to Italy on behalf of white civilization not to stir up anew antagonism between white and black in Africa. "The long memory of Black Africa never forgets and never forgives an injury or an injustice," he said.[36] Now an exception to the general rule of silence was made by the outspoken speech of the Haitian representative who, on October 10, 1935, told the other delegates, "Great or small, strong or weak, near or far, white or colored, let us never forget that one day we may be somebody's Ethiopia."

*International Reactions*

The effect on international opinion was considerable. In a world where most people with colored skins hoped for a modicum of stability and progress, the system of international security which had been born out of the "war to end war" was being breached by yet another European aggression—this time against the oldest black-skinned realm in the world. Deep-rooted fears, antagonisms, and prejudices were stirred. Throughout India, both Muslim and Hindu, among the peoples of Africa, in the black ghettoes of North America, feelings flamed out openly. Supporters of the League rallied to those who sympathized with Ethiopia on grounds of racial kinship. In Egypt and South Africa, in Marseilles and on the West Coast of the United States, dockers refused to load, and crews refused to sail in, ships bound for Italy.

The opponents of Italy's action placed their hopes in particular on the application of sanctions that would cut off Italy's oil supplies, thus halting the Italian Army and grounding Italian planes. Italy was understood at the outset to have only two months' supply of oil in East Africa, so that it was expected that the sanctions would prove effective. Indeed, Mussolini himself appears to have become apprehensive, and to have sought to hasten the military campaign while at the same time striving to delay the anticipated diplomatic action in Geneva. De Bono, in command of the Italian operations in Ethiopia, was felt to be moving too

35. *The Origins of the Second World War* (1961).
36. On September 23, 1960, Dr. Kwame Nkrumah, President of the Republic of Ghana, speaking to the United Nations General Assembly, said, "Africa does not seek vengeance. It is against her very nature to harbour malice."

slowly, and in November, 1935, he was replaced by Pietro Badoglio. Meanwhile—acting out a charade, it was suspected, in collusion with the French Foreign Minister, Laval—Mussolini threatened France, moving Italian troops up to the French frontier, and hinting that he might bomb the French Riviera. These actions, coupled with a threat to withdraw Italy from the League,[37] played upon the fears of another world war that had haunted Europe since 1918, thus resulting in a weakening of resolution among some of those opposed, or nominally opposed, to Italy's attempt to seize Ethiopia.

The gamble, if gamble it was, worked. The application of oil sanctions was delayed. The immediate action by the League that had been anticipated was postponed, and in December, 1935, Sir Samuel Hoare, the British Foreign Secretary, visited Paris to confer in secret with Laval. Hardly was the meeting over than the French press published details of the secret agreement that been reached in the "Hoare-Laval Plan." According to the plan Ethiopia would have ceded areas totaling about 60,000 square miles to the Italians, receiving in return a 3,000 square-mile area that would have given her an outlet to the Red Sea.[38] In addition the southern half of Ethiopia—an additional 160,000 square miles—would have become "a zone of economic expansion and settlement reserved to Italy." Any sovereignty Ethiopia would have retained under such an arrangement would have been purely nominal.

The outcry that greeted the premature revelation of the plan was overwhelming. It was all the greater because in September, 1935, doubtless with the forthcoming British elections in mind, Sir Samuel Hoare had delivered to the League "the most ringing assertion in favour of collective security ever made by a British statesman."[39] The League members who had placed their faith in the United Kingdom and France now learned that this faith had been betrayed, and that, moreover, pressure to accept the plan had been applied to the Emperor of Ethiopia by the two powers. The consequences were far-reaching. It mattered little that both Hoare and Laval were separately obliged to resign, or that both Italy and Ethiopia openly rejected the plan. What was important was that the League had received its deathblow, and had received it from the very powers which had been regarded as its greatest friends. The League was now seen by all to be no deterrent to aggression.

"The relief in Germany, the dismay in America, were unmistakable."[40] By February 1936, oil sanctions were technically ready to be put into

---

37. Italy gave notice of withdrawal, effective two years later, in December, 1937.
38. Commenting upon the unfairness of such an exchange, the London *Times* referred to Ethiopia's proposed share as constituting no more than "a corridor for camels."
39. A. J. P. Taylor, *The Origins of the Second World War* (1961).
40. F. P. Walters (formerly Deputy Secretary-General of the League of Nations), *A History of the League of Nations*, Vol. II (1952), p. 672.

effect, but member governments of the League, their collective morale now impaired, asked for more time for reflection. Meanwhile, the Italian armies had begun at last to move. As the Italian air force sprayed mustard gas over Ethiopian soldiers and Ethiopian villagers alike, Badoglio's forces advanced. The Ethiopian forces often fought with outstanding bravery, but jealousy between Ethiopian commanders, combined with the fact that Ethiopia had been deprived of arms, left the final outcome in no doubt. The Ethiopians with their swords and spears, and a few firearms, found themselves confronted with a concentration of fire-power such as they had never expected. The final conflict between the Italian army and the Ethiopian forces—the latter under the personal command of their Emperor, who, despite his evident courage, was driven sadly to observe "I am no soldier"—took place at the battle of Ashangi, which lasted from March 31 to April 3, 1936, and resulted in an Italian victory. On May 2 Haile Selassie left Ethiopia, and on May 6 Badoglio entered the Ethiopian capital, Addis Ababa. The war was over. On May 9, 1936, Mussolini, standing on the balcony of the Palazzo Venezia in Rome, announced the foundation of the Fascist empire, with the King of Italy taking for himself and his successors the title of Emperor of Ethiopia.

A final episode remained to be played out, however, before the chapter was closed. While Ethiopians and League supporters had charged Italians with the use of mustard gas, and with indiscriminate bombing of Ethiopian villages from the air, the Italians had accused the Ethiopians of using dum-dum bullets,[41] of emasculating captives and the slain, and of practicing slavery. In the heated atmosphere created by these charges and countercharges, the Emperor of Ethiopia, on June 30, 1936, appeared in person to address the League of Nations Assembly. Lord Avon (then Anthony Eden) later described his behavior as being

as always, brave, calm and dignified. In that great audience, his was probably the only mind at rest. He had done all he could, and gazed in quiet contempt at the hysterical Fascist journalists, hurling vulgar abuse, who had to be removed from the gallery.[42]

"I, Haile Selassie, Emperor of Ethiopia," he said, "am here today to claim that justice which is due to my people and the assistance promised to it eight months ago when fifty nations asserted that aggression had been committed." Asking whether Ethiopia was to be abandoned to the aggressor, and whether the member states of the League were "to set up the terrible precedent of bowing before force," he concluded with his

41. Bullets pierced before firing, so that they would "pancake" upon impact, thus inflicting severe internal wounds.
42. *The Memoirs of Anthony Eden, Earl of Avon: Facing the Dictators. 1923–1938* (1962), p. 437.

final question: "What reply should I take back to my people?" The delegates, conscience-stricken when they were not hostile, listened for the most part in grave embarrassment, saying nothing. In effect the Emperor already knew their unspoken answer. As he left the rostrum he muttered a nine-word prophecy that was all too soon to be realized: "It is us today. It will be you tomorrow."

# Chapter 14

# The Civil War Renewed

*If I try to gauge my work, I must consider, first of all, that I've contributed, in a world that had forgotten the notion, to the triumph of the idea of the primacy of race.* —Adolf Hitler (October 21–22, 1941)

[*President Franklin D. Roosevelt of the United States of America, and Prime Minister Churchill of the United Kingdom*] *respect the right of all peoples to choose the form of government under which they will live; and wish to see sovereign rights and self-government restored to those who have been forcibly deprived of them.* —The Atlantic Charter (August 14, 1941)

HAILE SELASSIE'S PROPHECY was fulfilled. War came. As the League of Nations, its policy betrayed by its creators, grew progressively demoralized, Adolf Hitler, leader of a renascent and militaristic Germany, established an aggressive policy of expansion that sapped the power and prestige of those who had been the victors at Versailles. France and the United Kingdom realized that they would soon be obliged either to make a stand against German expansion, or else prepare to surrender in their turn. Having reneged on their obligations to protect Czechoslovak independence in 1938 and 1939, they made a stand at last when German troops invaded Poland on September 1, 1939. War between the Allies and Germany then began on September 3. The white-skinned nations were at each other's throats again.

Although it has since been called the "Second World War," the war, in effect, initially was not a second one so much as a resumption of the first. The years between the wars can be seen as years of armistice rather than of peace—years in which the Allies, seeing themselves as victors, grew complacent and somnolent, while Germany, having suffered the consequences of its first defeat, gathered its strength for a renewal of the struggle, and for a reversal of the terms of the Treaty of Versailles.

Germany, beyond question, had wrongs to complain of.[1] The agreement that peace negotiations would be based on President Wilson's Fourteen Points had not been respected. The peace terms imposed on Germany were not designed to bring justice and stability to Europe, but, to a considerable degree, to exact vengeance for the losses and sufferings endured by the Allies in the First World War. Yet it was only a question of time before circumstances would permit Germany to attempt to turn the tables on her adversaries. For, as A. J. P. Taylor has pointed out, "the treaty [of Versailles] was designed to provide security against a new German aggression, yet it could work only with the co-operation of the German government."[2] The paradox was compounded by the circumstance that by the very fact of concluding an armistice with the German government, the Allies tacitly recognized Germany unity. First, this ensured that eventually Germany had merely to have the provisions of Versailles revoked in order to regain a dominant place in Europe. Second, it permitted the German military to argue later on that they themselves had not in fact failed in any way, but that they had been "stabbed in the back" by sinister forces inside Germany itself. As a united Germany would eventually come to overshadow the whole of Europe, the seeds of a second conflict were thus, in a sense, sown by the Allies themselves at the very moment of victory. Had they continued their victorious advance into German territory they would have made the failure of the German military manifest to all. Had they divided Germany into separate states, they would then have been able indefinitely to maintain the hegemony to which they laid claim.

However, they did none of these things. They feared that a collapse in Germany as absolute as those which had occurred in Austria and Russia might have resulted in the extension of Bolshevik rule to Germany. Instead Germany was to be made into a barrier against Bolshevism. Money, above all from the United States, was consequently poured into Germany to hasten its revival. The presumption was that a prosperous Germany would be a peaceful Germany. But Germany was being humiliated as well as strengthened. Other factors, too, were at work. The suf-

1. The terms of the Treaty of Versailles were nevertheless less rigorous than those which Germany imposed upon Russia in the Treaty of Brest-Litovsk. Versailles, as William L. Shirer has put it, "left the Reich geographically and economically largely intact," whereas Brest-Litovsk deprived Russia of a territory "nearly as large as Austria-Hungary and Turkey combined, with 56,000,000 inhabitants, or 32 per cent of her whole population; a third of her railway mileage, 73 per cent of her total iron ore, 89 per cent of her total coal production; and more than 5,000 factories and industrial plants." (See *The Rise and Fall of the Third Reich: A History of Nazi Germany*, 1959, pp. 90–91.)
2. *The Origins of the Second World War* (1963), p. 28.

ferings of the war, the vindictiveness that was visited upon the German people by the Allies not only by Versailles but also by the continuation of the wartime blockade, the moral confusion produced by inflation, and the psychological shock produced by the depression that followed, sowed dragon's teeth that were later to produce an unforeseen harvest. It was logical that Germany should revive, that wrongs inflicted should be resented, and that the restrictions imposed should one day be repudiated. Nobody, however, foresaw the particular final form that these developments would assume. Nobody foresaw that the government of a major European power would be seized by a racial psychosis without precedent in Christian times.

The racial psychosis was itself a form of xenophobia. Germany's hardships and losses had, in fact, been caused in part by a web of circumstance, and in part by the obtuseness of the Emperor and the military caste. With certain variations the sufferings of the other combatant European nations sprang from similar causes. In Russia and in Austria the court and the military machine had been swept away as a result of the war. France and the United Kingdom were largely spared recriminations because victory and vengeance diverted emotions that might otherwise have been directed against the wartime leaders whose mistakes had led to such incalculable and ghastly results. Germany, however, was not in a position so easily to dispose of the emotions aroused by the war. Virtually landlocked, and therefore inclined to be isolationist rather than cosmopolitan in its world view, Germany tended to blame alien influences, rather than its own leadership, for the ills afflicting it. The German militarists, aware that popular vengeance might be visited upon them as it had been upon their counterparts in Russia, also encouraged public opinion to seek "foreign" scapegoats, at home as well as abroad.

## The Nazis

So it came about that, with the complicity of part of the German army and police, with the backing of European and American financiers and industrialists seeking to build a strong and anti-Bolshevik Germany, and with the enthusiastic support of a substantial section of German opinion, the National Socialist German Workers (Nazi) Party emerged as a powerful political force. Nationalist it was, but socialist it was not.[3] Its leader, the son of an Austrian customs official, was named Adolf Hitler.

3. In 1920 the Nazi party had proclaimed a 25-point program of which points 11, 12, 13, 14, 16, and 18 had been socialistic in character—Point 11, for example, demanding the abolition of incomes unearned by work, and Point 13 the sharing with the state of industrial profits. When substantial business interests began to finance the party, however, nothing more was heard of these points, despite the fact that in 1926 Hitler declared them to be "unalterable." It would appear that they had been primarily adopted in the first place to appeal to the mood of the times, and to sow dissension among the Nazi's left-wing opponents.

Born in 1889 at Braunau am Inn in Austria, on the Austro-German frontier, Hitler had aspired to be a painter, but his efforts went practically unrewarded. After some years of poverty spent in Vienna, he had served with apparent bravery as a corporal in the German Army on the Western front in the First World War. Embittered and opportunistic, chauvinistic and loquacious, he found his vocation in politics, for which he was soon seen to have a genius. Such qualifications were sufficient for the interests seeking such a man to combat the advance of Communism in Germany. As Dietrich Eckart, one of Hitler's mentors in Munich, the city in which he laid the foundations of his career, reportedly put it in 1919:

> We need a fellow at the head who can stand the sound of a machine gun. The rabble need to get fear into their pants. We can't use an officer, because the people don't respect them any more. The best would be a worker who knows how to talk. . . . He doesn't need much brains, politics is the stupidest business in the world, and every marketwoman in Munich knows more than the people in Weimar [then the seat of the German government]. I'd rather have a vain monkey who can give the Reds a juicy answer, and doesn't run away when people begin swinging table legs, than a dozen learned professors. He must be a bachelor, then we'll get the women.[4]

At first the Nazi movement made little progress. On November 11, 1923, it attempted a coup—popularly known as the Munich Beer Hall Putsch—which proved abortive. As a result Hitler was confined for thirteen months in the fortress prison of Landsberg am Lech, during which time he wrote the first volume of his political testament *Mein Kampf* ("My Struggle"). It was published in 1925, while the second and final volume appeared in 1926. In *Mein Kampf*, a lengthy and somewhat formless dissertation, the main tenets of the Nazi movement were set down. Like Hitler himself, and like the Nazi movement, *Mein Kampf* was hardly noticed at first. Determined organization and skillful propaganda, backed by substantial financing, were soon, however, to make all three famous.

The betrayal of the German national interest by the signature of the Treaty of Versailles was the point of departure of the Hitlerian thesis. In comparing the terms of Brest-Litovsk with those of Versailles, Hitler spoke of the "actual boundless humanity of the one treaty compared to the inhuman cruelty of the second." Versailles must be repudiated. New slogans were proclaimed: "Give us arms!" "Germany will either be a world power or there will be no Germany." More, however, than a simple return to the frontiers of 1914 was involved. The restoration of these frontiers could not be achieved by "wheedling and begging," but "could be achieved only by blood." But state boundaries were "made by man

---

4. Cited by Konrad Heiden, one of Hitler's biographers who worked in Munich as a newspaperman at this time. See Adolf Hitler, *Mein Kampf* (1943), footnote p. 687. Hitler, incidentally, forbade the publication of an authorized English translation of his work.

and changed by man," and to spill blood for a mere return to the pre-war status quo would be a useless sacrifice. New goals, too, must be envisaged. "The boundaries of 1914 mean nothing at all for the German future." Or, more strongly:

No people on this earth possesses so much as a square yard of territory on the strength of a higher will or superior right. Just as Germany's frontiers are fortuitous frontiers, momentary frontiers in the current political struggle of any period, so are the boundaries of other nation's living space.

A new era was at hand, in which the earth was being gradually divided up among giant states—England "which calls nearly a quarter of the earth's surface its own," the American Union, Russia, China, France. Never had the position of the German Reich been as unfavorable, except at the beginning of its history two thousand years earlier. Indeed, it was now sinking into insignificance. Therefore the National Socialist movement must change Germany's direction.

We stop the endless German movement to the south and west, and turn our gaze towards the land in the east. At long last we break off the colonial and commercial policy of the pre-war period and shift to the soil policy of the future.

If we speak of soil in Europe today, we can primarily have in mind only Russia and her vassal border states. . . .

Our task, the mission of the National Socialist movement, is to bring our own people to such political insight that they will not see their goal for the future in the breath-taking sensation of a new Alexander's conquest, but in the industrious work of the German plow, to which the sword need only give soil.

The practice of such a policy implied new alignments. "The inexorable mortal enemy of the German people is and remains France. It matters not at all who ruled or who will rule . . ." On the other hand, "if we look about us for European allies . . . there remain only two states: England and Italy." Italy's natural sphere was the Mediterranean. Encouraged to expand there, she would ensure the safety of Germany's southern frontier. England, on the other hand, was a natural rival of France. Providing that Germany abandoned its former colonial policy, which had brought it into conflict with England, there was no reason why England should not support an alliance with Germany, if only because the two countries shared a common interest in opposing France. With the French danger neutralized, both nations would, however, be free safely to pursue their historic goals—England over the seas, and Germany toward the East.

On the subject of Afro-Asian nationalism, Hitler was scathing. After the First World War there had been a "League of Oppressed Nations."

Chiefly involved were representatives of various Balkan states, and some from Egypt and India, who as individuals always impressed me as pompous big-mouths without any realistic background. But there were not a few Germans, especially in the nationalist camp, who let themselves be dazzled by such inflated Orientals and readily accepted any old Indian or Egyptian student from God knows where as a "representative" of India or Egypt. These people never realized that they were usually dealing with persons who had absolutely nothing behind them, and above all were authorized by no one to conclude any pact with anyone, so that the practical result of any relations with such elements was nil, unless the time wasted were booked as a special loss.

Indeed, Hitler not only felt little sympathy with "such elements," but, on the contrary, felt sympathy for their imperial masters. "I, as a man of Germanic blood," he wrote, "would, in spite of everything, rather see India under English rule than any other." He complained that "some Asiatic jugglers, for all I care they may have been real 'fighters for Indian freedom,' who at that time [1920–1921] were wandering around Europe, had managed to sell otherwise perfectly reasonable people the *idée fixe* that the British Empire, which has its pivot in India, was on the verge of collapse at that very point." Such an idea, to Hitler, was out of the question. Before the First World War he recalled that German propaganda had depicted the Englishman as shrewd and perfidious but "unbelievably cowardly," adding that

the fact that a world empire the size of the British could not be put together by mere subterfuge and swindling was unfortunately something that never occurred to our exalted professors of academic science. . . . I remember well my comrades' looks of astonishment when we faced the Tommies in person in Flanders. After the first days of battle the conviction dawned on each and every one of them that these Scotsmen did not exactly jibe with the pictures they had seen fit to give us in the comic magazines and press despatches.

He himself had no intention of being similarly deceived a second time, and stated that "if anyone imagines that England would let India go without staking her last drop of blood, it is only a sorry sign of absolute failure to learn from the World War, and of total misapprehension and ignorance on the score of Anglo-Saxon determination." Quite as lamentable, he felt, were the hopes placed in "any mythical uprising in Egypt," and added that "as a folkish man, who appraises the value of men on a racial basis, I am prevented by mere knowledge of the racial inferiority of these so-called 'oppressed nations' from linking the destiny of my own people with theirs."

In effect, it was Hitler's racial philosophy, which accompanied and complemented his foreign-policy goals, that gave a new dimension to a program that, apart from the declaration of intent to take Eastern land "by the sword," nevertheless contained elements of a German foreign policy that would have been no more irrational than that of other powers. Whereas he himself never faced the task of defining precisely the racial concepts that he used, Hitler nevertheless proclaimed the superiority of the Aryan race,[5] with whose presence, he said, "human culture and human civilization on this continent [Europe] are inseparably bound up." The "folkish philosophy" that he upheld "by no means believed in an equality of races, but along with their difference . . . recognizes their higher or lesser value and feels itself obligated, through this knowledge, to promote the victory of the better and stronger, and demand the subordination of the inferior and weaker in accordance with the eternal will that dominates this universe."

This view necessarily implied a racial hierarchy in which the Germans were seen as the most admirable species of the Aryan genus, while, at the other extreme, the African Negroes represented the lowest level of the hierarchical scale.

> From time to time, illustrated papers bring it to the attention of the German pettybourgeois that some place or other a Negro has for the first time become a lawyer, teacher, even a pastor, in fact a heroic tenor, or something of the sort. . . . It doesn't dawn on this depraved bourgeois world that this is positively a sin against all reason; that it is criminal lunacy to keep on drilling a born half-ape until people think they have made a lawyer out of him, while millions of members of the highest culture-race must remain in entirely unworthy positions; that it is a sin against the will of the Eternal Creator if His most gifted beings by the hundreds of thousands are allowed to degenerate in the present proletarian morass, while Hottentots and Zulu Kaffirs are trained for the intellectual professions. For this is training exactly like that of the poodle, and not scientific "education." The same pains and care employed on intelligent races would a thousand times sooner make every single individual capable of the same achievements.

Even so, however, he felt that Africans were superior, within their limitations, to the products of racial crossing. The "tearing down of racial barriers," he held, would result in the loss of the best part of the higher element, leaving at last "nothing but a unified mash." The mission of humanity would then be over.

> Anyone who does not want the earth to move toward this condition must convert himself to the conception that it is the function above all of the Germanic states first and foremost to call a fundamental halt to any further bastardization.

Germans, then, had a mission to combat "mongrelization," as the standard-bearers of racial purity. This did not, however, mean a policy of "Germanization." If a Negro or a Chinese learned German, this did not make him a German.

> Only too frequently does it occur in history that conquering people's outward instruments of power succeed in forcing their language on oppressed peoples, but that after a thousand years their language is spoken by another people, and the victors

---

5. The Aryans were an ancient race believed to have originated between the Caspian and the North Sea, who later invaded the Iranian plateau and northern India. The Aryan language is a subgroup of the Indo-European family of languages, and many modern languages contain elements of it. Gobineau, author of *L'Inégalité des Races Humaines* (1853–1855), contended that Aryan-descended peoples were superior to others, thus bringing the name "Aryan" back into more general use.

thereby actually become the vanquished. . . . Nationality or other race does not lie in language but in blood.

In Europe, Hitler held, the natural enemy of Germany, both strategically and ideologically, was France. For just as Germany represented the defender of racial purity, so did France symbolize the policy of racial intermixture.

> Racially she [France] is making such progress in negrification that we can actually speak of an African state arising on European soil. . . . If the development of France in the present style were to be continued for three hundred years, the last remnants of Frankish blood would be submerged in the developing European-African mulatto state. An immense self-contained area of settlement from the Rhine to the Congo, filled with a lower race gradually produced from continuous bastardization.

While Hitler often referred disparagingly to "Orientals," from an early age he claims to have had a sympathy for the Japanese. As a boy at the time of the Russo-Japanese war, "for national reasons," he sided with the Japanese against "Austrian Slavdom." His early sympathy for Japan became, however, at a later date an integral part of his political philosophy. He noted that England had formed a mutually beneficial alliance with Japan in 1902 at a time when Germany was allying itself with what he regarded as a moribund Austria. He also noted that while Japanese and British interests coincided, they conflicted with those of the United States—and hence sensed a U.S.-British split in the making which, he felt, Germany would have done well to exploit earlier.

"British statesmen," Hitler said, "gaze with trepidation towards a period in which it will no longer be said: 'Britannia rules the waves!' But instead: 'The seas for the Union!' "

With respect to Japan itself, however, Hitler's attitude remained fundamentally ambiguous. Hitler was developing a new ideology, based on racial egoism, and such an ideology, by its nature, could not ultimately by sympathetic to a non-Germanic group. While a Japanese alliance might be useful to Germany, he denied that Japanese culture was in itself important. Aryan culture alone was responsible for Japan's success:

> In a few decades, the entire east of Asia will possess a culture whose ultimate foundation will be Hellenic in spirit and Germanic technology just as much as in Europe. Only the *outward* form—in part at least—will bear the features of Asiatic character. It is not true, as some people think, that Japan adds European technology to its culture; no, European science and technology are trimmed with Japanese characteristics. The foundation of actual life is no longer the special Japanese culture, although it determines the color of life—because outwardly, in consequence of its inner difference, it is more conspicuous to the European—but the gigantic scientific-technical achievements of Europe and America; that is, of Aryan peoples. . . . If beginning today all further Aryan influence on Japan should stop, assuming that Europe and America should perish, Japan's present rise in science and technology might continue for a

short time; but even in a few years the well would dry up, the Japanese special character would gain, but the present culture would freeze and sink back into the slumber from which it was awakened seven decades ago by the wave of Aryan culture. Therefore, just as the present Japanese development owes its life to Aryan origin, long ago in the gray past foreign influence and foreign spirit awakened the Japanese culture of that time. The best proof of this is furnished by the fact of its subsequent sclerosis and total petrifaction.

Despite such qualifications, the logic of his other convictions nevertheless drove Hitler to adopt a pro-Japanese stance. A key element in his political philosophy was the idea that international Jewry constituted a threat to the individual nations and nationalities of the world. Japanese nationalism, which had successfully resisted foreign domination, therefore appeared as Germany's natural ally in Asia.

The Jew knows only too well that in his thousand years of adaptation he may have been able to undermine European peoples and train them to be bastards, but that he would scarcely be in a position to subject an Asiatic national state like Japan to this fate. Today he may mimic the German and the Englishman, the American and the Frenchman, but he lacks the bridges to the yellow Asiatic. And so he strives to break the Japanese national state. . . . And so he incites the nations against Japan as he once did against Germany.

### Hitler's Anti-Semitism

Hitler's antagonism toward the Jews, which was first aroused in his youth, grew over the years until it became an obsession which knew no bounds. By his own account he was not at first hostile to Jews, and occasionally found himself repulsed by the tone of the anti-Semitic pamphlets that he read. Later, however, he became increasingly anti-Semitic, until at last his hatred of Jews became implacable. *Mein Kampf* expressed the violence of his feelings:

Was there any form of filth or profligacy, particularly in cultural life, without at least one Jew involved in it? . . . This was pestilence, spiritual pestilence, worse than the Black Death of olden times, and the people was being infected with it!

The Jews were "scribblers who poison men's souls like germ-carriers of the worst sort," they were responsible for the German collapse of 1918, they were the originators of Marxism, and the leaders of Social Democracy, they controlled the American stock exchange, and directed the vice traffic. The Jews were a "race of dialectical liars," who were impelled to "lie and lie perpetually as the inhabitants of northern countries are impelled to wear warm clothing." They were without true culture, since what they accomplished in art was "either patchwork or intellectual theft." They were cowards. It was argued that they were nomads, but this was false, for the Jew was not a nomad but "a parasite in the body of other nations." The Jew's "life within other peoples can only endure for any length of time if he succeeds in arousing the opinion that he is not a people but a 'religious community' though of a special sort." Left alone in the world the Jews would "stifle in filth and offal." The Jew, nevertheless, represented "the mightiest counterpart to the Aryan."

> If, with the help of his Marxist creed, the Jew is victorious over the other peoples of the world, his crown will be the funeral wreath of humanity and this planet will, as it did thousands[6] of years ago, move through the ether devoid of men.
>
> Eternal Nature inexorably avenges the infringement of her commands.
>
> Hence today I believe that I am acting in accordance with the will of the Almighty Creator: *by defending myself against the Jew, I am fighting for the work of the Lord.*

Two questions come to mind in connection with Hitler's obsession with the Jews. First, who in fact were the Jews? Second, why should Hitler have chosen them as his ultimate adversaries?

The Jews were, of course, a Palestinian people of Hebrew origin. They had—like another ancient people, the gypsies—become widely scattered over the centuries. However, whereas the gypsies had remained nomadic and virtually illiterate, the Jews had, at an early stage, become both literate and city-dwelling. Forming small colonies in many countries, they participated, when allowed to do so, in the national life of the different states in which they dwelt. They claimed descent from Jacob, a Biblical figure who may or may not have been a mythical personage. The diaspora, or the dispersion of the Jews, had begun in the eighth century B.C., when they were for a time driven into exile after their Palestinian homeland (from a part of which, the province of Judea, the word "Jew" derives) had fallen under Babylonian rule. By the first century B.C. the greatest center of the diaspora had become the city of Alexandria, from where, favored by Alexander the Great, the Jews settled throughout the Mediterranean region. After the final extinction of the Jewish state in 70 A.D., the hegemony of international Jewry passed successively from Babylon and Persia to Arab (later Christian) Spain, and then to France and Germany, before passing, in the nineteen century, to Poland and Russia. In the early part of the twentieth century, this hegemony was in the process of moving from Europe to the United States. In all epochs the Jews, either because of religious, social, or cultural antagonisms, or because of the seemingly occult power that their international connections could on occasion give them, were the objects of intermittent persecutions. Driven from country to country down the centuries, their seemingly endless migratory story was summed up in the legend of the "Wandering Jew," condemned eternally to seek rest without finding it.

6. "Thousands" was changed to "millions" in the second edition.

Throughout their long and well-nigh timeless pilgrimage, however, the Jews were sustained by the hope of an eventual ingathering of the exiles.

The answer to the second question—why should Hitler have chosen the Jews as his ultimate adversaries—can be given with less certainty. Or, rather, it can be answered in different ways—for example, in historical, psychological, or ideological terms.

Historically, Hitler might be regarded as yet another in a series of leaders who from time to time had gained support by diverting contemporary discontents against the Jews—a successor to such as, for example, one Rindfleisch who, in 1298, had launched an anti-Jewish campaign which began in Franconia and then spread to Austria and Germany, resulting in the deaths of large numbers of Jews, and the destruction of 140 Jewish communities. Seen in this perspective Hitler, in the twentieth century, would have saved the German military caste from the consequences of the defeat of 1918 by diverting the anger of the German people from their own leadership to the Jews. In order to achieve this a myth evidently had to be created—the myth of the "Jewish betrayal," of the "stab in the back." As with all myths there was evidently some coloring of truth admixed with the propaganda. The German military caste in general, like the French,[7] had never favored the Jews, so that in consequence there was little reason to expect the Jews to play a prominent role in Germany's military efforts. Moreover, the entry of the United States into the war in 1917 and the British support extended to the Zionist movement in the same year were both factors which influenced most Jews to look with more favor on the Allied rather than the German cause.

Seen from the standpoint of Hitler's personal psychology, other aspects appear. He himself stated in *Mein Kampf* that it was the anti-Semitism of the leaders of the Christian Social Party and the Pan-German Party in Vienna which first inspired his own anti-Semitism. Why it should then have developed to such an extent one can only speculate. Once the idea was instilled in him, and proved politically useful, he may simply have come not only to use it but also to depend on it to such an extent that it became a part of his personality. Then again, he was by nature both an absolutist and a visionary. Perhaps it was because, despite dispersion and persecution, the remarkable circumstance that the Jews had nevertheless preserved their cohesion throughout the centuries appealed, albeit in a negative way, to the visionary in him. Here, for him, was a worthy foe—a foe whose origins were as remote as those of the quasi-mythical Nibelungs. Then yet again, anti-Semitism was psycho-

---

7. The circumstances of the Dreyfus case will be recalled. Napoleon's own attitude, dealt with below, provides, of course, a special exception.

logically necessary to his creed, for every ideology has its dogma, its one unquestioned unchallengeable leverage point from which it seeks to move the world, a point that is held, if necessary, in the face of logic.

Ideologically, Hitler, being anti-Slav, had an incentive to be anti-Communist, since twentieth-century Moscow had taken the place of nineteenth-century Paris as the headquarters of the international revolution. In his earlier years he had included socialist aims in his declared creed, but, as we have seen, as he secured substantial backing from industrialists and financiers, and as his anti-Soviet policies hardened, these were quietly permitted to drop into limbo. While proclaiming his sympathy with workers, Hitler nevertheless saw Communism as a Jewish conspiracy. "In Russian Bolshevism," he said, "we must see the attempt undertaken by the Jews in the twentieth century to achieve world domination." Here again, mixed in with his distorted assertions, there was a coloration of verifiable truth. A natural sympathy had existed between radicalism and Jewry from the time of the French Revolution. In 1791, for example, revolutionary France had accorded full rights of citizenship to all the Jews living within its borders, and this same liberal policy had been reaffirmed by Napoleon. The Jews, who for centuries had been persecuted by the Church, and obliged to pay revenues to the aristocracy in return for protection, naturally rallied to the revolutionary cause which abolished the restrictions placed upon them, and opened up new opportunities. Some of the revolutionaries had entertained doubts, but, as A. L. Sachar has put it:

> The fervent loyalty of the Jewish population to the principles of the Revolution was the clearest answer to those who had opposed Jewish rights. The emancipated people outdid themselves in their devotion to what had at last truly become for them *"la patrie."* Those who could enlisted in the Guard, others poured out their treasures, and all prayed for the success of the Revolution against enemies at home and abroad. The very candelabra of the synagogues were sold to contribute to the war fund.[18]

Napoleon, whose own personal attitude to Jews was ambiguous, later conceived an idea whereby Jews might prove as useful to the Revolution abroad as they had been at home. Having called together the leaders of the Jewish communities in France in 1806, he formed them into a body named the Sanhedrin, after the Sanhedrin, or ecclesiastical and legislative tribunal, of the ancient Jewish state. This measure, he hoped, would serve to rally the whole of Jewry to his support. Although his interest in the Sanhedrin was distracted by other projects and events, a coincidence of interest between the international revolution and international Jewry had nevertheless been demonstrated.

---

8. *A History of the Jews* (1958), p. 279. Some synagogues were, nevertheless, like some of the churches, burned during the anti-religious excesses of the "Reign of Terror," which began in 1793. It has been suggested that these excesses may have been financed by royalists abroad in order to discredit the Revolution in other countries.

While the Jewish communities were able to maintain at last some of their gains in the period of reaction that followed Napoleon's downfall, and while they had at last, in effect, entered the mainstream of European life, Jewish interest in change, whether evolutionary or revolutionary, remained. Many Jews, for evident reasons, rallied to the revolutionary cause in Czarist Russia, and some of them, such as Leon Trotsky (whose original name was Davyd Leontievich Bronstein), rose to high position under Bolshevism. These circumstances were enough to enable Hitler to convince many people of the existence of a sinister and far-reaching international plot engineered by the Jews. Was not the leading Communist theoretician "the Jew Karl Marx"? Indeed he was.

> With the sure eye of the prophet [wrote Hitler, Marx had] recognized in the morass of a slowly decomposing world the most essential poisons, extracted them, and, like a wizard, prepared them into a concentrated solution for the swifter annihilation of the independent existence of free nations on this earth. And all this in the service of his race.

### Zionism

The liberalism of the nineteenth century had been a concomitant of the new doctrine of nationalism. In a nationalist age it was perhaps not surprising that a Jewish form of nationalism—Zionism—should make its appearance. Throughout Jewish history the myth of the eventual return to Jerusalem had persisted. After the gains of the Napoleonic era, however, it seemed for a time as though the Jews in Europe would at last become assimilated by the various nations. But a series of circumstances brought into existence a new movement, Zionism, that sought to establish a Jewish homeland in Palestine. Although there had been some precursors, the effective founder of the Zionist movement was Theodore Herzl, an Austrian journalist who, in 1896, published his ideas in a book entitled *The Jewish State*. Herzl proposed that Palestine should be obtained from the Sultan of Turkey, and that an autonomous Jewish state should be established there under Turkish suzerainty. As a result of the publication of his book, the first Zionist Congress met in Basle, Switzerland, in 1897, and adopted a program which began: "Zionism aims at establishing for the Jewish people a *publicly recognized* and *legally secured* home in Palestine." In pursuance of this aim Herzl obtained audiences with the Pope, the Kaiser, the Sultan of Turkey, and others. His labors served to publicize the scheme, although by the time of his death in 1904 little practical progress had been made. One result, however, was an official offer from the British government of lands in Uganda to serve as a Jewish homeland. The suggestion had been that of the British Colonial Secretary, Joseph Chamberlain, who had envisaged Jewish settlers raising sugar and cotton there. The offer aroused such divided emotions within the Zionist movement,[9] however, that finally it was not accepted.[10]

Meanwhile, the failure of the Russian revolutionary upsurge of 1905, as well as the series of pogroms which followed, resulted in the emigration of numbers of Russian Jews to Palestine. By 1914 about 90,000 Jews from Russia and other countries had settled there. The outbreak of the First World War resulted in renewed persecutions of Jewish minorities, particularly in Eastern Europe. This circumstance, together with the British need to obtain Jewish support for the Allied war effort, particularly in the United States, inspired the Balfour Declaration of November 2, 1917.[11] This took the form of a letter from the British Foreign Secretary, A. J. Balfour, sent with the approval of the Cabinet to Lord Lionel Walter Rothschild, President of the Zionist Association, which stated

> His Majesty's Government view with favour the establishment in Palestine of a national home for the Jewish people, and will use their best endeavours to facilitate the achievement of this object, it being clearly understood that nothing shall be done which may prejudice the civil and religious rights of existing non-Jewish communities in Palestine, or the rights and political status enjoyed by Jews in any other country.

The Declaration was enthusiastically received by Jews all over the world. The French and Italian governments had also previously approved the Declaration, and President Wilson, having been apprised of it, had signified his personal agreement. Although the term "national home" was vague, General Smuts of South Africa, then a member of the British Imperial War Cabinet, Lord Robert Cecil, another Cabinet member, and Mr. Winston Churchill all foresaw the establishment of a Jewish state— "on the banks of the Jordan a Jewish state under the protection of the British Crown," as Churchill put it. Despite the fact that when Allenby's troops entered Palestine to replace the Turks, they carried, in Arthur Koestler's phrase, "the Balfour Declaration in one pocket and Wilson's Fourteen Points in the other," the Allied governments, one by one, endorsed the Declaration, and in 1922 both houses of the U.S. Congress adopted a resolution favoring "the establishment in Palestine of a national home for the Jewish people, it being clearly understood that nothing shall be done which may prejudice the civil and religious rights of the Christian and all other non-Jewish communities in Palestine, and

9. Although Jewish advocates of the scheme argued that the East African settlement—which would have enjoyed autonomy under a Jewish Governor—would only represent a temporary emergency refuge (or a *Nachtasyl*—a "shelter for the night"), other Zionists attacked the scheme bitterly as a betrayal of the Zionist ideal. Paradoxically the most convinced "Ugandists" in the Zionist movement were the few Jews who had already settled in Palestine, and who believed that conditions in East Africa would have to be better than those that they were facing.

10. A later suggestion that a homeland be established in Guyana similarly came to nothing.

11. In addition, the British appear to have taken into consideration the long-term advantages of establishing a pro-British population within the vicinity of the Suez Canal, through which the economic lifeline of the British Empire then ran.

that the Holy Places and religious buildings and sites in Palestine shall be adequately protected."

Meanwhile, in 1920 the Supreme Council of the Peace Conference met at San Remo, and decided that the Balfour Declaration should be incorporated into the Peace Treaty with Turkey, and that the League of Nations Mandate for Palestine should be given to Britain. Already, after the Balfour Declaration had been published, a Zionist Commission, consisting of representative British, French, and Italian Jews (later to be joined by Russian and American Jews), had traveled to Palestine to advise the British authorities there on all matters relating to the Jews. The Palestine Mandate was adopted by the League on July 24, 1922, and entered into force on September 29, 1923. It recognized the Zionist Organization as "an appropriate Jewish Agency for the purpose of advising and co-operating with the Administration in matters affecting the Jewish National Home and the interests of the Jewish population in Palestine."

The Zionist Commission had found that by the end of the war the number of Jews in Palestine had been reduced from 90,000 to about 55,000. However, the way was now clear for a further influx of settlers, with financing from sympathizers abroad. Although the rate of immigration fluctuated in the years that followed, between October, 1919, and September, 1939, a total of 326,000 Jewish emigrants entered Palestine, and a new political situation developed. Land was legally acquired by the newcomers, but, often being purchased from the frequently corrupt *effendi* class, some members of which were absentee landowners, its transfer to what was regarded as alien ownership aroused deep resentment among the Arab peoples, despite the indirect benefits conferred by the introduction by the immigrants of more modern methods of agriculture, medicine, and education. Distrust was further fanned by friction over the Holy Places. As a result serious "disturbances"—a euphemism which in practice meant riots, massacres, and outbreaks of guerrilla warfare between Arabs and Jews—occurred, first in 1920, 1921, and 1929, and then continuously from 1936 to 1939.

Between the two world wars the British government, swayed by considerations that sometimes favored Arabs and sometimes Zionists, vacillated in its stance. Both sides consequently became alienated from Britain, and the British government found itself brought into some international disrepute for its failure to maintain order.

Particularly distressing from the Zionist viewpoint was the British White Paper of May 17, 1939, published when Nazi persecution of the Jews in Germany and in Austria was reaching fresh heights. The White Paper stated that "fear of indefinite Jewish immigration is widespread among the Arab people, and that this fear has made possible disturbances which have given a serious setback to economic progress." It was therefore proposed to admit 75,000 more immigrants within the next five years—bringing the number of Jews up to approximately one-third of the total population of Palestine—after which no further immigration would be permitted without Arab approval. The White Paper was patently a tactical move, seeking to counter the danger of a Nazi-Arab alliance developing—an alliance that would have threatened not only British interests in the Middle East, but also Britain's very presence there.

Hitler, for his part, had specifically expressed his opinion of the concept of a "national home" for the Jews in Palestine in *Mein Kampf*:

> While the Zionists try to make the rest of the world believe that the national consciousness of the Jew finds its satisfaction in the creation of a Palestinian state, the Jews again slyly dupe the dumb Goyim [Gentiles]. It doesn't even enter their heads to build up a Jewish state in Palestine for the purpose of living there; all they want is a central organization for their international world swindle, endowed with its own sovereign rights and removed from the intervention of other states; a haven for convicted scoundrels and a university for budding crooks.

Meanwhile, as the outbreak of the Second World War approached, Nazi Germany increased its persecution of German Jews. As early as March 12, 1930, the German National Socialist Party had introduced in the Reichstag the following addition to Article 218 of the Criminal Code:

> Whoever undertakes artificially to restrict the natural fertility of the German people to the injury of the nation, or by word, writing, print, picture, or in any other way to assist such attempts, or whoever by mating with members of the Jewish blood-community or of the colored races contributes or threatens to contribute to the corruption and disintegration of the German people shall be punished by imprisonment for racial treason.

By the end of 1933 over fifty concentration camps had been set up for Jews and political opponents of the Nazi regime, and on September 15, 1935, the "Nuremberg Laws" were enacted, which forbade both marriage and extramarital relations between Jews and "Aryans," and added other restrictions. Professions were progressively closed to Jews, and many businesses refused to cater to their needs. A further thirteen decrees which supplemented the Nuremberg Laws in the years that followed excluded the Jews from virtually every facet of normal life. On November 9, 1938, with the encouragement of the Nazi government, there occurred a savage pogrom, called the *Kristallnacht*—"the Night of Broken Glass"—in which many Jews were killed, and Jewish houses, shops, and synagogues were smashed or burned. It was perhaps the *Kristallnacht*, more than any other single event, which signaled to Europe that a new and dark spirit was abroad that would eventually challenge virtually every European institution.

The Jewish crisis in Germany created, in effect, a climate that helped to precipitate the war. Yet, finally, after the Nazi-Soviet Pact of August, 1939, it was the German invasion of Poland on September 1, 1939, in which the opening shots were fired that heralded the onset of the Second World War. However, Hitler's concentration on the anti-Semitic issue in particular and the racial issue in general transformed what might have been simply a continuation of the first "white civil war" into a conflict which produced the most profound ideological, ethical, and ethnic repercussions.

## The World at War

The war that began in Europe on September 1, 1939, became a world war with the Japanese attack on the U.S. Pacific Fleet in Pearl Harbor on December 7, 1941. The Axis powers, particularly Germany in Europe, and later Japan in Asia, gained impressive victories in the earlier stages before their main Allied opponents—the United Kingdom, the Soviet Union, and the United States—could organize themselves for war. Once the latter had done so, however, the eventual defeat of the Axis became a question of time. Both in time and in space the two war zones—the European and the Asian theaters respectively—remained separate, although evidently interrelated. The war in the West lasted from September 1, 1939, to May 9, 1945,[12] that in the East lasted from December 7, 1941, to August 9, 1945. Before both phases had been concluded, the changes that the war brought were to affect African and Asian peoples in new ways, causing ancient peoples and societies to glimpse new possibilities for themselves. As in the time of the French Revolution, new shock waves, transmitting violence and change, were to shake the remotest provinces of old continents, ultimately breaking the pattern of colonial rule that Europe had fastened upon faraway peoples.

In the First World War Africa had experienced little direct involvement. In the Second World War, however, its strategic status was at stake following the collapse of France before the German attack launched in May, 1940. General Charles de Gaulle of France, opposing the contemplated surrender, advised the French government to adopt as a last resort "the African solution," by which he meant the regrouping of French forces on the African continent. But the French government rejected his advice and surrendered to Germany on June 22, 1940.[13]

12. The unconditional surrender to the Allies, enacted at Rheims on May 7, 1945, was ratified in Berlin on May 9, 1945.
13. The French government left Paris in June to establish itself briefly first at Tours, and then at Bordeaux, before taking up its seat in Vichy. The U.S. Ambassador in Paris, William Bullitt, remained in the city when the Germans entered it, instead of following the government to which he had been accredited. According to Robert Murphy, then a member of his staff, Bullitt felt he had a tradition to uphold, since U.S. Ambassadors had remained in the capital during the crises of 1870 and 1916, whereas other emissaries had left. As a result of Bullitt's decision, during the vital week of June 10 to 17, at the end of which the French asked for an armistice, there was no American

De Gaulle, finding refuge in England, had resolved nevertheless to continue the war. On June 18, four days before the surrender, he called on all French officers and men "who are at present on British soil, or may be in the future," to rally to him so that the "flame of French resistance" should not die. A stream of Frenchmen came to join de Gaulle, but the movement stopped when in July it was learned that the British Mediterranean Fleet, fearful that French ships might fall under German control, had attacked the French squadron at Mers-el-Kebir in Algeria. At the same time the attitude of many of the authorities in the French Empire changed from one of hesitation to outright opposition to de Gaulle and Britain. De Gaulle announced, nevertheless, that his Free French forces had resumed the fight, adopting the Cross of Lorraine as their symbol. On June 28 he was publicly recognized by the British Cabinet as "leader of the Free French."

De Gaulle's decision to continue the war precipitated a crisis throughout the French Empire. Previously dependent on Paris, the authorities in the various colonial territories were now faced with a choice between the French government in Vichy, collaborating with Hitlerian Germany but still controlling a part of the homeland, or de Gaulle's Free French in London, now tarnished in French eyes by their association with the authors of the Mers-el-Kebir attack.

North Africa remained under Vichy control, with sentiments in favor of the Free French being rigidly suppressed, but, in de Gaulle's words, "Coloured Africa presented quite other possibilities." Particularly in French Equatorial Africa an undercurrent of opinion in favor of de Gaulle and of the continuation of the war was in evidence. Deciding first of all to rally the Equatorial bloc of territories to his cause, de Gaulle began by sending his emissaries to Lagos, capital of the British colony of Nigeria, with orders to concert their efforts from there. Results were not long delayed. The first—and most difficult—public step was taken by Félix Eboué, the black Guyanese-born Governor of Chad, who, on August 26, 1940, proclaimed at Fort-Lamy the adherence of the territory to de Gaulle. The following day, August 27, the mandated territory of the Cameroun—a former German colony whose reversion to German control was feared by the French colonists—also joined the Free French, to be followed on the day after, August 28, by Brazzaville, capital of the French Congo and the administrative center for the whole of French Equatorial Africa. The territory of Ubangi immediately followed, leaving Gabon as the only Equatorial territory still under Vichy control.

ambassador to the French government, which, according to de Gaulle, conveyed the impression to the French that "the United States no longer had much use for France." U.S. Secretary of State Hull, in his memoirs, wrote that if Bullitt had followed the French government, "it is possible, if not probable, that that Government would have taken the fleet, gone to North Africa, and continued the fight from there."

French West Africa, however, continued to adhere to Vichy. De Gaulle and the British Prime Minister, Churchill, therefore concerted a plan to send an Anglo-French expedition to Dakar, administrative seat of French West Africa, in the hope that it would rally to the Allies. But the expedition proved abortive. On September 23, 1940, the expedition, led by de Gaulle on the French side, arrived at Dakar in a dense fog. The fog prevented the population of Dakar from seeing their ships—a sight, it was hoped, that would produce a moral effect which would discourage resistance. Two further events also affected the success of the enterprise. First, there appeared to have been a leak of information from de Gaulle's London headquarters, with the result that Vichy was apparently forewarned of the plan. Second, Vichy had dispatched a naval force from Toulon bound for Equatorial Africa. The British naval authorities at Gibraltar had allowed this force to pass through the Straits unchallenged,[14] with the result that it had arrived in Dakar before the Franco-British force. An indecisive conflict between the two sides then followed, at the end of which de Gaulle and the British decided to withdraw. De Gaulle then requested that he be placed ashore at Conakry, from where he intended to advance on Dakar overland.

The British, however, refused to proceed with the Dakar affair, and Admiral Cunningham, who was faced with the necessity of returning rapidly to European waters, instead landed de Gaulle and his forces at Douala in the Cameroun,[15] where they received an enthusiastic welcome. From here de Gaulle proceeded to tour the Equatorial territories. In Chad, in "an atmosphere of tense excitement," he met with Eboué, who, said de Gaulle, gave him "his loyalty and confidence, once for all." Visiting the desert posts in Chad, de Gaulle told the troops there that he was counting on them one day to cross the Sahara, seize the Fezzan, and reach the Mediterranean—at which news, he said, he could see "stupor plain upon their faces," since they had previously only envisaged repulsing German or Italian attacks upon Chad itself. De Gaulle then visited Leopoldville, capital of the Belgian Congo, thus in his person reinforcing those elements opposed to "the spirit of capitulation." He then organized the capture of the remaining Vichy territory, Gabon, which came under Free French control in November, 1940.

De Gaulle then returned to London, having appointed Félix Eboué as Governor-General of Equatorial Africa. The appointment of a black man to this position symbolized the coincidence of African and Free French interests on the continent, while at the same time underlining

14. Part of the reason for inaction lay in the fact that London was then under almost continuous bombardment by the German Luftwaffe, a circumstance that led to work stoppages as a result of which an important cipher was delayed. (See Winston Churchill, *The Second World War*, Vol. 2, 1949, pp. 425–427.)

15. To Winston Churchill this circumstance recalled the events of 1655 when Cromwell sent a naval and military expedition to seize San Domingo which, failing in its aim, instead captured Jamaica.

the contrary coincidence of interest between the Vichy government and Nazi Germany. For had not de Gaulle, in making the appointment, shown himself to be at variance with Hitler's view that "the white man is destined to rule"? Testimony to the effectiveness of de Gaulle's actions at this time was later paid by the South African Prime Minister, Marshal Smuts, who told de Gaulle in Cairo in 1942:

If you, de Gaulle, had not rallied Equatorial Africa, I should never have been able to hold South Africa together. Once the spirit of capitulation had triumphed at Brazzaville, the Belgian Congo would have succumbed in its turn, and from then on those elements in my country which oppose our military alliance with England would certainly have taken the upper hand and contrived a collaboration with the Axis powers. German hegemony would have been established from Algiers to the Cape.[16]

In fact, however, Africa did not bulk large in Hitler's strategic calculations. As he had said in *Mein Kampf*, he was primarily interested in obtaining land in Eastern Europe for German settlement—land that would be taken from the Slavs. He dreamed not of an African empire, but of a self-sufficient Europe, with Berlin as its center, importing nothing from overseas but coffee and tea, and living beneath German hegemony. "If it were only a question of conquering a colony, I'd not continue the war a day longer," he said. "For a colonial policy to have any sense one must first dominate Europe."[17] Yet German domination of the Eastern lands would take a colonial form, as he repeatedly made clear. "The Russian space is our India," he said. "Like the English we shall rule this empire with a handful of men." And again: "To exploit the Ukraine properly—that new Indian empire—I need only peace in the West." Peace in the East, however, was not envisaged:

Asia, what a disquieting reservoir of men [he observed to his table companions on September 25, 1941]. The safety of Europe will not be assured until we have driven Asia back behind the Urals. No organised Russian state must be allowed to exist west of that line. . . . The danger would be still greater if this space were to be Mongolised. Suddenly a wave comes foaming down from Asia and surprises a Europe benumbed by civilisation and deceived by the illusion of collective security! . . . A permanent state of war on the Eastern front will help to form a sound race of men, and will prevent us from relapsing into the softness of a Europe thrown back upon itself.

Toward the course of events outside Europe itself, he preserved a certain detachment:

If the British Empire collapsed today, it would be thanks to our arms, but we'd get no benefit, for we wouldn't be the heirs. Russia would take India, Japan would take Eastern Asia, the United States would take Canada. I couldn't even prevent the Americans from gaining a firm hold in Africa.

16. *The Complete War Memoirs of Charles de Gaulle: 1940–1946* (1964), p. 323.
17. "In any case," he added, "the only colony I'd like to have back would be our Cameroons —nothing else." These statements, and others cited, are from *Hitler's Secret Conversations: 1941–1944* (1953). The text of these conversations was edited by Martin Bormann from shorthand notes taken down at mealtimes by a Nazi party official, usually Heinrich Heim.

And yet again: "It is ridiculous to think of a world policy as long as one does not control the Continent." Even Egypt and the control of Suez did not strike him as of primary importance. "For us the sphinx has no particular attraction . . ." Let the Italians have it. Suez would be useful to them because of their possessions in Eritrea and Ethiopia. Also if Italy had Egypt she would stay out of the Caucasus, a region in which Germany alone should have vital interests. Nor was there any immediate necessity for a conflict with Japan. Japan and Germany both needed "fifty to a hundred years for purposes of digestion: we for Russia, they for the Far East."

Hitler's contempt for "primitive peoples" in Africa and Asia (even of his Japanese allies he commented that "it goes without saying that we have no affinities"), and his relative disinterest in events outside the confines of Europe led to his disregarding opportunities that others judged to be favorable for Germany. He had a landlocked mind, and did not exhibit on a world scale the imaginative flair that he had shown in Europe. Some of Hitler's associates, such as Marshal Goering and General Guderian, for example, tried to persuade him, immediately after the French collapse, to send German forces through Spain and into Morocco while the French were still in a state of shock—but Hitler, apart from his discussions with Franco, to which we shall return, would have none of it. As a German diplomat in Morocco told an American colleague early in 1941, "Herr Hitler does not seem aware that this area exists. He always looks in every direction except south." The south, presumably, was to be the Italian sphere. Hitler's gaze, as always, was turned to the East.

What might have been the consequence of a more pressing German interest in Africa is revealed by an observation made in 1941 by the French General Weygand. "Opening Africa to Germany," he wrote, "means in the last analysis giving to Germany a unique opportunity to continue the war for ten years."[18] What held Hitler back, in the last resort? Perhaps he was afraid that by venturing beyond Europe proper the German people would be brought too closely into contact with African peoples, and so risk losing their "racial purity."

### The Liberation of Ethiopia

In the meantime, it was the Italians, rather than the Germans, who showed the greater interest in Africa. When Mussolini's Italy entered the war on the side of Germany on June 10, 1940, new prospects as well as new dangers appeared on the African continent. Immediately affected

18. According to Peter Tompkins, the Deutsche Bank and several German industrial firms had a controlling interest in the Trans-Africa Company, which was based on plans to build trans-Sahara rail links between the Mediterranean and both Dakar and Nigeria, thus opening up West Africa and permitting it to become a staging area for operations first in South America and later in the United States. (See *The Murder of Admiral Darlan*, 1965, p. 259.)

was the Emperor of Ethiopia, Haile Selassie, then living in exile in the city of Bath, England. On June 25, 1940, he arrived in Alexandria, Egypt, having traveled directly from England by seaplane. From there he proceeded toward the Sudan, only to find himself halted at Wadi Halfa on the Sudanese frontier. Up to this time the Emperor had believed that the liberation of Ethiopia was imminent. He was soon to be acquainted with the complexities of the situation.

The Italians had been experiencing difficulties in Ethiopia. As a British official, R. E. Cheesman, later wrote,

> Naboth's vineyard viewed from within was not what it had seemed from a distance. Minerals which could have justified the lavish expenditure on sea bases, public works, roads and bridges, had not been found in quantities that would repay the cost of the necessary machinery; the expected discovery of oil had not been made; trade was negligible; public security was nonexistent.[19]

Not only were the Ethiopian guerrillas active against the Italians, but from May 10, 1940, on—a month before Italy entered the war—they had been receiving arms and supplies from the British. The British authorities in the Sudan, however, viewed support of these guerrillas not as the first step in the liberation of Ethiopia, but as a method of keeping the Italians occupied on their own side of the frontier, so that they would be discouraged from attacking the Sudan. The Italians had over a quarter of a million troops in Ethiopia, as well as a modern air force, whereas the British in the Sudan had only 9,000 men and some old planes. So sure were the British authorities in the Sudan that their own defeat was at hand that they were primarily concerned that the coming transfer of power to the Italians should take place as smoothly as possible. The private assurances that they received from the Italian Viceroy in Ethiopia, the Duke of Aosta, that Italy did not intend to jeopardize the work of the British in the Sudan, must therefore have seemed auspicious to them. News of the imminent arrival of Haile Selassie, on the contrary, filled them with alarm—the Kaid of the Sudan, the British General Platt, remarking angrily that it would "stir up a hornet's nest."

When it became clear that Churchill had approved the Emperor's journey, Haile Selassie was permitted to enter the Sudan. Here, however, he soon found himself a semi-prisoner of the local British authorities, many of whom apparently felt that if Ethiopia was to be freed from Italian rule it would only be in order that it might pass under British administration. General Platt at one point stated that if the Emperor was to return to his country, it would only be "as part of my baggage." The same colonial approach was evident in the decision by the British authorities in Kenya to treat the numerous Ethiopian refugees who entered the territory as de jure Italian prisoners of war, and to set them to work making roads in consequence.

19. Leonard Mosley, *Haile Selassie: The Conquering Lion* (1965), p. 232.

It was the Emperor himself who found the way out of the impasse. By asking for a treaty of alliance and friendship between Ethiopia and the United Kingdom he drew the attention of highly placed Britons (among them Anthony Eden, Minister of War) who then proceeded to override the views of the local authorities. No treaty was concluded, but the Emperor was recognized as the leader of a war of liberation, and his freedom of movement restored. The forces that were to liberate Ethiopia now began to gather. Already Ethiopians had begun to cross the frontier to rally to the Emperor, thus forming the basis of a Patriot Army. The erstwhile roadmakers were brought to the Sudan from Kenya, and put into uniform. British, French, South African, and Australian officers were assigned to the embryo army. An addition to the Emperor's entourage was also made in the form of Colonel Wingate, an eccentric Scot with strong religious convictions and Zionist sympathies, who had also committed himself to the Emperor's cause. At length preparations were complete, and the offensive began. Operations were begun in January, 1941, by British and Indian troops against the Italian forces that had entered parts of the Sudan in July, 1940. Then, on January 20, 1941, the Emperor himself crossed the frontier into Ethiopia on his way back to his throne.

In the campaign which followed, Allied forces converged on Ethiopia to help the Ethiopian Patriots and guerrillas against the Italian occupiers. Some came, like the Emperor, from the Sudan, while others entered from Kenya to the south. In March the British, coming across the Red Sea from Aden, also landed troops from Berbera to recapture British Somaliland, which had been taken from them by the Italians the previous year. A determined stand was for a time made by the Italians at Keren in their adjacent colony of Eritrea. After the capture of Keren, however, by British-Indian forces, the capital of Eritrea, Massawa, surrendered on April 8, 1941. Advancing from the south a combined force of East and South Africans outflanked the Italians and captured Addis Ababa. On May 5, 1941, Haile Selassie returned in triumph to the city into which the Italians had entered five years before to the day. The Duke of Aosta surrendered with the remnants of his army on May 17. Further fighting continued in other parts of the country, in which Congolese troops under Belgian command, who entered Ethiopia in the course of the summer, also participated. A final Italian stand was made at Gondar, but by November, 1941, all was over. Mussolini's dream of an African empire had melted away.

One Englishman who participated in the campaign later commented on its complexities as follows:

> The collapse of the Italian armies in Ethiopia has always been to me a complete mystery. . . . They were beaten by a tiny army of raw askaris officered chiefly by amateurs such as myself, and two brigades of South Africans which hardly once got

into action. Such fighting as was done was done by the K.A.R. [King's African Rifles], the West Africans and the Ethiopian Patriots. . . . There was no lack of individual personal bravery on the part of the Italians. . . . I can only conclude that, as an army, they did not have faith in their cause.[20]

Mussolini's dominion might be gone, but another threat to Ethiopia's independence still existed. Although in February, 1941, Anthony Eden had announced that the British government "would welcome the re-appearance of an independent Ethiopian state and recognise the claim of Haile Selassie to the throne," adding that Britain had no territorial ambitions in "Abyssinia" (as Eden persisted in calling it), other officials had other ideas. A faction in which the South-African-born Sir Philip Mitchell figured prominently, and which was generally known as the "Cromerite" group, clearly envisaged Ethiopia's future as that of a British dependency. Sir Philip, a former Governor of Uganda, established an Occupied Enemy Territory Administration (O.E.T.A.), based in Nairobi, and took the view that Haile Selassie could not exercise his imperial functions until a peace treaty had been signed with Italy—a delaying tactic that was clearly designed to give the British administrators from Kenya and the Sudan time to consolidate their hold on Ethiopia. Again, it was Anthony Eden who stubbornly refused to yield to Mitchell's representations. Meanwhile, in Addis Ababa itself the Ethiopian supporters of the Emperor, aware of the Cromerite intrigues and plagued by the arrogant behavior of South African troops in the capital, began to question Haile Selassie's leadership. The Emperor thereupon sent a telegram to Churchill, who replied by giving him assurances that Ethiopian independence was not in question. These assurances were subsequently formalized in the Anglo-Ethiopian Agreement of January 31, 1942, which recognized the Emperor as Head of State, but retained for the British certain extra-territorial privileges, notably military control of the Ogaden region. The Cromerites were embittered by defeat. During the earlier days of the Italian occupation, Ethiopian technicians had been among those massacred by Graziani's forces. Now, however, it was the Italians who provided much necessary technical service. The Cromerites, noting that Ethiopians and Italians were now virtually making common cause against them, had their revenge by expelling the Italians, despite both Ethiopian and Italian protests. The period that followed was particularly difficult for Ethiopia. In consequence of Cromerite spite, however, Britain forfeited much sympathy, and when a new Anglo-Egyptian Treaty was concluded in 1944, almost all British privileges were withdrawn.

Why, it might be asked, did Eden so resolutely resist Mitchell's urgings to pursue a policy of imperial expansion? The answer is that

20. John Seymour, *One Man's Africa* (1956).

Eden was responsible for safeguarding British interests in their entirety, whereas Mitchell sought only on a regional basis what he viewed as British advantage. The Atlantic Charter, proclaimed on August 14, 1941, stated, at the most authoritative level, that as a guiding principle of national policy the United Kingdom, no less than the United States, wished to see sovereign rights and self-government restored to those who had been forcibly deprived of them. If this did not apply to the ancient empire of Ethiopia, the first victim of Fascist aggression, then the words were meaningless, and British motives as suspect as those of Britain's opponents. Furthermore, at this time embattled Britain depended primarily on the support of the United States for its survival, and British imperialism was distasteful both to the people and to the government of the United States. This distaste was constantly finding public expression. For example, a short time later, on October 12, 1942, the editor of *Life* magazine in the United States published an open letter to the British people which asked them to "Quit fighting a war to hold the empire together," and to join the United States and the Soviet Union in fighting the real war. Moreover, apart from alienating both American and Soviet sympathies at a vital juncture, a British annexation of Ethiopia would have jeopardized the tacit, if not the active, support of the populations inhabiting British-controlled territories throughout Africa and Asia, whose loyalties the British would have to depend on not only in the struggle against Germany and Italy in Europe, but also in the coming struggle against Japan. Finally, even in Britain itself a large number of people favored Ethiopian independence, and to have ended that independence would have impaired British morale and disrupted British unity at a time when Britain was fighting for its life. So Ethiopian independence was restored and upheld. The fact was taken by the world at large and by the nationalist movements of Africa and Asia in particular as a gage for the future, a sign of a change of heart, a promise of better times ahead.

## The Brazzaville Conference

General de Gaulle, some of whose Free French troops had also participated in the Ethiopian campaign, also recognized the new spirit that was abroad in colonial affairs. Later, in January, 1944, he was to convoke at Brazzaville a conference of French administrators, among them Félix Eboué, to consider the future of the French territories in Africa, and the conditions under which their populations lived.

Conditions in the French colonies had left much to be desired. The various territories, apart from those of French North Africa which were treated separately, were associated together in two large groupings—Afrique Occidentale Française, or French West Africa, known as A.O.F.

and established in 1904, and Afrique Equatoriale Française, or French Equatorial Africa, known as A.E.F., and established in 1910. Until the Second World War both A.O.F. and A.E.F. were controlled by a skeletal French administration that could do little more than maintain itself while providing some additional benefits for French homeland interests. So skeletal was the administration that, for example, in 1925 less than fifty Frenchmen lived in Fort-Lamy, capital of Chad. *La corvée* (forced labor) was openly exacted throughout the French possessions. Particularly in A.E.F., the least advanced of the two regions, and the one in which the concessionaire system had been permitted to operate, endemic abuses had led to recurrent scandals. Traveling through the relatively more advanced territories of A.O.F. in 1934, Geoffrey Gorer, the English anthropologist, commented on the administration as follows:

> Most of the French administrators I met were not bourgeois turned "gentilhomme": they were petits bourgeois turned Cæsar. The results were equally deplorable for rulers and ruled. An evilly disposed or cowardly man can create almost intolerable misery; I was in two areas in which the negroes would run and hide if possible at the approach of a white man.[21]

He added that when a village failed to pay its taxes, the administration stepped in "brutally and ruthlessly" by sending African soldiers. He was also "universally informed that the only treatment that negroes can understand is physical violence," adding that "It is certainly the only treatment they ever get."

New efforts, evidently, were needed if the new spirit symbolized by the promise of the Atlantic Charter were not to threaten a continuation of the French presence in tropical Africa. De Gaulle's speech at the opening of the Brazzaville Conference reflected this situation:

> Without wishing to exaggerate the urgency of the reasons impelling us to broach these African questions at once, we believe that the events now sweeping the world oblige us not to delay.

Having hailed France's effort in Africa, he noted that even before the war "had appeared the necessity of establishing here on new foundations the conditions of Africa's development, those of the progress of its inhabitants and those of the exercise of its sovereignty."

How much more urgent this was today, he said, "since the war, which will have been, in large share, an African war, is being fought to determine the nature of man's condition and since, beneath the action of the psychic forces it has everywhere unleashed, every population looks ahead and questions itself as to its destiny."[22]

In the conference which followed, proposals of an administrative, economic, and social nature were made that were to lay the foundations

21. *Africa Dances* (1962), p. 89.
22. *The Complete War Memoirs of Charles de Gaulle: 1940–1946*, p. 512.

for postwar reforms. Again in de Gaulle's words, "The route was traced and needed only to be followed."

## The Struggle in the Arab Lands

Brazzaville, however, still lay in the future when the struggle between the Allies and the Axis unfolded in the Arab lands. It was a European struggle in which the Arab peoples, swayed by the changing fortunes of war, sought to further the cause of their own independence as best they might.

In many of the Arab countries of North Africa and the Middle East the Axis powers did not need to create opposition to the Allies, since the independence movements opposed to British and French hegemony were already initiated. Furthermore, Arab opposition to the Zionist settlements in Palestine coincided with the anti-Jewish policy of the Fascist governments.

Upon the outbreak of war, those Arab leaders in Palestine who were pro-German, and notably the Grand Mufti of Jerusalem, had taken refuge in Iraq. The British mandate over Iraq had ended in 1932 when Iraq joined the League of Nations, but Britain had maintained several military bases in the country. Although nominally neutral, Iraqi sentiment tended to favor Germany in consequence. German influence in the country grew stronger until in March, 1941, an openly pro-German Prime Minister, Rashid Ali, came to power. Britain immediately reinforced her base in Basra, after which tension rose, fighting began, and the German Luftwaffe arrived on the northern airfields of Iraq. The German general in command of operations was informed by Hitler that "the Arab Freedom Movement is, in the Middle East, our natural ally against England. In this connection the raising of rebellion in Iraq is of special importance." Speedy British action in landing Indian troops at Basra, however, led to the suppression of the revolt. A call by the Grand Mufti to other Arab countries to rise against Britain in a holy war went unheeded. Eventually, in January, 1943, Iraq was to enter the war on the Allied side.

After the German air force began to use Vichy-held Syria in May, 1941, British and Free French forces entered the country. Fighting ended in July when the Vichy administration applied for an armistice. Some influential British saw in this circumstance, however, a chance for Britain to replace France in Damascus and Beirut. The campaign was therefore marked by a growing political rivalry between the Free French and the British, which took the form of a competition to receive credit for offering independence to the Arab populations. The Free French, upon entering Syria, declared that it was the intention of France to end the League of Nations mandate and to conclude treaties with independent states. Britain associated itself with this policy in a separate declaration. Although the full attributes of independence were not to be granted until after the war, an independent Syria was nevertheless proclaimed in September, 1941, and an independent Lebanon in November. In these two countries, at least, the European civil war had directly benefited the Arab peoples.

Egypt, however, the strategic heartland of the Arab countries, remained under British occupation. Despite the concessions to British sovereignty made in the Anglo-Egyptian Treaty of 1936, the ultimate arbiter in Egypt during the war remained Britain. Particularly after the Iraqi revolt of 1941, however, a strong pro-Axis undercurrent became evident in Egyptian opinion. Although Egypt remained nominally neutral, such neutrality meant little when armies from the British Commonwealth were gathering on its soil, when British aircraft, routed through Takoradi in the Gold Coast, were being flown to Egyptian fields in anticipation of battles to come, and when, after Italy's entry into the war in 1940, Italian forces were entering Egypt from the west.

Egyptian nationalist emotions and calculations were consequently strongly engaged in the vicissitudes of the fighting between the Allies and the Axis that, between 1941 and 1943, ranged through the length of North Africa from Egypt to Tunisia. In November, 1941, the British drove the Italians out of Egypt and 500 miles back into Libya. In 1942, however, the German Afrika Corps, under General Rommel, counterattacked, eventually driving the British back to El Alamein in Egypt. Although the British were later to gain the upper hand once more, advancing from El Alamein until at last they achieved victory in Tunisia, Rommel's successes meanwhile created a new surge of pro-Axis sympathy among the Egyptians. The Egyptian court, foreseeing an Axis victory, sought to have a government installed that would preserve friendly links with the Axis powers. This was strongly opposed by the British, however. The British Ambassador to Cairo, Lord Killearn, went so far as to issue an ultimatum to King Farouk, demanding that a government with the pro-British Nahas Pasha, a member of the Wafd party, be installed. When the King hesitated, the Ambassador arrived at the palace with British troops and armored vehicles, whereupon the King gave way. The old alliance between the British and the Egyptian monarchy had broken down, and in its place a new alliance between the British and the Wafd was formed at the expense of the monarchy. Association with the British, however, was to undermine the authority of the Wafd with the Egyptian people.

Ever since Turkey, at the end of the First World War, had begun to modernize and had relinquished the caliphate, Egyptian opinion had been split between on the one hand those, including members of the

Wafd, who favored following Mustafa Kemal's example, and on the other hand those conservatives who favored a return to Muslim orthodoxy. The conservatives grouped themselves around Sheikh Hassan el-Banna, who had founded the Muslim Brotherhood in 1928. Sheikh Hassan believed not only in religious orthodoxy, but also in the restoration of the caliphate in Egypt, and the emergence of Egypt as the leader among the Arab peoples. When, in the 1930s, the Brotherhood became politically active, it also aimed at liberating Egypt from British and other foreign influences. During the war Sheikh Hassan, who had a commanding personality, secretly built up the organization of the Brotherhood, despite efforts by the police to suppress it.[23] The Brotherhood thus became a powerful instrument for the propagation of Egyptian nationalism, and its activities at this time did much to prepare the way for the events which were to take place in the country after the war. So strong, indeed, did nationalist feeling become that throughout the war internal security in Egypt was a constant preoccupation of the British. As the war progressed a climate of militant nationalism developed, so that when, in 1945, Prime Minister Ahmed Maher (who succeeded Nahas Pasha) announced Egypt's entry into the war on the Allied side—a step that he favored in view of the advantages that it would later confer upon Egypt, including the right to founder-membership in the United Nations—he was promptly assassinated. The nationalist awakening that the First World War had brought to Turkey, the Second World War was bringing to the Arab countries.

A clear sign of the Arab awakening was the formation of a pan-Arabic organization. This was the League of Arab States, which, after a preliminary conference held in Alexandria, Egypt, from September 28 to October 8, 1944, formally came into existence on March 22, 1945. The League, which grouped together Egypt, Syria, Lebanon, Iraq, Transjordan, Saudi-Arabia, and Yemen in a loose confederation, aimed at strengthening relations, co-ordinating policies, and advancing the interests of all the Arab countries.

Meanwhile, to the west, Morocco, Algeria, and Tunisia, as we have said, had remained under Vichy control. During and after the war external national rivalries, similar in nature to those which were manifest in Syria, were to make the three countries, and especially Morocco, the scene of a struggle for predominance.

### Spanish Aspirations

After the Vichy surrender of June, 1940, Spain began to aspire to increase its North African holdings. General Franco had first come to

---

23. Some observers have held the view that Sheikh Hassan's postponement of his demand for the appointment of a caliph took place in order to give himself time to consolidate his position so that he personally might become caliph.

power as a result of a conspiracy which had begun with an army mutiny in Spanish Morocco.[24] Many of the colonists in French Morocco, some of whom were of Spanish origin, showed strong sympathies for Franco, and sent delegations to co-ordinate their political activities with his. After making some tactical advances to the Moroccan nationalist movement, in order to occupy diplomatic ground that might otherwise have fallen to his Spanish Republican adversaries, Franco showed his hand. Following the Vichy surrender of June, 1940, Spain occupied the international zone of Tangier, and permitted German influence to become strongly established there. At the same time Franco formulated his demands. As the asking price for entering the war, he let Hitler know, he wanted Gibraltar, French Morocco, part of Algeria including Oran, and various expansions of territory in the Spanish African colonies. He also asked for military and economic assistance, and indicated that the Spanish entry into the war should be delayed until after a German landing in Britain. Hitler found these demands high, particularly since they would alienate many of the French in North Africa, who would almost certainly set up a hostile government there in consequence—a government that, disposing of a powerful fleet, military forces, and gold reserves, could cause the Axis much embarrassment. Negotiations dragged on. The Germans asked for a base in the Canary Islands, a proposal that Franco, influenced perhaps by Britain's continued and unexpected defiance, refused to discuss.

At length Hitler met with Franco at Hendaye in the Pyrenees on October 23, 1940. He found Spanish objectives "absolutely out of proportion to their strength," and later told Mussolini that, rather than endure another such meeting, he would "prefer to have three or four of my teeth out." Franco, it seemed, feared the loss of his Atlantic islands and of the Spanish colonies in Africa to the British Navy. Later, pressed to enter the war and to permit German troops to pass through Spain to attack Gibraltar, Franco, mindful of British successes in Libya, refused to move until the Axis powers had captured Suez. When German pressure upon him was increased, Franco reinforced Spanish forces holding the Pyrenees frontier. Hitler turned away to prepare his attack on the Soviet Union. The matter was carried no further. With the Anglo-American landings in Morocco on November 8, 1942, Spanish hopes of easy gains in North Africa were at an end.

## North African Nationalism

The outbreak of the war provided the French with an opportunity to increase repression of the North African nationalist movements. The

24. The Moroccan nationalists had advance news of the conspiracy, and sent a delegation to warn the Republican government of its danger, as well as to ask for "democratic freedoms" for themselves "to enable them to organize in self-defense." But the Spanish Republic, believing that this was no more than nationalist agitation, ignored the warning.

Moroccan nationalists had, in 1939, rallied to the support of the Sultan of Morocco, Sidi Mohamed Ben Youssef, whose "wish was that Morocco should be considered as a belligerent state, fighting against racialism and the persecution of peoples, so that he might be able to press national demands in the name of these principles after the war."[25] He maintained the same essential approach throughout the vicissitudes of the war. German attempts to establish friendly links with the Moroccan National-ist Party by promising greater freedom after a German victory met with little success, however, since the Moroccans judged the true German intention to be "the foundation of a German empire based on the racial superiority of Aryans."[26]

In Morocco, however, where General Noguès was Resident-General, martial law was proclaimed; the Sultan remained a virtual prisoner in his palace at Rabat; and prominent nationalists were subject to arrest or exile. In Algeria Messali Hadj, who had been released in August, 1939, was rearrested in October, and finally brought to judgment in 1941, when he was fined 30 million francs, and sentenced to sixteen years hard labor, as well as to twenty years in exile.[27] In Tunisia, the smallest and relatively the most advanced of the three countries, the nationalist movement was also the most militant. Habib Bourguiba of the Neo-Destour had already been arrested, but his countrymen did not remain inactive. Tunisian nationalists launched a campaign to discourage army enlistment—a campaign that resulted in such a lack of enthusiasm for the war that force had to be employed to compel Tunisian troops to embark for Europe. Elsewhere in the country mutiny threatened and sabotage was rife.

The shock of the German victory in France and of the Vichy sur-render which followed, shattered French unity. As Hitler was to observe on May 13, 1942,

> The thing that strikes me above all in the present-day policy of the French is the fact that, because they were anxious to sit on every chair at the same time, they have not succeeded in sitting firmly on any one of them. The explanation is that the soul of the country has been torn asunder. In the Vichy Government alone a whole heap of tendencies is apparent.[28]

One of these tendencies was represented by General Weygand who, as Delegate-General in French Africa, exerted supreme authority over Vichy-held territory on the continent. In this capacity Weygand became a political rallying point for those who wished to continue the war against Germany. Although he was at odds with de Gaulle, and although

25. 'Alal al-Fasi, *The Independence Movements in Arab North Africa* (1954), p. 199.
26. *Ibid.* This evaluation was based on the results of a visit to European countries, including Germany, by Ahmed Balafrej, Secretary-General of the Moroccan Nationalist Party, for the purpose of ascertaining ultimate German intentions concerning North Africa.
27. He was released in 1946.
28. *Hitler's Secret Conversations*, p. 386.

he declined British proposals of aid, his presence in North Africa made Berlin so nervous that finally, in November, 1941, the German government threatened to occupy the whole of France and to let the French population starve unless Marshal Pétain secured Weygand's return to France from Africa—a threat which produced the desired result. Another leading Vichy personality, Pierre Laval, espoused, on the other hand, a policy of collaborating with Germany, although, like Franco, he had reservations concerning how far such collaboration should go. A more opportunistic approach was that of the French Admiral Darlan, who, initially a proponent of collaboration with Germany, sought to change sides when he realized that Germany was ultimately going to lose the war. The Vichy government, in sum, found itself in a position of ambiguity from which it could not safely extricate itself in any direction. Again it was Hitler who accurately described the situation:

> There are . . . only two possible courses which French policy can pursue . . .
> (a) She must renounce her metropolitan territory, transfer her seat of Government to North Africa and continue the war against us with all the resources of her African colonial empire, or
> (b) She must join the Axis Powers, and thus save the greater part of her territory. She must intervene in Central Africa and ensure for herself possessions there, which will compensate her for the loss of the territories which she will inevitably have to cede, when the peace treaty is signed, to Germany, Italy and Spain.[29]

Unable to choose between these two alternatives, Vichy's future in Africa was to be decided by the Anglo-American landings of November 8, 1942, and in France by the German invasion of the Unoccupied Zone which took place three days later on November 11, 1942.

## The Anglo-American Landings

British interest in French North Africa was strong, but as Britain had her hands full at home and abroad, it did not take the form of territorial ambition. Instead Britain appeared primarily concerned as to how the turn that events might take in North Africa would affect developments elsewhere. These other concerns included the preservation of Britain's communications through the Mediterranean, via Gibraltar and Malta to Suez, both for the long-term maintenance of the route to India and the East, and for the immediate maintenance of a shorter supply-line to the desert battlefields than that which ran via West Africa or around the Cape. Also of concern was the preservation of Britain's command of the seas, and the security of Britain's African colonies, both of which would have been jeopardized had Morocco fallen under Axis control. Apart from the 1940 attack on the French ships at Mers-el-Kebir, Britain moved cautiously until, in 1942, the Anglo-American landings at last took place.

29. *Ibid.*

Robert Murphy, however, cites a French informant who told him at the time that some British officials aimed at the decomposition of French Africa, whereas others wanted to strengthen the French position on the continent so that it might, at a vital moment, influence the outcome of the war.[30] He added that the British never did resolve this internal difference of approach.

It was United States interest, however, which provided both a new and a decisive element in the complex North African situation. The fact that the United States was a neutral power until the date of the Japanese attack on Pearl Harbor in December 7, 1941, permitted American diplomats enough time in which to exert an influence on the Vichy government that was favorable to the Allied cause. Complexities were added, however, not only by the attitudes of the different Vichy officials involved, but also by a divergence of view between American and British strategists. In strategic terms, Britain sought to involve Anglo-American power in the Mediterranean region as a whole, with a view to safeguarding the route through Suez. As Churchill complained, however, "United States Chiefs of Staff disliked very much the idea of committing themselves to large operations beyond the Straits of Gibraltar."[31] American interest was felt to be to prevent the Atlantic, rather than the Mediterranean, coastline of North Africa from falling into hostile hands, and at all costs to ensure that Dakar did not become a potential staging area for launching an attack on the Americas. With this objective in view, there was a disinclination to lose American lives for the purpose of pulling British imperial chestnuts out of the fire.

American contacts with French officials did not, as was hoped, lead to the Vichy government joining the United States against Germany. When the Anglo-American landings at last took place in Morocco and Algeria, however, fighting, thanks to American diplomatic preparation, was minimal. On November 9, 1942, the day after the landings, German and Italian troops arrived in Tunisia, and were soon in action against Allied forces. After some months of fighting, Allied troops thrusting east from Algeria at length linked up with British and Gaullist French forces advancing west from Libya, and compelled the Axis troops finally to surrender in Tunis on May 13, 1943. The fighting in Africa was at an end.

Meanwhile, factional intrigues had complicated Allied unity in North Africa. The French Admiral Darlan, apparently having advance knowledge of the Anglo-American invasion, happened to find himself in Algiers at the time that it occurred. After his assassination on December 24, 1942, however, a power struggle for French political supremacy took

30. *Diplomat Among Warriors* (1965), p. 97.
31. *The Second World War*, Vol. 4 (1950), p. 529.

place between Generals de Gaulle and Giraud—a struggle from which de Gaulle emerged, in June, 1943, as the uncontested French leader in North Africa.

Considerable Franco-American friction nevertheless developed as a result of the landings. Apart from the fact that the unpliable de Gaulle encountered considerable American opposition, many Frenchmen resented what they regarded as American interferences in the French North African sphere of influence. The most publicized instance of such "interference" concerned the dinner that U.S. President Franklin D. Roosevelt gave in honor of the Sultan of Morocco. As Morocco was the only place in the world where the United States still retained extra-territorial privilege, on the day of the landings President Roosevelt had sent a message to the Sultan expressing the hope that he would support the expedition. The message was intercepted and delayed by the French General Noguès, after which President Roosevelt, during his visit to Casablanca for his conference with Churchill, de Gaulle, and Giraud in January, 1943, held a dinner in the Sultan's honor. At the dinner, at which Noguès, in his capacity as the Sultan's Foreign Minister, was present, Roosevelt expressed sympathy with colonial aspirations for independence, and proposed that after the war Morocco and the United States should co-operate economically. Noguès was outraged. A proponent of French imperialism, he had opposed the ideal of Anglo-American intervention in North Africa on the ground that if Morocco became a battlefield it would be lost to France—a prediction that he now saw beginning to come true. However, the United States, for its part, had not forgotten that, as a signatory of the 1906 Algeçiras Convention which had admitted the privileged position of France in Morocco, it had acquired a recognized and legitimate interest in the area.

Another instance of American interest was not, however, brought to French attention. Not long after the landings seventeen American officers, of whom one or two spoke French and none spoke Arabic, arrived in Algiers for the purpose (as they thought) of administering French North Africa, which they had divided into seventeen regions after receiving instruction in administration at Charlottesville, Virginia. The American authorities in North Africa did not, however, permit them to take up their appointments, and they dispersed. Such contretemps, in the words of the American diplomat Robert Murphy, arose from the fact that "Roosevelt could never quite make up his mind whether we had 'occupied' or 'liberated' French Africa."[32]

The Allied landings permitted Moroccan nationalists to become more active. The events of the war, the proclamation of the Atlantic Charter, and the independence accorded in Syria and Lebanon, all undermined

32. *Diplomat Among Warriors*, p. 167.

French authority and decided many nationalists to work actively for independence. One of the most important developments in this connection was the establishment of links with Egypt, which were formalized in 1943 in the League for the Defense of Morocco in Egypt, a Moroccan organization which worked for independence and Arab unity. Of even more consequence was the founding, at a conference held in Rabat on January 11, 1944, of the Istiqlal Party, which abandoned the conciliatory gradualism of its predecessor, the National Party, and openly demanded Moroccan independence under the Sultan Mohamed V, as well as Morocco's affiliation with the signatories of the Atlantic Charter. A copy of the Istiqlal Covenant, drawn up at this time, was presented to the French Resident-General, who, like other French administrators, was astounded by its contents. Shortly thereafter leading nationalists were arrested on the grounds that the independence movement was supported and encouraged by the Axis. A wave of repression followed in which Senegalese troops were employed against the nationalists. From this time on the battlelines between France and Moroccan nationalism were drawn, ready for the struggle which lay ahead.

Events in Tunisia were not dissimilar to those in Morocco. At the time of the Vichy surrender a Tunisian nationalist delegation presented a memorandum to the Bey of Tunis requesting the termination of French occupation. The members of the delegation were arrested by the French Resident-General, but later released following the Bey's intercession on their behalf. In 1942 Habib Bourguiba, the Neo-Destour leader, who had been imprisoned in France since 1938, was released. He was welcomed by the Fascist government in Rome, but declined to identify himself with the Axis cause. Instead he spent the remaining war years traveling intermittently between Tunisia and the Middle Eastern countries, seeking international support for Tunisian independence. Meanwhile, in June, 1942, a new and markedly nationalist Bey had succeeded to the throne, and began to press the French for reforms. After the Allied victory in Tunis in May, 1943, however, the local French administration profited from the period of confusion to execute or to imprison many leading nationalists, and, at the instance of General Giraud, the Bey himself was ousted from the throne and sent into exile, in which, in 1948, he subsequently died. Clandestine nationalist activity aiming at ultimate independence nevertheless continued.

In Algeria two nationalist tendencies had been in evidence. Messali Hadj and his party had advocated independence, while Ferhat Abbas and others had favored reform within the French system. As already mentioned, Messali Hadj had been sentenced to prison in 1941, while his party had been driven underground. Ferhat Abbas, however, after the Vichy surrender of 1940, tried to persuade Marshal Pétain to institute reforms in Algeria—a plea that went unheard. After the Allied landings and the promulgation of the Atlantic Charter, Ferhat Abbas, in December, 1942, sent a "Message to the French authorities," which stated, in part:

This is not a war of liberation of all peoples without distinction of race or religion. Despite the promises which have been made to them, and the sacrifices which they have undergone, the native populations of Algeria are still deprived of the liberties and rights which others enjoy.

It concluded by asking for reforms, and for the convening of a conference that would include Muslim representation, whose purpose would be to draft a law establishing a new relationship between Muslim and European in Algeria. After General Giraud had dismissed the message with the observation that he waged war, not politics, Ferhat Abbas and other Muslim leaders published, on February 12, 1943, a "Manifesto of the Algerian People," which proposed granting Arabs and Berbers equal rights with Europeans, but which did not mention independence. The French Governor-General agreed to study the Manifesto as a basis for future reforms. Two further events then transpired. First, an Arab and Kabyle delegation, on March 26, 1943, added a Supplement to the Manifesto which increased Muslim demands. Second, political changes led to the appointment of General Catroux as French Governor-General, as well as to the accession to political power in French North Africa of General de Gaulle. While recognizing the situation that existed, Catroux nevertheless felt obliged, in order to preserve French unity in a time of crisis, to defend French privilege. He rejected the Manifesto and its Supplement, after which, French authority having been asserted, General de Gaulle, in December 1943, made concessions, which were enacted in the Ordinance of March 7, 1944. These included the admission of "several tens of thousands" of Muslims to the rights of French citizenship, as well as other reforms that represented an advance within the framework of a policy of assimilation.

But the reforms did not satisfy either the French *colons*, most of whom opposed all Muslim advance, or the Algerian nationalists, most of whom demanded progress toward independence, rather than assimilation. On March 14, 1944, both Ferhat Abbas and his party and the followers of Messali Hadj united to form *Les Amis du Manifeste et de la Liberté* ("The Friends of the Manifesto and of Freedom") (A.M.L.), an organization which opposed the Ordinance and promulgated the concept of an Algerian nation within an autonomous federal French republic. By March, 1945, however, the A.M.L., influenced among other things by the formation of the League of Arab States as well as by prevalent pan-Arabic sentiment, fell under the control of its Messalist wing. In consequence the A.M.L. revised its aims, reserving to the future Algerian state the right to join any grouping that it wished.

After this, tension rose rapidly between Algerian nationalists and French *colons*. On May 8, 1945, in the province of Constantine, the tension broke into violence, which soon became widespread. The day before the Germans had surrendered to the Allies at Rheims, and an Arab victory parade was held at Sétif, with French authorization. The carrying of banners was, however, apparently prohibited, and the prohibition was broken. "Long Live Independent Algeria" and similar slogans were displayed, and the Algerian flag was flown. When the French attempted to remove the banners and the flag, street fighting broke out, which, during the night, turned into insurgency, leading to the deaths of Europeans. Massive French reprisals then took place, in which the French Air Force, the Foreign Legion, and Senegalese troops participated. The French authorities admitted that about 1,500 Muslims had been killed, but others placed the total much higher.[33] According to 'Alal al-Fasi, "the engagements resulted in the death of one hundred Frenchmen while Muslim dead and wounded ran into tens of thousands." The action represented a declaration, in the starkest possible terms, that the French authorities did not intend to countenance Algerian independence after the war. The effect of the Constantine tragedy, however, was to create a gulf between the French and the Algerians that, despite many attempts, was not to be bridged until, at infinitely greater cost, Algerian independence, years later, was at last to become an admitted fact.

In the West the second white civil war thus drew to an end, concluding with Hitler's death in a flaming Berlin in May, 1945. The war had deeply harrowed not only Europeans but also the Arab and African countries. The promise implicit in the Atlantic Charter had raised high hopes for the political advancement of dependent peoples. Among the politically conscious populations of the African colonies the hope was now for reform. Among the Arab peoples, however, the demand was for freedom.

33. The U.S. Army newspaper *Stars and Stripes* reported that 10,000 had been "killed or wounded." The U.S. and British governments notified the French of their condemnation of the massacres.

# Chapter 15

# "The Greater East Asia War"

*The purposes of war with the United States, Great Britain, and the Nether-lands are to expel the influence of these three countries from East Asia, and to establish a sphere for the self-defense and self-preservation of our Empire, and to build a New Order in Greater East Asia.* —"The Essentials for Carrying Out the Empire's Policies," distributed at the Japanese Imperial Conference (September 6, 1941)

ON DECEMBER 7, 1941, when Japan went to war with the United States, the war in Europe became merged into a world conflict. Japan, an Asian power which had challenged and beaten Czarist Russia in 1904–1905, which had ousted Germany from China's Shantung province in 1914, and which had successfully invaded Man-churia in defiance of the League of Nations in 1931–1932, was now bidding for supremacy in Eastern Asia.

Underlying the Japanese challenge to the United States and to the European colonial powers in Asia was the question of China. Although the British, as we have seen, had tacitly encouraged Japan in its Chinese adventure, the United States, for its part, did not feel so accommodating. For it was Japan's intention to dominate China as Britain dominated India, and, moreover, also to exclude its American and European rivals from Chinese territory. It became the intention of the United States and its allies to prevent this from happening. And this fundamental difference over the future of China eventually made war inevitable.

Both for geographical and for historical reasons the war itself was primarily between Japan and the United States. For one thing the United States traditionally showed far less hesitation in becoming involved in Asia than it did in Europe. For another, as the American diplomat George F. Kennan has put it, "the problem of whether [Japan] had also to be ranged against us in the war . . . was of course primarily our problem, not that of the French and the British."[1] On the Japanese side, also, grievances felt were primarily, although not exclusively, felt against the United States. It was the United States, Japan believed, which had detached Britain from its alliance with Japan. It was the United States which had engineered the terms of the 1922 Nine Power Pact which restricted Japanese naval strength. It was the United States which urged the League of Nations to impose the Stimson Doctrine of economic sanctions against Japan at the time of the Manchuria Incident, and which later gave material and moral support to Chiang Kai-shek in his resistance to the extension of Japanese influence over China. There was even a suspicion that U.S. recognition of the Soviet Union in 1933 had been motivated by a desire to disrupt Russo-Japanese amity.

Nor, it was felt, were these simply economic or strategic expressions of unfriendliness to Japanese aspirations. American hostility also included racial aspects. Was it not the United States which, at Versailles, had opposed the inclusion of the Japanese proposal of a nondiscrimination clause in the League of Nations Covenant? Was it not the United States Congress which in 1924 passed the Immigration Act that classified Japanese as "ineligible aliens," while permitting other countries immigration quotas? Moreover, since Japan's surplus population, as Asians, had been denied entry to America, it was only natural for Japan to turn to the Asian mainland to seek an outlet—but here again it found its aspirations opposed by the same United States. Where, then, was Japan to find an outlet for its population which, from 1930 on, was increasing at the rate of about a million a year? How was the Japanese economy to become self-sustaining? Japan was convinced that practical answers had to be found to these questions, yet all that the United States seemed to do was oppose Japanese solutions in the name of abstract principles. As the years went by, and the ultimate collision point between the two countries drew nearer, fresh and more immediate grievances were added to those of long standing.

We have already seen how events had served to strengthen the role of the military within the Japanese polity.[2] After the success of the invasion of Manchuria in 1931–1932, the hand of the militarist faction, which

1. *American Diplomacy* (1951), p. 81.
2. See Chapter 13, p. 366.

held that preparation for an inevitable war with the Western powers was a necessity for Japan, was further strengthened. An important component of the faction was the Kwantung Army in Manchuria. Originally merely a garrison force for the Kwantung Leased Territory and the South Manchuria Railway Zone, the Army came to regard itself as the chosen instrument of Japan's manifest destiny, and, as such, a law unto itself answerable to none. It was the Kwantung Army which had precipitated the Manchuria Incident, and which later played a major role in other events leading up to the "China Affair" which began in 1937. Moreover, General Hideki Togo, first Minister of War and Premier at the time of the outbreak of war with the United States, was himself a former chief of staff of the Kwantung Army. So strong did the proponents of military expansion become in Japan itself that in the years before the outbreak of war they came to dominate all other parts of the body politic—business, government, even the court, although the Army was second to none in its expressions of devotion to an Emperor who was, nevertheless, expected to stay out of politics. Even in the realm of opinion the Kempei, or military police, often made their presence felt. Only the Navy, at times, was in a position to advance policies which might disagree with those approved by the Army.[3] In former years the Genro, a body of elder statesmen responsible to the Throne, had exercised control over the high command and the government alike, but after the First World War the Genro had not been replaced as they died, so that this check had been allowed to lapse.

Testimony to the degree of army supremacy that subsequently developed was later given, so far as one department of government was concerned, by Togo Shigenori, who recounted his experience upon taking up his appointment as Foreign Minister in October, 1941, as follows:

> The extent of military interposition into and predominance in our diplomacy was emphatically borne in upon me when I learned that . . . copies of purely diplomatic correspondence went habitually to the military authorities, a procedure which seemingly had been followed since the Manchuria Incident. The Foreign Ministry, needless to say, received none of the telegrams of the Army or the Navy, not even those dispatched by their attachés in the diplomatic missions abroad.[4]

### The "China Affair"

We have already seen how the "incident" at the Marco Polo Bridge on the outskirts of Peking on July 7, 1937, marked the opening of an undeclared war between Japan and China. Both sides sent reinforcements after the initial clash, and soon Japan was struggling to detach

---

3. Winston Churchill observed that "In the nineteenth century the Japanese Army was trained by German instructors, and the Navy by the British. This left lasting differences of mentality." [*The Second World War*, Vol. 3 (1950), p. 581.]

4. *The Cause of Japan* (1956), p. 60.

the northern provinces of China, and to assert its dominance over them, as it had already converted Manchuria into the Japanese-dominated state of Manchuko.

China did not, however, as Japan had hoped, quickly yield. The Japanese troops were not able, at the outset, to break out of their enclave at Shanghai until they had sent for reinforcements. Only then were they able to advance upon and to capture the Chinese capital of Nanking, which they took in December, 1937. During the fighting Japanese planes attacked British and American naval ships on the Yangtze River, sinking the U.S. gunboat *Panay*. Following the capture of Nanking, the sack of the city and the massacre of many of its inhabitants by the Japanese Army shocked international opinion. American opinion in particular was affected. Until then the American public had remained somewhat indifferent to developments in Asia, but these two events did much to focus attention on Japan and its policies, as well as to engender sympathy for China. Refusing to yield, the Chinese government moved to Hankow, and when that was threatened—it eventually fell to the Japanese on October 25, 1938—west to Chungking in Szechuan Province, where it remained for the rest of the war.

The Japanese now held all the coastal cities, and most of Northern China, including Peking and Tientsin, but found themselves faced with continued Chinese resistance and growing Western hostility. To have advanced on Chungking would have stretched Japanese communication lines dangerously far. Even as it was, the Japanese had difficulty in holding down the areas they had occupied, being subjected to intermittent attacks by Chinese guerrillas. The fact could not be hidden that a stalemate had been reached—a stalemate that was to endure for years. Seeking to end it, the Japanese persuaded Wang Ching-wei, a close associate of Chiang Kai-shek, to set up a Chinese government devoted to the establishment of peace and friendship with Japan. Wang had tried to persuade Chiang to come to terms with the Japanese, arguing that China would undergo a "rebirth" by participating in a new East Asian economic order, but, on December 26, 1938, Chiang rejected the suggestion in the following words:

> We must understand that the rebirth of China is taken by the Japanese to mean destruction of an independent China and creation of an enslaved China. The so-called new order is to be created after China has been reduced to a slave nation and linked up with made-in-Japan Manchukuo. The aim of the Japanese is to control China militarily under the pretext of anti-Communism, to eliminate Chinese culture under the cloak of the protection of Oriental culture, and to expel European and American influences from the Far East under the pretext of breaking down economic walls.

Wang's "Chinese" government was nevertheless proclaimed at Nanking on March 30, 1940, but, until his death shortly before the end of the war, it remained dependent on the Japanese, and therefore never achieved general recognition.

The international disapproval of the Japanese attack upon China had little immediate effect. The Assembly of the League of Nations declared that Japan was an aggressor and a treaty-breaker, since, apart from having agreed to the Paris (Kellogg-Briand) Pact renouncing war as an instrument of national policy, Japan was also a signatory of the nine-power Treaty of Washington of 1922, and therefore had agreed "to respect the sovereignty, the independence, and the territorial and administrative integrity of China." The United States supported the League's position, but when Franklin D. Roosevelt, in a speech made on October 5, 1937, suggested placing aggressor nations "in quarantine," the American public, still wishing to avoid involvement in foreign broils, was unenthusiastic, and the proposal was quietly dropped.

A meeting—which Japan refused to attend—of the signatories of the Treaty of Washington, to which ten other powers were also invited, was held in Brussels in October and November, 1937. However, as none of the participants was prepared to use force, those assembled contented themselves with declaring Japan to be an aggressor, and then disbanded. In response to the Brussels Conference the Japanese Premier, Prince Konoe, stated that the Washington Treaty merely provided others with a pretext for interfering in Eastern Asia. The following year, on November 1, 1938, Japan announced that its new policy was henceforth to be based on the establishment of a "New Order in East Asia," which would take the form of a political, economic, and cultural union between Japan, Manchukuo, and China—a concept that was later, in November, 1940, to be institutionalized in the form of an economic bloc entitled the "Greater East Asia Co-Prosperity Sphere." A short time after the "New Order" announcement was made, Prince Konoe also declared that the interference of third powers in the Japanese dispute with China would no longer be tolerated.

France and Britain, preoccupied with Hitler's growing power in Europe, were in no mood to be drawn into a quarrel with Japan in Asia. The Soviet Union, however, which had signed a nonaggression pact with China, and which was supplying China with arms, did not feel able to show the same degree of detachment, particularly since Japan had signed the Anti-Comintern Pact on November 25, 1936. A series of Russo-Japanese clashes had subsequently occurred between forces of the Kwantung Army on the one hand and those of the Special Red Banner Army of the Far East on the other. The first clash, which took place in 1937 over possession of islands in the Amur River, was won by the Japanese. In 1938 a second clash took place at Changkufang on the ill-defined Korean-Siberian frontier, and was concluded after diplomatic negotiations resulting in agreement by both sides to withdraw their forces. In the summer of 1939, however, a third and far more serious conflict developed in the Nomonhan region. Although nominally it began as a border dispute between Japanese-backed Manchukuo on the one hand and Soviet-backed Outer Mongolia on the other, Japanese and Soviet forces were soon drawn in, and, in an undeclared four-month war in which were fought the first large-scale battles in which tanks were used by both sides, many thousands were killed. After the Nazi-Soviet Pact of August, 1939, had shattered the basis on which Japanese foreign policy had been conducted, however, the fighting was ended, and the border dispute was eventually settled after a boundary commission had made its recommendations.

In China, meanwhile, the Japanese attack resulted in a united front being formed between Chiang Kai-shek's Kuomintang and the Chinese Communist Party. In practice this meant that the Kuomintang received a modicum of Soviet aid, while the Chinese Communist guerrillas harassed the Japanese behind their own lines. Although the alliance was relatively harmonious in the first two years of the war, strains later developed until at last, in early 1941, an open clash occurred between Kuomintang forces and the Chinese Communist New Fourth Army, in which the Kuomintang was victorious. This event signaled the end of the alliance. From that time on the Chinese Communists represented a third force in the military struggle between Japan and the Kuomintang government.

Internal differences, meanwhile, divided Japan's policy-makers. Shortly before the 1937 "Incident," Japanese general elections had been held which seemed to indicate an impulse toward moderation. But after the "Incident"—which was followed by the massacre of a number of Japanese living in China—the Japanese military and their ultranationalist supporters were able to create a climate favoring violence as an instrument of foreign policy. New differences, however, now arose. The Army saw the Soviet Union as Japan's primary enemy, and therefore favored preparations for a move by land to the north, whereas the Navy saw the United States as the primary threat, and therefore favored preparations for moves to the south and east. The struggle between these two schools of thought continued intermittently, with the Army advocating the conclusion of an anti-Soviet military alliance with Hitler, and the Navy opposing such close commitment. Although the Army was dominant within the government, tension in 1939 between the two services reached such a degree that the naval ministry was supplied with machine guns and defended by a battalion of marines to fend off a possible army attack. The incessant argument between the two viewpoints was still proceeding within the Japanese Cabinet when, in August 1939, it was interrupted by the news that the Nazi-Soviet Pact had been concluded. For the Japanese government, as one commentator put it, "the experience was like opening a mail box and having a pack of hornets dash out."[5] A basic assumption upon which Japanese policies had been based appeared suddenly to have collapsed.

The war that quickly followed in Europe found Japan feeling betrayed. In 1936 it had signed the Anti-Comintern Pact with Germany, and now Germany had compacted with the common enemy. Moreover, Germany was now at war with Britain and France, just as Japan was embroiled with China, leaving the Soviet Union with its hands free to intervene against Japan at any time of its choosing. The Japanese Army in particular—partisans of an alliance with Germany—had been made to feel foolish. But the Army could not now retract without losing ascendancy within Japan itself. More than ever it sought to extricate itself from its predicament by hustling Japan further along the path of military self-assertion. In this course it was strengthened by the argument that as a European war had once more broken out, the time was ripe for Japan to move against European dominion in Asia.

The war in China, meanwhile, was at a virtual standstill, with hostilities proceeding only in a desultory fashion. Attention now turned to the question of supplies. With the coastal cities in Japanese hands, China, apart from the trickle of supplies from the Soviet Union, could only obtain those materials that it could move along the newly built "Burma Road," which, running from the Burmese frontier to Yunnan, was subjected to intermittent Japanese air attack. Japan itself, still dependent on others, had been obtaining supplies and raw materials, particularly scrap iron, steel, and oil, from the United States. Upon the outbreak of war Japan warned other powers to stop supplying China—a warning that the United States, still pledged to recognize China's sovereignty and territorial integrity, rejected. At the same time Japan increased its own purchases in the United States. The United States, however, was growing increasingly hostile to Japan. Rising Japanese pressure to exclude Americans, as well as other Westerners, from Japanese-held areas of China was causing resentment. The occupation, early in 1939, of the island of Hainan as well as of the Spratly Islands—territories that had previously been claimed by the French—had also been taken as a sign that Japan was making preparations for expansion in the South Pacific. When, in June, 1939, the United States gave the six months' notice required to end the U.S.-Japanese Treaty of Commerce and Navigation, the way was cleared for the imposition at any time of a U.S. embargo upon trade with Japan. Apprehensive that the embargo might be imposed, Japan accordingly began to display interest in, if not to exert pressure upon, the Dutch East Indies, whose oil fields could help to meet its

5. Herbert Feis, *The Road to Pearl Harbor* (1950), p. 34.

needs. A marked sign of growing U.S. concern at this time was the removal, in April, 1940, of the base of the U.S. fleet from San Diego in California to Pearl Harbor in Hawaii—a move that brought it halfway across the Pacific and about 2,000 miles nearer to Japan.

The pace of events was, at this point, quickened by the news from Europe. When Holland was overrun by German troops, Japanese demonstrations of interest in the Dutch East Indies greatly increased. At the time of the French surrender Japan asked France for the right to maintain military observers in Indochina to ensure that no supplies were entering China from there—a demand to which France, unable to receive help from either Britain or the U.S., felt obliged to accede. Indications also began to accumulate that inside the Japanese government interest in expansion to the north had given way to the policy of expansion to the south. Thus on June 29, 1940, the Japanese Foreign Minister, Arita, speaking on the radio, declared:

> The countries of East Asia and the regions of the South Seas are geographically, historically, racially, and economically very closely related. . . . The uniting of all these regions in a single sphere on a basis of common existence, insuring thereby the stability of that sphere, is a natural conclusion.

Thus, adjusting to what it conceived to be the new fact of German-Soviet friendship, the Japanese government evolved a new basic policy, which was approved on July 26 and July 27, 1940. Instead of preparing for a northward move, every effort was to be put forward to end the "China Incident"; Japan would endeavor to secure passage of its troops through Indochina, as well as obtaining use of airfields there; finally, when conditions were favorable—that is to say, when the "China Incident" was ended—Japan would resort to arms in the south, while avoiding hostilities until the time was ripe.

The new basic policy was applied, in part, in September, 1940, when Japan increased its pressure on Indochina while at the same time concluding the Tripartite Pact of Mutual Assistance with the Axis Powers, apparently under the impression that this would deter the United States from any hasty anti-Japanese reactions.[6] The French were in a palpably weak position, and on September 23, 1940, Japan, giving several reasons for its action, occupied the Tonkin province of Indochina,[7] and then proceeded to back Thailand's demand upon the French for the return of

6. Matsuoka, the new Foreign Minister, argued that Americans of German and Italian ancestry would influence the U.S. against entering the war. In 1920–1921 General Kojiro Sato had advanced a similar argument, commenting that in the First World War not only German-Americans but also 15,000,000 "colored people (including mixtures)" had "not necessarily been truly patriotic." (See Robert J. C. Butow, *Tojo and the Coming of the War,* 1961, p. 169.)

7. De Gaulle, from his West African vantage point, followed these events mournfully. He was later to write: "To me, steering a very small boat on the ocean of war, Indochina seemed like a great ship out of control, to which I could give no aid until I had slowly got together the means of rescue. As I saw her move away in the mist, I swore to myself that I would one day bring her in." (See *The Complete War Memoirs of Charles de Gaulle: 1940–1946,* 1964.).

two more provinces—Laos and Cambodia. Again the French were obliged to yield. The U.S., however, on September 26, 1940, had embargoed the supply to Japan of scrap iron and steel as well as of aviation gasoline. The following day, September 27, the Japanese signed the Tripartite Pact. Both sides were moving nearer to war. On the initiative of the Japanese, negotiations were begun with Washington to find a basis for agreement—negotiations that were to continue fruitlessly until war, at last, began. Foreseeing the trend, Japan concluded a Neutrality Pact with the Soviet Union on April 13, 1941, in order to secure itself from any threat from the north. Preparations for the move to the south, meanwhile, continued. Once more, however, Japan, by following the German example, was to find itself deceived. On June 22, 1941, Germany attacked the Soviet Union. So convinced had the Japanese government become that German-Soviet friendship now prevailed that it had earlier discounted reports that the event was impending.

In mid-1941 two further events occurred that were to make war inevitable. In July the Japanese Army moved in force from Northern into Southern Indochina, thus placing itself in a position either to cross Thailand and Burma into India, or else to move against Malaya and the islands of the south. The United States, Britain, and the Netherlands responded by freezing all Japanese assets, thus cutting off trade relations of all kinds with Japan. But Japan could not remain economically isolated. Above all oil was needed. As it was, Japan had only enough for two years of peace, and the Navy only enough for eighteen months of war. Thus whereas even until June, 1941, the Navy had acted as a restraining influence, its dependence on oil now led it also to consider a resort to force. For unless Japan could capture the oil fields of the Dutch East Indies within a reasonably short time, its situation would become desperate. As one Japanese source expressed it, the situation of the nation was that of a fish in a pond from which the water was being gradually drained away.[8] Japan now faced the choice of either abandoning its claims and gains, or else of going to war. Nobody doubted which alternative would be chosen. The only question was—how soon?

## Pearl Harbor

By a series of policy decisions, Japan moved ineluctably toward war. Deadlines were set to permit diplomacy a final opportunity to gain acceptable concessions. As the hope of obtaining them was, however, slim indeed, at the same time military preparations for war moved forward. At an imperial conference held on September 6, 1941, it was decided that if by early October Japanese demands had not been met, hostilities

8. See Robert J. C. Butow, *Tojo and the Coming of the War*, p. 245.

would be launched against the United States, Britain, and the Netherlands.[9] The only way to avoid war would be for the United States to end its economic blockade and for Japan to negotiate a settlement of the "China Incident," but neither side was by now in the mood for conciliation or concession. Further arguments continued among Japanese policymakers, however, until on November 1, at another conference, the September 6 decision was more insistently reaffirmed, with the time limit for diplomacy to produce results now being extended until November 30. During the month of November, both the U.S. and Japanese positions hardened, with Japan presenting its "final proposals" on November 20, and the United States replying on November 26 with proposals that suggested a renegotiation of the Nine-Power Pact of 1922. On December 1, 1941, at yet another imperial conference, the final decision was made. There was to be war.

The element of risk in the war that was now to begin was acknowledged by both the Japanese Army and Navy, but it was felt that Japan's situation was such that the inherent risks would have to be accepted. Isoroku Yamamoto, Commander-in-Chief of the Japanese Navy, entertained more doubts than his colleagues about the wisdom of the enterprise, believing that if the war were to be protracted, Japan could not win. Only by striking a surprise blow, he believed, could enough time be gained to give Japan a chance of victory. He therefore planned to bomb the United States Fleet at its anchorage at Pearl Harbor in Hawaii. Already on November 26, 1941, a task force under Admiral Nagano had sailed from the Kurile Islands toward its target. The date of the attack was to be December 7 (December 8, Japanese time). To ensure surprise, such secrecy was maintained that even many senior officials of the Japanese government knew nothing of the impending event.

Under the Third Hague Convention of 1907, hostilities were not to begin between parties without prior notification.[10] Instructions were sent

9. The Emperor Hirohito, who presided at such conferences, usually remained silent. On this occasion, however, he broke the silence to read a short Japanese poem:

> "All the seas in every quarter
> Are as brothers to one another.
> Why, then, do the winds and waves of strife
> Rage so turbulently throughout the world?"

Those present, most of whom were working toward war, were thunderstruck by the Emperor's surprising intervention. Debate still continues as to whether the poem expressed Hirohito's true sentiment, or whether he was placing himself on record as favoring peace lest the war should turn out badly.

10. The U.S. representative at the Hague Conference, General Porter, had declared that the U.S. interpretation was that notification would not be required in case of a war of self-defense. Togo Shigenori, formerly Japanese Foreign Minister, later argued that if Japan believed the war to be one of self-defense, then no notification would have been necessary. (*The Cause of Japan*, p. 207). However, the Japanese notification was not a declaration of war, but a long statement of the Japanese position, concluding with the observation that in view of the American government's attitude, Japan could only consider that "it is impossible to reach an agreement through further negotiations."

to the Japanese negotiators in Washington to delay such notification until the last moment. But, because of clerical difficulties created by the degree of secrecy exacted,[11] the Embassy staff did not succeed in fulfilling their instructions to deliver the notification by 1 P.M. on Sunday, December 7, Washington time. Instead the Japanese emissaries handed over the document to U.S. Secretary of State Cordell Hull at 2:20 P.M. This was too late. At 12:45 P.M., Washington time, the Japanese aircraft in the Pacific had left their carriers and were flying toward Pearl Harbor. Just over half an hour later, when Pearl Harbor was, as one of the Japanese pilots afterwards remarked, "asleep in the morning mist," bombs and torpedoes from the first wave of attacking planes had begun to fall on the ninety-four American ships at anchor below. Surprise was complete.[12] Some two hours later, when the last plane left, six capital ships had been sunk or destroyed, many other ships sunk or damaged, and 149 American planes smashed. Japan was now the strongest power in the Pacific.

The news was carried swiftly to an astonished world. President Roosevelt called December 7, 1941, "a date which will live in infamy." Prime Minister Churchill, in London, found the event "of so startling a nature as to make even those who were near to the centre gasp."[13] At his headquarters in East Prussia Hitler, "completely surprised," went in the middle of the night to tell his generals the news. In Japan the people were "generally intoxicated with victory."[14] Declarations of war followed quickly—the U.S. Congress declaring war on Japan on December 8, Britain having done so a few hours earlier. Three days later, on December 11, Germany and Italy, in accordance with the Tripartite Pact, declared war on the United States. Neutrality was over: the war had become world-wide, even although Japan and Germany were failing to co-ordinate their actions.

The British Admiral Fisher, who had advised the Japanese at the time of the battle of Tsushima in 1905, had said that one should "hit first, hit hard, and keep on hitting." At Pearl Harbor the Japanese had hit first and hard. They were now to continue raining blows down upon their opponents. On the same day that Pearl Harbor was attacked, Japanese planes effectively destroyed U.S. air power in the Philippines, while

---

11. For security reasons diplomats, unused to typing, were obliged to type the 4,000-word document.
12. While the U.S. government had many indications—among others those from intercepted and deciphered Japanese communications—that a Japanese attack was imminent, its targets were not known. British and Dutch possessions were believed to be in more imminent danger than American-held territories or bases. The impression that Pearl Harbor would not be in danger was reinforced by the erroneous belief of Commander McCollum, Chief of the Far Eastern Section of the American Naval Intelligence Service, that the American fleet was not in Pearl Harbor. President Roosevelt apparently anticipated some blow, and permitted it to fall first so that the United States would have "a clean record," but he also did not conceive that the Fleet in Pearl Harbor could be in danger. A series of circumstantial accidents prevented the Americans from apprehending the danger in time. (See Ladislas Farago, *The Broken Seal*, 1967.)
13. *The Second World War*, Vol. 3, p. 605.
14. Togo Shigenori, *The Cause of Japan*, p. 227.

other American or British-held territories similarly came under Japanese attack. Thailand was invaded, and quickly surrendered. Japanese troops swept into Malaya and kept moving southward. Like an avalanche Japanese progress continued. On December 10, 1941, the Japanese sank the British battleships *Repulse* and *Prince of Wales* off the Malayan coast, thereby removing the last threat to their command of the southern seas. On December 25 the British possessions of Hong Kong and Sarawak fell into Japanese hands. More successes were to be obtained in 1942. On February 15 the Japanese, after moving down the Malayan coast in a series of amphibious operations, captured Singapore, whose defenses had inexplicably not been prepared on the landward side. By March a major objective—the vital oil fields of the Dutch East Indies—had been captured. Meanwhile the Japanese had been making progress in the Philippines, where they had landed in December. The American forces had fallen back on the Bataan peninsula, and established headquarters on the rocky island of Corregidor, but were unable to hold either. In April about 12,500 Americans and 60,000 Filipinos surrendered in the Bataan peninsula, and the following month a further 11,000 Americans and 50,000 Filipinos surrendered on Corregidor. General MacArthur of the American Far East Command had earlier been ordered to fall back upon Australia and establish new headquarters there. By this time the Japanese had also captured Java, Sumatra, Bali, Timor, and countless other islands, and had also reached New Guinea. By June they had overrun Burma. India to the west, Australia to the south, and Hawaii to the east were all now directly threatened. Never, since white world dominion had been established, had it faced such a challenge.

The Japanese success focused white Western attention upon Japanese society and culture which, until then, had been, relatively speaking, little regarded. With bitterness and fear prevalent, it was not surprising that most attention was paid to those aspects of Japanese society which appeared the most unfamiliar and the least acceptable to Westerners. Japanese politeness was represented as innate hypocrisy. The cult of Bushido, the code of the samurai, popularized by the military-minded faction, was seen as a sinister force inhibiting normal ethical development. The practice of *hara-kiri*—a form of honorable suicide committed to clear one's name—was seen as both ridiculous and distasteful. But, above all, it was the difference in the conventions of methods of waging war that envenomed the atmosphere. In Japanese eyes honor was bound up with fighting to the death, whereas to Westerners surrender was, under many circumstances, justifiable. Ruth Benedict has attempted to express this difference in statistical form. In the campaign in North Burma, she reported, the proportion of captured to dead among Japanese troops was 142 to 17,166—or one prisoner to every 120 dead. Among Western armies, however, the proportion of prisoners to dead was usually about four to one.[15] To become a prisoner was thus, to the Japanese, to become dishonored. In consequence American prisoners were seen by the Japanese as disgraced, and could hardly expect, in the Japanese view, to receive the kind of treatment to which "complete" men would be entitled. Prisoners were thus subjected to forced marches[16] and harsh handling of a kind that they would not have received had they been captured by European belligerents. This created much resentment, and led to the propagation of the thesis, in the emotional wartime atmosphere, that the Japanese were "barbarian," and, by their alien and inhumane behavior, had placed themselves beyond the pale of human kind.

Western resentment against the Japanese, which was to a large degree colored by the knowledge that Japan was undermining the structure of white hegemony in Asia, was focused to a considerable extent upon Hideki Tojo, Premier of Japan at the time of the outbreak of war. Tojo, who, as we have seen, was a military martinet with a dislike of foreigners, had earlier held the post of Chief of Staff of the Kwantung Army, and then of Minister of War. Short of stature and humorless, he had shown administrative ability, and had consistently advocated a policy of expansion, even at the cost of war. In the view of Western propagandists and publicists, however, he was a second Hitler, driven by demented ambition and thirsting for blood, representing to them the very incarnation of the threat with which Western power was faced.

> More than any other [wrote a leading American magazine in 1944], this walking venom sac embodies the fanaticisms and ferocities of his race, for even as he forced war with China and the United States, so he is waging both wars with a barbarity unknown since man quit running on all fours.[17]

On the Japanese side, also, animosity toward Western leaders was often evident—President Roosevelt, for example, being referred to as the "Would-be Lord High Protector of the Universe." On December 23, 1941, the Japan *Times and Advertiser* of Tokyo, attacking the Anglo-American alliance, commented:

> The fetid breath of the dying British Empire poisons all who come in contact with it. Those who would arrest the inevitable decay of the moribund old monster are themselves contaminated and rushed to an untimely grave. . . .

In place of the dominance of the "moribund old monster," Japan decreed a policy of "Asia for the Asians," and assiduously publicized it in such Japanese-occupied territories as Burma, Malaya, the Philippines,

---

15. *The Chrysanthemum and the Sword* (1946), pp. 38–39.
16. Many of the prisoners captured in the Bataan peninsula died in the course of the "Bataan Death March" which followed, and which consequently became particulary notorious in Western countries.
17. *Collier's,* February 5, 1944, p. 60. As Butow has pointed out, Tojo was not responsible for the outbreak of the "China Incident."

and the Indonesian archipelago. Even in British-held India and Ceylon the same gospel was surreptitiously spread, creating new stirrings beneath the surface which added fervor to the already-existing nationalist doctrines.[18]

## These "United Nations"

Immediately after the outbreak of war with Japan, Churchill traveled to the United States where, in Washington, he and President Roosevelt, together with their staffs, had planned the strategy of the war. A Grand Alliance was to be formed, to which allied combatant nations could adhere, and these "United Nations"—as they were to be known—were to end the war first by ensuring the defeat of Germany and Italy in Europe, and then by defeating Japan in the Pacific. This meant that for a time—and above all in 1942—the Anglo-Americans and their allies in the Pacific would necessarily remain on the defensive.

Indeed, as 1942 progressed, and as defeat followed defeat, apprehension grew for the safety of both Australia and Madagascar. The Allies had been unable or unwilling to believe that an Asian nation could successfully challenge a white nation in battle, and were now suffering the consequences of this conceit.[19] The Australians, in particular, were deeply concerned. Their military strength was scattered, with three divisions away in Egypt and a fourth in Singapore. Moreover, more than half of the Australian population lived in seacoast cities which appeared vulnerable to a Japanese onslaught. Especially since primacy had been assigned to the European theater, the Australians felt neglected, and even before the fall of Singapore in February, 1942, a certain amount of Anglo-Australian recrimination occurred—a recrimination that was not lessened when, later the same month, the Australian Prime Minister, John Curtin, refused Churchill's pressing request that an Australian division be sent to help resist the imminent Japanese advance into Burma. The Australians, haunted by visions of Australia with its white population passing under Japanese control, for a time resolutely refused to commit further forces abroad, and insisted that all their available troops return forthwith to prepare the defense of their homeland. However, when the United States assumed primary responsibility for the defense of the Pacific, including Australia, and sent American reinforcements to the continent, Australian apprehensions were progressively removed.

Meanwhile the British and the white South Africans were particularly concerned about the possibility of a Japanese move westward across the

18. Rash Bihari Bhose, an advocate of Pan-Asianism from Bengal, had found refuge in Japan as early as 1916, and since had worked actively for the Pan-Asian cause. Bhose, who died in 1945, enjoyed the protection of the powerful Toyama Mitsuru, founder of the Black Dragon Society.

19. As Churchill, speaking of the Japanese successes, admitted, "The efficiency of the Japanese in air warfare was at this time greatly underestimated both by ourselves and by the Americans." (*The Second World War*, Vol. 3, p. 619.)

Indian Ocean. Should the Allies lose control of the sea and the air in this region, dire consequences might follow. Japan might seize Ceylon, after which India might, as it were, fall of its own weight. Madagascar, too, might be seized, after which the British position in the Middle East might be undermined by the cutting off of supplies passing round the Cape route. Even the loss to the British of oil supplies from Abadan could prove disastrous, for without this oil, Churchill told Roosevelt on April 15, 1942, "We cannot maintain our position either at sea or on land in the Indian Ocean area." Furthermore, had a junction been effected between the Japanese and the Axis forces fighting in North Africa and the Middle East, the war might well have been over for the Allies.

But the Japanese, while they had plans for the establishment of bases in Ceylon and Madagascar, had already achieved, or were about to achieve, their main objectives in the Pacific, and had no strategy worked out in combination with the other Axis powers to bring the war to an end. This failure to co-ordinate, which stood in marked contrast to the close degree of co-operation established on a world-wide scale by the American and British commands, more than any other single factor was to lead to the final defeat of the Axis powers. The Germans were set upon their drive to the east against Russia, whereas the Japanese were primarily concerned with their struggle against the United States. The degree of failure to combine Japanese and German efforts was later demonstrated by the testimony given to the International Military Tribunal at Nuremberg after the war by the German Foreign Minister, Ribbentrop, which exposed German ignorance of Japanese intentions. "Japan," said Ribbentrop, speaking of the Japanese entry into the war, "did neither the one thing we wanted (attack Singapore) nor the other (attack the U.S.S.R.); rather she did a third thing. She attacked the United States at Pearl Harbor."

After the Pearl Harbor attack, there had been some attempt to establish a theoretical framework for at least a degree of military co-ordination. On January 18, 1942, a military agreement was reached in Berlin between Germany, Italy, and Japan, by the terms of which their respective spheres of military operation were defined. The Japanese sphere was to be the waters eastward from about 70° E. longitude to the west coast of the American continent, as well as the continent and islands—Australia, the Netherlands East Indies, and New Zealand—which are situated in these waters, as well as the Asian continent east of about 70° E. longitude. It was further agreed that if Anglo-American naval forces should concentrate their efforts in the Atlantic, then Japan would send some naval forces into the Atlantic to co-operate with the German and Italian fleets, whereas if the Anglo-Americans concentrated primarily on the Pacific, then Germany and Italy would likewise send naval reinforcements there. Indian Ocean operations beyond the agreed-upon limit—and by this operations against Madagascar, which lay to the west of the demarcation line, were doubtless envisaged—would be subject to future agreement.

At first it appeared to the Allies that the westward movement that they feared was about to begin in earnest, for in the first days of April, 1942, a Japanese naval force, including aircraft carriers, under the command of Admiral Nagumo, the victor of Pearl Harbor, was detected heading for Ceylon. In anticipation of such a development the British had hastily assembled as many planes on the island as they could muster. On April 5, 1942, Japanese dive bombers attacked Colombo, sinking ships in the harbor as well as attacking and sinking two British cruisers at sea further south. The following day Trincomalee, the main base of the British Eastern Fleet, situated on the northeast coast of Ceylon, was also attacked. Fortunately for the British, however, they had already dispersed much of their naval strength beforehand, so that it was out of harm's way. Moreover, the unexpected strength of the British in the air over Ceylon, where they inflicted considerable losses upon the attacking squadrons, was sufficient to discourage the Japanese, who then withdrew. The British, although they did not realize it at the time, had merely experienced a probing raid, and not a prelude to a landing. Instead of moving westward the Japanese were now, instead, to move south and east.

The British and the white South African government, meanwhile, were concerned about the possibility of Vichy-held Madagascar falling, or being surrendered, to the Japanese. To forestall such an eventuality a British and South African force was landed on Madagascar at Diego Suarez on May 5, 1942, despite the armed opposition of the Vichy French. It soon transpired, however, that although the Vichy authorities were violently hostile to the Allies, the Madagascan population was not. Several months of armed truce then ensued, during which the British sought to obtain assurances from the Vichy Governor-General that he would not at any time permit the Japanese to land. When no such assurances could be obtained from him, hostilities were resumed, after which the capital of Tananarive fell to South African troops on September 23, 1942. The Vichy Governor-General and his remaining forces surrendered on November 5. Meanwhile the British, who much to his displeasure had not informed General de Gaulle beforehand of their intention to land in Madagascar, attempted to obtain concessions from him regarding the French position in the Middle East or North Africa in return for handing Madagascar back to French control. When de Gaulle refused to countenance such a bargain, an agreement was signed on December 14, 1942, that returned the island and its dependencies to French control under a Gaullist administration.

*The Greater East Asia Co-Prosperity Sphere*

By May, 1942, it had become clear that Japan had secured its immediate strategic objectives by seizing control of Southeast Asia and of the East Indies. Believing that an effective Allied counteroffensive would prove too great a burden to be undertaken, the Japanese now expected that eventual negotiations would finally result in a compromise peace that would accord them the greater part of their gains. In the meantime Japan faced the problem of consolidating its hold over the vast area that it had conquered.

Particular attention was paid by the Japanese to the task of destroying the myth of white omnipotence throughout their newly acquired territories. Apart from systematically disseminating anti-European propaganda which condemned the European colonizers as exploiters of Asia and the Asians, the Japanese also went out of their way to inflict public humiliations upon white prisoners, so that any potential authority that they might still possess would be destroyed. Thus, for example, a Singapore newspaper, the *Syonan Times*[20] of February 25, 1942, commented:

> Today in Syonan, and wherever the victorious Nippon armies have brought the New Order, Europeans may be seen, nude to the waist, doing jobs that Asians only were made to do before. Many of them cut ludicrous figures slouching their way through work which even Asian women are able to tackle with greater ability.

Japan's Greater East Asia sphere now consisted of Korea (annexed in 1910), Manchukuo (occupied in 1931), the Philippines, the Netherlands East Indies, Malaya, Burma, Thailand, Indochina, and parts of war-torn China itself. A different situation prevailed, however, in each territory —Korea, for example, was subjected to direct rule; Burma was accorded a titular independence on August 1, 1943; and Indochina, until March 9, 1945, continued to be administered by the French colonial authorities, virtually on suffrance.

On November 1, 1942, the Japanese, by imperial decree, established a Greater East Asia Ministry. The Ministry was established on the insistence of General Tojo and the military, in the face of objections from the Japanese Foreign Ministry, headed by Shigenori Togo. Togo, rather than see the functions of his Ministry thus circumscribed, resigned. The new Ministry, however, did not itself possess much power, but formed, as it were, an agency halfway between the Foreign Ministry and the military administrators. Its declared aims were the Nipponization of the occupied territories, and the dissemination of cultural propaganda. Its greatest success occurred in November, 1943, when it organized a

---

20. *Syonan,* or *Shonan,* meaning "light of the South," was the name given by the Japanese to Singapore. The newspaper, which had previously been the *Straits Times,* continued to be published in English throughout the war.

Greater East Asia Assembly in Tokyo that was attended by representatives from Manchukuo, China, Thailand, Burma, and the Philippines. At this conference a communique, dated November 5, was issued which laid the blame for the war on American and British ambitions to enslave East Asia. It stated that the participants would co-operate to ensure the stability of the region and to construct an order of common prosperity, pledging mutual respect for one another's sovereignty and independence, while also respecting one another's traditions and developing "the creative faculties of each race." It also promised economic co-operation and expressed a determination to work for the abolition of racial discrimination, for the promotion of cultural intercourse, and for the opening of resources throughout the world.

Behind this facade complex problems beset the *Dai Toa Kyokeiken* (Greater East Asia Co-Prosperity Sphere). For one Japan itself had varying interests. The oil of the Netherlands East Indies was essential to the Japanese economy. Malayan tin and rubber, also, was needed. The Philippines, on the other hand, could not be left unoccupied lest it constitute a threat in the rear to Japan's southward advance.

Yet, seen from the viewpoint of the nationalist movements in each separate country, other aspects also emerged. In Manchuria, where Japanese control had been consolidated, the fiction of independence was nevertheless maintained. The "Chinese Central Government" at Nanking, led by Wang Ching-wei, was, as we have already seen, likewise fictitiously independent, so that its conclusion of "peace" with Japan on November 30, 1940, no less than its declaration of war against the United States and Britain on January 9, 1943, in no way altered the situation. Of more significance, however, were the agreements reached between the Wang Ching-wei government and Japan—agreements which promised mutual co-operation as equals in the establishment of a Greater East Asia; which promised that Japanese troops would be withdrawn from China when the war ended; and which renounced the Japanese claim to station troops in China under the Protocol dating from the time of the Boxer Rebellion. By reaching these agreements with Wang, the Japanese were, in effect, offering terms to the Chiang Kai-shek government in Chungking—terms which, if accepted at the price of Chiang's renunciation of his alliance with the West, would have brought the "China Incident" to a final end. But Chiang anticipated Japan's ultimate defeat, and remained obdurate in his refusal to consider the matter.

Relations between Japan and Thailand were governed by a Treaty of Alliance, signed on December 21, 1941, which contained secret provisions under which Japan promised to help Thailand regain her lost provinces, while Thailand, for its part, promised to give Japan assistance in its war with the United States and Britain. Thailand declared war on the two allies on January 25, 1942. In the period which followed, Japanese forces were stationed in Thailand; large prisoner-of-war camps were established there; and Bangkok became the headquarters for the Japanese-backed *Azad Hind,* or Free India movement. Economic difficulties nevertheless arose between the Japanese and their Thai hosts, and Thai opinion was only partially appeased by Japanese help in 1943 in enabling, as promised, Thailand to secure the return of four provinces that the British had detached in 1909 in order to make them a part of Malaya. Later, however, when the fortunes of war began to turn against Japan, and Tojo fell from power in July, 1944, Thailand's pro-Japanese leader, Luang Pibul, likewise lost office. After this the new Thai administration, maintaining an atmosphere of ambiguity in which contacts with the Allies no less than relations with the Japanese were maintained, moved steadily in the direction of a de facto neutrality.

Pro-Japanese currents had been in evidence in Burmese politics even before the Japanese invasion. The invasion itself, however, was followed by a period of confusion during which the Japanese were obliged to disband the Burma Independence Army that they had had trained, as it was creating disturbances in the country instead of pacifying it. On August 1, 1942, a Burmese coalition government, headed by Ba Maw, was set up in Rangoon. Ba Maw believed that co-operation with the Japanese would result in early independence, and in fact Burmese independence was declared one year later on August 1, 1943, with Burma declaring war on the United States and Britain at the same time. The Japanese Army remained the final political arbiter, however, with the result that as time progressed complaints of Japanese severity and of exploitation became increasingly frequent. It was in 1943 that the Allied counteroffensive, aiming at the recapture of Burma, began to materialize, and in 1944 the Japanese hold on the country became increasingly precarious. By 1945 the Japanese position began to collapse, a process that was hastened by the decision of Aung San, the Burmese Minister of Defense, to go over to the Allied side and to place his forces at the disposal of the British. Ba Maw, meanwhile, sought refuge in Japan.

In the Philippines the situation was somewhat different from that in the other occupied territories. After 300 years of Spanish rule, the population, and especially the educated Filipinos, owed more to their European than to their Asian cultural heritage. Moreover, according to the Tydings-McDuffie Act of 1934, adopted by the United States Congress, the Philippines was to receive full independence in 1946. The appeal of Japan's policy of "Asia for the Asians" was, therefore, largely inapplicable. On the other hand independence would result in placing the Philippines outside the United States tariff barrier, thereby threatening the future of the islands' sugar industry. While Japan already obtained sugar from Taiwan, she was nevertheless interested in the raw cotton and the iron ore that the Philippines could produce. There were some Filipinos, consequently, who foresaw the islands' economic future lying with Japan. The shock of the Japanese invasion was, however, all the greater because both Filipinos and Americans underestimated Japan's military capability.[21] Filipino troops, despite a lack of equipment, fought under U.S. command until they were overwhelmed. Under the Japanese occupation, however, the Filipino politicians were divided. Some, including President Quezon, had left for the United States. Others remained, either to resist, or else to co-operate with the Japanese.

Having secured control, the Japanese authorities strove to introduce Nippongo—the Japanese language—into general use, and to promote the production of cotton rather than of sugar as the main export crop. It was their hope that the Philippines would become a partner in the Greater East Asia Plan. Toward the end of 1942 they encouraged the formation of an Association for Service to the New Philippines, known as the *Kalibapi,* with the help of which a new constitution was eventually drawn up. Elections for a national assembly were held in September, 1943, with José Laurel becoming President. On October 14, 1943, the independence of the Philippines was proclaimed, and, on the same day, a pact of Alliance concluded with Japan. The relationship with Japan nevertheless remained strained. The Japanese were dissatisfied because the Philippines would not declare war on the United States, while the Filipino population frequently showed resentment at the treatment they received from the Japanese occupation forces. Indeed, the population at large remained generally apathetic so far as the new order was concerned, while a number of small groups, some of whom remained in touch with the Americans, conducted sporadic guerrilla action. As American fortunes in the war waxed, so Filipino enthusiasm for the Japanese partnership waned. It was with the greatest difficulty that, after American aircraft had attacked the islands in August and September, 1944, the Japanese at last prevailed upon the Laurel administration to declare war on the United States. The declaration remained, nonetheless, a technicality, since the will to fight on the side of the Japanese was generally lacking. With the approach of the American forces, who recaptured Manila in March, 1945, the administration set up by the Japanese finally crumbled away.

In Indo-China, as we have seen, the Japanese, after the fall of France, introduced their forces peaceably in two stages, occupying the whole of the country by July, 1941. But, since the Japanese lacked sufficient administrators for the many East Asian countries they occupied in 1942,

21. The U.S. General MacArthur, as military adviser, had, before Pearl Harbor, discouraged the Philippines from buying military equipment before independence, stating that until then it was the United States that was responsible for the defense of the islands.

they permitted the French, represented by the Vichy Governor-General, Admiral Decoux, to remain, despite the paradoxical spectacle of a European colonial power continuing to function in a region where the proclaimed policy was "Asia for the Asians." It was, nevertheless, an uneasy alliance of convenience, barely tolerated by the younger Japanese military, who often did what they could to lower French prestige and undermine the administration's authority. The Annamese nationalist movement, for example, was given a degree of encouragement by the Japanese, with the Cao Dai movement in particular—representing a fusion of European and Asian philosophic and religious themes—receiving their support. Meanwhile, Japan's Asian rival, China, did not remain indifferent to events in Indochina. China informed Vichy that, if necessary, it would claim the same rights as Japan in Indochina. However, when the French pointed out that any Chinese action would only result in Japan assuming full control—an event that might prove disadvantageous to both China and her supporter the United States—no more was heard of the matter. Instead the Chinese contented themselves with extending support and providing refuge to various Annamite groups who formed themselves into a coalition under the leadership of Ho Chi Minh, former leader of the Indochinese Communist Party. This coalition, which included both communists and nationalists, in 1942 took the name of the Viet Minh, opposed both Japanese and French control, and sought independence for Annam, in pursuance of which it organized uprisings in Indochina.

In 1944 the authority of Vichy was replaced by that of de Gaulle's provisional government in Paris—a development that undermined Decoux's position. An American invasion was also feared by the Japanese. These circumstances led, on March 9, 1945, to a Japanese coup d'état which ended French rule. Decoux was captured, and most of the French taken prisoner—some of them then being massacred by the Japanese. A French contingent in Tonkin province managed to make a fighting retreat into China. Meanwhile, in place of the French, the Japanese supported the authority of the Emperor Bao Dai in Annam, and of King Norodom in Cambodia, while Cochin-China, Laos, and Tonkin were placed under Japanese administration. Bao Dai, however, did not enjoy the support of the Viet Minh, who continued to fight against the Japanese. After the fall of Japan, Bao Dai abdicated on August 22, 1945, and was succeeded by a government headed by Ho Chi Minh. In Hanoi on September 2, 1945, Ho Chi Minh's government repudiated French rule and proclaimed independence.

### Indonesia

The Netherlands East Indies, with its oil fields, was, together with Malaya, a primary objective of Japan, which intended that it should become a vital part of the Greater East Asia Co-Prosperity Sphere. Should a compromise peace be concluded with the United States and its allies, some other territories might be yielded up, but the East Indies would remain Japanese. To this end the Japanese made every effort to consolidate their hold on the archipelago. Batavia, the capital, where the Japanese military administration had established its headquarters, was renamed Djakarta. A centralized administrative system, resembling that of Japan itself, was introduced. The Dutch population was interned, and the Dutch officials replaced by Japanese. Dutch property and assets, including mines and factories, were seized. The Dutch language was replaced by Japanese and Indonesian. The result of all these efforts, however, was not so much to replace Dutch with Japanese influence, as to strengthen Indonesian nationalism. The population, for example, found Japanese hard to learn, and resorted increasingly to the use of the Indonesian language. To their surprise, also, the Indonesians found that under Japan, instead of Dutch colonial exploitation being replaced with an enlightened Asian rule, a new oppressive system, both inefficient and corrupt, was introduced. Furthermore, because the Japanese were ignorant of local conditions, the Japanese administrators had to lean heavily on Indonesian assistance—a circumstance that, although this was not the intention, resulted in the Indonesians acquiring administrative experience in their own right.

The Japanese, for their part, were opposed to Indonesian nationalism. Although they released Indonesian leaders, such as Sukarno and Mohammed Hatta, who had been imprisoned or exiled by the Dutch, what they sought was to obtain their collaboration, not to grant Indonesian independence. Indeed, while using the nationalists to foster anti-Western sentiment, the Japanese at the same time forbade the display of the Indonesian flag and the singing of the national anthem. The Japanese attitude was expressed in the decision of the Imperial Conference held on May 31, 1943, which decreed that Indonesia should be treated as Japanese territory, but that the Indonesians should be permitted to participate in the administration. In November, 1943, Sukarno, while on a visit to Tokyo, discreetly appealed to Tojo to grant the same independence to Indonesia that Burma and the Philippines had received. The appeal was rejected. However, as the tide of war began to turn against Japan, the Japanese, while increasingly distrustful of the growing strength of the nationalists, nevertheless began to make concessions to nationalism. In September, 1944, they agreed in principle that Indonesia should be granted eventual independence. Further concessions were being prepared, but were largely rendered inapplicable by the advance of the Allies, who landed in Borneo in July, 1945. On August 11, 1945, hastening to salvage whatever anti-Western support they could obtain, the Japanese informed Sukarno that independence was to be granted the following month, September. Four days later, however, on August 15, the Japanese surrender was announced. But the momentum of progress toward independence had already been established, and this last development merely accelerated it. On August 17, 1945, with the tacit consent of the Japanese, the independence of Indonesia was proclaimed from Sukarno's own house.

Malaysia—renamed Malai—like Indonesia was destined by the Japanese to become an integral part of the new Greater East Asia. Like Indonesia, also, it was placed under military administration and declared to be Nipponese territory. Here, however, Japanese policy supported the Malays rather than the Chinese or Indian populations of the peninsula. To this end the island of Sumatra was detached from the Indonesian complex and declared, for a time, to be a part of Malaya. The Japanese also adopted a conciliatory attitude toward the Muslim religion, and retained the local sultans in their positions, although with reduced stipends.

Nevertheless, as in Indonesia, the Japanese language was not easily accepted; Malay, Chinese, Thai, and Indian languages, and even English, were preferred. The substantial Chinese population, which included all political tendencies, was generally opposed to the prospect of Japanese hegemony, and reacted in the cities with various kinds of passive resistance. In the interior, however, resistance to the Japanese was conducted by the Communist Anti-Japanese Malaya Peoples Party. The Japanese sought to apply a policy of "divide and rule" by playing on the differences between Malays, Chinese, and Indians, but, as elsewhere, in time the Malays, despite the favor shown to them, grew disenchanted with the new order. The Japanese, while obtaining access to Malayan rubber and tin, could nevertheless not absorb the full output, so that the economy was disrupted. To offset the economic effects of this the Japanese strove to make Malaya self-sufficient by encouraging more local food production but, despite their efforts, they were unable to prevent food scarcity. Thus despite the anti-Western sentiment that had been strengthened by the Japanese interregnum, the peoples of Malaysia, following the Japanese surrender in August, 1945, were glad to see relations with the Allies restored, not only for economic reasons, but also because they were thus spared the ordeal of seeing Malaya become the scene of a bloody contest between the Eastern and Western belligerents.

## The Partnership that Failed

All this, however, still lay in the future. Six months after Pearl Harbor, Japan was still reaping the fruits of its victories. Diplomatically, nevertheless, the position of the Soviet Union—at war with Germany but not with Japan—remained anomalous. The German government, especially in 1942, tried repeatedly to prevail upon the Japanese to enter the war against the Soviet Union. But Japan, having already taken the strategic decision to strike southwards instead of to the north, was unwilling to do so. Moreover, with two wars already on her hands—one with Chungking and the other with the Allies—Japan felt that she could do no more. Rather than enter the war against the Soviets herself, Japan would have preferred to see peace concluded between Germany and the Soviet Union —a peace which would have permitted Germany to turn her full strength against the Western Allies. The Japanese therefore attempted, with tacit Italian support, to play the role of mediator between the two belligerents, whose sprawling armies were locked in combat across the face of Eastern Europe. The idea of concluding such a peace was rejected, however, first by Hitler, and then later, when the fortunes of war began to turn against Germany, by the Soviet government. The struggle was to be fought out to the end.

The United States, for its part, favored a Soviet attack upon Japan. But so long as the Soviet Union was fighting for its existence against the German armies on its soil the matter was out of the question.

On October 30, 1943, Stalin told Cordell Hull, the U.S. Secretary of State, that when Germany was defeated the Soviet Union would enter the war against Japan. This promise was later formalized in an agreement between the Soviet, U.S., and British leaders, signed at Yalta on February 11, 1945, according to the terms of which the Soviet Union would enter the war against Japan "two or three months after Germany has surrendered" on several conditions—inter alia that the status quo in Outer Mongolia be preserved; that the Kurile Islands, the southern part of Sakhalin, and the adjacent islands be handed over to the Soviet Union; that the port of Dairen be internationalized, with Soviet interests there being recognized as pre-eminent; and that Port Arthur be leased to the Soviets as a naval base. In due course the agreement was to be honored.

The Japanese premise—as we have mentioned—was that a negotiated peace would permit Japan to retain the greater part of her conquests. But the Allies had no intention of negotiating. Following the Cairo Conference—attended by Roosevelt, Churchill, and Chiang Kai-shek— from November 22–26, 1943, it was announced on December 1 that the war was to be pursued until Japan surrendered unconditionally. It was also declared that Japan was to be stripped of all possessions acquired since 1895. Specifically Manchuria, Formosa, and the Pescadores were to be restored to China, and Korea was to be granted independence. At the Cairo Conference, moreover, China itself—represented by Chiang Kai-shek—was for the first time accorded great power status.[22]

22. The point that the Allies supported the emergence of a strong and sovereign China had already been driven home in January, 1943, when the United States and Britain had both concluded treaties with China which called for an immediate end to extraterritoriality and provided for the return of the legation quarter in Peking as well as the international settlements in Shanghai and Amoy to Chinese control. The United States also agreed not to station troops or gunboats in China, and inland trade and navigation rights were relinquished. On December 17, 1943, the United States laws prohibiting Chinese immigration were amended to permit a small annual quota of Chinese immigrants to enter the United States.

Western determination not to negotiate was also emphasized in other ways. With the slogan "Remember Pearl Harbor," the memory of what was regarded as the treachery attending the outbreak of the war was kept alive. What was viewed as Japanese callousness toward human life also strengthened Allied determination to efface the threat that had arisen to Western rule. The decision to give primacy in the war to the defeat of Germany was deeply resented by many American military men in the Pacific, who in the meantime faced long months and years of bitter and dangerous struggle with insufficient resources. Since this faction saw the war with Japan in which they were engaged as primary, and viewed American involvement in the European theater as something akin to a betrayal of the national interest, they regarded the concept of negotiations with Japan as virtually treasonable. Beyond all other considerations, however, was the fact that the sudden and surprising Japanese onslaught had injured the pride, self-esteem, and self-image of the whites, so that there arose a determination to repair these injuries. Whereas the Japanese might regard themselves as white, to many Western whites the Japanese, being different, were considered "yellow," and for this reason alone had to be "put back in their place" in the color hierarchy. This could only be done by inflicting a resounding military defeat upon the Japanese.

Unlike those of Japan, the military problems of the Western Allies were immediate rather than long-term. The Allies had first of all to halt the Japanese advance, and obtain time to mobilize their resources. Once this was done the war could proceed to its appointed conclusion. Until May, 1942, however, the Japanese advance continued. But in that month the Japanese, instead of moving west across the Indian Ocean to effect an eventual junction with their German allies, moved south to attempt to cut off Australia. On May 7 and 8, 1942—that is, beginning the very day after the American forces in the Philippines had surrendered at Corregidor—the Japanese were engaged by American naval and air forces in the Coral Sea, about 500 miles from the northeast coast of Australia. The immediate Japanese aim was to send a task force round the southeast tip of New Guinea to capture Port Moresby. After a sharp conflict in which the Americans suffered the heavier losses, the Japanese decided to retreat. American power had, albeit with difficulty, blocked what had for a time promised to become an open road to Australia.

The following month a powerful Japanese force moved eastward across the Pacific bound for Midway Island, which protected the approach to Hawaii. Had the Japanese captured Midway, Pearl Harbor might have been rendered untenable as a base, after which the west coast of the United States would have been open to the threat of air attack. Small wonder that some Japanese even spoke of eventually reaching Washington. More practically, success at Midway would have greatly enhanced Japan's chances of victory in the Southeast Pacific. But Japanese hopes were dashed. The attacking force was intercepted by American aircraft carriers, from whose decks planes launched a three-day battle. The American air crews suffered cruel losses; thirty-five out of forty-one torpedo bombers which flew in for the first attack were shot down. But Japanese losses were to prove more grievous, for American dive bombers arrived, eventually sinking all the four aircraft carriers sailing with the Japanese armada, as well as damaging several battleships and cruisers. For their part the Americans suffered the loss of one aircraft carrier. The conflict ended with the Japanese force fleeing homeward.[23]

After the battle of Midway, which took place on June 4, 1942, and was one of the most decisive of the war, the Americans regained the initiative, moving from defense to attack. The American strategy was to take the form of a long-sustained and hard-fought struggle to move toward Japan, wresting, at heavy cost, island after island from Japanese control. The process was hastened by the American tactic of "leapfrogging"—moving, in amphibious operations, to outflank heavily defended Japanese positions, which had then to be abandoned. The long road which was to end in Tokyo began at Guadalcanal and other islands of the Solomons group, which lay athwart the communication line between the United States and Australia. Here the Americans landed Marines on August 7, 1942, opening a bitterly contested campaign into which naval and air forces were thrown by both sides. After the outcome had hung in the balance, the fighting turned in favor of the Americans in November, 1942, and on February 9, 1943, the Japanese evacuated Guadalcanal.

Meanwhile, bitter fighting had also been taking place in the forests and mountain ranges of New Guinea, where American and Australian forces, based on Port Moresby, succeeded in occupying the Papuan peninsula up to the Huon Gulf by the end of January, 1943. Slowly and painfully the Allies were advancing. Most of the ships sunk at Pearl Harbor had also been raised and refitted. The American forces in the Pacific were building up their strength.

The first half of 1943, nevertheless, marked a lull in the Pacific war, with the principle activity consisting of the American recapture from the Japanese of the Aleutian Islands in the North Pacific. By mid-1943, however, the Allies were ready to take the first steps in executing their Pacific strategy, which was to advance along the land bridge which stretched from New Guinea to the Philippines. First, however, it was

23. Isoroku Yamamoto, the Japanese Commander-in-Chief, retired to his cabin on the homeward voyage, and did not emerge until port was reached. The U.S. victory was due in part to the fact that before the battle began the Americans had deciphered the codes being used by the Japanese, and were thus able to make the necessary disposition of their forces.

necessary to neutralize the threat posed to the northern flank of this "bridge" by the Japanese occupation of New Britain and the remaining Solomons, as well as of the Gilbert, Marshall, and Caroline islands. In the phase that now opened, these aims were slowly and systematically to be achieved. On occasion—as in the advance along the New Guinea coastline—the "leapfrogging" technique proved successful. In other circumstances, however, as at Tarawa in the Gilbert group, American forces waged costly battles to win territory from the Japanese who, strongly entrenched, fought to the death.

Meanwhile, in the Asian mainland, the Japanese hold on Burma was weakening. The Allied campaign to recapture the country began in December, 1943, when U.S. General Joseph Stilwell entered the northern region with two Chinese divisions. The following month, January, 1944, the British, entering Burma from India, began to advance down the Arakan coast. In February a Japanese counterattack failed, and the British General Orde Wingate (who had already distinguished himself in Ethiopia) flew in behind the Japanese lines and began to operate with guerrilla forces known as Chindits. Although Wingate himself was killed in an air crash in March, 1944, the Chindits, arriving by glider, were able to help Stilwell and his forces by cutting the Japanese communication lines. The Japanese, however, occupied themselves by mounting an attack upon India itself, opening their offensive in March. The attack was halted in April, at Kohima, on Indian soil. In June, 1944, 60,000 British and Indian soldiers who had been encircled on the Imphal Plain were relieved after Chiang Kai-shek had sent troops from China to threaten the Japanese flank. The Japanese advance in the West had reached its high watermark. The Allied campaign in Burma was now to gather momentum. Despite the fact that the Chinese troops were recalled from Burma to counter a new Japanese offensive in China, by January, 1945 the Allies had advanced far enough to reopen the old Burma Road to China, closed since 1942. In March, 1945, the Allies defeated the Japanese at the battles of Mciktila and Mandalay. On May 2, 1945, the Burma campaign culminated in the recapture of Rangoon, which fell to an Allied amphibious assault before other Allied forces, advancing from the north, could arrive.

In the Pacific, meanwhile, American forces were moving closer to Japan itself. On June 15, 1944, the Americans landed at Saipan in the Marianas, thus embarking upon the conquest of a chain of island stepping stones leading directly to the Japanese homeland. Thus menaced, the Japanese attempted to regain the initiative by launching a major air attack from their carriers against the American fleet. In the Battle of the Philippine Sea, which opened on June 19, 1944, over 345 Japanese planes were shot down, with the loss of only 17 American aircraft. After this reverse the Americans were able to secure possession of the major islands of the Mariana group—Saipan, Tinian, and Guam. From airfields in the Marianas the Americans were then soon in a position to begin bombing southern Japan.

The Americans were now able to turn their attention to the Philippines, where they landed on the island of Leyte on October 20, 1944. General MacArthur, disembarking with President Osmena of the Philippines, by declaring "People of the Philippines, I have returned!" was able to fulfill a vow that he had earlier made. The Japanese response to the American landings, however, developed into the greatest naval battle in history—in reality three separate engagements—known as the Battle of Leyte Gulf, which took place on October 25, 1944. This massive engagement, in which the entire Japanese fleet was involved, ended in an American victory. By the end of the year two of the Philippine islands —Leyte and Samar—were in American hands. Bitterly contested, the American advance in the Philippines continued in 1945. Landings on Luzon took place on January 9, while the city of Manila, a scene of destruction, was recaptured by the Americans and Filipinos on March 4. Other islands, including Panay, Palawan, and Mindanao, also fell before the Japanese surrender.

Elsewhere in the Pacific, American amphibious forces at heavy cost captured another island—Iwo Jima, where Japanese resistance ended on March 14. An even heavier struggle was to be waged on Okinawa, the first island to be assaulted forming a part of the Japanese homeland. After American troops had landed there on April 1, 1945, heavy fighting raged until June, with the Japanese resisting with a stubborn defiance that resulted in the loss of over 12,000 American lives. Moreover Japanese pilots, with heroic bravery, employed *kamikaze* tactics. The name *kamikaze* (Divine Wind) was chosen in allusion to the wind that had supposedly been sent in 1281 A.D. by the sun goddess Amaterasu to blow away the ships of Kublai Khan that had then been on their way to invade Japan. The Kamikaze Corps of pilots were trained to crash their planes, filled with high explosive, into the Allied naval vessels—which they did at the cost of their own lives but with deadly effect. Thirty-two American vessels were sunk and others heavily damaged. Okinawa was nevertheless taken.

The growing toll of defeats suffered by the Japanese inevitably produced internal consequences. Following the fall of Saipan on July 7, 1944, the Tojo government resigned, and was replaced by that of General Koiso. Food, clothing, and other necessities became increasingly scarce. There was difficulty in obtaining fuel for aircraft. As steel became scarce, ships were built of wood instead. Moreover, Tokyo and other Japanese cities soon came under heavy air attack. On the night of March 9, 1945, U.S. planes from the Marianas attacked Tokyo with 2,000 tons of incendiary bombs. Flying in low they started fires which, whipped by a strong wind, created such a conflagration that in a single night over 100,000 Japanese died, and over 250,000 buildings were destroyed. Pearl Harbor was being avenged. On April 5, 1945, the Koiso Cabinet, in its turn, resigned, being replaced by that of Admiral Suzuki. Japan's fortunes nevertheless inevitably continued to decline. On the very day of Koiso's resignation the Soviet government gave one year's notice that the Neutrality Pact which it had signed with Japan would not be renewed. Even as the Japanese tried to come to terms with Moscow in return for further guarantees of Soviet neutrality, Japan's ally Germany surrendered on May 7. As Japanese cities were being turned into shambles by aerial bombardment, and Allied forces in Europe were diverted to the Pacific, it became increasingly clear to the Japanese leaders that the war was now lost. In accepting defeat, however, many members of the military faction who had advocated the war also personally faced the prospect of death, either at their own hands or at those of the Allies. At an imperial conference held on June 8, 1945, it was determined that Japan would fight to the end. Whatever was said in public, nevertheless, many influential Japanese were coming to feel that the war must be ended as soon as possible. Even in late 1944 Swedish representatives had been tentatively sounded out on the possibilities of mediation. Now, on July 13, 1945, the Japanese government officially requested the Soviet Union to mediate with the Allies. The Soviets were evasive, however, replying that nothing could be done until after the imminent Potsdam Conference.

## Potsdam

The political leaders of the United States, the Soviet Union, the United Kingdom, and the Republic of China met at Potsdam, Berlin, in July. Stalin represented the Soviet Union, Churchill the United Kingdom, and Chiang Kai-shek China, but the United States was now represented by President Harry S. Truman, the successor to Roosevelt, who had died on April 12, 1945. Even as the leaders were meeting, however, news of events bore in upon them, affecting the basis of their deliberations. Churchill and Stalin were informed by the Americans that a new weapon —the atomic bomb, immeasurably greater in destructive power than all previous weapons of war—had been successfully exploded in the New Mexican desert. Before the event the British, on July 4, 1945, had already assented in principle to the use of the new weapon should it prove successful. The final decision concerning its use therefore now lay with President Truman. The conference at Potsdam, at this juncture, was interrupted by the British general election in which, somewhat unexpectedly for many, Churchill was defeated, being replaced as Prime Minister by the British opposition leader Clement Attlee. On July 26, 1945—the day of Churchill's resignation—the United States, the United Kingdom, and China, the three conferring powers who were at war with Japan, published an ultimatum to Tokyo which concluded as follows:

We call upon the Government of Japan to proclaim now the unconditional surrender of all the Japanese armed forces, and to provide proper and adequate assurances of their good faith in such action. The alternative for Japan is complete and utter destruction.

The Japanese were not warned in any way of the new form of destruction with which they were threatened. The terms of the ultimatum were received by radio by the Japanese, and a censored version of them was published in the Japanese press.[24] The ultimatum made no reference, however, to the Japanese Emperor, as the U.S. Secretary of State, Cordell Hull, an ardent republican, had strongly urged that no assurances on the future of the monarchy should be given. It has since been argued that if any such assurance had been included, the ultimatum would then have been accepted. It would not then have been necessary for the Allies to use the atom bomb, or to accept Soviet support in the war in return for territorial concessions. It was upon this point that peace now turned, for the supporters of the Emperor, as distinct from the military faction, feared that without such an assurance the way would be cleared for the accession to power of a Communist or pro-Communist regime in Japan. Premier Suzuki therefore announced that he would "ignore" the ultimatum. The Allies, meanwhile, made ready to unleash "complete and utter destruction" upon the Japanese, in preparation for which two atomic bombs were delivered to an American air base at Saipan in the Mariana Islands.

At 8:15 A.M., on August 6, 1945, the first atomic bomb was dropped from a lone B-52 bomber, the *Enola Gay*, over the city of Hiroshima, where the Second Japanese Army was then based. Over 60,000 Japanese, both soldiers as well as civilians of all kinds, were killed, and many more contaminated in various degrees with radiation. Hardly had Japan and other nations begun to grasp the new reality of the atomic age to which the war had given such an awe-inspiring birth, than a second atomic explosion took place. On August 9, 1945, another U.S. plane, the *Bock's*

24. Some of the more acceptable clauses were deleted in the censored version, presumably so as not to weaken the martial determination of the Japanese nation before the government had itself reached a decision.

*Car*, failing to obtain a clear sight of its primary target in the city of Kokura on the island of Kyushu, flew instead to Nagasaki, over which it exploded the second atomic bomb, killing 36,000 more Japanese. A few hours earlier the Soviet Union, in accordance with its Yalta pledge to begin hostilities in Asia within two or three months of the conclusion of the war in Europe, declared war against Japan, sending troops through Manchuria into northern Korea.

On August 10, 1945, the Japanese government gave a qualified acceptance to the Potsdam Declaration—that is to say they accepted the Potsdam terms "with the understanding that the said Declaration does not comprise any demand which prejudices the prerogatives of His Majesty as a Sovereign Ruler." This was, in effect, the same guarantee that the Japanese had attempted to obtain from the Allies earlier, and in which no interest had been shown.

The following day, August 11, 1945, the U.S. Secretary of State replied that the authority of the Emperor and of the Japanese State should be subject to the Supreme Commander of the Allied Powers, General MacArthur, and that the Emperor would be required to authorize and to ensure the signature of the surrender terms necessary to carry out the provisions of the Potsdam Declaration.

On August 14, 1945, the Japanese government finally accepted the Potsdam Declaration, the Emperor, Hirohito, issuing an imperial rescript on the surrender.[25] The rescript informed the Emperor's subjects that since the Allies had "begun to employ a new and most cruel bomb" the acceptance of the Potsdam Declaration had been ordered. Regret was also expressed to "our allied nations of East Asia, who have consequently co-operated with the Empire toward the emancipation of East Asia."

The instrument of the surrender of Japan was then signed by the Allied and Japanese representatives on September 2, 1945, on board the U.S. battleship *Missouri* lying in Tokyo Bay. The Greater East Asia War was over. To defeat Japan the Western world had resorted to using the atomic bomb, a weapon so utterly destructive that it surpassed all previous engines of war in lethal capacity, making no distinction between adult and child, male or female, civilian or soldier—wiping out a city at a single stroke. Yet though seemingly representing the ultimate in weaponry, the nuclear bomb, while casting a pall of fear over the world, in the act of being used also revealed the limitations of physical power alone. Japan was defeated. But of all the territories that Japan had freed from European domination, such as Burma, Malaya, Indonesia, and the Philippines, only one, Indo-China, was much longer to remain subject to

25. The announcement by the Emperor was recorded on August 14, 1945, for broadcast to the public the following day. During the night of August 14–15, a group of army officers, opposed to surrender, attempted a coup d'etat, in which they strove to seize and destroy the recording. The attempt, however, failed, and the broadcast was consequently made on August 15, 1945.

the direct imposition on its soil of Western power by means of military force. Even in India itself—the keystone of the entire British Empire, which had been threatened but not conquered by Japan—imperial power was soon to come crashing down. Japan had lost the battle. But Asian nationalism had won the war. Even the atomic bomb could not change that.

# Chapter 16

# From Hiroshima to Bandung:

# The Decline of

# Western Domination in Asia

*Colonialism in all its manifestations is an evil which should speedily be brought to an end.* —From the final communique of the Asian African Conference held in Bandung (April 18–24, 1955)

**THE COLONIAL SYSTEM** by means of which Europe had been able to dominate Asia had been shattered by the Japanese during the Greater East Asia War. The damage, moreover, was irreparable. A transformation of relationships, no less than of institutions, consequently began as soon as the war ended, gathering a momentum that was not to be lost until not only Asia but also most of Africa had witnessed the ending of colonial rule.

Preparations for the "new world" that was to emerge from the ruins of war had been continuing ever since Churchill and Roosevelt had proclaimed the Atlantic Charter on the battleship U.S.S. *Augusta* on August 14, 1941, thereby pledging, in paragraph three of the Charter, to "respect the right of all peoples to choose the form of government under which they will live," as well as expressing their wish "to see sovereign rights and self-government restored to those who have been forcibly deprived of them." On January 1, 1942, representatives of twenty-six nations, meeting in Washington, subscribed to the purposes and principles of the Atlantic Charter. With respect to paragraph three, however, subsequent interpretations varied; some understood it to apply only to the European family of nations, and others understood its application to be universal. Despite this ambiguity, however, the acceptance of the principle that colonies might aspire to eventual independence gained ground. As an international civil servant was later to express it:

The view that the liberation of the colonies was an essential objective gained recognition throughout the war. In London, the American Ambassador Winant said it. The Queen of the Netherlands said it. Field Marshal Smuts said it. British and Americans combined at a Canadian Conference of the Institute of Pacific Relations to say it. Australia and New Zealand made a pact at Canberra to mark the ethical purpose of their domination of Pacific territories. Many of the statements were hedged with restrictions or escaped into vague generalizations. But the compulsion was growing to speak of colonial liberation as a war aim.[1]

Among dependent peoples, moreover, a climate of expectation was engendered by the widespread impression that, when reduced to its essence, the cause that the Allies defended was that of freedom, and that this Western ideal inherently guaranteed eventual self-government for dependent peoples. Few among Allied propagandists, at a time when the allegiance of Arabs, black Africans, and Asians was in question, would have gainsaid them, even if they had wished to do so. In effect the content of the word "freedom," to European minds, was associated with the restoration of independence to European countries which had been conquered by Nazi Germany. Beyond the boundaries of Europe itself, however, the identification of freedom with the Allied cause was largely due to the publicity given to the "Four Freedoms" of which President Franklin D. Roosevelt had spoken to the United States Congress in his State of the Union address on January 6, 1941. These freedoms, which Roosevelt proclaimed to be objectives for the people of the United States, and ultimately for the peoples of the world, were freedom of speech and expression, freedom of every person to worship God in his own way, freedom from want, and freedom from fear. Despite the fact that no mention was made of freedom from colonial rule, American opposition to "imperialism," especially with respect to India, was sufficiently well known to make many believe that such mention was only omitted by the President to avoid embarrassing Britain and its European allies at a time when they were fighting for their own independent existence. In private, Roosevelt did not hesitate to raise the question of freedom for subject peoples when Churchill visited Washington shortly after Pearl Harbor. As Lord Moran tells it:

The friendly atmosphere of the White House was sharply broken one day after Roosevelt had given his views on India's future. There was a violent explosion, and we had Mr. Churchill's own word that the President did not venture again to raise the subject when they met. But in his correspondence Roosevelt did not exercise the same self-denying ordinance.[2]

1. Wilfrid Benson, "The International Machinery for Colonial Liberation," from *New Fabian Colonial Essays* (1959), p. 224.
2. *Churchill: Taken from the Diaries of Lord Moran* (1966), p. 33.

Because of the potentially strong emotions that could be aroused, colonial questions were not specifically raised until a late stage in the discussions of the postwar international settlement. At Yalta the Americans, in the Woodrow Wilson tradition, had suggested establishing an international trusteeship system for all dependent territories. The concept had, however, been resolutely opposed by Churchill, who had forcefully told Roosevelt and Stalin, "I will not consent to a representative of the British Empire going to any conference where we will be placed in the dock and asked to defend ourselves. Never, never, never."

At the San Francisco Conference on International Organization a compromise was worked out and the United Nations Charter was drawn up. By this time United States defense interests concerned with the Pacific islands, won at heavy cost from the Japanese, had brought about a modification of the original American position—a modification which was, moreover, supported by the Soviet Union. Australia, which had a Labor administration, however, together with China and the Philippines, advocated the assumption of international responsibility for the advancement of colonial peoples, especially for those of the Pacific. As not enough support could be found for the Australian position, however, an agreement was finally reached which left it to each administering authority to decide whether the principle of international supervision should be accepted for any given territory. Thus, the powers administering former League of Nations mandates which had not yet become independent were given the opportunity to conclude Trusteeship Agreements with the United Nations concerning these territories. For other non-self-governing territories[3] the responsibility of the administering authorities was limited to informing the Secretary-General of the United Nations, under the provisions of Article 73(e) of the Charter, of the economic, social, and educational—but not political—conditions in the territories. A Declaration Regarding Non-Self-Governing Territories, contained in Chapter XI of the Charter, established three principles regarding the administration of the territories in question: first, that nations ruling other peoples are accountable to the world community for the "sacred trust" they have accepted; second, that their primary obligation is to promote the advancement of the inhabitants; and third, that the administration of the territories should contribute to the maintenance of world peace and security.

The Charter, which included arrangements for international peacekeeping under the U.N. Security Council, was duly agreed to by fifty-one nations, and came into force on October 24, 1945. Trusteeship agreements were then concluded with the United Nations by the various ad-

3. In drafting the Charter the administering powers opposed the use of the word "colonies." The ensuing terminological deadlock was broken when the Chinese delegation proposed, instead, the term "non-self-governing territories."

ministering powers. The United Kingdom thus assumed responsibility, in conjunction with the United Nations, for Tanganyika, British Togoland, and the British Cameroons; France for French Togoland and the French Cameroons; Belgium for the twin kingdoms of Ruanda and Urundi;[4] Italy for Somaliland; Australia for Nauru and New Guinea; and New Zealand for Western Samoa. The United States was later, in 1947, to assume similar responsibility for what was designated as the strategic trust territory of the Pacific Islands, consisting of the former Japanese-mandated islands of the Marshalls, Marianas (with the exception of Guam), and the Carolines. Only South Africa refused to sign an agreement for the mandate of South West Africa. In 1946 the South African representative informed the United Nations that as the League of Nations had ceased to exist,[5] and as the territory was sparsely populated and unable to support itself, and as a referendum had shown that the majority of its inhabitants desired incorporation with South Africa, South Africa proposed to annex the territory. The validity of the referendum was challenged by other U.N. member states, and the United Nations General Assembly consequently rejected the proposed annexation, recommending instead that South West Africa be placed under the international trusteeship system. This South Africa declined to do, with the result that a deadlock over the future of the territory ensued, with South Africa continuing, de facto, to administer it.

The composition of the United Nations itself, at the outset, was hardly an accurate reflection of the profound change that had occurred in the colonial world since the days of the League of Nations. Eleven African or Asian states—Afghanistan, China, Egypt, Ethiopia, India, Iraq, Japan, Liberia, Persia, Turkey, and South Africa[6]—had been members of the League. Among the signatory members of the United Nations, however, the number of African or Asian states had only risen to thirteen, for, although Lebanon, the Philippines, Saudi Arabia, and Syria had joined, Japan had been defeated in the war and so was automatically excluded, and Afghanistan did not join until the following year. Thus in 1945, African and Asian representation in the United Nations was barely over a quarter of the total membership. Within a mere five years, however, African and Asian membership was to increase to one-third,[7] after which the following decade was to culminate in a far more dramatic increase.

4. The territories were jointly designated as "Ruanda-Urundi" during the period of their dependent status. After independence in 1962 they were named "Rwanda" and "Burundi."

5. The League of Nations, at its last session, held on April 18, 1946, decided that the League would cease to exist as from the following day.

6. "Persia" was to be designated as "Iran" after 1935. Evidently not all "African or Asian" states were necessarily anti-colonial. India, for example, in the days of the League, represented the British Raj, while South Africa, both in the days of the League and of the United Nations, has represented the white minority who control the state. Moreover Haiti, an anti-colonial state with a colored population, belongs to the "Latin-American" grouping.

7. By September, 1950, U.N. membership had risen to sixty states, of which twenty were situated in Africa or Asia.

Yet, while this transformation still lay in the future, the underlying circumstances which were to bring it about had already come into being.

## Independence for India

With the return of peace, the time had come to redeem wartime promises. One such promise had been the guarantee given to the nationalists by the United Kingdom to grant independence to India.

In effect, India had been dragged willy-nilly into the war. The Indian National Congress was opposed to Fascism abroad, but was more naturally concerned with eliminating British imperial rule at home. It had protested when, in the summer of 1939, the British had dispatched Indian troops to the Middle East. When, on September 3, 1939, the war had begun, the Viceroy, without consulting any Indian representative body, had declared that India too was at war. As Jawaharlal Nehru later commented, "One man, and he a foreigner and a representative of a hated system, could plunge 400 millions of human beings into war, without the slightest reference to them."[8] On September 4, 1939, the Congress Working Committee issued a statement condemning Fascism and Nazism, and offering to co-operate with the British—providing that co-operation was not obtained by compulsion, but was a co-operation established "between equals by mutual consent." "India," the statement said in part, "cannot associate herself in a war said to be for democratic freedom when that very freedom is denied to her, and such limited freedom as she possesses, taken away from her."

Congress was opposed, however, by the Muslim League, led by Mohammed Ali Jinnah. Congress claimed to represent Muslims as well as Hindus, but the great majority of India's Muslims supported the League, which stood for the establishment of an autonomous Muslim state in those areas in which the Muslim population was predominant. Unlike Congress the Muslim League supported the British war effort, and encouraged Muslims to join the armed forces. In consequence, although Hindus outnumbered Muslims by almost three to one in the country as a whole, 65 percent of the Indian Army troops who fought in the Second World War in Africa and Asia and in the Italian campaign in Europe, were Muslims.

Gandhi, meanwhile, who opposed war as he opposed all forms of violence, found himself in disagreement with Congress, which was proposing to co-operate with the British in the war in return for India's freedom. Gandhi himself, technically, had resigned from Congress in 1934, but his moral authority over Congress in most matters remained unchallenged. Members of Congress therefore found themselves in a

8. *The Discovery of India* (1946), p. 432.

painful dilemma when they felt themselves obliged to diverge from his leadership, as they did in this instance. Although deprived of his support, no less than that of the Muslim League, Congress nevertheless entered into a contest of will with the British government in which the British strove to elicit Indian co-operation in the war on their own terms, whereas the Indian Congress held out for a commitment to independence. In the course of this contest Congress members resigned from the provincial governments, obliging the British to rule directly, as in the nineteenth century. As the danger of disturbances consequently grew, the British, under the Defence of India Act, adopted as a war measure, intensified repression so that numbers of nationalist leaders, often as a result of conscious choice taken in the spirit of *satyagraha*, found themselves imprisoned. The fall of France, in 1940, increased the pressure upon the British government, and Congress took the opportunity to offer the British complete co-operation in return for a declaration of Indian independence after the war, coupled with the immediate formation of a national government. The British did not, however, respond favorably. In consequence Gandhi and Congress were able to join forces once more to launch, in 1940 and 1941, a symbolic civil disobedience campaign in the course of which many nationalists were imprisoned.

The entry of Japan into the war in December, 1941, transformed the situation once more. Nehru and other Congress leaders felt that, with Japanese invaders at the gates of India, to advocate a policy of nonviolence was entirely impractical. Gandhi, however, continued to advocate nonviolence—even at the price of submission to Japanese rule. Britain, which had remained impervious to the situation in India so long as war was raging in the European theater, felt obliged to review its position once Japan was in the war.

It was not, however, solely the success of Japanese arms that led the British to this difficult conclusion. As we have seen, President Roosevelt was showing interest in India's independence, and Chiang Kai-shek, during a good-will visit to India in February, 1942, had called for the transfer of "real political power" to the Indian people, so that they might resist the Japanese. The fall of Rangoon to the Japanese on March 8, 1942, brought matters to a head. On March 10, Roosevelt suggested to Churchill that a temporary Dominion government be established in India along the lines of the American Articles of Confederation. Despite Churchill's disgust at the suggestion (after all it was only a year earlier, in the summer of 1941, that he had declared, "I have not become His Majesty's first minister to preside over the liquidation of the British Empire"), the logic of events no less than the persuasion of his ally drove him to act. On March 11, 1942 he announced that he was sending a

Cabinet mission, headed by Sir Stafford Cripps, to India to make proposals for a settlement.

The negotiations between Cripps and the various Indian groups—which included not only Congress and the Muslim League, but also the Hindu Mahasabha,[9] the Sikhs, the Untouchables, the princes, and other minority groups—opened on March 25, and broke down eighteen days later. The "Cripps Offer," upon which the negotiations were based, proposed full Dominion status for India after the war with the right of secession from the Commonwealth. A constituent assembly would be established immediately after the war was over, with delegates from British India being elected by the lower houses of the provincial legislatures, and delegates from the princely states being appointed by the princes. The British then undertook to accept the resulting constitution, provided only that any province would be accorded the right not to accede to the new Dominion if it so wished. So long as the war lasted, however, no constitutional change would occur, but the formation of an all-party national government would be encouraged, with the British retaining control of defense.

Negotiations were for the most part with Congress. Congress objected that the right of any province not to accede in effect granted the Muslim League what it sought, and could also lead to the fragmentation of the entire Indian grouping. Objection was also made to the inclusion of "non-representative elements," such as the princes' delegates, participating in the constitution-making process. The Muslim League, for its part, and for entirely different reasons, also declared itself dissatisfied, and asked for further clarifications. It appeared, nevertheless, that the various parties were on the brink of agreement when a stiffening of positions occurred that led to the collapse of the talks. After Churchill had remonstrated with Cripps for going too far, and Gandhi had recommended that Congress reject the Cripps offer, there was no more to be said. Cripps returned to London. Congress, seized by a mood of bitterness, mulled over the next step to be taken, with individual members suggesting surrender to the Japanese as a possibility. In April, Congress adopted a resolution, inspired by Gandhi, advocating nonviolent resistance to the Japanese. Indian emotions were, however, rising fast and sought expression.

### "Quit India"

Sensing the mood of the moment, Gandhi challenged the British *Raj* with a new slogan—"Quit India!" The British, he suggested, should leave India at once so that a free India could—whether violently or nonviolently —mobilize its strength to resist the Japanese advance. The slogan imme-

9. A militantly conservative Hindu organization.

diately struck the imagination of large masses of the population. The next step, clearly, could be the launching of a mass civil disobedience campaign—a campaign, moreover, that would bring the British *Raj* crashing down as the Japanese advanced. Fierce discussions broke out between individual members of Congress before, on August 8, 1942, Congress adopted a "Quit India" resolution which resolved "to sanction . . . the starting of a mass struggle on non-violent lines on the widest possible scale." The struggle, it was specified, would "inevitably" be under the leadership of Gandhi. The resolution spurred the British to counteraction. On August 9, 1942, Gandhi was arrested and imprisoned in the Aga Khan's palace in Poona, while all twelve members of the Congress Working Committee, including Nehru, were arrested and imprisoned in Ahmadnagar Fort in Bombay Province. These imprisonments were to continue until June 15, 1945.

The arrests sent a wave of anger through India which resulted in the most serious uprising against British rule since the days of the Indian Mutiny in 1857. The August Revolt, as it became known, was harshly repressed by the British within a few weeks. Demonstrations and strikes led to rising tensions, with the police firing many times upon crowds of demonstrators. Police stations were then attacked, trains derailed, and telephone lines cut. Hundreds were killed in the course of these disturbances. Congress was outlawed and about 100,000 nationalists imprisoned. The time for compromise was past. The British and the nationalists alike could no longer reach accommodation, but faced each other in stark confrontation. "Do or Die" ["Karo ya Maro"] had been the *mantra*[10] that Gandhi had given to the nationalists the day before his arrest, asking that "every non-violent soldier of freedom" write the slogan on paper or cloth and fix it to his clothing so that, in case of his death, his attachment to nonviolence should be known. "We shall either free India or die in the attempt," he had told them. "We shall not see the perpetuation of our slavery."

Throughout history there is no comparable example of a nationalist such as Gandhi leading a great country toward its freedom in such an unusual spirit of nonviolent sacrifice. The confrontation was all the more poignant in view of the striking contrast between the two leaders—Churchill and Gandhi—whose wills were in conflict. Churchill, essentially, was a man of the eighteenth century, the time of imperial expansion. Like the Europeans of the eighteenth century, too, he possessed a romantic nature, in which poetry and moral courage on the one hand were combined with fleshly indulgence on the other. He was dedicated to the greatness of the British Empire. Gandhi, for his part, belonged to no era. Small, bent, and often weak from fasting, his ascetic nature had

10. A saying to be recited or sung.

severed any attachment that would have bound him to one age rather than to another, were it not to the eternal age of poverty, which has retained its characteristics beyond time. Spiritual simplicity and social concern, together with a sharp tactical sense, had combined to make him the revered leader of millions. In one thing, however, he resembled Churchill. His will was indomitable. In June, 1945, when the Nazis had been at last defeated, Churchill resigned to permit elections to be held in Britain. Gandhi's tenacity, after more than a thousand days of imprisonment, had at last begun to yield results.

Much had happened during those thousand days. The war with Japan had disrupted the food distribution system, and in 1943 and 1944 famine—"ghastly, staggering, horrible beyond words"[11]—came to Bengal and eastern and southern India. It was the worst famine in 170 years of British rule. According to the official estimate—and it was undeniably conservative—one and a half million people died, and four and a half million more suffered greatly.[12] The British *Raj* had proved incapable of averting the disaster, and this circumstance generated even stronger pressures for change than those that already existed. Meanwhile, when the war had ended in Europe, British attention was turned to the conflict with Japan, and thus to India, which was to be the main base of British operations. At this juncture Churchill, his long struggle with Hitler ended, resigned. In the last resort Churchill had been concerned with the course of events in Europe, and had remained fundamentally disinterested if not ignorant[13] about conditions elsewhere. The great barrier to the official recognition of the new situation that had come into being in India during the war was thus removed. Change was now to come rapidly. On June 14, 1945, new constitutional proposals for India were announced by the British government, and on the following day Nehru and other nationalist leaders were released from prison. Gandhi himself, for health reasons, had been released the previous year —on May 6, 1944.

To discuss the new consitutional proposals, over twenty nationalist leaders, including Gandhi and Jinnah, met in conference at Simla on June 25, 1945, at the invitation of the Viceroy. Conflict developed, however, between the Muslim League, which claimed the right to appoint all Muslims on the Viceroy's Executive Council, and the Indian National Congress, which claimed ultimate authority as the main national organi-

11. Jawaharlal Nehru, *The Discovery of India* (1946), p. 4.
12. The Department of Anthropology of Calcutta University estimated that in Bengal alone about 3,400,000 deaths resulted from famine.
13. Testimony to Churchill's Eurocentrism is to be found in Lord Moran's diaries. On July 5, 1953, Moran reported Churchill as stating "Korea does not really matter. . . . I'd never heard of the bloody place till I was seventy-four. . . . It's Germany, not Korea, that matters." And again, at a later date: "I'd never heard of this bloody place Guatemala until I was in my seventy-ninth year." *Churchill: Taken from the Diaries of Lord Moran* (1966), p. 451 and p. 603.

zation. After the Viceroy had failed to reconcile the two views, the conference ended in deadlock on July 14, 1945.

On July 26 the British Labour government took office. In August the Viceroy was called home to London for a review of the situation in India, after which it was announced that general elections would be held, both for the central and for the provincial legislatures. Provincial autonomy was to be restored after the elections, and a constituent assembly would be convened. The Viceroy's Executive Council was also to be reconstituted.

The elections themselves were held early in 1946. In eight of the eleven provinces Congress won large majorities. Jinnah and the Muslim League, however, had campaigned against Hindu domination and in favor of a separate Muslim state—Pakistan. Muslim voters in both the central and provincial elections rallied overwhelmingly to the League, thereby belying the claim of Congress to speak for the entire nation. Almost all the seats reserved for Muslims were won by the Muslim League. The conflict, formerly between British imperialism and Indian nationalism, had now, with the emergence of Muslim separatism, become a three-cornered struggle.

Meanwhile, popular discontent with continuing foreign rule had found a focus in the trial by the British-Indian government of members of the former Japanese-sponsored Indian National Army (I.N.A.). The I.N.A., under the leadership of the late Subhas Bose (who had died in August, 1945), had in 1943 found its recruits in Indian prisoner-of-war camps. After Bose had formed a Provisional Government of Free India, in the name of which he had declared war on the United Kingdom and the United States in October, 1943, the strength of the I.N.A. had risen to 20,000. However, after it had suffered defeat at the battle of Imphal in April, 1944, it had virtually disintegrated. Yet when in November, 1945, leading members of the former I.N.A. were put on trial at the Red Fort in Delhi, Indian national pride was offended. Officials who had been unable to prevent hundreds of thousands if not millions of deaths in the famine of the previous year were, it was argued, as guilty of war crimes as any member of the I.N.A. Although Congress members had differed with the I.N.A.'s partisans, they had nevertheless respected them, and now proceeded to form an I.N.A. Defence Committee. Nehru commented: "Whatever their failing and mistakes . . . they are a fine body of young men . . . and their dominating motive was love for India's freedom." The I.N.A. leaders were convicted but, because of the weight of popular opinion in their favor, the sentences were suspended. As a result the accused became popular heroes, to the detriment of British prestige.

In the winter of 1945–1946, also, discontent in the Indian armed forces led to outbreaks of mutiny. Mutiny, in effect, was to prove the straw that broke the British camel's back. Mutiny first occurred at the Royal Air Force base at Dum Dum, near Calcutta, and then at other stations, both in India and in the Middle East. On February 18, 1946, a major mutiny broke out at the headquarters of the Royal Indian Navy in Bombay, from where it spread to other bases. Although the mutinies were to prove short-lived, their effects were incalculable. On February 19—the day after the Bombay outbreak had begun—the British government announced that a Cabinet mission was to be sent to India. On March 15, 1946, the British Prime Minister Clement Attlee gave further details concerning its utimate aims:

> India herself must choose what will be her future Constitution. I hope that the Indian people may elect to remain within the British Commonwealth. . . . But if she does so elect, it must be by her own free will. . . . If, on the other hand, she elects for independence, in our view she has a right to do so.

He added that, on the crucial issue of the relationship between the Muslims and Hindus, while minorities should be able to live free from fear, "we cannot allow a minority to place a veto on the advance of the majority." The main barrier to independence had now been removed. From now on discussions were to center not on "whether" but on "how" independence was to come.

On March 24, 1946, a British Cabinet mission, again headed by Sir Stafford Cripps, arrived in New Delhi. In the consultations that followed it was agreed by Muslim and Hindu alike that India would be a unitary state with the central government assuming responsibility for defense, foreign affairs, and communications. The country would, however, be divided into three administrative groups—Group A, comprising those areas in which the Hindus were in the majority; Group B, comprising areas in which the Muslims were in the majority; and Group C, consisting of Bengal and Assam in which the Muslims had a small majority. The agreement was, however, to prove brittle. Although the Congress Party had approved the plan, its presidency had passed from Azad to Nehru.[14] Nehru was then invited by the Viceroy, Lord Wavell, to form an interim government. On July 10, 1946, Nehru—who had previously voted for acceptance of the Cabinet Mission's plan—gave a press conference which effectively destroyed the limited degree of trust upon which the plan had been based.[15] He stated that Congress was "com-

---

14. A majority of Congress would have chosen Sardar Vallahbhai Patel, who according to the habitual principle of rotation would have obtained the presidency. Gandhi, however, persuaded Patel to step down in favor of Nehru—who, Gandhi apparently felt, could, with his British background, play an invaluable role at the time when power was to be transferred from British to Indian hands.

15. Brecher describes Nehru's press conference as "one of the most fiery and provocative statements in his forty years of public life." (Michael Brecher, *Nehru: A Political Biography*, 1959, p. 316.)

pletely unfettered by agreements and free to meet all situations as they arise." On the question of minorities he said that Congress would accept no interference, and certainly not that of the British. On the subject of Groupings A, B, and C he declared "This grouping business approached from any point of view does not get us on at all."

Nehru's press conference meant the end of the Cabinet Mission's plan, even though the plan continued in theoretical existence for a few months more. Whether or not the plan could in fact have succeeded became, after July 10, an academic question. On July 27, 1946, the Muslim League, at Jinnah's request, withdrew its acceptance of the plan. Congress, at Wavell's urging, adopted a resolution reiterating its support of the plan and deprecating Nehru's statement. But the damage was done. On previous occasions Jinnah had found that Congress pledges to him had not been honored, and this time, when so much was at stake, he saw no reason to fly in the face of past experience. Instead he asked members of the Muslim League to "bid goodbye to constitutional methods." August 16, 1946, was then proclaimed "Direct Action Day," in which Muslims would demonstrate their determination to partition India and achieve a separate Pakistan.

### The Calcutta Riots

With apparent encouragement from a Muslim League politician, Shaheed Suhrarwardy, Premier of Bengal, who was not averse to demonstrating his local power,[16] murderous rioting broke out in Calcutta—a city with a Muslim majority—on the morning of August 16, 1946. Violence was at first only the work of organized squads of terrorists known as goondas, but in the atmosphere of tension that had been created, it spread like contagion until it became general. The riots lasted from August 16 to 19, with an estimated 4,000 persons being killed, and thousands more wounded. The Calcutta *Statesman* of August 20, 1946 commented: "This is not a riot. It needs a word found in mediaeval history, a fury." Unfortunately, the senior British military official in the region was attending a conference in London, and in his absence the British Governor, Sir Frederick Burrows, allowed himself to be persuaded on the first day that the riots had subsided. Only when, on the second day, the Hindus began to retaliate against the Muslim population was the British Army at last called in to attempt to restore order.

The riots increased bitterness throughout the subcontinent. One of the first results was a quarrel that took place on August 27, 1946, between on the one hand the British Viceroy, Lord Wavell, who had just

16. On August 5, 1946, under the pen name of Shaheed, the Premier wrote an article containing the words "Bloodshed and disorder are not necessarily evil in themselves, if resorted to for a noble cause."

returned from Calcutta, and on the other hand Gandhi and Nehru. The rift between the two sides opened wide after the Viceroy informed the two Hindus that unless they accepted the Cabinet Mission plan, he would, since India was on the verge of civil war, rescind the decision to permit Congress to form an interim government.

In retaliation against this threat, Gandhi and Nehru immediately used their influence with the British Labour Party in London, many members of which were temperamentally more sympathetic to Indian nationalists than to Conservative Party appointees such as Wavell. But already informed by Wavell that he wished to delay the installation of the Interim Government, the British Prime Minister, Clement Attlee, refused to approve this recommendation. Instead he ordered Wavell to install the Interim Government forthwith, which was done on September 2, 1946. From this time onward Wavell's effectiveness as Viceroy was ended.

On September 7, 1946, Nehru, as Vice-President of the Viceroy's Executive Council, outlined the policy objectives of the nascent Indian government which, in the shadow of the British *Raj*, was coming into being. At home Congress would strive for communal harmony, the raising of living standards, and the removal of the stigma of Untouchability. Abroad his foreign policy would be based on nonalignment with the big powers; would support colonial emancipation; would oppose racism; and would seek to promote friendship with Britain and the Commonwealth, as well as with the United States and the Soviet Union, while seeking to establish friendly links with Asian countries, and especially with China and the countries of Southeast Asia.

Hindu-Muslim tensions, meanwhile, deepened. In the aftermath of the Calcutta riots, communal disturbances spread to other parts of Bengal, as well as to Bihar. Before long Gandhi was to proceed to the troubled areas on a mission of reconciliation. On October 15, 1946, the Interim Government was reconstituted with the participation of the five Muslim League representatives. This step, however, only signaled the opening of a new theater of conflict between Congress and the League. A conference was held in London in December, supposedly to clear the way for the Constituent Assembly which, as the British government had promised in 1945, was now to be convened. The Muslim League members, still determined to establish an independent Pakistan, refused to participate in it. Without them, and without the Indian princes, the Assembly nevertheless began its work on the formulation of a Constitution a few days after the London conference had ended in deadlock.

In January, 1947, the focus of the Indian crisis moved to the Punjab, where 16 million Muslims and 12 million non-Muslims coexisted. Each of the three principal communities—Muslim, Hindu, and Sikh—had created its own private army. When the Punjab government banned these armies, the Muslim League launched a civil disobedience campaign in protest. From this moment on the situation in the Punjab began to deteriorate.

On February 20, 1947, Prime Minister Attlee announced that Wavell would be replaced as Viceroy by Admiral Viscount Mountbatten. At the same time he also announced that power would be transferred to an Indian government by June, 1948. Now it was official. The British were to leave India. Even a target date had been set.

### Mountbatten's Arrival

Mountbatten arrived in India on March 22, 1947. Earlier in the month events in the Punjab had gone out of control, with ferocious riots and murders taking place not only in cities such as Lahore, Amritsar, and Rawalpindi, but in country areas as well. Nehru had from the beginning been inclined to underestimate the intensity of the desire of Muslims for a separate Pakistan. By now, however, many members of Congress were coming to feel that the partition of India was the only way to avoid a devastating civil war, and before long Nehru too showed signs of moving to accept this view. This change on his part may have been influenced by his visit to the Punjab, which led him to comment that he had "seen ghastly sights," and "heard of behaviour by human beings that would degrade brutes." Prominent among the Congress leaders who were beginning to consider partition was Sardar Patel, the party strong man who obtained the organization's contributions from Indian millionaire backers. Patel had been dismayed by the budget introduced by Liaquat Ali Khan, the Muslim League member responsible for finance in the Interim Government. The budget, which taxed the profits of the rich, was highly unpopular with the backers of Congress, and thus also exposed the contradictions in the claim of Congress to be a socialist party. If this was to be the kind of price to be paid for a unitary India, Patel felt, then it was too high. Already he had drafted a resolution, approved by the Congress Working Committee on March 8, 1947, which proposed partitioning the Punjab into two states, one Muslim and one Hindu, with the Sikhs being permitted to join whichever they chose. Once the principle of partition was admitted in the Punjab, it could clearly be given general application.

Within a few days of his arrival, the new Viceroy, who had already won fame for his decisiveness in the Burma campaign, had conferred with the principal Indian and Muslim leaders, had made up his mind what was to be done, and had begun, with subtle certainty, to move toward his goal. Like Patel he had privately decided that, with the threat of chaos quickly materializing, partition was the only possible answer to the growing Indian crisis. Mountbatten quickly succeeded in establishing an atmosphere of friendship and trust with Nehru. Gandhi, a proponent of a unitary India, when consulted by Mountbatten proposed that Jinnah should be called upon to form a government to rule India— with or without Hindu participation, and subject to a viceregal veto. Mountbatten promised to consider this plan if it were also approved by Congress. Privately he felt it unworkable, and it soon transpired that Congress thought so too. Gandhi, outmaneuvered for once, thereupon returned to his work of reconciliation, thus effectively removing himself as a serious obstacle to the achievement of partition.

Mountbatten, unlike his predecessor, enjoyed strong backing from London, not to speak of additional powers that he could exercise at his own discretion. Until now, however, a unitary India had been the pro-claimed aim of the British. In May, 1947, nevertheless, the British Cabinet approved a draft plan, drawn up by Mountbatten and his staff, under the terms of which not only would India be partitioned, but power would be handed over to a federal rather than to a central government. The plan had not, however, been seen, much less approved, by either the Muslim League or the Congress leaders. While the plan was being considered in London, Mountbatten, on vacation at Simla in India, showed it privately to Nehru. Nehru found it unacceptable. The neces-sary compromise was thereupon found by V. P. Menon, Reforms Com-missioner in the Indian government, whose views had not previously been taken into account by Mountbatten's staff because he was an Indian. Menon recommended that two central, rather than federal, governments be established, and that both of them—rather than merely Pakistan—be accorded Dominion status[17]—an arrangement that possessed the added virtue of ensuring co-operation by both Indians and British, and thus increased the chances of maintaining stability during the difficult period of transition to independence. Furthermore, in return for accepting Do-minion status, India would be granted its independence much earlier than June 1, 1948. After independence, moreover, both India[18] and Pakistan could abandon Dominion status and leave the Commonwealth at any time they chose.

The new draft plan, which was worked out at Simla, was taken to London by Mountbatten, and approved by the British Cabinet in place

17. Mountbatten had previously assumed, erroneously, that Dominion status would be un-acceptable to an independent India.

18. It was proposed to create two states, to be called "Hindustan" and "Pakistan." Congress, however, found "Hindustan" unacceptable, choosing to retain the name "India," thereby empha-sizing that independent India was the legitimate successor to the British *Raj*, rather than a new country. Thus India did not have to be admitted to the United Nations as it was already a founder member. Pakistan, however, as a newly created country, had to apply, and was admitted to the United Nations on September 30, 1947.

of the one previously submitted. From this moment on events moved forward pell-mell, as if of their own volition. As Mountbatten was later to observe, when he spoke in Karachi on the very eve of independence:

History seems sometimes to move with the infinite slowness of a glacier and sometimes to rush forward in a torrent. Just now, in this part of the world . . . we are carried onwards in the full flood. There is no time to look back. There is only time to look forward.

On June 2, 1947, Mountbatten met in conference at New Delhi with the Congress, the Muslim League, and Sikh leaders. The following day the leaders broadcast to their peoples that agreement had at last been reached. Nehru, in his speech, stressed that he had no doubt that the proposals represented the best course, although he commended them, he said, "with no joy in my heart." He added, with humility:

We are little men serving great causes, but because the cause is great some of that greatness falls upon us also.

On June 14, 1947, Mountbatten held a press conference at which he announced that the date of independence would be August 15, 1947—an item of news that allegedly startled even the British Prime Minister, who had not expected the date to be so soon.[19] History was now accelerating indeed.

Among the many problems which now had to be faced were two that demanded urgent attention—the question of the future of the princely states, and the question of the demarcation of boundaries between India and Pakistan.

The princely states, numbering about 600, varied in importance from Hyderabad, which had a population of 14 million, to several small states in Western India with a population of approximately 900 each. Altogether the land area of the princely states accounted for about two-fifths of the Indian subcontinent, and contained about 80 million inhabitants. Some of the veteran British officials, opposed as they were to the whole concept of a free India, would have preferred that the treaties which these states had independently concluded with Britain should lapse only on the day of Indian independence—a circumstance that would have created great confusion, and could have led to what Nehru called the "Balkanization" of India. Fears were expressed that, as V. P. Menon put it, "the ship of Indian freedom would founder on the rock of the States."[20] But Sardar Patel and V. P. Menon combined forces and secured the cooperation of the Viceroy to try to persuade the princes to adhere to either

19. It has been suggested that the Viceroy chose a date much earlier than anyone had expected in order to avoid the risk of another power moving into the vacuum.
20. *The Story of the Integration of the Indian States* (1956), p. 91.

Pakistan or India in advance of independence. This approach was largely successful, with considerable numbers of princes adhering to one or the other after Mountbatten, at a meeting with them on July 25, 1947, had persuaded them that by doing so at that time they could obtain the best conditions for themselves. They were also, however, swayed by other considerations—not the least of which was the knowledge that, should they not agree, Congress might be in a position to incite disaffection within their borders after independence came, at which moment they would have nowhere else to turn for support. A few princes, nevertheless, refused to sign. The Nizam of Hyderabad—the largest of the states—was one of these. Although Hyderabad itself became independent on the same day as India and Pakistan, Indian troops took over the state shortly thereafter, permitting the Nizam to remain in a titular position.

More serious was the refusal of the state of Jammu and Kashmir to the north of India—adjoining India, Pakistan, China (and Tibet), the Soviet Union, and Afghanistan—to align itself with either India or Pakistan. Even by the day of independence, the Maharajah, who was a Hindu ruling over a state which possessed a Muslim majority, had declined to accede to either side. In October, 1947, however, Pakistan claimed the state on the grounds first that it had a Muslim majority, and second that it had economic ties with Pakistan. On October 20, 1947, Pathan tribesmen from Pakistan entered the state in support of the Azad (Free) Kashmir movement. The Maharajah thereupon signed an instrument of accession to India, and called in Indian troops, whereupon fighting ensued. By January 1, 1949, however, a cease-fire, under United Nations supervision, had come into force, at which time Pakistan held the lesser and India the greater part of the territory. Although the United Nations called for a plebiscite to determine the State's future allegiance, India refused to withdraw from the territory that it occupied, with the result that no plebiscite was held.

Meanwhile, by the terms of the India Independence Act, which was introduced into the British House of Commons on July 4, 1947, and which received the royal assent on July 18, the British made constitutional provision for the transfer of power. Arrangements for demarcating the frontiers of India and Pakistan were also going forward under the jurisdiction of a Boundary Commissioner, Sir Cyril Radcliffe, a British lawyer who had no previous knowledge of India, and who was therefore held to possess the necessary objectivity for his difficult task. Within a few weeks he had completed his work, transmitting the results—which both India and Pakistan had agreed to accept—to the Viceroy on the eve of independence.

India and Pakistan duly became independent on August 15, 1947. The ceremonies, however, which among other things signaled the end of British rule that had lasted, in some places, since the eighteenth century, were haunted by the knowledge that the crisis was not yet over. On the following day, August 16, the Radcliffe Boundary Awards were published. For days communal violence had been growing as independence had approached, and now the publication of the Awards was the signal for a major upheaval, with resident populations attacking and murdering minorities who, as refugees, sought to flee east to India or west to Pakistan as the case might be.

It was in the Punjab that the greatest problem existed, for here partition necessarily involved a large-scale exchange of populations. Matters were made worse by the fact that the shrines of the non-Muslim Sikhs were located in the Western Punjab, where they were in a minority. The circumstance added to the frenzy that now broke out. Columns of refugees were attacked by one side or the other as they attempted to march toward safety. Refugee trains were stopped and attacked—eventually, in some instances, arriving at their destinations crammed with dead passengers. A special force that had been created to maintain order found that, because of its ethnic composition, its emotions were so involved that it could not function effectively. The riots spread to Delhi, where Nehru, distraught, courageously rushed in person into the riot areas to attempt, by his presence, to help restore order. Trouble had also been anticipated in Bengal, but here Gandhi, as Mountbatten afterwards said, achieved single-handed what 50,000 soldiers had been unable to do in the Punjab, and the peace was kept. In the Punjab and elsewhere, however, 600,000 were killed, and between 14 and 16 million persons driven from their homes as refugees. The price that was paid for independence saddened Hindu, Muslim, Sikh, and British leaders alike, and arguments long continued as to whether, or how, the tragedy might have been averted.

When all was over, nevertheless—and the troubles did not die down until the end of the year—the overwhelming fact remained that Indian and Pakistani independence had been gained at last. Other events, such as Gandhi's assassination by a Hindu extremist in January, 1948, and the Kashmir war of the same year, could not detract from the impression made by this fundamental reality, which signaled to the entire colonial world that the twentieth century could be one not only of promise but also of fulfillment. Hitler had said that England would not let India go "without staking her last drop of blood." Many others, too, had thought so. They had been demonstrably wrong. Further assumptions had now necessarily to be questioned. If Britain was not to keep India, then what was to be the fate of Britain's other possessions? What of the other colonial powers? What, in fact, was to be the fate of colonies everywhere? The world was evidently spinning in a new direction.

## Ceylon and Burma

With India freed, two other British-ruled countries, Ceylon and Burma, quickly followed her into independence.

Ceylon's transition to independence was remarkable for the fact that its progress was entirely constitutional, involving no open collisions between Ceylonese nationalism and the British colonial authorities. To some extent this was because the liberation movement—as Gunnar Myrdal has put it—"never really reached down, as it did in India . . . to touch the mass of the people." As we have seen, even before the Second World War Ceylon had attained a greater degree of representative government than virtually any other British colonial territory, with its entire Cabinet, from 1936 until 1942, being Sinhalese.[21] Further reforms had, moreover, been promised. In 1943 the British gave assurances that Ceylon would obtain internal self-government after the war, and in the same year the Ceylonese ministers, among whom D. S. Senanayake was prominent, drafted a constitution. This constitution was, with various amendments, approved by a British Royal Commission led by Lord Soulbury, which visited the island in 1944–1945. The new constitution came into force in 1946, giving the island internal self-government but reserving ultimate British control over defense and external relations. With a Labour government in power in London, and with India on the verge of independence, further advance was soon to follow. Under the Ceylon Independence Act of 1947, the remaining powers reserved to the British were transferred to the Ceylonese legislature, and Ceylon was accorded Dominion status. Under the terms of the Act it thus attained its independence on February 4, 1948. Mr. Senanayake, who had led the negotiations for Ceylonese independence, and who had taken particular pains to secure equitable representation for his country's minority groups, such as the Tamils, became the first Prime Minister.

In Burma, where, at the end of the war, Allied forces had driven out the Japanese with the help of the Burmese under Aung San, a different situation prevailed. Burma had declared its own independence on August 1, 1943, and the British, in 1945, were hardly in a position to consider attempting a reconquest of the country, even had they wished to do so. The principal political force in Burma at this time was Aung San's Anti-Fascist Peoples' Freedom League (A.F.P.F.L.). Aung San himself, as Minister of Defense, had been in contact with Lord Louis Mount-

---

21. The Sinhalese compose the majority of the Ceylonese population, with the Tamils constituting the largest minority.

batten during the Burma campaign, and had arranged for the Burmese to support the Allied war effort. After the war, however, the British Governor, Sir Reginald Dorman-Smith, returned to Burma, from which he had earlier been driven into "exile" in India by the Japanese advance. Dorman-Smith created a fourteen-member executive council of which two members were British, and five more were Burmese appointed by himself. When the A.F.P.F.L., which had overwhelming popular support, refused to accept this arrangement, the Governor excluded all A.F.P.F.L. members from the council. Disorders then began, and a widespread strike occurred in Rangoon. The Labour government in London became concerned at the turn that the situation had taken, and replaced Dorman-Smith as Governor with Sir Hubert Rance, a former member of Mountbatten's staff and a friend of Aung San. In October, 1946, Aung San and his associates were admitted to the executive council, which, from this time on, was dominated by the A.F.P.F.L., with Aung San acting as virtual Prime Minister.

The British pledged to grant independence to Burma after elections to a constituent assembly had been held, and a constitution drafted. The A.F.P.F.L. won the elections, and Aung San prepared to form a Union of Burma, to which end he secured the assent of the various hill tribes, with the exception of the Karens. On July 19, 1947, however, Aung San and several of his associates were murdered at a Cabinet meeting by a partisan of U Saw, the prewar prime minister of Burma, who had just been released from the internment in which he had been placed by the United States for attempting to contact the Japanese at the time of Pearl Harbor. Sir Hubert Rance then chose U Nu, Deputy Prime Minister of the A.F.P.F.L., to take Aung San's place as Burmese leader of the executive council. On October 17, 1947, a treaty was signed in London between the British and the Burmese, and was enacted by the British Parliament on December 10, 1947. Under the terms of the treaty the Union of Burma was to come into existence with a parliamentary constitution based on adult suffrage, and with separate constitutional provision made for the Shans, Kachins, Karens, and Chins. Burma then became independent on January 4, 1948,[22] choosing to remain outside the British Commonwealth.

Independence did not, however, spell the end of trouble for the new government. Various internal disturbances took place, of which the most serious was an uprising of the Karens. Matters were also complicated by the establishment within the borders of Burma of a Kuomintang division, under the command of General Li Mi, which had entered the country from the Yunnan province of China. Eventually, however, U Nu's

22. Independence was proclaimed at 4:20 A.M. for astrological reasons.

government was able to assert its authority. Burma was admitted to the United Nations on April 19, 1948, after which it followed a foreign policy of neutralism and nonalignment, resembling that pursued by India.

## Indonesia

As we saw earlier, the Japanese occupation of Indonesia had strengthened Indonesian nationalism, and on August 17, 1945, two days after the Japanese surrender, Indonesian independence had been unilaterally proclaimed. It was to be five years, however, before the country's independence was to become internationally recognized.

From the outset the situation was confused. At first the Japanese troops, who had instructions to remain where they were until they could hand over to the Allies, attempted to suppress the Indonesian revolution. Allied troops landed on September 29, 1945—the British in Java and Sumatra, and the Australians in East Indonesia—with instructions to prepare the way for the return of the Dutch. When British forces, including Indian contingents, fought the Indonesians at the battle of Surabaya on November 10, 1945, Indian nationalist leaders denounced the British for using Indian forces to suppress an Asian nationalist movement. Australia, too, which had a Labour government, showed itself sympathetic to the Indonesian cause. When it became evident that the other Allied troops would eventually have to withdraw, the Dutch used the intervening period to increase their forces.

On November 15, 1946, when the British were about to withdraw, the Dutch and the Indonesians initialed the Linggadjati Agreement, which was then signed on March 25, 1947. By the terms of this pact the Dutch recognized, de facto, the Republican government of Indonesia as controlling Java and Sumatra. The pact also called for co-operation between Indonesians and Dutch in establishing the United States of Indonesia, to be composed of East Indonesia, Borneo, and the Republic, and which was to come into being on January 1, 1949. The agreement was, however, interpreted differently by the two sides. The Dutch—who at this time had the support of the United States, which now no longer necessarily saw eye to eye with the Soviet Union on colonial questions—regarded themselves as in control of Indonesia until 1949, and therefore felt themselves free to establish further states. The breakdown of the agreement led to an ultimatum being issued by the Dutch, followed by a Dutch attack on the forces of the Republic, launched on July 20, 1947.

With the resumption of fighting a United Nations Good Offices Committee was formed, which offered its services to bring the two sides together. The Dutch, however, did not hasten to avail themselves of the proposed opportunity. The United Nations committee, nevertheless, persuaded the Dutch to accept the Renville Agreement, which was concluded on January 17, 1948, and by the terms of which the Dutch agreed to a cease-fire, while accepting the principle of free elections in states under their control. By the end of the year the Dutch had created a total of fiften states, each of which sent a delegate to a Dutch-sponsored federal consultative assembly. International concern about Indonesia was, however, growing. Neither side respected the Renville Agreement, and sporadic guerrilla warfare continued. For the Dutch matters were made more difficult by such actions as that of the government of newly independent Ceylon, which in 1949 refused to allow Ceylonese facilities to be used in the sending of more Dutch troops to Indonesia. For the Indonesian Republic, on the other hand, difficulties were increased by a Communist uprising which took place in Maidun on September 18, 1948.

On December 18, 1948, in a last attempt to settle matters by force, the Dutch launched a second major attack, supported by tanks, aircraft, and paratroops. Djakarta, the capital of the Republic, was seized by them, and the Republic's two leading figures, President Sukarno and Prime Minister Hatta, were captured. The Republic nevertheless continued to function, and to inflict military losses upon the Dutch. The United Nations called for a cease-fire, and for the release of the Republican leaders, but without result. On January 28, 1949, therefore, the Security Council called upon the Dutch to discontinue fighting, as well as upon the Indonesians to cease guerrilla warfare. The Dutch were to release the captured leaders and transfer sovereignty to the United States of Indonesia by July 1, 1950, after holding free elections to a constituent assembly which would then draft a constitution. As the Dutch military position was weakening, the Netherlands proposed that the Indonesian nationalists be invited to a Round Table Conference to be held at the Hague on March 12, 1949. But the nationalists refused to attend. By now, moreover, United States opinion had hardened against the Dutch, and the U.S. government came to view the accession of Indonesia to independence as inevitable. The U.S. Senate further threatened to cut off financial aid to the Netherlands, which had been extended under the Marshall Plan, unless the Dutch complied with the Security Council resolution. Under these combined pressures the Dutch released the nationalist leaders on condition that the guerrilla warfare end. A cease-fire was arranged for August 1, 1949, and the Round Table Conference then opened on August 15. At the conference the two sides agreed to the establishment of a federal government of the United States of Indonesia, with the Netherlands and Indonesia as two separate independent states being further united under the Dutch Crown.[23] Sukarno was then elected as President of the new federal government of Indonesia. Sovereignty was

23. The Netherlands-Indonesian Union, never a vital link, was dissolved on August 10, 1954.

transferred to Indonesia, which thus became independent on December 27, 1949.

Independence was not, however, the end of the story. Some Dutch refused to accept the fait accompli, and disturbances continued. A prominent part in them was played by a Dutch captain, R. P. P. Westerling, who obtained the co-operation of the Sultan of West Borneo, mobilized a number of troops from the Netherlands East Indies who had not yet been disbanded, and with them attacked Bandung on June 23, 1950. Similar disturbances occurred in the South Moluccas on April 25. The uprisings were suppressed, but under these strains the federal Republic of the United States of Indonesia disintegrated, with all but two of the participating states dissolving themselves, after opting for unitary rule. Negotiations with the two remaining states then led to the formation of a single unitary state, the Republic of Indonesia, which came into being on August 17, 1950, and which was then admitted to the United Nations on September 28, 1950.

Two further events affecting the Dutch relationship with Indonesia were, years later, to be settled in favor of Indonesia. First, certain provisions of the Round Table Agreements proved in practice to favor the Dutch rather than the Indonesian interest. As a result Indonesia unilaterally abrogated the Round Table Agreements on April 9, 1956. Second, Indonesia laid claim to Netherlands New Guinea (West Irian). No agreement was reached at the time of independence, however, and for years the question lingered, being raised repeatedly at the annual sessions of the United Nations General Assembly. Eventually, through the good offices of the United Nations, and as a result of pressures exerted by the United States, agreement was reached between the Netherlands and Indonesia on August 15, 1962, on the transfer of the territory to Indonesia. On May 1, 1963, therefore, the territory was transferred to Indonesia jurisdiction with the stipulation that a referendum was to be held in ten years' time to decide the territory's permanent status.

## The Cold War

Despite the progress of these various countries to independence, a vast new crisis was to gather over Asia as a result of the Soviet-American conflict that became generally known as the "Cold War."[24] Although the prolonged contest—which never resulted in a clash of arms involving Soviet and American troops—was soon to assume a pronounced ideological aspect, in its origin it stemmed, rather, from the strategic situation that ensued after the collapse of Germany had upset the balance of power in Europe.

24. The expression "The Cold War" became current after a book of that title by the American writer Walter Lippmann was published in 1947.

At the war's end the Soviet sphere of influence, extending roughly to the line to which the Soviet troops had advanced, included the whole of Eastern Europe. Western Europe, economically disorganized, physically devastated, and with two of its major countries—France and Italy—influenced by large pro-Soviet Communist parties, consequently lay virtually open to conquest. The imbalance of power was further aggravated by the fact that whereas Soviet armed forces after the war were kept at a strength of between five and six million men, American forces were reduced from a strength of some twelve million to just over half a million by 1948.

This radical reduction of American strength, carried out in response to electoral demand, took place before any postwar settlement had been concluded. The security of Western Europe, therefore, depended in the first place on the hope that relations with the Soviets would be amicable, and in the second place on the fact that, in the last resort, the United States possessed nuclear weapons.

The Soviet Union, however, like the Czarist state to which it was the successor, was a great continental power which had frequently suffered from attacks that had devastated its territory and decimated its population. As a result it was conditioned to suspect the motives of other great powers that might be in a position to attack it once more. Consequently it attempted to surround its borders with a defensive bulwark of small and compliant states. The expansion of Soviet influence in pursuit of this essentially defensive aim—an expansion which continued until 1948—was mistaken by the United States as the realization of the earlier stages of a conspiratorial plan for world revolution. Such developments as the unwillingness of the Soviet Union to withdraw its troops from Northern Iran in March, 1946[25] the occurrence of a Communist-led attempt to seize power in Greece in February and March, 1947,[26] the refusal of the Soviets and their Eastern European allies to co-operate in the European Recovery Program in July, 1947, the creation of the Cominform[27] on September 22, 1947, the failure of the Soviets and the Western powers to reach agreement over the future of Berlin in December, 1947, followed by the unsuccessful Soviet blockade of Berlin which lasted from June 1948, to May 1949—all increased the conviction of key elements

25. By the Anglo-Soviet-Iranian treaty of January 29, 1942, Soviet troops were due to withdraw from Northern Iran six months after the end of the war. The Soviets became involved with an Iranian separatist movement, and proved reluctant to withdraw, only doing so after the question had been taken up by the United Nations Security Council.

26. Stalin, in concert with Churchill, had agreed that Greece, after the war, would remain within the British sphere of influence. He kept his word. He opposed Yugoslav support of Communist guerrillas in Greece. Had the Communists prevailed in Greece, it would have been against Stalin's will.

27. The "Cominform" (Communist Information Bureau) was an organization designed to co-ordinate Communist policy in Europe outside the Soviet sphere. It was thus the successor to the Comintern ("Communist International"), which, founded by Lenin in 1919, had been dissolved—much to the relief of the Western powers—in 1943.

in the United States, as well as much of the American public at large, that a dangerous world conspiracy was ripening.

On the Soviet side, meanwhile, such American responses as the Truman Doctrine of March 12, 1947 (which, while specifically intended to assume economic and military responsibility in Greece and Turkey in place of the British, nevertheless proclaimed as a universal principle that "it must be the policy of the United States to support free peoples who are resisting attempted subjugation by armed minorities or by outside pressures"), and the Marshall Plan for European economic recovery, announced on June 5, 1947, were both seen as "the embodiment of an American design to enslave Europe."[28] In addition to such Soviet reactions was the knowledge that the United States possessed the atomic bomb, and that some American military men were advocating its use in a pre-emptive attack upon the Soviet Union.

Instead of recognizing and resolving the practical details of the conflict of interest which was dividing them in Europe, the two parties gave way to their fears. Stalin, for his part, "appears to have seen a likelihood of military attack by the United States,"[29] while President Truman, on the other hand, seems to have believed that such a world crisis had occurred that, as he put it, "at the present moment in world history nearly every nation must choose between alternative ways of life"[30]—namely Western democracy and revolutionary Communism. This mutual misreading of the opponents' aims, in which both parties attributed to the other not so much the desire as the practical intention to secure world domination, led first to the perpetuation of the division of Europe into two opposing camps, and, second, to the aggravation of a latent ideological quarrel to such a point that it would soon produce far-reaching, unsought, and undesirable consequences in Asia. Moreover, by the time the Soviet Union detonated its first atomic explosion in the summer of 1949—thus, as it were, adding fuel to the flames by communicating to Washington and other capitals the feeling of insecurity already experienced by Moscow—the Cold War had achieved a momentum of its own.

### The Civil War in China

In China, meanwhile, a civil war had developed between the Kuomintang, led by Chiang Kai-shek, and the Chinese Communists, who were under the leadership of Mao Tse-tung. The United States had, in the course of the struggle against Japan, become deeply involved in Chinese affairs, supporting the Chiang Kai-shek government. But, despite

28. A. A. Zhdanov of the U.S.S.R. at the Conference of Communist Parties held in Silesia, Poland, on September 22, 1947.
29. Louis J. Halle, *The Cold War as History* (1967), p. 147.
30. President Truman's "Message to Congress," March 12, 1947.

substantial American aid to the Kuomintang, the civil war was, nevertheless, eventually to be won, in 1949, by the Chinese Communist forces.

As we have seen, in 1943 the Western powers had abandoned their extraterritorial rights in China, together with other external vestiges of domination remaining from imperial days. At the Cairo Conference of December, 1943, moreover, China had also, for the first time, been accorded great-power status at the insistence of the United States. At Yalta in 1945, however, in return for an assurance that the Soviet Union would enter the war against Japan, the Soviets were granted the same position of influence in Northern China and Manchuria that had belonged to the Czarist state until its defeat by the Japanese in 1904–1905.[31] This restoration of influence was later accepted by the Kuomintang government in the terms of a Treaty of Friendship and Alliance between the Soviet Union and the Chinese Republic, signed on August 14, 1945, the day before the Japanese surrender.

However, once the Allies had entered the war against Japan in 1941, the Kuomintang had seen little reason to exert itself unduly against the Japanese—who, for their part, were militarily occupied elsewhere. Repeated American urgings to attack the Japanese had little effect upon the Chiang Kai-shek government. Indeed, at one moment in 1943 it appeared more likely that the Kuomintang troops would march west to subdue the Dalai Lama in Tibet, rather than east against the Japanese. As it proved, no energetic move was made in either direction. From 1941 to 1944 it became apparent that Chiang Kai-shek's policy was to avoid battle and, by frightening Washington with the prospect of an imminent collapse of Republican China, to induce the United States to provide large quantities of arms and money. The arms and money were, indeed, forthcoming, although as time progressed President Roosevelt became increasingly disillusioned with his Chinese ally—particularly after December, 1943, when Chiang demanded a $1,000,000,000 loan from the United States, thus, as the U.S. Department of the Army's official war history[32] expressed it, insisting on "making the Americans literally pay to fight in China."

Although the billion-dollar loan was not forthcoming, a substantial proportion of the not inconsiderable sums that were sent found their way into the bank accounts of a corrupt officialdom. The quantities of United States arms and ammunition that were, with difficulty, flown to Chiang's forces over a section of the eastern Himalayas (popularly known as "The Hump") were mostly stockpiled by the Kuomintang for later use against Chinese Communists and other domestic opponents—instead

31. See Chapter 15, p. 458.
32. Charles F. Romanus and Riley Sutherland, *The United States in World War Two, China-Burma-India Theater* (U.S. Department of the Army).

of being used against the Japanese. Kuomintang troops, meanwhile, in preparation for the civil conflict that it was felt would later occur, began to ring the territory held by the Chinese Communists in Northern China.

Churchill, at about this time, took the view that to consider China as one of the world's four great powers was "an absolute farce," and he would only promise that he would be reasonably polite about "this American obsession." "The latest information from inside China," he wrote on August 23, 1944, "points to the rise already of a rival Government to supplant Chiang Kai-shek, and now there is a Communist civil war impending there."[33]

During most of the war years the U.S. commander in the China-Burma-India (C.B.I.) war theater was General Joseph W. Stilwell, who also acted as Chiang Kai-shek's chief of staff. Relations between the two men became strained. United States air bases had been constructed in China from which bombing raids were launched against Japan. Stilwell had contended that these bases could only be defended if the Chinese Nationalist army was reorganized. His recommendations did not fall upon receptive ears, as in his subordinates Chiang valued personal loyalty to himself above competency. The result was that when the Japanese, in their first major action in China since the Allies had entered the war, launched large-scale ground attacks against the bases in April 1944, they defeated Chinese Nationalist troops who outnumbered them by far. In Honan province the local Chinese population, having suffered from Nationalist exploitation, even rose up to help the Japanese kill the Kuomintang forces. By September, 1944, the U.S. bases in Eastern China were lost to the Japanese, and this brought the dispute between Chiang and Stilwell to a head. On October 18, 1944, President Roosevelt agreed to Chiang's request that Stilwell be recalled. Writing later Stilwell was to comment:

> I judge Kuomintang and Kungchantang [Communist Party] by what I saw: Kuomintang: Corruption, neglect, chaos, economy, taxes, words and deeds. Hoarding, black market, trading with enemy.
> Communist programme . . . reduce taxes, rents, interest. Raise production and standard of living. Participate in government. Practice what they preach.[34]

After its entry into the war on August 8, 1945, the Soviet Union sent troops into Manchuria to take over from the Japanese. Throughout most of Northern China the Chinese Communist troops were already in control, while the Nationalist forces were mostly in the West. Manchuria—which the Soviet troops were by agreement to occupy for three months—remained, however, the key to the future, for reasons which, apart from

33. *The Second World War* (1953), p. 701.
34. *The Stilwell Papers*, edited by Theodore H. White (1948), pp. 315–322.

its strategic location, are clear from the following description of it by the American diplomat William C. Bullitt:

> Manchuria is the finest piece of territory in Asia. As large as France and Germany combined, containing in its valleys agricultural land as rich as any in the world, where wheat, corn, soya beans, and all our Northern crops grow superbly; holding great deposits of coal and iron, and even gold; having immense wealth in forests and in waterpower both developed and undeveloped; containing before the war 70 per cent of Chinese industry but populated by only forty million people and offering immense possibilities for further settlement of overcrowded Chinese farmers, Manchuria is vital for the future development of China.[35]

Between August, 1945, and March, 1946—the date at which Soviet troops were finally withdrawn (having in the meantime removed most of Manchuria's industrial plant equipment to the Soviet Union)—a race took place between Communist and Nationalist troops to take over control from surrendering Japanese troops and thereby acquire fresh stocks of arms. The preliminary symptoms of the Cold War were, at this time, beginning to appear, and here, as elsewhere, American and Soviet aims differed, with the Soviets seeking to hand over control in Manchuria to the Chinese Communists, and the United States seeking to help the Chinese Nationalists overcome their geographical handicap by transporting the Kuomintang troops to Manchuria both by air and by sea. The rival forces, therefore, both found themselves installed in the region.

Despite a fundamental American commitment to Chiang Kai-shek, United States policy, however, was not to back the Nationalists in a civil war, but to reconcile Nationalist and Communist factions so that a united and democratic government could be established. Difficult as this task was, it was further complicated by a difference of view among Americans—a difference which has still not been resolved—as to whether the Chinese Communists were Communists only in name, or whether they were acting on orders emanating from Moscow. Expressed otherwise, it could be said that the same ambiguity became apparent toward China that had been evidenced toward Russia. Were the Communists in each country motivated primarily by ideology, or primarily by nationalism? Nobody, it seemed, could answer the question once and for all.

United States Major-General Patrick J. Hurley, for example (sent out as Ambassador to China in September, 1944),[36] on February 4, 1945, reported from Moscow that he understood the Soviet attitude toward the Chinese Communists to include the following points:

> (1) The so-called Chinese Communists are not in fact Communists at all.
> (2) The Soviet Government is not supporting the Chinese Communists.[37]

---

35. "Report to the American People on China," *Life*, October 13, 1947.
36. Hurley recommended that Stilwell be replaced. Stilwell's place was later taken by General Albert Coady Wedemeyer.
37. *United States Relations with China*, U.S. Department of State Publication 3573 (1949), p. 93.

A similar view had already been communicated to U.S. Ambassador W. Averell Harriman when, in June, 1944, Stalin told him "The Chinese Communists are not real Communists. They are 'margarine' Communists."[38]

A contrary view was to be expressed by, among others, William C. Bullitt who, in 1949, demanded that "the abundant evidence of the subservience of the Chinese Communists to Moscow" be published in the United States.[39]

In effect it would appear that, despite ideological affinities, Stalin did not anticipate that the Chinese Communists could gain power in China, and did not believe, either, that the United States would permit them to do so. This view is substantiated by the Yugoslav writer Milovan Djilas, who reported that in 1948 Stalin privately stated:

> True, we, too, can make a mistake! Here, when the war with Japan ended, we invited the Chinese comrades to reach an agreement as to how a modus vivendi with Chiang Kai-shek might be found. They agreed with us in word but in deed they did it in their own way when they got home: they mustered their forces and struck. It has been shown that they were right and not we.[40]

All the evidence, therefore, points to the conclusion that at the end of the war with Japan both the United States and the Soviet Union aimed at the formation of a coalition between Chiang and the Communists. On the American side Vice-President Henry A. Wallace, Ambassador Hurley, and General George C. Marshall successively attempted to achieve this end. General Marshall, who was appointed as President Truman's special representative in China on November 27, 1945, came the closest —at least in appearance—to success. As a result of his efforts a truce was arranged between the hostile Nationalists and Communists, and agreement was reached on governmental organization, on a National Assembly, and on a draft Constitution. On March 11, 1946, General Marshall left Chungking for consultations in Washington in the belief that his mission had been successful. By the time he returned to China on April 18, 1946, however, agreement had vanished, and fighting had begun. The basis of trust between the two sides had been too frail, and mutual determination to gain control in Manchuria had been too strong. Despite all of Marshall's efforts the fighting spread and intensified. By September, 1946, it had become clear that China was engaged in civil war. Leaving China on January 7, 1947, with failure openly admitted, Marshall blamed both sides for the fighting, but, in doing so, if anything he laid greater stress upon the role of the Nationalist government in which, he said "reactionaries . . . have evidently counted on substantial American support regardless of their actions."

38. Emily Hahn, *China Only Yesterday* (1963), p. 392.
39. "Report to the American People on China," *Life,* October 13, 1947.
40. *Conversations with Stalin* (1962), p. 182.

The two Chinese leaders whose forces now confronted each other differed greatly. In age and origins the differences were not, however, marked ones. Chiang, the son of a farmer, was born in 1888 in Chikow, in Chekiang province, while Mao, the son of a peasant and grain merchant, was born in 1893 in Shaoshan in Hunan. Both, too, were military men—Chiang from early choice, and Mao from political necessity. There, however, the resemblances ended. Chiang, slim and well-groomed, habitually wearing a smart military uniform, was a well-known figure throughout the world. Mao, unkempt and somewhat ungainly, was not widely known abroad. Chiang, while describing himself as a revolutionary, had married into the most powerful family in China, and attempted to defend the status quo. Mao, a revolutionary in fact, whose first wife had been executed by the Nationalists, had been hunted and harried from province to province with a price on his head. Chiang was a Confucian traditionalist who had become converted to Christianity (Methodism) at the time of his marriage. Mao, whose mother had been a Buddhist, had dabbled in many ideas, including anarchism, before becoming a Marxist. In the last resort Chiang relied upon troops and guns, whereas Mao relied upon the support of China's peasant masses.

Yet perhaps the most significant difference between them lay in their approach to military strategy. Chiang tended to value the form of control more than control itself—being satisfied with towns captured, territory seized (at least nominally on the map), and the amount of foreign aid obtained. Mao, for his part, was only satisfied with the substance of power. He recognized that China was an agricultural nation, and cared little whether towns were won or lost, so long as losses were inflicted upon the enemy. He prized mobility above territorial gains, and preferred the support of the Chinese population to aid obtained from abroad. This fundamental difference—Chiang's preoccupation with form, as distinct from Mao's preoccupation with substance—was, inevitably, to give Mao victory. For the peoples of China, who had known no stable peace since the 1840s, longed for the peace and prosperity that they had never known in their lifetimes to be re-established. Chiang's supporters, fanning out over China from the half-dozen provinces of the west in which they had been pent up during the war years, began to institute a system of repression and exploitation on a scale that had hitherto been unthinkable. Mao's Communists, promising to better the lot of the agricultural workers as well as the middle-class by effecting reforms, lowering taxes, and abolishing corruption, proposed to build a new China, free at last not only from warlords but also from the humiliation of foreign control. The issue, when it was finally joined, stood in no doubt. China had at last awakened, and the days of its subjugation were numbered. Irrespective of ideology, the victory of Mao and the defeat of

Chiang would mean that the most populous country not only in Asia but in the entire world would have broken the shackles of Western domination.

The Nationalists began by making mistakes in both Manchuria and Taiwan. The Manchurians found themselves being considered as "collaborators" with the Japanese, not as fellow Chinese, and then being treated accordingly. The possibility that, under such circumstances, the Manchurians might find Communist rule preferable was not, apparently, considered. In Taiwan the Nationalists who took over from the Japanese —who had been established there for half a century—similarly aroused widespread resentment by plundering the island of its accumulated wealth. Throughout China too, despite large American credits granted for reconstruction, the self-interest of the Nationalist officials was placed before the general welfare, so that popular discontent grew stronger.

The "Third Revolutionary Civil War,"[41] as it was called by the Communists, opened in July, 1946—the month in which the Communists renamed their forces the "People's Liberation Army" (P.L.A.). To begin with the Nationalists made much apparent progress, seizing many towns in the North and in Manchuria. The Communists, however, were meanwhile consolidating their strength in the countryside. The lessons that had been learned in the war against Japan were now to be applied against the Nationalists.

In January, 1947, at a time when the Nationalists did not anticipate any Communist action because of the cold, the P.L.A., in Manchuria, launched the first of a series of attacks that later grew in strength. In the spring the Nationalists riposted by capturing the former Communist stronghold of Yenan, only to find that the Communists had moved instead in strength into Shansi province. The Communists then proceeded to advance in Manchuria, dashing Kuomintang hopes for a victory there, and beginning to entrap the Nationalist forces not only in Manchuria but also in Northeast China. Chiang Kai-shek, however, despite the warnings of his American advisers, who pointed out that his lines of communication there were becoming dangerously extended, insisted that the Nationalists retain Manchuria at all costs. The Communist position, meanwhile, grew patently stronger, nor could the situation of the Nationalists be improved by superficial actions, such as publicising overly optimistic figures of Nationalist troop strength, removing the Nationalist capital from Chungking to Nanking, or changing the title of the Nationalist military headquarters back to its old name, the "Bandit Suppression Headquarters." As the American O. E. Clubb, U.S. Consul-General in Peking during this period, later expressed it, "The Nanking regime had

41. The "First Revolutionary War" took place from 1921 to 1927, and the "Second Revolutionary War" from 1927 to 1938.

some appreciation of its difficult position but patently counted on American aid, not domestic reforms, to save it from any extremity."[42] It would also appear that Chiang was counting on another circumstance to transform his losing cause into a winning one—an outbreak of a third world war, between the United States and the Soviet Union. Despite the growing tensions of the Cold War, this hope was not, however, to be realized.

Heavy fighting in Manchuria and elsewhere resulted in a further deterioration of the Nationalist position. Some Nationalist troops were now beginning to defect to the Communists. In June, 1948, moreover, the Communists passed from guerrilla to open warfare, inflicting a heavy defeat on the Kuomintang forces outside Manchuria at Kaifeng in Honan province, thereby obtaining much American equipment[43] in addition to the Japanese arms and supplies that they already possessed. The P.L.A. now paused to prepare for the next phase. When they struck it was to win another victory, at Tsinan in Shantung. In Manchuria, meanwhile, Chiang Kai-shek belatedly tried to extricate his forces, many of whom were now prepared to defect to Mao Tse-tung. Large numbers of Nationalist troops surrendered—notably on November 1, 1948, at Mukden —and great stockpiles of American stores passed into Communist hands. Within a few days Chiang had lost the whole of Manchuria.

Immediately after the fall of Mukden, the battle of Hwai-Hai took place in Central China, raging for sixty-five days, from November 7, 1948, to January 12, 1949. One of the great battles of the twentieth century, it resulted in a crushing defeat for Chiang Kai-shek, who lost over half a million men, in addition to the 400,000 and more that he had just lost at Mukden. Shortly before the battle was over, on January 8, 1949, Chiang, realized that the game was lost and asked for the intervention of the United States, British, French, and Soviet governments, expressing the "sincere desire" of the Nationalist government "for a peaceful settlement with the Chinese Communist Party" (now no longer referred to as "bandits"). The power position on which such a settlement might have been based had, however, now disappeared, and although the Chinese Communists put forward an eight-point peace plan, Chiang found it unacceptable. The various governments to whom Chiang had appealed declined, moreover, in the course of the next few days, to intervene. On January 21, 1949, Chiang—who had been elected President of the Kuomintang National Assembly on April 18, 1948, resigned his presidency. His resignation was, however, a feint, and he covertly undercut his

42. *Twentieth Century China* (1964), p. 284.
43. In December, 1936, Mao Tse-tung had written: "Our basic directive is to rely on the war industries of the imperialist countries and of our enemy at home. We have a claim on the output of the arsenals of London as well as of Hanyang, and, what is more, it is to be delivered to us by the enemy's own transport corps. This is the sober truth, not a joke. (*Strategic Problems of China's Revolutionary War*, 1936.)

successor, General Li Tsung-Jen, who vainly attempted to rally the Nationalist cause south of the Yangtze River, while Chiang occupied himself by removing the Nationalist gold reserves and a substantial body of the Nationalist forces to Taiwan.

The back of the Nationalist cause was now broken, and all that remained was for the P.L.A. to take over control of the rest of China. Tientsin had fallen on January 15, 1949, and Peking itself on January 31. On April 20 Mao's forces crossed the Yangtze, and on April 22 Nanking fell, obliging the Nationalists to move their capital south to Canton. On May 27 the Communist forces entered Shanghai, from which they had been driven in 1927. Further surrenders and capitulations followed in other provinces, with Canton itself falling, at last, on October 14, 1949. Even before that had happened, however, on October 1, 1949, Mao Tse-tung in Peking had proclaimed the establishment of the People's Republic of China, and had himself been elected its first Chairman. The two greatest states in Asia—India and China—were now indisputably in control of their own destinies.

### The Korean War

The fact that a single national government had at last gained control over the whole of mainland China was, to most Western observers, obscured by the fact that ideologically the new regime was Communist.[44] The American and West European governments, who had been growing increasingly preoccupied with the Cold War in Europe, now judged that, Communist expansion having been contained in Europe, the Communists had now turned to Asia to strike, indirectly, at the West. In this connection much mention was made of a quotation, supposedly from Lenin, but now believed to be spurious, to the effect that "the road to Paris lies through Peking." Many Westerners feared that the saying might prove true, and that militant Communism might thus triumph in the European heartland.

The Communist victory in China was credited by most Westerners to Stalin, rather than to Mao, and phantom visions of a resurgent colonial world of black, brown, and yellow men, seeking vengeance for past wrongs, real and imagined, and acting under the direction of the Kremlin, bent on world power, began to be entertained. It was at this juncture, when Soviet and Western mutual distrust was at its height, that the Korean War of 1950–1953 broke out. While much remains obscure about the origins of the Korean War, it is clear that apparent misunder-

---

44. Controversy still continues as to whether primacy should be given to the Chinese or to the Communist attributes of the Peking regime. The nature of international relations would appear to ensure, however, that in any nation the national interest finally takes supremacy over ideological preoccupation, of whatever kind.

standings by both sides were largely responsible for the conflict occurring at all.

It had been agreed at the Cairo Conference in 1943 that Korea, after the war, would be an independent state. At Potsdam in 1945 Truman and Stalin had agreed that Korea should become independent after a five-year period of trusteeship.[45] After the entry of the Soviet Union into the war against Japan on August 8, 1945, Soviet troops from the north and American troops from the south occupied Korea. By agreement between the respective chiefs of staff, the territory was, for mutual convenience, arbitrarily divided by the 38th parallel into two military zones, pending further arrangements. Stalin and Roosevelt had earlier agreed that all foreign troops should be withdrawn from Korea. The Soviets prepared for this eventuality by training Korean troops in the Soviet Union. The United States, for its part, made no political preparations. In December, 1945, the United States, the United Kingdom, and the Soviet Union agreed in Moscow that a provisional government should eventually be established on democratic principles in Korea, and a joint Soviet-American Commission was set up to make the necessary preliminary arrangements and recommendations. It was also confirmed that China, the Soviet Union, the United Kingdom, and the United States should administer Korea as a Trust Territory for a period of five years. However, it soon became clear that the Koreans, having been under Japanese rule since 1905, were by no means disposed to accept any further foreign tutelage, even in the benevolent form of a transitional trusteeship administration. Instead the Koreans considered themselves to have been librated, and proposed to exercise their sovereignty forthwith.

In 1946, with differences between the United States and the Soviet Union, no less than between the various Korean factions, the talks between the two great powers became deadlocked. In the North the Korean Communists were effectively in power, whereas in the South different factions, bitterly divided, strove to gain the ear of the United States command. Eventually Syngman Rhee, a Korean politician of conservative bent, born in 1875, who had highly placed friends in Washington, and who had spent a lifetime agitating for independence, obtained the support of the United States. As a result of an election held in South Korea in May, 1947, which was "less an expression of preference by the electorate than a victory of terrorization by violence or intimidation,"[46] Syngman Rhee became President of the Republic of Korea on July 20, 1947. In the North the Communists were not slow in following this example, establishing the Democratic People's Republic of Korea on Sep-

45. Roosevelt had earlier proposed—and Stalin had agreed—that Korea should be placed under trusteeship for twenty or thirty years.
46. Nathaniel Peffer, *The Far East: A Modern History* (1958), p. 458.

tember 9, 1947. North and South Korea were thus each equipped with a separate government, and the division of the country was consequently now formalized. With the Cold War intensifying, moreover, there seemed little possibility of its imminent reunification.

Strategically the Korean peninsula represented a vital link between the Chinese mainland and the islands of Japan. Until 1945 American strategists had necessarily thought only in terms of the defense of China. With the Americans now responsible for the defense of Japan, the situation was reversed, but this was not immediately noticed by the United States, and the new importance that Korea held for them tended to be overlooked. Short of troops, following its precipitate demobilization, the United States sought and obtained Soviet consent for foreign troops to be withdrawn from Korea. Soviet troops accordingly withdrew from the North by December, 1948, and United States troops from the South by June, 1949.

American military planning at this time was concerned with only one possible eventuality—a third world war, nuclear in character, between the United States and the Soviet Union. In case of such a war it was decided in Washington that the defense of Korea would not be attempted. The publicizing of the American decision not to defend Korea in the event of nuclear war was, however, apparently interpreted by the Kremlin as a diplomatic hint that the United States would not defend Korea under any circumstances—a "hint" that was wrongly interpreted as amounting to an invitation to solve the Korean dispute by permitting North Korean troops to take over the South.[47] On no less than three occasions prominent Americans indicated in public statements, outlining American commitments in this part of the world, that Korea was excluded from the zone for which America accepted military responsibility. In an interview with a British journalist, later reported in the New York Times, General Douglas MacArthur stated in Tokyo on March 1, 1949, that the American line of defense in the Pacific "starts from the Philippines and continues through the Ryukyu Archipelago . . . Then it bends back through Japan and the Aleutian Island chain to Alaska." On January 12, 1950, U.S. Secretary of State Dean Acheson told the National Press Club in Washington that "the defensive perimeter runs along the Aleutians to Japan and then goes to the Ryukyus." Finally in May, 1950, U.S. Senator Tom Connally, Chairman of the Senate Foreign Relations Committee, stated that the Soviet Union could seize South Korea without United States intervention because Korea was not "very greatly important."

47. George F. Kennan, the American diplomat, has taken the view that the American decision to conclude a peace treaty with Japan to which the Soviet Union was not a party, and at the same time to conclude an agreement to retain U.S. bases in Japan, "probably had an important bearing on the Soviet decision to unleash the attack in Korea." (*Memoirs: 1925–1950*, 1967, p. 395.)

On June 25, 1950, the North Korean Army crossed the 38th parallel to seize the southern part of the country. The news, which came as a surprise to Washington, created consternation and alarm. Fears were expressed that if the Communists were permitted to unify Korea by force they would be sufficiently encouraged to seek to unify Germany in the same way. Meeting in Washington on the nights of June 25 and June 26, 1950, President Truman and his advisers decided that North Korea's aggression must be resisted.

Since 1945 it had been the general assumption in the United States that peace could be kept by reliance in the first instance on the United Nations, and in the second instance on American possession of nuclear weapons. Conventional warfare, therefore, was seen as a thing of the past. This assumption—which, as we noted, had underlain the hasty demobilization of 1945—was now challenged by the Korean crisis. The United Nations had already been concerned with Korea, and in 1948 had sanctioned the holding of elections in the South, but had not been able to influence the situation north of the 38th parallel, in view of Soviet insistence that matters could be settled by the application of the Moscow Agreement of 1945. United Nations diplomacy, therefore, would prove impotent if it were not backed by force. When it came to force, quite apart from the fact that the Soviets had produced a nuclear explosion in 1949, the United States was not psychologically prepared to resort to nuclear weapons in 1950. Force, it therefore became evident, would have to assume more conventional forms.

To Truman it appeared that not only American will but also the new United Nations organization was being tested. The League of Nations had failed to act in the face of aggression. "In my generation," he thought, "this was not the first occasion when the strong had attacked the weak. I recalled some earlier instances: Manchuria, Ethiopia, Austria. I remembered how each time that the democracies failed to act it had encouraged the aggressors to keep going ahead."[48]

On June 25, 1950, the U.N. Security Council, meeting at the request of the United States, declared that the North Korean action constituted a breach of the peace, called for a withdrawal of North Korean forces to the 38th parallel, and called upon member states to render every assistance to the United Nations in execution of the Security Council decision. Paradoxically the resolution would presumably have been vetoed by the Soviet Union had not the Soviets been boycotting the Council at the time in protest against the United Nations' failure to seat the People's Republic of China in place of the representatives of the Chiang Kai-shek regime.

On June 27, 1950, President Truman ordered General MacArthur,

48. *Memoirs by Harry S. Truman*, Vol. Two (*Years of Trial and Hope*) (1956), pp. 332–333.

then commanding U.S. forces in the Far East from his headquarters in Tokyo, to send air and sea support to South Korea. (The United States, despite Truman's distaste for "the methods used by Rhee's police to break up political meetings and control political enemies," had signed a defense agreement with South Korea on January 26, 1950.) At the same time Truman ordered the United States Seventh Fleet to prevent any attack on Taiwan, and called on the Chiang Kai-shek regime to cease all air and sea operations against the mainland. "The determination of the future status of Formosa [Taiwan] must await the restoration of security in the Pacific, a peace settlement with Japan, or consideration by the United Nations."[49] On the same day, the U.N. Security Council adopted a second resolution, recommending that U.N. members "furnish such assistance to the Republic of Korea as may be necessary to repel the armed attack and to restore international peace and security in the area." Truman's South Korean action had thus received United Nations sanction, although his action in intervening in the Chinese civil war had not. In effect, Truman was at that time acting on the incorrect assumption that China was a satellite of the Soviet Union, and that consequently the Korean and Chinese situations were directly connected. It now seems virtually beyond doubt that the Chinese were not initially involved,[50] and, indeed, the Chinese appear to have been taken as much by surprise by the North Korean action as was President Truman.

On June 30, 1950, Truman authorized the use of United States ground troops in Korea, and on July 7, 1950, the Security Council recommended that U.N. members sending military forces to that country "make such forces and other assistance available to a unified command under the United States of America." It requested the United States "to designate the commander of such forces," and authorized the unified command "at its discretion to use the United Nations flag in the course of operations . . . concurrently with the flags of the various nations participating." President Truman appointed General MacArthur to the unified command, to which a total of fifteen nations eventually contributed troops.[51]

Legally the action taken by the unified command was United Nations action. In practice, however, the United States made the decisions, and provided almost 90 percent of the troops. As one commentator has expressed it:

> In terms of international politics and of international organization . . . it fell crucially short of being a real United Nations operation. It was not under the executive

49. Statement by President Truman on the Korean Question, June 27, 1950.
50. See the report of a study by the Rand Corporation, commissioned by the United States Air Force to examine why China entered the Korean War, appearing in the Toronto *Globe and Mail* on February 22, 1961, and cited in *The Wall Has Two Sides,* by Felix Greene (London, 1962), p. 282–283.
51. Forces were contributed by Australia, Belgium, Canada, Colombia, Ethiopia, France, Greece, Luxembourg, the Netherlands, New Zealand, the Philippines, Thailand, Turkey, the United Kingdom, and the United States.

control of the United Nations; the Secretariat had no part in its organization or deployment; it was not financed by the United Nations, nor did the United Nations determine in any but the broadest terms the conditions and objectives of its employment. The response to the appeal to all Member States to furnish assistance was generally poor. One member, the United States, was the self-appointed Atlas of the operation, without whose broad shoulders all would have failed.[52]

The United States contributed about a quarter of a million men as compared with about 36,000 contributed by other nations.

The war itself began with successes for the North Koreans, who, well organized and equipped, swept southward until for a moment it seemed they might overwhelm all opposition. In August, 1950, however, American and South Korean troops succeeded in maintaining a position based on Pusan at the southern tip of the peninsula. On September 15, 1950, moreover, General MacArthur, repeating the amphibious tactics that had proved so successful against the Japanese, landed a force at Inchon behind the North Korean lines. The North Koreans were obliged to fall back behind the 38th parallel, retreating in confusion and suffering many losses. Having thus seized the initiative, MacArthur was loath to abandon it. It had hitherto been the general assumption that the aim of the unified U.N. force was to defeat the attackers, and to restore the status quo ante bellum, after which a political settlement might be made. In the flush of success, however, this assumption was now to be challenged by MacArthur and his political supporters.

Even before the Inchon landings on September 15, Chu Teh, Commander-in-Chief of the Chinese People's Liberation Army, had stated, on August 1, 1950, "We definitely come to the relief of the Korean people and definitely oppose the American government's aggression in Korea." On August 17, moreover, the New York *Times* reported that Mao Tsetung and Soviet Foreign Minister Molotov had agreed in Peking that if United States forces crossed the 38th parallel, China would send troops into Korea. Chinese preparations for such a contingency were, no doubt, not discontinued when, on August 25, 1950, the U.S. Secretary of the Navy, Francis Mathews, stated that the United States should wage a "preventive war."

On October 1, 1950, matters developed further. On that date South Korean troops crossed the 38th parallel; General MacArthur ordered North Korean forces to lay down their arms, while in Peking Chou Enlai declared that "The Chinese people definitely cannot tolerate foreign aggression, and cannot allow imperialists recklessly to aggress against their own neighbor and disregard it . . . Whoever would . . . foolishly think to settle arbitrarily any Eastern question directly related to China will

52. Herbert Nicholas, "U.N. Forces and Lessons of Suez and Congo: An Appraisal," *International Military Forces: The Question of Peacekeeping in an Armed and Disarming World*, edited by Lincoln P. Bloomfield (1964), p. 107.

certainly break his head and spill his blood." Two days later, to dispel any lingering doubts as to the Chinese position, Chou En-lai informed the Indian Ambassador in Peking, K. M. Pannikar, that China would intervene if United Nations forces crossed the 38th parallel. General MacArthur, however, disregarded these warnings, or belittled them as propaganda. He succeeded in obtaining from the authorities in Washington on September 27, 1950, authorization to operate north of the 38th parallel, provided that "there has been no entry into North Korea by major Soviet or Chinese Communist forces, no announcement of intended entry, nor a threat to counter our operations militarily in Korea."[53] On October 7, 1950, therefore, the first United States forces crossed the parallel and began to drive north to the Manchurian border. On the same day the U.N. General Assembly adopted Resolution 367 (V), which inferentially authorized the action by recommending that "all appropriate steps be taken" to ensure stability "throughout" Korea, as well as the holding of elections under U.N. auspices for the establishment of a unified, independent, and democratic government.

On October 15, 1950, President Truman met with MacArthur on Wake Island in the Pacific, at which time MacArthur assured the President that victory was won in Korea, and that the Chinese Communists would not attack the United States forces. North Korean resistance, he said, would be over by Thanksgiving (November 23, 1950).

On the next day, October 17, the first Chinese units crossed the Yalu River, which separates Manchuria from Korea, thereby entering the Korean war. They had the status of "volunteers," thus avoiding any legal entanglement of China in the war. The presence of Chinese soldiers was not realized by the United States, however, for some days. Indeed, on October 24, 1950, MacArthur, disregarding instructions that only Korean forces be allowed in the vicinity of the Chinese and Soviet frontiers, ordered his forces to advance into these areas, citing "military necessity," as well as a previous direction that he "feel unhampered" in his northward advance, for his action. Even as late as the end of October the U.S. Far East Command was still discounting reports of Chinese intervention as "unconfirmed."

The awakening to reality was a rude one. As U.S. General Matthew B. Ridgway later expressed it: "Then the blows fell and fell with such devastating suddenness that many units were overrun before they could

---

53. The wording of this proviso is strange, as certainly both MacArthur and the Truman administration knew of the Chinese warnings. The U.S. Joint Chiefs of Staff appear to have been chary of giving MacArthur clear orders, knowing he might disobey them if he chose, and may therefore have taken refuge in ambiguity. The Truman administration, for its part, would not have wished to deter the man who had just won victory at Inchon, particularly since he was known to be in touch with the opposition (Republican) party, which would not fail to make political capital out of any apparent failure to exploit what superficially appeared to be a promising situation for the United States.

quite grasp what had happened."[54] On November 1 many American soldiers—some of whom had been engaged in planning details of a victory
march to be held in Tokyo—heard for the first time the "wild clamor" of
the Chinese bugles which signaled attack.

On November 7, however, a lull in the fighting began. U.S. troops had
reached the Yalu River. On November 24 MacArthur announced the
launching of a general offensive to end the war, stating at about the
same time that his troops would be "home by Christmas." This proved
to be a false prophecy. The Chinese opened a counteroffensive on November 26, attacking with forces about 200,000 strong. On November 28
MacArthur was obliged to admit that he faced "an entirely new war," and
reported that his command faced conditions "beyond its control and its
strength." Soon the U.N. forces were being driven southward with heavy
losses, with whole divisions put to rout.[55] Not until the end of January
could the retreat be stopped, by which time the U.N. forces were all
south of the 38th parallel, and the South Korean capital of Seoul had
been lost.

In early 1951 the conflict, long latent, between President Truman,
pursuing a policy of containment of the Communist nations, and General
MacArthur, who wished to expand the war to China, even at the risk of
involving the Soviet Union and thus precipitating a third world war,
developed into an open clash. On March 19, 1951, a draft presidential
statement had been prepared which would, it was hoped, make possible
a negotiated settlement in Korea. General MacArthur was notified the
following day that the statement was to be made shortly.

Before it could be given, however, MacArthur, on March 24, 1951,
made a statement of his own which, while professing his readiness to talk
"with the Commander-in-Chief of the enemy forces," also contained this
declaration:

> The enemy . . . must by now be painfully aware that a decision of the United
> Nations to depart from its tolerant effort to contain the war to the area of Korea, through
> an expansion of our military operations to all its coastal areas and interior bases, would
> doom Red China to the risk of imminent military collapse.

MacArthur's "offer," rejected by the Chinese on March 29, effectively
foreclosed the possibility that Truman's offer could meet with any success. On April 11, 1951, Truman consequently relieved MacArthur of his
commands, appointing General Ridgway in his place. MacArthur's dismissal, and the policy dispute underlying it, provoked bitter recrimina-

54. *The Korean War* (1967), p. 54.
55. On November 30, 1950, when it was clear that the fortunes of war were turning against
the United Nations forces, President Truman hinted that use of the atomic bomb was being considered
—a prospect that disquieted the allies of the United States, who sought assurances that nothing of
the kind was contemplated.

tions in the United States—recriminations that left deep scars on the body politic. Stating that "there is no substitute for victory," MacArthur implied that victory had been denied him because of limitations placed on his actions by the Truman administration—mentioning particularly the denial of permission to bomb air bases inside Manchuria. Meanwhile, in Korea, both sides continued to attempt to break the deadlock by periodically launching bloody and useless attacks that cost countless lives.

On June 23, 1951, meanwhile, the Soviet representative at the United Nations, Jacob Malik, proposed that discussions for a cease-fire be opened —a suggestion that was supported two days later by the *People's Daily* in Peking. President Truman responded to the suggestion, and talks were opened at Kaesong, on July 10, between North Korean and American representatives. The talks proved to be lengthy, and on October 25, 1951, were moved to a new site at Panmunjon. Meanwhile the war went on.

The United States presidential election the following year was strongly influenced by the circumstances of the Korean war, which subjected American public opinion to a kind of frustration that it had not known before. The promise of the Republican candidate, General Dwight D. Eisenhower, to "go to Korea" suggested that a new approach to the problem could be made, and thus struck a sympathetic chord in the ears of his hearers. The MacArthur slogan that "there is no substitute for victory"—implying, as it did, that an expansion of the war to China was necessary and desirable—was not stressed in the electoral campaign. Eisenhower was elected on November 4, 1952, and on December 2, 1952, shortly before taking office, redeemed his promise by visiting Korea, where he talked with American military leaders, as well as with Syngman Rhee and members of the South Korean government. As as a result of this visit Eisenhower decided that the war should be ended rather than expanded.

However, since the Republican administration wished to take a more aggressive stance toward Peking than its Democratic predecessor, in his State of the Union Address of February 2, 1953, Eisenhower announced that the United States Seventh Fleet, while continuing to protect Taiwan from a Chinese Communist invasion, would no longer "be employed to shield Communist China" from attack by Chiang Kai-shek. Earlier—although Truman had rejected MacArthur's urgings that he accept Chiang Kai-shek's offer to send 33,000 Chinese Nationalist troops to fight in Korea—Truman had nevertheless, in May, 1951, sent a U.S. military mission to Taiwan to rehabilitate the Nationalist forces there. Thus the United States, which had already refused to recognize the Peking regime, and which had supported United Nations Resolution 498 (V) of February 1, 1951, in which the General Assembly found that "the Central People's Government of the People's Republic of China, by giving direct aid and assistance to those who were already committing aggression in Korea and by engaging in hostilities against United Nations forces there, has itself engaged in aggression in Korea," now openly identified itself with the cause of Nationalist China, thus widening still further the gulf that already separated Washington from Peking.

In accordance with Eisenhower's decision to end the war, new U.S. efforts to achieve a cease-fire were made on February 22, 1953. For a time it seemed that no response would be forthcoming. Then, on March 5, 1953, the startling news of Premier Stalin's death became known—an event so momentous that it called into question, at least for a time, many of the assumptions on which Western policies and attitudes toward the Communist countries had been based. When the initial shock had subsided, however, progress toward a settlement was relatively rapid. In May the North Koreans reached agreement with the Americans on the release of prisoners of war—an issue which had long constituted a stumbling block to a cease-fire. After some difficulty was experienced in persuading Syngman Rhee to accept the agreement, the cease-fire agreement ending the Korean war was finally signed on July 27, 1953. The war had cost South Korea an estimated 843,000 casualties of all kinds, North Korea an estimated 520,000 casualties, the United States about 136,000, and China about 900,000. The heavy loss of life among Korean civilians could not be computed, although losses among other nationalities fighting beneath the U.N. flag were minimal. Apart from the death and destruction that this accidental war had caused, it also profoundly embittered Chinese-American relations, making the resolution of other differences between the two nations infinitely more difficult.

## The War in Indochina

After the Japanese surrender on August 15, 1945, the future of Indochina was once more called into question. On August 19, 1945, Ho Chi Minh's Viet Minh guerrillas had seized Hanoi. The following week the Emperor Bao Dai, in the palace at Hué, had been obliged to abdicate, after which, on September 2, 1945, the Democratic Republic of Vietnam (D.R.V.N.) had been proclaimed. Vietnam thus became the second Communist state to be established in Asia—Outer Mongolia, which had been proclaimed a People's Republic in 1924, having been the first.[56]

At Teheran and at Potsdam, however, arrangements had been made for Chinese forces to occupy the north and for British Commonwealth forces to occupy the south of Vietnam. The French, meanwhile, in March, 1945, had announced that after the war it was their intention to form a

56. Following a plebiscite, held on October 20, 1945, which resulted in a vote in favor of independence, China, by previous agreement with the Soviet Union, recognized the independence of the Mongolian People's Republic on January 5, 1946.

five-state Indochinese Federation—composed of Tonkin, Annam, Cochin-China, Laos, and Cambodia—within the French Union. Despite obstacles placed in their way by the United States—at that time following an anti-colonial policy which included aiding the Viet Minh—the French succeeded in re-establishing themselves in both Northern and Southern Vietnam by March, 1946. In so doing they experienced no difficulties in taking over from the British in the South, but in the North the Chinese, in return for withdrawing, demanded and obtained the renunciation of the special rights hitherto accorded to France in China, as well as the French acceptance of Chinese rights in the port of Haiphong.

The French were thus left confronting one another. Despite their opposition to colonial rule, the Viet Minh were nevertheless, at this time, virtually obliged to come to terms with the French. Vietnam had suffered from a major famine in the winter of 1945–1946, as a result of which about a million Vietnamese died. In addition to this, the attitude of the United States toward the Viet Minh changed. Hitherto the Viet Minh had enjoyed American support, extended through the Office of Strategic Services (O.S.S.), a semi-clandestine agency. By March, 1946, however, the United States had become anxious to prevent a Communist administration from establishing itself in France, and had therefore, at least overtly, changed to a policy of supporting French colonial rule. The Viet Minh, in consequence, appeared to have no other recourse but to seek a modus vivendi with France.

At first it appeared that such a modus vivendi might be reached after the Viet Minh and the French military, on March 6, 1946, signed an agreement recognizing the Republic of Vietnam as a free state within the French Union. It was then agreed that the French troops stationed in Northern Vietnam should be progressively replaced over a period of five years by Viet Minh forces, who would be trained and equipped by the French. The French High Commissioner in Indochina, Admiral d'Argenlieu, with the support of French conservative interests based in Cochin-China, regarded this development with apprehension. In order to undercut the Viet Minh position, d'Argenlieu—without the authorization of Paris, where the French Communist Party enjoyed considerable influence—announced on May 30, 1946, that he would recognize the establishment of a "Republic of Cochin-China." The new French puppet state was consequently officially proclaimed on June 2, 1946.

These unexpected developments occurred as Ho Chi Minh was in the process of embarking for France on a French warship with the intention of concluding final accords in Paris. Inured as he was to vicissitudes, both political and personal, d'Argenlieu's action nevertheless took Ho by surprise.

Born in the village of Kim-Lien in central Vietnam in the early 1890s,[57] Ho—whose true name was believed to be Nguyen Ai-Quoc[58]— had been attracted by nationalist ideals from an early age. He traveled to Europe—probably in 1911 or 1912—and later visited both African and North American ports, serving as a kitchen boy on various French ships. His travels removed any illusions that he might have entertained concerning the superiority of Europeans over the inhabitants of other continents. His varied experiences, which brought him a breadth of view surpassing that of most other nationalist leaders in colonial countries, included working as a pastry cook for Escoffier, the celebrated French chef, then at the Carlton Hotel in London, as well—it is alleged—as living for a time in New York's Harlem. At the end of the First World War, as an enthusiastic adherent of the ideals of self-determination proclaimed in Woodrow Wilson's Fourteen Points, Ho attended the Versailles Peace Conference, but failed to obtain the audiences that he sought with Wilson and other leaders. It was shortly after this that Ho, on December 30, 1920, became a founding member of the French Communist Party. From this moment on he emerged both as a leading advocate of colonial emancipation, and as a dedicated Communist. Ho consequently enjoyed the unusual distinction of successfully blending in his single personality both the Communist and nationalist elements— a circumstance that was not without influence on the development of the Vietnamese nationalist movement.

Ho's subsequent career took him to the Soviet Union, China, and many other countries. Unlike other political leaders, he wrote little, and then only some unremarkable colonial pamphlets.[59] It was rather as a political activist that he excelled. In 1921 he created the Intercolonial Union in Paris; in 1923 he helped to create the Krestintern (Peasant International) in Moscow; and in 1925 in Canton he founded the League of Oppressed People of Asia—an organization that was the Comintern's principal agency in Eastern Asia. From Canton, too, he organized the political and military training[60] of young Vietnamese to prepare them for a revolutionary role in their own country. Forced to flee from China after Chiang Kai-shek's break with Moscow, Ho for a time disappeared into a world of secrecy, first traveling in Europe, and then working among the Vietnamese of Thailand in the disguise of a Buddhist monk.

57. His birth date was on May 19, but doubt persists as to whether the year was 1890, 1891, or 1892.

58. Nguyen That Thanh and Nguyen Van Thanh are other variants of his true name that have been cited. Ho Chi Minh, in the course of his political career, has also employed a number of aliases. (See Bernard Fall, *The Two Viet-Nams*, 1963, p. 83.)

59. One of his pamphlets, presumably based upon his experiences in Africa and North America, was entitled *La Race Noir* (The Black Race). Published in Moscow in 1924, it dealt with American and European racial attitudes and practices.

60. Some Vietnamese received military training at Chiang Kai-shek's military academy at Whampoa, while others received political training, either in Moscow, or directly from Ho himself.

He was then called upon to end factional fights among Indochinese Communists by forming a unitary Indochinese Communist Party in 1930. Arrested by the British authorities in Hong Kong in 1931, he was released in 1932, eventually returning to Moscow for a period. By 1938 he was in China once more, and in 1940 returned to Vietnamese soil for the first time in thirty years. In 1942 he was apparently arrested by the Chinese, but was released in 1943, allegedly after the Americans had intervened on his behalf.

In 1944, when a Chiang Kai-shek-sponsored "Provisional Republican Government of Viet Nam" was formed, Ho received a ministerial portfolio. In the turbulent period that followed, Ho relied primarily on American support until, at last, American policy toward Indochinese nationalism changed, obliging him to try to come to terms with the French.

This, then, was the man who opened talks with the French at Fontainebleau near Paris in July, 1946. The talks, however, though they confirmed the accords of March, 1946, did not advance. Ho, relying on the strength of French Communist influence in Paris, took too rigid a position, while in Indochina itself d'Argenlieu continued working against the Viet Minh while, at the same time, the Chiang Kai-shek-supported faction of Vietnamese nationalists accused Ho and the Viet Minh of becoming tools of the French. A modus vivendi was nevertheless agreed upon, on September 16, 1946, by Ho and the French, and the intention was proclaimed of renewing the talks in January, 1947. By then, however, it would be too late. Tension had been rising in Vietnam itself, and incidents began to occur. Following the French seizure of a Chinese junk with a cargo of contraband, which was brought into Haiphong harbor on November 20, 1946, the Viet Minh in Haiphong launched two attacks on French soldiery, killing thirty-one men. The French decided to strike back, and demanded that the Viet Minh evacuate the Chinese quarter of Haiphong—moving to the attack when they refused to do so. When the shooting began, thousands of Vietnamese, mostly civilians, left the city for the safety of the countryside. The French cruiser *Suffern*, anchored offshore, mistook the crowds for Viet Minh insurgents and opened fire on them, with the result that over 6,000 Vietnamese civilians were either killed by the gunfire or trampled to death. Political efforts to restore the situation after this catastrophe failed. On December 19, 1946, the Viet Minh launched a general uprising against the French. The war in Indochina, which was to last eight years, had begun.

From the outset the French held the towns, while the Viet Minh controlled most of the countryside. The French attempted to reconquer the country by fighting a colonial war on the classic pattern they had developed in North Africa. This consisted first of all in seizing control of the towns and the main communication routes, and then proceeding to "pacify" the country by dividing it up in a grid pattern, and then systematically "raking over" the entire area, district by district, to rid it of their opponents. The guerrilla tactics of the Vietnamese, adapted from those advocated by Mao Tse-tung, however, created difficulties for them that they did not know how to solve. Even superior French fire-power, and the use of aircraft and napalm, proved insufficient to daunt the Viet Minh. The establishment of the Communists in Peking in 1949, moreover, permitted the Viet Minh to seek sanctuary across the Chinese border, where they retrained and re-equipped their forces before returning to the attack. The French military, from the outset, had not had large enough forces at their disposal, and discovered that the political mood in France, where the war was unpopular, did not permit them to obtain the reinforcements they required. By 1949, the French had been placed on the defensive.

Realizing that in the last resort they were losing support in Indochina because they were opposing an increasingly popular nationalism, the French, earlier that year, had attempted to ameliorate their position by making limited political concessions. By the Elysée Agreement of March 8, 1949, the Emperor Bao Dai of Annam had been recognized by the French as Chief of State of a Vietnam that was independent as an Associated State of the French Union. Laos and Cambodia, both of which had been constitutional monarchies since 1947, were also, in 1949, granted similar status as Associated States. But the changes did little to help the French. Bao Dai was already criticized widely for self-indulgence, and his frequent absences in France still further discredited him with the Vietnamese people. It was evident that he ruled in name only.

In all three associated states, it was clear that so long as the French military presence remained, it would be the French, rather than the supposedly independent governments that had been established, who would make decisions. This did not prevent the United States and the United Kingdom from extending de jure recognition to the new French-sponsored Vietnamese government in February, 1950. By this time, however, the Ho Chi Minh government, secure in the knowledge that the Chinese Communist army had now reached its northern frontier, had issued an appeal to the world for diplomatic recognition. The appeal was made on January 14, 1950, and was soon followed by recognition being extended by China, the Soviet Union, and their allies.

Meanwhile, the French military position continued to deteriorate. In October, 1950, heavy fighting took place in North Vietnam. As Bernard Fall wrote, "When the smoke cleared the French had suffered their greatest colonial defeat since Montcalm died at Quebec."[61] Although the government in Paris would not yet admit it, the French had lost the war.

Another factor, however, was now to result in the French continuing their involvement, and eventually being subjected to further catastrophic defeat—the outbreak of the Korean War. At the behest of the Eisenhower administration, which took the view that the Korean and Indochinese wars were two facets of the same conflict, Washington and Paris entered into agreements that interrelated the two wars, and, at least implicitly, ensured that neither party would terminate hostilities without the consent of the other.[62] In consequence the French—who had nevertheless seen the large quantities of United States equipment lost to the Communists in North Korea in 1950 being used to arm several Viet Minh divisions in 1951—recalled, on the insistence of the United States, a delegation that was being sent to Rangoon in 1952 to negotiate with the Viet Minh. This did not, however, prevent the U.S., under the Eisenhower administration, from negotiating a cease-fire in the North Korean war in 1953 without consulting with its French ally. As a result, the French, who might have gained much better peace terms in 1952 than they were to obtain in 1954, from 1953 on had to continue a colonial war in which their opponents enjoyed the undivided support of Communist China. Predictably the outcome was a disastrous French defeat, which occurred at Dien Bien Phu in 1954.

Dien Bien Phu was an isolated strongpoint in northwest Vietnam, near the Laotian border, supplied by air, and garrisoned by 15,000 men. The Viet Minh had hitherto practiced guerrilla warfare, but now openly threw four divisions against Dien Bien Phu. The situation of the French in Indochina had now become so serious that they informed the Eisenhower administration that unless the United States intervened they would be obliged to abandon the country. This news precipitated an intense debate in American governmental circles as to whether the United States should intervene to prevent Southeast Asian territories from falling into Communist hands like a row of collapsing dominoes, or whether it should acquiesce in a French withdrawal. The United States, represented by Secretary of State John Foster Dulles, suggested united action following the formation of a new Western alliance, the South East Asia Treaty Organization (S.E.A.T.O.). The British, however, who did not relish a general Western involvement in Indochina that would amount to a resumption of the fighting in Asia which had ended with the Korean war

---

61. *Street Without Joy: Insurgency in Indochina 1946–1953* (1961), p. 30.
62. Bernard Fall wrote: "It has not been admitted publicly that the two allies exchanged formal agreements guaranteeing that neither would conclude a peace without the other." (See *The Two Viet-Nams*, 1963, p. 122.)

cease-fire, declined to support general military intervention. Instead it was decided to await the outcome of the conference that was to be held in Geneva between the Soviet, British, Chinese, and American Foreign Ministers to attempt to reach a settlement of the Korean problem and the Indochinese war. Scenting victory, the Viet Minh, on the eve of the conference, launched a massive attack on the French and Vietnamese troops at Dien Bien Phu. After great gallantry on both sides, the French surrendered on May 8, 1954. "Dien Bien Phu" now became a name to conjure with—the first great battle within living memory in which colonial peasant insurgents had beaten a Western colonial power which had been armed with all the conventional resources that modern technology could provide. Dien Bien Phu spelled the death of the old mystique of Western omnipotence. Describing the Viet Minh artillery attack, the French commander in Indochina, General Navarre, said it had been "worse than anything since Verdun."

Earlier that year, in January and February, 1954, a conference had been held in Berlin, between the Soviets and the Western powers, at which it had been decided that a five-power conference should be convened in Geneva on April 26, first, to seek "a peaceful settlement of the Korean question," and second, to discuss the "problem of restoring peace in Indochina." The participants in the subsequent Geneva Conference on Far Eastern Problems were France, the United Kingdom, China, the Soviet Union, and the United States, as well as the "three associated states"—Laos, Cambodia, and Vietnam, with Vietnam being represented both by the French-supported government of Bao Dai, and the Viet Minh. Korea was discussed until June 15, 1954, without any settlement being reached, after which the Indochinese question was taken up.

By July 21, 1954, a general settlement on Indochina was arrived at. Separate cease-fire agreements were signed, covering Vietnam, Cambodia, and Laos. Both French and Viet Minh troops were to be withdrawn from Cambodia, while in Laos the Pathet Lao forces which had supported the Viet Minh were to be integrated into the Laotian army. In Vietnam general elections were to be held by July, 1956, to reunify the country, and no foreign troops were to be permitted either north or south of the cease-fire line that divided the country at about the 17th parallel. This arrangement was subscribed to by all the participants with the exception of the government of Vietnam and of the United States. The United States made a separate unilateral declaration, in which it stated that it would "refrain from the threat or the use of force to disturb" the Geneva Agreements, and also declared that it would view any renewal of the aggression in violation of the agreements "with grave concern and as seriously threatening international peace and security."

Although for the time being peace was restored, it was not to prove durable. After the conclusion of the Geneva Agreements, the place of France in South Vietnam, was increasingly taken by the United States. On June 19, 1954, Ngo Dinh Diem, a Catholic who had opposed both the French and the Viet Minh, and who had the support of the United States, had been appointed Premier of the Bao Dai government. On October 24, 1954, President Eisenhower sent a letter to Diem, stating that United States assistance would be extended directly to the South Vietnamese government in the expectation that certain "needed reforms" would be undertaken.[63] In 1955 direct American assistance began and the United States began to send military advisers to South Vietnam. This new assumption of American responsibility in Southern Vietnam took place, moreover, within a new framework. On September 8, 1954, a South East Asia Collective Defence Treaty establishing the South East Asia Treaty Organization (S.E.A.T.O.) had been signed at Manila by Australia, France, New Zealand, Pakistan, the Philippines, Thailand, the United Kingdom, and the United States, with Cambodia, Laos, and South Vietnam being associated with its key provisions through a protocol to the treaty so as not to infringe the terms of the Geneva Agreements. The United States, moreover, which had been the principal sponsor of the new collective defense treaty, stated that it was its understanding that the "aggression by means of armed attack" referred to in the treaty referred specifically to Communist aggression. The treaty entered into force on February 19, 1955. On October 23, 1955, Bao Dai was deposed by a popular referendum held in South Vietnam, and on October 26 Diem proclaimed a republic, and became its President. France had now been effectively replaced by the United States.

Arguing that South Vietnam had not signed the 1954 agreements, the Diem administration refused to hold elections in July, 1956. This decision was made in the knowledge that—as President Eisenhower was later to reveal in his memoirs[64]—it was generally agreed that if elections had been held throughout Vietnam at the time of the fighting, Ho Chi Minh would have obtained about 80 percent of the vote. The Diem administration was thus upheld in its refusal to hold elections by the United States government, which viewed the primary necessity as being the containment of Communism, and not the according of the right of self-determination to an Asian people. In January, 1957, the International Commission for Supervision and Control (I.C.S.C.), which had been established by the Geneva Agreements, and which was composed of Canadian, Indian, and Polish members, stated that neither North nor South

63. This letter, which was frequently cited as the point of departure of the United States commitment in Vietnam, in effect, did no more than express willingness to extend aid in developing a strong and viable state. (See *Vietnam and Beyond,* by Don R. and Arthur Larson, 1965.)
64. See *Mandate for Change: 1953–1956* (1963), p. 372.

Vietnam had been fulfilling their obligations under the 1954 agreements. From this time on the position deteriorated once more, with guerrilla warfare developing in South Vietnam. From small beginnings an undeclared war was now to gather momentum—a war into which the United States would find itself increasingly drawn, and that by the 1960s would assume substantial proportions. India, Pakistan, Ceylon, China, and other Asian states might have seen their independence won and Western domination withdrawn, but in Vietnam the most powerful nation of the West, the United States, would—despite external criticism and internal dissension—increasingly seek to frustrate the realization of aspirations that were nationalist as well as Communist. A new dimension was thus to be added, in the years ahead, to the long-drawn-out struggle of Asian nations to gain their independence.

The British, meanwhile, had been experiencing difficulties in Malaya, to which they had returned in 1945. In June, 1948, a Communist-backed uprising had begun, and had developed into a guerrilla war against British rule. In some ways this insurgent movement resembled the Hukbalahap peasant revolt which had developed in the Philippines after the Second World War, and which had come under Communist leadership. In both Malaya and the Philippines armed resistance by guerrilla forces continued for about a decade before being finally suppressed—by joint British and Malayan forces in Malaya, and by U.S. and Filipino forces in the Philippines. Suppression of the Malayan uprising was, however, facilitated by the fact that the insurgents were mostly drawn from the Chinese minority of the population—a circumstance which not only made their identification easier, but which also permitted the British to rely upon the Malayan and Indian population, which comprised about 53 percent of the total.

In 1946 the British had formed the Malayan Union, but on February 1, 1948, this was succeeded by the Federation of Malaya, grouping together about eleven separate states. The ethnic divisions in the country, however, slowed down, although they did not halt, an inevitable progress toward independence. This delay did not displease the British, who meanwhile obtained much-needed dollar exchange from the exploitation of Malayan tin and rubber. In 1952, however, the principal Malayan party, the United Malays National Organization (U.M.N.O.) and the Malay Chinese Association (M.C.A.) formed the Alliance Party—later also to be joined by the Malayan Indian Congress (M.I.C.). In general elections held in July, 1955, the Alliance won fifty-one of the fifty-two seats in the Legislative Council, and Tunku Abdul Rahman, a Malayan prince, was appointed chief minister. The Federation acceded to independence within the Commonwealth on August 31, 1957, with Tunku as Prime Minister.

*Bandung*

Independence had now spread throughout the greater part of Asia. The Asian colonial epoch was now a thing of the past, even although some of its symbols and vestiges still remained. In order to strengthen and reaffirm their independence, as well as to exorcise fears of a return to subjection, Asian and African governments met in a conference at Bandung in Indonesia from April 18 to 24, 1955.

The concept of the conference had emerged a year earlier when, meeting in Colombo, Ceylon, in April, 1954, five Asian prime ministers— U Nu of Burma, Sir John Kotelawala of Ceylon, Nehru of India, Dr. Ali Sastroamidjojo of Indonesia, and Mohammed Ali of Pakistan had formulated recommendations to the Geneva Conference concerning the ending of the war in Indochina. At that time Sastroamidjojo had proposed that a larger conference of Asian and African nations be held to discuss problems of common concern. The suggestion was approved when the Prime Ministers reconvened at Bogor, Indonesia, on December 28 and 29, 1954.

The Bandung Conference itself was attended by representatives of twenty-nine states—including twenty-three independent Asian states (Afghanistan, Burma, Cambodia, Ceylon, China, India, Indonesia, Iran, Iraq, Japan, Jordan, Laos, Lebanon, Nepal, Pakistan, Philippines, Saudi Arabia, Syria, Thailand, Turkey, North Vietnam, South Vietnam, and Yemen), four independent African states (Egypt, Ethiopia, Liberia, and Libya), and two African states—the Gold Coast and the Sudan—that were expected to attain independence shortly. The Central African Federation, where a small European minority dominated an African majority, was the only state invited that declined to attend. Without explanation a number of controversial countries—including North and South Korea, Taiwan, and Israel—were not invited. Similarly omitted were such interested European or European-governed countries as South Africa, Australia, New Zealand, and the Soviet Union. However, observers attended the conference from the nationalist movements of Algeria, Morocco and Tunisia, as well as from the African National Congress (A.N.C.) of South Africa, the South African Indian Congress, and from Malaya and West Irian. The Grand Mufti of Jerusalem also attended, as did Archbishop Makarios of Cyprus. American Negro interest in the conference was represented by the presence, in an unofficial capacity, of U.S. Congressman Adam Clayton Powell. Altogether the official governmental delegates alone represented populations numbering almost one and a half billion people.

News that the conference was to be held generated concern, if not alarm, in Washington and some other Western capitals. The U.S. publication *Newsweek* commented on January 1, 1955:

> Everybody knows what must come to pass between Asia and the West, the yellow and the white. It is imbecile folly to close our eyes to the inevitable. . . . All the world understands that the gravest crisis in the destiny of the earth's population is at hand. . . .

It then proceeded to forecast "an Afro-Asian combination turned by Communists against the West. The problem, according to those who have to deal with it today and tomorrow, is to prevent its formation."

Washington was particularly concerned by the fact that the Peking government was represented while the governments of European origin were excluded. The displeasure of U.S. Secretary of State John Foster Dulles, who saw some of the Asian member states of S.E.A.T.O. now forming a new allegiance that was evidently not anti-Communist, was made manifest in his statement in Washington, D.C., on March 8, 1955, in which he said "Three of the Asian parties to the Pacific Charter, Pakistan, the Philippines, and Thailand, may shortly be meeting with other Asian countries at a so-called Afro-Asian conference." Admiral Carney, the U.S. Chief of Naval Operations, predicted that the Chinese Communists would probably attack the islands of Quemoy and Matsu, held by the Chiang Kai-shek forces, timing the opening attack on Matsu to coincide with the Bandung Conference. Earlier, in Lisbon, Portugal, the *Diario Popular* had commented on March 3, 1955, "this spectacular conference is actually a kind of vast whirl of panic, as happens in ant hills on the approach of some collective danger." It went on to observe that the task of the West was to calm "the immense flock before it delivers itself up to a bad shepherd." More discerning was the observation of Walter Lippmann, who on March 1, 1955, had stated, "What this is, to put it plainly, is the most formidable and ambitious move yet made in this generation to apply the principle of Asia for the Asians."

The news of the conference also sent a tremor of consciousness throughout much of the non-European world. An American Negro writer, Richard Wright, told his wife that he felt he must go to Bandung. "I know," he said, "that people are tired of hearing of these hot, muddy faraway places filled with people yelling for freedom. But this is the human race speaking."[65]

Many others felt as he did. They felt, too, that the conference would help to change the political emphasis in Asia from a Western-backed crusade against Communism to what Asians regarded as the fundamental problems of colonialism and discrimination. But, whatever the reaction to the news of Bandung—whether of hope or of fear—the event

65. *The Color Curtain* (1956), p. 15.

itself loomed large in the imagination, symbolizing as had nothing else in the twentieth century, or indeed before, the reality of a resurgent Asia determined to take its place upon the world's stage.

Bandung itself, a city with a population of about a million, stands about 120 miles to the south of Djakarta. Here, on April 18, 1955, the opening address of the conference, entitled "Let a New Asia and a New Africa Be Born," was given by President Sukarno of Indonesia. Touching on the themes that were to dominate "this first intercontinental conference of colored peoples in the history of mankind," he recalled that many of the delegates present had met in Belgium three decades earlier to attend the Conference of the League Against Imperialism, and welcomed representatives of many different religions to Bandung. Other speeches by heads of state and others followed, after which much of the conference's work was concluded in closed sessions.

On April 24, 1955, a communique was issued that represented the only tangible result of the meeting. The communique stressed such themes as economic co-operation, and the necessity of developing nuclear energy for peaceful purposes, the need for promoting African and Asian cultures which had frequently been suppressed under colonial rule, and the fact that the Conference believed that "Asian and African cultural co-operation should be developed in the larger context of world co-operation." The fundamental principles of human rights as outlined in the United Nations Charter were upheld, and it was decided that colonialism in all its manifestations was an evil that should speedily be brought to an end. The denial of the right of self-determination to the peoples of North Africa was noted, and the Conference declared its support for them, as well as for the rights of the Arab people of Palestine, and for the stand taken by the peoples of African, Indian, and Pakistani origin in South Africa. The admission of various African and Asian states to the United Nations was urged, and at the same time it was furthermore specified that United Nations membership should be universal. Stress was also laid upon the imperative necessity of achieving disarmament and the control of nuclear weapons. No direct mention, at any point in the communique, was made to the immediate policy aims of the largest power present at Bandung—China. Western fears that China would thus obtain the support of the conference for an attempt to gain control of Taiwan, or that it would form a new anti-Western bloc of colored nations, were thus seen to be without foundation.

The communique subscribed to by the twenty-nine participating states concluded by enumerating ten principles, as follows:

> Free from mistrust and fear, with confidence and goodwill towards each other, nations should practice tolerance and live together in peace with one another as good neighbors and develop friendly cooperation on the basis of the following principles:

1. Respect for fundamental human rights and for the purposes and principles of the Charter of the United Nations.

2. Respect for the sovereignty and territorial integrity of all nations.

3. Recognition of the equality of all races and of the equality of nations large and small.

4. Abstention from intervention or interference in the internal affairs of another country.

5. Respect for the right of each nation to defend itself singly or collectively, in conformity with the Charter of the United Nations.

6. (a) Abstention from the use of arrangements of collective defence to serve the particular interests of any of the big powers.[66]

(b) Abstention by any country from exerting pressures on other countries.

7. Refraining from acts or threats of aggression or the use of force against the territorial integrity or political independence of any country.

8. Settlement of all international disputes by peaceful means, such as negotiation, conciliation, arbitration or judicial settlement as well as other peaceful means of the parties' own choice, in conformity with the Charter of the United Nations.

9. Promotion of mutual interests and cooperation.

10. Respect for justice and international obligations.

At Bandung the nations of Asia and the nations of Africa for the first time joined hands. It was clearly an event of historic and intercontinental moment. Yet, while virtually all the nations of Asia were now independent, virtually all of Africa was still subject to colonial rule. The final act in the drama had still to unfold.

66. This clause clearly reflected Asian dissatisfaction with the establishment of S.E.A.T.O. seven months earlier. Significantly the three principal Asian signatories of the S.E.A.T.O. pact—Pakistan, the Philippines, and Thailand—all subscribed to the Bandung communique.

# Chapter 17

# The African Awakening

*Over two hundred millions of our people cry out with one voice of tremendous power—and what do we say? We do not ask for death for our oppressors; we do not pronounce wishes of ill-fate for our slave-masters; we make an assertion of a just and positive demand; our voice booms across the oceans and mountains, over the hills and valleys, in the desert places and through the vast expanse of mankind's habitation, and it calls out for the freedom of Africa; Africa wants her freedom; Africa must be free.* —Kwame Nkrumah to the Fifteenth United Nations General Assembly (September 23, 1960)

DESPITE THE DOCTRINES of such innovators as Marcus Garvey, J. E. K. Aggrey, and W. E. B. Du Bois, Africa in 1945 was still regarded by the generality of mankind, African and non-African alike, as an inevitably subject continent. Europeans and Africans usually assumed that it had no culture or history to speak of, and that it was consequently not to be taken seriously by the technologically advanced countries, except as a source of raw materials. The general attitude toward Africa and its inhabitants was perhaps typified by the view of Arnold J. Toynbee who, after distinguishing twenty-one separate civilizations that had emerged in the course of human history, concluded that when mankind was classified by color, "the only one of the primary races ... which has not made a creative contribution to any of our twenty-one civilizations is the Black Race."[1] African students in the United States often found themselves neglected or avoided by American Negroes who,

---

1. *A Study of History*, Vol. One (London, 1934), p. 233. Toynbee also observed, however, that because (in his opinion), no such contribution had yet been made, it was unjustifiable to conclude that a contribution would not be made in the future.

because of the prevalent notions, had become convinced that the African past was, if anything, something to be ashamed of, and the African present something from which to dissociate themselves. So prevalent even in Africa itself was the view, later to be identified with the Afrikaaner Nationalist government in South Africa, that black Africans were innately inferior and thus incapable of aspiring to the state of civilization attained by Europeans, that there was no thought of new African states acceding to independence except, perhaps, in the remote future—the twenty-first century, for example.

In 1945 only four independent states were in existence on the African continent—Liberia, which had retained its independence despite the vicissitudes of the interwar years; Ethiopia, which, thanks to the Allied victory over European Fascism had seen its independence strengthened as well as restored; Egypt, ruled by a British-sponsored monarchy; and the Union of South Africa, where a white minority government ruled under the aegis of the internationally honored but aging Field Marshal Smuts.

In October, 1945, an anti-colonial conference was held in Manchester, England, which was to mark the beginning of a new era in Africa—an era in which, after a mere fifteen years, the greater part of Africa was to become freed from colonial rule. This development, in turn, was to modify, if not to transform, not only the generally held view of Africa as an inherently inferior continent, but also to change the self-image of many Africans, making possible aspirations that would have seemed unrealistic in the extreme a short generation earlier. The conference that signaled this new departure in African affairs was the Fifth Pan-African Congress, primarily organized by a Guyanese expatriate, Dr. Peter Millard, and attended by some, such as Jomo Kenyatta of Kenya, Kwame Nkrumah of the Gold Coast, and George Padmore of Trinidad, whose names were later to become closely associated with the independence movement in Africa. Appropriately the conference was presided over by Dr. W. E. B. Du Bois, then seventy-three, who had been the moving spirit of the first four Pan-African Congresses.[2]

Unlike the preceding congresses, however, which had been largely intellectual in character, the Fifth Pan-African Congress was militant in tone, and could claim to represent the beginnings of a colonial mass movement. The moment was propitious. A Labour administration had just acceded to power in the United Kingdom. The Second World War, in the process of dislocating the habitual patterns of life, had brought a new understanding of their situation to many colonial peoples. New leaders were now arising to voice new claims, and, in Manchester, some of those from Africa, deriving strength from one another's support, as-

2. See Chapter 13, p. 405.

sembled together to present a co-ordinated program. Complete independence for the peoples of West Africa was demanded. Far-reaching reforms were demanded for the peoples of East and Central Africa, including the abolition of racially discriminatory laws, and the introduction of universal adult suffrage. The projected imposition of a European-dominated Central African Federation upon the peoples of Nyasaland and the Rhodesias was warned against. Self-government for the peoples of Kenya, Uganda, Tanganyika, Somaliland, and Zanzibar was demanded, and support was pledged to the African inhabitants of the High Commission Territories of Bechuanaland, Basutoland, and Swaziland in resisting South African annexation. The apartheid policy of the Union of South Africa, which restricted voting rights to whites, was condemned, and it was stated that South Africa manifested the same racist characteristics which had been evident in the recently defeated Fascist countries, where the "master race" ideology had been prevalent. The demand of the peoples of Tunisia, Algeria, Morocco, and Libya for independence were endorsed, and the abolition of the Anglo-Egyptian condominium in the Sudan was demanded, together with the right of the Sudanese to independence from both British and Egyptian rule. Reference was also made to the situation in the Caribbean and to the race problem in the United States.

Greetings were sent to the governments and peoples of Ethiopia, Liberia, and Haiti, as well as to the peoples of India and Indonesia, both then struggling toward the consummation of their independence. Greetings were also sent to the Vietminh of Indochina, under the leadership of Ho Chi Minh. The hope was also expressed that before long the free nations of Asia as well as Africa would stand united to consolidate and to safeguard their liberties and independence from the restoration of Western imperialism, as well as from the dangers of Communism.

The Congress concluded by challenging the colonial powers to honor the principles of the Atlantic Charter, declaring that

> The delegates believe in peace. How could it be otherwise, when for centuries the African peoples have been the victims of violence and slavery? Yet if the Western world is still determined to rule mankind by force, then Africans, as a last resort, may have to appeal to force in the effort to achieve freedom, even if force destroys them and the world. We are determined to be free.

### The White Stronghold

If nascent African nationalism, at that time, was growing stronger in Northern and Western Africa, the bastion of the philosophy of white domination remained the Union of South Africa. As if to compensate for the coming advance toward self-determination elsewhere on the continent, in 1948 the white South African electorate returned the South African Nationalist Party to power—a party which espoused the doctrine of *apartheid,* or separation of the races.

The access to power of the Nationalist Party, under the leadership of Dr. D. F. Malan, was the open culmination of a political trend that, often in semi-secrecy, had long been gathering momentum. In 1936, as we noted earlier,[3] Field Marshal Smuts, leader of the United Party, had concurred in the decision to deprive Africans of the vote. The change from Smuts to Malan was, from the viewpoint of the African majority, therefore more one of degree than of kind. Yet, while the United Party, empirical and opportunistic in its approach to politics, was not above sacrificing African interests to gain other advantages for itself, the Nationalist Party of Malan possessed an ideological basis which, far from being empirical, was akin to the Fascist philosophies that had emerged on European soil between the two world wars. Emphasis was, above all, placed on blood and racial purity, while other cultural circumstances ensured that the doctrine that was now to emerge on African soil appeared in a different guise, representing a modification of its European forerunners. Its character, for example, was Christian Nationalist, rather than National Socialist. Its rationale was once succinctly expressed in a Nationalist Party pamphlet published in March, 1948, two months before the elections that brought the Nationalists to power:

Either we must follow the course of equality, which must eventually mean national suicide for the white race, or we must take the course of separation (apartheid).

The rise of the Nationalist Party had been given impetus by the work of the Afrikaner Broederbond (Band of Brothers), an organization that, originally founded in 1918, had become a secret society in 1924. Co-ordinating activities among Afrikaners, it sought to ensure that its members advanced to key positions in South African society so that they could the better promote the interests of the Afrikaner *volk*, and oppose those of the English-speaking population of South Africa. Many, if not most, of the leading Nationalist politicians were members of the Broederbond, just as, earlier, many had also been strongly influenced by the Nazi movement in Germany. While opposed to South Africa's entry into the war against Germany, the Nationalists had been unable to prevent it.[4] After the fall of France, another Afrikaner society, the Ossewa Brandwag (Oxwagon Guardian), which had originally been founded in 1938, and which was quasi-military in character, came into prominence. The Kommandant-Generaal of the Ossewa Brandwag, (or "O.B.," as it was known), J. F. J. van Rensburg, expressed the ethos of his movement when he commented "As against the spirit of the French revolution which wanted

3. Chapter 13, p. 409.
4. South Africa entered the war after a parliamentary vote, taken on September 4, 1939, of 80 in favor and 67 opposed.

to break away from every lord and master has come the new cry of urgency in the world: 'Give us a master! Give us bonds which tie us to a stable way of life.'" Another prominent figure in the O.B., who held the rank of general, was Balthazar Johannes Vorster, later (in 1966) to become Prime Minister of South Africa. In 1942, the year of his arrest by the authorities of the day under wartime emergency regulations, Vorster expressed in his own words the relationship between the dominant Afrikaner philosophy, and that of the European Fascist movements:

> We stand for Christian Nationalism which is an ally of National Socialism. You can call this anti-democratic principle dictatorship if you wish. In Italy it is called Fascism, in Germany German National Socialism, and in South Africa Christian Nationalism.[5]

Rivalry between the O.B., which had become a mass movement, and the Nationalist Party itself, however, soon developed. From the contest the Nationalist Party under the leadership of Malan emerged victorious. Malan's hope of consequently negotiating with Hitler after the defeat of the Allies was not, however, to be realized.[6] Political power, nevertheless, was not to be denied him. The parliamentary arm of the O.B. was the Afrikaner Party. By contesting the 1948 elections in alliance with the Afrikaner Party, and by advocating the policy of *apartheid*, Malan and the Nationalists were to win the elections,[7] thus driving Smuts and the United Party from power. South Africa was now set on the road leading toward racial segregation and totalitarian control.

In the years that followed a body of legislation was to be enacted that aimed at the separation of the races, and the application of discriminatory measures favoring those with white skins in general, and the Afrikaner population in particular. Marriages between whites and nonwhites were rendered illegal; censorship was established; a racial register was established, classifying the population in three main categories—Europeans, Coloured persons, and Africans; a "Suppression of Communism Act" was introduced, defining communism in such broad terms that virtually any person who displeased the government could be prosecuted under its provisions; the land set aside for the use of each racial group was clearly demarcated, with the best land available, as well as the greater part of the total area, being reserved for whites. Numerous other

---

5. Quoted in *The Rise of the South African Reich,* by Brian Bunting (Harmondsworth, 1964), p. 88.
6. German documents captured by the Allies after the Second World War, the contents of which were disclosed in the South African Parliament in May, 1946, revealed that the view had been communicated to Malan from the German Foreign Minister, von Ribbentrop, that Germany wanted to live in friendship with the Afrikaner people. South West Africa would have to be returned to Germany, but South Africa would, in return, be given the British High Commission territories of Bechuanaland, Basutoland, and Swaziland. Furthermore Germany would raise no objection to South Africa's annexation of Southern Rhodesia. South Africa, also, would be regarded as the "leading white state in the South African living space." (*Ibid.,* p. 89.)
7. The Nationalist Party obtained seventy seats; the United Party sixty-five; the Afrikaner Party nine; the Labour Party six; and Native Representatives three.

legislative acts governed virtually every other aspect of life—such as entertainment, employment, education, and military service. South Africa, in effect, was to be transformed into a garrison state—the one state in the world, after the fall of Nazi Germany, openly to uphold, at any cost, the theory and practice of white supremacy. The fact that, by 1951, out of a total population of 12,671,000, only 2,641,000 were white[8] was not considered of primary importance. Racial purity, and not the greatest good of the greatest number, was from now on to be the determining factor in South Africa, so far as the Nationalist Goverment was concerned.

The formal adoption of a policy of *apartheid* created a strain on the relations between South Africa and most of the other states of the world. From the point of view of the other states, the South African problem assumed three different aspects—first the question of *apartheid* within South Africa itself; second the question of the treatment by the government of South Africa's Asian minority; and third the question of the future status of South West Africa, which had been a League of Nations mandate administered by South Africa.

Concerning the question of *apartheid* there appeared to be little that other states could do. Although the policy of *apartheid* was clearly at variance with the ideals proclaimed in the United Nations Charter, South Africa, as a founder member of the United Nations, appeared to be protected from overt outside influences by Article 2, Paragraph 7, of the Charter, which stated that "nothing contained in the present Charter shall authorize the United Nations to intervene in matters which are essentially within the domestic jurisdiction of any state or shall require the Members to submit such matters to settlement under the present Charter."[9] In 1952 the United Nations nevertheless established a Commission on the Racial Situation in the Union of South Africa, but in 1955 South Africa temporarily withdrew from United Nations activities in protest against "United Nations interference" which the Commission's

8. Among the "non-white" population in 1951, 8,560,000 were Africans, 366,000 were Asians, and 1,103,000 were Coloured.

9. The Charter also stated, however, that this principle should not prejudice the application of enforcement measures under Chapter VII of the Charter, which dealt with Security Council action with respect to threats to the peace, breaches of the peace, and acts of aggression. It is also of interest that although the United Kingdom, the leader of the Commonwealth, was later to argue that because of Article 2, Paragraph 7, the United Nations could not even discuss *apartheid*, it did not take this view in 1945. In that year a White Paper (Command Paper 6666), entitled "A Commentary on the Charter of the United Nations," was presented to the British Parliament by the Foreign Secretary soon after the conclusion of the San Francisco Conference. It stated: "Articles 10, 13, and 14 extend the power of the General Assembly to discuss and make recommendations concerning any matter which affects the peace of the world or the general welfare of nations. The duty of making recommendations for the purpose of assisting in the realization of human rights and fundamental freedoms is specifically laid upon it. . . . The General Assembly will have a real part to play in the maintenance of international peace and security. Criticism of any power, large or small, will be completely free in that body, and it is there that world opinion will very largely be formed . . . it can both lay down general principles and "recommend measures for the peaceful adjustment of any situation, regardless of origin, which it deems likely to impair the general welfare or friendly relations between nations."

work represented. Because of pressure exerted by South Africa's allies the Commission was discontinued in the same year, but South Africa did not resume participation in the United Nations until 1958.

The question of the treatment of South Africa's Asian minority was, however, another matter. In 1927 the Cape Town Agreement had been concluded between the South African and Indian governments, by the terms of which the Indian government, then evidently British-controlled, had agreed to assist voluntary repatriation of Indians living in South Africa, while the South African government, for its part, had pledged to help those Indians who remained in South Africa to improve their standards of living and their civilization. Few Indians, however, had returned to India, while the numbers of those remaining in South Africa had steadily increased. The South African government had then, in 1943 and 1946, enacted legislation which discriminated against Indians, particularly with respect to land ownership and occupation.

The United Nations General Assembly, which took up the question in 1946, adopted over the years a series of resolutions declaring that the treatment of the Indian (and, after independence, also the Indo-Pakistani) minority in South Africa should be in conformity with international obligations between India and South Africa. Various attempts to promote negotiations between the two countries were made, and in 1950 it was agreed that their representatives should meet at a round-table conference. Before the conference could be held, however, it became clear that a measure extending the principle of residential segregation, and discriminating against both the Asian and African populations in South Africa, was to be enacted beforehand.[10] India therefore refused to participate in the conference. Subsequently, South Africa ignored United Nations-sponsored efforts to promote any further negotiations. The United Nations, however, continued to discuss the question annually until 1962 when, on the insistence of the African states, India and Pakistan withdrew their demand that the United Nations should consider the treatment of Indians and Indo-Pakistanis by the South African government as an agenda item separate from the question of the policy of *apartheid* practiced by the South African government. From that time on, therefore, so far as the Afro-Asian approach to the question was concerned, the treatment of Asians in South Africa became merged with the question of *apartheid* in general.

## South West Africa

The question of the future status of South West Africa—which, as we saw earlier had been mandated to South Africa by the League of Na-

10. The Group Areas Act of 1950.

tions in 1919—was posed when, in 1946, South Africa, unlike all the other League mandatory powers, refused to conclude a Trusteeship Agreement with the United Nations concerning its mandated territory of South West Africa. Instead South Africa sought to incorporate South West Africa as part of the Union of South Africa.[11] In so doing South Africa claimed that the mandate agreement had lapsed when the League of Nations ceased to exist, and that the United Nations had not inherited the responsibilities of the League.

In 1946 South Africa also conducted a referendum in South West Africa in order to justify its proposed annexation. A document to be signed was circulated among the chiefs and headmen of the various tribal units in the territory which stated that the people had been happy and had prospered under South African rule; that the people did not wish any other government or people to rule them; and that they would like their country to become part of South Africa. South African spokesmen also misrepresented the situation to the South West Africans, allowing the impression to prevail that the people were voting to be placed under the protection of the British Crown, and to avoid being transferred to the jurisdiction of some new and perhaps unknown foreign power. In consequence 208,850 of the "non-white" of South West Africa voted for incorporation, and 35,520 against, while 56,870 were not consulted. However, even though this evidence was presented to the United Nations by Smuts himself, the majority of United Nations delegates declined to sanction the proposed annexation, which, they claimed, would be a retrogressive step, at variance with the ideals for which sacrifices had been made during the war that had just ended. The trusteeship system should not become a system of plunder. The referendum, moreover, had been a dubious consultation.

Thirty-seven nations then voted that the United Nations should not accede to the proposed incorporation, with none voting against, and nine nations abstaining. The South African government was also invited to submit a trusteeship agreement. This, however, South Africa did not do, although it announced that incorporation was not contemplated at that time, and submitted a report on its administration of South West Africa for the previous year, 1946. Subsequently, after the Nationalist Government had come to power in South Africa, it was announced in 1949 that no trusteeship agreement would be made, and that no more reports or information would be supplied. At the same time South West Africa was given representation in the South African Parliament.

11. As early as 1933 the proposal had first been made in the Legislative Council of South West Africa that "South West" (as the territory was colloquially known), should be incorporated as a fifth province of the Union. The majority of the members of the League of Nations Mandates Commission had, however, taken the view that the proposal was inadmissible, although discussion on the question continued until 1937.

At the time that the referendum had been conducted in 1946, Frederick Mahareru, Paramount Chief of the Hereros—the South West African tribe which had been decimated, while under German rule in the early years of the century, by order of General Von Trotha—had received letters from the elders of his tribe concerning the referendum. Their gist was summed up by a line in one of the letters: "Come quickly, the heritage of your father's orphans is about to be taken from them."

Frederick Mahareru was then living across the frontier in Bechuanaland, under British protection. He asked an English clergyman, Michael Scott, to visit South West Africa to investigate the situation. Scott found that the peoples of South West Africa did not wish to be incorporated into South Africa, and also discovered the questionable fashion in which the referendum was conducted. Subsequently Scott, at the request of a number of South West African chiefs, including Hosea Kutako of the Hereros, who was living in South West Africa, appeared before the Trusteeship Committee of the United Nations General Assembly as the spokesman of the Herero people. In the years that followed Scott persisted in his representations at the United Nations, despite efforts by the South African government and its friends to discredit him, thereby perhaps doing more than any other single individual to expose the conflict between the values guiding the actions of the Nationalist government of South Africa and the ideals by which other United Nations members aspired to live. Thus, over a period of years, the South African government, which had in 1945 been treated as a government much like any other, was obliged to witness a steady erosion of its international reputation.

In an effort to reverse this trend, South Africa, from 1955 to 1958, withdrew from the United Nations, while retaining its membership in the organization. From the point of view of its own interests this proved to be a mistake. When South Africa returned to the United Nations once more in 1958, it was only to discover that, during its absence, opinion had hardened against it.

South Africa, nevertheless, ignoring growing United Nations opposition, continued to control South West Africa. This fact remained unaltered, despite the appearance within the territory of African nationalist movements, and despite the adoption by the United Nations of a series of adverse resolutions.[12] Only by armed force, it appeared, could South Africa be compelled to relinquish its grip on the territory.

Meanwhile, the legal status of South West Africa was the subject of judgments by the International Court of Justice. On July 11, 1950, the Court ruled that legally South West Africa was still under the League of Nations mandate assumed by South Africa after the First World War,

12. In one of these, adopted in 1962, the Assembly requested the United Nations Secretary-General "to take all necessary steps to establish an effective United Nations presence in South West Africa."

and that South Africa alone was not competent to modify the international status of the territory. The Court further found that whereas South Africa was not obliged to place the territory under the trusteeship system of the United Nations, any change in the legal status of South West Africa would require the consent of the United Nations. In 1960 the governments of Ethiopia and Liberia—both of which had been members of the League of Nations—brought a complaint against the government of South Africa for alleged breaches of its obligations under the mandate. The Court, however, after deciding in 1962 that it had jurisdiction to adjudicate in the case, on July 18, 1966, ruled that the complaint of the Ethiopian and Liberian governments was rejected, as they had not established any legal right or interest in the subject matter of their claim. Thus, while theoretically a complaint could still be lodged against South Africa for having violated the terms of the mandate, in practice no other former League members, with or without "any legal right or interest" in the matter, came forward to complain.[13]

### The Former Italian Colonies

At the end of the Second World War the question of the future of Italy's former African colonies, captured in the course of the fighting, was posed. Ethiopia, restored to independence, presented no problem. But what was to become of Libya, Eritrea, and Italian Somaliland? At the Paris Peace Conference, held in 1947, Italy renounced all claims to these three territories, and under Article 23 of the Italian Peace Treaty, the disposition of the four colonies was to be determined by France, the United Kingdom, the United States, and the Soviet Union within one year—which was to say by September 15, 1948. As the four powers could not, however, agree, the question was referred to the United Nations General Assembly. The Assembly subsequently decided, on November 21, 1949, that Libya (comprising Cyrenaica, Tripolitania, and the Fezzan) should be constituted as an independent sovereign state not later than January 1, 1952; that Italian Somaliland should for a period of ten years be placed under the United Nations trusteeship system, with Italy as the administering authority, being aided by an Advisory Council consisting of representatives of Colombia, Egypt, and the Philippines, after which the territory should become an independent sovereign state; and that, with respect to Eritrea, a five-member Commission (consisting of representatives of Burma, Guatemala, Norway, Pakistan, and South Africa) should be established to ascertain the wishes of the inhabitants,

13. Subsequently, in 1967, the United Nations established a Council for South West Africa, which was directed to proceed to South West Africa to take over administration of the territory and to ensure the withdrawal of South African personnel. As South Africa refused the Commission entry, it was unable to fulfill its mandate. All that the United Nations could do was to change the name of the territory to "Namibia," which it did on June 12, 1968.

and to examine the question of the disposal of Eritrea. In consequence Libya became an independent kingdom, under the rule of King Mohammed Idris El-Senussi, on December 24, 1951; Eritrea federated with Ethiopia, as an autonomous unit under the Ethiopian Crown, on September 15, 1952; and Italian Somaliland, after ten years of trusteeship, merged with the British Protectorate of Somaliland to become the independent state of Somalia on July 1, 1960. Libya was admitted to the United Nations on December 14, 1955, and Somalia on September 20, 1960.

## The Creation of Israel

In the years after the Second World War progress toward independence in Northern Africa was to stand in contrast with the lack of it in Southern Africa.

Contemporary strategists, at that time, reflecting the habit of mind that dismissed "Africa South of the Sahara" as of small account, frequently categorized Northern Africa as part of the Middle East. In effect the developments that were to follow would prove not only that the Arab countries were interrelated, but also that a wider regional interrelationship also existed, linking happenings in the Middle East with those throughout the African continent.

In the Middle East the defeat of Hitler had created a new situation in Palestine. Hitherto, under the terms of the British White Paper of May 17, 1939, which had clearly been issued with the intent of blocking a possible Arab-Nazi entente, Jewish immigration was to halt completely by 1944, while further Jewish land acquisition was virtually prohibited. However, once the power of the Third Reich had been smashed, the situation altered. The threat of an Arab-Nazi entente disappeared, while Zionists throughout the world, freed from the threat of Hitlerism, were now able to concentrate their efforts on founding an independent Jewish state in Palestine. The first step toward this goal was to secure the abolition of the restrictions imposed by the White Paper. In achieving this end the Zionists were aided by sympathetic public opinion in the United States.

On June 18, 1945, about six weeks after Germany's capitulation, the Jewish Agency, on behalf of the surviving Jews of Europe, applied to the British authorities in Palestine for 100,000 immigration permits. Although some members of the British Labour government, which came into office in July, had spoken during their election campaign in favor of further Jewish immigration into Palestine, the application was not granted. A letter from U.S. President Truman to the British Prime Minister, Clement Attlee, urging that "the 100,000" be admitted to Palestine, also remained unanswered. In practice, however, while not repudiating the White

Paper, the British began to permit Jewish immigration once more, although only to the extent of 1,500 persons a month. Essentially, despite the advent of the Labour government, British policy in the Middle East remained unaltered, being made not by the government in power but by "the Foreign Office and the Arab experts."[14] This policy aimed at giving the Jews in Palestine a "guaranteed minority status," but curbing Jewish immigration so as to prevent the emergence of a Jewish state. Thus it was intended to retain the confidence of the Arab states which, it was believed, might otherwise turn to the Soviet Union, as they had once been tempted to turn to Germany. The Soviet Union would be prevented from extending its influence into a region that, apart from containing oil supplies vital to Western economy, was also traversed, through the Suez Canal, by the principal sea lane linking Europe and Asia.[15]

Britain thus became the major obstacle in the path of the Zionists, with the result that the British became subjected to mounting Zionist pressure. The pressure took two principal forms. First it was exercised indirectly through United States public opinion, which in turn affected American governmental policy. Second it was exercised directly through underground military action in Palestine itself. In the United States the Zionists strove to make a connection between a change in British policy toward Palestine and the loaning of United States funds to the United Kingdom. In Palestine the Haganah (the Jewish Defense Force) moved into action against the British mandatory authorities, notably on the night of October 31, 1945, when it blew up some hundred bridges and junctions throughout the territory. Its subsequent actions were supplemented by those of two small but effective dissident Jewish terrorist groups—the Irgun (National Military Movement), and the Stern group (Fighters for the Freedom of Israel).

On November 13, 1945, the situation altered slightly. The British Foreign Secretary, Ernest Bevin, while reaffirming British adherence to the White Paper, announced that a commission—subsequently entitled the "Anglo-American Committee of Enquiry Regarding the Problems of European Jewry and Palestine"—was to be formed. It was also intimated that, if its recommendations were unanimous, the British government would comply with them. On April 20, 1946, the Committee published its report, recommending unanimously that the 100,000 permits be issued, that the restrictions on Jewish purchase of land be abolished, and that the British mandate be extended under the United Nations trustee-

14. See Arthur Koestler, *Promise and Fulfillment: Palestine 1917–1949* (London, 1949), p. 118.

15. It was argued at the time by some British military authorities that the Jewish military forces in Palestine had become so strong in relation to Arab strength that the United Kingdom, from the point of view of realpolitik, would have been better advised to permit the foundation of a Jewish state forthwith. Subsequent military developments proved that the facts, at least, upon which this argument were based were accurate.

ship system. The emergence of a Jewish state in Palestine was, however, rejected, and the possible partition of Palestine into Arab and Jewish areas was not mentioned. Prime Minister Attlee, however, instead of complying with the recommendations, stated that it would not be possible to admit so many immigrants to Palestine without U.S. help, and that the recommendations could not be followed until the Jewish "illegal armies" (that is, the Haganah and other organizations) had been "disbanded and their arms surrendered." In view of the fact that the armies of the Arab League would meanwhile have remained in existence the Zionists found this second condition unacceptable, so the deadlock persisted in an atmosphere of mounting tension.

Following a major strike by the Haganah on June 16, 1946, the British authorities in Palestine on June 29 attempted to suppress the "illegal armies" by arresting a large number of Jews and beginning military operations against the Jewish settlements. From this time on an intermittent warfare raged between the British authorities on the one hand, and the Haganah and other Jewish organizations on the other. British officialdom in London and elsewhere remained, however, deeply divided on the best policy to follow in Palestine in particular and the Middle East in general. After various suggested solutions were inconclusively advanced, one after another, the British Foreign Secretary finally announced, on February 18, 1947, that as the Palestine mandate had become unworkable, the problem would be submitted to the judgment of the United Nations.

The United Nations, which took up the question on April 28, 1947, appointed a U.N. Special Commission on Palestine (U.N.S.C.O.P.), which, after visiting the territory, presented a majority report to the Second United Nations General Assembly. The report recommended termination of the mandate; the partition of Palestine into two separate states, one Jewish and one Arab, linked by an economic union; and the creation of a separate enclave for Jerusalem under the supervision of the U.N. Trusteeship Council.[16] On November 29, 1947, after an impassioned debate and the exercise of much diplomatic pressure, the U.N. General Assembly approved the majority report's recommendations by a vote of 33 in favor, with 13 opposed, and 10 abstentions.[17] A U.N. Commission for Palestine was created to help in the establishment of the two

16. The minority report recommended the establishment of an independent bi-national Jewish-Arab state composed of two autonomous national sectors.
17. Those voting in favor of this decision were Australia, Belgium, Bolivia, Brazil, Byelorussian Soviet Socialist Republic, Canada, Costa Rica, Czechoslovakia, Denmark, the Dominican Republic, Ecuador, France, Guatamala, Haiti, Iceland, Liberia, Luxembourg, the Netherlands, New Zealand, Nicaragua, Norway, Panama, Paraguay, Peru, the Philippines, Poland, Sweden, the Ukrainian Soviet Socialist Republic, the Union of South Africa, the Union of Soviet Socialist Republics, the United States of America, Uruguay, and Venezuela. Those voting against were Afghanistan, Cuba, Egypt, Greece, India, Iran, Iraq, Lebanon, Pakistan, Saudi Arabia, Syria, Turkey, and Yemen. Those abstaining were Argentina, Chile, China, Colombia, El Salvador, Ethiopia, Honduras, Mexico, the United Kingdom, and Yugoslavia.

projected states, as well as to ensure governmental continuity, and to maintain law and order in co-operation with the British. The United Kingdom, however, insisted that the maintenance of law and order was its sole responsibility, and declined to permit the Commission to enter Palestine until two weeks before the final British withdrawal from the country, due to take place on May 14, 1948. By that time, the situation had deteriorated so far that the United Nations was unable, under the circumstances, to play its intended role.

Throughout most of 1947 violence between the Jewish organizations and the British authorities in Palestine had steadily increased. After the United Nations vote of November 29, however, a virtual civil war broke out between the Jews and the Arabs, with the British, for the most part, standing aside while upholding the fiction that they were maintaining law and order. In the earlier part of 1948, as the date of the British withdrawal approached, both the Jews and the neighboring Arab states openly began to prepare for war. On May 13, 1948, the British naval blockade of Palestine was at last lifted, and on the following day the mandate ended and the British withdrew. On that same day, May 14, the state of Israel was proclaimed in the Jewish sector of Palestine.

A few hours later, on May 15, 1948, five Arab states—Syria, Lebanon, Egypt, Iraq, and Jordan[18]—attacked Israel with the intention of destroying it. The Arab forces, numbering altogether between 30,000 and 40,000, were opposed by Jewish fighting units numbering about 15,000, supported by 30,000 civil defense forces, and about 6,000 Stern and Irgun partisans.[19] The fighting that followed, interrupted by a series of truces, continued intermittently until January 7, 1949, by which time the Israeli forces had not only proved they could survive such an attack, but had also expanded the frontiers of the new state beyond the limits originally set by the United Nations. By this time, too, the Arab forces, beset by rivalries, had become discouraged. In the final weeks of the war the Israelis, striking southward, were able to drive the Egyptians from Palestinian soil. The time had come to end the war.

Earlier, United Nations efforts at mediation had received a setback when, on September 17, 1948, the U.N. mediator, Count Folke Bernadotte of Sweden, was assassinated by a Jewish terrorist group generally assumed (though this has not been confirmed) to be a part of the former Stern organization. His successor, Ralph Bunche, an American Negro, was subsequently able to mediate an armistice. After the fighting ended on January 7, 1949, armistice agreements were concluded between

---

18. On June 17, 1946 the name of "Transjordan" was changed to that of the "Hashemite Kingdom of Jordan." The name "Jordan," rather than "Transjordan" came into general use only in 1949, however.

19. In June, 1948, the Haganah, the Stern group, and the Irgun were merged into the Israeli Defense Army.

Israel and individual Arab states: with Egypt on February 24, 1949; with Lebanon on March 23; with Jordan on April 3; and with Syria on July 20. Meanwhile, on May 11, 1949, Israel had been admitted to membership in the United Nations. The United Nations, nevertheless, in the face of both Arab and Jewish opposition, was unable to effect the internationalization of Jerusalem, thus leaving the city partly under Jewish and partly under Arab control. As for the Arab sector of Palestine (the so-called "West Bank"), instead of becoming a separate state it was annexed by the King of Jordan, whose troops had occupied it.

## The Egyptian Revolution

The Egyptian reverse in the Arab-Israeli war of 1948–1949 precipitated an internal crisis in Egypt that eventually led to the downfall of the monarchy and the emergence of a revolutionary nationalist government free of British influence.

The main political forces in Egypt after the Second World War were the monarchy, the various Wafdist factions (including the Saad Wafd[20]), the Muslim Brotherhood, and the British. Unnoticed at that time was a secret army organization headed by a young officer named Gamal Abdel Nasser. The monarchy and the Wafdists, while opposed to each other, were both deeply tainted by corruption. The Wafdists, however, maintained ambiguous relations with the British, while at the same time often bidding for popular support by launching verbal attacks against the British influence which weighed on the country as a whole. Less compromising was the Muslim Brotherhood which, under the leadership of Sheikh Hassan el-Banna, was consistently opposed to the British presence in Egypt.

At the end of the Second World War the necessity of adjusting Anglo-Egyptian relations was evident to all. In 1945 the Egyptians had asked the British for negotiations to revise the 1936 treaty, and the British had agreed. The 1936 treaty[21] had accorded the British the right to station 10,000 troops in the Canal Zone, but because of the exigencies of the war, the British had stationed over 80,000 troops there, as well as forces in Cairo and Alexandria, all of which they showed no signs of withdrawing.[22] Also at issue was the future of the Sudan, still ruled in theory by an Anglo-Egyptian Condominium—as provided for by the agreements concluded in 1899 and 1936—but in practice administered by the British. Egypt was also anxious to reach an agreement over the use of the Nile waters, concerning which Sudanese and Egyptian interests were in con-

20. The Saad Wafd, which had broken away from the Wafd, took its name from the party's founder, Saad Zaghloul, to whose original principles it claimed to have returned.
21. See Chapter 13, p. 397.
22. The British claimed that the postwar threat of Soviet expansion into the Middle East necessitated maintaining these large forces in the Canal Zone.

flict. The negotiations were opened in 1946, but broke down before the end of the year over the question of the Sudan. The Egyptian government understood the proposed phrase "unity between the Sudan and Egypt under the common Crown of Egypt" as meaning permanent unification between Egypt and the Sudan, with the Sudanese being permitted a measure of autonomy, whereas the British, while recognizing many interests in common between Egypt and the Sudan, refused to conclude any agreement which would prevent the Sudanese from determining their own status in the future.

The Egyptian government, therefore, even before the humiliation of the 1948–1949 campaign, had been denied success over the treaty revision. The result of the failure of the war against Israel was to increase popular dissatisfaction with the Wafdists and King Farouk,[23] while contributing instead to the popularity of the Muslim Brotherhood. Perhaps for this reason the Brotherhood's leader, Sheikh Hassan, was assassinated on February 13, 1949, and shortly thereafter the Brotherhood was subjected to severe repression by the Wafdist administration. Under such circumstances the decline in prestige of both King Farouk and the Wafdist politicians was steady. Popular discontent became acute when it was subsequently revealed, in the course of investigations, that during the war against Israel corrupt contractors had knowingly supplied the Egyptian Army with defective weapons.

Seeking a way out of its difficulties, the Egyptian government again turned its attention to renegotiating a treaty revision with the British. When the same differences over the Sudan reappeared, the Egyptian government, on October 8, 1951, announced that it had unilaterally abrogated both the 1899 Condominium Agreement and the 1936 Treaty—an action which produced protests from both the British and the British-controlled Sudanese government, who claimed that the agreements could not be unilaterally abrogated. At the same time the Egyptians proclaimed Farouk as King of both Egypt and the Sudan. Tension then rose swiftly between Egypt and the United Kingdom, with the British further reinforcing their troops in the Canal Zone. The Wafd government, which had replaced a Saad Wafd administration in the elections of December 1950, had made no preparations for a conflict with the British. It therefore found itself obliged to rely on the Muslim Brotherhood which, restored to official favor, was rearmed and encouraged to engage in guerrilla activities against the British. In addition the British troops in the Canal Zone were subjected to a boycott which deprived them of Egyptian food and labor.

These actions led the British to respond with a campaign of limited offense. On January 25, 1952, after a local one-hour ultimatum had ex-

23. King Farouk also lost much public esteem by divorcing the popular Queen Farida in 1948.

pired, the British attacked an Egyptian auxiliary police headquarters at Ismailia, killing forty-three of the occupants. This event roused Egyptian opinion to a fury, directed against the Wafd government no less than against the British. On the following day, January 26, mobs attacked British and Jewish establishments of various kinds in Cairo, burning down Shepheard's Hotel and other buildings. The riots did not subside until the Egyptian Army was called in to clear the streets. The Wafd government fell from power, and efforts to form a new administration met with prolonged difficulties. Finally, on the night of July 22, 1952, a secret officers' organization within the Egyptian Army staged a coup d'etat.

The new force which had appeared upon the scene, an outgrowth of a "Free Officers' Committee" led by Colonel Gamal Abdel Nasser, established itself as a Revolutionary Council. For a time, however, the new government that was installed was headed by Mohamed Neguib, a general who had conducted himself creditably during the Arab-Israeli war, and who had been elected president of the Officers' Club a few months earlier, despite the opposition of King Farouk.

The first decision that the new government faced was what to do with King Farouk. After a discussion, in which the alternatives of execution or exile were considered, it was decided to exile him. An ultimatum was accordingly sent to him which, after stating that because of his protection "treacherous and corrupt people have been able to amass shameful fortunes and waste public funds while the people continued prey to hunger and want," demanded his abdication in favor of his heir apparent, Prince Ahmed Fuad, then a small child. Farouk was also required to leave the country by 6 P.M. on July 26, 1952. Accepting the ultimatum, the King, together with Queen Narriman, Prince Fuad, and their entourage, duly left the country in the royal yacht, onto which as many valuables as possible at such short notice had been loaded. The monarchy was kept in existence for a few months longer to discourage monarchist intrigues against the new regime before it had had time to consolidate its power. It was finally abolished, however, on June 18, 1953. So ended the Mohamed Ali dynasty that had ruled Egypt, at least in name, for a century and a half.

The new government had assumed that it would be sufficient for it to assume power for all to be well. As Nasser was later to observe, he had imagined that "the whole nation was ready and prepared, waiting for nothing but a vanguard to lead the charge against the battlements, whereupon it would fall in behind in serried ranks, ready for the sacred advance towards the great objective. And I had imagined," he wrote, "that our role was to be this commando vanguard. I thought that this role would never take more than a few hours."[24] But, he continued, how different was the reality from the dream. Order, unity, and work were needed, but only chaos, dissension, and sloth were in evidence. "Every man we questioned had nothing to recommend except to kill someone else. Every idea we listened to was nothing but an attack on some other idea."

Despite such discouragements, however, the new government set about its task of purging the nation of corruption. Here a paradox appeared. On the one hand the new administration sought national unity. On the other hand, however, in order to consolidate the political revolution against imperial control upon which it had embarked, a social revolution was required. Speaking of the difficulties that this situation created, Nasser was later to comment:

> It was not within our power to stand on the road of history like a traffic policeman and hold up the passage of one revolution until the other had passed by in order to prevent a collision. The only thing possible to do was to act as best we could and try to avoid being ground between the millstones.

With such a congestion of problems, the new government was not reluctant to see a solution to the problem of the Sudan, to which Neguib (himself half-Sudanese by birth), brought a fresh approach. Whereas the United Kingdom had supported self-determination for the Sudan, while Farouk had opposed it, demanding instead Egypto-Sudanese unity under the Egyptian Crown, Neguib now also declared himself in favor of self-determination. Although there were signs that the British, taken by surprise by so sudden a change in the Egyptian position, would have preferred the Sudan to remain under their tutelage for a decade longer, they nevertheless, on November 2, 1952, reached agreement with the Egyptians that a period of self-government for the Sudan should begin immediately, to be followed by self-determination. A formal joint agreement between Egypt and the United Kingdom was then concluded in Cairo on February 12, 1953, by the terms of which the Self-Government Statute for the Sudan that the British had drawn up was recognized as an interim constitution, while the Sudanese right, after a short transitional period, to choose whether they wanted union with Egypt or national sovereignty, was recognized. A Sudanese Parliament, empowered to decide the future form of government, was subsequently elected in November, 1953. The National Unionist Party emerged as the dominant force in the parliament, which then proceeded to supervise the "Sudanization" of the administration, which was completed by July 31, 1955. By November, 1955, both British and Egyptian military forces were with-

24. This quotation from Nasser, and others which follow, are from *Egypt's Liberation: The Philosophy of the Revolution*, by Gamal Abdel Nasser (1955).

drawn from the Sudan, while on January 1, 1956, the Sudan itself acceded to independence and national sovereignty. One of the first results of the nationalist revolution in Egypt was to hasten the independence of the Sudan.

In Egypt, meanwhile, the revolutionary regime was encountering further difficulties. Complications had arisen because the Muslim Brotherhood, while sharing many of the aims of the Revolutionary Council, nevertheless represented a rival movement. In January, 1954, the government felt obliged to suppress the Brotherhood. So strong a movement could not, however, be disposed of overnight. Only after members of the Brotherhood had attempted, in October 1954, to assassinate Nasser, was the movement decisively crushed. Moreover, in November, 1954, Neguib, whom, it was believed, the Brotherhood had planned to make use of, was removed from office and, for a time, imprisoned. Henceforth Nasser alone was to assume control of Egypt's destiny.

Nasser, who was before long to play a role on the world stage as well as in Egypt, was a dedicated and somewhat ingenuous nationalist. Both in personality, social background, and purpose he had much in common with Colonel Arabi who, seventy years earlier, had also had recourse to the Egyptian Army in an attempt to bring about a nationalist revolution.[25] Born on January 15, 1918, in the small town of Beni Mor, in Asiut Province, Upper Egypt, where his father had been in the postal service, Nasser had been sent to Cairo for his education at the age of eight. Like many others of his generation, even as a boy, he had dreamed of ending the British occupation. Later he was to tell how, in those days, when he would see an airplane in the sky he would cry out *Ya 'Azeez, Ya 'Azeez! Dahiya Takhud al-Ingleez!* ("Oh, Almighty God! May disaster take the English!")[26]

In part because of his boyhood participation in anti-British riots, Nasser had not at first been allowed to enter, as he desired, the Military College. When, however, after the 1936 Treaty, it was decided to expand the Egyptian Army he had at last been able to obtain his wish, entering the College in 1937, and being commissioned in 1938. Although at that time King Farouk was still popular, Nasser had already, in his mind, identified imperialism, monarchy, and feudalism as three related evils that had to be fought.

A tall, quiet, and diligent student, Nasser soon began to exert an influence on his colleagues. Almost instinctively he began to work toward the formation of a secret group of like-minded people, a group that was

25. See Chapter 7, p. 166.
26. Nasser observed that he was later to discover that the phrase—or rather its echo—had come down to twentieth-century Egyptians from the days of the Mamelukes, when their forbears had used a similar phrase against the Turk: *Ya Rabb, Ya Mutajelle, Ahlik al 'Uthmanli!* ("O God, the Self-Revealing! Annihilate the Turk!")

later to become the Society of Free Officers. The Society itself, which was founded in 1939, was cellular in structure, so that the identity of its members was the better protected. For a time it experimented with political assassination as a technique to free Egypt from its ills. Nasser later described his own involvement in one such attempted assassination, in which a proposed victim had been ambushed upon his return home. As Nasser had driven away from the scene after the shots had been fired, he had heard sounds of screaming and wailing. "I heard a woman cry," he wrote, "a child terrified, and a continuous, frightened call for help." Upon his own return home Nasser had thrown himself down on his bed and, after a sleepless night, had decided that the method of achieving their aim had to be changed. The way should not be, negatively, to eliminate those who stood in the way, but rather, positively, to bring forward those who could build.

During the Second World War Nasser continued to strengthen the Free Officers' group. Outraged by the British move against the palace in February, 1942, members of his group had contacted the Germans, whose army was then in the Libyan desert striving to enter Egypt. Some of these contacts were, however, discovered, arrests were made, and for a time the group—whose existence was still not known to the authorities —had to lie low. Nasser himself obtained a transfer to the Sudan. Later he entered the Army Staff College. In the Arab-Israeli war of 1948–1949 Nasser fought with particular distinction, first being wounded in the fighting, and then returning to take part in the battle of Faluja, despite his wound. It was at this time that he recruited the final members of the Free Officers' group which, in 1952, was to seize power. After the establishment of the Revolutionary Council Nasser, whose abstemious personal life contrasted vividly with the licentiousness of that of Farouk, continued to live, together with his wife and family, in the same house that he had previously inhabited.

In his book *The Philosophy of the Revolution*, after considering the place of the Egyptian national revolution in history, Nasser considered the place of the Egyptian nation itself in the world. Egypt's place, he said, lay within three circles. The first and most important circle was that of the Arab world. The second circle was that of the African continent, for not only was Egypt a part of Africa, but also it was linked to the heart of Africa by the Nile, the life artery of Egypt. The third circle was that of the Islamic world, which linked Egypt not only with parts of Africa and most of the Middle East, but also with Indonesia, parts of China, several other Asian countries, and even with the Soviet Union, which had a Muslim population of 40 million.

With his authority unchallenged, and with the Sudanese question, despite minor abrasions, essentially disposed of, it now became possible for Nasser to reach agreement with the British on the Canal Zone. On October 19, 1954 a new Anglo-Egyptian Treaty was signed, by the terms of which British forces were to evacuate the Canal Zone within twenty months, while the British base there would be maintained for seven years by British civilian technicians. During this time it was also agreed that it could be readied for war should there be an armed attack on Egypt, on Turkey, or on any signatory state of the Arab Joint Defense Treaty. Anglo-Egyptian relations had, it seemed, at last been placed on a normal basis.

### The Struggle for North African Independence

Nationalism, never far under the surface in the Maghreb since its occupation by the French, had been stimulated by the events of the Second World War. In particular the implications of the collapse of France in 1940, and the publication of Western war aims, gave North African nationalists food for thought. In 1942, for example, Ferhat Abbas, the Algerian politician, having been influenced by his contacts with Robert Murphy, the United States special envoy in Algeria at that time, read the Atlantic Charter "with rising excitement and began to have second thoughts about the moderation he had so assiduously exhibited."[27] The Sultan of Morocco, for his part, was able to brood over the implications of his meal with President Roosevelt in January, 1943— an occasion at which the President, in the presence of the French, after expressing sympathy with colonial aspirations, had spoken of the possibility of economic co-operation between Morocco and the United States after the war.[28] The Tunisian leader Habib Bourguiba, meanwhile, who spent many of the war years in French prisons, was less concerned with Allied promises than with ensuring that Tunisia would not find itself "in the camp of the vanquished." Although courted by the Axis powers he judged that Germany would not win the war, and that therefore Tunisian nationalist help for the Allies must be unconditional. "It is a question of life and death for Tunisia," he wrote to a colleague. "It is an order I give you. Do not question it."[29]

Despite the hopes that had been awakened, nationalist prospects nevertheless looked bleak in 1945. When peace returned Bourguiba appeared to co-operate with the French but, in the face of French hostility, fled to Cairo, a center from which he hoped to enlist international but, above all, Arab support for Tunisian independence. Ferhat Abbas, after the French repression of Algerian nationalism in May, 1945,[30] was arrested. Messali Hadj was in exile. Sultan Mohammed ap-

27. Ronald Segal, *African Profiles* (Harmondsworth, 1962), p. 291.
28. See Chapter 14, p. 454.
29. *African Profiles*, p. 314.
30. See Chapter 14, p. 457.

peared powerless to influence events. Furthermore, the large settler populations in each of the three territories—numbering perhaps approximately 240,000 out of a population of 3,600,000 in Tunisia; 400,000 out of eight million in Morocco; and one million out of nine million in Algeria—constituted a powerful factor inhibiting change.

Difficult as the situation appeared to the nationalists of North Africa, external forces nevertheless favored them. The war had brought the United States out of its traditional isolation, and now the United States and the Soviet Union were moving toward an apparent global confrontation. Despite its links with the United States, France nevertheless had the second largest Communist Party in Western Europe[31]—a circumstance which made it conceivable that, in the event of war, France might be occupied by Soviet forces. From this it followed that United States bases established in North Africa might enjoy greater security than those in Europe itself—provided that the North African populations remained well disposed to the United States. The best way to ensure this was evidently to support North African nationalism, even though this would have to be done covertly for fear of straining Franco-American relations. A pro-nationalist policy, moreover, had the advantage, from the United States point of view, of stealing the thunder of the Communist movement, which appeared to be the logical champion of those struggling for independence from colonial rule. In practice, however, North African nationalists found that links with the French Communist Party proved only of marginal value to their cause, while, in return, they were called upon to devote considerable energy to forwarding Communist-backed causes in France or elsewhere that were unrelated to the independence struggle. As a result of this a certain disillusion with Communist affiliations became evident among the nationalists, despite the realization that the potential threat to colonial rule exercised by Moscow was a powerful spur goading the Western powers to permit concessions to be granted—concessions that would not otherwise, in all likelihood, have been made.

The nationalist demand for independence first made itself felt in Tunisia. In part this was due to the fact that, like Morocco but unlike Algeria, it was a protectorate—a circumstance which in itself gave nationalism a recognition that was at least theoretical. In part this was also due to the fact that Tunisia was the most Westernized, and therefore the most politically conscious, of the three countries. Bourguiba, in his travels abroad, had been somewhat disappointed by what he felt was the quality of the support and understanding that Tunisia had received from the Arab League countries. Meanwhile, in Tunisia, after an appeal for internal autonomy by eighty moderate nationalist notables had been

31. Italy had the largest.

rejected by the French, moderates and Neo-Destour members joined together in September, 1946, to demand independence. In 1949 Bourguiba, after traveling to many countries including the United States and the United Kingdom, returned to Tunis, despite the risk of arrest, and was greeted by popular acclaim. Once more he began to press the French for reforms. In 1951, when Robert Schuman became Prime Minister of France, Tunisia was promised internal autonomy by progressively negotiated stages. Resistance to this program developed, however, from French *colons* in Algeria as well as in Tunisia, and on December 15, 1951, the French government, after refusing to establish a Tunisian parliament, announced that it could not institute any further reforms. On January 18, 1952, Bourguiba—who had meanwhile again traveled to the United States and to other countries, and who was preparing to have Tunisia's case placed before the United Nations Security Council by African and Asian states, was arrested once more. He was, for a time, held in the interior of Tunisia, but was then transferred to La Galite, a small island off the coast where, the French felt, the risk of his being rescued by the Tunisians was less.

When Bourguiba's arrest became known a general strike was called by the Tunisian trade union movement, the Union Générale des Travailleurs Tunisiens (U.G.T.T.). The French made further arrests, after which widespread unrest developed into a state of virtual insurrection, with terrorist groups operating in the southern part of the country. The murder, on December 5, 1952, of Farhat Hached, a Tunisian labor leader, presumably by French terrorists, still further aggravated the Franco-Tunisian crisis, and also produced repercussions in Morocco and Algeria. France was thus increasingly faced with the choice of either accepting the possibility of Tunisian independence, or of continuing to rule by force alone.

Morocco, too, before long was to confront France with the same stark choice. Unlike Tunisia, where the Bey retained only a shadow of his former powers,[32] Morocco possessed a popular sultanate with a pro-nationalist sultan. In 1947, on the occasion of his visit to Tangier, a part of the Sherifian Empire, the Sultan Mohammed had proclaimed the affiliation of Morocco with the Arab world, and had demanded that Morocco's nationalist aspirations be recognized forthwith. This statement resulted in the Moroccan nationalist movement, represented above all by the Istiqlal party, rallying to him. Mohammed was only able to exert pressure on the French, however, by refusing to sign certain decrees. Determined to oust him, the French attempted to undermine his power by supporting some of his rivals, in particular a Moroccan noble named

---

32. The Tunisian monarchy was abolished, after independence, on July 25, 1957.

El Glaoui. Eventually, in 1953, El Glaoui and other rural nobles staged a demonstration against the Sultan, thus providing the French with the excuse they needed to act against him. On August 20, 1953, the Sultan, together with his family, was deposed and exiled first to Corsica, and later to Madagascar. Just as Bourguiba's arrest and exile had plunged Tunisia into a state of unrest, so the exiling of the Sultan Mohammed threw Morocco into a turmoil. The Sultan's popularity was greatly enhanced, while the noble with whom the French had attempted to replace him, Moulay Arafa, went in fear of his life and was obliged to remain immured within his palace. Throughout the country, meanwhile, terrorism grew stronger, and a Moroccan Army of Liberation was formed to fight the French.

By 1954 the French felt obliged to make concessions. Apart from the strain of continuing the war in Indochina, they now also faced growing insurrection in both Tunisia and Morocco. In May, 1954, Bourguiba was taken from La Galite to France itself, and in July, as the Geneva Conference on Indochina drew to an end, he was taken to the vicinity of Paris. The French administration was plainly about to attempt to resolve some of its African, as well as its Asian, problems. On July 31, 1954, the French Prime Minister, Pierre Mendès-France, visited Carthage in Tunisia, where he solemnly recognized the right of Tunisia to autonomy, and proposed negotiations for a convention to determine the conditions of autonomy. A Neo-Destour government was then formed, and Bourguiba was officially released so that he might participate in the negotiations. The following year, on June 1, 1955, by which time the negotiations had been concluded, Bourguiba returned in triumph to Tunisia. A Franco-Tunisian Convention, which permitted a qualified autonomy, was signed two days later in Paris.

With the ending of the war in Indochina, and with progress toward a Tunisian solution visible, it appeared, for a few weeks in 1954, as if France might win some respite from her colonial troubles. French hopes of such a respite were soon to be dashed, however. In the early hours of November 1, 1954, armed attacks were launched by guerrilla forces against police stations, military posts, railways, radio stations, and telephone exchanges at many different points in Algeria. The seven-year Algerian war, which was to surpass in violence, suffering, and duration both the Tunisian and Moroccan conflicts, had begun.

Throughout 1955 while Tunisia remained relatively calm, the situation in Morocco became more aggravated. Serious anti-French riots occurred in August, while in November the Moroccan Army of Liberation began to attack French positions in the Riff Mountains. At this point the French government gave way. The Sultan Mohammed returned from exile, and was once more granted recognition by the French.[33] Furthermore, by the Declaration of La Celle St. Cloud, which replaced the 1912 Treaty of Fes, the principle of independence for French Morocco was also recognized. Independence itself followed on March 2, 1956. Nor was the remainder of the Sherifian Empire to remain for long under alien control. On April 7, 1956, the Spanish relinquished control of their Moroccan protectorate, while on October 29, 1956, the international status of Tangier was ended with the consent of France, Spain, the United Kingdom, the United States, Italy, Belgium, the Netherlands, Sweden, and Portugal. Both territories were restored to Morocco.

The access to independence of Morocco made it impossible for the French to continue to deny independence to Tunisia, which was accordingly granted on March 20, 1956. Independence also helped to solve an internal problem that had arisen for Bourguiba who, since the signing of the Franco-Tunisian accord of June 3, 1955, had found himself attacked by Salah Ben Youssef, the Secretary-General of the Neo-Destour who, now turned political rival, criticized him for accepting anything less than total and immediate independence. Salah Ben Youssef's position had led to some internal dissension and some acts of violence but, after Ben Youssef had been expelled from the Secretary-Generalship of the party, the majority of Tunisians had rallied to Bourguiba. Salah Ben Youssef was obliged to flee abroad to Cairo. His movement was subsequently suppressed.[34]

Tunisia's independence was still for a time, however, to remain qualified. French troops stationed in the country were only withdrawn after de Gaulle came to power in France in 1958, and even then the military and naval base at Bizerte remained in French hands. Only after a serious clash between Tunisians and French in 1961 had caused much loss of life did the French finally agree in 1963 to hand over Bizerte, thus finally granting Tunisia sovereign control over the whole of its territory.

## The Suez Crisis

Until 1956 the chain of colonialism which bound the dependent countries of Africa had been slowly and logically unraveling at the gradual pace of historic evolution. The whisper of new times was beginning to spread throughout the continent. Apart from those Asian and African countries which had recently achieved sovereignty, the British West African colony of the Gold Coast had been promised its independence. Whole populations were coming to realize that the hope of better days lay ahead. The British were frequently praised for conceding inde-

33. Recognition was not only forthcoming from the French. El Glaoui, on his knees, asked the Sultan's pardon for his past actions.
34. Salah Ben Youssef was assassinated in West Germany in August, 1961.

pendence before popular demand for it had mounted so high that violence resulted. The French, on the other hand, were blamed for holding on too long, so that needless bloodshed ensued. But, with or without violence and at whatever pace, the process of decolonization continued.

In 1956, however, an astonishing human aberration disrupted the pattern, causing a political phenomenon that was later to be known as the "Suez crisis," or the "Suez affair." This extraordinary episode, which none could have predicted, caused an upheaval that was to have far-reaching consequences, for the dependent territories no less than for the prestige of the colonial powers.

The key figure in the Suez crisis was the British Prime Minister, Anthony Eden. The successor to Winston Churchill, Eden was only too conscious that comparisons must inevitably be drawn between him and his famous predecessor. Hence he apparently had a predisposition—and was encouraged—to act in what he conceived to be the Churchillian manner. A skilled and experienced negotiator, he was, nevertheless, essentially a tactician rather than, like Churchill, a strategist.[35] Goaded by criticism from some members of his own Conservative party, who accused him of lacking in firmness, he attempted to act out of character to demonstrate that he too could be forceful. Instead of demonstrating firmness, however, he became merely obstinate, persisting in a course of action when reason would have led him to abandon it. As, in addition, his health was poor, his sense of judgment appeared also to have been affected. When, on March 1, 1956, King Hussein of Jordan dismissed the British Chief of Staff of the Jordanian Army, Glubb Pasha, Eden jumped to the conclusion that Nasser, rather than King Hussein, was to blame for this blow to British prestige. Cairo Radio, indeed, had been attacking Glubb Pasha, but the reason for Glubb's dismissal was simply that Hussein wished to control Jordan's forces himself. Even though Eden later admitted this, in the meantime the animus that he had conceived against Nasser became deeply rooted, and he decided that, at the first opportunity, he would bring about Nasser's downfall, preferably by force. The opportunity was not long to be delayed.

In the United States elections were due in November, 1956, so that in consequence, the Republican administration was unduly sensitive to domestic pressure. One form this pressure took was a demand by United States cotton-growing interests that the U.S. government cut off aid, promised in December, 1955, to Egypt for the Aswan Dam project. This project, which was to be financed partly by the United States, partly by the United Kingdom, and partly by the World Bank,[36] would not only have provided hydroelectric power for industry, but would also have

35. See Anthony Nutting, *No End of a Lesson: The Story of Suez* (1967), p. 25.
36. The International Bank for Reconstruction and Development.

stored enough irrigation water to treble Egypt's cotton crop. It was bad enough, the cotton lobby argued, that U.S. taxpayers were called upon to pay for aid to countries abroad: when such aid created direct competition with the American cotton industry, it was asking for too much. John Foster Dulles, the United States Secretary of State, accordingly informed the Egyptian Ambassador in Washington on July 19, 1956, that the U.S. was canceling its promised aid. Two days later the British also withdrew support for the scheme. The World Bank's share, it was also clear, would not be forthcoming.

Nasser's reply came in the form of an announcement made on July 26, 1956: Egypt was nationalizing the Suez Canal Company, and from the Canal's revenues would raise the money needed to construct the Aswan Dam.

The canal, most Britons felt, was the United Kingdom's lifeline. One commodity that flowed through the canal was oil. When Bulganin and Khrushchev, the Soviet leaders, had visited London a few months earlier, Eden had specifically told them that the uninterrupted supply of oil was vital to the British economy, and that Britain, if necessary, would fight for it. He now had the public justification that he sought for an attack upon Nasser. Furthermore Churchill himself remarked to Eden on July 30: "We can't have this malicious swine sitting across our communications."[37] Eden had already contacted the French with a view to acting jointly against Egypt. The French, too, sought Nasser's downfall not only because of the canal, but also because he was supporting the Algerian insurgents, and thus impeding a French victory in Algeria. By August 8, 1956, Eden had approved a secret plan, later also agreed to by the French Prime Minister, Guy Mollet, whereby an ultimatum would be presented to Egypt, which would then be rejected, after which force could be used. However, as it was discovered that neither France nor the United Kingdom was militarily prepared, the plan had to be delayed. Military preparations were begun. The United States, meanwhile, sought to stabilize the situation, and co-operated in diplomatic initiatives to restore the status quo.

The first such initiative was the convening in London on August 16, 1956, of a twenty-two nation conference which brought together the principal maritime powers, the canal users, and the signatories of the Constantinople Convention of 1888.[38] Eighteen of these twenty-two powers—with Ceylon, India, Indonesia, and the Soviet Union dissenting —then agreed to propose to Egypt that the operation of the canal should be entrusted to an international agency of which Egypt should be a

37. Hugh Thomas, *Suez* (1966, 1967), p. 37.
38. The signatories were Great Britain, Germany, Austria-Hungary, Spain, France, Italy, the Netherlands, Russia, and Turkey.

member. The Australian Prime Minister, Robert Menzies, was then dispatched to Cairo to present the proposals to Nasser. Menzies arrived in Cairo on September 3, 1956, and conferred with Nasser for six days. Nasser pointed out that the Suez Canal Company had always been Egyptian, and that therefore Egypt was within its rights in nationalizing it. He denied that any crisis existed, beyond that created by the threats of the British and the French. Menzies left Cairo empty-handed.

The next initiative came from Dulles, who proposed that a Suez Canal Users Association (SCUA) be formed. Dulles apparently sought by this scheme to preserve appearances, rather than to obtain results. Eden, however, hoped that it would involve the United States in a project which would, if need be, eventually be backed by force. If Egypt had the right to nationalize the canal, the legal justification for force would be found in the 1888 Constantinople Convention which provided in its first article that "The Suez Maritime Canal shall always be free and open, in time of war as in time of peace, to every vessel of commerce or of war, without distinction of flag." As the British anticipated that the Egyptians would not be able to operate the canal without the French and British pilots employed by the Company, the convention would therefore have been violated, and force could then be used.

The divergence between the British and American interpretations of the purpose of SCUA was, however, exposed to public gaze when, on September 13, 1956, Dulles, at a press conference, stated that he knew nothing of any plan "to shoot a way through the canal. If force was interposed by Egypt, then "the alternative for the United States is to send our vessels round the Cape." He added: "I want to say right now that it is fantastic that anyone should wish to impose some undesirable regime on Egypt, and we won't do it, certainly not as far as the United States is concerned." If smaller nations could not afford to send ships round the Cape, then the United States would help them with loans. The news of Dulles's conference was met with jubilation in Cairo, grim anger in London, and bitterness in Paris. The Anglo-French position did not improve when, after British and French pilots left their jobs with the Suez Canal Company on September 15, Egyptian pilots, despite expectations to the contrary, continued to operate the canal. Meanwhile, the revenues obtained from British and French ships passing through the canal continued to be paid to the old Suez Canal Company in Paris, while United States and other ships paid dues—which had, by mid-August, amounted to 35 per cent of the total—to Nasser's new company.

Relations between Eden and Dulles had always been poor. After the press conference they became almost openly hostile. Dulles had not forgiven Eden for thwarting him, while at the same time winning a personal triumph, at the Geneva Conference in 1954.[39] He had now had a measure of revenge: Eden referred to him, in private conversation at this time, as "that terrible man."

Nevertheless, toward the end of September it seemed, on the surface, as if the worst of the crisis was over. SCUA had met but, with the United States and the United Kingdom divided, and with Nasser's pilots running the canal as usual, there seemed to be nothing to discuss. Eden and Mollet had announced that the dispute with Egypt was to be submitted to the United Nations Security Council. Matters, it seemed, were falling into everyday patterns. Appearances were, however, deceptive. Virtually from the outset France and Israel, without the knowledge of the British, had been secretly combining. Early in September the French had reportedly informed the Israeli Prime Minister, David Ben-Gurion, that if Israel wished to continue to enjoy French support, then Israel must attack Egypt—at a date conveniently close to the United States elections on November 6, 1956, thus, because of the risk of alienating the Jewish vote, preventing the United States administration from protecting Nasser in any way. Ben-Gurion had for some time wished to wage a preventive war against Egypt, but had hitherto been unable to do so because of the Tripartite Declaration of France, the United States, and the United Kingdom, dated May 25, 1950, which bound the three signatories to take action if necessary, both within and outside the U.N., to prevent either the Arab states or Israel from violating frontiers or armistice lines. But, with both France and the United Kingdom themselves preparing to violate frontiers, and with France encouraging Israel to attack, the Tripartite Declaration was already—although this was not generally known —a thing of the past. Ben-Gurion's time to strike had also come.

British military preparations had meanwhile been moving forward: it was now time, the French felt, to bring the British into the plot that was being woven. Eden was approached on September 23, 1956, and reacted favorably. After further diplomatic conversations with the French he informed his Cabinet, on October 3, that "the Jews had come up with an offer" to attack Egypt, thus providing the British and the French with an opportunity to intervene jointly. The intervention, already known as "Operation Musketeer," would result, he confidently expected, in the recapture of the canal. The plan, however, was to be kept as secret as possible, above all from the United States.

Meanwhile, in New York, following efforts by the United Nations Secretary-General, Dag Hammarskjold, the U.N. Security Council on

39. Dulles sought to pursue a policy of raising tension until a confrontation between the Communist powers and the Western powers resulted—i.e., the policy known as "brinkmanship." Rejecting this approach, Eden sought to avoid confrontation through negotiating a compromise settlement—as was done at Geneva.

October 13, 1956, unanimously agreed that any settlement of the Suez question should meet the following requirements:

1. There should be free and open transit through the Canal without discrimination, overt or covert—this covers both political and technical aspects;
2. The sovereignty of Egypt should be respected;
3. The operation of the Canal should be insulated from the politics of any country;
4. The manner of fixing tolls and charges should be decided by agreement between Egypt and the users;
5. A fair proportion of the dues should be allotted to development;
6. In case of disputes, unresolved affairs between the Suez Canal Company and the Egyptian Government should be settled by arbitration with suitable terms of reference and suitable provisions for the payment of sums found to be due.

The way now seemed clear for a general settlement of the dispute, no matter what hard bargaining took place over the details. Eden by now, however, had no intention whatsoever of accepting the six principles. His heart was in the plot.

After further meetings, final arrangements were made. Wishing nevertheless to maintain the appearance of virtue, the British did not begin to move militarily until the Israeli attack had actually begun. This delay, in itself, was to prove fatal to the scheme.

The Israeli attack upon Egypt began at about 4 P.M. on October 29, 1956, at which time Israeli troops crossed the frontier, while Israeli paratroops dropped about thirty miles east of Suez. Rumors of tension on the Jordan-Israeli frontier had previously been disseminated to mislead Egyptian and international opinion. The following day, October 30, the British and French issued a previously prepared joint ultimatum that called on the two belligerents to stop fighting and to withdraw their forces to a distance of about ten miles on each side of the Suez Canal. In addition the Egyptians were asked to allow Anglo-French forces to move "temporarily"[40] into Port Said, Ismailia, and Suez. If within twelve hours the belligerents had not undertaken to comply with the ultimatum, British and French forces would, it was stated, seize the canal and its terminal ports. Israel, which had not yet advanced to within ten miles of the canal, was delighted to accept the ultimatum; Egypt, naturally, refused to do so.

The British then, on October 31, instructed their armed forces to proceed with "Operation Musketeer," and to occupy Port Said, Ismailia, and Suez. The French air force was already in action. British ships then began to lumber slowly toward Egypt from Malta, while other craft set out from Algiers and Southampton. On the evening of the same day,

40. There was a precedent for the use of this word. Prime Minister Gladstone described the British occupation of Egypt in 1882 as "temporary," although the occupation lasted for over seventy years.

October 31, British aircraft, operating from Malta, Cyprus, and aircraft carriers, began a forty-eight-hour bombardment of Egyptian airfields. When the bombing began, Nasser, realizing that the British had indeed now resorted to force, disengaged Egyptian troops who were in action against the Israelis in the Sinai peninsula, and withdrew them to prepare for Anglo-French landings in the vicinity of Port Said and Alexandria. The Egyptians then sunk over forty ships filled with concrete to block the canal, and also blew up three oil-pumping stations. The Anglo-French gamble had thus provoked the very situation that it had sought to avoid —the blocking of the canal, and the cutting off the flow of oil to Western Europe.

Meanwhile, trouble was brewing for Eden in several places. Until the day of the Israeli attack, international attention had been captured by developments in Hungary, where a popular uprising had taken place. The Middle East crisis, however, soon replaced Hungary as the focus of concern. Reactions to the Anglo-French action were soon forthcoming from the United Nations, the British Parliament, Moscow, and Washington.

At the United Nations the Security Council, finding itself blocked by the veto power of both the British and the French,[41] called for an emergency special session of the General Assembly, which was accordingly convened on November 1, 1956. Prime Minister Eden had earlier said "I would rather have the British Empire fall in one crash than have it nibbled away." Now it almost looked as though he had brought the crash about. The Indian government informed Canada, Australia, and New Zealand that India would be obliged to quit the Commonwealth if their governments presented a "white" united front together with the United Kingdom at the United Nations. Nor was India alone. Ceylon and Pakistan took the same position. Perhaps to help prevent the breakup of the Commonwealth, the United States at this juncture took the lead at the United Nations in presenting a resolution urging "all parties now involved in hostilities" to agree to a cease-fire. The resolution was adopted on November 2 by a vote of 64 to 5 with 6 abstentions. Those opposing the resolution were, apart from France and the United Kingdom, Australia, New Zealand, and Israel.

In London the British Parliament was in turmoil. Although the conspiracy with France and Israel could not be seen, it could be strongly smelled. There were, moreover, many gaps and inconsistencies in Eden's public explanations. So high did emotions rise that on November 1, 1956,

---

41. Under Article 27 of the U.N. Charter, Security Council decisions, at that time, required seven votes out of eleven, including "the concurring votes of the permanent members"—the Republic of China, France, the Soviet Union, the United Kingdom, and the United States. In the Assembly itself, however, the entire U.N. membership could vote, and the five permanent members of the Security Council possessed no veto.

when Eden was unable to tell the British House of Commons whether or not Britain was at war, and consequently whether or not the Geneva Convention applied to the developing conflict in Egypt, the uproar became so great that for the first time in over thirty years a session of Parliament had to be suspended. Eden, shaken by the unexpected strength of the opposition to his policy, both at home and abroad, showed increasing signs of strain. Ashen-faced, he looked the sick man that he was.[42] The British press, with one or two exceptions, was critical of him. On November 4, mass demonstrations against "Eden's war," sponsored by the Labour Party, took place in London—the noise of which was so great that the French Foreign Minister, Pineau, and the French Minister of Defense, Bourges-Manory, who were even then conferring with Eden at 10 Downing Street, became alarmed.

In New York the Canadians had abstained in the United Nations vote calling for a cease-fire. Instead, Canada had proposed that a United Nations peace-keeping force be formed to separate the combatants until a settlement could be reached. On November 5, 1956, the Assembly asked United Nations Secretary-General Hammarskjold to submit a plan for such a force within forty-eight hours "to secure and supervise the cessation of hostilities." The note of urgency was not misplaced. Israel, having obtained its objectives, including the breaking of the Egyptian blockade of the Israeli port of Elath on the Red Sea, was not inclined to incur further odium by continuing hostilities. Both Israelis and Egyptians were, moreover, in the position demanded by the Anglo-French ultimatum. Fearful that the stated raison d'être of the expedition would therefore vanish, the British, goaded on by the impatient French, were hurrying to land before it was too late. Thus no sooner had Israel announced that fighting with the Egyptians had ceased than French and British paratroops began to drop near Port Said. In Port Said itself Egyptian loudspeaker vans informed the populace that World War III had begun, and that London and Paris had been hit with missiles.

Officials in London, Paris, and Washington became, in fact, apprehensive that this last fantasy might become transformed into reality, for, on the evening of November 5, the British, the French, and the Israelis each received a note from Bulganin informing them that the Soviet Union was ready to crush them with "every kind of modern destructive weapon"—a statement that was reinforced by ominous news of Soviet military preparations. Thus, while the Anglo-French forces captured Port Said on November 6, and, using tanks, began to move southward toward Suez, pressures that were to bring the operation to a halt were swiftly building up.

42. The United States Secretary of State, John Foster Dulles, was also admitted to hospital at about this time.

Whether influenced by the Soviet threat or not, the United States now gave the United Kingdom a demonstration of its economic power. Speculation against sterling, which had begun some weeks earlier, had developed into a run on the pound. Since the Israeli attack began on October 29, the drain on the pound had reached critical proportions, with sterling reserves dropping by £100 million in a single week. Moreover, with the Middle East oil supply cut off, Britain would now have to obtain its oil from the United States—and could only do so if the United States extended credit. This the United States declined to do unless Britain not only observed the cease-fire, but was also seen to be withdrawing its forces. If, however, there was a cease-fire by midnight that very night—November 6—then the United States, which effectively controlled the International Monetary Fund, would ensure that Britain received a £300 million loan from the fund in order to save the pound. Britain was thus placed in the position of the proverbial donkey, with the difference that the carrot would be given if it stopped (or, even better, retreated), and the stick applied if it advanced. Furthermore, if it was not accepted, some members of the British Cabinet would resign. Faced with problems of such dimensions, and feeling ill in mind and body, Eden felt obliged to comply with the wishes of the United States. He telephoned the French Prime Minister, Guy Mollet, to inform him of his decisions. As the French felt that they could not continue alone, the invading forces were thereupon stopped in their tracks. The great expedition that was to restore the imperial prestige of Britain and France in Africa and Asia was now ignominiously halted. As one veteran British diplomatist grimly commented, "Our smash and grab raid got stuck at the smash."[43] All that now remained was to have the troops evacuated, have the United Nations Emergency Force brought in, have the canal cleared, the damage repaired, an agreement patched up, and the post mortems conducted.

Peace was accordingly restored, and the necessary adjustments made. Israel withdrew behind her former frontiers; the British and the French troops were withdrawn by December 22, 1956; the canal, now under unchallenged Egyptian control, was reopened on April 9, 1957; Eden went to Jamaica to recuperate and, soon after his return, resigned; petrol rationing was introduced in Britain; a de facto settlement was reached on terms less favorable for Britain and France than would have been obtained had a settlement been accepted along the lines of the Six Principles offered (and supposedly accepted) at the U.N. Security Council in October; the Anglo-American alliance was reknit—but with

43. *Harold Nicholson: The Later Years: 1945–1962*, Vol. Three of *Diaries and Letters*, edited by Nigel Nicholson (1968), p. 318.

a difference. Dulles found it hard to forgive the British for undermining the moral position of the Western countries, as well as shattering Western unity, at the very moment when the Soviet Union was exposed to international criticism because of its repression of the Hungarian uprising. France, meanwhile, found itself no nearer the victory it sought over the Algerian nationalists. As for Egypt, as the British official Anthony Nutting put it:

> By making Nasser a martyr and a hero, we had raised him to a pinnacle of power and prestige unknown in the Arab world since the beginning of the eighteenth century, when Mohammed Ali defied the combined pressures of the Ottoman Sultan and of Lord Palmerston's England to enthrone himself as the independent ruler of renascent Egypt.[44]

Finally, however, perhaps the most important result of the Suez crisis was to rid the would-be imperialist faction in Britain of some of their delusions of grandeur by demonstrating that British power was no longer what it had been. With its maritime trappings the whole Suez adventure was clearly an anachronism—a nineteenth-century episode played out in the nuclear weapon age. The history of Britain's imperial incursion into Egypt had indeed repeated itself—but this time as farce. Meanwhile, the coming generation of Western politicians could ponder and mark the lessons of Suez—one of which was that the day of the old imperialism had gone by. Rather than challenge the rising tide of Afro-Asian nationalism it was advisable, instead, for the colonial powers to accommodate themselves to the new times.

### The Birth of Ghana

After the Suez fiasco, the time was ripe for Britain to show another face to the world. Fortunately for Britain, an occasion for doing so was present. Less than three months after the last British troops left Egypt, the British West African colony of the Gold Coast was due, on March 6, 1957, to become the independent state of Ghana. The imagination of people in many lands was struck by the unexpectedness of this development. For Britain, imperial by nature, to free one of its colonies without undue compulsion was as much a reversal of usual behavior as for a man to bite a dog. Furthermore, for so long had black Africans been considered a subject people that this proposed transformation of condition had in it the universal elements of those legends in which those of low degree are exalted.[45] The fact that the Prime Minister of the new

---

44. *No End of a Lesson: The Story of Suez* (1967), p. 171. Nutting, Minister of State for Foreign Affairs in the Eden administration, resigned in protest against Eden's Suez adventure at the beginning of November, 1956.

45. Aladdin, King Cophetua (a legendary African king) and the Beggarmaid, Dick Whittington, the Golden Fish—not to speak of such "rags to riches" stories as those popularized by Horatio Alger —are among those that come to mind.

state, Kwame Nkrumah, in his own person, illustrated the dramatic metamorphosis, contributed to the power of the living myth that was thus created.

Kwame Nkrumah, the son of a goldsmith,[46] was born at Nkroful, a village near the coast in the western region of the Gold Coast, on an uncertain date that was later tentatively fixed as September 18, 1909.[47] After a German Roman Catholic priest had taken an interest in his early education, he later studied at Achimota College, near Accra. At Achimota, moreover, Nkrumah studied under Dr. Aggrey, who first stimulated his nationalism. In 1930 Nkrumah graduated from Achimota and became a teacher. In 1935, with financial help from an uncle, he traveled to the United States. It was to be over twelve years before he again returned to the Gold Coast—years which, in his own words, were "years of sorrow and loneliness, poverty and hard work."[48]

In the United States he graduated from Lincoln University in 1939, then obtained further qualifications from the University of Pennsylvania. To pay his way, however, he was obliged to undertake many odd jobs —working in a soap factory, as a dishwasher on a shipping line plying to Mexico, as an assistant lecturer in philosophy, and in a shipbuilding yard in Chester, Pennsylvania. He was also active in other ways—he became a Freemason, was elected President of the African Students Association of America and Canada, and established connections with various political movements in order to study political organization. From C. L. R. James, a Trotskyite from Trinidad, for example, he learned how an underground movement worked.

In May, 1945, Nkrumah left the United States for London. Upon his arrival he was met by George Padmore, the radical political organizer and journalist, who was also from Trinidad. Almost immediately the two became involved in preparations for the Fifth Pan-African Conference that was to be held in Manchester in October, 1945.[49] After the conference, the West African Nationalist Secretariat was established, and Nkrumah was appointed as its secretary. He was also involved in the organization of two West African conferences in London, visiting Paris beforehand to solicit the support of French-speaking West Africans— such as Sourou-Migan Apithy of Dahomey, Leopold Senghor and Lamine Gueye of Senegal, and Houphouet-Boigny of the Ivory Coast—and to discuss plans for a Union of West African Socialist Republics with them. In the midst of these political activities, further studies could only be followed intermittently. He did, however, publish a short book entitled

46. Nkrumah's opponents later challenged his own account of his parentage, claiming instead that he was the son of another man.
47. As *Kwame* means "Saturday's child," this name was one indication taken into account in fixing the date.
48. *Ghana: The Autobiography of Kwame Nkrumah* (1957), p. xiii.
49. See Chapter 17, pp. 545–546.

*Towards Colonial Freedom.* Finally he received a letter from a compatriot, Ako Adjei, whom he had known both in the United States and in Britain, and who had now returned to the Gold Coast. Ako Adjei offered him the job of general secretary of the principal nationalist party in the country, Dr. J. B. Danquah's United Gold Coast Convention (U.G.C.C.). Nkrumah accepted the offer, and left England to return to his homeland on November 14, 1947.

The Gold Coast, since the end of the Ashanti wars at the turn of the century, had had a relatively tranquil colonial history. Earlier, the British settlements on the coast had been administratively separated from Sierra Leone and given their own separate government in 1850. The southern region of the country had been a crown colony since 1874, while inland the Ashanti region and the northern territories had been proclaimed a British protectorate in 1901. In the colony itself, legislative and executive councils, nominated by the Governor, had been established as early as 1850, although the first African—John Sarbah, a merchant—had not been appointed to a council until 1888. In 1897 the Aborigines Rights Protection Society, supported by a coalition of chiefs and of educated Africans, was formed to oppose a projected British measure that would have alienated "Stool lands"—lands vested in the African chieftainships—to the British crown. After the society had sent a delegation to London, the measure was withdrawn, and the land remained under African control.[50]

In 1916 the Legislative Council was given greater African representation, although it was not until 1925—following agitation by the West African National Congress, led by two African barristers, J. Caseley-Hayford and T. Hutton Mills—that the principle of elected representation was first introduced. Disturbed by the growing influence of the Africans, however, the British succeeded in breaking up the coalition which until then had united the African chiefs and the emerging African middle class. In 1946, however, the Governor, Sir Alan Burns, introduced the "Burns Constitution," under which the protectorate, as well as the colony, was represented on the Legislative Council. At the same time African representation on the council was increased to eighteen seats out of thirty-one, with five of the eighteen being elected from towns on a restricted franchise. The Gold Coast consequently now had the most advanced constitution in tropical Africa, since the Africans formed a majority on the council—even though British authority was not thereby threatened, since most African members were still effectually controlled by the Governor.

50. As George Padmore has pointed out, this was primarily due to the fact that West Africa, unlike Eastern and Southern Africa, was unsuited to European settlement. "The mosquitoes," he wrote, "saved the West Africans, not the eloquence of the intellectuals." (*The Gold Coast Revolution*, London, 1953, p. 38.)

It was to this situation, then, that Kwame Nkrumah returned at the end of 1947. He immediately set about organizing the U.G.C.C. so as to give it a broader popular base throughout the country. He was also in touch with ex-servicemen who, having seen better conditions abroad, were not satisfied with returning to their prewar social condition. At about this time the price of imported goods rose sharply, so that an African boycott of European stores was begun. An ex-servicemen's demonstration was also held. When, on February 28, 1948, the ex-servicemen attempted to march to Christiansborg Castle, the Governor's seat, they were fired upon, and two of them were killed. Riots then broke out in which the inmates of the central prison in Accra were freed, and European and Syrian stores in Accra and other towns were looted. In suppressing the riots twenty-nine Africans were killed, and over 200 injured. Blaming the U.G.C.C. for having encouraged the demonstrations and the boycott, the British then arrested the principal U.G.C.C. leaders, including Nkrumah—who was, to some extent, held responsible by his colleagues for having taken actions which had resulted in their imprisonment. He was consequently demoted to party treasurer, but, when released, resumed his political activity, among other things founding a nationalist publication, the *Accra Evening News*, in September, 1948.

The British, meanwhile, disturbed by the violence which had erupted in what had previously been one of their most peaceful colonies, appointed an all-African committee under the chairmanship of Justice J. H. Coussey to advise on further constitutional changes. The Coussey Committee presented its report on October 26, 1949, recommending governmental reforms that would increase African influence in the formulation and carrying out of policies, and that would transform the colonial administration into a parliamentary system resembling that of Britain. By the time the report appeared, however, other developments had occurred.

The imprisoned U.G.C.C. leaders had been popularly known as the "Big Six." Tension had grown up between Nkrumah and the other five —tension which was not diminished when the five were appointed to the Coussey Committee and Nkrumah was not. Furthermore Nkrumah came from a poor and isolated region of the country, whereas the others belonged to, or were affiliated with, the rising professional class in the capital. Significance was also attached to the fact that when arresting Nkrumah, the British had found in his possession an unsigned British Communist Party card that he had acquired in London. The other U.G.C.C. leaders would like to have expelled Nkrumah from the party, but hesitated to do so because of his reputation throughout the country, and his following among the youth, whom he had organized into a movement called the Committee on Youth Organization (C.Y.O.). The rift between Nkrumah and the U.G.C.C. nevertheless occurred when, on June 12, 1949, the C.Y.O. broke away to form the Convention People's Party (C.P.P.), under Nkrumah's leadership. A new slogan was also proclaimed. Whereas the Coussey report called for self-government, the C.P.P. called for "Self-Government Now."

On November 20, 1949, the C.P.P. called a "Ghana Representative Assembly"[51] in Accra, attended by a large number of people, reportedly numbering 80,000, who represented fifty organizations, including trade unions, farmers' organizations, women's organizations, and educational, cultural, and youth groups. The Assembly rejected the Coussey report, calling for immediate self-government—which it defined as "full Dominion status within the Commonwealth." On January 8, 1950, Nkrumah then launched a Positive Action campaign for immediate self-government, a campaign that was based on Gandhian techniques of nonviolence, involving the withdrawal of co-operation with the British. Disturbances, however, soon broke out, whereupon the British declared a state of emergency, and arrested the principal C.P.P. leaders, including Nkrumah, who was imprisoned on January 21, 1950.

While Nkrumah remained in prison, the British announced the terms of a new constitution, under which popular elections based on universal suffrage were held on various dates in early February, 1951. As a result, the C.C.P. won 29 out of 33 elected country seats, and all 5 of the elected town seats. Nkrumah himself, whose name had been entered as a candidate, even though he was in prison, was among those elected. The C.P.P. then asked the Governor, as an act of grace, to release him. He was, accordingly, released on February 12, 1951, and was immediately surrounded by enthusiastic crowds. The following day the Governor, Sir Charles Arden-Clarke, instructed him to form a government. A Cabinet was formed, headed by Nkrumah himself with the title of Leader of Government Business. The new Legislative Assembly met on February 20, 1951. The period of violence and confrontation was over. From this time on the Gold Coast's evolution toward independence was to be constitutional and pacific. On March 21, 1952, Nkrumah's title was changed to Prime Minister. The C.P.P. continued to press for more self-government, and, after a White Paper on constitutional reform was

51. The name "Ghana," recalling the medieval kingdom of that name in the Western Sudan, had been popular in nationalist circles in the Gold Coast since the 1930s, if not earlier. Objection was taken to the name "Gold Coast," since it had evidently been given by European seamen who had come to the shores of Africa for gain. Some scholars maintained that there was no evidence to support the claim that the Akan peoples were descended from the inhabitants of ancient Ghana, asserting instead that it was the Mandingo people of Guinea who were so descended. Others claimed, however, that the Akan-Ghana link was supported by verbal tradition.

published, Nkrumah, on July 10, 1953, in a motion approved unanimously by the Assembly, asked the United Kingdom to grant independence to the Gold Coast.

Elections were again held in June, 1954, and yet again in July, 1956, both of which were won by the C.P.P. Clearly the C.P.P. administration expressed the popular will. However, yet another problem remained—the future of the United Nations Trust Territory of Togoland under British administration. Since 1919 the territory had been administered by the British as an integral part of the Gold Coast. A United Nations plebiscite, held on May 9, 1956, established that a majority of the population chose to unite with an independent Gold Coast, rather than to continue under United Nations trusteeship. Thus another obstacle barring the road to independence was removed. Finally, on September 17, 1956, the Governor informed Nkrumah that the date of the independence of the Gold Coast had been set. It was to be March 6, 1957.[52] On that date independence was accordingly proclaimed, amid scenes of wild rejoicing. In his speech, delivered shortly after midnight, in the first minutes of the new nation's existence, and with the national flag unfurled for the first time, Nkrumah indicated that, so far as he, at least, was concerned, Ghana's independence was only a step in a longer journey. "We have done with the battle," he said, "and we again re-dedicate ourselves in the struggle to emancipate other countries in Africa, for our independence is meaningless unless it is linked up with the total liberation of the African continent."[53]

## The First Conference of Independent African States

Many countries had been represented at Ghana's independence celebrations,[54] although, because of the tensions between London and Cairo, Egypt was not invited to send a representative. Congratulations were sent to Accra from every continent. As one Ghanaian official observed, "For one reason or another, the rest of the world seemed to be nearly as excited as we were about this black country that had become the first in Sub-Saharan Africa to graduate from a purely colonial status into independent nationhood."[55] Indeed, the unexpectedness of the British action in according Ghana its independence, standing in stark contrast, as it did, with the rigid and unbending attitude of the French, then deeply involved in the murderous Algerian conflict, stirred wonder, as well as hopes for a new international climate in which relations between

52. March 6 was chosen as the date for independence because it marked the anniversary of the Bond of 1844—an agreement concluded between the British Governor of Cape Coast castle and eight Fanti chiefs, defining the limits of British authority. W. E. F. Ward comments that the Bond "is regarded by modern Gold Coast politicians as their Magna Carta." (*A History of Ghana*, London, 1958), p. 194.

53. *I Speak of Freedom: A Statement of African Ideology* (London, 1961), p. 107.

54. The United States was represented by Richard M. Nixon, then Vice-President.

55. Alex Quaison-Sackey, *Africa Unbound: Reflections of an African Statesman* (1963), p. 5.

the colonial countries and their former European rulers need not be exacerbated. Emotionally, too, Britain's action was reassuring. If rationality, imagination, and generosity could be shown in the creation of the Ghanaian state, then one day, surely, the same qualities would be exhibited toward other African countries. The struggle for freedom that undoubtedly lay ahead need not be a struggle to the death.

Some suspicion was expressed that the gesture was, perhaps, too good to be true. This was not, it was felt, the way that the world worked. Perhaps Nkrumah had become a British puppet. In fact, however, this was not so. Nkrumah remained an African nationalist. On April 17, 1957, a few weeks after Ghana's independence, Nkrumah wrote to the heads of the governments of all the independent African states, including the Union of South Africa, proposing that a conference of these states be convened to discuss matters of mutual concern. The conference was accordingly held in Accra from April 15 to April 22, 1958, with representatives from Ethiopia, Ghana, Liberia, Libya, Morocco, the Sudan, Tunisia, and the United Arab Republic[56] attending, as well as observers, from nationalist organizations throughout the continent, including the Algerian Front de Libération Nationale (F.L.N.). South Africa, however, declined to attend.

The conference laid down the outlines of a joint policy for the liberation of African countries from colonial rule—a policy that, novel as it appeared at the time, was to be consistently reaffirmed at all similar gatherings in the future. The conference expressed deep concern over the bloodshed in Algeria, and called upon France to recognize the right of the Algerian people to independence; it noted with abhorrence the statement in which the Prime Minister of South Africa declared that he would continue the policy of *apartheid*; it set April 15 of every year as Africa Freedom Day; reaffirmed loyalty to the United Nations Charter[57] and to the Principles of the Bandung Conference; established an informal group to co-ordinate efforts to prepare for future conferences; resolved that the study of African culture, history, and geography should be encouraged; and closed with a declaration of unity among the participating countries, solidarity with the dependent peoples of Africa, and friendship with all nations.

Meanwhile the nationalist movements elsewhere on the continent were also struggling to progress. Encouraged by Ghana's independence, the remaining three British West African colonies—Nigeria, Sierra Leone, and Gambia—looked forward to slow but certain constitutional advances toward their own independence. Of the three the vast territory of Ni-

56. On February 1, 1958, Egypt and Syria had united under the name of the United Arab Republic. The name was retained by Egypt after Syria left the union in September, 1961.
57. Ghana had been admitted to the United Nations on March 8, 1957, two days after independence.

geria was potentially the most important. Administrative and tribal divisions within Nigeria, however, created problems that precluded the relatively rapid advance to independence that Ghana had known. Nigerian nationalism had been stimulated to a great extent by Dr. Nnamdi Azikiwe—popularly known as "Zik." An Ibo from Eastern Nigeria, born in 1904, he had, like Nkrumah, visited the United States, and, also like Nkrumah, had worked at many odd jobs there, and encountered racial discrimination. He had also studied journalism and, upon returning to Africa, had spent three years in the Gold Coast, where he had edited a nationalist publication, the *African Morning Post,* which had influenced Nkrumah. Returning to Nigeria in 1937, he had founded a chain of newspapers, of which the best known was the *West African Pilot,* which had broken new ground in African journalism.

Less radical than Nkrumah—perhaps because his American experience had largely been gained before the Depression—"Zik" had been impressed by the doctrines of Booker Washington,[58] and, by applying them, had amassed a fortune. Consequently, unlike most African politicians, he had a financial foundation on which to build when he entered politics. In 1944 he established the Nigerian National Council, which was later to become the National Council of Nigeria and the Cameroons (N.C.N.C.). Advocating a federation of eight states as the most hopeful formula for an independent Nigeria, he found himself in constant opposition to the British, who advocated the division of the country into three regions. In 1945 the *West African Pilot* was banned by the British, and "Zik" went into hiding for a time in the belief that the British were attempting to have him assassinated. After these incidents, "Zik" became increasingly well known both in Nigeria and abroad. However, constant feuding with the British over the form that an independent Nigeria would take, rather than over the simple issue of independence, as well as feuds with other Nigerian movements, such as the Action Group in Western Nigeria, led by Chief Obafemi Awolowo, prevented "Zik" from achieving the kind of success that Nkrumah had been able to win in Ghana. Lack of unity in Nigeria, in effect, proved the stumbling block which made it possible for the British repeatedly to delay advances toward independence. The dynamic spirit of nationalism consequently became mired down in constitutional complexities that seemed to drag on interminably.

### British East Africa

Different circumstances, again, prevailed in the three British East African territories of Kenya, Uganda, and Tanganyika.

58. See Chapter 13, p. 406.

In Kenya the outstanding nationalist leader was Jomo Kenyatta.[59] After visiting England in 1929, Kenyatta returned there again from 1931 to 1946, during which time he both learned and taught at the London School of Oriental and African Studies, as well as studying anthropology under Professor Bronislaw Malinowski at the London School of Economics. In 1938 he published *Facing Mount Kenya*, an anthropological treatise on the Kikuyu tribe. He also traveled in Europe, and spent some time in the Soviet Union, where he studied at Moscow University. After participating, with Nkrumah and others, in the Fifth Pan-African Congress in Manchester in 1945, he returned to Kenya in 1946 to find that the Kikuyu Central Association, of which he had been the general secretary, had been proscribed by the British. He therefore formed the Kenya African Union (K.A.U.), which included representatives of other tribes, as well as the Kikuyu.

The primary political problem in Kenya had been the land question. In the early years of the century a series of natural disasters, such as an outbreak of smallpox, a famine, and a plague of locusts, had depopulated the fertile highlands of the Kikuyu. The British, seeing the land unused, had alienated much of it for white settlement. Subsequently, the population of the Kikuyu had increased markedly, creating growing pressure on the remaining land available, as well as bringing the interests of the African and settler communities into opposition. Economic and social conditions among the Kikuyu, in particular, deteriorated steadily, and became so bad that traditional and family authority was undermined, while crime and violence increased. British attempts to rule the Kikuyu indirectly through tribal chiefs—although traditionally the tribe had been governed by elders, and not chiefs—merely added a further vexatious complication. Finally, in 1950, sporadic outbreaks of violence occurred, which the British claimed were organized by a secret Kikuyu society known as *Mau Mau*. By 1952 the violence had developed into an open rebellion. On October 22, 1952, Kenyatta and five other Kenyans were arrested by the British, and later charged with managing Mau Mau. A state of Emergency was proclaimed, and the Kenya African Union, which then had a membership of about 150,000, was banned. Kenyatta, subjected to a trial that departed from accepted legal norms, was sentenced on April 8, 1953, to seven years' imprisonment. Meanwhile terrorism, unleashed by both the African rebels and the British counterinsurgency forces, swept those parts of the country that were affected.

The so-called "Mau Mau movement," which was primarily directed against pro-European Africans, rather than against Europeans themselves, was based on a secret organization which gave a new form to

59. In his early years Kenyatta was known as Kamau wa Ngengi.

some ancient animistic rites and customs, including oath-taking. Unlike other forms of African nationalism, therefore, it was deprived of international sympathy and support, if only because, representing a return to an ancient tribal past, it was hard to identify with. Apart from the fact that it helped to discourage further European immigration, and forced some settlers to leave, it constituted, primarily, a rejection of the contemporary world, rather than an effective liberation movement. In this sense it might fairly be compared to the medieval Jacquerie, the peasant uprising which took place in Beauvais, France, in May, 1358, when, after the cycle of war, famine, and taxes had become too great to be borne, the peasants, rejecting even God and his church, proclaimed that they would "kill all the nobles in the world"—and then proceeded to kill in crude and shocking fashion such members of the nobility, men, women, and children alike, as they could seize. Mau Mau and the Jacquerie were both movements of protest. Both were woven from the same plain cloth of rural despair. Both, too, were doomed to be defeated.

By 1956 the rebellion had been suppressed by the British. In April, 1959, Kenyatta was freed from prison, but remained in restricted residence in the remote Northern Frontier Province. Not until 1961, after elections had at last given Africans a majority in the Legislative Council, was Kenyatta restored to liberty. Meanwhile, in Kenya itself, constitutional advance, which had been paralyzed during the Emergency, slowly gained momentum once more, as new African parties and organizations were formed. So clearly, after the Emergency, was the country evolving toward independence that those European settlers who were unwilling to remain under African majority rule began to sell their land and emigrate elsewhere.

In Uganda evolution toward independence was hindered by the problem of the relationship between the kingdom of Buganda and the rest of the country. Nationalism in Buganda itself was a powerful force, and, to the Baganda people, was personified by their ruler, the Kabaka, Mutesa II. Despite constitutional reforms introduced in 1953, differences between the Kabaka, who sought to have Buganda given eventual independence as a separate state, and the British Governor of Uganda, Sir Andrew Cohen, who sought to develop Uganda as a unitary state, became so acute that, on October 30, 1953, the Governor sent the Kabaka into exile in London. This development so aroused the Baganda nation that Buganda was thrown into a turbulence from which it only emerged after the restoration of the Kabaka on October 17, 1955—an event that was marked by three days of rejoicing. After the Kabaka's return a federal relationship between Buganda and the rest of the country was established.

In Tanganyika the outstanding nationalist leader was Julius Nyerere, a softspoken Catholic of short stature who, despite an unassuming manner, achieved results by quiet persuasion, constantly and logically pursued. A member of the small Bazanaki tribe, Nyerere had been a schoolteacher before traveling to Edinburgh, Scotland, where he studied liberal arts from 1949 to 1952. In 1953 Nyerere became President of the Tanganyika African Association and, in 1954, of the Tanganyika African Nationalist Union (T.A.N.U.). In 1955 he appeared as a petitioner at the United Nations, asking the British to establish a target date—distant if necessary—for the independence of his country. In this way he opened a lengthy dialogue with the British administration that was to establish his position as the main nationalist spokesman in Tanganyika. The British had nominated him as a member of the Legislative Council, but he resigned in December, 1957, because of "lack of progress." Subsequently, in September, 1958, he accepted "tripartite" election proposals made by the British, according to which separate African, Asian, and European seats were allocated to the Legislative Council, although voting was by the electorate as a whole. In the subsequent elections T.A.N.U., campaigning for independence and a non-racial democracy, and sponsoring African, Asian, and European candidates, won a substantial majority. Progress to independence was only a matter of time.

## The Central African Federation

If the British West African had made the greatest progress toward independence, followed by the British East African territories, it was in British Central Africa that African nationalism encountered the most serious obstacles. In Southern Rhodesia a substantial number of white settlers had established themselves, while in Northern Rhodesia the copper mines, controlled by British and American companies, constituted an economic interest that seemed unlikely to favor eventual African control of the territory. Only in the smaller agricultural colony of Nyasaland did the road to African advancement seem less encumbered. All three territories, moreover, were landlocked, and so isolated from the outside world, being surrounded by the Belgian Congo and Tanganyika to the north, Portuguese territories to east and west, and—apart from the even more isolated Bechuanaland—by the Union of South Africa to the south. Belgians, Portuguese, and South African administrations were all hostile to African advancement to independence.

Furthermore, as if this were not enough, in 1953, against the will of the African populations, and at the instigation of the white Rhodesian minority, Britain had joined together Northern Rhodesia, Southern Rhodesia, and Nyasaland to form the Federation of Rhodesia and Nyasaland —or, as it was generally known, the Central African Federation. The idea of the federation had been conceived by the white Prime Minister of

Southern Rhodesia, Sir Godfrey Huggins (later Lord Malvern), who sought to detach Northern Rhodesia and Nyasaland from the control of the British Colonial Office (which to some extent constituted itself as a guardian of African interests), and, by means of the federation, to place them under the control of the white minority in Rhodesia. In order to disarm critics of this constitutional maneuver, much stress was placed on the fact that the federation would be dedicated to "multi-racialism," despite the lack of guarantees to protect African or Asian interests.

In 1955 Huggins, who had acted as the first federal Prime Minister, retired, yielding his place to a colleague, Sir Roy Welensky, a former railway worker and trade unionist, famous for once having been the heavyweight boxing champion of Rhodesia. Welensky, the son of a Lithuanian Jewish father and of an Afrikaner mother, had influential friends in London, among whom he campaigned assiduously in an attempt to secure complete independence from Britain, as well as Dominion status, for the Federation. Both in Britain itself, therefore, where argument and counterargument concerning the Federation raged intermittently, and in the territories of the Federation, where African politicians and their followers were subjected to repressive legislation, the cause of African nationalism assumed a defensive, rather than an aggressive, character. Welensky had declared himself opposed to adult suffrage in 1958, when a new constitution for Northern Rhodesia was proposed.

In 1959 demonstrations by the Africans against the imposed Federation were to become so widespread that a state of Emergency was to be proclaimed in both Southern Rhodesia and Nyasaland. African opposition to Federation was represented by such leaders as Harry Nkumbula and Kenneth Kaunda in Northern Rhodesia, Joshua Nkomo in Southern Rhodesia, and Dr. Hastings Banda—who returned to his homeland, after many years abroad, in 1958—in Nyasaland. All of them, at one time or another, were to experience imprisonment before, finally, the Federation was to be dissolved on December 31, 1963. For ten years the Federation had successfully constituted an artificial barrier to the political progress of the African majority.

## French Africa

Throughout the years when many African territories south of the Sahara were moving toward independence, the Algerian war, which was to last from 1954 to 1962, was to continue its cruel course in the north, thereby providing, as it were, a sinister counterpoint to the other themes that were being heard. By the time de Gaulle was, in one of his greatest achievements, to conduct negotiations that were to result in the signing of a cease-fire agreement with the Algerian F.L.N. at Evian-les-Bains in Switzerland on March 18, 1962—an agreement that was to open the door to Algerian independence—large numbers of Algerians and French would have been killed, a countryside devastated, and incalculable suffering caused.

Apart from the Maghreb, the vast hinterland of French Africa, stretching from Cape Verde to the Congo, was divided into twelve colonies, to which were added the two United Nations Trust Territories of French Togoland and the French Cameroons. Sometimes France found it convenient to administer its colonies in two large groupings—l'Afrique Occidentale Française, or French West Africa (A.O.F.), comprising Senegal, Mauritania, Guinea, the French Soudan, the Ivory Coast, Niger, Upper Volta, and Dahomey, and l'Afrique Equatoriale Française, or French Equatorial Africa (A.E.F.), comprising Chad, the French Congo, Gabon, and Ubangui-Chari. At other times, however, it had proved more practicable to govern each territory primarily through its separate colonial administration. African nationalism in the territories—strongly tinged with the politics of Paris as well as with the culture of France itself—reflected the same ambiguity, sometimes adopting local and sometimes regional forms.

The most striking regional approach to the politics of nationalism had occurred when, at Bamako in October, 1946, Houphouët-Boigny of the Ivory Coast had organized the Rassemblement Démocratique Africain (R.D.A.), an interterritorial party which aimed to "free Africa from the colonial yoke by the affirmation of her personality and by the association —freely agreed to—of a union of nations." The R.D.A., of which Houphouët-Boigny was President, was, at this time, supported and advised by the French Communist Party. By 1950, however, tension between the R.D.A. and the French administration began to erupt into sporadic violence. Houphouët-Boigny accordingly announced, in October of that year, that the R.D.A. was severing its links with the Communists, and would remain "a purely African party." After this the territorial influence of the R.D.A. declined for a time, but later acquired a strength that stemmed from a well-organized party machinery, rather than from revolutionary ideology.

Houphouët himself, by the early 1950s, had clearly emerged as the single most influential politician in French-speaking Africa south of the Sahara—with the possible exception of Léopold Sédar Senghor of Senegal. Born on October 18, 1905, at Yamoussoukro in the Ivory Coast, Houphouët was the son of a prominent Baoulé planter, and received medical training in Dakar before entering politics in 1944 by organizing an African planters' trade union. In 1945 he founded the Parti Démocratique de la Cote d'Ivoire (P.D.C.I.) and later was elected in November, 1945, and June, 1946, as representative for the Ivory Coast and for Upper Volta in the French Constituent Assembly in Paris. A coalition between the French Communist Party and the French African representatives at the Assembly, in which Houphouët played an active role, resulted in a series of reforms being adopted, including the abolition of the forced labor regime that had hitherto prevailed, the adoption of guarantees of freedom of meeting and association, and the extension of French citizenship to inhabitants of "France Overseas." A draft French constitution favoring African advancement was nevertheless rejected by the French people in May, 1946. A second draft constitution allowing for the representation of the colonial peoples in the central governing institutions in Paris, but overweighting the representation first in favor of France as opposed to the colonial areas, and then in favor of Europeans as opposed to African or other peoples, was then approved in October, 1946, thus bringing the French Union into being. As, however, the new constitution did not favor colonial emancipation, Houphouët responded by organizing the R.D.A.

Senegal, traditionally, had been the most favored of French African colonies, and when, in 1950, Houphouët broke with the Communists and came to terms with the French government, he demanded, and secured from Paris, favored treatment for the Ivory Coast, rather than for Senegal. Henceforth a tide of investment for development flowed toward the Ivory Coast, bringing it new economic life. As early as November, 1946, Houphouët had been elected to the French National Assembly, and in 1951 he was once more re-elected.

When, in the years that followed, French-speaking Africa was deeply stirred by the news that the British intended to grant independence to the Gold Coast, Paris felt obliged to make a substantial concession to African nationalism. Thus, when Houphouët took office in a French Socialist government in 1956, he was called upon to play a major role in drafting a new measure, the *loi-cadre* (enabling law) of June 23, 1956. This act, which laid down general principles for reform, made it possible for specific measures to be proclaimed as necessary, simply by decree. Among other reforms, universal suffrage was introduced in the French African territories, while in each individual territory executive councils, having a majority of elected members, were established. In this way it was hoped not only not to fall too far behind the British in permitting constitutional progress, but also to prevent the insurgence in France's African colonies of the violence that had wrecked French institutions in Southeast Asia, and that was even then wrecking them in North Africa, where the Algerian war continued. From this time on Houphouët's career flourished in Paris, no less than in the Ivory Coast, where he had become Mayor of Abidjan in November, 1956. After holding a ministerial portfolio in the Cabinet of the French Prime Minister, Guy Mollet, at the time of the Suez invasion, he subsequently served as a Minister of France until 1959, when, because of developments in Africa, he resigned in order to return to the Ivory Coast once more.

The developments in Africa stemmed from the Algerian war which, after the failure of the Anglo-French attack on Egypt in 1956, continued its cruel and seemingly interminable course. Eventually, in the summer of 1958, it led to a crisis within the French parliamentary system that resulted in the dramatic return to power in Paris of General de Gaulle. In September, 1958, de Gaulle held a referendum that led to the establishment of the Fifth French Republic. Under its constitution the French Union was to be transformed into the French Community. The Community represented a further decentralization of power in French Africa, even though France still maintained control over the whole. From the African standpoint, the new Constitution, which granted local autonomy, made much possible—but not independence. A rejection of the Constitution by any territory would nevertheless, it was made clear, be equivalent to a declaration of independence from France.

The referendum was held on September 28, 1958, throughout the territories of French Africa, no less than in the mother country. In addition to France itself, all the French African territories approved the constitution of the Fifth Republic with the single exception of Guinea, where Sékou Touré, leader of the principal nationalist party, the Parti Démocratique de Guinée (P.D.G.), had urged the electorate to vote "no" on the day of the referendum. While visiting Guinea a few weeks earlier, in August 1958, de Gaulle had declared:

> I say here, even louder than elsewhere, that independence is available to Guinea, she can have it; she can have it on 28 September by saying "no" to the proposition that is put to her, and in saying this I guarantee that Paris will raise no obstacle to it.

De Gaulle kept his word. On October 2, 1958, Guinea was proclaimed an independent republic, with Sékou Touré as its President.

France wished, however, to make an example of Guinea. For if Guinea succeeded in maintaining its independence, then all the other French African territories would similarly demand independence. If, however, Guinea's bid for independence ended in disaster, and Guinea was obliged to turn to France for aid and protection, then further evolution toward independence in French Africa would be indefinitely postponed. In its attempt to oblige Guinea to renounce its independence, the French government withdrew all French administrators, technicians, teachers, doctors, and other professionals from the new republic. All French property that could aid the Guineans was destroyed or otherwise rendered useless. Telephones were torn out of offices. Even medical supplies were destroyed. Guinea had chosen independence: let Guinea see what independence without French support meant.

Instead of returning to the French fold, however, Sékou Touré traveled instead to Accra, where, on November 23, 1958, he signed a joint declaration with Kwame Nkrumah of Ghana, stating that, on behalf of their respective governments, and subject to ratification, they had agreed to constitute their two states as the nucleus of a Union of West African states. At the same time it was agreed that, with the approval of the Ghanaian parliament, which was subsequently forthcoming, Ghana would advance Guinea the sum of $28 million, "to afford Guinea such technical and administrative aid as may be necessary to strengthen the new state." This development aroused the greatest interest abroad. The French tended to conclude that the British, working through the medium of the Ghana government, were trying to take advantage of the situation by attempting to wrest Guinea out of the franc currency zone and into the sterling zone. The British, for their part, complained that Ghana had not given them sufficient forewarning of their action, which affected the Commonwealth. The territories of French Africa, sensing that their own futures were now also at stake, followed the situation with keen concern, and in some instances sent some of their trained personnel to help the Guineans. They also began, one after the other, to opt for the privilege, given by the Constitution of the Fifth Republic, to become "Autonomous Republics" within the French Community. Finally, on December 12, 1958, Guinea was admitted to the United Nations, where its application to the Security Council was approved by ten votes out of eleven, with only France abstaining. Guinea's admission was accepted as proof that it had surmounted the crisis into which France's action had plunged it at the moment of independence.

The effect of Guinea's admission to the United Nations, and the subsequent international interest that was aroused, was to convince the political leaders of almost all the territories of French Africa to demand independence. By the end of 1959 it was clear that in 1960 Africa would witness a veritable stampede toward independence. France, unable to bring the Algerian rebellion to a conclusion, was accordingly obliged to prepare to accord independence to those states that wanted it.

### 1960—Anno Mirabile

1960 was indeed to prove the most remarkable year in the history of the African continent—a year without precedent. When the year opened Africa was still, for the most part, under colonial tutelage. When the year closed an era had passed, and the outlines of an entirely new era had come into view.

The year began with the granting of independence, on January 1, 1960, to the U.N. Trust Territory of the Cameroons under French administration. The occasion was not entirely a happy one, for the French had earlier prevented elections from being held with the participation of the largest and most militant of the African parties, the Union of the Population of Cameroun (U.P.C.), and had banned the party. An uprising had subsequently taken place and, while the principal U.P.C. leader, Ruben Um Nyobe, who had Communist affiliations, had been ambushed and shot, regions of the country were still in a state of turmoil. In 1959, after a lengthy debate, the United Nations, against the wishes of the independent African states, had refused, by a narrow margin, to call upon France to hold further elections before independence was granted. But independence, even under such circumstances, was independence still.

Meanwhile, the transformation that was so clearly to take place in French Africa, as well as internal developments within the Congo itself, had affected Belgian policy toward the Congo. On January 4, 1959, violent rioting had broken out in Leopoldville, capital of the Belgian Congo —rioting which clearly indicated that nationalist feeling was sweeping the Congo so strongly that Belgium could not long maintain it in a state of dependency, even by force. Belgian and Congolese leaders, meeting at a round-table conference in Brussels, subsequently agreed, on January 27, 1960, that the Congo itself should become independent on June 30, 1960.

Hardly had the import of this announcement been adequately digested when a new event impressed itself upon the consciousness of the world. Upon March 21, 1960, at Sharpeville in South Africa, police opened fire on Africans who had been demonstrating against the pass laws,[60] killing sixty-six and wounding hundreds more. World-wide condemnation of South Africa's *apartheid* policies resulted, and the U.N. Security Council adopted a resolution deploring the incident, as well as South Africa's policies and actions. It was in this atmosphere that, on April 9, 1960, an English-born South African farmer shot Prime Minister Henrik F. Verwoerd twice in the head, but failed to kill him. For a moment South African history—like Prime Minister Verwoerd's life—hung in the balance. A mood of doubt and introspection swept over South Africa's white community. A state of Emergency was declared. Between March 25 and April 14, South Africa's gold and foreign exchange reserves dropped by over $36 million. The president of the Johannesburg Chamber of Commerce urged the government to take a new approach to Africans, based on consultations with them. Other influential voices spoke in the same vein. For a moment it seemed that South Africa itself might be preparing to abandon its policy of *apartheid*, and to begin moving toward a system based on universal adult suffrage for all races. Instead, white South Africa hesitated, and, while hesitating, in effect de-

60. The pass laws, requiring Africans to carry identification papers when entering urban areas, constitute the principal mechanism employed in operating the South African system of *apartheid* (racial segregation).

cided to await the next turn of events—and to build up military strength. Events in the Congo were, before long, to confirm the South African government in its decision not to abandon *apartheid*. 1960, a turning point in African history, was for South Africa a turning point which failed to turn.

On April 27, 1960, the U.N. Trust Territory of Togo under French administration acceded to independence, under the premiership of Sylvanus Olympio, a former businessman who had enjoyed the distinction of being the first African petitioner ever to appear before the United Nations. Togo's independence was but the prelude to the independence of other French African territories, some of which had been negotiating the terms of their emancipation for some time. On June 3, however, to the dismay of the French, even Houphouët-Boigny of the Ivory Coast, whom they had regarded as their staunchest African ally, suddenly demanded unconditional independence for the Ivory Coast, as well as for three other states—Dahomey, Niger, and Upper Volta—that were linked with it in a grouping known as the *Conseil de l'Entente*. There was an explosion of rage in Paris at this unexpected "treachery," followed by a sudden silence in official circles which was only broken, a few weeks later, by the announcement that Houphouët's demand would be met.

Meanwhile, on June 20, 1960, the Federation of Mali, composed of the two territories of Senegal and the Soudan, became independent. Then, within a single week, three further states were proclaimed independent—Madagascar on June 26, the Belgian Congo on June 30, and Somalia, comprising the U.N. Trust Territory of Somaliland under Italian administration, and the British protectorate of Somaliland,[61] on July 1. At this juncture, however, the rapid passage of one African state after another from dependence to sovereignty was interrupted by events that were to plunge both Africa and the world into a major crisis.

Shortly after the proclamation of the independence of the Belgian Congo—or, as it was to become known, the Republic of the Congo (Leopoldville)—disturbing reports of violent events began to emanate from the new state. On July 6 it was reported that the 25,000-member Force Publique, responsible for the maintenance of order, was in revolt against its Belgian officers. On July 7 reports alleged that Belgian women were being violated by the Congolese. On July 8 many of the Belgian communities in the Congo succumbed to panic, with the result that crowds of frightened Belgians fled across the Congo river to Brazzaville, seeking to return to Europe. The Congolese government announced its decision to dismiss all Belgian officers in its employ, while at the same time Belgium began to fly troops into the Congo, allegedly to protect Belgian

---

61. British Somaliland had become independent on June 26, thus existing as an independent unit for five days before becoming a part of Somalia.

lives. On July 11, 1960, Moise Tshombe, the Provincial Premier of Katanga, the Congo's richest province, where mining and industry were the most developed, and Belgian investment the most significant, announced that Katanga had seceded from the Congo. On the same day Premier Khrushchev of the Soviet Union accused Belgium and its allies of seeking to return the Congo to colonial status "under the guise of suppressing riots." On July 12 the Prime Minister of the Congo, Patrice Lumumba, requested the United States to send troops to the Congo, but the request was rejected by President Eisenhower. The following day, July 13, with Belgian troops attacking Leopoldville airport, Lumumba asked President Nkrumah of Ghana to send Ghanaian troops to help him. At the suggestion of Dag Hammarskjold, Secretary-General of the United Nations, it was agreed that the Ghanaian troops, together with more from other African states, might be sent to the Congo under U.N. auspices. On July 14, accordingly, the U.N. Security Council decided to send United Nations forces to the Congo, and appealed to Belgium to withdraw from the new state. Each day that followed brought further news of events—diplomatic, military, and political—while the principal powers concerned continued to trade accusations of bad faith. Meanwhile, on July 21, 1960, Ghanaian and Tunisian troops arrived in the Congo, precursors of contingents from other countries who were, together, to comprise the forces of the U.N. Operation in the Congo (O.N.U.C.).

From this time on, while Lumumba sought, with U.N. help, both to secure the expulsion of the Belgians and to end the secession of Katanga, the major powers sought to avoid the incipient confrontation between the Soviet Union and the United States in the Congo that now threatened the world with the specter of nuclear war. The weeks that followed were of the utmost confusion. The confusion became worse compounded when, on September 5, 1960, Joseph Kasavubu, the President of the Congo Republic, dismissed Lumumba as Prime Minister. Subsequently, Lumumba was kidnaped and, in 1961, murdered in Katanga under mysterious circumstances—a development which profoundly disturbed the African and Asian countries, since they recalled that it was he who had first called upon the United Nations for help, yet, after the arrival of United Nations forces, the U.N. had not only been tainted by some of the intrigues that led to his political downfall, but had also not even been able to prevent his murder. After this it was only slowly, and with painful effort, that the Congo was able to emerge from the state of anarchy into which these and other events had plunged it. In so complex a situation one fact could clearly be seen. The tide of African independence, which had spread over the African continent and had begun to move southward, had been temporarily halted in the Congo.

The Congo itself, after further trials, was to retain its independence and its territorial integrity, and subsequently other African states—such as Kenya, Uganda, Tanganyika, Zanzibar, Northern Rhodesia (under the name of Zambia), Nyasaland (under the name of Malawi), as well as Bechuanaland (under the name of Botswana), Basutoland (under the name of Lesotho), and Swaziland—were also to gain independence,[62] and be admitted to the United Nations. But the effective movement of African nationalism toward the south as a challenge to the power of the white minority in Southern Africa, had been paralyzed for some years, despite guerrilla uprisings that were subsequently to occur in Angola and Mozambique, not to speak of the West African territory of Portuguese Guinea.

Meanwhile, as the 1960 Congo crisis had developed, the territories of the French Community had continued to accede to independence—Dahomey on August 1, Niger on August 3, Upper Volta on August 5, Ivory Coast on August 7, Chad on August 11, the Central African Republic (formerly Ubangui-Shari) on August 13, the Republic of the Congo (Brazzaville)—formerly the French Congo—on August 15, and Gabon on August 17. Subsequently, on September 20, 1960, Cameroun, Togo, Madagascar, Somalia, the Congo (Leopoldville), the Congo (Brazzaville), Dahomey, Niger, Upper Volta, the Ivory Coast, Chad, Gabon, and the Central African Republic were all admitted to the United Nations. Since, in August, 1960, Senegal had seceded from the Mali Federation, and the former French Soudan, on September 22, 1960, took, instead, the name of the republic of Mali, it was not until September 28, that Senegal and Mali, former partners in the defunct federation, could also be admitted to U.N. membership. On October 1, 1960, moreover, Nigeria, too, attained independence, being admitted to the U.N. on October 7. Mauritania, which became independent on November 28, 1960, was, however, not to be admitted to the U.N. until October, 1961, by which time Sierra Leone, which was to become independent on April 27, 1961, would also have been admitted.

The emancipation of so many countries—sixteen African states in a single year—from the colonial dependency in which they had been held subject, clearly signified the rejection of the colonial formula as relevant to the contemporary world. While further territories nevertheless remained, for a time, as dependencies, the United Nations, as a whole, by adopting a Declaration on the Granting of Independence to Colonial Countries and Peoples on December 14, 1960, clearly reflected the international attitude toward colonialism, as well as proclaiming United Na-

---

62. After Tanganyika had become independent on December 9, 1961, Uganda became independent on October 9, 1962, Zanzibar on December 10, 1963, and Kenya on December 12, 1963. Tanganyika and Zanzibar united to become the United Republic of Tanganyika and Zanzibar on April 26, 1964, after which its name was changed to the United Republic of Tanzania on October 29, 1964. Malawi obtained independence on July 6, 1964, Zambia on October 24, 1964, Botswana on September 30, 1966, Lesotho on October 4, 1966, and Swaziland on September 6, 1968.

tions policy on the subject. The first three operative paragraphs of the Declaration, which were taken in part from the Final Communique of the 1955 Bandung Conference, read as follows:

The General Assembly . . . Declares that:

1. The subjection of peoples to alien subjugation, domination, and exploitation constitutes a denial of fundamental human rights, is contrary to the Charter of the United Nations, and is an impediment to the promotion of world peace and co-operation.

2. All peoples have the right to self-determination; by virtue of that right they freely determine their political status, and freely pursue their economic, social and cultural development.

3. Inadequacy of political, economic, social or educational preparedness should never serve as a pretext for delaying independence.

By the adoption of the Declaration, Africa received international moral sanction for its recovery of the freedom it had for so long been denied.

# Chapter 18

# Conclusion: The World in the Melting Pot

*In perusing the pages of our history, we shall scarcely meet with a single great event, in the lapse of seven hundred years, which has not turned to the advantage of equality.* —Alexis de Tocqueville

"NONE CAN SAY," wrote Alexis de Tocqueville, reflecting upon nineteenth-century democracy, "which way we are going, for all terms of comparison are wanting." His insight is as relevant to our times as it was to his own. He added that his *Democracy in America* had "been written under the impression of a kind of religious dread produced in the author's mind by the contemplation of so irresistible a revolution" which had advanced for centures in spite of amazing obstacles, and which was still proceeding in the midst of the ruins it had made. Indeed, could it be checked by the efforts of a single generation? Was it credible that "the democracy which has annihilated the feudal system, and vanquished kings, will respect the citizen and the capitalist? Will it stop," he asked, "now that it is grown so strong, and its adversaries so weak?" Evidently, he felt, the answer was "No." Implicit in his thesis, also, was the spread of democracy to the limits of Christendom. Today democracy's seed has been widely sown beyond those limits, and its slow but irrevocable processes set in motion.

While foreseeing the future extension of the democratic revolution which had convulsed the Europe and elevated the America of his day, de Tocqueville did not specifically connect it with the question of color. Now, however, the connection is becoming increasingly apparent as the idea of democracy and the ideal of equality of condition begin to ferment in the lands of Africa, Asia, and Latin America, albeit often with paradoxical results, such as the seizure of power by new tyrants. In part this dream of equality has local effects—undermining alike the ancient power of mandarin, maharajah, and tribal chief, and the more recent power of comprador and white administrator. In part it has international application, affecting relations between the rich countries of Europe and of North America and the poor and largely neglected territories to the south where men of color are in the majority.

There are, of course, those who believe that this difference of condition has no particular significance, and that the world has always been much the same, part rich, part poor. This, however, is a misconception. Superficially, the world may still appear to be the same, but a decisive change has occurred. The poor all over the world now *know* that they are poor, and—perhaps more important—that possibilities of change and betterment exist. Every Western weekly magazine, with its pages of advertising, which makes its way to the lands of the south carries a revolutionary message. Consumer goods are available to the many. Why not to all? From which follows a corollary that is often given sinister connotations: "Who, then, prevents it?"

The possibility of a collision occurring between the rich and the poor lands, the onset of an international racial conflict that slowly gathers momentum, is becoming increasingly clear. Yet the pattern of events to come still remains obscure. Will the disadvantaged colored majority arise in an irresistible tide, sweeping away the last vestiges of white control from their lands while attempting to beleaguer the white homelands of the north? Will the whites, astutely employing bribery and force as the situation requires, maintain the present status quo indefinitely? Or will the whites, rallying the forces that have previously been dissipated in the white civil wars, unite in an attempt to reimpose an open hegemony —a neocolonialism without a mask—on the colored lands? Different factions may severally attempt all of these things. Indeed, so many combinations of circumstance are possible, so many possibilities of new developments, good and bad, loom ahead that, again to refer to de Tocqueville, sight is troubled and reason fails. All the more reason, therefore, to prepare for the future. To prepare for it means marshaling the relevant facts of the past record of race relations—and this is what this book has attempted to do.

History rarely moves along simple and direct paths. Mankind in the mass, it often appears, seems incapable of foreseeing disaster until the first cataclysms have actually occurred. Only then do men come to appreciate that the danger is a present one, and not a theoretical abstraction bruited about by fools or rogues for reasons that are either invalid or unworthy. Only lessons, it sometimes seems, that have been paid for with blood are truly learned. Often, too, the lesson is not learned the first time, but must be repeated. To become indelible it must sear society to the depths. Nor can the process be rushed simply because the conclusion seems clear to some. It is rightly said that one thing leads to another. So the events of history are linked together, unfolding one by one in a complex yet remorseless sequence that only comes to seem inevitable after the event. In this book we have followed one sequence from early times down to 1960, when the adoption by the United Nations of the Declaration on the Granting of Independence to Colonial Countries and Peoples effectively marked the death rattle of the old colonial era. Since then, while it is true that some countries and peoples have continued under colonial tutelage, this tutelage has nevertheless been exercised without the moral sanction of the majority of the governments and peoples of the world. 1960 therefore provides us with a convenient termination point for our story, particularly since the events of the ensuing decade represent only the first part of an entirely new phase.

These events, nevertheless, cannot be completely ignored, even though it is my intention to avoid, so far as possible, entering into current controversies.

In Africa the sudden granting of independence to the Congo by Belgium in 1960, without the necessary preparation for the transfer of power, resulted in chaos and created an opportunity for the white minority administrations of Southern Africa and allied interests to halt the southward spread of the African independence movement. Although with the help of the United Nations a fragile form of government was restored to the Congo, this did not happen before the nascent confidence of many Europeans and Americans in African forms of government had been injured, or before the U.N.'s own reputation had been damaged and the life of its Secretary-General, Dag Hammarskjold, lost in Africa under circumstances that, despite an official inquiry, still remain obscure. A line of demarcation between black and white administration was thus drawn across Southern Africa—a line that, despite the turmoil engendered by an African nationalist uprising in Portuguese-administered Angola in 1961, followed by similar outbreaks in Portuguese-administered Mozambique and Portuguese Guinea, has since been effectively maintained. Subsequently, a series of political assassinations of African nationalist leaders as well as outbreaks of major tribal conflict—in Nigeria, where the Eastern region declared its secession as the state of Biafra, and in the Sudan, where the Southern provinces attempted to secede from the Arab-controlled government in Khartoum—shattered the facade of African stability, and publicly weakened the African nationalist cause. After a few brief years of brave confidence it became clear that African administrations, although no longer uniquely dependent as in colonial days upon the goodwill of European or American capitals, now enjoyed a degree of autonomy that was still severely circumscribed. The overthrow of the principal African nationalist leader, Kwame Nkrumah of Ghana, in February, 1966, drove the lesson home.

In Asia a less uniform pattern has developed. Ideological convulsions have occurred in Indonesia and China, while in India an increasing population has meant increasing misery which, in turn, has strengthened the centrifugal forces threatening the integrity of the Indian state. Japan, on the contrary, has consolidated and strengthened its economic power. Southeast Asia has, however, been overshadowed by the conflict in Vietnam where the aberration of again committing American troops to the Asian mainland has produced even more fateful sequels than those which followed General MacArthur's ill-starred excursion towards the Yalu, with which we dealt in Chapter 16. Vietnam, moreover, has generated yet further consequences that will eventually be as far-reaching as they are now unpredictable. Apart from the wide-ranging effect upon a new generation of Americans, not the least of these further consequences will be the effect upon race relations in Asia, Africa, and America. In Asia the spectacle of the American Goliath attempting to club an Indochinese David into submission after the French giant had abandoned the attempt, has hardly reassured other Asian nationalists about either the intelligence or the good intentions with which the affairs of the leading power of the Western world are sometimes conducted. That the Vietnamese combatants may also be Communist is not, to Asians, the main issue. What is of ultimate consequence is that—despite the recent arbitrary division of Vietnam into two parts—it is, after all, their country. Meanwhile in Africa the unproductive drain upon the international economy symbolized by Western military expenditure on Vietnam—a drain which has alarmingly increased the plight of African nations, whose economies are usually the first to suffer when either international trade or aid are reduced —has increased the bitterness and sense of frustration which would, even without the Vietnam episode, have proved an obstacle to mutually beneficial cooperation between African states and the West. Similar economic effects have occurred in Latin America, and suspicions of Western motives have sufficiently sharpened to permit a new type of military nationalism to make its appearance upon the scene. In North America the connection between the Vietnam war, in which many American Negroes have fought and died for their country, and the struggle to secure equitable treatment for black American citizens within the Union itself has been sufficiently striking for a new consciousness of the problem to have been awakened. Here it is not yet clear whether the ultimate outcome of the new situation will be a widening of the existing gap between black and white in America—a result which would clearly be accompanied by increased violence—or a more equitable adjustment of the status quo. All that can be said for the moment is that at no time since the Civil War have Americans—young and old, black and white, defenders and attackers of the present status quo—become so preoccupied with the question of race relations. Pessimists would echo the words of de Tocqueville apropos the question of race relations: "The inhabitants of the United States may retard the calamities which they apprehend, but they cannot now destroy their efficient cause." Optimists, on the other hand, would hope that such calamities are not inevitable.

Impinging upon the political patterns that the past has led us to expect, however, are new developments that call all previous assumptions into question. Prominent among these are firstly the rapid increase in world population, and secondly the possibilities and dangers unlocked by technological progress.

The world's population, which took long centuries to reach a billion —approximately in 1850—had increased to two billion by 1930. By 1960 —within a mere thirty years—it had increased to three billion, and is expected to reach four billion by 1980, if not before. Whereas these figures are evidently unreliable, given the inexactitude of censuses, they nevertheless reflect an unprecedented development affecting human life on earth. Within a few short years population increase in certain countries —notably India—may be expected to have outstripped food if not living space. According to some estimates, a cycle of major world famines may be expected to begin some time between 1975 and 1984. The political effects of the population increase will therefore profoundly modify all existing assumptions concerning international affairs, including existing assumptions about race relations. One long-standing article of faith that is likely to find itself challenged is the slogan, backed by the sanction of religion, that the hungry shall be fed. Military calculations will also be modified by the rate of population increase. In international negotiations the vast Chinese population, comprising about one quarter of mankind, already weighs heavily in the scale. By the year 2,000—should the present rate of population increase be maintained—Asians alone will number close to four of the six billion or more people who will then comprise mankind. In the face of such an unprecedented and overwhelming phenomenon, all calculations—including those based on the lessons of the past—will appear inconsequential.

As population grows, so man's reliance on machines, rather than on other men, increases. Computers, for example, are justifying far-reaching decisions that, while they may or may not prove to be rational from a human point of view, can at least be mathematically proven. Thus, just as our political system in its present form—producing at best only indifferent results—will find itself challenged if not overwhelmed by the pressures of demography, so it is reasonable to predict that other institutions, financial, economic, military, and social, will also find themselves challenged if not transformed out of recognition by computer technology. The effect of this—that is to say, the effect of calculations not yet made, in an emotional and political climate not yet established, using machines not yet built—upon race relations is also evidently entirely unpredictable. Theoretically at least, it is nevertheless conceivable that the two great unknowns—the respective effects of demographic increase and of technological development—which now veil the future from us could, when the veil is lifted, show themselves to be interrelated in a way which could help to avert some crises that might otherwise ensue. A technology which, instead of employing resources to probe outer space, could first adapt itself to the efficient exploitation of the resources of the seas and oceans could go far to stem the impending disasters which can now be discerned more clearly with every passing year. We have not even mentioned the potential effects in peace as in war of discoveries made in nuclear physics or in biology. De Tocqueville was undoubtedly right when he declared that "a new science of politics is indispensable to a new world." Yet today what is needed is not only a new science of politics but a whole new world culture as a framework for dealing with the problems ahead. Yet for the need for such a culture to be evident is one thing, and for it to come into being is another. The problem of race relations, many feel, bars the path toward such a culture like a huge and insurmountable barrier. In effect, however, upon close examination, it may be noted that what are described as "racial problems" often prove instead to be primarily problems of cultural difference. It was generally accepted in England, for example, at the time of the imperial Raj, that an Indian maharajah, if rich enough and endowed with an Oxford or Cambridge education, might to the eye appear swarthy, but could not be considered colored. Cultural differences, nonetheless, are by no means to be underrated. Differences in diet, differences in religion, differences in language, differences in custom, differences in historic memories and traditions, differences in ways of signaling or expressing pleasure, displeasure, surprise, or other emotions, differences in ideas of what is right or wrong, or of what is one's own due, or one's due to another—all these factors, and more, raise strong barriers against cultural unity. Nor is there any quick and easy way in which such barriers can be surmounted. Those who would overcome such barriers by ignoring them—or seeking to melt them away, as it were, in a blaze of good will—far from promoting any substantial advance are rather preparing eventual disillusion for themselves and perhaps for others.

Yet, this much said, signs of progress can be seen. The increasing ineffectiveness of nation states would seem to indicate that the time for larger groupings—groupings that economics, technology, and the necessity of collective defense alike necessitate—is fast approaching. Yet before such a larger grouping can be formed, its component parts, if the grouping is to prove durable, must, paradoxically, affirm their separate identities before consenting to submerge them in the larger whole. Thus, in a slightly different context, the recent assertion of the black racial heritage and black racial pride among the black minority in North America appears as a necessary prelude not to the formation of a separate black culture, but rather to the ultimate entry of black Americans into American culture upon the basis of equality.

Yet, important as it undoubtedly is to those immediately concerned, the question of race relations in North America is no more than a minority problem and, as such, distinct from, although related to, the larger problem of race relations in the world as a whole. In this larger context particular interest attaches to the possibilities of the emergence of societies capable of forming component parts of a world culture. Perhaps the earliest example of the emergence of a society with such a potential occurred with the birth of Haiti, where a colonial society, composed mostly of masters and slaves, was transformed by the fusion of French and African elements into a new cultural entity. The political and human disasters that ensued, the subsequent isolation of the island republic, and the dwindling of its economic growth, are circumstances that do not alter the fact that a phenomenon of great significance occurred. Similarly with the birth of Ghana a neo-African culture was seen to have come into being, formed out of British and African elements and attuned to the modern world. Apart from appropriating what it required from British culture, the new Ghanaian form did not deny but on the contrary affirmed its African origins.

Different racial ideals of female beauty are seen by some as forming an insurmountable obstacle to the emergence of a common world culture. On this subject deep emotions are stirred, as it is so closely related to the question of racial intermarriage, which occasionally occurs, and will no doubt always continue occasionally to occur as a somewhat isolated phenomenon. Yet when the ideal of beauty is carefully considered, the obstacle may be seen to be not so forbidding as might at first appear. It is not a question here of imagining that mankind might ever be made over into one huge endogamous kith group, but rather that the different races of mankind might not appear as irredeemably alien to one another. On such a subject it is, of course, impossible to generalize, and the French proverb that "tastes and colors are beyond discussion" is particularly appropriate. But it might be noted in passing that the Hollywood ideal of American or European beauty which was projected in the 1930s and 1940s in a way that often seemed so exclusive as to be inimical to other racial types now appears distinctly dated. Today other types of beauty are also projected on film, while new generations of African and Asian women are sometimes able to adopt styles that have more universal appeal than those of the past.

Finally, in facing the problems that are to come, it would appear that no solutions will be found so long as we consider ourselves the prisoners of history, whether past or future. No guilt, for example, attaches to whites now alive because there was once a transatlantic African slave trade, just as no shame attaches to blacks now alive because blacks once also participated in that trade, or were enslaved by it. Similarly, we are not limited in our future actions by abstract laws of politics, economics, or fate. Our destiny still lies in our hands and is subject to our will. The world, as never before, needs change, and yet, paradoxically, has never before been so wearied of change. Yet change will come. If we fail to meet its challenge the fault will be ours alone.

# Select Bibliography

Adams, Henry. *Historical Essays*. London: T. Fisher Unwin, 1891.

'Alal al-Fâsi. *The Independence Movements in Arab North Africa*. Wash. D.C.: American Council of Learned Societies, 1954.

Allen, James S. *Reconstruction: The Battle for Democracy, 1865–1876*. New York: International Publishers, 1937.

Aptheker, Herbert. *American Slave Revolts*. New York: International, 1963.

Arkell, Anthony J. *A History of the Sudan, from the Earliest Times to 1821*. London: The Athlone Press, 1955.

Anon. *La Chanson de Roland*, trans. Dorothy L. Sayers. Harmondsworth, Mdx.: Penguin Books, 1963.

Ardouin, C. N. Celigny. *Essais sur l'Histoire d'Haiti*. Port-au-Prince, Haiti: T. Bouchereau, 1865.

Arendt, Hannah. *On Revolution*. Viking Press, 1963.

Ascherson, Neal. *The King Incorporated: Leopold II in the Age of Trusts*. Doubleday & Co., 1963.

Atkinson, William C. *A History of Spain and Portugal*. Harmondsworth, Mdx.: Penguin Books, 1960.

Eannes de Azurara, Gomes. *The Chronicle of the Discovery and Conquest of Guinea*, trans. C. R. Beazley. London: Printed for the Hakluyt Society: 1896–1899.

Baker, Ray Stannard. *Woodrow Wilson and World Settlement*. Garden City, N.Y.: Doubleday, Page & Co., 1922.

Barnett, Anthony. *The Human Species: A Biology of Man*. Harmondsworth, Mdx.: Penguin Books, 1961.

Barth, Heinrich. *Travels and Discoveries in North and Central Africa*. London: Ward, Lock & Co., 1890.

Batsell, Walter R. *The United States and the System of Mandates*. Worcester, Mass., N.Y.C.: Carnegie Endowment for International Peace, 1925.

Beaglehole, John C. *The Exploration of the Pacific.* Stanford, Calif.: Stanford University Press, 1947.

Beatty, Charles R. L. *Ferdinand de Lesseps of Suez.* Harper & Bros., 1956.

Bemis, Samuel Flagg. *A Diplomatic History of the United States.* Henry Holt & Co., 1950.

Benedict, Ruth. *The Chrysanthemum and the Sword: Patterns of Japanese Culture.* Boston: Houghton Mifflin Co., 1946.

Benson, Mary. *The African Patriots: The Story of the African National Congress of South Africa.* London: Faber & Faber, Ltd., 1963.

Benson, Wilfrid. "The International Machinery for Colonial Liberation," in *New Fabian Colonial Essays* (A. C. Jones, ed.) New York: Praeger, 1959.

Billington, Ray Allen. *The Westward Movement in the United States.* Princeton, N.J.: Van Nostrand Co., 1959.

Bourret, Florence M. *Ghana: The Road to Independence, 1919–1952.* Stanford, Calif.: Stanford University Press, 1960.

Bovill, Edward W. *The Golden Trade of the Moors.* London: Oxford University Press, 1958.

Bradford, Ernie. *A Wind from the North: The Life of Henry the Navigator.* Harcourt, Brace & Co., 1960.

Brecher, Michael. *Nehru: A Political Biography.* London: Oxford University Press, 1959.

Bryce, Viscount James. *Race Sentiment as a Factor in History.* London: University of London Press, 1915.

Bulfinch, Thomas. *The Age of Chivalry and Legends of Charlemagne, or Legends of the Middle Ages.* New York: Mentor Classics, 1962.

Bunting, Brian P. *The Rise of the South African Reich.* Harmondsworth, Mdx.: Penguin Books, 1964.

Burns, Sir Alan C. *Colour Prejudice.* London: Allen & Unwin, 1948.

Butow, Robert J. C. *Tojo and the Coming of War.* Princeton, N.J.: Princeton University Press, 1961.

Camoens, Luis de. *The Lusiads.* (Translated by Leonard Bacon). New York: Hispanic Society of America, 1950.

Cary, Joyce. *The Case for African Freedom and other Writings on Africa.* Austin: University of Texas Press, 1962.

Carlyle, Thomas. *The French Revolution.* New York: Modern Library, n.d.

Carter, Gwendolen M. *The Politics of Inequality: South Africa since 1948.* New York: Frederick A. Praeger, 1958.

Churchill, Sir Winston S. *The Second World War.* London: Cassell, 1948–1954.

Clark, Charles M. H., ed. *Select Documents in Australian History: 1788–1850.* Sydney: Angus & Robertson, 1950.

———. *Select Documents in Australian History: 1851–1900.* Sydney: Angus & Robertson, 1955.

Clark, Charles M. H. *A Short History of Australia.* Sydney, Australia: Tudor Distributors, 1963; New York: Mentor Books, 1963.

Clarkson, Thomas. *History of the Rise, Progress, and Accomplishment of the Abolition of the African Slave Trade by the British Parliament.* London: John W. Parker, 1839.

Clendenen, Clarence and Duignan, Peter. *The United States and the African Slave Trade: 1619–1862.* Stanford, Calif.: Stanford University Hoover Institute on War, Revolution and Peace, 1963.

Clubb, O. Edmund. *Twentieth Century China.* New York: Columbia University Press, 1964.

Collier, John. *The Indians of the Americas.* New York: W. W. Norton & Co., 1948.

Collingwood, Robin G. *Roman Britain.* Oxford: Clarendon Press, 1932.

Columbus, Christopher. *Four Voyages to the New World. Letters and Selected Documents.* New York: Corinth Books (Citadel Press), 1961.

Condliffe, John B. *New Zealand in the Making.* London: Allen & Unwin, 1959.

Conrad, Earl. *Harriet Tubman, Negro Soldier and Abolitionist.* Wash., D.C.: The Associated Publishers, Inc., 1942.

Coon, Carleton S. *The Origin of Races.* New York: Alfred A. Knopf, Inc., 1962.

———. *The Races of Europe.* New York: The Macmillan Co., 1939.

Corey, Lewis. *The House of Morgan.* New York: Grosset & Dunlap, 1930.

Crawford, Raymond M. *Australia.* New York: Hutchinson's University Library, 1952.

Darwin, Charles. *The Descent of Man.* New York: Modern Library, n.d.

Davidson, Basil. *The African Awakening.* New York: The Macmillan Co., 1955.

———. *Black Mother: The Years of the African Slave Trade.* Boston: Little, Brown & Co., 1961.

Davidson, Basil, ed. *The African Past: Chronicles from Antiquity to Modern Times.* Little, Brown & Co., 1964.

Dawson, Christopher H. *The Making of Europe: an Introduction to the History of European Unity.* New York: Meridian Books, 1956.

Defoe, Daniel. *The Life, Adventures, and Piracies of the Famous Captain Singleton.* London: J. M. Dent, 1906.

de Gaulle, Charles. *The Complete War Memoirs of Charles de Gaulle: 1940–1946.* Simon & Schuster, 1964.

Diaz del Castillo, Bernal. *The Conquest of New Spain,* trans. J. M. Cohen. Harmondsworth, Mdx.: Penguin Books, 1963.

Djilas, Milovan. *Conversations with Stalin.* Harcourt Brace & World, 1962.

Donnan, Elizabeth. *Documents Illustrative of the Slave Trade to America* (4 vols.). Wash., D.C.: Carnegie Institution of Washington, 1930–1935.

Donnelly, Ignatius. *Atlantis: The Antediluvian World.* New York: Gramercy Publishing Co. (division of Crown Publishers), 1949.

Dostoevsky, Feodor. *The Diary of a Writer.* New York: Charles Scribner's Sons, 1949.

Douglass, Frederick. *Life and Times of Frederick Douglass Written by Himself.* New York: Collier Books, 1962.

Duignan, Peter and Clendenen, Clarence. *The United States and the African Slave Trade: 1619–1862.* Stanford, Calif.: Stanford University Hoover Institute on War, Revolution and Peace, 1963.

Du Bois, W. E. B. *John Brown.* New York: International Publishers (centennial edition), 1962.

———. *The Souls of Black Folk.* New York: Fawcett Publications, 1961.

———. *The World and Africa.* New York: International Publishers, 1965.

Dunne, Finley Peter. *Mr. Dooley at His Best.* New York: Charles Scribner's Sons, 1938.

Easton, Stewart C. *The Rise and Fall of Western Colonialism.* New York: Frederick A. Praeger, 1964.

Eden, Anthony. *The Memoirs of Anthony Eden, Earl of Avon: Facing the Dictators, 1923–1938.* New York: Houghton Mifflin Co., 1962.

Eisenhower, Dwight D. *Mandate for Change: 1953–1956.* New York: Doubleday & Co., 1963.

Emerson, Rupert. *From Empire to Nation: The Rise to Self-Assertion of Asian and African Peoples.* Cambridge: Harvard University Press, 1960.

Fage, John D. *An Introduction to the History of West Africa.* Bronxville, N.Y.: Cambridge Publishers, 1959.

Fage, John D. and Oliver, Roland. *A Short History of Africa.* Harmondsworth, Mdx.: Penguin Books, 1962.

Fairservis, Walter A. *The Origins of Oriental Civilization.* New York: New American Library, 1959.

Fall, Bernard B. *The Two Viet-Nams.* New York: Praeger, 1963.

———. *Street without Joy: Insurgency in Indochina: 1946–1954.* Harrisburg, Pa.: Stackpole Co., 1961.

Farago, Ladislas. *The Broken Seal: The Story of Operation Magic and the Pearl Harbor Disaster.* New York: Random House, 1967.

Farmer, Bertram H. *Ceylon: A Divided Nation.* New York: Oxford University Press, 1963.

Farwell, Byron. *The Man Who Presumed: a Biography of Henry M. Stanley.* London, N.Y.: Longmans, Green, 1957.

Feis, Herbert. *The Road to Pearl Harbor.* Princeton, N.J.: Princeton University Press, 1950.

Filler, Louis. *The Crusade Against Slavery: 1830–1860.* New York: Harper & Row, 1960.

Flint, John E. *Sir George Goldie and the Making of Nigeria.* London: Oxford University Press, 1960.

Foxcroft, Edmund J. B. *Australian Native Policy.* Melbourne and London: Melbourne University Press in assn. with Oxford University Press.

Franklin, John Hope. *From Slavery to Freedom.* New York: Alfred A. Knopf, 1947.

Freyre, Gilberto. *The Masters and the Slaves: A Study in the Development of Brazilian Civilization.* New York: Alfred A. Knopf, 1963.

———. *New World in the Tropics: The Culture of Modern Brazil.* New York: Vintage Books, 1963.

Friedlander, Ludwig. *Roman Life and Manners under the Early Empire.* London: G. Routledge & Sons, Ltd., 1910–13.

Frobenius, Leo. *The Voice of Africa.* London: Hutchinson & Co., 1913.

———. *African Genesis* (with Douglas C. Fox). New York: Stackpole Sons, 1937.

Gandhi, Mohandas. *Gandhi, an Autobiography: The Story of My Experiments with Truth.* London: Phoenix Press, 1949.

Genovese, Eugene D. *The Political Economy of Slavery: Studies in the Economy and Society of the Slave South.* New York: Pantheon Books, 1965.

Girodias, Maurice (with Peter Singleton-Gates). *The Black Diaries: An Account of his Diaries and Public Writings.* New York: Grove Press, 1959.

Gobineau, Joseph Arthur, comte de. *The Inequality of Human Races.* New York, 1915.

Goodrich, Luther Carrington. *A Short History of the Chinese People.* New York: Harper & Row, 1963.

Gorer, Geoffrey. *Africa Dances: A Book about West African Negroes.* New York: W. W. Norton Co., 1962.

Greenidge, Charles W. W. *Slavery.* London: Allen & Unwin, 1958.

Gross, Felix. *Rhodes of Africa.* New York: Frederick A. Praeger, 1957.

Hahn, Emily. *China Only Yesterday, 1850–1950: A Century of Change.* New York: Doubleday & Co., 1963.

Halle, Louis J. *The Cold War as History.* London: Chatto & Windus, 1967.

Hanke, Lewis. *South America*. Princeton: Van Nostrand, 1959.

Hart, Henry H. *Sea Road to the Indies*. New York: Macmillan Co., 1950.

Herodotus. *The Persian Wars*. New York: Modern Library, 1942.

Herskovits, Melville J. *The Myth of the Negro Past*. Boston: Beacon Press, 1958.

Hitler, Adolf. *Mein Kampf*. Boston: Houghton Mifflin Co., 1943.

———. *Hitler's Secret Conversations: 1941–1944*. New York: Farrar, Straus & Giroux, 1953.

Hobson, John A. *Imperialism: A Study*. Ann Arbor: University of Michigan Press, 1965.

Hodgen, Margaret T. *Early Anthropology in the Sixteenth and Seventeenth Centuries*. Phila.: University of Pennsylvania Press, 1964.

Hoover, Herbert C. *Years of Adventure, 1874–1920* (vol. I of *Memoirs*) New York: Macmillan Co., 1951.

House, Col. Edward M. *The Intimate Papers of Colonel House*. Boston and New York: Houghton Mifflin Co., 1926–28.

House, Col. Edward M., and Seymour, Charles, eds. *What Really Happened at Paris: the Story of the Peace Conference, 1918–1919*. New York: Charles Scribner's Sons, 1921.

Howard, C., ed. (Introduction by J. H. Plumb). *West African Explorers*. London, etc.: Oxford University Press, 1951.

Huizinga, Johan. *The Waning of the Middle Ages*. Garden City, N.Y.: Doubleday Anchor Books, 1954.

Ibn Batutah. *Travels in Asia and Africa: 1325–1354*. London: G. Routledge & Sons, Ltd., 1929.

James, Cyril L. R. *The Black Jacobins*. New York: Vintage Books, 1963.

Johnston, Sir Harry H. *The Negro in the New World*. London: The Hakluyt Society at the Universities Press, 1958–62.

———. *A History of the Colonization of Africa by Alien Races*. Cambridge: Cambridge University Press, 1913.

Josephson, Matthew. *The President-Makers*. New York: Harcourt Brace & Co., 1940.

Kelen, Emery. *Peace in Their Time: Men Who Led Us In and Out of War, 1914–1945*. New York: Alfred A. Knopf, 1963.

Kennan, George F. *American Diplomacy, 1900–1950*. New York: New American Library (Mentor Books), 1952.

———. *Memoirs: 1925–1950*. Boston: Little Brown & Co., 1967.

Kennedy, Malcolm. *A Short History of Japan*. New York: Mentor Books, 1964.

Kiewit, Cornelius W. de. *The Anatomy of South African Misery*. London and New York: Oxford University Press, 1956.

Kimble, George T. *Geography in the Middle Ages*. London: Methuen & Co., Ltd., 1938.

Kingsley, Mary H. *Travels in West Africa*. London and New York: Macmillan and Co., 1897.

Kinross, John Patrick Douglas Balfour, 3d baron, Lord. *Ataturk: A Biography of Mustafa Kemal*. New York: William Morrow and Co., 1965.

Klingberg, Frank W. (editor). *A History of the United States from 1865 to the Present*. New York: Meridian Books, 1962.

Klose, Nelson. *A Concise Study Guide to the American Frontier*. Lincoln: University of Nebraska Press, 1964.

Koestler, Arthur. *Promise and Fulfillment: Palestine, 1917–1949*. New York: Macmillan Co., 1949.

Korngold, Ralph. *Citizen Toussaint*. Boston: Little, Brown & Co., 1944.

Kropotkin, Peter. *Mutual Aid*. London: William Heinemann, 1915.

Lacroix, General Pamphile A. de, Comte. *Mémoires pour Servir à l'Histoire de la Révolution de Saint-Domingue*. Paris, 1820.

Larson, Dan R., and Larson, Arthur. *Vietnam and Beyond*. Durham, N.C.: Rule of Law Research Center, Duke University, 1965.

Laver, James, *Nostradamus*. Harmondsworth, Mdx.: Penguin Books, 1952.

Lecky, W. E. H. *A History of European Morals, from Augustus to Charlemagne*. London: Watts & Co., 1930.

Legum, Colin. *Pan Africanism: A Short Political Guide*. New York: Frederick A. Praeger, 1965.

Lenin, V. I. *Selected Works* (12 vols.), *Vol. VI*. New York: International Publishers, 1943.

————. *Imperialism: The Highest Stage of Capitalism*. New York: International Publishers, 1939.

————. *The Right of Nations to Self-Determination*. New York: International Publishers, 1951.

Lewis, Meriwether, and Clark, William. *The Journals of Lewis and Clark. A New Selection*. New York: Mentor Books, 1964.

Lhote, Henri. *The Search for the Tassili Frescoes: The Story of the Prehistoric Rock Paintings of the Sahara*. New York: E. P. Dutton & Co., 1959.

Lissner, Ivar. *The Silent Past: Mysterious and Forgotten Cultures of the World*. New York: G. P. Putnam's Sons, 1962.

Little, Kenneth. *Behind the Color Bar*. 1950.

Little, Tom. *Egypt*. New York: Frederick A. Praeger, 1958.

Lloyd, Christopher. *The Navy and the Slave Trade: The Suppression of the African Slave Trade in the Nineteenth Century*. London and New York: Longmans, Green & Co., 1949.

McBurney, Charles B. *The Stone Age of Northern Africa*. Harmondsworth, Mdx.: Penguin Books, 1960.

McHenry, John P. *A Short History of Mexico*. Garden City, N.Y.: Doubleday & Co., 1962.

McKitrick, Eric L., ed. *Slavery Defended: The Views of the Old South*. Englewood Cliffs, N.J.: Prentice-Hall, 1963.

Macmillan, William M. *The Road to Self-Rule: A Study in Colonial Evolution*. New York: Praeger, 1960.

Madariaga, Salvador de. *The Fall of the Spanish American Empire*. New York: Collier Books, 1963.

Mannix, Daniel P. (in collaboration with Malcolm Cowley). *Black Cargoes: A History of the Atlantic Slave Trade, 1518–1865*. New York: Viking Press, 1962.

Mathiez, Albert. *The French Revolution*. New York: Russell & Russell, 1962. Paris, 1922–27.

Méneval, Claude Francois de, Baron. *Memoirs of Napoleon Bonaparte*. New York: P. F. Collier & Son, 1910.

Menon, Vapal Pangunni. *The Story of the Integration of the Indian States*. New York: Macmillan Co., 1956.

Meyerowitz, Eva. *Akan Traditions of Origin*. London: Faber & Faber, 1952.

————. *The Divine Kingship in Ghana and Ancient Egypt*. London: Faber & Faber, 1960.

Michelet, Raymond. *African Empires and Civilisations* (Foreword by Nancy Cunard). London: Panaf Service Ltd., 1945.

Montagu, Ashley. *Man's Most Dangerous Myth: The Fallacy of Race.* New York: Columbia University Press, 1942.

Moon, Parker T. *Imperialism and World Politics.* New York: Macmillan Co., 1927.

Moorehead, Alan. *The White Nile.* New York: Harper & Row, 1962.

———. *The Blue Nile.* New York: Harper & Row, 1962.

Moran, Charles McMoran Wilson (1st baron), Lord. *Churchill: The Struggle for Survival, 1940–1965, Taken from the Diaries of Lord Moran.* Boston: Houghton Mifflin Co., 1966.

Morel, Edmund D. *Red Rubber: The Story of the Rubber Slave Trade Flourishing on the Congo in the Year of Grace 1906.* London: T. Fischer Unwin, 1906.

Morison, Samuel Eliot. *Admiral of the Ocean Sea: A Life of Christopher Columbus.* Boston: Little, Brown & Co., 1942.

Mosley, Leonard. *Haile Selassie: The Conquering Lion of Judah.* Englewood Cliffs, N.J.: Prentice-Hall, 1965.

Murphy, Robert D. *Diplomat Among Warriors.* New York: Pyramid Books, 1965.

Myrdal, Gunnar. *Asian Drama: An Inquiry into the Poverty of Nations.* New York: Pantheon Books, 1968.

Nasser, Gamal Abdel. *Egypt's Liberation: The Philosophy of the Revolution.* Washington, D.C.: Public Affairs Press, 1955.

Nehru, Jawaharlal. *The Discovery of India.* New York: Anchor Books, 1960.

Nerval, Gérard de. *Les Illuminés.* Vol. 4 of *Oeuvres Complètes.* Paris: Lèvy Frères, 1868–1881.

Nicolson, Sir Harold G. *Harold Nicolson: The Later Years: 1945–1962.* Vol. III of *Diaries and Letters.* New York: Atheneum Publishers, 1968.

Nkrumah, Kwame. *Ghana: An Autobiography.* New York: Thomas Nelson and Sons, 1957.

———. *I Speak of Freedom: A Statement of African Ideology.* New York: Frederick A. Praeger, 1961.

Nutting, Anthony. *No End of a Lesson: The Story of Suez.* New York: Clarkson N. Potter, 1967.

Oliver, Roland and Fage, John D. *A Short History of Africa.* Harmondsworth, Mdx.: Penguin Books, 1962.

Padmore, George. *Pan Africanism or Communism? The Coming Struggle for Africa.* London: Dennis Dobson, 1956.

Pannikar, Kavalam Madhara. *Asia and Western Dominance: A Survey of the Vasco da Gama Epoch of Asian History, 1498–1945.* London: Allen & Unwin, 1953.

Parkman, Francis. *The Jesuits in North America.* Boston: Little, Brown & Co., 1963.

———. *La Salle and the Discovery of the Great West.* New York: Signet Classics, 1963.

Parrinder, Geoffrey. *West African Religion.* London: The Epworth Press, 1949.

Parry, John H. *The Establishment of the European Hegemony: 1415–1715; Trade and Exploration in the Age of the Renaissance.* New York: Harper & Bros., 1961.

Pauléus Sannon, Horace. *Histoire de Toussaint L'ouverture.* Port-au-Prince, Haiti: A. A. Héraux, 1920.

Pedraza, Howard J. *Borrioboola-Gha: The Story of Lokoja and the First British Settlement in Nigeria.* London: Oxford University Press, 1960.

Peffer, Nathaniel. *The Far East: A Modern History.* Ann Arbor: University of Michigan Press, 1958.

Pendle, George. *A History of Latin America.* Harmondsworth, Mdx.: Penguin Books, 1963.

Penrose, Boies. *Travel and Discovery in the Renaissance: 1420–1620.* New York: Atheneum Publishers, 1962.

Perham, Margery F. *Lugard: The Years of Adventure: 1858–1898.* London: Collins, 1956.

———. *The Colonial Reckoning.* London: Collins, 1963.

Pirenne, Henri. *Economic and Social History of Mediaeval Europe.* New York: Harcourt Brace & Co., 1937.

———. *Mohamed and Charlemagne.* New York: Meridian Books, 1957.

Plumb, John H. and Howard, C. *West African Explorers.* London, etc.: Oxford University Press, 1951.

Polo, Marco. *Travels of Marco Polo the Venetian.* Garden City, N.Y.: Garden City Books, 1948.

Prescott, William H. *The Conquest of Mexico and the Conquest of Peru.* New York: Modern Library, n.d.

Price, Thomas and Shepperson, George. *Independent African: John Chilembwe and the Origins, Setting and Significance of the Nyasaland Native Uprising of 1915.* Edinburgh: Edinburgh University Press, 1958.

Quaison-Sackey, Alex. *Africa Unbound: Reflections of an African Statesman.* New York: Frederick A. Praeger, 1963.

Rattray, R. S. *Religion and Art in Ashanti.* Oxford: Clarendon Press, 1927.

Reade, William Winwood. *The Martyrdom of Man.* London: Jonathan Cape, 1872.

Reid, J. M. *Traveller Extraordinary: The Life of James Bruce of Kinnaird.* New York: W. W. Norton & Co., 1968.

Richmond, Anthony H. *The Colour Problem.* Harmondsworth, Mdx.: Penguin Books, 1955.

Ridgway, Matthew B. *The Korean War.* New York: Doubleday & Co., 1967.

Rocker, Rudolf. *Nationalism and Culture.* Los Angeles: Rocker Publications Committee, 1937.

Rogers, Joel A. *Sex and Race* (3 vols.) New York: J. A. Rogers, 1941, 1942, 1944.

———. *The World's Great Men of Color.* New York: J. A. Rogers, 1947.

———. *Nature Knows No Color Line.* New York: J. A. Rogers, 1952.

Runciman, Sir Steven. *Byzantine Civilization.* Cleveland: World Publishing Co., 1956.

Sachar, Abram Leon. *A History of the Jews.* New York: Alfred A. Knopf.

Schiffers, Heinrich. *The Quest for Africa: 2,000 Years of Exploration.* New York: G. P. Putnam's Sons, 1957.

Schurz, William Lytle. *Latin America: A Descriptive Survey.* New York: E. P. Dutton & Co., 1964.

Scott, Michael. *A Time to Speak.* New York: Doubleday & Co., 1958.

Seaver, George. *David Livingstone: His Life and Letters.* New York: Harper Bros., 1957.

Segal, Ronald. *African Profiles,* Harmondsworth, Mdx.: Penguin, 1962.

Seligman, Charles G. *Races of Africa.* London, New York: Oxford University Press, 1957.

Seymour, Charles and House, Col. Edward M. *What Really Happened at Paris.* New York: Charles Scribner's Sons, 1921.

Seymour, John. *One Man's Africa.* New York: The John Day Co., 1956.

Shepperson, George and Price, Thomas. *Independent African.* Edinburgh: Edinburgh University Press, 1958.

Shirer, William T. *The Rise and Fall of the Third Reich: A History of Nazi Germany.* New York: Simon & Schuster, 1959.

Sinclair, Keith. *A History of New Zealand.* London and New York: Oxford University Press, 1961. Harmondsworth, Mdx.: Penguin Books, 1959.

Singleton-Gates, Peter, and Girodias, Maurice. *The Black Diaries: An Account of Roger Casement's Life and Times with a Collection of His Diaries and Public Writings.* New York: Grove Press, 1959.

Slocombe, George. *A Mirror to Geneva.* London: Jonathan Cape. 1937.

Smith, Edwin W. *Aggrey of Africa: A Study in Black and White.* London: Student Christian Movement, 1929.

Smith, William. *A New Voyage to Guinea.* London: J. Nourse, 1744.

Smuts, Jan Christian. *Africa and Some World Problems.* Oxford: Clarendon Press, 1930.

Spaulding, Robert K. *How Spanish Grew.* Berkeley: University of Calif. Press, 1962.

Stalin, J. V. *Marxism and the National Question,* in *Works,* Vol. 2. (13 vols.) Moscow: Foreign Languages Publishing House, 1953.

Stampp, Kenneth M. *The Peculiar Institution: Slavery in the Ante-Bellum South.* New York: Alfred A. Knopf, 1956.

Stoddard, Theodore Lothrop. *The French Revolution in San Domingo.* Boston: Houghton Mifflin Co., 1914.

———. *The Rising Tide of Color Against White World Supremacy.* New York: Charles Scribner's Sons, 1921.

Stowe, Harriet Beecher. *Uncle Tom's Cabin.* New York: Washington Square Press, 1963.

Sykes, Sir Percy. *A History of Exploration.* New York: Harper Torchbooks, 1961.

Taylor, A. J. P. *The Origins of the Second World War.* New York: Premier Books, 1963.

Teilhard de Chardin, Pierre. *Le phenomène humain.* Paris: Editions du Seuil, 1955.

Thomas, Hugh. *Suez.* Harper & Row, 1967.

Thomas, John L., ed. *Slavery Attacked: The Abolitionist Crusade.* Englewood Cliffs, N.J.: Prentice-Hall, 1965.

Thucydides. *The Peloponnesian War.* Harmondsworth, Mdx.: Penguin Books, 1954.

Tompkins, Peter. *The Murder of Admiral Darlan: A Study in Conspiracy.* New York: Simon & Schuster, 1965.

Tocqueville, Alexis de. *Democracy in America.* New York: Schocken Books, 1961.

———. *The Old Regime and the French Revolution.* Garden City, N.Y.: Doubleday Anchor Books, 1955.

Togo, Shigenori. *The Cause of Japan.* New York: Simon & Schuster, 1956.

Townsend, Mary Evelyn. *The Rise and Fall of the German Colonial Empire, 1884–1918.* New York: The Macmillan Co., 1930.

Toynbee, Arnold J. *A Study of History, Vol. I.* London and New York: Oxford University Press, 1934.

———. *Civilization on Trial.* New York: Oxford University Press, 1948.

Trimingham, J. Spencer. *Islam in West Africa.* Oxford: Clarendon Press, 1959.

Truman, Harry S. *Memoirs, Vol. II. Years of Trial and Hope.* New York: Doubleday & Co., 1956.

United Nations. Official Records of the General Assembly (1946 to date).

———. Official Records of the Security Council (1946 to date).

Upthegrove, Campbell L. *Empire by Mandate: A History of the Relations of Great Britain with the Permanent Mandates Commission of the League of Nations.* New York: Bookman Associates, 1954.

Walbank, T. Walter. *Contemporary Africa: Continent in Transition.* New York: Van Nostrand Co., 1956.

Walters, Francis P. *A History of the League of Nations*. London, etc.: Oxford University Press, 1952.

Ward, W. E. F. *A History of Ghana*. London: Allen & Unwin, 1958.

Washburn, Wilcomb E. (editor). *The Indian and the White Man*. New York: New York University Press, 1964.

Wells, H. G. *A Short History of the World*. London: Cassel and Co., Ltd., 1922.

White, Theodore H., ed. *The Stilwell Papers*. New York: William Sloan Associates, 1948.

Williamson, James A. *Cook and the Opening of the Pacific*. London: English Universities Press, 1946.

Wiltgen, Ralph M. *Gold Coast Mission History: 1471–1880*. Techny, Ill.: Divine Word Publications, 1956.

Wint, Guy. *The British in Asia*. London: Faber & Faber, 1947.

Wright, Richard. *The Color Curtain: A Report on the Bandung Conference*. Cleveland and New York: World Publishing Co., 1956.

# Index